Detention and Occupation in International Humanitarian Law

The Library of Essays in International Humanitarian Law
Series Editors: Michael N. Schmitt and Wolff Heintschel von Heinegg

Titles in the Series:

The Development and Principles of International Humanitarian Law
Michael N. Schmitt and Wolff Heintschel von Heinegg

The Scope and Applicability of International Humanitarian Law
Michael N. Schmitt and Wolff Heintschel von Heinegg

The Conduct of Hostilities in International Humanitarian Law, Volume I
Michael N. Schmitt and Wolff Heintschel von Heinegg

The Conduct of Hostilities in International Humanitarian Law, Volume II
Michael N. Schmitt and Wolff Heintschel von Heinegg

Detention and Occupation in International Humanitarian Law
Michael N. Schmitt and Wolff Heintschel von Heinegg

The Implementation and Enforcement of International Humanitarian Law
Michael N. Schmitt and Wolff Heintschel von Heinegg

Detention and Occupation in International Humanitarian Law

Edited by

Michael N. Schmitt

US Naval War College, USA

Wolff Heintschel von Heinegg

Europa-Universitat Viadrina, Germany

Routledge
Taylor & Francis Group
LONDON AND NEW YORK

First published 2012 by Ashgate Publishing

2 Park Square, Milton Park, Abingdon, Oxfordshire OX14 4RN
711 Third Avenue, New York, NY 10017

Routledge is an imprint of the Taylor & Francis Group, an informa business

First issued in paperback 2018

British Library Cataloguing in Publication Data
Detention and occupation in international humanitarian law.
– (The library of essays in international humanitarian law)
1. Humanitarian law. 2. Prisoners of war – Legal status, laws, etc. 3. Detention of persons. 4. Military occupation.
I. Series II. Schmitt, Michael N. III. Heintschel von Heinegg, Wolff.
341.6'7–dc23

Library of Congress Control Number: 2011946162

ISBN 978-0-7546-2937-5 (hbk)
ISBN 978-1-138-37864-3 (pbk)

Contents

Acknowledgements

The editors and publishers wish to thank the following for permission to use copyright material.

Cambridge University Press for the essays: Jelena Pejic (2005), 'Procedural Principles and Safeguards for Internment/Administrative Detention in Armed Conflict and Other Situations of Violence', *International Review of the Red Cross*, **87**, pp. 375–91. Copyright © 2005 International Committee of the Red Cross; Eyal Benvenisti (2008), 'The Origins of the Concept of Belligerent Occupation', *Law and History Review*, **26**, pp. 621–48. Copyright © 2008 Board of Trustees of the University of Illinois.

Chatham House for the essays: Richard R. Baxter (1950), 'The Duty of Obedience to the Belligerent Occupant', *British Year Book of International Law*, **27**, pp. 235–66; R.Y. Jennings (1946), 'Government in Commission', *British Year Book of International Law*, **23**, pp. 112–41.

Copyright Clearance Center for the essays: Derek Jinks (2004), 'The Declining Significance of POW Status', *Harvard International Law Journal*, **45**, pp. 367–442. Copyright © 2004 Harvard University Law School; Howard S. Levie (1961), 'Prisoners of War and the Protecting Power', *American Journal of International Law*, **55**, pp. 374–97. Copyright © 1961 American Society of International Law; Richard A. Falk (1973), 'International Law Aspects of Repatriation of Prisoners of War during Hostilities', *American Journal of International Law*, **67**, pp. 465–78. Copyright © 1973 American Society of International Law; Adam Roberts (1990), 'Prolonged Military Occupation: The Israeli-Occupied Territories since 1967', *American Journal of International Law*, **84**, pp. 44–103. Copyright © 1990 American Society of International Law; Adam Roberts (2006), 'Transformative Military Occupation: Applying the Laws of War and Human Rights', *American Journal of International Law*, **100**, pp. 580–622. Copyright © 2006 American Society of International Law; Elbridge Colby (1925), 'Occupation under the Laws of War: I', *Columbia Law Review*, **25**, pp. 904–22. Copyright © 1925 Columbia Law Review Association, Inc.; Elbridge Colby (1926), 'Occupation under the Laws of War: II', *Columbia Law Review*, **26**, pp. 146–70. Copyright © 1926 Columbia Law Review Association, Inc.

International Law Review for the essay: Sean D. Murphy (2007), 'Evolving Geneva Convention Paradigms in the "War on Terrorism": Applying the Core Rules to the Release of Persons Deemed "Unprivileged Combatants"', *George Washington Law Review*, **75**, pp. 1105–164.

Oxford University Press for the essays: Adam Roberts (1985), 'What is a Military Occupation?', *British Year Book of International Law*, **55**, pp. 249–305. Copyright © 1985 Adam Roberts; Marco Sassòli (2005), 'Legislation and Maintenance of Public Order and

Civil Life by Occupying Powers', *European Journal of International Law*, **16**, pp. 661–94. Copyright © 2005 EJIL.

Public Domain: Lassa Oppenheim (1917), 'The Legal Relations between an Occupying Power and the Inhabitants', *Law Quarterly Review*, **31**, pp. 363–70.

Every effort has been made to trace all the copyright holders, but if any have been inadvertently overlooked the publishers will be pleased to make the necessary arrangement at the first opportunity.

Series Preface

Over half a century ago, Sir Hersch Lauterpacht, then Whewell Professor of International Law at the University of Cambridge, observed that 'if international law is the vanishing point of law, the law of war is at the vanishing point of international law'. He was wrong. While it is true that the law of war, or international humanitarian law as it has become known, is particularly vulnerable to the vagaries of political, social and economic influences, it has nevertheless proven itself a robust normative regime that positively shapes man's most destructive undertaking – warfare. No other body of law can be credited with saving more lives or alleviating as much suffering.

These six volumes comprise a collection of particularly significant works on humanitarian law. They are intended for use by scholars, practitioners and students who seek to better understand the topics addressed herein, together with their lineage. Just as importantly, they allow users to begin to separate the wheat from the chaff. The proliferation of publications in the field, in part a sad reflection of the fact that armed conflict remains so horribly pervasive, as well as the digitization that facilitates access to journals that would not otherwise be readily available, often results in information overload. A Ministry of Defence legal adviser looking for background material to address a situation involving belligerent occupation will, for instance, uncover scores of articles. The student writing a dissertation on the law of targeting or a scholar penning an article on detention will find him- or herself buried in material. Unfortunately, some of what they unearth will prove misguided, out of context or simply wrong. This collection will not break down these obstacles in their entirety. But it does afford a useful starting-point by offering topically arranged humanitarian law journal essays that have been thoroughly vetted by many of the top experts in the field.

In this regard, a few words on the process used to choose the essays are helpful. It began with the selection of those subjects that we believed comprised the *sine qua non* of international humanitarian law – development, principles, scope, application, conduct of hostilities, detention, occupation, implementation and enforcement. We then contacted over 60 recognized humanitarian law experts, both academics and seasoned legal advisers. They were provided the topics and asked in a very open-ended fashion to identify pieces they considered 'classics', believed to be 'essential' in a compilation of this nature, have found to be especially influential, used regularly in their work or deserved greater attention on the basis of their quality and insights. The experts were asked to pay particular attention to those essays that may have been 'forgotten' over time, but merited 'rediscovery'. Many of them responded in depth. We also benefited from the work of a five-member team from Emory Law School's International Humanitarian Law Clinic which conducted an exhaustive literature review to locate essays relied on regularly by writers – the 'usual suspects', if you will. Finally, as editors we took the liberty of adding a few pieces to the pool *sua sponte*.

Armed with a daunting inventory of candidates for inclusion, we began the difficult task of whittling it down. Many essays proved to be consensus choices among the experts; often the Emory team had also identified them. These provided the skeleton for the project. We then fleshed out the collection based on two key factors: quality assessments by the experts and topic coverage. The latter criterion proved particularly central to the process, for our objective was to produce a collection that not only contained thoughtful and influential works, but also addressed most key humanitarian law topics.

Beyond esteem factors and topical relevance, some essays were selected on account of their temporal significance, that is, having been written at key junctures in the development of international humanitarian law. As an example, the collection includes pieces written in the immediate aftermath of the First and Second World Wars and the attacks of 11 September 2001. Others were published soon after adoption of the 1949 Geneva Conventions or the 1977 Additional Protocols. We hope they both afford insight into the perspectives at play as humanitarian law was evolving and provide a context for understanding the genesis of contemporary norms.

In the end, we were unable to include many insightful and influential works. Exclusion was frequently a mere matter of being cursed with too many good choices on a particular topic. Although no reader is likely to be entirely satisfied with the essays included, or comfortable with the omission of others, we hope the rigorous selection process has resulted in a collection that is both useful and enlightening.

This project would not have been possible without the help of many supporters. We are, of course, deeply indebted to the many international experts who took time from their busy schedules to offer recommendations and comments over the course of the three-year effort. Although we cannot possibly name them all, particular appreciation is due to Ken Anderson, Yutaka Arai, Louise Arimatsu, Laurie Blank, Gabriella Blum, Bill Boothby, Ove Bring, Claude Bruderlein, Knut Dörmann, Alison Duxbury, William Fenrick, Dieter Fleck, Steven Haines, Agnieszka Jachec-Neale, Dick Jackson, Marie Jacobsson, Claus Kress, William Lietzau, Noam Lubell, Lindsay Moir, John Murphy, Sean Murphy, Mary Ellen O'Connell, Bruce Oswald, Hays Parks, Stephen Pomper, Jean-Francois Queguiner, Noelle Quenivet, Adam Roberts, A.P.V. Rogers, Peter Rowe, Joseph Rutigliano, Robert Sloane, Dale Stephens, Ken Watkin and Sean Watts.

We are equally indebted to the brilliant group of young scholars at Emory Law School, whom we dubbed our 'IHL Detectives' – Flora Manship, Carmel Mushin, Jeannine Privat, Nandini Rao and, in particular, Benjamin Farley. Their ability to identify and locate 'lost treasures' of humanitarian law was awe-inspiring. All have since graduated, and we wish them the very best in their professional careers.

Three people deserve special mention and gratitude. Laurie Blank, Director of the Emory's International Humanitarian Law Clinic, ably and tirelessly supervised her team. Beyond supervision, she also devoted an enormous amount of her own time to the substance and administration of the project. At European University Viadrina, Kaya Kowalski took on the task of collating materials and later working with us as we made the final selections for the collection. She was unflappable in the face of our long and sometimes contentious deliberations and always exceptionally good-natured and professional. Finally, we thank our editor at Ashgate, Valerie Saunders, who showed the patience of Job throughout.

We hope this collection proves valuable in the years to come. For our part, it was a fascinating endeavour.

MICHAEL N. SCHMITT
Newport, Rhode Island, USA

and

WOLFF HEINTSCHEL VON HEINEGG
Frankfurt (Oder), Germany

Introduction

This volume addresses two subjects that have re-emerged in the twenty-first century as flashpoints of international humanitarian law: detention and belligerent occupation.

Detention

Detention is one of the oldest and most heavily codified topics in this body of law. After all, it must be recalled that humanitarian law began not as an effort to protect the civilian population, but was instead intended to mitigate the suffering of combatants. This was natural because it was not until the twentieth century that conflict among ordinary people became prevalent. Indeed, only in the Second World War did the number of civilian casualties in a conflict finally exceed military deaths.

The issue of prisoners of war (POWs) was addressed in the 1874 non-bonding Brussels Declaration. Its codified lineage can be traced back to the 1899 and 1907 Hague Conventions (II and IV respectively), which contained 17 provisions related to prisoners of war. During the inter-war years, the 1929 Geneva Convention on prisoners further developed the norms regarding prisoners. In light of the suffering of prisoners during the Second World War, the 1949 Geneva Convention (III) Relative to the Treatment of Prisoners of War was adopted. Also noteworthy was the inclusion of protections for civilian detainees in the 1949 Fourth Geneva Convention. In 1977 these conventions were supplemented by a number of articles on prisoners of war in Additional Protocol I.

Despite this extensive record of codification, unresolved issues remain. For instance, the Korean and Vietnam conflicts raised questions as to non-consensual repatriation of prisoners. Twenty-first-century conflicts such as Afghanistan, Iraq and the so-called 'global war on terror' have also infused the topic of detention with controversy. The issues range from the status of fighters captured on and off the battlefield to their treatment. Part I of this volume explores these and related matters. The five essays should be read in conjunction with those in *The Conduct of Hostilities in International Humanitarian Law*, Volume I, which deals with the status of individuals involved in an armed conflict.

In 'The Declining Significance of POW Status' (Chapter 1), Derek Jinks, of the University of Texas, examines the effects of denial of prisoner-of-war status. Traditionally, such a denial was deemed to have 'drastic protective and policy consequences' (p. 4). Jinks argues to the contrary, asserting that 'the gap in protection for those classified as POWs and those not so classified (e.g., those designated "unlawful combatants") is closing' (ibid.). In particular, he suggests that '[t]he only gaps that persist are: (1) that POWs are "assimilated" into the legal regime governing the armed forces of the detaining state; and (2) that POWs enjoy "combatant immunity"' (ibid.).

Jinks's analysis focuses on the war in Afghanistan. Early on in that conflict, the United States determined that captured detainees were unlawful combatants who did not qualify as prisoners of war. Specifically, it asserted that neither captured Taliban nor al Qaeda fighters met the requirements for status under the Third Geneva Convention. In a position that has since moderated, the United States therefore concluded that it had 'the right to treat the detainees in any way it deems appropriate – unencumbered by international legal obligation' (p. 6). Many disagreed with the US position, arguing not only that it was wrong as a matter of law, but also that, in any event, the procedure for resolving doubt set forth in the Convention (an 'Article 5 Tribunal') should have been employed.

For Jinks, the distinction was less than momentous from both a protective and a policy perspective. He observes that all persons in enemy hands are entitled to Common Article 3 and Article 75 of Additional Protocol I protections and that under Articles 4 and 5 of the Fourth Geneva Conventions enemy aliens are entitled to humane treatment and fair trial rights. He also takes the position that unlawful combatants are 'presumptively covered by the full protections of the Geneva Conventions – even if some of these protections may be suspended when (and so long as) necessary to protect state security' (p. 59), a level of protection that he characterizes as closely approximating that accorded to POWs. It must be noted that, as pointed out in *The Conduct of Hostilities in International Humanitarian Law*, Volume II, the issue of whether unlawful combatants fall under the protection of the Fourth Geneva Convention is as yet unsettled.

There are, of course, certain differences. For instance, the Third Geneva Convention is highly detailed, with violation of certain of its provisions constituting grave breaches. By contrast, violations of Common Article 3, which sets forth protections in abstract terms, and those in Article 75 of Additional Protocol I are not grave breaches. In addition, numerous key states are not party to Protocol I, although the United States now considers its protections to be of customary character.

Jinks suggests that two major developments have narrowed the apparent gap between the protective regimes. First, 'abstract provisions have acquired a more concrete meaning through the elaboration of general humanitarian principles such as "humane treatment," "torture," and "essential judicial guarantees"'. Second, 'the conditions under which the identified alternative schemes apply have been broadened' (p. 60).

He cites the example of the Fourth Geneva Convention's nationality criterion, tracing its relaxation through the case law of the International Criminal Tribunal for the Former Yugoslavia. Human rights law also serves to imbue the provisions with substance – for example, through the 'elaboration and concretization of non-derogable rights' (pp. 62–63) and the clarification of fair trial rights. Moreover, '[a]lthough the lower threshold of applicability for Common Article 3 remains poorly defined, there is now an emerging consensus on the upper threshold: Common Article 3 applies in both non-international and international armed conflict' (pp. 64–65).

The key remaining differences derive from 'a curious feature of the POW Convention – that POWs must be "assimilated" into the armed forces of the detaining state' (p. 69). According to Article 102 of the Convention, prisoners of war 'can be validly sentenced only if the sentence has been pronounced by the same courts according to the same procedure as in the case of members of the armed forces of the Detaining Power'. This means, *inter alia*, that they may not be tried in special civilian or military courts, such as military commissions.

More importantly, prisoners of war enjoy combatant immunity – that is, they may not be punished for their acts of participation in the conflict so long as those acts do not constitute war crimes. This distinction is controversial. Some commentators argue that those who do not enjoy prisoner-of-war status 'may be prosecuted upon capture for their very act of participation in the hostilities (even if they otherwise scrupulously observed the rules of war)' (p. 70). Jinks disagrees, arguing that there are sound policy reasons 'to accord all captured combatants immunity for their otherwise lawful warlike acts' (ibid.). He contends that '[i]f all captured combatants failing to satisfy the requirements for POW status are subject to prosecution for any warlike acts, the law provides irregular fighters with no incentive to comply with its dictates' (ibid.). One's position on this issue determines in part whether Jinks's conclusion that 'POW status carries *no significant, unique protective consequences*' holds water (p. 78, emphasis in original).

Howard Levie, then Legal Adviser at the US European Command and later Professor Emeritus at Saint Louis University, examines a 'significant, but inadequately recognized' aspect of prisoner-of-war detention in 'Prisoners of War and the Protecting Power' (Chapter 2). A protecting power is 'a state which has accepted the responsibility of protecting the interests of another state in the territory of a third, with which, for some reason, such as war, the second state does not maintain diplomatic relations' (p. 79).

The notion is an ancient one, first appearing in the Capitulations of the Ottoman Empire in the sixteenth century. In the nineteenth century the practice was widely employed during the 1870–71 Franco-Prussian War, the first conflict in which protecting powers represented all the belligerents. Protecting powers were active in most subsequent conflicts through the First World War. The 1929 Geneva Convention Relative to the Treatment of Prisoners of War was the first international instrument negotiated during peacetime to formally recognize the institution. It applied during the Second World War, but neither the USSR nor Japan was party to it. The fact that there were few neutral powers of significance during the conflict also weakened its application, especially since the same neutral nation sometimes represented opposing belligerents. The lessons of the Second World War influenced further development of the institution in the 1949 Third Geneva Convention, as well as inclusion of the practice in the other three conventions. For instance, the Third Geneva Convention makes designation of protecting powers 'at least a moral obligation' (p. 87), whereas the comparable 1929 Convention provision simply raised the possibility of designation.

Protecting powers must be neutral states that enjoy diplomatic relations with both the 'Power of Origin' (of the prisoners) and the detaining power. A neutral becomes a protecting power upon request of the power of origin and approval of the detaining power; more than one state may be so designated for a belligerent, and a neutral may serve as a protecting power for multiple states, as in the case of Switzerland in the Second World War. Either diplomats or other nationals may serve as representatives.

The Third Geneva Convention does not delineate powers and duties with great specificity. The keystone duty, set out in Article 8, is to 'safeguard the interests of the Parties to the conflict'. It was generally agreed at the Diplomatic Conference which drafted the 1949 Convention that this entitled protecting powers to 'verify whether the convention was being properly applied and, if necessary, to suggest measures on behalf of prisoners of war' (p. 94). Accordingly, the convention permitted them, *inter alia*, to visit places of detention, have access to prisoners, visit locations of prisoner transport, interview prisoners and prisoner representatives without witnesses, assist in the settling of disputes, inspect financial records, inspect disciplinary punishment records and find counsel for prisoners facing judicial proceedings. Protecting powers are also a conduit for communication between the power of origin and the detaining power. As stated in Article 8, in performing their duties, the protecting powers must 'take account of the imperative necessities of security of the State wherein they carry out their duties'.

According to the Third Geneva Convention, the International Committee of the Red Cross (ICRC) also shoulders certain powers and duties vis-à-vis prisoners of war. In the event that a protecting power is no longer able to serve (for instance, because it becomes a belligerent) and no substitute can be found, the detaining power may request or accept the services of the organization, although, since it is not a state, it acts in its humanitarian capacity rather than a protecting power as such. Even beyond this specific circumstance, the ICRC, or 'any other impartial humanitarian organization may, subject to the consent of the Parties to the conflict concerned, undertake [humanitarian activities] for the protection of prisoners of war and for their relief'. Indeed, the ICRC and the protecting power may act in parallel.

In 'International Law Aspects of Repatriation of Prisoners during Hostilities' (Chapter 3) Richard Falk, of Princeton University, considers the return of prisoners during an ongoing conflict. He wrote this essay following the release of three US prisoners of war in 1972 to mark North Vietnam's National Day. Soon after their release, the US Department of Defense announced that none of the men would be reassigned to duties that related to the continuing conflict.

A threshold issue is the applicability of the Third Geneva Convention. North Vietnam claimed that it was not bound by the treaty because it had issued a reservation to Article 85: 'Prisoners of war prosecuted under the laws of the Detaining Power for acts committed prior to capture shall retain, even if convicted, the benefits of the present Convention'. The United States objected to the reservation. Falk also questions whether the Third Geneva Convention applied beyond Common Article 3 because 'it remains unclear whether North Vietnam would be bound to treat the armed conflict as one of international character bringing the whole of the Convention into play' (p. 107).

In any event, the Third Convention did not deal with repatriation to a belligerent state during hostilities. Rather, it addressed repatriation of the sick and wounded, repatriation to a neutral country, repatriation at the close of hostilities (also governed by the 1907 Hague Regulations) and return of dead prisoners of war. Falk looks to these provisions for guidance. He reasons that if repatriated wounded and sick personnel may not 'be employed on active military service' pursuant to Article 117, neither may repatriated able-bodied prisoners. As to whether the article extends to using repatriated prisoners 'to engage in official or semiofficial pro-war propaganda' (p. 108), Falk argues that such a prohibition is a reasonable interpretation, and one that was accepted by the US government in the form of an assurance by President Nixon that 'the men shall do nothing further to promote the American war effort in Indochina' (ibid.).

The incident also raised the issue of the role played by humanitarian organizations in repatriation. During the conflict, anti-war activists formed the Committee of Liaison with Families of Servicemen Detained in North Vietnam to facilitate acquiring information about prisoners of war and to deliver mail to and from them. Until the 1973 Paris Peace Accords, the North Vietnamese would deal only with this group, and not US government officials, on prisoner matters; it was accordingly designated by the North Vietnamese to serve as 'the social organization' responsible for escorting the released prisoners back to the United States.

Falk queries whether the protections afforded by the Third Geneva Convention encompass the activities of such a group. Article 9 contemplates, subject to the consent of the parties, impartial humanitarian organizations which undertake humanitarian activities for the benefit of prisoners. Article 10 sets forth the circumstances in which a detaining power may allow a humanitarian organization to assume protecting power functions (impartially). Falk argues that the Committee qualified as a humanitarian organization encompassed by these provisions. Although not formally appointed by North Vietnam and anti-war by design, it *de facto* acted as such, and its performance of humanitarian activities was by nature non-partisan. As to the absence of US consent (Article 9), the United States did nothing to actively frustrate the group's activities. Thus, use of the Committee was, for Falk, consistent with the Third Convention.

Falk offers five observations drawn from his analysis of the incident:

> (1) The humanitarian objectives of the Convention may have to be realized in a flexible manner that is responsive to the characteristics of a particular armed conflict;
>
> (2) A private organization of nationals of the 'enemy' state may be more acceptable to the Detaining Power in certain situations than either the International Committee of the Red Cross or a neutral or even a friendly third power government;
>
> (3) The Geneva system is comprehensive enough to provide general guidelines of relevance even in relation to a form of repatriation not specifically covered by the existing treaty;
>
> (4) Treaty revision efforts should take explicit account of the possibility of repatriation of healthy prisoners to the enemy belligerent during the period of active hostilities;
>
> (5) Repatriated prisoners should also be entitled to humanitarian protection once returned to their country of nationality and should be removed from any further relationship, direct or indirect, to an armed conflict in progress. (p. 115)

He concludes that the incident amounted to a 'precedent with international law relevance', for in the absence of treaty law directly on point it 'provides guidelines and experience as to repatriation during hostilities to a belligerent power, and affirms the capacity of a nongovernmental organization of private citizens to play a direct role in this process' (p. 116).

Although the treatment of prisoners of war was the foundation upon which the international humanitarian law of detention was built, in modern conflict the law governing the status and treatment of civilian detainees has loomed large. This is especially so in light of those involving occupation and insurgencies. In 'Procedural Principles and Safeguards for Internment/ Administrative Detention' (Chapter 4), Jelena Pejic, Legal Adviser at the International Committee of the Red Cross, examines deprivation of liberty for security reasons in armed conflicts and other situations of violence.

Pejic defines internment or administrative detention (terms she uses interchangeably) as 'the deprivation of liberty of a person that has been initiated/ordered by the executive branch – not the judiciary – without criminal charges being brought against the internee/administrative detainee' (pp. 117–18). It is an aspect of conflict situations that is highly problematic. She points out that '[t]here is often no mechanism in place to review, initially and periodically, the lawfulness of internment/administrative detention or, if there is one, its lack of independence prevents it from effectively examining cases' (p. 118). Other problem areas include the relative absence of legal assistance in challenging detentions and the difficulty of securing access to one's family.

The law on internment is set forth in Article 3 Common to the 1949 Geneva Conventions, the Fourth Geneva Convention, Article 75 of Additional Protocol I (for parties thereto), Additional Protocol II and customary law. Pejic also draws on human rights law, both in its binding sense and as a source of 'soft law'. She supports her position in this regard by noting that the International Court of Justice has deemed the rights of persons interned for security reasons to be a matter of both international humanitarian law and human rights law. In addition, the Additional Protocols acknowledge the applicability of human rights law in certain circumstances.

Pejic's essay is especially useful in setting forth the principles and practices that govern such detention. Various general principles can be identified from the applicable law. Internment/administrative detention is an exceptional measure that can only be ordered on a non-discriminatory case-by-case basis and it must cease as soon as the reasons for it no longer exist. It must also conform to the principle of legality. Those subject to internment/administrative detention are entitled to an array of procedural safeguards. They include the rights to: information about the basis for their predicament; be held in a recognized place of internment/detention; challenge the detention/internment; have the detention/internment reviewed by an independent and impartial body (including subsequent periodic review) and have legal representation; have contact with family; receive medical care; and have ICRC access.

In Chapter 5, 'Evolving Geneva Convention Paradigms in the "War on Terrorism"', Sean Murphy, of George Washington University, considers the controversies that erupted in light of US detention practices following the 11 September 2001 terrorist attacks. He perceptively notes that although

> ... the Geneva Conventions and the laws of war more generally comprise a sophisticated regulatory regime, ...like all law, the inevitable imprecision in the rules presents opportunities for governments to exploit gray areas so as to augment governmental authority and to avoid sensible interpretations that will protect individuals from overreaching governmental power. (p. 135)

Murphy cautions that '[s]uch exploitation ... severs the rules from their ethical foundation and loses sight of their underlying object and purpose' (p. 135).

In reaching his conclusion, Murphy recounts the historical development of the issue, noting that the problem of dealing with 'guerrilla' forces has 'bedeviled' international humanitarian law from at least the time of Francis Lieber (p. 136). Two paradigms emerged – one for international armed conflict, the other for non-international hostilities – which eventually found expression in the 1949 Geneva Conventions and their 1977 Additional Protocols.

Events subsequent to the attacks of 9/11 deviated from this neat binary scheme. For the sake of analysis, Murphy addresses three contemporaneous conflicts: (1) the Northern Alliance against the Taliban; (2) the United States-led coalition against Afghanistan; and (3) the United States against al Qaeda. As he notes:

> By considering each of these conflicts ... it becomes apparent why many roads in contemporary armed conflict can lead to application of the minimum standards of Common Article 3, rather than the full range of protections contained in the 1949 Geneva Conventions as a whole. (p. 148)

The first conflict was clearly non-international prior to the launch of Coalition operations in October 2001. At that point, two possible characterizations of the conflict present themselves: an international armed conflict involving all parties and a continuing non-international armed conflict coexistent with an international armed conflict between the Coalition states and the Taliban. Murphy finds the first option less than compelling because 'the 1949 Geneva Conventions were not designed to impose obligations (other than those contained in Common Article 3) on nonstate actors' (p. 152). The second is also problematic because 'it envisages two completely separate sets of rules governing allied armed forces that may be fighting side-by-side, perhaps even inviting the more-regulated forces to shift certain responsibilities to the less-regulated force so as to avoid significant laws-of-war obligations' (p. 153). Once the Taliban were ousted from power, the international armed conflict ended, and Coalition forces were present in support of the non-international armed conflict between the remnants of the Taliban and the new Afghan transitional government. As Murphy notes, this seems an odd result given that 20,000 US combat troops remained in the country.

At least until the Taliban lost control of the government and most of the country, the second conflict was clearly international. The United States took the position that members of the Taliban's armed forces lacked prisoner-of-war status because they did not meet the Third Geneva Convention criteria (see the discussions in *The Conduct of Hostilities in International Humanitarian Law*, Volume II). Murphy highlights the debates in the international humanitarian law community over whether the criteria apply to members of the armed forces, taking the view that they do. He supports the United States' controversial blanket determination that all members of the Taliban armed forces failed to meet the criteria, but argues that it erred 'in making sure that the persons in its custody *were in fact part of the Taliban (or al Qaeda)*, rather than a wayward tourist or relief worker' (p. 161, Murphy's emphasis).

If the Third Geneva Convention did not reach the Taliban, did they enjoy the benefits of the Fourth? In other words, are the Third and Fourth Conventions seamless, as claimed by the ICRC? Ultimately, Murphy concludes, they are not. However, he accepts the International Court of Justice's claim in *Nicaragua* that Common Article 3 rules constitutes a 'minimum yardstick' applicable in all conflicts. Thus, captured Taliban fighters were entitled to the limited protections it affords.

The most significant normative quandaries arose with regard to the third conflict. Since al Qaeda is not a state, the international armed conflict paradigm is ill-fitting. In that the conflict is transnational, it equally does not accord well with characterization as a non-international armed conflict. This paradox has led some – for instance, the ICRC – to conclude that the situation does not qualify as an 'armed conflict' at all in the way in which that term is used in international humanitarian law, but is instead mere international criminality.

Arguments that international humanitarian law governs hostilities between the United States and al Qaeda rely on a number of observations and propositions. First, Article 3 is not limited to 'internal' armed conflicts. Instead, it refers to conflicts 'not of an international character', which can be interpreted as conflicts with entities other than a state. Second, the phrase 'in the territory of one of the High Contracting Parties' in the article can be broadly interpreted as referring to hostilities in the territory of any party. Third, the extension of the protections of Additional Protocol I to conflicts with certain non-state actors, such as those involving colonial domination, illustrates a trend towards a broad reach of international humanitarian law. This approach underpinned the US Supreme Court's position in *Hamdan* v.

Rumsfeld, although that case involved an individual detained on the battlefield in Afghanistan during the US conflict with the Taliban. Murphy concludes that the debate will continue, with some arguing for fuller application of the protections of the Geneva Conventions and others opposing even the application of Common Article 3.

Despite concluding that treaty law offers little protection to irregular forces, Murphy nevertheless observes that 'the historical trend is one that has favored development of certain core protections for all persons engaged in armed conflict' (p. 170), particularly in customary law. He singles out Article 75 of Additional Protocol I as 'an appropriate touchstone for determining the rights of non-state actors' (p. 175) and argues that there is 'strong evidence' that its terms now reflect customary law (p. 176). Since the publication of Murphy's essay, the United States has adopted exactly this position.

Also problematic in the conflict is the duration of captivity issue. Combatants may normally be held for the 'duration of hostilities', a position apparently adopted by the US Supreme Court in *Hamdi* v. *Rumsfeld*. But Murphy notes that Article 75(3) provides that 'such persons shall be released with the minimum delay possible and in any event as soon as the circumstances justifying the arrest, detention or internment have ceased to exist'. Of course, if the detainees have committed criminal offences, they may be tried and subsequently held to serve their sentence. The mechanism for making the determination is, by reference to Article 75, the periodic review process for decisions on internment set forth in the Fourth Geneva Convention. The United States has set up just such a system.

Murphy concludes that '[w]ith respect to the Taliban detainees, the United States, its allies, and the government of Afghanistan should be permitted to continue the detentions so long as the individuals remain a threat' (p. 191), which may be until conclusion of the hostilities. As to the al Qaeda detainees, 'the United States must continue to engage in periodic reviews of the threat posed by each individual detainee' (p. 192). Factors to consider include the passage of time, age, health, psychological condition and relationship to al Qaeda.

Occupation

Part II of this volume turns to belligerent occupation, a subject of particular contemporary relevance. Following the occupations that occurred during and after the Second World War, the Israeli occupation of Egyptian, Jordanian and Syrian territory in the aftermath of the 1967 Six-Day War continued to draw attention to the topic. Those occupations were, and remain, unique in that certain of the territories remain occupied, the Golan Heights and parts of the Israeli capital of Jerusalem have been annexed, sections of the occupied territory are no longer claimed by the original state in possession, and Israel has unilaterally withdrawn from Gaza. Recent conflicts have also served to focus attention on occupation law issues. For instance, questions arose not only on whether all states maintaining forces in Iraq qualified as occupying powers, but also about the Security Council's authority to end an occupation as a matter of law when it appeared to be ongoing as a matter of fact.

Eyal Benvenisti, of Tel Aviv University, examines occupation law's lineage in 'The Origins of the Concept of Belligerent Occupation' (Chapter 6). The modern law of occupation can be traced back to the late nineteenth century. Benvenisti identifies two theoretical approaches underpinning its development. The first emphasizes the principle of humanity (the distinction between combatants and civilians). Maturing from the writings of Vattel, Grotius and others into the Rousseau–Portalis doctrine, this approach held that non-combatants should not be harmed unless involved in the conflict. It led to such occupation rules as the prohibition on taking private property.

National self-determination, a by-product of the French Revolution, serves as the basis for the second approach. According to this concept, a state's territory belongs to the citizenry and thus cannot be transferred by 'the prince'. This premise eventually resulted in replacement of the notion of transfer by conquest with that of temporary control through occupation, followed by return of sovereignty.

Drawing on these ideas, the law of occupation began to take shape. The Lieber Code, for instance, permitted occupation authorities to only make new law 'as far as military necessity requires' and to 'acknowledge and protect ... religion and morality; strictly private property; the persons of the inhabitants, especially those of women; and the sacredness of domestic relations'. The Code ignored the sovereignty issue, for it was intended for application in a civil war.

In Europe, the Franco-Prussian War focused attention on the issue, with Prussian demands for the annexation of Alsace and Lorraine evoking much debate. Articles 2 and 3 of the Brussels Declaration of 1874 delicately addressed the subject by providing that an occupier 'shall take all the measures in his power to restore and ensure, as far as possible, public order and safety' and 'shall maintain the laws which were in force in the country in time of peace, and shall not modify, suspend or replace them unless necessary'.

The issue of occupation was taken up again at the 1899 Hague Peace Conference, with discussions marked by a sharp division between would-be occupiers and those likely to be occupied. Ultimately, the 1907 Hague Regulations strengthened the Brussels Declaration's approach in favour of occupied states by providing, in Article 43, that the occupant 'shall take all steps in his power to re-establish and insure, as far as possible, public order and safety, while respecting, unless absolutely prevented, the laws in force in the country'. Thus, by the dawn of the twentieth century, occupation was understood as a temporary condition designed to maintain order and civil well-being pending a return of responsibility and authority to the occupied state.

Benvenisti notes that the Hague provisions 'represented a delicate balance that both provided for a civilian population brought under the control of an occupant and safeguarded the interests of the ousted government for the duration of the occupation' (p. 197). Of particular significance in the context of recent occupations is that occupation law traditionally sought to safeguard the interests of the ousted state pending conclusion of a peace treaty. This aim has been subjected to increasing pressure, for such interests are often exercised to the detriment of the population, as in the case of Saddam Hussein's Iraq. It clearly conflicts with contemporary notions of promoting governance and human rights.

In his two-part essay, 'Occupation under the Laws of War' (Chapters 7 and 8), Elbridge Colby, a US army officer and early twentieth-century law of war scholar, addresses the occupation of territory *flagrante bello*, as well as that which occurs after a cessation of hostilities, but before peace is concluded. Such situations amount to 'belligerent occupation' – 'conditions of war exist, ... the occupation is founded on force, [and] the laws are laws of war' (p. 227). Part I of the essay provides a valuable insight into perspectives on occupation pre-dating the Second World War and on the resulting Fourth Geneva Convention of 1949.

Colby emphasizes that the commencement of occupation is determined *de facto*, not *de jure*. According to Article 42 of the 1907 Hague Regulations, '[t]erritory is considered occupied when it is actually placed under the authority of the hostile army'. While mere raids into enemy territory do not suffice because there is no attempt to establish administration, the 'actual size and distribution of the occupying forces are immaterial' (p. 229). The issue is instead one of 'effectiveness', with the extent of occupation determined by an occupying force's 'effectiveness in permanently eliminating the authority of the original government and continuously maintaining the authority of the occupant' (ibid.). Since the test is factual, an occupation proclamation need not be issued.

In the same way in which an occupation commences upon the occasion of a particular factual situation, so it ends. If the occupation forces are expelled, the occupation ceases, although the simple fact of some degree of armed opposition to the occupant's forces does not suffice. But '[o]ccupation does cease definitely when a military reverse or a strategic withdrawal permits the original officials to return and institute again the functions and processes of their administration' (p. 231). It also ends with a peace treaty, whatever the fate of the occupied territory by operation of the treaty. In that regard, Colby distinguishes a peace treaty from an armistice, which, as that term was used at the time, signifies an agreed temporary cessation of hostilities pending conclusion of a final peace treaty. As it is also temporary in nature, a ceasefire would likewise fail to terminate an occupation, absent any provision for withdrawal of the forces maintaining the occupation.

Historically, territorial occupation was a form of 'conquest'. Since conquest transferred sovereignty, an occupant acquired title to the territory. Over time, 'occupation became more and more merely a means of war instead of an end of war. It was in purpose as well as fact belligerent, an act of war, without necessarily any prospects of permanence' (p. 233). Colby attributes this shift to the influence of Rousseau and Locke, as well as practices during the French Revolution. A technical legal debate ensued over whether sovereignty actually passed to the hands of the occupant, if only temporarily. Colby concludes that, whatever the answer, 'for the time being it is enemy territory, so far as the ousted nation is concerned' (p. 236).

The essay is replete with scepticism regarding limits placed on the occupant's actions. The 1907 Hague Regulations, for instance, require the occupant to respect the laws in force in the occupied country, 'unless absolutely prevented' (Article 43). But Colby suggests that this and other limitations of the Regulations 'can be avoided on a just plea of military necessity, of reprisals, or of superior orders and national policy' (p. 237). Labelling the Hague Convention and its annexed Regulations 'scant' and 'superficial', he concludes that:

> ... such things are left in vague and general terms – and therefore meaningless since they can be interpreted in various ways and always in view of that elastic doctrine of military necessity – to 'the principles of the laws of nations, the usages among civilized peoples, the laws of humanity, and the dictates of public conscience.' (p. 238)

These are fascinating comments in light of the fact that, decades later, the Nuremberg Tribunal and International Court of Justice would find the Hague Regulations reflective of customary international law. His comments are likewise interesting in view of the extensive refashioning of the Iraqi government following the 2003 conflict, which Adam Roberts has labelled, in his essay (Chapter 9), 'transformative occupation'.

In Part II of the essay, Colby examines the legal status of the population in occupied territory. He notes that, in light of the 'overthrow' of domestic authorities, '[e]veryone in the territory is subject to [the military commander's] rule, natives, his own nationals, and neutrals ...Whatever the theoretical legal status of the inhabitants may be, the fact is that they are controlled by the occupant' (pp. 245, 246). Thus, '[t]he inhabitants remain citizens of their original state; but they are like those who live in a foreign land and who, for a time and in certain limits, submit to another power' (p. 248).

Such control derives, according to Colby, not solely from the need to maintain law and order, but also from 'the necessity of maintaining the "firm occupation"' (p. 246). This perspective tracks with his characterization of belligerent occupation as a military operation. It further derives from his recognition that '[b]y tradition and training, the inhabitants must be expected to sympathize with the ousted government' and, therefore, they 'will only be prevented from ...overt acts [against the occupants] by threats of superior force, indeed, by threats of personal force' (p. 247).

The relationship between the inhabitants is another matter. It theoretically remains unchanged by occupation, either in fact or law. The Hague Regulations requirement for retention of the existing legal regime reflects this premise. But Colby argues that the authority behind the government, and of the judiciary in particular, is that of the occupying power. 'It is based upon the fact of military occupation and the necessity for a proper conduct of further military operations together with the necessity for some rule in the territory' (p. 257).

In light of the abuses committed by occupying authorities during the Second World War, the Fourth Geneva Convention scaled back this authority. For instance, Article 54 provides that '[t]he Occupying Power may not alter the status of public officials or judges in the occupied territories', while Article 64 requires the general retention of penal laws and the judiciary. So we see in Colby's essay a way-station in the law of occupation. He writes at a time (1925–26) when the sovereignty transfer premise was under challenge, but the general authority of the occupying authorities remained expansive despite purported limitations to the contrary in the Hague Regulations. In the post-Second World War period, the law evidenced a steady march towards limits on occupant authority.

Adam Roberts, of Oxford University and presently President of the British Academy of Art and Sciences, offers a post-Additional Protocols analysis of the subject in 'What is a Military Occupation?' (Chapter 9). Roberts notes that cases since the Second World War have raised difficult questions of law, such as the extent to which occupations that do not fit the mould envisaged in the Hague Regulations and the Fourth Geneva Conventions are subject to the rules set forth therein, the effect of a 'rejection' of the status by one of the parties to the conflict and whether there is but a single form of military occupation. Yet, he begins with sage advice, 'not to get into definitional and legalistic quibbling if one can avoid it' (p. 272). For Roberts, a 'fair rule of thumb' is that 'every time the armed forces of a country are in control of foreign territory, and find themselves face to face with the inhabitants, some or all of the provisions of the law on occupation are applicable' (ibid.).

As noted, the Hague Regulations set forth a simple factual test for occupation, the placing of territory under the authority of the hostile army. The assumption has traditionally been that this occurs during war and involves the occupant exercising authority through its armed forces. But events preceding and during the Second World War necessitated a more precise definition. For instance, the occupation of Czechoslovakia and Denmark met with little resistance, and the administration of the countries was largely exercised through indigenous governments. As a result of such departures, Common Article 2 of the Fourth Geneva Convention extended coverage to 'all cases of partial or total occupation of the territory of a High Contracting Party, even if the said occupation meets with no armed resistance'. With regard to the existence of a 'war' proper, according to the treaty it matters not whether war is declared or even recognized; so long as armed conflict (a factual determination) or occupation exist, the treaty applies. Additional Protocol I 'close[s] a tiny technical loophole' by referring to 'alien occupation'. This term is '"meant to cover cases in which a High Contracting Party occupies territories of a State which is not a HCP, or territories with a controversial international status"' as with the West Bank and Gaza (p. 276).[1]

Although occupation begins when the invading force 'actually exercises authority', Roberts highlights the prevailing view that 'the rules which apply to occupied territory should also be observed as far as possible in areas through which troops are passing and even on the battlefield' (p. 278). Occupation generally ends when the occupying forces depart, as was the case in 1955 with the withdrawal of Allied forces from Austria and the final withdrawal of Israeli forces from the Sinai in 1982. But, it may also cease if forces remain, as in the case of a treaty allowing for the presence of foreign forces. Examples include Japan, East Germany and West Germany. The termination of occupation can also be factual. For instance, the Soviet army in Hungary was labelled an army of occupation by the UN General Assembly in 1956 (in response to its suppression of the uprising), but over time the characterization was dropped despite the continued presence of Soviet troops. Finally, it may terminate upon the lawful transfer of sovereignty over the territory or because resistance to the occupation becomes so widespread that the invader loses the ability to control it.

Roberts proffers a typology of occupation, which, although meant to be 'neither exhaustive nor definitive' (p. 282), provides a useful tool for characterizing occupations and their consequences. There are three broad categories. Wartime and post-war occupations include belligerent occupation, occupation of neutral territory, occupation of allied territory, armistice occupation, post-surrender occupation, and occupation one year after military operations. Peacetime occupations include forcible peacetime occupation and peacetime occupation by consent. Occupations falling outside these categories include occupation of territory whose status is disputed or uncertain, occupation with an indigenous government in post, subsequent occupation, multilateral occupation, UN occupation, occupation of territory for which the UN is responsible, occupation by a non-state entity, illegal occupation and trustee occupation.

Certain situations are distinct from military occupation. For instance, a state may not occupy its own territory, as in a case of liberating enemy-occupied territory and creating a military government pending the return of the civil authorities. However, Roberts notes that elements of occupation law may apply, for instance, when the inhabitants resist the returning forces. Occupation law may also be relevant during a non-international armed conflict; he points to the example of the US Civil War. But, in general, he concludes that 'governments are not only reluctant to be viewed as maintaining an occupation in their own territory or in that with which they are constitutionally linked, but are also likely to reject the application of the law on occupation' (p. 319).

---

[1] Citing M. Bothe, K. Partsch and W. Solf, W., *New Rules for Victims of Armed Conflicts*, The Hague: Martinus Nijhoff, 1982, pp. 51–52.

Having surveyed the various genre of occupation, Roberts offers certain 'markers which may help to indicate the existence of an occupation, or may suggest the need for occupation law to be applied' (p. 322). They include:

> (i) there is a military force whose presence in the territory is not sanctioned or regulated by a valid agreement, or whose activities there involve an extensive range of contacts with the host society not adequately covered by the original agreement under which it intervened; (ii) the military force has either displaced the territory's ordinary system of public order and government, replacing it with its own command structure, or else has shown the clear physical ability to displace it; (iii) there is a difference of nationality and interest between the inhabitants on the one hand and the forces intervening and exercising power over them on the other, with the former not owing allegiance to the latter; (iv) within an overall framework of a breach of important parts of the national or international legal order, administration and the life of society have to continue on some legal basis, and there is a practical need for an emergency set of rules to reduce the dangers which can result from clashes between the military force and the inhabitants. (pp. 322–323)

Finally, with regard to the array of situations that might constitute an occupation, Roberts rejects the position that the law should bear only on classic belligerent occupations and argues that '[a] better approach … is to accept that the law on occupations is formally applicable to, and capable of being applied in, a wide variety of situations' (p. 326). The law's provisions are broad enough to be applied generally. Moreover, it is flexible, with its obligations and rights dependent on such factors as the security situation or on special arrangements between the occupants and the occupied. He concludes that:

> The condition of international society being what it is, the practical need for a body of law derived largely from the law of war, and providing … a yardstick for the activities of armed forces *vis-à-vis* the inhabitants of foreign territories, is likely to remain. (p. 327)

In light of this conclusion, Roberts' essay on transformative occupation, reproduced as the final chapter of this volume, is especially relevant.

The essays next turn to distinct aspects of occupation law. Lassa Oppenheim, the Whewell Professor at Cambridge University, deals with the central issue of occupation in 'The Legal Relations between an Occupying Power and the Inhabitants' (Chapter 10). He wrote the essay while the First World War was being fought. In an earlier essay he had rejected the premise that the inhabitants owe the occupant any duty of allegiance, although he notes that, at least at the time the essay was written, '[i]t cannot be said at all that the nature of these relations is everywhere clearly recognized and well defined' (p. 329). Oppenheim identifies three points on which commentators generally agreed:

> Firstly … through military occupation the authority over the territory and the inhabitants only *de facto*, and not by right, and only temporarily, and not permanently, passes into the hands of the occupant … Secondly … since the occupant is *de facto* in authority, he has a right of administration over the territory, with the consequence that all administrative acts which he carries out in accordance with the laws of war must be recognized by the legitimate government after occupation ceases. Thirdly … while the occupation lasts, the inhabitants have to render obedience to the occupying power. (pp. 329–30)

For Oppenheim, the 'kind' of power exercised by the occupant is 'mere military authority' (p. 330); occupation is but an element of military operations. The 1907 Hague Regulations significantly limit this authority by requiring occupants to ensure public order and safety, refrain from altering local laws unless prevented by military necessity, collect money (tax) only for military necessities or the requirements of local administration and so forth. Moreover, inclusion of the Martens Clause meant that acts not specifically addressed are not necessarily lawful.

As to the obligation of obedience, as distinct from allegiance, Oppenheim emphasizes that it cannot derive from domestic law because the territory was seized against the will of the state. To the extent that inhabitants are bound by domestic norms that remain in place, their obedience is a product of their relationship with their own government, even though enforced by the occupation authorities. Nor do the inhabitants owe obedience by virtue of international law, since that body of law governs only (at the time in question) the rights and obligations of states, not individuals. Oppenheim concludes that to the extent an obligation of obedience exists, it derives from:

> ... the martial law of the occupying power *ipso facto* imposed upon the inhabitants by the military occupation of the territory. They owe obedience to him because he holds them in the hollow of his hand; he will crush them if they are not obedient ... His authority is based, not on any law, but on his force; it rests on his bayonets, and on the good will, if any, of the inhabitants. No other law than the martial law of the occupant is at the background... (p. 334)

This can only be the case, for:

> States will never consent to a law-making international treaty proposing a rule by which they would be prevented from asking the inhabitants of such of their territory as may come under enemy occupation to rise in arms and drive the occupant out. (p. 335)

Richard Baxter, at the time a member of the US army's Judge Advocate General's Corp, deals with the same topic in his 1950 essay, 'The Duty of Obedience to the Belligerent Occupant' (Chapter 11). Baxter benefited from both the occupation experience during and after the Second World War and the recent adoption of the Fourth Geneva Convention. His is therefore a fascinating bookend to Oppenheim's essay.

Traditionally, inhabitants of occupied territory were understood as bearing an obligation of obedience to the occupant; violations of the duty were considered 'war treason' or 'war rebellion'. The 'ruthlessness and disregard for international law which have characterized the conduct of belligerent occupations during two world wars' (p. 337) merited reconsideration of the continued existence of such a duty. Although the Fourth Geneva Convention profited from these post-Hague Regulation experiences, Baxter notes that '[t]he fundamental question of the relationship existing between the inhabitant and the occupying Power remains for the most part a problem of the common law of war and is illuminated only fitfully by explicit provisions of the new Geneva Convention' (ibid.).

Prior to the development of occupation law, conquered territory became that of the occupying state. Accordingly, its occupants owed that state a duty of allegiance. With the 1907 Hague Regulations, this theory (and the related theory of temporary allegiance) had definitively died. Article 45 of the Regulations, which resembled similar provisions in the

1874 Brussels Declaration and the 1880 Oxford Manual, expressly prohibits compelling the population of an occupied territory to swear allegiance to the enemy occupant. Article 68 of the Fourth Geneva Convention obliquely acknowledges that nationals of occupied states owe no such duty of allegiance to the occupying power. Baxter dismisses any theory that municipal law imposes an obligation of this nature, although he does accept the possibility that 'it lies within the competence of a state to impose such a duty if it believes this course to be desirable' (p. 360).

War treason, a term first set forth in its contemporary sense in the Lieber Code, 'involves the commission of hostile acts, except armed resistance and possibly espionage, by persons other than members of the armed forces properly identified as such' (p. 346). The classic example involved Germany's prosecution of Nurse Edith Cavell, who facilitated the escape of British and French soldiers and Belgians of military age from occupied territory during the First World War. Although war treason did not occupy a prominent place in subsequent codification efforts, the notion was the subject of lively academic discussion and found its way into military manuals; it typically extended beyond occupied territory into any area where the civilian population was collocated with enemy military forces.

Baxter suggests that during the Second World War 'occupation practices often so far exceeded the bounds of legally permissible conduct' (p. 353) that it is difficult to draw any conclusions from them. Generally, though, none of the belligerents made much use of the concept. Instead, they simply promulgated proclamations and decrees describing the conduct expected of the occupied population.

War rebellion is a concept that also first found modern expression in the Lieber Code. It is distinguished from war treason in the sense that, unlike the latter, it is not individual in character. Rather, it refers to 'uprisings in arms by groups of persons' (p. 355). The line between it and a *levée en masse*, which involves an uprising of the population to meet an invader, is ill-defined, although the latter occurs in the face of prospective occupation, rather than during occupation itself.

Baxter, drawing on the experiences of the war just concluded, posits that the prospect of war rebellions has diminished. In modern warfare, the occupant is much more likely to face guerrilla warfare, sabotage and individual attacks than a general uprising. As a result, he suggests that 'the conventional concept of war rebellion has, like war treason, passed into desuetude both in the practice of belligerents and in the substantive law applied by war crimes tribunals' (p. 357). This position is supported by the extension of prisoner-of-war status to members of qualifying resistance movements.

He concludes that the concepts of an international law duty to obey the occupant, war treason and war rebellion 'serve neither the interests of the occupying Powers nor of the occupied population' (p. 368). The law therefore can be restated as follows:

> 1. Subject to the general limitation of reasonableness and the specific limitations imposed by the Hague Regulations and the [Fourth] Geneva Convention … international law permits a belligerent occupant to prohibit and punish, but does not itself prohibit, conduct by the inhabitants of occupied areas which is hostile to him or which is inconsistent with the security of his forces or administration.
>
> 2. In conformity with the Geneva Civilians Convention, the occupant must announce in advance those acts which he will penalize. The occupying Power must be recognized to have a wide range of legislative competence to forbid acts which may reasonably be considered to imperil his safety.

> 3. Like the spy, the individual who commits hostile acts or acts inconsistent with the security of the occupant may not be penalized for such acts after he has joined or rejoined the armed forces of his own state. (p. 368)

The other side of the coin is that occupiers shoulder obligations for the benefit of the population. In 'Legislation and Maintenance of Public Order and Civil Life by Occupying Powers' (Chapter 12), Marco Sassòli, of the University of Geneva, examines Article 43 of the 1907 Hague Regulations. It provides:

> The authority of the legitimate power having in fact passed into the hands of the occupant, the latter shall take all the measures in his power to restore, and ensure, as far as possible, public order and safety, while respecting, unless absolutely prevented, the laws in force in the country.

The Nuremberg Tribunal and the International Court of Justice have specifically recognized the provision as customary. This essay employs the occupation of Iraq as its foil.

Sassòli interprets the phrase 'public order and safety' broadly as referring to civil life, which encompasses not only security, but also 'social functions, ordinary transactions which constitute daily life' (p. 372). The requirement of maintenance does not impose an obligation of achieving particular results, but rather merely requires using all means at an occupant's disposal to achieve them. He suggests that '[p]ublic order is restored through police operations, which are governed by domestic law and international human rights law, and not through military operations governed by IHL on the conduct of hostilities' (p. 373). By way of example:

> [A] response by US forces to an RPG attack upon one of their convoys in the midst of Baghdad may … be considered to be covered by the law on the conduct of hostilities, while their firing upon a car failing to stop at a checkpoint is covered by human rights law applicable to police operations. (pp. 373–4)

Sassòli argues in this regard that:

> Although both the US and Israel deny it, UN practice and judicial decisions clearly indicate that international human rights law binds an occupying power with respect to the population of an occupied territory. (p. 374)

This is, of course, a less than settled issue. Assessing Coalition conduct during the early days of the occupation, when looting was widespread, he concludes that Article 43 was violated. He also opines that excessive force was used during policing activities.

Article 43 prohibits an occupying power from either 'extending its own legislation over the occupied territory' or 'acting as a sovereign legislator' (p. 376). Examining the relationship between Article 43 and relevant provisions found in the Fourth Geneva Convention, Sassòli notes, *inter alia*, that an occupant, albeit limited in its legislative authority, may change existing laws in order to meet its occupation responsibilities, as in cases where the pre-existing law would serve improper ends or interfere with orderly government. Similarly, an occupant may not alter institutions of government, for they are based in the law of the occupied state. That said, institution may be changed '"where a political system constitutes a permanent threat to the maintenance and safety of the military forces of the occupant so that there is an 'absolute necessity' to abolish it"' (p. 379).[2] De-Nazification of Germany following the Second World War epitomizes this caveat. Sassòli also contends that the provisions regarding institutional change are humanitarian in nature and, therefore, changes made in the spirit of humanitarianism are acceptable. For example:

> That the Coalition established an Interim Governing Council in Iraq, laid ground for a federalist constitutional system, abolished the Ba'ath Party and its system of government and tried to introduce a free-market economy, was … not as such a violation of IHL …. (p. 381)

Taking an in-depth look at Article 43, its legislative history and other relevant treaty law, Sassòli offers certain conclusions regarding the scope of the prohibition on an occupant legislating. The occupant is only empowered to legislate for the period of occupation and thus any change 'should be commensurate with the transitional and temporary nature of the occupation' (p. 381). Military necessity (especially ensuring the security of occupation forces) and the well-being of the civilian population, as well as the need for law essential for the implementation of international humanitarian law, justify legislation by the occupant. Laws that are contrary to international human rights law can be set aside, and arguably laws may be passed to safeguard human rights, as was done in Iraq to prohibit child labour.

Sassòli takes a liberal view of the authority to legislate to maintain civil life. Thus, he finds acceptable regulations which, for instance, fix prices or secure the equitable distribution of food and other commodities, call up members of the population for police duties designed to maintain order or for firefighting and, as in the case of Iraq, stabilize currency. On the other hand, he highlights the risk of abuse of such authority in order to refashion economic and social life, especially in long-term occupations. In this regard, he claims the Coalition went too far in simplifying public contracts and liberalizing trade and foreign investment. Finally, an occupant may legislate when authorized by the UN Security Council, although Sassòli asserts that this right was exceeded in the case of Iraq.

The essay also contains both a useful discussion of the end of occupation, especially with regard to Iraq, and an extremely rich discussion of occupation in the context of peace operations. Sassòli concludes with a cautionary note that occupants which are 'either less active in restoring and maintaining public order and civil life or go further in terms of legislation, encounter serious problems among the population concerned or the international community' (p. 401).

The volume concludes with an examination of three particularly unique occupations. The first, the Allied occupation of Germany, is considered by Robert Jennings of Cambridge University and former President of the International Court of Justice in his 1946 essay, 'Government in Commission' (Chapter 13).

Following Germany's unconditional surrender, the country was divided into four zones of occupation controlled by the United States, the United Kingdom, the Soviet Union and France; each was placed under the authority of a commander-in-chief designated by the respective

[2] Citing E.H. Schwenk, 'Legislative Power of the Military Occupant Under Article 43, Hague Regulations', *Yale Law Journal*, **54** (1944–45), pp. 393–413, at p. 403.

occupant. Berlin was also divided into zones, but governed by an Inter-Allied Governing Authority. The occupiers established a Control Council, operating under the principle of unanimity, for the governance of the whole of Germany. This arrangement proved somewhat unwieldy, involving, as it did, two distinct sources of authority – the zone commander for issues regarding his area and the Control Council for matters affecting the entirety of Germany.

The four Powers issued a formal statement announcing that the measures were temporary, meant to operate only while Germany was carrying out the basic requirements of its unconditional surrender. As de-Nazification proceeded, they increasingly involved Germans in administration of the zones. However, the Germans were 'in every way completely under the authority of the Zone Commanders-in-Chief and the Control Commission' (p. 410).

The Allies claimed, by virtue of the unconditional surrender, '"supreme authority with respect to Germany, including all the powers possessed by the German Government, the High Command, and any State, municipal, or local government authority"' (p. 411).[3] This raised the question of whether Germany continued to exist as a state in international law. Jennings asserts that it did, for 'supreme authority' could not be equated to 'full sovereignty' (p. 412). Supreme authority is assumed for particular purposes, it is provisional, and the Allies made no claim of annexation; in other words, it falls short of authority incident to sovereignty. In coming to this conclusion, Jennings acknowledges that 'draw[ing] a distinction between government and state and assum[ing] plenary powers of government unaccompanied by annexation of the state is admittedly unprecedented' (p. 413). But in Jennings's view, because Germany was a state with 'a long history of independence' (p. 414), a presumption of its continued existence attached – one that could not be rebutted in international law by a temporary assumption of all governmental power.

He adds that, since neither a peace treaty had been concluded nor had there been a cessation of the *animus belligerandi*, a state of war continued to exist between Germany and the Allies; after all, war in the technical sense is a conflict between states, not governments. This situation permitted the Allies to treat Germany as an enemy state and to conduct Germany's foreign relations 'in accordance with the Allies' own state of belligerency' (p. 415). Jennings notes that:

> The prolongation of the state of war after the assumption of supreme authority over the whole territory of the enemy is indeed to claim the best of both worlds; the conqueror enjoys the rights conferred by his conquest yet stops short of permitting his conquest to resolve the state of war. (p. 415)

In that Germany continued to exist as a state, 'it follows that Germany remains a subject of international law capable of relations with third states, and continuing to bear rights and duties *vis-à-vis* third states' (pp. 416–17). Despite this juridical reality, the Allies conducted foreign relations on its behalf. Any liabilities incurred and rights acquired by the Allies on behalf of Germany during this period 'inhere in the German state and not in the Allied states' (p. 418). Yet, the Allies bear some state responsibility for their actions in governing Germany, thereby raising the 'nice question whether a third state's right of redress lies against the state of Germany or against one or all of the Allied states' (p. 418).

As to existing treaty relations and obligations, the occupants declared that '"[t]he Allied Representatives will give directions concerning the abrogation, bringing into force, revival

3 Citing *The Times*, 4 April 1946.

or application of any treaty, convention or other international agreements … to which Germany is or has been a party"' (p. 418).[4] In a typical occupation, such matters would be the responsibility, to the extent possible in the circumstances, of the occupied state's government. Where, as in this case, the occupant assumes all governmental authority, Jennings suggests that 'as regards third states, there would seem to be no valid reason why the occupying Powers should assume all the rights of government without incurring the corresponding liabilities' (p. 419), In particular, 'there should be no room for doubt that treaties which secure rights of third states against German property or territory will be binding on the Allied Representatives on the ordinary principles of *res transit cum suo onere*' (ibid.).

Jennings's approach to judicial reform is quite liberal. Again, it is the assumption of all governmental authority that is, for him, the deciding factor. The Hague Regulations had provided that the laws in force should be respected unless absolutely prevented by the circumstances. Jennings accepts that the law in force in Germany remains the German municipal law, but then asserts that 'the Control Council, being the Government of Germany, is fully competent to change or modify this law in any way' (p. 423). He also makes a point that would later resonate during the occupation of Iraq. Noting that much of the pre-existing German municipal law 'was a denial of the most elementary principles of natural law and justice', he contends that the Allied government of Germany 'is not merely competent to modify those laws but is under a plain duty to do so' (ibid.).

In much the same way as the occupation of Germany departed from traditional understandings of occupation, so too do does the Israeli experience in the occupied territories. In 'Prolonged Military Occupation' (Chapter 14), Adam Roberts examines this situation, which by the time he wrote this essay had gone on for more than two decades. It continues today. Roberts asks whether the fact that an occupation is prolonged alters the legal regime governing it and concludes that to the extent there are departures from the accepted legal norms, the occupant bears the burden of demonstrating that the commitments in question do not apply.

The essay begins with a survey of the law of occupation, the key aspects of which need not be repeated. What is critical to the issue of prolonged occupation, though, is that the law views occupation as provisional, ending either through expulsion of the occupying forces or with termination of the conflict and accompanying change of status through negotiation. Despite this, the post-Second World War period witnessed numerous prolonged occupations, such as the Allied occupations of Germany and Japan, South Africa's occupation of Namibia and the Turkish occupation of Northern Cyprus. None of the treaties bearing on occupation contains any limit on the duration of an occupation, although the Fourth Geneva Convention does provide that certain of its provisions cease to apply after one year of occupation. Roberts notes that the latter provision has not proven significant, especially since it was essentially abrogated in Additional Protocol I for states party to the instrument.

The Israeli case is highly complex. Following the 1967 war, Israel found itself occupying the West Bank, the Gaza Strip, East Jerusalem, the Golan Heights and the Sinai Peninsula. East Jerusalem and part of the Golan Heights were later brought under Israeli law, although they are still seen as occupied by some members of the international community. The Sinai and a section of the Golan Heights were returned to Egypt and Syria after an extended occupation of the areas. Since Roberts wrote the essay, all Israeli forces have withdrawn from

[4] Citing Control Council Proclamation No. 2 of 20 September 1945.

Gaza; nevertheless, many experts argue that it remains occupied. The Palestinian Authority exercises considerable authority in the still-occupied West Bank.

Over time, the views of states, international organizations, non-governmental organizations and groups within the occupied territories, especially Palestinian groups, have evolved. The Israeli Supreme Court has proven especially active in dealing with cases involving the rights and duties of both Israel and the inhabitants of the occupied territories, and the International Court of Justice has likewise considered the situation in the context of the security fence built by Israel. Despite this complicated history, the conclusions drawn by Roberts as to prolonged occupation remain relevant.

He is pessimistic about the prospect of securing international agreement on a treaty to address the unique circumstance of prolonged occupation. In light of this difficulty, international organizations should, according to Roberts, play a central role during long-term occupations:

> They can remind all concerned of their obligations under international law; indicate which policies, or international legal provisions, remain not merely applicable but in urgent need of being applied; interpret legal provisions in light of new circumstances; suggest appropriate action where there is a conflict between legal principles or provisions; engage in fact-finding or arbitration in respect of particular issues; and provide peacekeeping or observer forces to facilitate total or partial withdrawals by the occupant. (p. 485)

This role is all the more essential because there are multiple challenges to the application of classic occupation law during prolonged occupations. For instance, international bodies have taken the position that during a prolonged occupation, 'especially if it extends into something approximating peacetime, an occupant cannot exercise the draconian powers that may be permissible in a shorter occupation' since 'the interests and wishes of the inhabitants must be accorded greater weight' (p. 485). The role of foreign states in assisting a resistance movement is equally an issue that has proven especially difficult to resolve in cases of prolonged occupation.

The relevant treaties appear to be based on the premise that the previous status of the territory as part of a particular state is clear, which is not the case with the Israeli-occupied territories. They also fail to deal adequately with issues peculiar to prolonged occupations, such as long-term economic development and the treatment of resistance movements. Such shortcomings are not a basis for discarding the law. Instead, they augur for flexible interpretation sensitive to its underlying purposes. And, of course, human rights law enjoys greater play during a prolonged occupation.

With respect to the Israeli-occupied territories, Roberts notes that both sides have reason to be dissatisfied with occupation law's classic framework. The 'Israelis could argue that the law on occupation has provided a safety net, enabling the Palestinians to escape the consequences of their leaders' folly, or that of some Arab governments, in not negotiating seriously about the future of the territories' (pp. 486–87), while '[a] concern widely shared by Palestinians is that the law on occupation has afforded Israel a cloak of legitimacy' (p. 487). Despite these concerns, the Hague Regulations and the Fourth Geneva Convention undeniably remain of consequence, for they address a range of issues, such as the treatment of detainees and the legality of settlements and deportations, that continue to characterize occupations extending over years. And Israel has shown that it can be innovative in applying the law. It has banned capital punishment, 'which shows that the duty in Article 43 of the Hague Regulations to respect "unless absolutely prevented, the laws in force in the country" need not be a bar to progressive legislation' (p. 488). Similarly, the right of the occupied population to petition the Supreme Court with respect to acts of the occupying forces is a positive measure not envisioned in the classic treaty law.

Roberts is modest in his expectations. He sagely concludes that 'the law on occupation cannot conceivably eliminate the fundamental conflict between the Israeli occupants and the Palestinian inhabitants', but it can 'mitigate some of the worst effects of that conflict, ... remind all concerned of the provisional status of the occupation and deter further drastic steps that would militate against an eventual settlement' (p. 492).

The final essay in this volume, also by Adam Roberts, asks when it is legitimate for an occupying power, in the name of creating the conditions for a more democratic and peaceful state, to introduce fundamental changes in the constitutional, social, economic, and legal order within an occupied territory._ To an extent, this was a question posed by Oppenheim. In 'Transformative Military Occupation' (Chapter 15), Roberts addresses the issue head-on in the context of the dramatic transformation of Iraq during the Coalition occupation that began in 2003.

The issue arises because 'of the cautious, even restrictive assumption in the laws of war ... that occupying powers should respect the existing laws and economic arrangements within the occupied territory, and should, therefore, by implication, make as few changes as possible' (p. 493). It is a 'conservationist principle' that 'stands in potential conflict with the transformative goals of certain occupations' (ibid.). Roberts asserts that this conflict can be mitigated through application of human rights law, 'which offers principles and procedures that can help to define the means and ends of an occupation' and through the involvement of international organizations, particularly the United Nations, that can 'assist in setting or legitimizing certain transformative policies' (ibid.). He tempers these assertions by cautioning that transformation is not an end in itself, for '[o]nly in exceptional circumstances are occupations likely to bring about a successful democratic transition in a society' (ibid.). Moreover, the fact that transformative policies may be pursued in the framework of the *jus in bello* cannot lead to the conclusion that there is, under the *jus ad bellum*, a 'general right to invade other sovereign states with the stated purpose of reforming their political systems in a democratic direction' (p. 494). Therefore, '[t]he question of whether an occupant is entitled to transformative goals is in principle distinct from the question of the original reason for the intervention' (ibid.).

An occupant's authority derives from its factual control over the territory, not from an express legal right. Occupation law recognizes the notion of *de facto* control as a basis for governing the state to the necessary and proper extent. 'Transformation, which necessarily involves handing over power to authorities that come from within the territory, threatens 'the underlying assumption that the occupying power maintains a structure of authority and responsibility within the territory' (p. 498). But Roberts notes that, '[a]lthough many of the wide variety of governmental arrangements imposed by occupying powers undoubtedly differ from what is envisaged in the Hague Regulations and the Fourth Geneva Convention, states have been reluctant to conclude that in every case such practices are unlawful' (p. 499), especially when the aim is the introduction of constitutional democracy.

Also central to traditional occupation law is the Hague Regulations requirement to respect the laws in force unless absolutely prevented from doing so. Practice has illustrated that this is not always possible, as in the case of law imposed by 'dictatorial or extremist' regimes (p.

500). Accordingly, the Fourth Geneva Convention slightly relaxed the law, such that changes necessary for the security of the occupant, to fulfilment by the occupant of its occupation duties or to the maintenance of orderly government were explicitly permitted. Transformative occupations provide further pressure for liberalizing this norm, and Roberts suggests that, if the Convention were written today, it would include scope for changes to realize fundamental human rights or the implementation of transformative purposes that have been approved by the UN Security Council.

Although occupations were historically subject only to international humanitarian law, today human rights law is of growing relevance. Roberts describes a clear trend towards increasing applicability of this body of law during occupations, one that steps beyond 'a simple confrontation between the *lex generalis* of human rights law and the *lex specialis* of the laws of war' (p. 507). Certain important matters during long-term occupations, such as employment or educational discrimination, are dealt with in depth only in human rights law. Similarly, human rights law sets forth for individual complaints or redress that are absent in the law of occupation. Thus, 'international human rights standards may not merely fill in gaps in the laws of war, but also provide procedures for assisting in the implementation of key provisions of those laws' (p. 507). Today, '[t]he general principle that human rights law can apply to military occupations is ... widely, but by no means universally, accepted' (p. 508). In this regard, Roberts draws attention to the actions of UN bodies, the International Court of Justice's *Wall* Advisory Opinion and domestic court decisions taking this approach.

In Iraq, transformation was an unambiguous goal of the occupation. This purpose was especially explicit in work of the Coalition Provisional Authority. In addition, the Security Council, while calling on the occupants to comply with the relevant international law, adopted a number of resolutions with clear transformative intent. For example, Resolution 1483 instructed the UN Special Representative to cooperate in efforts to 'restore and establish national and local institutions for representative government', promote human rights and foster 'international efforts to promote legal and judicial reform'.

Roberts observes that during the occupation, 'the inevitable legal interplay between the contending imperatives of conservation and reform played out mainly in favor of drastic change' (p. 527). While some of the changes, such as introduction of a new currency, were useful and well received, others proved controversial. In particular, de-Ba'athification, the dissolution of numerous governmental entities and the decision to allow foreign investors to own Iraqi companies without reinvesting profits created negative unintended effects. These and other changes fuelled the insurgency, for '[a]ny attempt at a major restructuring of society was likely to provoke opposition, especially when a large segment of that society – in this case the Sunni Muslim population – saw reforms as threatening a long-established pattern of political and economic dominance' (p. 528). On the positive side, significant political reform was achieved in a short period.

In June 2004 the occupation ended not by traditional means, but rather as a result of Security Council Resolution 1546. Despite the continued presence of the Multi-National Force MNF), the 'new situation ... was not just an occupation by another name' (p. 530). In particular, the new Iraqi government enjoyed the right to demand the withdrawal of foreign troops. Yet, remnants of occupation-type norms remained. As an example, the Resolution's preamble noted the commitment of all forces 'promoting the maintenance of security and stability in Iraq to act in accordance with international law' and cautioned that, while the interim government assumed full responsibility and authority, it should refrain 'from taking any actions affecting Iraq's destiny beyond the limited interim period'.

It is incontrovertible that '[t]he idea of military intervention with a transformative purpose stands in tension with the existing system of international law as it applies to states' (p. 532). Nevertheless, Roberts concludes that 'experience suggests that even overtly transformative occupants would be wise to recognize the strength and continuing validity of the law on occupations in general, and the conservationist principle in particular' (p. 533). Indeed:

> Numerous errors in the occupation of Iraq arose from the failure to recognize that the laws of war can play a valuable role in focusing attention on certain perennial problems of armed conflicts and occupations – such as looting and the management of economic life – and do so in a sensible and constructive way. (p. 533)

MICHAEL N. SCHMITT

Part I
Detention

[1]

The Declining Significance of POW Status

Derek Jinks*

What is the significance of prisoner-of-war (POW) status?[1] Drawing on the substance, universal acceptance, broad-based institutionalization, and enforce-

---

* Visiting Professor of Law, University of Chicago Law School; Associate Professor of Law Designate, Arizona State University College of Law. M.Phil., Yale University, 1999; J.D., Yale Law School, 1998; M.A., Yale University, 1998; B.A., University of Texas at Austin, 1991. Thanks to Adam Cox, Jack Goldsmith, Ryan Goodman, Bernard Harcourt, Howard Levie, Martha Nussbaum, Eric Posner, Kal Raustiala, David Sloss, Cass Sunstein, Adrian Vermeule, and John Yoo for helpful comments. The project also benefited from the comments of participants in the faculty seminar at Arizona State College of Law, the faculty workshop at Saint Louis University School of Law, and the faculty workshop at the University of Chicago Law School.

1. The four 1949 Geneva Conventions, by their terms, protect specific categories of persons. Each Convention defines, in some detail, the categories of persons protected by its substantive terms. *See* GENEVA CONVENTION FOR THE AMELIORATION OF THE CONDITION OF THE WOUNDED AND SICK IN ARMED FORCES IN THE FIELD, Aug. 12, 1949, 6 U.S.T. 3114, 75 U.N.T.S. 31 [hereinafter GENEVA CONVENTION I]; GENEVA CONVENTION FOR THE AMELIORATION OF THE CONDITION OF WOUNDED, SICK AND SHIPWRECKED MEMBERS OF ARMED FORCES AT SEA, Aug. 12, 1949, 6 U.S.T. 3217, 75 U.N.T.S. 85 [hereinafter GENEVA CONVENTION II]; GENEVA CONVENTION RELATIVE TO THE TREATMENT OF PRISONERS OF WAR, Aug. 12, 1949, 6 U.S.T. 3316, 75 U.N.T.S. 135 [hereinafter POW CONVENTION] (the third of the Geneva Conventions); GENEVA CONVENTION RELATIVE TO THE PROTECTION OF CIVILIAN PERSONS IN TIME OF WAR, Aug. 12, 1949, 6 U.S.T. 3516, 75 U.N.T.S. 287 [hereinafter CIVILIANS CONVENTION] (the fourth of the Geneva Conventions). These definitions of "protected persons" are dense and are riddled with ambiguities and obscure terms of art. *See, e.g.*, Neil McDonald & Scott Sullivan, *Rational Interpretation in Irrational Times: The Third Geneva Convention and the "War on Terror,"* 44 HARV. INT'L L.J. 301 (2003) (noting the interpretive difficulties occasioned by Article 4 of the POW Convention). The text of these provisions, coupled with the duration and intensity of the drafting debates on them at the Diplomatic Conference, strongly support two conclusions: (1) the Conventions writ large do not have broad, general applicability—the categories of protected persons are discrete; and (2) states could not agree, with great precision, on how best to delimit these categories. As a consequence, states retained substantial interpretive wiggle room on a question made central in the protective schemes of the Conventions—the question of who is protected. The POW Convention and the interpretive controversies arising out of the war on terrorism exemplify these difficulties. Article 4(A) of the POW Convention, in relevant part, defines "prisoners of war" as follows:

> Prisoners of war, in the sense of the present Convention, are persons belonging to one of the following categories, who have fallen into the power of the enemy:
>
> 1. Members of the armed forces of a Party to the conflict as well as members of militias or volunteer corps forming part of such armed forces.
>
> 2. Members of other militias and members of other volunteer corps, including those of organized resistance movements, belonging to a Party to the conflict and operating in or outside their own territory, even if this territory is occupied, provided that such militias or volunteer corps, including such organized resistance movements, fulfill the following conditions:
>
> (a) That of being commanded by a person responsible for his subordinates;
>
> (b) That of having a fixed distinctive sign recognizable at a distance;
>
> (c) That of carrying arms openly;
>
> (d) That of conducting their operations in accordance with the laws and customs of war.
>
> 3. Members of regular armed forces who profess allegiance to a government or an authority not recognized by the Detaining Power.

ment machinery of the Geneva Convention for the Protection of Prisoners of War ("POW Convention"), conventional wisdom maintains that denial of POW status to combatants has drastic protective and policy consequences. Contrary to this conventional wisdom, this Article argues that denial of POW status carries few protective or policy consequences, and that the gap in protection for those classified as POWs and those not so classified (e.g., those designated "unlawful combatants") is closing. The only gaps that persist are: (1) that POWs are "assimilated" into the legal regime governing the armed forces of the detaining state; and (2) that POWs enjoy "combatant immunity." The scope and significance of these gaps are, however, also diminishing—from both a protection and policy perspective. The Article further argues that this emerging "protective parity" has important implications for humanitarian law and policy: (1) it clarifies and consolidates debates about coverage gaps in the Geneva law; (2) it recasts debates about the proper procedure for determining "status" in humanitarian law (procedurally, POW status might be understood only as an affirmative defense to any prosecution for simple participation in hostilities); and (3) it underscores the escalating inefficiencies of approaches that calibrate treatment based on complex status determinations (and, in doing so, provides an explanation of why some states—including the United States—expressly incorporate elements of "protective parity" into their military policy). Finally, the Article offers a normative defense of "protective parity"—emphasizing whether it can be reconciled with the principle of distinction.[2]

Conventional wisdom maintains that denial of POW status to captured combatants has drastic consequences for the scope of applicable humanitarian protections. Indeed, the prevailing view is that denying captured enemy combatants POW status places them "at the mercy of the detaining power."[3] The ground-breaking Lieber Code of 1863, issued by President Abraham Lincoln as General Order 100 governing the conduct of U.S. forces in the Civil War, provided that persons engaged in hostilities without satisfying the requirements for POW status could be captured and summarily shot.[4] The

---

POW Convention, art. 4(A), §§ 1–3.

2. *See infra* Part V.

3. Capt. Michael W. Brough, *The POW in a Time of Terrorism: An Investigation into Moral Status*, *in* JSCOPE 2003: Joint Services Conference on Professional Ethics (2003), *available at* http://www.usafa.af.mil/jscope/JSCOPE03/Brough03.html (last visited Apr. 23, 2004). *See also* Maj. Richard R. Baxter, *So-Called 'Unprivileged Belligerency': Spies, Guerrillas, and Saboteurs*, 28 Brit. Y.B. Int'l L. 323, 328 (1951). Baxter concluded:

> The correct legal formulation is, it is submitted, that armed and unarmed hostilities, wherever occurring, committed by persons other than those entitled to be treated as prisoners of war or peaceful civilians merely deprive such individuals of a protection they might otherwise enjoy under international law and place them virtually at the power of the enemy . . . . International law deliberately neglects to protect unprivileged belligerents because of the danger their acts present to their opponent . . . . [Privileged belligerents] have a protected status upon capture, whilst other belligerents not so identified *do not benefit from any comprehensive scheme of protection*.

Id. at 343 (emphasis added).

4. U.S. Dep't of War, Instructions for the Government of the Armies of the United States in the Field

Hague Regulations of 1907 provided that the rights and obligations of war applied only to persons satisfying the criteria for POW status.[5] Although no U.S. court has had occasion to address the question directly, some courts have suggested that the government may treat "unlawful combatants" summarily.[6] Many foreign courts have expressly supported this view.[7] Similar views are espoused by many commentaries,[8] including several important treatises on the laws of war.[9] In short, it is generally believed that the denial of POW

---

by Order of the Secretary of War, General Orders No. 100, art. LVII (1863).

5. HAGUE CONVENTION NO. IV RESPECTING THE LAWS AND CUSTOMS OF WAR ON LAND, Oct. 18, 1907, 36 Stat. 2277, 1 Bevans 631 [hereinafter HAGUE CONVENTION] (Hague Regulations are annexed to the Convention).

6. *See, e.g.*, *Ex parte* Quirin, 317 U.S. 1, 34 (1942).

7. *See, e.g.*, Mohamed Ali and Another v. Public Prosecutor, 42 I.L.R. 458 (Malay., Judicial Comm. of the Privy Council, 1968) (ruling that accused saboteurs were not entitled to protection under laws of war, including fair trial rights, because they were not entitled to POW status); Military Prosecutor v. Omar Mahmud Kassem and Others, 42 I.L.R. 470 (Israeli Military Ct. at Ramallah, 1969) (holding the same for a group of guerrilla fighters).

8. *See, e.g.*, Brough, *supra* note 3 ("Captured combatants who are not POWs are devoid of [Geneva Convention] protection, and they are at the mercy of the Detaining Power. The Detaining Power may agree to treat the captives as if they were POWs (as President Bush declared he would do for Afghan detainees), but they are not bound by international agreement to do so . . . ."); McKeogh has written that

> The formal approach to combatancy of the Hague Regulations yielded a clear delineation of the categories of combatant and civilian. However, this clear delineation also meant that there was a gap between the two lawful categories of combatant and civilian. There was a third category of person in war: the unlawful combatant. Those who did not abide by the rules set out in the [Hague Regulations defining lawful combatants] were unlawful combatants and were accorded *no protection*.

COLM MCKEOGH, INNOCENT CIVILIANS: THE MORALITY OF KILLING IN WAR 137 (2002) (emphasis added); *see also* INGRID DETTER, THE LAW OF WAR 148 (2d ed. 2000) ("Unlawful combatants . . . though they are a legitimate target for any belligerent action, are not, if captured, entitled to any prisoner of war status . . . . They are often summarily tried and enjoy no protection under international law."); Draper has written that:

> Civilians participating in combat ceased to be immune from attack. They might be killed in combat, and, on capture, were liable to be treated as marauders and executed summarily at the discretion of the captor commander . . . . [T]heir very participation, however conducted, was in itself a violation of the law of war, or, alternatively, conduct that put them outside its protection and left them at the mercy of the enemy.

G.I.A.D. Draper, *The Status of Combatants and the Question of Guerrilla Warfare*, *in* REFLECTIONS ON LAW AND ARMED CONFLICTS 206, 208 (Michael A. Meyer & Hilaire McCoubrey eds., 1998); Richard R. Baxter, *The Duties of Combatants and the Conduct of Hostilities (Law of the Hague)*, *in* INTERNATIONAL DIMENSIONS OF HUMANITARIAN LAW 93, 106 (Henry Dunant Institute, UNESCO ed., 1988) (arguing that unlawful combatants "upon capture were not entitled to be treated either as prisoners of war or as peaceful civilians"; and that they "fell outside the protected categories . . . .").

9. *See, e.g.*, GEORG SCHWARZENBERGER, II INTERNATIONAL LAW AS APPLIED BY INTERNATIONAL COURTS AND TRIBUNALS: THE LAW OF ARMED CONFLICT 115–17 (1968) (arguing that unprivileged belligerents are in the same position as "spies," and as such, are entitled only to the "minimum requirements imposed by the standard of civilization"—which, he suggests, includes the right to "a [standardless] trial"); JULIUS STONE, LEGAL CONTROLS OF INTERNATIONAL ARMED CONFLICT 549 (1954) (maintaining that the distinction between unprivileged and privileged combatants "draws the line between those personnel who, on capture, are entitled under international law to certain minimal treatment as prisoners of war, and those not entitled to such protection. 'Non-combatants' who engage in hostilities are one of the classes deprived of such protection . . . . Such unprivileged belligerents, though not *condemned* by international law, are not protected by it, but are left to the discretion of the belligerent threatened by their activities."); 2 L. OPPENHEIM, INTERNATIONAL LAW: A TREATISE 257 (H. Lauterpacht ed., 1952) (1905) (arguing that unlawful combatants are "liable to be treated as war criminals and shot."); J. M. SPAIGHT, WAR RIGHTS ON LAND 37 (1911) ("[W]ar law has a short shrift for the non-combatant who

status carries drastic protective consequences for captured combatants—some suggesting that denial of this status leaves captured combatants *unprotected* by the law of war.[10]

The controversy concerning the legal status of captured Taliban and Al Qaeda fighters reflects this conventional wisdom. The United States has expressly advanced the conventional view in this context, and has determined that these detainees do not qualify for POW status. This view deprives them of protection under humanitarian law. Of course, the U.S. position has been sharply criticized by allied governments, inter-governmental organizations, prominent human rights and humanitarian law organizations, and foreign courts.[11] This criticism, however, centers on the merits of the U.S. POW status determination and the procedures used to make that determination.[12] In classifying the detainees as unlawful combatants, the United States, it seems, asserts the right to treat the detainees in any way it deems appropriate—unencumbered by international legal obligation. For example, Secretary of Defense

violates its principles by taking up arms."); *id.* at 35–72 (outlining long history of summary treatment accorded unlawful combatants). EMMERICH DE VATTEL, THE LAW OF NATIONS 481 (Luke White trans., 1792) (1758) ("A nation attacked by such sort of [unlawful combatants] is not under any obligation to observe towards them the rules of wars in form.").

10. The "law of war" encompasses two distinct bodies of rules: the *jus ad bellum*—rules governing when use of force is lawful—and the *jus in bello*—rules governing the conduct of war. "International humanitarian law" refers to the corpus of *jus in bello* (and perhaps some rules, such as the prohibitions on "genocide" and "crimes against humanity," formally outside the *jus in bello*). The *jus in bello* itself has two principal subdivisions: "Geneva law" and "Hague law." Geneva law, embodied principally in the four 1949 Geneva Conventions and the two 1977 Additional Protocols, prescribes an extensive body of detailed rules governing the treatment of the victims of armed conflict. *See* GENEVA CONVENTION I, *supra* note 1; GENEVA CONVENTION II, *supra* note 1; POW CONVENTION, *supra* note 1; CIVILIANS CONVENTION, *supra* note 1; PROTOCOL ADDITIONAL TO THE GENEVA CONVENTIONS OF 12 AUGUST 1949, AND RELATING TO THE PROTECTION OF VICTIMS OF INTERNATIONAL ARMED CONFLICTS, opened for signature Dec. 12, 1977, 1125 U.N.T.S. 3 [hereinafter ADDITIONAL PROTOCOL I]; PROTOCOL ADDITIONAL TO THE GENEVA CONVENTIONS OF 12 AUGUST 1949, AND RELATING TO THE PROTECTION OF VICTIMS OF NON-INTERNATIONAL ARMED CONFLICTS, *opened for signature* Dec. 12, 1977, 1125 U.N.T.S. 609 [hereinafter ADDITIONAL PROTOCOL II]. Hague law, embodied principally in the 1899 and 1907 Hague Conventions, governs the means and methods of warfare, tactics, and the general conduct of hostilities. *See, e.g.*, HAGUE CONVENTION, *supra* note 5. This is not to say that Geneva law includes no rules governing means and methods of warfare, or that Hague law includes no rules governing the treatment of war victims; indeed, each treaty series includes elements of the other. This terminology, although conceptually imprecise, emphasizes the distinction between the two kinds of regimes—one governing the treatment of persons subject to the enemy's authority (Geneva law), the other governing the treatment of persons subject to the enemy's lethality (Hague law). In contemporary parlance, "international humanitarian law" embraces the whole *jus in bello*, in both its "Geneva" and "Hague" dimensions. *See generally* DETTER, *supra* note 8, at x–xviii (surveying these terminological issues).

11. *See* JENNIFER ELSEA, TREATMENT OF BATTLEFIELD DETAINEES IN THE WAR ON TERRORISM 1–5 (2003) (documenting the storm of controversy surrounding the POW issue); Mark A. Drumbl, *Victimhood in our Neighborhood: Terrorist Crime, Taliban Guilt, and the Asymmetries of the International Legal Order*, 81 N.C. L. REV. 1, 10 n.24 (2002) (same); Bryan Bender, *Red Cross Disputes US Stance on Detainees*, BOSTON GLOBE, Feb. 9, 2002, at A1 (stating that the International Committee of the Red Cross (ICRC) considers "both the Taliban and Al Qaeda fighters held by US forces . . . to be prisoners of war."); Tamara Lytle, *Taliban, Al-Qaeda Captives Arrive as Rights Groups Fret*, ORLANDO SENTINEL, Jan. 12, 2002, at A1.

12. *See generally* Sean Murphy, *Decision not to Regard Persons Detained in Afghanistan as POWs*, 96 AM. J. INT'L L. 475 (2002) (summarizing debates). *See also* John Mintz, *Debate Continues on Legal Status of Detainees*, WASH. POST, Jan. 28, 2002, at A15; John Mintz, *On Detainees, U.S. Faces Legal Quandary*, WASH. POST, Jan. 27, 2002, at A22.

Donald Rumsfeld stated that the United States would, as a matter of *policy*, treat the detainees humanely, but made clear that the United States was under no legal obligation to do so.[13] In addition, the formal proclamation of the U.S. policy concludes that the detainees are not protected by the Geneva Conventions, and that, as a consequence, the treatment to be accorded the detainees is solely a matter of policy.[14]

Predictably, the POW controversy has persisted and intensified. Indeed, the controversy has reached such proportions that it threatens to compromise the "war on terrorism."[15] Perhaps even more importantly, disagreement concerning the scope and content of fundamental humanitarian rules might impede cooperative security arrangements in general.[16]

The heart of this controversy is whether the detainees—enemy combatants captured in Afghanistan—are entitled to POW status as defined in the POW Convention.[17] Consider the details of the debate. The official U.S. government position is that neither Taliban nor Al Qaeda fighters qualify as POWs because they fail to satisfy international standards defining lawful combatants.[18] In short, the United States maintains that assignment of POW status in this case would be incorrect as a matter of law and imprudent as a matter of policy. Specifically, the United States argues that neither group of captured fighters satisfies the express requirements of the POW Convention, and that POW protections would impede the investigation and prosecution of suspected terrorists.[19] Of particular concern on the policy front are

---

13. *See* U.S. Dep't of Defense News Transcript, Sec'y Rumsfeld Media Availability en Route to Camp X-Ray (Jan. 27, 2002), *available at* http://www.defenselink.mil/news/Jan2002/t01282002_t0127sd2.html (last visited Apr. 15, 2004).

14. Fact Sheet, White House Press Office, Status of Detainees at Guantanamo (Feb. 7, 2002), *available at* http://www.whitehouse.gov/news/releases/2002/02/20020207-13.html [hereinafter Status of Detainees at Guantanamo] (last visited Apr. 15, 2004).

15. Because international cooperation is crucial to the effectiveness of U.S. antiterrorism policies, transnational disagreements about the treatment of detainees assume enormous importance. Routine aspects of transnational law enforcement have been complicated by the controversy. For example, some states are reluctant to extradite suspected Al Qaeda (or Taliban) fighters to the United States without assurances that they will not be held at Guantanamo. And, because the prisoners at Guantanamo are nationals of several co-belligerent states, the controversy has triggered diplomatic disputes between the United States and several important allies in the war against terrorism (including the United Kingdom and Australia). *See generally* Harold Hongju Koh, *On American Exceptionalism*, 55 STAN. L. REV. 1479 (2003); Manoocher Mofidi & Amy Eckert, *"Unlawful Combatants" or "Prisoners of War": The Law and Politics of Labels*, 36 CORNELL INT'L L.J. 59 (2003).

16. Following the controversy surrounding the treatment of the Guantanamo detainees, coalition military planning has involved sensitive negotiations on the proper interpretation of Geneva law. For example, prior to the invasion of Iraq, the United Kingdom sought and received assurances from the United States that all captured fighters would be treated in accordance with the POW Convention. George Jones & Ben Rooney, *U.S. "Will Adhere" to Geneva Convention*, LONDON DAILY TELEGRAPH, Feb. 4, 2003.

17. POW CONVENTION, *supra* note 1, art. 4.

18. *See* Press Release, Dep't of Defense, DoD News Briefing: Secretary Rumsfeld and Gen. Myers (Feb. 8, 2002), *available at* http://www.defenselink.mil/news/Feb2002/t02082002_t0208sd.html (last visited Apr. 15, 2004); Status of Detainees at Guantanamo, *supra* note 14.

19. For a summary of the government's position, see Mike Allen & John Mintz, *Bush Makes Decision on Detainees*, WASH. POST, Feb. 8, 2002, at A1; Murphy, *supra* note 12. *See also* Joyce Howard Price, *Detain-*

(1) restrictions on the interrogation of POWs;[20] (2) the criminal procedure rights of POWs (which might preclude trial by special "military commission");[21] and (3) the right of POWs to release and repatriation following the cessation of hostilities.[22] In short, the United States has concluded that the detainees are "unlawful combatants" (or "unprivileged belligerents") and thus not protected by the Geneva Conventions.[23]

Critics of the U.S. policy, on the other hand, argue that (1) the U.S. determination that the detainees are not POWs is flawed because it relies on a misreading of the POW Convention; and that (2) the United States must, irrespective of the merits of their classification, treat the detainees as POWs until a "competent tribunal" has determined that they do not qualify for POW status. The first criticism questions the U.S. interpretation of Article 4 of the POW Convention—relating to the identification of persons entitled to POW status (the "Article 4 issue").[24] The second criticism, on the other

---

ees Not POWs Insists White House, WASH. TIMES, Jan. 27, 2002, at A1 (discussing interrogation rationale); Rowan Scarborough, *Geneva Rules for Taliban, not al Qaeda*, WASH. TIMES, Feb. 8, 2002, at A1 (discussing repatriation and military tribunals rationales); Rowan Scarborough, *Powell Wants Detainees To Be Declared POWs; Memo Shows Differences with White House*, WASH. TIMES, Jan. 26, 2002, at A1 (discussing leaked memo from White House Counsel Alberto Gonzales in which he states that the war against terrorism "renders obsolete Geneva's strict limitations on questioning of enemy prisoners . . . .").

20. Under the POW Convention, the detaining authority may not subject POWs to coercive questioning, and POWs are required to provide only name, rank, and serial number to interrogators. *See* POW CONVENTION, *supra* note 1, arts. 17–18; Jeremy Rabkin, *After Guantanamo: The War over the Geneva Conventions*, NAT'L INTEREST 15 (Summer 2002) (defending denial of POW status to Taliban and Al Qaeda detainees, in part, on this ground); Ruth Wedgwood, *Al Qaeda, Terrorism, and Military Commissions*, 96 AM. J. INT'L L. 328 (2002) (same).

21. *See* Military Order of November 13, 2001: Detention, Treatment, and Trial of Certain Non-Citizens in the War Against Terrorism, 66 Fed. Reg. 57,833, at 57,834 (Nov. 16, 2001), *reprinted in* 10 U.S.C. § 801 (2001) [hereinafter Military Order]. It is a fair reading of the POW Convention that POWs facing criminal charges are entitled to trial by court-martial or regular civil court. *See* POW CONVENTION, *supra* note 1, arts. 99, 102; Laura Dickinson, *Using Legal Process To Fight Terrorism: Detentions, Military Commissions, International Tribunals, and the Rule of Law*, 75 S. CAL. L. REV. 1407, 1423–24 (2002); Neal Kumar Katyal & Laurence Tribe, *Waging War, Deciding Guilt: Trying the Military Tribunals*, 111 YALE L.J. 1259, 1263–66 (2002) (concluding, in view of rights recognized in the POW Convention, that the Military Order must cover only unlawful belligerents); Daryl A. Mundis, *The Use of Military Commissions To Prosecute Individuals Accused of Terrorist Acts*, 96 AM. J. INT'L L. 320, 324–26 (2002); Diane F. Orentlichter & Robert Kogod Goldman, *When Justice Goes to War: Prosecuting Terrorists Before Military Commissions*, 25 HARV. J.L. & PUB. POL'Y 653, 659–63 (2002); Jordan Paust, *Antiterrorism Military Commissions: Courting Illegality*, 23 MICH. J. INT'L L. 1 (2001) [hereinafter Paust, *Courting Illegality*]. Under this view, denying POW status would appear to leave open the possibility of trying detainees before military commissions for violations of the law of war. For an evaluation of this claim in view of the arguments developed herein, see *infra* Part IV.C.1.

22. *See* POW CONVENTION, *supra* note 1, arts. 117–18 (recognizing the right to repatriation); Joan Fitzpatrick, *Jurisdiction of Military Commissions and the Ambiguous War on Terrorism*, 96 AM. J. INT'L L. 345, 353 (2002) (suggesting that this right is one procedural consequence of denying POW status); Rabkin, *supra* note 20 (defending denial of POW status to Taliban and Al Qaeda detainees, in part, on this ground); Wedgwood, *supra* note 20 (same).

23. In addition, the U.S. government asserts that the Geneva Conventions do not, in any case, apply to Al Qaeda fighters—because that group is a non-governmental, criminal organization not party to the treaties. *See* Status of Detainees at Guantanamo, *supra* note 14 ("Al-Qaida is not a state party to the Geneva Convention; it is a foreign terrorist group. As such, its members are not entitled to POW status.").

24. *See, e.g.*, Paust, *Courting Illegality*, *supra* note 21, at 2–6. Recall that Article 4 of the POW Convention identifies several categories of persons protected by the Convention. *See* POW CONVENTION, *supra*

hand, questions the U.S. interpretation of Article 5 of the treaty, which establishes presumptive POW status in all cases of "doubt" and prescribes the procedure for determining the legal status of captured fighters (the "Article 5 issue").[25]

---

note 1, art. 4. This provision, although somewhat detailed, leaves many crucial questions unresolved. For example, it is difficult to discern the degree to which these provisions protect irregular forces incorporated into the regular armed forces of a state. Whether or when these provisions protect members of private armed groups—including terrorist organizations—is also unclear. With respect to Article 4, one important question is whether the four criteria expressly applied to "militia and other volunteer corps" in paragraph (A)(2) also limit the scope of paragraph (A)(1) concerning members of the armed forces. That is, there is some question whether members of the regular armed forces must have a command structure, wear uniforms, carry arms openly, and generally comply with laws of war to qualify for POW status. As the current POW controversy illustrates, states and commentators take divergent views on this question. *See, e.g.*, George H. Aldrich, *New Life for the Laws of War*, 75 AM. J. INT'L L. 764, 768–69 (1981) (arguing that Article 4(A)(2) criteria apply only to certain "irregular" armed forces and that "[m]embers of regular, uniformed armed forces do not lose their [POW] entitlement no matter what violations of the law their units may commit, but the guerrilla unit is held to a tougher standard . . . ."). Moreover, the text and drafting history lend some support to both views. *See, e.g.*, G.I.A.D. DRAPER, THE RED CROSS CONVENTIONS 52 (1958); 1 HOWARD S. LEVIE, THE CODE OF INTERNATIONAL ARMED CONFLICT 13–14 (1986); RICHARD I. MILLER, THE LAW OF WAR 29 (1975). Indeed, there is good reason to doubt that standard interpretive methods can resolve this disagreement decisively. On the one hand, paragraph (A)(1) covers members of the "armed forces" of a state, and the drafting history of the provision suggests that this language covers only members of the *regular* armed forces. Hence, some have concluded that the four criteria of (A)(2) are implicitly embedded in (A)(1) because *regularization* of forces requires, at a minimum, these four characteristics. *See generally* HOWARD S. LEVIE, PRISONERS OF WAR IN INTERNATIONAL ARMED CONFLICT 34–59 (U.S. Naval War College, International Law Studies, Vol. 59, 1977). On the other hand, the text of (A)(1) does not make reference to "regular" armed forces. Indeed, it extends coverage to "members of militia and other volunteer corps forming part of" the armed forces. Inexplicably, this reference to "militia and other volunteer corps," unlike the reference in (A)(2), is not qualified by the four criteria. This textual anomaly suggests that the four criteria apply only to "militia and other volunteer corps" not part of the "armed forces" of the state, and that captured fighters covered by (A)(1) are POWs irrespective of whether they satisfy the four criteria.

25. *See, e.g.*, Inter-American Commission on Human Rights [hereinafter Inter-Am C.H.R.], *Legal Status of the Detainees at Guantanamo Bay To Be Determined by a Tribunal* (Inter-Am. C.H.R., Mar. 12, 2002), *reprinted in* 23 HUM. RTS. L.J. 15 (2002) (granting, in part, petitioners' request for precautionary measures, and urging the United States "[to] take the urgent measures necessary to have the legal status of the detainees at Guantanamo Bay determined by a competent tribunal [in accordance with POW Convention, Article 5]"); Yasmin Naqvi, *Doubtful Prisoner-of-War Status*, 84 INT'L REV. RED CROSS 571 (2002). It is difficult, in many cases, to discern easily whether a captured combatant satisfies the requirements of Article 4—a point well understood by the drafters of the Convention. To address this problem directly, the POW Convention establishes that captured combatants, when their status is unclear, are presumptively entitled to POW status. Article 5 of the POW Convention provides that,

> [s]hould any doubt arise as to whether persons, having committed a belligerent act and having fallen into the hands of the enemy, belong to any of the categories enumerated in Article 4, such persons shall enjoy the protection of the present Convention until such time as their status has been determined by a competent tribunal.

POW CONVENTION, *supra* note 1, art. 5. Although this provision takes a useful approach—identifying a default rule—the application of the rule is qualified and the conditions under which it applies are poorly defined. More specifically, the applicability of Article 5 is triggered by "doubt" regarding the status of captured persons. The problem is that the text and drafting history provide little guidance on the meaning of this critical term. Once again, the current controversy illustrates that states and commentators define the term differently. *See* Naqvi, *supra* note 25 (surveying drafting history). Of course, the United States maintains that the status of Taliban and Al Qaeda detainees was not in doubt. *See, e.g.*, Katharine Q. Seelye, *Detainees Are Not P.O.W.'s, Cheney and Rumsfeld Declare*, N.Y. TIMES, Jan. 28, 2002, at A6 (quoting Secretary of Defense Rumsfeld that "[t]here is no ambiguity in this case").

Two important points follow from this discussion. First, the current debate turns on competing interpretations of the qualifications for POW status and the procedures for assessing the status of individual combatants. Each interpretation enjoys non-trivial textual and historical support. Indeed, it is well understood in humanitarian law circles that the 1949 Geneva Conventions did little to resolve the long-standing dispute over whether and when irregular forces should qualify for lawful combatant status.[26] Some commentators note that the vagueness of the qualifications for this status, coupled with the ascendancy of irregular forces and guerrilla tactics, strongly suggests that belligerents will interpret these criteria "so as to eliminate most irregulars from their protection."[27] Because these indefinite criteria invite "deliberate misconstructions," the regime's extension of POW status to some irregulars may be "disregarded completely."[28] Second, the scope and content of the controversy make clear that both sides build upon the claim that POW status determinations carry significant protective and policy implications. All sides of the POW controversy, therefore, rely upon or presume that the conventional wisdom is, at least in part, correct.

The conventional view, however, requires substantial qualification. Without question, the Geneva Conventions guarantee POWs several important rights and privileges. It is a mistake, however, to infer from this proposition that the denial of POW status carries significant detrimental consequences for the scope and content of detainee rights. In fact, careful analysis of the text, structure, and history of the Geneva Conventions demonstrates that the Conventions provide a robust rights regime for all war detainees. Indeed, the rights extended to all detainees include those rights that the U.S. government suggests may undermine the war on terrorism.[29] In this Article, I argue that, irrespective of whether war detainees are assigned POW status, humanitarian law accords protections that mirror, in most important respects, the rights accorded POWs.[30] In short, I argue, contrary to conven-

---

26. *See, e.g.*, JUDGE ADVOCATE GENERAL'S SCHOOL, U.S. ARMY, A TREATISE ON THE JURIDICAL BASIS OF THE DISTINCTION BETWEEN LAWFUL COMBATANT AND UNPRIVILEGED BELLIGERENT 83 (1959) [hereinafter JAG, TREATISE] ("The changes wrought in the field of belligerent qualifications by the Geneva Convention of 1949, while they represent important innovations, did not reach the crux of the ['unlawful combatant'] problem."); KARMA NABULSI, TRADITIONS OF WAR: OCCUPATION, RESISTANCE, AND THE LAW 241 (1999) ("By the end of the Geneva negotiations in 1949, significant progress had been made in the codification of the laws of war . . . . However, the question of the distinction between lawful and unlawful combatants remained essentially unresolved.").

27. JAG, TREATISE, *supra* note 26, at 84–85.

28. *Id.* at 82.

29. *See supra* text accompanying notes 19–23 (surveying U.S. rationales for treatment of war detainees).

30. In the interest of clarity, an important note on the scope of this analysis is in order. In this Article, I consider only the scope and content of protection accorded under *humanitarian law*. Some would, no doubt, argue that *international human rights law* protects "unlawful combatants" in all circumstances, and that these protections are, in all crucial respects, similar to POW rights recognized in the laws of war. *See, e.g.*, Fitzpatrick, *supra* note 22; Paust, *Courting Illegality*, *supra* note 21. Although this claim, on the merits, is one worthy of sustained reflection (a matter I will take up in subsequent work), the scope and content of humanitarian law nevertheless remains an important, open question. Indeed, over-reliance on

tional wisdom, that denying detainees POW status has no significant protective consequences, and, as a consequence, yields no important policy advantages to the detaining state. The text, structure, and history of the Geneva Conventions strongly support two conclusions: (1) Geneva law protects unlawful combatants; and (2) this protection very closely approximates that accorded POWs. Moreover, several recent developments in humanitarian law and policy suggest that this minimal protective gap is closing. The trajectory of international humanitarian law reflects an emerging "protective parity" across combatant status categories. This protective parity recasts debates about the legal status of unlawful combatants.

The argument is organized as follows: Part I outlines the direct protective consequences of POW status and explicates the general features of POW rights. Part II canvasses the rights of unlawful combatants—individuals who participate in hostilities without satisfying the minimum legal requirements to do so. In that Part, I analyze important structural features of the Geneva Conventions that have been underexamined (or, more commonly, misunderstood or misrepresented) in the current controversy. Part III clarifies the application of these overlapping protective schemes to varying categories of unlawful combatants. In Part IV, I argue that the Geneva Conventions, properly understood, afford POWs little in the way of unique procedural protections. In addition, I maintain that several overlapping developments suggest that even the limited significance of POW status is declining. By way of illustration, I discuss the implications of this analysis for the current POW controversy and, more specifically, U.S. anti-terrorism policy. Finally, I offer some preliminary reflections on the conceptual integrity and normative attractiveness of protective parity in humanitarian law.

---

human rights law as the source of protection for war detainees is problematic in several respects. Although it is beyond the scope of this Article to analyze this issue fully, consider a few deficiencies of human rights law vis-à-vis humanitarian law. First, international human rights law is not institutionalized in national law and policy to the same extent as humanitarian law. National military policy—embodied in national legislation, military manuals and formal military training—incorporates directly the requirements of humanitarian law. *See, e.g., infra* text accompanying notes 44–48 (describing the level of institutionalization of the POW Convention). Second, humanitarian law enjoys a more robust enforcement regime. For example, all serious violations of the laws of war give rise to individual criminal liability, and many violations of the laws of war come within the subject matter jurisdiction of special national and international tribunals. *See, e.g.*, KRIANGSAK KITTICHAISAREE, INTERNATIONAL CRIMINAL LAW (2001); STEVEN R. RATNER & JASON S. ABRAMS, ACCOUNTABILITY FOR HUMAN RIGHTS ATROCITIES IN INTERNATIONAL LAW: BEYOND THE NUREMBERG LEGACY (2d ed. 2001). Third, the content of humanitarian law is both more detailed and more narrowly tailored to the realities of armed conflict. *See, e.g.*, G.I.A.D. Draper, *Humanitarian Law and Human Rights*, *in* REFLECTIONS ON LAW AND ARMED CONFLICTS (Michael A. Meyer & Hilaire McCoubrey eds., 1998). Fourth, the applicability of human rights law, particularly in international armed conflict, may be limited by "derogability, territorial scope, or . . . jurisdiction." Gerald L. Neuman, *Humanitarian Law and Counterterrorist Force*, 14 EUR. J. INT'L L. 283, 292 (2003).

I. The Protective Consequences of POW Status

In one sense, the significance of POW status is obvious to any student of international humanitarian law. After all, POWs enjoy substantial international legal protection pursuant to the POW Convention.[31] These protections include: (1) the right to humane treatment (including important limitations on coercive interrogation tactics);[32] (2) due process rights;[33] (3) the right to release and repatriation upon the cessation of active hostilities;[34] and (4) the right to communication with (and the institutionalized supervision of) protective agencies.[35] The POW Convention also prohibits reprisals against POWs[36] and precludes the use of POWs as slave labor.[37] In addition, POWs may not be prosecuted for their participation in the hostilities—that is, they are entitled to "combatant immunity."[38] Moreover, the POW Convention makes clear that POW rights are inalienable[39] and non-derogable.[40] Finally, the Convention requires that states suppress the mistreatment of POWs by investigating, prosecuting, and punishing individuals responsible for "grave breaches" of the Convention.[41]

Nearly all states have now ratified this treaty,[42] and many have incorporated its protections directly into domestic law.[43] Several influential national

31. POW Convention, *supra* note 1.

32. *Id.* art. 13 (humane treatment); *see also id.* art. 17 (rules concerning interrogation), 21–48 (rules governing conditions of confinement).

33. *Id.* arts. 99–108.

34. *Id.* arts. 118–19.

35. *Id.* arts. 8–11.

36. *Id.* art. 13.

37. *Id.* arts. 49–57.

38. This privilege is, as a formal matter, extra-conventional in that the Geneva Conventions do not expressly accord any such privilege. It is nevertheless universally recognized. *See, e.g.*, Waldemar A. Solf & Edward R. Cummings, *A Survey of Penal Sanctions Under Protocol I to the Geneva Conventions of August 12, 1949*, 9 Case W. Res. J. Int'l L. 205, 212 (1977) ("[T]hose who are entitled to the juridical status of 'privileged combatant' are immune from criminal prosecution for those warlike acts which do not violate the laws and customs of war but which might otherwise be common crimes under municipal law."); Maj. Geoffrey S. Corn & Maj. Michael L. Smidt, *"To Be or Not To Be, That Is the Question": Contemporary Military Operations and the Status of Captured Personnel*, Army Law., June 1999, at 14 (arguing that combatants, as privileged belligerents, are entitled to "a blanket of immunity for their pre-capture warlike acts"); United States v. List, 11 Trials of War Criminals 757, 1228–29 (1948). Moreover, the privilege may be inferred from several provisions of the POW Convention. *See* POW Convention, *supra* note 1, arts. 82, 87–88.

39. POW Convention, *supra* note 1, art. 7.

40. *Id.* art. 5 (providing that the Convention "shall apply to the persons referred to in Article 4 from the time they fall into the power of the enemy and until their final release and repatriation").

41. *Id.* arts. 129–31.

42. *See* ICRC, *States Party to the Geneva Conventions and Their Additional Protocols: Geneva Conventions of 12 August 1949 and Additional Protocols of 8 June 1977*, *available at* http://www.icrc.org/Web/eng/siteeng0.nsf/htmlall/party_gc/$File/Conventions%20de%20GenSve%20et%20Protocoles%20additionnels%20ENG-logo.pdf (last visited Mar. 7, 2004) (documenting 191 ratifications). *See also* Annotated Supplement to the Commander's Handbook on the Law of Naval Operations 490 n.47 (Naval War College, Int'l L. Studies vol. 73, A.R. Thomas & James C. Duncan eds., 1999) ("[The POW Convention] is the universally accepted standard for treatment of [POWs]; virtually all nations are parties to it and it is now regarded as reflecting customary law.").

43. *See* ICRC, International Humanitarian Law, National Implementation Database, *available at*

military manuals direct their armed forces to observe unconditionally the obligations embodied in the POW Convention.[44] These obligations are now also formally accepted by several international organizations supervising multinational force deployments, including the United Nations[45] and the North Atlantic Treaty Organization (NATO).[46] These rules, unlike many international legal protections, have teeth: they are accompanied by an elaborate criminal enforcement regime. Under the POW Convention, for example, the mistreatment of persons entitled to POW status constitutes a "grave breach" of international humanitarian law[47]—giving rise to individual criminal liability[48] and so-called "universal jurisdiction" over perpetrators.[49] The criminalization of violations of POW rules is now also recognized in many national penal codes,[50] as well as several important international agreements concerning the scope of international criminal law—including the Interna-

---

http://www.icrc.org/ihl-nat.nsf/WebLAW2?OpenView (last visited Mar. 7, 2004) (providing excerpts of implementing national legislation from over 50 countries).

44. *See, e.g.*, DEP'T OF THE ARMY, FM 27-10: DEPARTMENT OF THE ARMY FIELD MANUAL: THE LAW OF LAND WARFARE, ch. 3 (1956) [hereinafter FM 27-10] (U.S.), *available at* http://www.osc.army.mil/others/Gca/files/FM27-10.pdf (last visited Apr. 23, 2004); JUDGE ADVOCATE GENERAL OF CANADA, LAW OF ARMED CONFLICT MANUAL (2001), *available at* http://www.forces.gc.ca/jag/training/publications/loac_man_e.asp (last visited Mar. 7, 2004); MANUAL OF MILITARY LAW, PART III: THE LAW OF WAR ON LAND (1958) (U.K.); THE HANDBOOK OF HUMANITARIAN LAW IN ARMED CONFLICTS (Dieter Fleck ed., 1999).

45. *See* United Nations Secretariat, Secretary General's Bulletin, Observance by United Nations Forces of International Humanitarian Law, U.N. Doc. ST/SGB/1999/13 (Aug. 6, 1999), *available at* http://www.un.org/peace/st_sgb_1999_13.pdf (last visited Mar. 7, 2004).

46. *See* NATO Parliamentary Assembly, Civilian Affairs Committee, Res. 287 (15 Nov. 1999), *available at* http://www.naa.be/archivedpub/resolutions/99-amsterdam-287.asp (last visited Apr. 23, 2004). As part of the IFOR/SFOR mandate under the Dayton Accords, NATO agreed to enforce the substantive commitments of the parties, including the commitment to observe the 1949 Geneva Conventions. *See* Stabilization Force, Framework Agreement, Annex 1A (authorizing forces to enforce the agreement), Annex 6 (outlining human rights obligations of the parties and enumerating the 1949 Geneva Conventions as part of the applicable law), *available at* http://www.nato.int/sfor/basic/gfap.htm (last visited Apr. 23, 2004). This institutional commitment to the Geneva Conventions is not surprising given that all NATO states are party to the four 1949 Conventions. Indeed, the only real difficulty regards the applicability of the 1977 Protocols to the Conventions in NATO operations. *See infra* note 357 (discussing this issue).

47. *See* POW CONVENTION, *supra* note 1, arts. 129–31.

48. *Id.*; *see also* JORDAN J. PAUST ET AL., INTERNATIONAL CRIMINAL LAW 3–15, 27–43 (2d ed. 2000) (describing the emergence of individual criminal responsibility in the laws of war).

49. Although I use the phrase "universal jurisdiction," I invoke it in a limited sense. Of course, the "grave breach" regime of the Geneva Conventions does not formally confer "universal jurisdiction." Rather, the Conventions require states to prosecute or extradite persons accused of grave breaches. *See* POW CONVENTION, *supra* note 1, arts. 129–31; *see also* Edward M. Wise, *Aut Dedere aut Judicare: The Duty To Prosecute or Extradite*, *in* II INTERNATIONAL CRIMINAL LAW: PROCEDURAL AND ENFORCEMENT MECHANISMS 15 (M. Cherif Bassiouni, ed.) (2d ed. 1999). These provisions do not purport to confer on states jurisdictional authority they would not otherwise enjoy. Rather, the "prosecute or extradite" obligation is aimed at securing international cooperation in the suppression of serious violations of the Conventions. *Id.* at 17–19.

50. *See, e.g.*, ICRC, *supra* note 43; Coalition for the Int'l Criminal Court, National Legislation Database (providing full text of national war crimes legislation from over 35 states), *available at* http://www.iccnow.org/resourcestools/ratimptoolkit/nationalregionaltools/legislationdebates.html (last visited Mar. 7, 2004).

tional Criminal Court[51] and the International Criminal Tribunal for the Former Yugoslavia.[52] In short, the inquiry proposed above yields an incontestable, yet deceptively simple answer: the designation of a captured combatant as a POW carries significant protective consequences.

Discerning, on the other hand, the *unique* protective significance of POW status presents several complications. What are the protective consequences of *denying* POW status? The problem is a thorny one in part because international humanitarian law also accords substantial legal protection to other status categories. For example, the Geneva Conventions provide detailed legal protection to "civilians"—a term of art in humanitarian law. As I shall explore in detail below,[53] the Geneva Convention Relative to the Protection of Civilian Persons in Time of War ("Civilians Convention") entitles "civilians" to protections that, in most respects, are identical to those provided by the POW Convention.[54] In addition, the Civilians Convention enjoys the same international acceptance,[55] formal institutionalization,[56] and enforcement regime as does the POW Convention.[57] The upshot is that the denial of POW status in many cases arguably carries no unique protective consequences.[58]

Of course, many persons captured in time of war do not neatly fit into the category of "civilians." The central difficulty is what protections apply, and which should apply, to persons who have directly participated in hostilities,

---

51. *See* ROME STATUTE OF THE INTERNATIONAL CRIMINAL COURT, art. 8, July 17, 1998, 37 I.L.M. 999 (1998) [hereinafter ICC Statute].

52. *See* S.C. Res. 808, U.N. Doc. S/RES/808 *annexed to* The Secretary-General, *Aspects of Establishing an International Tribunal for the Prosecution of Persons Responsible for the Serious Violations of International Humanitarian Law Committed in the Territory of the Former Yugoslavia*, U.N. Doc. S/25704, art. 2 (May 3, 1993), *reprinted in* 32 I.L.M. 1159 (1993).

53. *See infra* Part II.A (discussing the Civilians Convention). The Geneva Conventions also prescribe important protections for sick and wounded combatants. *See* GENEVA CONVENTION I, *supra* note 1; GENEVA CONVENTION II, *supra* note 1. However, the definition of persons protected by these treaties makes clear that only persons who, if captured, would qualify for POW status are covered by the treaty. *See* GENEVA CONVENTION I, *supra* note 1, art. 4; GENEVA CONVENTION II, *supra* note 1, art. 4.

54. *Compare* POW CONVENTION, *supra* note 1, arts. 21–42, 46–88 *with* CIVILIANS CONVENTION, *supra* note 1, arts. 79–149; *see also infra* Part II.A (summarizing the most important protections); ICRC, COMMENTARY: IV GENEVA CONVENTION RELATIVE TO THE PROTECTION OF CIVILIAN PERSONS IN TIME OF WAR 4–5 (Jean S. Pictet ed., 1958) [hereinafter ICRC, COMMENTARY IV] ("In general . . . the regulations applicable to civilians reproduce almost word for word the regulations relating to prisoners of war.").

55. *See* ICRC, *States Party*, *supra* note 42.

56. *See, e.g.*, ICRC, National Implementation Database, *supra* note 43; Coalition for the Int'l Criminal Court, National Legislation Database, *supra* note 50. *See also* sources collected in notes 42–46 (incorporating both POW Convention and Civilians Convention).

57. *See, e.g.*, CIVILIANS CONVENTION, *supra* note 1, art. 146 (establishing "grave breach" regime for Civilians Convention); *see also* sources collected in notes 47–52 (establishing enforcement mechanisms for both POW Convention and Civilians Convention).

58. As I analyze in detail below, there is one cluster of POW rights that arguably provides unique protective benefits. Under the POW Convention, POWs are, for protective purposes, "assimilated" into the armed forces of the detaining power. *See* POW CONVENTION, *supra* note 1, arts. 82, 84, 87, 88, 95. As a consequence, POWs are subject to the same substantive law as the armed forces of the detaining power (giving rise to combatant immunity), and POWs are entitled to the same trial procedures as the armed forces of the detaining power (precluding the use of special military commissions to try POWs). *See infra* Part IV.C (assessing these claims).

yet failed to satisfy the requirements for POW status. Such persons, often called "unlawful combatants" or "unprivileged belligerents," pose an important challenge to the laws of war. The concern is that the conceptual and normative structure of humanitarian law requires a sharp distinction between combatants and civilians (or non-combatants), strongly suggesting that persons taking up arms in time of war are not properly considered civilians. According to this view, combatants either qualify for POW status or fall outside the protective schemes of humanitarian law.[59] In addition, this so-called "rule of distinction" supports establishing minimum organizational and individual requirements for combatants so as to ensure that combatants, as a practical matter, remain sufficiently distinguishable from civilians. Combatants failing to satisfy these minimum requirements arguably are not properly classified as POWs (or "lawful combatants"). The important point is that the "rule of distinction" arguably necessitates a restrictive definition of both civilian status and, by implication, POW status.

Two additional points underscore the centrality of these issues. First, these tensions in humanitarian law likely will escalate over time. The number of combatants arguably falling outside the protective umbrella of international humanitarian law is substantial and likely to remain so. Irregular or guerrilla forces are commonplace in contemporary conflicts, and typically they do not satisfy the minimum requirements for POW status. Second, the potential gaps in humanitarian law are poorly understood, because of both the evolving character and the complexity of its overlapping protective schemes. In this regard, systematic analysis of the legal situation of "unlawful combatants" would clarify the unique protective significance—or lack thereof—of POW status. If POW status matters, it will matter most in the case of unlawful combatants. Because they are not POWs (by definition), and because their civilian status is also problematic, the legal situation of unlawful combatants provides an opportunity to explore the contours of humanitarian law generally.

I next offer detailed consideration of the rights accorded unlawful combatants in Geneva law—that is, individuals who participate in hostilities without satisfying the requirements for POW status. There are, in general, two widely endorsed approaches to this issue: (1) international law does not protect unlawful combatants; or (2) international law provides some relatively modest protection to "unlawful combatants," but these protections are substantially below those accorded POWs. Part II evaluates the plausibility of these two approaches through a systematic analysis of other protective schemes that arguably apply to unlawful combatants.

59. It should also be noted that Geneva law provides some important protections for all persons subject to the authority of a belligerent state. *See infra* Parts II.C, II.D (discussing Common Article 3 of the four Geneva Conventions [hereinafter Common Art. 3] and Article 75 of Additional Protocol I); *see also infra* Part IV (analyzing several important recent developments implicating the scope and content of these provisions).

II. Unlawful Combatants and Geneva Law

In this Part, I identify four sources of potentially applicable humanitarian rules. The Geneva Conventions provide multiple discernible sources of procedural rights protections—only one of which is taken into account in the current controversy. First, the Geneva Conventions establish a dense network of guarantees for the four categories of "protected persons."[60] The categories of "protected persons" include POWs and civilians (a much broader category), and both are entitled to extensive procedural rights protections and other guarantees.[61] Second, the Conventions also prescribe the minimum procedural rights required in the prosecution of individuals charged with violating the substantive rules of the Conventions.[62] Third, the Conventions identify the minimum humanitarian protections applicable to all persons rendered *hors de combat*—that is, all persons no longer taking active part in the hostilities.[63] Finally, Article 75 of Additional Protocol I recognizes several important protections that apply to all persons "in the power of" a belligerent state.[64]

In this sense, international humanitarian law provides at least four sources of detainee rights, each with a distinct field of application. Humanitarian protections therefore apply to four categories of persons: (1) "protected persons" under the four Geneva Conventions (including civilians as defined in the Civilians Convention); (2) all persons charged with violations of the laws of war; (3) all persons no longer taking active part in the hostilities; and (4) all persons "in the power of" a party to the conflict. Because of the breadth of these categories, most significant humanitarian protections apply to all detainees—including unlawful or unprivileged combatants.

A. *Civilians Convention (the Fourth Geneva Convention)*

The Civilians Convention provides detailed rules governing the treatment of "civilians" in armed conflicts, and the substance of these rules in most important respects mirrors the rights of POWs. These protections include: due process rights (including the right to fair trial in the event of criminal prosecution);[65] the right to humane treatment;[66] freedom from coercive interrogation;[67] freedom from discrimination;[68] the right to repatriation (in-

60. *See* Geneva Convention I, *supra* note 1 (sick and wounded on land); Geneva Convention II, *supra* note 1 (sick, wounded, and shipwrecked at sea); POW Convention, *supra* note 1; Civilians Convention, *supra* note 1.

61. Civilians Convention, *supra* note 1, arts. 65–78; POW Convention, *supra* note 1, arts. 82–108.

62. *See infra* Part II.B.

63. *See infra* Part II.C.

64. *See infra* Part II.D.

65. *See* Civilians Convention, *supra* note 1, arts. 64–76, 126, 146–47.

66. *Id.* arts. 27–34.

67. *Id.* arts. 31–32.

68. *Id.* arts. 1, 3, 27.

cluding the right to leave enemy territory voluntarily);[69] the right to internal camp governance;[70] and the prohibition on attacks directed against civilian objects (including strict prohibition of attacks on hospitals and other facilities providing essential services to the civilian population).[71]

Although the Civilians Convention broadly defines the class of persons protected by its substantive provisions, the scope of its application is limited in several important ways.[72] First, the full protections of the Convention extend only to persons who "find themselves . . . in the hands of a Party to the conflict or Occupying Power of which they are not nationals."[73] Second, the Convention writ large protects only the nationals of states party to the Civilians Convention.[74] Third, the full protections of the Convention do not apply to nationals of a neutral state or nationals of a co-belligerent state "while the State of which they are nationals has normal diplomatic representation in the State in whose hands they are."[75] Fourth, most provisions of the Convention apply only in (1) the territory of a party to the conflict, and (2) occupied territory.[76]

Moreover, the Civilians Convention by its terms applies *only* to persons *not* covered by the other Conventions (such as POWs).[77] That is, persons who do not qualify for POW status may nevertheless be "protected persons" under the Conventions. Furthermore, although the Geneva Conventions do not include an express definition of civilians, and despite the fact that it seems odd to characterize combatants as civilians, the text and drafting history of the Civilians Convention make clear that it does protect unlawful combatants (although to a lesser extent in some circumstances than non-combatant civilians), provided, of course, that they are enemy nationals.

1. *Applicability to Unlawful Combatants*

The Civilians Convention applies to all enemy nationals—including unlawful combatants—not protected by the other Conventions.[78] Although this

69. *Id.* arts. 35–38, 77, 132–35.

70. *Id.* arts. 101–04.

71. *Id.* arts. 13–26.

72. It is important to point out, however, that the Convention does offer some protection to all civilian persons. *See* CIVILIANS CONVENTION, *supra* note 1, arts. 13–26 (establishing minimal protections for civilians and civilian objects—such as hospitals—located in combat zones); *see also infra* Parts II.B, II.C (discussing penal repression regime and Common Article 3 of the four Geneva Conventions); *see also infra* Part IV (analyzing several important recent developments implicating the scope and content of these provisions).

73. CIVILIANS CONVENTION, *supra* note 1, art. 4. *See also infra* Part IV.B.1 (discussing recent developments that arguably relax these requirements).

74. CIVILIANS CONVENTION, *supra* note 1, art. 4 ("Nationals of a State not bound by the Convention are not protected by it.").

75. *Id.*

76. *Id.*

77. CIVILIANS CONVENTION, *supra* note 1, art. 4.

78. *Id.* Common Article 3, the provisions of Part II, and the penal repression regime are applicable irrespective of the nationality of the person in question. *See infra* Part III.C; *see also* Common Art. 3, *supra*

point is often overlooked in current debates,[79] it enjoys broad support in the legal literature,[80] contemporary international war crimes jurisprudence,[81] and national military manuals.[82] Nevertheless, some dissent persists because (1) the consensus view is often asserted without any sustained defense;[83] (2) the contrary view—that the Convention covers civilians as distinguished from combatants—enjoys some intuitive appeal;[84] (3) the "protected person" classification question overlaps with—and is, as a consequence, often confused with—classification questions that arise under the rule of distinction;[85] and (4) the Convention's derogation regime—invoked by some as definitive proof that the Convention covers unlawful combatants[86] and by others as definitive proof that it does not[87]—generates several conceptual complications.[88] Notwithstanding these points, the best reading of the Civilians Convention is that it covers unlawful combatants who satisfy its nationality and territoriality requirements, and that this coverage is subject to qualifications delimited in the Convention's derogation regime. Three points support these conclusions.

First, the text of the Civilians Convention suggests that it applies to unlawful combatants. Persons protected by the Convention are "those who, at any given moment and in any manner whatsoever, find themselves . . . in the

---

note 59; CIVILIANS CONVENTION, *supra* note 1, arts. 13–26, 146.

79. *See, e.g.*, Inter-Am. C.H.R., *Report on Terrorism and Human Rights*, OEA/Ser.L/-V/II.116, doc. 5 rev. 1 corr. (Oct. 22, 2002), *available at* http://www.cidh.oas.org/Terrorism/Eng/toc.htm (last visited Mar. 24, 2004); Knut Ipsen, *Combatants and Non-Combatants*, *in* THE HANDBOOK OF HUMANITARIAN LAW IN ARMED CONFLICTS, *supra* note 44, at 65, 67–68.

80. *See, e.g.*, MICHAEL BOTHE ET AL., NEW RULES FOR VICTIMS OF ARMED CONFLICTS: COMMENTARY ON THE TWO 1977 PROTOCOLS ADDITIONAL TO THE GENEVA CONVENTIONS OF 1949 261–63 (1982); HILLARE MCCOUBREY, INTERNATIONAL HUMANITARIAN LAW: MODERN DEVELOPMENTS IN THE LIMITATION OF WARFARE 137 (2d ed. 1998); Draper, *supra* note 8; George Aldrich, *The Taliban, Al Qaeda, and the Determination of Illegal Combatants*, 96 AM. J. INT'L L. 893 (2002); Knut Dormann, *The Legal Situation of "Unlawful/Unprivileged Combatants,"* 85 INT'L REV. RED CROSS 849 (2003); Frits Kalshoven, *The Position of Guerrilla Fighters under the Law of War*, 11 REVUE DE DROIT PÉNAL MILITAIRE ET DE DROIT DE LA GUERRE 55, 71 (1972); Esbjorn Rosenblad, *Guerrilla Warfare and International Law*, 12 REVUE DE DROIT PÉNAL MILITAIRE ET DE DROIT DE LA GUERRE 91, 98 (1973).

81. *See, e.g.*, Prosecutor v. Delalic, Case No. IT-96-21-T, Judgment, ¶ 271 (Nov. 16, 1998) ("If an individual is not entitled to the protections of the Third Convention as a prisoner of war (or of the First or Second Conventions) he or she necessarily falls within the ambit of Convention IV, provided that its article 4 requirements are satisfied.").

82. *See, e.g.*, FM 27-10, *supra* note 44, ¶ 73:

> If a person is determined by a competent tribunal, acting in conformity with Article 5, [POW Convention] (par. 71), not to fall within any of the categories listed in Article 4, [POW Convention] (par. 61), he is not entitled to be treated as a prisoner of war. He is, however, a "protected person" within the meaning of Article 4, [Civilians Convention] (Par. 247).

See also BRITISH MILITARY MANUAL, PART III: THE LAW OF LAND WARFARE art. 94 (1958) (U.K.).

83. *See, e.g.*, Draper, *supra* note 8; Kalshoven, *supra* note 80; Rosenblad, *supra* note 80. Baxter is the exception here. Baxter, *supra* note 3, at 326–28. I assess his line of reasoning in detail below. *See infra* Part II.A.2.b.

84. The relationship between these categories and the rule of distinction undergirds this intuition. As a consequence, this point ultimately collapses into the next. As I argue in the conclusion, this approach to the protective classification problem is misplaced. *See infra* Part V.

85. *See infra* Part V.

86. *See, e.g.*, Dormann, *supra* note 80.

87. *See, e.g.*, Baxter, *supra* note 3, at 338. *See also infra* Part II.A.2.b (analyzing Baxter's position).

88. *See infra* Part II.A.2; *see also infra* Part V.

hands of a Party . . . of which they are not nationals."[89] This is the strongest argument for the applicability of the Convention to unlawful combatants. The provision also makes clear that several categories of persons are not protected by the Convention. For example, nationals of a state "not bound by the Convention are not protected by it."[90] In addition, nationals of "neutral" or "co-belligerent" states are not protected by the Convention "while the State of which they are nationals has normal diplomatic representation in the State in whose hands they are."[91] And, as previously discussed, the Civilians Convention does not apply to persons protected by any of the other Conventions.[92] The provision does not, however, expressly limit the application of the Convention to persons taking no part in the hostilities.[93] Indeed, the Convention prescribes, in some detail, rules governing the treatment of civilians "suspected of or engaged in activities hostile to the State."[94] It is also important to note that the definitions of "protected persons" in the other Geneva Conventions are, without exception, quite detailed.[95] When read in light of the other Conventions, the Civilians Convention should not be interpreted as implicitly excluding from its protection a broad category of individuals otherwise satisfying its definition of "protected persons."

Second, the drafting history of the Civilians Convention makes clear that it protects unlawful combatants and that this protection is subject to important qualifications. At the Diplomatic Conference, some delegations, including those from the United Kingdom and Australia, expressed the view that unlawful combatants (spies or saboteurs, to be more precise) should not be protected by the Civilians Convention.[96] Others, including the Soviet Union, Scandinavian countries, and the International Committee of the Red Cross (ICRC), criticized this view.[97] Indeed, consider the amendment Australia proposed to Article 4: "Provided persons definitely suspected of or engaged in activities hostile to the security of the State or the Occupying Power shall not be entitled to such rights and privileges contained in this Convention, as this would be prejudicial to the security of such State or Power."[98] On the other side of the issue, the Soviet Union countered with a defense of the

---

89. CIVILIANS CONVENTION, *supra* note 1, art. 4.

90. *Id.*

91. *Id.*

92. *Id.*

93. *Id.*

94. *Id.* art. 5. I analyze the scope and content of these limitations below. *See infra* Part II.A.2.

95. *See* GENEVA CONVENTION I, *supra* note 1, art. 4; GENEVA CONVENTION II, *supra* note 1, art. 4; POW CONVENTION, *supra* note 1, art. 4

96. *See* 2A Diplomatic Conference Convened by the Swiss Federal Council for the Establishment of International Conventions for the Protection of War Victims, Apr. 21–Aug. 12, 1949, *Final Record*, 621–22 [hereinafter Diplomatic Conference]; ICRC COMMENTARY IV, *supra* note 54, at 52 ("Some people considered that the Convention should apply without exception to all the persons to whom it referred, while to others it seemed obvious that persons guilty of violating the laws of war were not entitled to claim its benefits.").

97. *See* 2A Diplomatic Conference, *supra* note 96, at 618–24, 814.

98. *See* 3 Diplomatic Conference, *supra* note 96, at 100.

ICRC's pre-Conference "Stockholm draft" (which would have extended the full benefits of the Convention to unlawful combatants)[99] and in the alternative proposed amendments to clarify that unlawful combatants were covered.[100] Both views were rejected by the Committee.[101] Instead, the Committee steered a middle course by adopting draft Article 3A (Article 5 in the final text), which made clear that although unlawful combatants are "protected persons," states may, in specified circumstances, deprive such persons of some of the protections of the Convention.[102] When the Soviet delegate made his final plea to the Plenary to reject the Committee's proposal,[103] several delegations responded that Articles 4 and 5, in their final form, reflected a "careful compromise solution" and urged the Plenary to endorse the Committee's recommendation.[104] The U.K. delegate rejected the Soviet Union's criticism of Article 5, in part, by pointing out that some important protections, including the right to humane treatment and fair trial rights of the Convention, would apply to persons covered by Article 5.[105] In the end, the Diplomatic Conference overwhelmingly approved the Committee's proposed text.[106] Indeed, even Australia, the original sponsor of the amendment that would have left unlawful combatants completely unprotected, indicated that it supported the compromise reflected in the final version.[107] In short, the drafting history demonstrates that the Conventions were designed to cover unlawful combatants and that the extent of this coverage was made subject to the limitations embodied in Article 5.[108]

Third, the text and structure of Additional Protocol I to the Geneva Conventions suggest that the Civilians Convention applies to unlawful combatants. Subsequent refinements of Geneva law demonstrate how states and other important international actors such as the ICRC interpreted the scope of the 1949 Conventions. By the 1970s, several leading commentators, many

99. *See* 1 Diplomatic Conference, *supra* note 96, at 113–30 (providing text of Stockholm draft). The drafting history of the "Stockholm draft" makes clear that the Civilians Convention would protect, to some extent, persons not protected by the other Conventions. *See also* ICRC, 17th International Red Cross Conference, Stockholm, Aug. 1948, *Draft Revised or New Conventions for the Protection of War Victims (No. 4A)*, 3; ICRC, Conference of Government Experts for the Study of the Conventions for the Protections of War Victims, Geneva, Apr. 14–16, 1947, *Report on the Work of the Conference of Government Experts for the Study of the Conventions for the Protection of War Victims*; ICRC, Preliminary Conference of National Red Cross Societies for the Study of the Conventions and of Various Problems Relative to the Red Cross, Geneva, July 26–Aug. 3, 1946, *Report on the Work of the Preliminary Conference of National Red Cross Societies for the Study of the Conventions and of Various Problems Relative to the Red Cross*.

100. 2A Diplomatic Conference, *supra* note 96, at 621–23.

101. *See* 2A Diplomatic Conference, *supra* note 96, at 814 (Committee Report to the Plenary).

102. *See* 3 Diplomatic Conference, *supra* note 96, at 101 (proposed by Austria, Sweden, Switzerland, and others).

103. *See, e.g.*, 2B Diplomatic Conference, *supra* note 96, at 377–79.

104. *See, e.g.*, 2B Diplomatic Conference, *supra* note 96, at 379 (U.S. delegate).

105. *Id.* at 380. Compare the delegate's remarks here with his remarks in the Committee where he insisted that no rights should apply to spies and saboteurs; the United Kingdom had clearly and unequivocally accepted the compromise. *See* 2A Diplomatic Conference, *supra* note 96, at 621–22.

106. 2B Diplomatic Conference, *supra* note 96, at 377, 384.

107. *Id.* at 382.

108. *See infra* Part II.A.3.

international organizations, and most states discerned important deficiencies and gaps in Geneva law.[109] Broad-based efforts to address these concerns culminated in the drafting of the Additional Protocols to the Conventions. One important and, in part, controversial development was the redefinition of lawful belligerency as part of the overall effort to make the rules governing international armed conflicts applicable to non-international wars of national liberation.[110] The relevant provisions of Additional Protocol I involve two conceptually distinct reforms: (1) these provisions relaxed the requirements for lawful combatant and POW status;[111] and (2) they clarified the protective consequences of failing to meet these relaxed requirements.[112] Although the advisability and proper interpretation of the first reform do not directly implicate the instant analysis,[113] the precise contours of the second clearly require further consideration.[114] Article 45 of Additional Protocol I provides in part:

---

109. *See* BOTHE ET AL., *supra* note 80, at 3–10 (describing background to the Conference); ICRC, COMMENTARY ON THE ADDITIONAL PROTOCOLS (Yves Sandoz et al. eds., 1987), at xxix–xxxv, 19–21; Christopher Greenwood, *Historical Development and Legal Basis of Humanitarian Law*, *in* THE HANDBOOK OF HUMANITARIAN LAW IN ARMED CONFLICTS, *supra* note 44, at 1, 24–26 (summarizing important developments in Additional Protocol I); FRITS KALSHOVEN, CONSTRAINTS ON THE WAGING OF WAR 72–137 (1987) (providing a more elaborate review of developments reflected in Additional Protocol I).

110. ADDITIONAL PROTOCOL I, *supra* note 10, arts. 1(4), 43–45.

111. *Id.* arts. 43–44.

112. *Id.* art. 45.

113. For critical evaluation of the Protocol's amendments of the definition of lawful combatants, see Hans-Peter Gasser, *An Appeal for Ratification by the United States*, 81 AM. J. INT'L L. 912 (1987), Abraham Sofaer, *The Rationale for the U.S. Decision*, 82 AM. J. INT'L L. 784 (1988).

114. Here I highlight only the interpretive relevance of Article 45. The substantive merits of this provision (and its companion provisions, Articles 43 and 44) are not important for these purposes. It should be noted that the United States is not party to either Additional Protocol. *See* Letter of Transmittal from President Ronald Reagan, PROTOCOL II ADDITIONAL TO THE 1949 GENEVA CONVENTIONS, AND RELATING TO THE PROTECTION OF VICTIMS OF NONINTERNATIONAL ARMED CONFLICTS, S. TREATY DOC. NO. 2, 100th Cong., 1st Sess., III (1987), *reprinted in* 81 AM. J. INT'L L. 910 (1987); George Aldrich, *Prospects for United States Ratification of Additional Protocol I to the 1949 Geneva Conventions*, 85 AM. J. INT'L L. 1 (1991). Although the U.S. recognizes many provisions of these treaties as customary international law (indeed, the United States expressly supports many provisions as good law and policy), it specifically objects to the redefinition of combatant status in Article 44. *See* Michael J. Matheson, *The United States Position on the Relation of Customary International Law to the 1977 Protocols Additional to the 1949 Geneva Conventions*, 2 AM. U. J. INT'L L. & POL'Y 419, 420 (1987); *see also* Aldrich, *supra*; Sofaer, *supra* note 113. The United States, however, views Article 45 "as either legally binding as customary international law or acceptable practice though not legally binding." Matheson, *supra*, at 420. Indeed, the U.S. military expressly acknowledges the centrality of the Protocols in the laws of war. *See, e.g.*, JUDGE ADVOCATE GENERAL'S SCHOOL, U.S. ARMY, *Legal Framework of the Law of War*, *in* LAW OF WAR WORKSHOP DESKBOOK 25, 32 (Brian J. Bill ed., 2000), *available at* http://www.jagcnet.army.mil/JAGCNETInternet/Homepages/AC/TJAGSAWeb.nsf/8f7edfd448e0ec6c8525694b0064ba51/9dc02ec45aba401d852569ad007c79df/$FILE/LOWW%20Master%20Document.pdf (last visited Apr. 23, 2004):

> Although the U.S. has never ratified either of these Protocols, their relevance continues to grow based on several factors:
>
> a. The U.S. has stated it considers many provisions of Protocol I, and all of Protocol II, to be binding customary international law.
>
> b. The argument that the entire body of Protocol I has attained the status of customary international law continues to gain strength.
>
> c. These treaties bind virtually all of our coalition partners.
>
> d. U.S. policy is to comply with Protocol I and Protocol II whenever feasible.

> Any person who has taken part in hostilities, who is not entitled to prisoner-of-war status and who does not benefit from more favourable treatment in accordance with the Fourth Convention shall have the right at all times to the protection of Article 75 of this Protocol. In occupied territory, any such person, unless he is held as a spy, shall also be entitled, notwithstanding Article 5 of the Fourth Convention, to his rights of communication under that Convention.[115]

Two aspects of this provision have bearing on the inquiry here. First, the provision conclusively establishes that *all* unlawful combatants are at least entitled to the minimum protections of Article 75, as analyzed in Part II.D. The drafting history of, and official commentary on, Articles 45 and 75 reveal that these provisions sought to clarify several general, structural characteristics of the 1949 Conventions (such as the relationship between the POW Convention and the Civilians Convention)[116] and to extend some minimum protections to persons expressly excluded from the scope of the Civilians Convention (such as nationals of co-belligerents, nationals of the detaining authority, and nationals of states not party to the Convention).[117] That is, these provisions were not designed to extend protection to unlawful combatants as such. Rather, they were drafted to protect a subset of all unlawful combatants otherwise not protected under the Conventions.

The affirmative protective consequences of this provision are, for the purposes of this line of analysis, less important than the second salient aspect of the provision: its implicit recognition that other Geneva rules may apply to some unlawful combatants. That is, the provision makes clear that the Civilians Convention protects, to some as-yet-undefined extent,[118] some unlawful combatants.[119] Of course, as previously discussed, the Civilians Convention writ large clearly would not apply to unlawful combatants who fail to satisfy the nationality or territoriality constraints of Article 4. The important point is that the inapplicability of the Convention in such cases is a function of the nationality of the person in question or the nature of the territory in which the person is detained—not the designation of any such person as an unlawful combatant.

These themes, and the growing influence of the Protocols, are addressed more systematically below. *See infra* Part IV.B.4.

115. ADDITIONAL PROTOCOL I, *supra* note 10, art. 45(3). The provision was adopted at the Diplomatic Conference by consensus. *See* 6 Diplomatic Conference on the Reaffirmation and Development of International Humanitarian Law, Geneva, 1974–77, *Official Record*, 155 CDDH/SR. 41 (1978).

116. *See* BOTHE ET AL., *supra* note 80, at 258–61.

117. *Id.*

118. As discussed *infra* in Part II.A.2, the scope of this protection is conditioned by Article 5 of the Civilians Convention. CIVILIANS CONVENTION, *supra* note 1, art. 5.

119. *See, e.g.*, BOTHE ET AL., *supra* note 80, at 261–62; Dormann, *supra* note 80, at 50.

2. *Limitations*

So far, the analysis offered above demonstrates only that unlawful combatants were covered by the Civilians Convention *to some extent*. Two potentially significant qualifications of this protection require further analysis. First, the protection accorded unlawful combatants under the Civilians Convention was expressly conditioned by the derogation regime of Article 5. As discussed above, Article 5 of the Civilians Convention, by its terms, applies to all unlawful combatants and arguably authorizes derogation of some Convention obligations. Recall that states may suspend some Convention rights if the detainee in question poses a threat to the security of the detaining state. The scope of this derogation power, however, is less clear. This Article 5 derogations, properly understood, are sharply limited. Second, the Civilians Convention may not provide any protection in "zones of active combat"—that is, on the battlefield. This is the interpretation of the Convention proposed by then-Major Richard Baxter in his famous article on the subject in the British Yearbook of International Law.[120] In this Part, I reject Baxter's claim because it is predicated on a cramped reading of the Convention and its drafting history—one that generates several interpretive and normative anomalies.

a. Article 5 of the Civilians Convention: The "Derogation" Provision

Application of the Civilians Convention to unlawful combatants is qualified by Article 5, the "derogation" provision. Specifically, this provision supplements the definition of "protected persons" provided in Article 4 by qualifying the applicability of the Civilians Convention to unlawful combatants. As a structural matter, Article 5 defines the scope of state authority to suspend the rights and privileges of persons otherwise protected by the Civilians Convention. Therefore, all categories of persons subject to Article 5 derogations are necessarily "protected persons" within the meaning of Article 4. In addition, all persons covered by Article 4 are "protected persons" *irrespective of whether their protection is qualified by Article 5*.[121] The provision authorizes states, subject to important limitations, to deny protections to individuals "suspected of or engaged in activities hostile to the security of the State [or the Occupying Power]."[122] In full, it provides that:

> [1] Where in the territory of a Party to the conflict, the latter is satisfied that an individual protected person is definitely suspected of or engaged in activities hostile to the security of the State, such individual person shall not be entitled to claim such rights and privileges under

120. *See* Baxter, *supra* note 3.

121. As I discuss above, this structural point is also important in discerning the territorial scope of the Convention.

122. CIVILIANS CONVENTION, *supra* note 1, art. 5.

> the present Convention as would, if exercised in the favour of such individual person, be prejudicial to the security of such State.
>
> [2] Where in occupied territory an individual protected person is detained as a spy or saboteur, or as a person under definite suspicion of activity hostile to the security of the Occupying Power, such person shall, in those cases where absolute military security so requires, be regarded as having forfeited rights of communication under the present Convention.
>
> [3] In each case, such persons shall nevertheless be treated with humanity and, in case of trial, shall not be deprived of the rights of fair and regular trial prescribed by the present Convention. They shall also be granted the full rights and privileges of a protected person under the present Convention at the earliest date consistent with the security of the State or Occupying Power, as the case may be.[123]

Although the provision clearly constitutes a broad authorization to derogate from the substantive commitments of the Convention, Article 5 conditions this authorization in several important respects. The provision establishes four types of constraints on the power to derogate: (1) derogations are permitted only in certain types of territory; (2) derogations are permitted only with respect to certain categories of persons; (3) derogations must be necessary to preserve certain state interests; and (4) derogations are permitted only with respect to certain rights and privileges.

First, the provision is subject to severe territorial restrictions. Indeed, the text suggests that it applies only in occupied territory and the territory of the detaining state.[124] That is, it does not expressly authorize derogations in non-occupied, enemy territory or in the territory of a co-belligerent. On this reading, the authority to derogate is most constrained in territory over which the derogating state exercises no sovereign or *de facto* authority. Conversely, this authority is at its apex in territory governed by the derogating state.

Indeed, the drafting history of the provision makes clear that it was motivated by concerns over *internal* security. The Swiss delegate introduced Article 5 by noting that "internal security was one of the main preoccupations of national leaders in time of war" and that "[i]t was essential . . . that the protection given by the Convention should not facilitate the subversive activities of 'fifth columnists.'"[125] Article 5 was introduced "[i]n order to guard against that danger."[126] The U.K. representative offered support for the provision by emphasizing that while his country "had given haven to refugees of all nationalities" and offered them the "same treatment as that accorded to its own citizens," the United Kingdom refused "to jeopardize the lives of its

123. *Id.*
124. *Id.*
125. 2A Diplomatic Conference, *supra* note 96, at 796.
126. *Id.*

own citizens . . . by omitting to take effective steps to counter, in time of war, the activities of those who abused its hospitality and conspired against its safety."[127] The delegate further stressed that "[i]t should be possible to counteract the dangers to which a country could be exposed to in wartime by the activities of traitors and saboteurs . . . by the adoption of effective measures against individuals suspected of giving assistance to the enemy."[128] The final drafting committee report to the Plenary emphasized "internal security" as the rationale for the provision, underscoring the necessity of Article 5 to counter effectively those "underground activities" that pose "a secret threat to the security of the State."[129] These statements demonstrate that the purpose of the first paragraph of Article 5 was to empower states to restrict, as necessary for state security, the rights and privileges of spies, saboteurs, and other enemy agents operating in the *home territory of a belligerent power*.[130]

Similar logic applies in the context of "occupied territory." Spies, saboteurs, and other unlawful combatants threaten the capacity of the military authority to administer occupied territory. Because the occupying forces must, under the terms of the Convention, assume many essential governmental functions, threats to military security are roughly analogous to threats to state security.[131] Hence, the second paragraph of Article 5, concerning occupied territory, authorizes derogations "where absolute military security so requires," whereas the first paragraph, concerning the home territory of a belligerent state, authorizes only derogations from rights the exercise of which would "be prejudicial to the security of [the] State."[132]

Second, derogations are permitted only with respect to certain persons—namely, those engaged in activity hostile to the state or occupying power. Derogation therefore requires that the detaining state know or have good reason to suspect that a particular individual has engaged in hostile acts.[133] This requirement, in general, poses no great difficulty in the case of unlawful combatants, who, by definition, have directly participated in hostilities against the detaining state. The important point for our purposes is that Article 5 is activated by the acts of, and directed to the treatment of, "indi-

---

127. *Id.* at 797.

128. *Id.* In the plenary debates, the U.K. delegate emphasized that Article 5 concerned

> [those] who have entered the country of the Home Power in time of peace and with their permission, and who have taken all that the country had to give them and have turned out to be conspirators and traitors in war-time against the country which has sheltered them.

2B Diplomatic Conference, *supra* note 96, at 380.

129. *Id.* at 814.

130. I do not mean to suggest that unlawful combatants are unprotected if captured in the home territory of the detaining state (or occupied territory). The point is only that the treatment accorded such persons is conditioned by the derogation regime of Article 5.

131. *See, e.g.*, 2B Diplomatic Conference, *supra* note 96, at 379–81 (demonstrating the analogy drawn by several delegates).

132. CIVILIANS CONVENTION, *supra* note 1, art. 5.

133. *Id.*

vidual persons."[134] As the ICRC Commentary points out, "[t]he suspicion must not rest on a whole class of people; collective measures cannot be taken under this Article; there must be grounds justifying action in each individual case."[135] That is, the provision requires individualized assessments with respect to (1) the applicability of Article 5 to any particular civilian, and (2) the necessity of specific derogations in each case.[136] The first of these requirements will obtain for each and every "unlawful combatant" because, by definition, such individuals have directly participated in the hostilities. The second, however, requires that the detaining state make individualized findings regarding the necessity of any contemplated derogations.

Third, the protections of the Convention may only be suspended if—and only for such time as—they are necessary to preserve state security in the territory of the derogating state or to preserve absolute military security of the occupying power in occupied territory.[137] This requirement limits sharply the range of permissible derogations. As the drafting history of Article 5 demonstrates, very few examples of lawful derogations were acknowledged:

> As soon as the subject [Article 5] came up for discussion at the Diplomatic Conference several delegations explained that in their opinion provision would have to be made for certain exceptions in the case of spies and saboteurs. They pointed out that the effectiveness of the measures taken to deal with enemy agents and saboteurs depended on the secrecy of the proceedings; it was inconceivable that a State which had arrested one or more enemy agents should be obliged to announce their capture and let the persons under arrest correspond with the outside world and receive visits; the situation was the same in the case of saboteurs and also, in occupied territories, in that of members of underground organizations.[138]

The ICRC Commentary concludes that:

> The rights referred to are not very extensive in the case of protected persons under detention; they consist essentially of the right to correspond, the right to receive individual or collective relief, the right to spiritual assistance from ministers of their faith and the right to receive visits from representatives of the Protecting Power and the International Committee of the Red Cross. The security of the State could not conceivably be put forward as a reason for depriving such persons of the benefit of other provisions . . . . It should, moreover, be noted that this provision cannot release the Detaining Power from its obligations towards the adverse

134. *Id.*
135. ICRC, COMMENTARY IV, *supra* note 54, at 55.
136. *Id.* at 55–56.
137. *Id.* at 56.
138. *Id.* at 52–53.

> Party. It remains fully bound by the obligation, imposed on it by Article 136, to transmit to the official Information Bureau particulars of any protected person who is kept in custody for more than two weeks. This is not, in fact, a right or privilege of the protected person, but an obligation of the Detaining Power.[139]

Although the significance of these derogable protections should not be minimized, the important point is that the necessity requirement constitutes an important limit on Article 5 derogations.[140]

Finally, and most important for the purposes of this analysis, Article 5 imposes two express limits on the scope of derogations: (1) the third paragraph limits the scope of the first two paragraphs by enumerating non-derogable rights; and (2) the second paragraph, by its terms, limits the scope of derogations in occupied territory to "rights of communication."

The third paragraph of Article 5 makes clear that "[i]n each case, such persons shall nevertheless be treated with humanity and, in the case of trial, shall not be deprived of the rights of fair and regular trial prescribed by the present Convention."[141] In short, the provision expressly identifies two categories of non-derogable protections—rights not subject to restriction even if the requirements of Article 5 are otherwise satisfied. These protections include: (1) the general right to "humane treatment" as defined in articles 27–29, 31–34 and 37;[142] (2) the prohibitions on forced deportations and transfers;[143] (3) the provisions prescribing minimum conditions of confinement;[144] (4) the provisions requiring adequate food and water, clothing, and medical treatment;[145] and (5) the fair trial rights identified in Articles 64–76 in occupied territory and Articles 71–76 in the territory of the belligerent state—made applicable to non-occupied territory by Article 126.[146]

In addition, the second paragraph, pertaining to derogations in occupied territory, only authorizes the suspension of "rights of communication."[147] These rights include the right to communicate with the Protecting Power, ICRC, or other humanitarian organizations.[148] This category of rights clearly also includes the right to visits from ministers and other spiritual advisors,[149] as well as the general right to correspondence with the outside world.[150] Ac-

---

139. *Id.* at 56.

140. *Id.* at 58.

141. Civilians Convention, *supra* note 1, art. 5.

142. *Id.* arts. 27–29, 31–34, 37.

143. *Id.* arts. 45–49.

144. *Id.* arts. 83–88.

145. *Id.* arts. 89–92.

146. *Id.* arts. 64–76, 126. The ICRC Commentary inexplicably misses this point, suggesting that "there are no special [fair trial] provisions applying to the territory of the conflict . . . ." ICRC, Commentary IV, *supra* note 54, at 58.

147. Civilians Convention, *supra* note 1, art. 5.

148. *Id.* arts. 30, 101, 143.

149. *Id.* art. 93.

150. *Id.* arts. 107–12; *see also* ICRC, Commentary IV, *supra* note 54, at 57 (stating that the provision

cording to this reading, Article 5 expressly limits potential derogations in occupied territory to these few rights.

Although this restrictive interpretation seems, at first glance, the most plausible reading of the second paragraph, interpretive difficulties become clear when the paragraph is read in light of the provision as a whole. As several commentators have pointed out, the central difficulty is how to square the text of the second paragraph with that of the third.[151] Recall that the third paragraph provides that "in each case"—that is, in the situations described in both the first and second paragraphs—all persons must be treated humanely and granted all fair trial rights recognized in the Convention. The interpretive puzzle is this: "If only provisions relating to communication can be derogated from, why is there a need to indicate as minimum protections humane treatment and fair trial?"[152] The solution typically offered is that the second paragraph is poorly drafted, and that it must constitute a broader authorization to derogate than the text read in isolation would suggest.

One possible alternative reading is that the second paragraph expressly identifies communication rights only to underscore their derogability in occupied territory. This interpretation is, however, unsatisfying for several reasons. First, it is predicated on the view that the provision cannot mean what it says—a view questioned below. Also, this interpretation does not adequately explain the textual discrepancies between the first and second paragraphs. For example, there is no good reason to suspect that the case for derogability of communication rights is stronger in occupied territory than in the home territory of the belligerent state; indeed, the opposite seems more accurate. This interpretation does not provide any convincing explanation for the lack of a "communication rights" clause in the first paragraph. Moreover, there is no good reason to conclude that the general security interest recognized in the second paragraph is an insufficient authorization to curtail any communication rights, even if the need to do so is greater in occupied territory.[153] This interpretation does not adequately explain the value added by the communication rights clause in the second paragraph, particularly since the drafting history suggests that the first paragraph targeted this category of rights.[154]

The problem with this strained reading is that it is founded on an impoverished reading of the plain text. Indeed, the interpretive puzzle itself issues from the conceptual mistake associated with this reading. The puzzle presumes that there is no meaningful overlap between communication rights

"obviously refer[s] to [rights governing] his relations with the outside world . . . .").

151. *See, e.g.*, DRAPER, RED CROSS CONVENTIONS, *supra* note 24, at 29–30; Dormann, *supra* note 80, at 64–66.

152. Dormann, *supra* note 80, at 66. The same puzzle applies, although in less acute form, to the interpretation of the first paragraph.

153. This is particularly puzzling given the lower security standard in occupied territory. See CIVILIANS CONVENTION, *supra* note 1, arts. 5, 41–43.

154. *See* ICRC, COMMENTARY IV, *supra* note 54, at 52–54.

and the rights protected by the third paragraph—humane treatment and fair trial rights. This view, however, does not withstand sustained scrutiny. First, some communication rights implicate "humane treatment." For example, the ICRC Commentary on Article 5 points out that "it would be really inhuman to refuse to let a chaplain visit a detained person who was seriously ill."[155] The important point is that Article 5 could be understood to authorize derogations of communication rights (second paragraph) unless doing so would constitute inhuman treatment (third paragraph). In addition, some communication rights are among the fair trial rights recognized in the Convention. For example, detainees facing criminal charges have the right to visit and communicate freely with defense counsel[156] and the right to communicate with the Protecting Power.[157] Therefore, the second paragraph of Article 5, on this reading, authorizes derogation from communication rights so long as all communication rights protected by the Convention's fair trial provisions are respected.

In short, the best reading of the second paragraph of Article 5, I submit, is that it authorizes derogations of *only* communication rights in occupied territory. Moreover, the scope of this authorization is conditioned by the third paragraph in that any deprivation of communication rights amounting to inhuman treatment or resulting in the denial of a fair trial is strictly prohibited.

b. Applicability to Non-Occupied, Enemy Territory

Irrespective of the scope of derogation authority, the Civilians Convention may not, in any case, apply in zones of active combat. Then-Major Richard Baxter famously defended this claim[158]—suggesting that Article 5 implicitly supports the conclusion that the Convention writ large does not apply on the battlefield.[159] The argument proceeds as follows: The drafting history

155. ICRC, COMMENTARY IV, *supra* note 54, at 56.

156. CIVILIANS CONVENTION, *supra* note 1, arts. 71–72; *see also id.* art. 126 (making articles 71–76 applicable in non-occupied territory).

157. *Id.* art. 74; *see also id.* art. 126 (making articles 71–76 applicable in non-occupied territory).

158. For much of the Cold War era, Baxter was one of the world's most prominent scholars of the laws of war. He was also principal author of the 1956 edition of the U.S. Army Field Manual 27-10, *supra* note 44, which implemented the Geneva Conventions into formal U.S. military policy.

159. Note that this claim is not inconsistent with the claim that the Civilians Convention applies to unlawful combatants. In Baxter's view, the Convention covers unlawful combatants, but only within certain categories of territory and not in the territory where protection is most needed—the battlefield on enemy territory. Many commentators have addressed the question of the status of unlawful combatants who have been captured, but little analysis has been dedicated to their status on the battlefield. *See, e.g.*, Draper, *supra* note 8, at 208; Dormann, *supra* note 80, at 48–52; Albert J. Easgain & Waldemar A. Solf, *The 1949 Geneva Convention Relative to the Treatment of Prisoners of War: Its Principles, Innovations, and Deficiencies*, 41 N.C. L. REV. 537, 549–51 (1962); Kalshoven, *supra* note 80, at 70, 74; John Cerone, *Status of Detainees in International Armed Conflict, and Their Protection in the Course of Criminal Proceedings*, ASIL INSIGHTS (Jan. 2002), *available at* http://www.asil.org/insights/insigh81.htm (last visited Mar. 6, 2004); Human Rights Watch, *Background Paper on Geneva Conventions and Persons Held by U.S. Forces* (Jan. 2002), *available at* http://www.hrw.org/backgrounder/usa/pow-bck.htm (last visited Mar. 6, 2004); Wayne Elliott, *POW's or Unlawful Combatants? September 11 and Its Aftermath*, CRIMES OF WAR PROJECT,

of Articles 4 and 5 demonstrates that combatants failing to qualify for POW status are covered by the Civilians Convention.[160] The scope of this coverage is governed principally by Article 5. The derogation authority recognized in Article 5, however, only extends to two types of territory (as previously discussed at length): (1) the home territory of the detaining power; and (2) occupied territory. Because Article 5 does not address non-occupied, enemy territory (in other words, zones of active combat), Baxter concludes that the Convention does not apply in this context. There are several problems—conceptual, textual, historical, and normative—with this line of argument.

Before evaluating the claim on the merits, some clarification is in order. The fundamental problem is that there are two ways to understand the foundation of the argument. Perhaps the claim is, at bottom, that the territorial scope of Article 5 evidences the intentions of the treaty's framers. This variant of the claim emphasizes the *interpretive significance* of Article 5. On the other hand, the claim may be that unlawful combatants are covered under the Convention *in virtue of* Article 5. Put differently, it is Article 5 itself which protects unlawful combatants, so any limitations on the scope of Article 5 would also limit the scope of protection accorded such persons. This variant of the claim emphasizes the *substantive significance* of Article 5. Both variants are fatally flawed, though for slightly different reasons.

The second variant—emphasizing the substantive significance of Article 5—is flatly implausible. It is inconsistent with the text, structure, and history of Articles 4 and 5. Recall that Article 5 supplements Article 4—the definition of "protected persons"—by limiting the applicability of the Civilians Convention to unlawful combatants. That is, Article 5 defines the scope of state authority to derogate from rights and privileges *otherwise protected* by the Civilians Convention. Unlawful combatants are covered under Article 4, and this coverage is, in turn, conditioned by the derogation authority conferred by Article 5. Moreover, the text of Article 5 does not, by its terms, confer rights; it authorizes restriction of them. In this sense, the text of Article 5 and its structural relation to Article 4 demonstrate that all persons subject to Article 5 derogations necessarily must be "protected persons" within the meaning of Article 4.

Read in its best light, therefore, Baxter's claim should be understood as something like the first variant identified above—emphasizing the interpretive significance of Article 5. This variant nevertheless is flawed in that it relies on a misreading of Article 5 and an impoverished reading of Article 4. Because I outlined in detail (and offered a sustained defense of) my interpretation of Article 5 in the preceding Part, this assessment of Baxter's view draws liberally on claims that are more fully developed above. Specifically, Baxter argues that

---

available at http://www.crimesofwar.org/expert/pow-elliott.html (last visited Mar. 6, 2004).

160. *See* CIVILIANS CONVENTION, *supra* note 1, arts. 4–5; *see also supra* Part II.A.1.

> [T]he failure of Article 5 to refer to areas where fighting is in progress outside occupied territory or the territory of the detaining state suggests that both Articles 4 and 5 were directed to the protection of inhabitants of occupied areas and of the mass of enemy aliens on enemy territory and that unlawful belligerents in the zone of operations were not taken into account in connexion with the two articles.[161]

The argument here, put differently, is that the text of Article 5 suggests that the Civilians Convention does not protect unlawful combatants in the "zone of operations." The logic behind this claim is not entirely clear. Baxter appears to be arguing that although Article 4 covers unlawful combatants, Article 5 recognizes that they present unique and grave security concerns, and that some of these concerns would be exacerbated by the protective scheme established in the Convention. Therefore, according to Baxter's view, Article 5 expressly authorizes states to deprive otherwise protected unlawful combatants of certain Convention rights under certain circumstances. Although this derogation authority is itself obviously significant, Article 5 is also important for what it does not say. More specifically, Article 5 authorizes derogation only in two types of territory: the home territory of the detaining power and occupied territory. Article 5 does not authorize derogation of Convention rights in non-occupied enemy territory—that is, the battlefield or, as Baxter called it, the "zone of operations." Because the security rationale undergirding Article 5 is, in Baxter's view, equally if not more applicable to the zone of operations, this textual gap is inexplicable if unlawful combatants are protected in such circumstances. Indeed, it suggests that, for Baxter, the framers did not even consider application of the Convention to unlawful combatants on the battlefield; if they had, Article 5 would have authorized derogation in such circumstances as well.

Although the Convention's drafting history provides non-trivial support for this line of reasoning, it is unsound. It rests on questionable or invalid assumptions, and it carries several anomalous interpretive implications.

First, Baxter's reading of Article 5 is unconvincing. Baxter expressly assumes that the territorial limitations in Article 5 are inexplicable if the Convention protects civilians on the battlefield in enemy territory, suggesting that the Convention must not apply in any case to such territory. His tacit claim is that the justification for derogation is as compelling (if not more so) on the battlefield (in enemy territory) as it is in occupied territory or the home territory of the belligerent state. But, as demonstrated above, Article 5 was designed to address problems of internal security and order maintenance.[162] That the provision authorizes no derogation in zones of active operations is therefore unsurprising. Additionally, the substantive protections accorded by the Convention suggest that derogation authority is in many respects unnec-

161. Baxter, *supra* note 3, at 328.
162. *See supra* Part II.A.1.

essary on the battlefield. The 1949 Geneva Conventions do not regulate the means and methods of warfare, nor do they protect all persons subject to the lethality of the enemy.[163] Rather, the Conventions govern only the treatment of "war victims" made subject to the authority of the enemy—the paradigmatic example being persons captured and detained. The Civilians Convention, in this sense, does not regulate the application of force on the battlefield, at home or abroad, against unlawful combatants or peaceful civilians. Therefore, persons covered by Article 5—persons committing hostile acts—may be targeted and killed on the battlefield irrespective of whether Article 5 applies. Finally, the individualized assessment contemplated by Article 5 suggests that valid derogation would prove difficult if not impossible on the battlefield. Recall that Article 5 requires an individualized determination as to whether and which derogation measures are necessary.[164] In other words, there is good reason to think that the Article 5 regime would not extend to circumstances in which its safeguards could not be implemented adequately.

Second, Baxter's interpretation of Article 4 is similarly unconvincing. He contends that the drafters of Article 4 did not contemplate its application in zones of combat. That is, Baxter claims that the Civilians Convention *writ large* is inapplicable to non-occupied, enemy territory—wherein it does not protect unlawful combatants or peaceful civilians. Rather, "protected persons" within the meaning of Article 4 are those who, in time of armed conflict or occupation, find themselves in the hands of an enemy state in either that state's territory or in territory occupied by that state.

This interpretation of the treaty's scope produces troubling anomalies when applied in other contexts. The sharp edge of this view is, of course, that the Conventions would afford no protection in zones of active operations in enemy territory. One problem is that Baxter does not offer any theory as to why the Conventions would be so limited. The claim cannot be that the special circumstances of the battlefield require special rules. After all, even on this view, the Conventions protect persons on the battlefield in the home territory of the detaining power, and the Conventions would also apply to the battlefield in the case of sporadic, guerrilla conflict in occupied territory. The claim cannot be that such circumstances did not occur to the delegates to the Diplomatic Conference—the record makes clear that they did.[165] The claim cannot be that excluding such territory from coverage reflects some judgment about whether the Convention should apply to unlawful combatants, for the delegates well understood that peaceful civilians often encounter the enemy in zones of active operations.[166] Ultimately, Baxter offers no

---

163. *See infra* Part III.D.
164. *See supra* Part II.A.1.a.
165. *See supra* Part II.A.1.
166. *See id.*; *see also supra* note 159.

reason why the Conventions would have been designed this way, and no good reason is readily apparent.

Moreover, there are good reasons to think that Article 4 is not limited in this way. The plain text of Article 4 suggests that it is not so limited; Article 4 defines protected persons as those who, "at any given moment and in any manner whatsoever" fall into the hands of the enemy.[167] In addition, Baxter's "implicit limitation" reading of this provision is discredited by comparing Article 4 of the Civilians Convention to the provisions defining "protected persons" in the other three 1949 Geneva treaties. Recall that the definitions of "protected persons" in the other Conventions are, without exception, quite detailed.[168] And the Civilians Convention itself prescribes, in some detail, rules governing the treatment of civilians "suspected of or engaged in activities hostile to the security of the State."[169] When read in light of the other Conventions, the Civilians Convention should not be interpreted as implicitly excluding from its protection a potentially broad category of persons otherwise satisfying its definition of "protected persons." The best reading of Article 4 is that it assigns "protected person" status to all individuals satisfying its express requirements. Indeed, Baxter's alternative reading—even assuming for the moment its textual and historical plausibility—introduces inexplicable asymmetries into the Conventions' application. For example, in Baxter's view, a belligerent would have greater freedom of action in dealing with unlawful combatants fighting for the enemy in an international armed conflict on foreign soil than it would on its home territory. In addition, Baxter's view suggests that when battles are fought on a state's territory, the state finds itself at a disadvantage vis-à-vis the belligerent who, by virtue of fighting on non-occupied enemy territory, enjoys greater latitude in dealing with irregular forces. In short, Baxter's tacit assumption that there are no plausible alternative readings of Article 5 proves inaccurate, and his interpretations of Articles 4 and 5 are flawed in several respects.

To summarize, the Civilians Convention protects unlawful combatants, and these protections closely resemble the rights accorded under the POW Convention. Although conventional wisdom suggests that these protections, even if applicable, are subject to severe derogation restrictions (Article 5) and territorial restrictions (Baxter's reading of the Convention), these restrictions, in fact, are illusory, overstated, and, in some respects, inconsequential.

B. *Penal Repression Regime of the Geneva Conventions*

In addition to the protections discussed above, the Geneva Conventions protect all unlawful combatants facing trial for war crimes. Indeed, the Con-

167. CIVILIANS CONVENTION, *supra* note 1, art. 4.

168. *See* GENEVA CONVENTION I, *supra* note 1, art. 4; GENEVA CONVENTION II, *supra* note 1, art. 4; POW CONVENTION, *supra* note 1, art. 4.

169. CIVILIANS CONVENTION, *supra* note 1, art. 5.

ventions prescribe a detailed inventory of procedural rights guarantees for prosecutions brought under its substantive provisions. That is, the Conventions provide for minimum procedural rights for any person charged with serious violations of its substantive rules irrespective of the person's status under the Conventions.[170]

Individuals prosecuted for violations of the Geneva Conventions, regardless of their status as "protected persons," must be provided with "safeguards of proper trial and defence, which shall not be less favourable than" those outlined in Articles 105 and following of the POW Convention.[171] Article 105 specifically provides for basic fair trial rights including: the right to counsel of the defendant's choice, the right to confer privately with counsel, the right to call witnesses, and the right to an interpreter.[172] These provisions also require, for example, that accused persons be granted the same right of appeal as that accorded members of the armed forces of the Detaining Power.[173]

Although these protections apply formally only to prosecutions for violations of the rules established in the Conventions, they should also apply in any prosecutions brought under the laws of war. First, there is no principled reason to apply these protections only to breaches of the Geneva Conventions. It is, after all, important to note that the "grave breach" provisions and illustrative "simple breach" provisions are the only express criminal prohibitions in the Conventions. Consequently, these criminal provisions also make explicit the minimum procedural rights to be accorded in any prosecution under the penal repression regime of the Conventions. Thus, the express criminal provisions necessitate an express procedural rights regime.

Second, the structure of the Geneva Conventions' penal repression regime suggests that these procedural rights should apply to all prosecutions under the laws of war. Recall that the Geneva Conventions require states to punish acts constituting "grave breaches."[174] The Conventions, however, also provide that states must discharge this obligation through formal criminal proceedings in which fundamental procedural rights are respected.[175] In this way, the Conventions make clear that these procedural rights condition the efforts of states to repress serious violations of the Conventions. In addition, the text of Common Article 3, which is common to all four Geneva Conventions, supports this view. By its terms, that provision prohibits the imposition of criminal punishment "without previous judgment pronounced by a

170. *See, e.g.*, CIVILIANS CONVENTION, *supra* note 1, art. 146.

171. GENEVA CONVENTION I, *supra* note 1, art. 49; GENEVA CONVENTION II, *supra* note 1, art. 50; POW CONVENTION, *supra* note 1, art. 129; CIVILIANS CONVENTION, *supra* note 1, art. 146.

172. POW CONVENTION, *supra* note 1, art. 105.

173. *Id.* art. 106.

174. *See* GENEVA CONVENTION I, *supra* note 1, art. 49; GENEVA CONVENTION II, *supra* note 1, art. 50; POW CONVENTION, *supra* note 1, art. 129; CIVILIANS CONVENTION, *supra* note 1, art. 146.

175. *See, e.g.*, CIVILIANS CONVENTION, *supra* note 1, art. 146.

regularly constituted court, affording all the judicial guarantees which are recognized as indispensable by civilized peoples."[176]

Finally, the structure of the Conventions as a whole suggests that fundamental judicial guarantees should apply to all prosecutions under the laws of war. As I have argued elsewhere, states enjoy wide discretion in triggering the application of the laws of war in both international and non-international armed conflicts.[177] This discretion promotes the humanitarian purposes of the Conventions by rendering the laws of war broadly applicable. At a high level of abstraction, the general structure of the Geneva Conventions may be discerned: the Conventions establish an extensive humanitarian code, including basic fair trial rights, with a low threshold of application. The Conventions, as a consequence, should not be read to provide states an anti-humanitarian incentive to recognize the existence of an armed conflict. That is, the substantive laws of war should be tightly coupled with the procedural rights recognized in the laws of war. Otherwise, the Conventions would give states an incentive to characterize hostilities as an "armed conflict" in order to decrease procedural rights protections. The danger is that loose coupling of procedure and substance would arguably empower states to implement exceptional, draconian procedural devices by invoking the existence of an "armed conflict." Therefore, any person charged with war crimes should receive, at a minimum, the fair trial protections established in the POW Convention.

C. *Common Article 3*

The Geneva Conventions also specify fundamental humanitarian protections applicable to all persons subject to the authority of a party to the conflict. The Conventions detail minimum protections to be accorded all persons no longer taking part in hostilities irrespective of: (1) the territory in which the affected person is located; (2) the nationality of the affected person; or (3) the character of the armed conflict. These principles, first codified in Common Article 3 of the Conventions, govern the treatment of persons no longer taking active part in the hostilities.[178] All such persons are entitled to humane treatment and, in the case of criminal charges, fair trial by "a regularly constituted court, affording all the judicial guarantees which are recognized as indispensable by civilized peoples."[179] It is important to note that this

176. Common Art. 3, *supra* note 59.

177. *See* Derek Jinks, *September 11 and the Laws of War*, 28 YALE J. INT'L L. 1 (2003) [hereinafter Jinks, *September 11*]; Derek Jinks, *The Temporal Scope of Application of International Humanitarian Law, Policy Brief*, HARVARD PROGRAM ON HUMANITARIAN POLICY AND CONFLICT RESEARCH (2003) [hereinafter Jinks, *Temporal Scope*], *available at* http://www.ihlresearch.org/ihl/Session3.pdf (last visited Apr. 10, 2004) (on file with the HARV. INT'L L.J.); *see also* POW CONVENTION, *supra* note 1, art. 2 (establishing that the Conventions apply if one of the states party to the hostilities determines that an "armed conflict" exists or if one state formally declares war).

178. It is important to note that the provision expressly covers persons who take up arms against the state and applies even to persons who do not lay down their arms voluntarily. Common Art. 3, *supra* note 59.

179. Common Art. 3(1)(d), *supra* note 59.

provision is, by its nature, applicable to unlawful combatants in that it governs the relations between states and informal armed opposition groups. The provision obligates states to apply, at a minimum, the following principles in armed conflicts "not of an international character":

> (1) Persons taking no active part in the hostilities, including members of armed forces who have laid down their arms and those placed "hors de combat" by sickness, wounds, detention, or any other cause, shall in all circumstances be treated humanely, without any adverse distinction founded on race, colour, religion or faith, sex, birth or wealth, or any other similar criteria. To this end, the following acts are and shall remain prohibited at any time and in any place whatsoever with respect to the above-mentioned persons:
> (a) violence to life and person, in particular murder of all kinds, mutilation, cruel treatment and torture;
> (b) taking of hostages;
> (c) outrages upon personal dignity, in particular humiliating and degrading treatment;
> (d) the passing of sentences and the carrying out of executions without previous judgment pronounced by a regularly constituted court, affording all the judicial guarantees which are recognized as indispensable by civilized peoples.
> (2) The wounded and sick shall be collected and cared for.[180]

Common Article 3, therefore, seemingly necessitates humane treatment and fair trial rights for all persons rendered *hors de combat* in non-international armed conflicts. Three issues require more sustained reflection. Does Common Article 3 apply only to non-international armed conflicts? What persons are protected by the provision? What legal protection does this provision afford? In Part II.C, I argue that Common Article 3: (1) applies to all armed conflicts; (2) covers unlawful combatants no longer taking active part in hostilities; and (3) confers on unlawful combatants important, even if abstract, legal protection. Although Common Article 3, when considered in isolation, does not provide a sufficiently precise body of rules to protect "unlawful combatants" effectively, this provision does establish a framework within which a more robust protective regime has evolved.

1. *Application to International Armed Conflicts*

In general, the laws of war are applicable only in the context of an international armed conflict between two or more nation states.[181] The full protections of the Geneva Conventions, for example, expressly apply only in

180. Common Art. 3, *supra* note 59.

181. *See generally* EDWARD KWAKWA, THE INTERNATIONAL LAW OF ARMED CONFLICT: PERSONAL AND MATERIAL FIELDS OF APPLICATION (1992).

"armed conflicts involving two or more High Contracting Powers."[182] Similarly, the Hague Conventions and their annexed Regulations are applicable only in case of war between two or more of the Contracting Powers.[183] Common Article 3, by its terms, applies only to armed conflicts "not of an international character."[184] The structure and history of the Conventions, however, make clear that the provision applies in *all armed conflicts*.

Traditionally, the laws of war did not apply to non-international armed conflicts.[185] These conflicts, even when prolonged and intense, were as a consequence exclusively governed by domestic law.[186] Interference by another state in such matters would have been deemed an unlawful intrusion into the internal affairs of the state[187] and might have been considered an act of war.[188] The atrocities perpetrated by the Nazi regime before and during World War II clearly demonstrated that internal matters presented grave threats to humanitarian principles.[189] The Spanish Civil War, which broke out in 1936, also suggested to many that existing international law inadequately regulated internal armed conflicts.[190]

Against the backdrop of these events and the general humanitarian trajectory of the laws of war,[191] broad support for some sort of international regulation of non-international armed conflicts crystallized prior to the Diplomatic Conference in Geneva.[192] Because states nevertheless resisted international regulation of wholly internal matters, there was little support at the Conference for the ICRC's pre-Conference proposal to make the entire text of the Geneva Conventions applicable to non-international conflict. Two alternative approaches enjoyed substantial support. One approach sought to apply all the rules of the Conventions to a narrow range of internal conflicts—those closely resembling interstate conflicts, such as the Spanish Civil War. A second approach sought to apply a more limited set of substantive principles to to a much broader range of conflicts.[193] On this view, the core principles

182. POW CONVENTION, *supra* note 1, art. 2.

183. HAGUE CONVENTION, *supra* note 5, art. 2.

184. Common Art. 3, *supra* note 59.

185. *See, e.g.*, Rosemary Abi-Saab, *Humanitarian Law and Internal Conflicts: The Evolution of Legal Concern*, *in* HUMANITARIAN LAW OF ARMED CONFLICT: CHALLENGES AHEAD 209, 210–11 (Astrid J. M. Delissen & Gerard J. Tanja eds., 1991).

186. *See* LINDSAY MOIR, LAW OF INTERNATIONAL ARMED CONFLICT 4 (2002) ("No international restraints were applicable, and the rebels had no rights or protection in international law . . . ."); HEATHER WILSON, INTERNATIONAL LAW AND THE USE OF FORCE BY NATIONAL LIBERATION MOVEMENTS 23–24 (1988); Richard A. Falk, *Janus Tormented: The International Law of Internal War*, *in* INTERNATIONAL ASPECTS OF CIVIL STRIFE 185, 197 (James N. Roseneau ed., 1964).

187. *See, e.g.*, Abi-Saab, *supra* note 185, at 216–17.

188. *See, e.g.*, Erik Castren, *Civil War*, 142(2) ANNALES ACADEMIAE SCIENTARIARUM FENNICAE, 1, 179–81 (1966).

189. *See, e.g.*, RATNER & ABRAMS, *supra* note 30, at 5–14 (describing the importance of these events for the development of international humanitarian law).

190. *See* NORMAN J. PADELFORD, INTERNATIONAL LAW AND DIPLOMACY IN THE SPANISH CIVIL STRIFE 18 (1939); Vernon A. O'Rourke, *Recognition of Belligerency in the Spanish Civil War*, 31 AM. J. INT'L L. 398 (1937); OPPENHEIM'S INTERNATIONAL LAW, *supra* note 9, at 270–72.

191. *See* Theodor Meron, *The Humanization of Humanitarian Law*, 94 AM. J. INT'L L. 239 (2000).

192. *See, e.g.*, Abi-Saab, *supra* note 185, at 211–12.

to a much broader range of conflicts.[193] On this view, the core principles of the Conventions would apply even in the context of armed conflicts not of an international character.[194]

The Diplomatic Conference, in the final text of Common Article 3, adopted the latter approach.[195] Utilizing language originally proposed as text for the preamble to the four Conventions, the drafters of the provision sought to invoke the core principles of the treaty that should pierce the veil of sovereignty and apply even in the absence of an international armed conflict. Indeed, the character of Common Article 3 was well understood by the drafters of the Conventions as evidenced by the ICRC Commentary:

> This minimum requirement in the case of a non-international armed conflict, is *a fortiori* applicable in international conflicts. It proclaims the guiding principle common to all four Geneva Conventions, and from it each of them derives the essential provision around which it is built.[196]

The purpose of Common Article 3 was, therefore, to "ensur[e] respect for the few essential rules of humanity which all civilised nations consider as valid everywhere and under all circumstances and as being above and outside war itself."[197] In short, "[i]t is both legally and morally untenable that the rules contained in common Article 3, which constitute mandatory minimum rules applicable to internal conflicts, in which rules are less developed than in respect of international conflicts, would not be applicable to conflicts of an international character."[198]

Indeed, the applicability of Common Article 3 to international armed conflicts is now recognized in the jurisprudence of the International Court of Justice (ICJ),[199] the International Criminal Tribunal for the Former Yugoslavia (ICTY),[200] the International Criminal Tribunal for Rwanda (ICTR),[201] and the Inter-American Commission for Human Rights.[202] It is U.S. military policy to apply Common Article 3 in all armed conflicts and even in situations not rising to the level of an "armed conflict," such as internal dis-

193. *See* 2B Diplomatic Conference, *supra* note 96, at 34–54; Moir, *supra* note 186, at 21–31.

194. Common Art. 3, *supra* note 59; ICRC, Commentary: III Geneva Convention relative to the Treatment of Prisoners of War, 31–34 (Jean de Preux ed., 1960) [hereinafter ICRC, Commentary III].

195. Abi-Saab, *supra* note 185, at 217.

196. ICRC, Commentary IV, *supra* note 54, at 14.

197. *Id.* at 44.

198. Prosecutor v. Delalic, Case No. IT-96-21-A, Judgment, ¶ 150 (Feb. 20, 2001) [hereinafter Celebici Case].

199. *See* Military and Paramilitary Activities (Nicar. v. U.S.), 1986 I.C.J. 14, 114 (June 27).

200. *See* Prosecutor v. Tadic, Case No. IT-94-1-I, Decision on the Defense Motion for Interlocutory Appeal on Jurisdiction, ¶ 87 (Oct. 2, 1995) [hereinafter Tadic Appeal].

201. *See* Prosecutor v. Akayesu, Case No. ICTR 96-4-T, Judgment, ¶ 601 (Sept. 2, 1998).

202. *See* Abella v. Argentina, Case 11.137, Inter-Am. C.H.R., Report No. 55/97, OEA/Ser.L/V/II.98, doc 6 rev. ¶¶ 155–56 (1997) [hereinafter Abella].

turbances.[203] The Judge Advocate General of the U.S. Army endorses this view as well.[204] Moreover, Additional Protocol I to the Geneva Conventions, now ratified by over 160 countries, clarifies that the protections codified in Common Article 3 apply, as a matter of positive international law, to all armed conflicts.[205] This avalanche of legal authority prompted the ICTY Appeals Chamber to proclaim that it is now "indisputable that common Article 3, which sets forth a minimum core of mandatory rules, reflects the fundamental humanitarian principles which underlie international humanitarian law as a whole, and upon which the Geneva Conventions in their entirety are based."[206]

2. *Applicability to Unlawful Combatants*

Common Article 3 governs the treatment of "[p]ersons taking no active part in the hostilities, including members of armed forces who have laid down their arms and those placed 'hors de combat' by sickness, wounds, detention, or any other cause."[207] In general, the provision covers "persons taking no active part in hostilities"—an expression that, by its terms, includes "members of the armed forces." Common Article 3 therefore clearly applies to civilians who have not engaged in hostilities and members of the armed forces no longer engaged in hostilities. The central question is whether it also covers civilians and irregular forces who, despite the fact that they no longer take active part in the conflict, did at some point participate in the hostilities.

On this issue, there are at least two potential readings of Common Article 3: (1) the provision applies to all persons no longer taking part in the hostilities (including members of the armed forces *hors de combat*); or (2) it applies to all persons who did not take active part in the hostilities at any point and members of the armed forces no longer participating in the fighting. The second reading suggests that the provision protects only noncombatants and lawful combatants no longer fighting and excludes unlawful combatants.

The general character of the provision and its full text strongly suggest, however, that the first reading (the provision covers all persons no longer

---

203. *See* Dep't of Defense, Dir. 5100.77, DoD Law of War Program, ¶ 5.3.1 (Dec. 9, 1998), *available at* http://www.dtic.mil/whs/directives/corres/pdf/d510077_120998/d510077p.pdf (last visited Apr. 9, 2004) (saying that the Heads of the DoD Components shall "[e]nsure that the members of their Components comply with the law of war during all conflicts, however such conflicts are characterized, and with the principles and spirit of the law of war during all other operations."). *See generally* Major Timothy P. Bulman, *A Dangerous Game Disguised as Enlightened Policy: United States Law of War Obligations in Military Operations Other than War*, 159 MIL. L. REV. 152 (1999).

204. *See* JUDGE ADVOCATE GENERAL'S SCHOOL, U.S. ARMY, *Protection of Civilians During Armed Conflict*, *in* LAW OF WAR WORKSHOP DESKBOOK, *supra* note 114, 123, 129.

205. ADDITIONAL PROTOCOL I, *supra* note 10, art. 75; *see also infra* Parts II.D, IV.B.4 (discussing Article 75 and its subsequent development).

206. Celebici Case, *supra* note 198, ¶ 143.

207. Common Art. 3, *supra* note 59.

engaged in hostilities) is the best interpretation. First, the purpose of Common Article 3 strongly suggests that it covers irregular combatants and others who have participated in the hostilities. As previously discussed, the provision makes some core principles of the Conventions applicable to *non-international* conflicts—that is, conflicts between states and sub-state, "irregular" armed groups—whose fighters have taken up arms against the state in question without the right to do so. In other words, the purpose of the provision was to humanize, to some extent, hostilities between states and "unlawful combatants." Indeed, the drafting history makes clear that states were primarily concerned that Common Article 3 would, if its threshold of application were too low, intrude on the sovereign prerogative of states to suppress internal rebellion.[208] The Inter-American Commission on Human Rights, one of the few bodies to address the issue directly, has held that:

> Common Article 3's basic purpose is to have certain minimum rules apply during hostilities for the protection of persons who do not or no longer take a direct or active part in the hostilities.... Individual civilians are...covered by Common Article 3's safeguards when they are captured or otherwise subjected to the power of an adverse party, even if they had fought for the other side.[209]

Second, the text of Common Article 3 strongly suggests that it covers "unlawful combatants." For example, the text of the provision flatly imposes obligations on all parties to the conflict—both the state group and the non-state, irregular armed group.[210] In addition, the text makes clear that its applicability in no way affects the "legal status" of the parties to the conflict.[211] At the 1949 Diplomatic Conference, states were concerned that application of the "laws of war" to insurgent forces would confer on the group international legal personality, and many states indicated that they could not support the provision at all absent some favorable resolution of this issue.[212] To address this concern, the text specifies that the application of the provision does not formally constitute "recognition of the belligerency" of the armed group, and that the applicability of the provision therefore does not confer on the non-state armed group lawful combatant status.[213] States supported this language so that members of an irregular armed group could be subjected to domestic criminal prosecution *for their very participation in the hostilities even if conducted in accordance with the laws of*

208. *See, e.g.*, Jinks, *September 11*, *supra* note 177.

209. *See* Abella, *supra* note 202, ¶¶ 176, 189. The ICTY endorses this interpretation as well. *See* Tadic Appeal, *supra* note 200, ¶ 616 (holding that persons captured by opposing forces were entitled to the protections of Common Article 3 "[w]hatever their involvement in hostilities prior to that time").

210. Common Art. 3, *supra* note 59.

211. *Id.*

212. For an excellent summary of the debate and the range of concerns represented therein, see MOIR, *supra* note 186, at 52–58.

213. *See, e.g.*, Jinks, *September 11*, *supra* note 177; Jinks, *Temporal Scope*, *supra* note 177.

war.[214] In short, Common Article 3 makes clear that, although entitled to its protections and subject to its obligations, unlawful combatants nevertheless remain unlawful combatants.

3. *Legal Protections*

Common Article 3 mandates that all persons protected by the provision "shall in all circumstances be treated humanely."[215] In general, this requirement directs the detaining authority to extend the protections of the Conventions' broad "humane treatment" provisions to all persons not taking active part in hostilities.[216] Although important, without any further specification this general requirement would nevertheless offer only modest legal protection. Several more specific prohibitions give the provision a more concrete character. The provision prohibits certain acts "at any time and in any place"—including murder, torture, cruelty, humiliating or degrading treatment, and punishment without fair trial—directed against these persons.[217] It also requires that parties to the conflict collect and provide care to the wounded and sick.[218]

Although these protections are pitched in abstract terms, it is plain that the provision accords substantial legal protection to "unlawful combatants." Similar to the protections accorded POWs, Common Article 3 expressly prohibits: (1) "violence to life and person," including torture and cruel treatment; and (2) "outrages upon personal dignity," including humiliating and degrading treatment.[219] The provision also mandates due process protections that in principle are difficult to distinguish from POW rights. Indeed, read in light of national practice and subsequent developments in humanitarian and human rights law, the protections of Common Article 3 closely approximate the most important protections accorded POWs.

---

214. Although Common Article 3 does not preclude such prosecutions, neither does it require or authorize them. As a consequence, any such prosecution would be brought under domestic law and not under the laws of war. This is an important point because it suggests that the law of war applicable in internal armed conflicts does not proscribe the very act of taking up arms against the state. *See, e.g.*, Baxter, *supra* note 3, at 339–40, 344.

215. Common Art. 3, *supra* note 59.

216. *See* POW CONVENTION, *supra* note 1, art. 13; CIVILIANS CONVENTION, *supra* note 1, art. 27.

217. In one sense, Common Article 3 identifies a category of "protected persons." That is, the conceptual structure of the provision is similar to that of the Conventions as a whole, which establish an elaborate code protecting certain categories of "protected persons," such as "prisoners of war" and "civilians." This similarity prompted the United States to suggest that the "grave breach" provisions of the Conventions, which criminalize certain acts directed against "persons protected by the Conventions," are also applicable to Common Article 3 violations. *See Amicus Curiae* Brief Presented by the Government of the United States of America, at 35–38, Prosecutor v. Tadic, Case No. IT-94-I-T, Opinion and Judgment (May 7, 1997) (on file with author). Despite the textual plausibility of this view, the drafting history of Common Article 3 and many commentators suggest otherwise. *See generally* MOIR, *supra* note 186.

218. Common Art. 3(2), *supra* note 59. I have argued elsewhere that the September 11 terrorist attacks constituted violations of Common Article 3 (even if Al Qaeda acted without the assistance of a state). *See generally* Jinks, *September 11*, *supra* note 177; Jinks, *Temporal Scope*, *supra* note 177.

219. *See* Common Art. 3, *supra* note 59.

With respect to due process rights, Common Article 3 prohibits "the passing of sentences and the carrying out of executions without previous judgment pronounced by a regularly constituted court, affording all the judicial guarantees which are recognized as indispensable by civilized peoples."[220] Although the substance of this rule is difficult to discern with precision, considerable evidence suggests that it embodies protections at least as robust as the POW rules. Without question, the rule prohibits the sort of "summary justice" that had all too often characterized quasi-judicial battlefield tribunals.[221]

In addition, the text of the provision suggests some important principles. For instance, the rule prohibits punishment without a "previous judgment"—suggesting that a formal adjudication is required.[222] Moreover, the body pronouncing this judgment must be "regularly constituted," suggesting that it must be established in law and must not be convened especially for the punishment of the adversary.[223] Furthermore, this body must be a "regularly constituted *court*," suggesting that there must be adequate safeguards in place to ensure the impartiality, independence, and fairness of the institution issuing the judgment.[224]

Moreover, the text of Common Article 3—specifically the reference to the opinions of "judicial guarantees which are recognized as indispensable by civilized peoples"[225] establishes an evolving standard that, *by design*, tracks customary international law in this area.[226] In addition to the developments embodied in Article 75 of Additional Protocol I (referenced above and detailed below), international human rights law has in the past fifty years elaborated a detailed body of due process norms that now arguably define the minimum requirements of procedural fairness. Several international human rights treaties,[227] declarations,[228] and resolutions[229] establish minimum

220. *Id.*

221. ICRC, COMMENTARY IV, *supra* note 54, at 224–26.

222. Common Art. 3(1)(d), *supra* note 59.

223. *Id.*

224. *Id.* (emphasis added).

225. Common Art. 3, *supra* note 59.

226. *See, e.g.*, MOIR, *supra* note 186 at 203–08 (arguing that the judicial guarantees of Common Article 3 must be understood in light of international human rights treaties); Jordan Paust, *Judicial Power To Determine the Status and Rights of Persons Detained*, 44 HARV. INT'L L.J. 503, 511–12 n.27, 514 (2003).

227. *See, e.g.*, CONVENTION AGAINST TORTURE AND OTHER CRUEL, INHUMAN OR DEGRADING TREATMENT OR PUNISHMENT, U.N. GAOR, 39th Sess., Supp. No. 51, at 197, U.N. Doc. A/39/51 (1984), *entered into force* June 26, 1987; Council of Europe, EUROPEAN CONVENTION FOR THE PROTECTION OF HUMAN RIGHTS AND FUNDAMENTAL FREEDOMS, arts. 5–7, Nov. 4, 1950, 213 U.N.T.S. 222, E.T.S. 5, *amended by* Protocol No. 3, E.T.S. 45, Protocol No. 5, E.T.S. 55, and Protocol No. 8, E.T.S. 118 [hereinafter ECHR]; INTERNATIONAL COVENANT ON CIVIL AND POLITICAL RIGHTS, arts. 9, 14–15, Dec. 19, 1966, 999 U.N.T.S. 171 [hereinafter ICCPR]; Organization of African Unity, AFRICAN CHARTER ON HUMAN AND PEOPLES' RIGHTS, arts. 3, 6–7, June 27, 1981, 21 I.L.M. 59 [hereinafter BANJUL CHARTER]; Organization of American States, AMERICAN CONVENTION ON HUMAN RIGHTS, arts. 7–9, Nov. 22, 1969, O.A.S. T.S. No. 36, 1144 U.N.T.S. 123 [hereinafter ACHR].

228. *See, e.g.*, UNIVERSAL DECLARATION OF HUMAN RIGHTS, arts. 9–11, G.A. Res. 217A, U.N. Doc. A/810 (1948) [hereinafter UDHR].

229. *See, e.g.*, BODY OF PRINCIPLES FOR THE PROTECTION OF ALL PERSONS UNDER ANY FORM OF

procedural protections for all individuals deprived of their personal liberty. Under Article 9 of the International Covenant on Civil and Political Rights (ICCPR), no one shall be "subjected to arbitrary arrest or detention" or "deprived of his liberty except on such grounds and in accordance with such procedure as are established by law."[230] This provision also specifies that "[a]nyone who is arrested shall be informed, at the time of arrest, of the reasons for his arrest and shall be promptly informed of any charges against him."[231] Article 9(3) provides that all persons arrested or detained on a criminal charge "shall be brought promptly before a judge or other officer authorized by law to exercise judicial power and shall be entitled to trial within a reasonable time or to release."[232] As interpreted by the U.N. Human Rights Committee, the provision requires at a minimum that an individual must be brought before a judge or other officer within "a few days."[233] Finally, the

---

Detention or Imprisonment, G.A. Res. 43/173, Supp. No. 49, at 298, U.N. Doc. A/43/49 (1988); Standard Minimum Rules for the Treatment of Prisoners, U.N. Doc. A/CONF/611, annex 1, E.S.C. Res. 663C, (XXIV) (July 31, 1957), U.N. ESCOR, Supp. No. 1, at 11, U.N. Doc. E/3048 (1957), *amended by* E.S.C. Res. 2076, (LXII) (May 13, 1977), U.N. ESCOR, Supp. No. 1, at 35, U.N. Doc. E/5988 (1977); Basic Principles on the Role of Lawyers, Eighth U.N. Congress on the Prevention of Crime and the Treatment of Offenders, Havana, Aug. 27–Sept. 7, 1990, U.N. Doc. A/CONF.144/28/Rev.1 at 118 (1990); Guidelines on the Role of Prosecutors, Eighth U.N. Congress on the Prevention of Crime and the Treatment of Offenders, Havana, Aug. 27–Sept. 7, 1990, U.N. Doc. A/CONF. 144/28/Rev.1 at 189 (1990); Basic Principles on the Independence of the Judiciary, Seventh U.N. Congress on the Prevention of Crime and the Treatment of Offenders, Milan, Aug. 26–Sept. 6, 1985, U.N. Doc. A/CONF.121/22/Rev.1 at 59 (1985).

230. ICCPR, *supra* note 227, art. 9, ¶ 1.

231. *Id.* art. 9, ¶ 2.

232. *Id.* art. 9, ¶ 3. Note that Article 9(3) of the ICCPR applies only to individuals arrested or detained on a *criminal* charge, while the other rights recognized in the Article apply to all persons deprived of their liberty. People awaiting trial on criminal charges should not, as a general rule, be held in custody. *See id.* art. 14, ¶ 3. Of course, international standards explicitly recognize some circumstances in which authorities may detain an accused pending trial. *See id.* art. 9, ¶ 3; *see also* ACHR, *supra* note 227, art. 7, ¶ 5; Body of Principles, *supra* note 229, princ. 39; Tokyo Rules: U.N. Standard for Minimum Rules for Non-custodial Measures, G.A. Res. 45/110, princ. 6, U.N. Doc. A/RES/45/110 (1990).

233. Hum. Rts. Comm., gen. cmt. 8, art. 9 (Sixteenth session, 1982), Compilation of General Comments and General Recommendations Adopted by Human Rights Treaty Bodies, U.N. Doc. HRI/GEN/1/Rev.1 at para. 2 (1994). Note that this provision does not explicitly recognize a right to counsel for all accused at this stage of the proceedings. The Human Rights Committee has stated, however, that "all persons arrested must have immediate access to counsel." Hum. Rts. Comm., *Concluding Observations on State Party Report: Georgia*, ¶ 28, U.N. Doc. CCPR/C/79/Add.74 (Apr. 9, 1997). *See also* Body of Principles, *supra* note 229, princ. 18, ¶ 1; Basic Principles on Lawyers, *supra* note 229, princ. 1 (stating that "[a]ll persons are entitled to call upon the assistance of a lawyer of their choice to protect and establish their rights and to defend them in all stages of criminal proceedings."); *id.* princ. 7 (requiring governments to ensure that all persons arrested or detained have access to a lawyer within 48 hours of arrest or detention); *id.* princ. 5 (providing that all persons arrested, charged or detained must be promptly informed of their right to legal assistance); *id.* princ. 8 (requiring authorities to ensure that all arrested, detained or imprisoned persons have adequate opportunities to be visited by, and to communicate with, their lawyers without delay, interception or censorship, in full confidentiality). It also has been widely recognized that prompt and regular access to a lawyer for all detainees is an important safeguard against torture, ill treatment, coerced confessions, and other abuses. *See, e.g.*, Hum. Rts. Comm., gen. cmt. 20, art. 7, ¶ 11 (44th session, 1992), U.N. Doc. HRI/GEN/REV. 1 at 30 (1994); U.N. Econ. & Soc. Council, Commission on Human Rights—Special Rapporteur, *Question of the Human Rights of All Persons Subjected to Any Form of Detention or Imprisonment, in Particular: Torture and Other Cruel, Inhuman or Degrading Treatment or Punishment*, ¶ 284, U.N. Doc. E/CN.4/1992/17 (Dec. 27, 1991) (*prepared by* P. Kooi-

ICCPR also provides for the right to habeas corpus, or *amparo*.[234] Under this provision, anyone deprived of liberty by arrest or detention has the right to "take proceedings before a court, in order that that court may decide without delay on the lawfulness of his detention and order his release if the detention is not lawful."[235] International human rights law also has established an extensive inventory of procedural rights for individuals facing criminal charges. The Universal Declaration of Human Rights,[236] the ICCPR,[237] the African Charter on Human and Peoples' Rights,[238] the Inter-American Convention on Human Rights,[239] and the ECHR[240] all include detailed fair trial provisions. Specifically, Article 14 of the ICCPR recognizes the right to "a fair and public hearing by a competent, independent and impartial tribunal established by law."[241] This provision enumerates the minimum procedural requirements of a "fair trial," including the right to be presumed innocent,[242] the right to be tried without undue delay,[243] the right to prepare a defense,[244] the right to defend oneself in person or through counsel,[245] the right to call and examine witnesses,[246] and the right to protection from retroactive criminal laws.[247] Because these principles are recognized in numerous widely ratified human rights treaties, several unanimously supported international

---

jmans).

234. ICCPR, *supra* note 227, art. 9, ¶ 4.

235. *Id.*

236. *See* UDHR, *supra* note 228, art. 10.

237. *See* ICCPR, *supra* note 227, art. 14.

238. *See* BANJUL CHARTER, *supra* note 227, arts. 7, 26. The African Commission on Human and Peoples' Rights has adopted a Resolution on the Right to Recourse Procedure and Fair Trial, Doc. No. ACHPR/COMM/FIN(XI)/Annex VII (Mar. 9, 1992), which elaborates on Art. 7(1) of the Banjul Charter and guarantees several additional rights, including: notification of charges, appearance before a judicial officer, right to release pending trial, presumption of innocence, adequate preparation of the defense, speedy trial, examination of witnesses, and the right to an interpreter.

239. *See* ACHR, *supra* note 227, art. 8.

240. *See* ECHR, *supra* note 227, art. 6.

241. ICCPR, *supra* note 227, art. 14, ¶ 1.

242. *See* ICCPR, *supra* note 227, art. 14, ¶ 2; ECHR, *supra* note 227, art. 6, ¶ 2.

243. *See* ICCPR, *supra* note 227, art. 14, ¶ 3(c); ECHR, *supra* note 227, art. 6, ¶ 1.

244. *See* ICCPR, *supra* note 227, art. 14, ¶ 3(d); ECHR, *supra* note 227, art. 6, ¶ 3(b).

245. Article 14 of the ICPR provides:

> In the determination of any criminal charge against him, everyone shall be entitled to the following minimum guarantees, in full equality . . . (d) To be tried in his presence, and to defend himself in person or through legal assistance of his own choosing; to be informed, if he does not have legal assistance, of this right; and to have legal assistance assigned to him, in any case where the interests of justice so require, and without payment by him in any such case if he does not have sufficient means to pay for it.

ICCPR, *supra* note 227, art. 14, ¶ 3; ECHR, *supra* note 227, art. 6, ¶ 3(c).

246. *See* ICCPR, *supra* note 227, art. 14, ¶ 3 ("In the determination of any criminal charge against him, everyone shall be entitled to the following minimum guarantees, in full equality.... To examine, or have examined, the witnesses against him and to obtain the attendance and examination of witnesses on his behalf under the same conditions as witnesses against him."); ECHR, *supra* note 227, art. 6, ¶ 3(d); ACHR, *supra* note 227, art. 8, ¶ 2(f).

247. *See* ICCPR, *supra* note 227, art. 15, ¶ 1 ("No one shall be held guilty of any criminal offence on account of any act or omission which did not constitute a criminal offence, under national or international law, at the time when it was committed.").

resolutions, and nearly all national constitutions, they arguably reflect the "judicial guarantees which are recognized as indispensable by civilized peoples."[248] In short, these principles confer due process rights equivalent to, if not greater than, those accorded to POWs in the POW Convention.

In addition, subsequent developments in humanitarian law also suggest that the Common Article 3 standard embodies substantial due process rights. Article 75 of Additional Protocol I[249] identifies the minimum rights of those who are not accorded any "more favorable treatment under the [Geneva] Convention or under this Protocol [I]," including fundamental due process rights that are "generally accepted principles of regular judicial procedures."[250] Article 75 requires, in all circumstances, trials by impartial and regularly constituted courts that, at a minimum, afford the presumption of innocence; the right to counsel before and during trial; the right of defendants to be present at proceedings, call witnesses, and examine witnesses against them; the right to be promptly informed of the charges or reasons for detention; the right to a public judgment; and the right of defendants not to testify against themselves or to confess their guilt, among other rights.[251]

The procedural rights recognized in the ICTY, ICTR, and the ICC—tribunals empowered to try persons for serious violations of humanitarian law, including war crimes—provide further evidence of a broad consensus as to the essential (or "indispensable") attributes of fair trials.[252]

D. *Article 75 of Additional Protocol I*

Building on the protective schemes identified above, Article 75 of Additional Protocol I and Article 6 of Additional Protocol II clearly establish minimum humanitarian protections applicable to all persons "in the power of" a belligerent state, irrespective of whether any such person participated in the hostilities.[253] Widely understood as the "gap filler" in Geneva law,[254] the "fundamental guarantees" provisions of the 1977 Protocols make clear that all persons subject to the authority of a belligerent are entitled to humanitarian protection.[255] Because the issue under consideration is whether

248. Common Art. 3, *supra* note 59.

249. *See infra* Part II.D.

250. ADDITIONAL PROTOCOL I, *supra* note 10, art. 75.

251. ADDITIONAL PROTOCOL I, *supra* note 10, art. 75(4).

252. *See generally* Paust, *Courting Illegality*, *supra* note 21 (summarizing these protections).

253. ADDITIONAL PROTOCOL I, *supra* note 10, art. 75; ADDITIONAL PROTOCOL II, *supra* note 10, art. 6.

254. *See* JUDGE ADVOCATE GENERAL'S SCHOOL, U.S. ARMY, *Protection of Civilians During Armed Conflict*, *in* LAW OF WAR WORKSHOP DESKBOOK, *supra* note 114, 123, 126–27.

255. As discussed above, the United States is not party to either Protocol. *See supra* note 114. I address in more detail the significance of this fact when I discuss various factors limiting the effectiveness of Article 75. *See infra* Part IV.B.3. Three points bear mentioning at this juncture. First, the United States does not object to Article 75 of Additional Protocol I or Article 6 of Additional Protocol II; indeed, the United States recognizes that these minimum protections are part of customary international law. *See infra* note 359. Second, the United States often does observe, as a formal matter, these provisions when it fights alongside other states (as part of a coalitional force) who are party to the treaties (such as the

and to what extent humanitarian law protects unlawful combatants in international armed conflicts, the analysis in this Part centers on Article 75 of Additional Protocol I. (The fundamental guarantees regime of Additional Protocol II mirrors this provision in all important respects.) The drafting history of Article 75 suggests that the provision was designed: (1) to clarify the scope and application of several fundamental guarantees recognized in the 1949 Conventions; (2) to extend greater protections to persons not covered by those Conventions—most notably, nationals of the detaining power, nationals of co-belligerents and neutrals, and stateless persons and refugees; and, by implication, (3) to condition the derogation powers conferred on states by Article 5 of the Civilians Convention by rendering a broader range of rights expressly non-derogable.[256]

Two points regarding the scope and content of Article 75 are relevant for present purposes. First, the text, structure, and drafting history of Additional Protocol I make plain that it covers unlawful combatants. Second, Article 75 provides specific and substantial protection, particularly to persons detained, arrested, or interned and to persons facing criminal charges. As mentioned previously and discussed more fully below, the substance of this provision is clearly modeled on—and, as a consequence, closely resembles—the substance of Common Article 3.

1. Applicability to Unlawful Combatants

The text and structure of Additional Protocol I demonstrate that Article 75 protects unlawful combatants.[257] As previously discussed, Article 45(3) of Additional Protocol I expressly makes the fundamental guarantees of Article 75 applicable to unlawful combatants.[258] That provision specifies that Article 75 constitutes the minimum humanitarian protection to be accorded combatants, although the provision acknowledges that some unlawful combatants are protected by the Civilians Convention.[259]

In addition, Article 75 arguably applies to unlawful combatants of its own force. This view is explicitly endorsed (though often without extended analysis) by many commentators.[260] In addition, by its terms, Article 75 covers all "persons who are in the power of a Party to the conflict and who do not benefit from more favourable treatment under the Conventions or

United Kingdom). *See infra* text accompanying note 357. And third, the United States is, notwithstanding its status as a global superpower, only one state. More than 160 states are party to the Protocols. *See infra* text accompanying note 356.

256. BOTHE ET AL., *supra* note 80, at 460–61.

257. ADDITIONAL PROTOCOL I, *supra* note 10, art. 75.

258. *Id.* art. 45(3).

259. *See supra* text accompanying notes 111–119 (analyzing Article 45).

260. *See, e.g.*, Inter-Am. C.H.R., *Report on Terrorism*, *supra* note 79; Draper, *supra* note 8; Dormann, *supra* note 80; Christopher Greenwood, *International Law and the War on Terrorism*, 78 INT'L AFF. 301, 338 (2002); Paust, *Courting Illegality*, *supra* note 21.

under this Protocol."[261] The drafting history strongly suggests that the "in the power of" formulation includes all persons subject to detention by a party to the conflict.[262] The formulation clearly encompasses all instances in which "the power has been exercised in order to limit the freedom of the persons enjoying protection."[263] This language leaves open the question of whether the formulation should apply only to persons in such circumstances, or whether it should also cover all persons residing in territory subject to the party's control. The best reading of the phrase seems to be that it encompasses all such persons. On this point, the ICRC Commentary concludes that "the expression covers not only persons who have fallen into the hands of a Party to the conflict, but also those over whom it exercises, or would be able to exercise, authority, for the sole reason that they live in territory under its control."[264]

Critics of this view might suggest that *combatants* fall outside the purview of Article 75 because this provision is included in Part IV of Additional Protocol I concerning protection of the *"civilian population."* However, this criticism is a non-starter because the definitions of "civilians" and "civilian population" in Additional Protocol I include all persons not classified as lawful combatants (as defined in Article 43 of the Protocol).[265] Nevertheless, it is important to address this potential line of criticism so as to distinguish the conceptual linkages between the "lawful combatant" scheme of Additional Protocol I—a matter of some controversy—and the "fundamental guarantees" scheme. Critics might suggest that application of Article 75 to unlawful combatants is predicated on the controversial reformulation of lawful combatant status in Articles 43–45. Successful linkage of these schemes therefore could: (1) arguably deprive Article 75, as applied to unlawful combatants, of customary international law status; and (2) encourage states actively opposing the unlawful combatants scheme to resist application of Article 75 to unlawful combatants. The United States, for example, is not party to the Additional Protocols and specifically objects to the lawful combat regime elaborated therein. As a consequence, conceptual clarity on this matter is crucial. A proper reading of two provisions illustrates that the regime established in Articles 43–45 has no significant protective conse-

261. ADDITIONAL PROTOCOL I, *supra* note 10, art. 75(1). The provision protects such persons "[i]n so far as they are affected by a situation" that constitutes an international armed conflict as defined in Article 1 of the Protocol. *Id.* Notably, Article 1 includes in the definition of international armed conflict so-called "wars of national liberation" even though these conflicts are, as a formal matter, non-international. *Id.* art. 1(4).

262. BOTHE ET AL., *supra* note 80, at 460; ICRC, COMMENTARY ON THE ADDITIONAL PROTOCOLS, *supra* note 109, at 837–38.

263. BOTHE ET AL., *supra* note 80, at 460; ICRC, COMMENTARY ON THE ADDITIONAL PROTOCOLS, *supra* note 109, at 837–38.

264. ICRC, COMMENTARY ON THE ADDITIONAL PROTOCOLS, *supra* note 109, at 838, ¶ 2912; *see also* BOTHE ET AL., *supra* note 80, at 460.

265. ADDITIONAL PROTOCOL I, *supra* note 10, arts. 43, 50.

quences with respect to rights recognized in Article 75. The difficulty is, of course, how best to classify irregular forces.

The important point here is that all such persons are entitled to protection equivalent to or greater than that recognized in Article 75. Any irregular fighters classified as "unlawful combatants," irrespective of whether the POW Convention standard or the Additional Protocol I standard is used, are classified as "civilians" for protective purposes by Additional Protocol I. If, on the other hand, any such fighters are lawful combatants, then they are entitled to POW protections, including combatant immunity. In short, no view on the proper content of the "lawful combatant" category implicates, as a conceptual matter, whether any affected persons are entitled, at a minimum, to protections equivalent to those established by Article 75.

2. *Legal Protections*

The substance of these rules tracks closely the substance of Common Article 3 of the 1949 Conventions.[266] By its terms, Article 75 requires humane treatment in all circumstances and requires that its protections be provided without any adverse distinction based on "race, colour, sex, language, religion, or belief, political or other opinion, or on any similar category." It also prohibits violence to the life, health, or well-being of all covered persons (including murder, torture, corporal punishment, and all "outrages upon personal dignity"), the taking of hostages, and collective punishments. Moreover, the provision requires several fundamental judicial guarantees in cases of arrest, detention, or internment.[267]

The inclusion of Article 75 in the Protocols, however, advances the protective scheme of Common Article 3 in two non-trivial respects. First, the Common Article 3 protections, made applicable in all armed conflicts by inference and implication, are expressly applied to international armed conflicts by Article 75.[268] Article 6 of Additional Protocol II makes this protective scheme applicable in non-international armed conflicts as defined in that treaty.[269] Second, Article 75 elaborates the "judicial guarantees" clause of Common Article 3 by enumerating several specific fair trial rights.[270] Article 6 of Additional Protocol II does the same for non-international armed conflicts.[271] Echoing the language of Common Article 3, Article 75 provides:

> No sentence may be passed and no penalty may be executed on a person found guilty of a penal offence related to the armed conflict except pur-

266. *See supra* Part II.C.2 (analyzing the legal protections accorded by Common Article 3).
267. Additional Protocol I, *supra* note 10, art. 75(3)–(7).
268. *Id.* art. 1.
269. Additional Protocol II, *supra* note 10, art. 6.
270. Additional Protocol I, *supra* note 10, art. 75(3)–(4).
271. Additional Protocol II, *supra* note 10, art. 6(3).

> suant to a conviction pronounced by an impartial and regularly constituted court respecting the generally recognized principles of regular judicial procedure . . . .[272]

Unlike Common Article 3, Article 75 of Additional Protocol I specifies many of these principles. They include: (1) provision of "all necessary rights and means of defence" (which almost certainly includes the right to counsel, the right to be present at the hearing, the right to compel process, the right to be informed of pending charges, the right to be accorded sufficient time and resources to formulate a defense, and the right to challenge alleged unfairness in the proceedings on appeal);[273] (2) the right to be presumed innocent;[274] (3) freedom from compelled self-incrimination;[275] (4) the right to be advised of rights and available post-conviction remedies;[276] (5) freedom from *ex post facto* application of the criminal law;[277] and (6) recognition of the principle of *non bis in idem*.[278] In summary, Article 75 of the First Additional Protocol: (1) protects unlawful combatants; and (2) provides detailed, substantial protection, particularly to persons detained and persons facing criminal charges.

III. Disaggregating the "Unlawful Combatant" Category: Permutations and Corresponding Protective Schemes in Geneva Law

The Geneva Conventions confer substantial protection on unlawful combatants. Because these protective schemes have varying fields of application, the Conventions protect differently situated unlawful combatants to varying degrees. As such, no single protective scheme governs the treatment of unlawful combatants to the exclusion of all others. Consequently, a complete analysis of the protections accorded unlawful combatants requires disaggregation of this category along the lines suggested by the protective schemes under investigation. In this Part, I analyze several axes along which protection may vary in order to graft some conceptual organization onto these disparate, yet partially overlapping, schemes. These variables include: (1) the character of the hostilities; (2) the nationality of the unlawful combatant; (3) the territory in which the unlawful combatant is found; and (4) the jurisdictional nexus between the belligerent state and the unlawful combatant.

272. Additional Protocol I, *supra* note 10, art. 75.
273. *Id.*
274. *Id.*
275. *Id.*
276. *Id.*
277. *Id.*
278. *Id.*

A. Character of the Hostilities

All unlawful combatants captured in non-international armed conflicts are entitled to Common Article 3 protections (and perhaps those of Article 6 of Additional Protocol II) *irrespective of their nationality or the territory in which they are found.*[279] Any such persons charged with war crimes are arguably entitled to the fair trial protections identified in the Conventions' penal repression regime.[280] No such persons, however, are entitled to POW or Civilian status under the Geneva Conventions. That is, the Conventions writ large apply only in the context of international armed conflicts and occupation.[281] Persons captured in situations that do not constitute an armed conflict within the meaning of Geneva law are not entitled to any protection under the Conventions. If they are charged with committing a war crime, the crime in question must have been committed in a past armed conflict; war crimes, by definition, only occur in armed conflicts.

TABLE 1: CHARACTER OF HOSTILITIES AND POTENTIALLY APPLICABLE PROTECTIONS

International armed conflict (or occupation)	• Civilians Convention • Common Article 3 • Article 75 of Additional Protocol I • Penal Repression Regime
"Wars of national liberation"	• Civilians Convention • Common Article 3 • Article 75 of Additional Protocol I • Penal Repression Regime
Other non-international armed conflicts	• Common Article 3 • Article 6 of Additional Protocol II (perhaps)
No armed conflict	None

B. Nationality of the Unlawful Combatant

For the most part, the applicable Geneva rules cover unlawful combatants irrespective of nationality considerations. For example, Common Article 3, Article 75 of Additional Protocol I, and the Conventions' penal repression protections apply without regard to the nationality of the combatant. The exception, of course, is the Civilians Convention. As discussed extensively in

279. *See* Common Art. 3, *supra* note 59; *see also supra* Part II.C (explicating the content and extent of Common Article 3 protections).

280. *See supra* Part II.B.

281. Common Article 2 of the Four Geneva Conventions.

Part III, the applicability of the Civilians Convention writ large—recall that one section of the treaty applies to all civilians—turns on rigid nationality requirements. Nationals of a state "not bound by the Convention are not protected by it."[282] In addition, nationals of "neutral" or "co-belligerent" states are not protected by the Convention "while the State of which they are nationals has normal diplomatic representation in the State in whose hands they are."[283]

TABLE 2: NATIONALITY AND POTENTIALLY APPLICABLE PROTECTIONS

Enemy national	• Civilians Convention • Common Article 3 • Article 75 of Additional Protocol I • Penal Repression Regime
National or co-belligerent or neutral	• Common Article 3 • Article 75 of Additional Protocol I • Penal Repression Regime
National of detaining power	• Common Article 3 • Article 75 of Additional Protocol I • Penal Repression Regime

C. *Territory Where Unlawful Combatant Is Found*

In general, Geneva law's territorial field of application is broad, encompassing the territory of all parties to the conflict as well as "occupied territory." Moreover, some protections, such as Common Article 3 and Article 75 of Additional Protocol I, apply without territorial restrictions. Nevertheless, the scope and content of some potentially applicable protective schemes vary by territory in important respects. Two points—one significant, the other less so—bear mention.

First, some specific protections of the Civilians Convention are applicable only in certain types of territory. As discussed previously, the Civilians Convention expressly limits the applicability of many protections to "occupied territory." It defines others in terms that make clear that the protections are applicable only in the home territory of a belligerent state. Of course, the significance of this variable protective scheme for the purposes of this analysis is sharply attenuated by Part III, Section IV of the Convention prescribing protections for all internees.[284] These protections—which closely resemble POW protections—are applicable in both "occupied territory" and the territory of the parties to the conflict.

282. CIVILIANS CONVENTION, *supra* note 1, art. 4.
283. *Id.*
284. *See* CIVILIANS CONVENTION, *supra* note 1, arts. 79–141.

Second, the derogation regime of Article 5 of the Civilians Convention, which applies in principle to all unlawful combatants, is subject to important territorial limitations. Recall that Article 5 applies only in occupied territory and the territory of the detaining state[285] and consequently does not expressly authorize derogations in non-occupied enemy territory or in the territory of a co-belligerent.[286] In addition, Article 5, by its terms, authorizes the suspension only of communication rights in "occupied territory."[287]

TABLE 3: TERRITORY AND POTENTIALLY APPLICABLE PROTECTIONS

Home territory of belligerent state	• Civilians Convention • Common Article 3 • Article 75 of Additional Protocol I • Penal Repression Regime
Territory of co-belligerent state	• Civilians Convention • Common Article 3 • Article 75 of Additional Protocol I • Penal Repression Regime
Non-occupied enemy territory	• Civilians Convention • Common Article 3 • Article 75 of Additional Protocol I • Penal Repression Regime
Occupied enemy territory	• Civilians Convention • Common Article 3 • Article 75 of Additional Protocol I • Penal Repression Regime
Territory of neutral state	• Common Article 3 • Article 75 of Additional Protocol I • Penal Repression Regime

285. *See* CIVILIANS CONVENTION, *supra* note 1, art. 5; *see also supra* Part II.A.2.
286. *Id.*
287. *Id.*

TABLE 4: TERRITORY AND THE SCOPE OF DEROGATION PERMITTED UNDER ARTICLE 5 OF CIVILIANS CONVENTION

Home territory of belligerent state	Paragraph (1) as limited by (3) and Art. 75 of Additional Protocol I: restrictions necessary to state security
Territory of co-belligerent state	No derogation permitted
Non-occupied enemy territory	No derogation permitted
Occupied enemy territory	Paragraph (2) as limited by (3) and Art. 75 of Additional Protocol I: restrictions only to communication rights
Territory of neutral state	Civilians Convention not applicable

D. *Jurisdictional Nexus Between Belligerent State and Unlawful Combatant*

The applicability of some Geneva law also turns on the character of authority that the belligerent state exercises over the would-be protected person. That is, states must exercise sufficient authority over an individual to trigger the application of some rules. This is, of course, not true for all Geneva rules. For example, Common Article 3 protects persons no longer taking active part in hostilities "in all circumstances."[288] In addition, many restrictions on the means and methods of warfare, particularly the prohibition on targeting civilians and civilian objects, do not require belligerents to exercise "authority" proper over the persons protected by their terms. Nevertheless, some protections require such a nexus between the protected person and the belligerent power against whom Geneva law is invoked. As previously discussed, the Civilians Convention, for example, protects "those who, at any given moment and in any manner whatsoever, find themselves . . . in the hands of a Party . . . of which they are not nationals."[289] In addition, Article 75 of Additional Protocol I governs the treatment of "persons who are *in the power of* a Party to the conflict."[290] Analogously, the fair trial rights recognized in the Conventions' penal repression regime apply only in the case of an actual exercise of criminal jurisdiction, alleging violations of the laws of war.[291]

288. Common Art. 3, *supra* note 59.

289. CIVILIANS CONVENTION, *supra* note 1, art. 4 (emphasis added).

290. ADDITIONAL PROTOCOL I, *supra* note 10, art. 75(1) (emphasis added). Recall that the provision protects such persons "[i]n so far as they are affected by a situation" that constitutes an armed conflict as defined in Article 1 of the Protocol. *Id.* Therefore, the requisite jurisdictional nexus must arise in connection with the armed conflict in question.

291. *See, e.g.*, CIVILIANS CONVENTION, *supra* note 1, art. 146; *see also supra* Part II.B (discussing this

These important requirements do not, however, present any significant difficulty for this analysis because, although the precise meaning of these requirements is somewhat unclear, the triggering conditions certainly include all circumstances in which the belligerent power arrests or detains the person in question.[292] Likewise, the problem does not arise in the context of the POW Convention because the nature of the obligations makes clear that the treaty governs only those circumstances in which a belligerent has captured and detained an enemy.

In the end, the applicability of the obligations analyzed in this Article does not vary by jurisdictional nexus because these rights, by their nature, protect persons in situations clearly satisfying each of these thresholds. The potentially applicable protections do nevertheless vary depending on whether the would-be protected person is subjected to criminal charges under the laws of war.[293] If such charges are brought, defendants are entitled to the fair trial rights recognized in the Conventions' penal repression provisions, as clarified and augmented by Article 75(7) of Additional Protocol I.[294] Also, the authority of belligerent states to detain captured combatants without criminal charge or trial does not vary significantly depending on the applicable rule. Common Article 3 does not purport to confer or condition the power to detain captured combatants. Article 75 of Additional Protocol I tacitly assumes that parties may detain combatants, requiring only that such persons "shall be released with the minimum delay possible and in any event as soon as the circumstances justifying the arrest, detention or internment have ceased to exist."[295] Moreover, the Civilians Convention clearly acknowledges the authority of state parties to detain protected persons without charge or trial, even though such measures are allowed "only if the security of the Detaining Power makes it absolutely necessary."[296] Note that this "necessity" standard is much more restrictive than the POW Convention's broad authorization to detain, wherein Article 21 provides that "[t]he Detaining Power may subject prisoners of war to internment."[297] This difference, however, is not significant for the purposes of analyzing the protections applicable to unlawful combatants because detention of any person properly so designated would, without question, satisfy the "necessity" requirement.

---

regime in detail).

292. *See* BOTHE ET AL., *supra* note 80, at 460; ICRC, COMMENTARY ON THE ADDITIONAL PROTOCOLS, *supra* note 109, at 837–38, 866–71.

293. *See, e.g.*, CIVILIANS CONVENTION, *supra* note 1, art. 146; *see also supra* Part II.B (discussing this regime in detail).

294. ADDITIONAL PROTOCOL I, *supra* note 10, art. 75(7).

295. *Id.* art. 75(3).

296. CIVILIANS CONVENTION, *supra* note 1, arts. 42, 79.

297. POW CONVENTION, *supra* note 1, art. 21.

TABLE 5: POTENTIALLY APPLICABLE PROTECTIONS IN CRIMINAL PROCEEDINGS

Charged with war crimes	• Civilians Convention • Common Article 3 • Article 75 of Additional Protocol I • Penal Repression Regime
Charged with other crimes	• Civilians Convention • Common Article 3 • Article 75 of Additional Protocol I

TABLE 6: AUTHORIZATION TO DETAIN COMBATANTS WITHOUT CRIMINAL CHARGE OR TRIAL

Prisoner of war	YES—until the cessation of hostilities (under POW Convention)
"Civilian"	YES—as long as necessary for state security until the cessation of hostilities (under Civilians Convention and Article 75 of Additional Protocol I)
Non-civilian, unlawful combatant (not covered by Civilians Convention)	YES—as long as necessary for state security until the cessation of hostilities (under Article 75 of Additional Protocol I)

E. *Illustrations*

Some concrete examples may help clarify the application of these overlapping schemes. Consider first the situation of an Afghan citizen captured in Afghanistan during Operation Enduring Freedom and detained at the U.S. military base in Kandahar, Afghanistan. Even if this fighter is an unlawful combatant; that is, he participated directly in the hostilities without the right to do so—he is covered by all the alternative protective schemes identified in this Article. He is protected by the Civilians Convention because he has "fallen into the hands of" a belligerent power of which he is not a national; that is, from the U.S. perspective, he is an "enemy national." Moreover, because he is not detained in the home territory of the United States, the Article 5 derogation regime authorizes only minimal security-based restrictions on his rights as a "civilian." Common Article 3 also protects him because he is no longer taking active part in hostilities—irrespective of the conditions surrounding his capture, the facts of his capture and subsequent detention render him *hors de combat*. Finally, Article 75 of Additional Protocol I obviously applies because he is "in the power of" the United States in virtue of his detention.

Next consider the situation of the same fighter detained at the U.S. Naval Base at Guantanamo Bay, Cuba. This change in circumstance has bearing only on the applicability of the Civilians Convention. As discussed previously, the substantive protections of the Civilians Convention writ large pertain only to occupied territory and to the territory of parties to the conflict. At first blush, it seems that Cuban territory falls outside both categories. More sustained reflection, however, suggests that Cuba is a party to the conflict within the meaning of the Civilians Convention. Hence, Guantanamo Bay would constitute the "territory of a party to the conflict."[298] More specifically, Cuba is arguably a co-belligerent for the purposes of determining the applicability of the Convention. As argued above, the category of co-belligerents is best understood as encompassing states that knowingly allow the systematic, conflict-related use of their territory by a belligerent state. Recall that this understanding of co-belligerency is most consistent with the obligations of neutrals in laws of war and the broad definition of "armed conflict" in Geneva law. This understanding avoids the perverse results that issue from a narrow interpretation of co-belligerency. Cuba, therefore, is a party to the conflict because it has allowed the systematic use of its territory by the United States in the prosecution of the war.[299] On this reading then, this

298. It is important to note that Guantanamo Bay is not, as a formal matter, "occupied territory" even though the United States exercises de facto authority over this territory for war-related purposes. Indeed, Article 3 of the lease agreement defines the character of U.S. authority in the territory in terms of "complete jurisdiction and control," notwithstanding Cuba's "ultimate sovereignty" over the lands. *See* AGREEMENT BETWEEN THE UNITED STATES AND CUBA FOR THE LEASE OF LANDS FOR COALING AND NAVAL STATIONS, Feb. 23, 1903, T.S. No. 418, art. 3, *available at* http://www.yale.edu/lawweb/avalon/diplomacy/cuba/cuba002.htm (last visited Mar. 13, 2004) [hereinafter AGREEMENT BETWEEN THE UNITED STATES AND CUBA]. When such authority is exercised by the military and the territory is made subject to military law, this situation indeed resembles "occupied territory." Recall that the touchstone of "occupation" is the exercise of "de facto" (as opposed to formal), "provisional" (as opposed to sovereign) authority. *See, e.g.*, HAGUE CONVENTION, *supra* note 5, art. 42; FM 27-10, *supra* note 44, ¶¶ 351–53. Nevertheless, the definition of "occupied territory" established in the Hague Regulations—and echoed in U.S. military manuals—excludes situations involving the administration of friendly or allied territory, except when such territory is recaptured from the enemy on behalf of the ally. *See, e.g.*, HAGUE CONVENTION, *supra* note 5, art. 42 (implying the capture of enemy territory by stating that "[t]erritory is considered occupied when it is actually placed under the authority of the *hostile* army") (emphasis added); FM 27-10, *supra* note 44, ¶ 354 (distinguishing friendly territory administered by United States in virtue of civil agreement); *Id.* ¶ 352(d) (providing that occupation rules apply only in the context of "belligerently occupied areas"); *Id.* ¶ 352(c) ("Occupation . . . is invasion plus taking firm possession of *enemy* territory . . . .") (emphasis added). *See also* Paust, *Courting Illegality*, *supra* note 21, at 18, 21, 25–26 (arguing that Guantanamo Bay is not "occupied territory" within the meaning of the Geneva Conventions because the territory was not acquired in war or other war-related circumstances); Jordan J. Paust, *Antiterrorism Military Commissions: The* Ad Hoc *Rules of Procedure*, 23 MICH. J. INT'L L. 677, 681 (2002) (same).

299. The lease agreement was signed with full knowledge that the United States would use the territory as a military base to facilitate force projection. Of course, the title of the agreement itself acknowledges that naval stations would be built there. *See* AGREEMENT BETWEEN THE UNITED STATES AND CUBA, *supra* note 298. Moreover, the agreement implements a Cuban constitutional provision concerning collective defense and, most interestingly, U.S. self-defense. The preamble of the lease provides that:

> The United States of America and the Republic of Cuba, being desirous to execute fully the provisions of Article VII of the Act of Congress approved March second, 1901, and of Article VII of the Appendix to the Constitution of the Republic of Cuba promulgated on the 20th of May, 1902, which provide:

hypothetical fighter would be protected by the Civilians Convention. According to this view, the Article 5 derogation regime would not authorize any restrictions on Convention rights because this hypothetical protected person is detained outside the territory of the United States.[300]

Other variants of the Guantanamo Bay scenario are also instructive. Consider the case of a Saudi national, Al Qaeda fighter otherwise in the same circumstances as the previous example. Because this detainee is not formally an enemy national, he is not protected by the Civilians Convention writ large. That is, he does not satisfy the nationality requirements of Article 4, in that he is the national of a neutral or co-belligerent state with which the United States has normal diplomatic relations.[301] Of course, Common Article 3 and Article 75 of Additional Protocol I would apply, as would the fair trial rights of the Conventions' penal repression regime if the detainee were subjected to war crimes charges.

The same analysis is in order if an otherwise similarly situated detainee were a U.S. citizen. Again, the Civilians Convention would not protect this detainee because he is not an enemy national.[302] By its terms, "protected

---

> ARTICLE VII. To enable the United States to maintain the independence of Cuba, and to protect the people thereof, as well as for its own defense, the Cuban Government will sell or lease to the United States the lands necessary for coaling or naval stations, at certain specified points, to be agreed upon with the President of the United States.

Id. pmbl.

300. Conversely, if such a detainee were held in U.S. territory, the same protective schemes would apply except that his rights under the Civilians Convention would be subject to the nominally broader derogation authority recognized in Article 5(1). *See* CIVILIANS CONVENTION, *supra* note 1, art. 5(1) (authorizing derogation from rights that would "if exercised in the favour of such individual person, be prejudicial to the security of such State"). The upshot is that such Guantanamo Bay detainees enjoy somewhat greater protection, not less, under the Civilians Convention than they would in U.S. territory. *See supra* Part II.A.1.a (explaining the rationale for augmented derogation authority in a belligerent state's home territory).

301. CIVILIANS CONVENTION, *supra* note 1, art. 4.

302. This may well constitute an important difference between the Civilians Convention and the POW Convention. That is, the POW Convention may apply irrespective of the detainee's nationality. The terms of Article 4 do not expressly make nationality variables relevant to defining "protected persons" under the Convention. POW CONVENTION, *supra* note 1, art. 4. Moreover, at least one U.S. court has held that U.S. citizenship is not a bar to POW status at the hands of U.S. forces. *See In re* Territo, 156 F.2d 142 (9th Cir. 1946). Note the date of this decision; the court accordingly analyzes the status question under the Hague Regulations and the 1929 POW Convention. Some commentators have supported this view. *See, e.g.*, LEVIE, *supra* note 24.

Despite the surface appeal of this interpretation, there are several non-trivial reasons to question its validity. Indeed, the majority of commentators reject this view. *See, e.g.*, OPPENHEIM, *supra* note 9. It should first be noted that the United States is an outlier on this issue—no other state recognizes POW status for its own nationals fighting on the side of its enemies. *See, e.g.*, LEVIE, *supra* note 24. Second, several provisions of the POW Convention clearly presume that the protected person is not a national of the detaining power. *See, e.g.*, POW CONVENTION, *supra* note 1, art. 87 (providing for leniency in punishment because POWs are not nationals of detaining power). Third, the drafting history of the POW Convention strongly suggests that it was intended to cover only enemy nationals. *See, e.g.*, 2A Diplomatic Conference, *supra* note 96, at 291–94 (illustrating in the context of debate on penal and disciplinary sanctions, that delegates simply assumed that POWs would not be nationals of the "Detaining Power"). In addition, the negotiations surrounding the Civilians Convention implicitly support the same conclusion. *See* 2A Diplomatic Conference, *supra* note 96, at 813–14 (summarizing debates in drafting committee). Given the controversy that arose surrounding the nationality requirements of the Civilians Conven-

persons" under the Civilians Convention are "those who, at any given moment and in any manner whatsoever, find themselves . . . in the hands of a Party . . . *of which they are not nationals*."[303] Nevertheless, the other surveyed protective schemes apply. Indeed, as demonstrated previously, both Common Article 3 and Article 75 of Additional Protocol I were designed in large part to close this very gap in Geneva law.[304] Likewise, the penal repression regime is not subject to any nationality restrictions. By its text, it applies "in all circumstances," and its drafting history clearly indicates that delegations considered the prosecution of one's own nationals the paradigmatic application of the "grave" and "simple" breach regimes.[305]

IV. The Declining Significance of POW Status

The Geneva Conventions protect unlawful combatants, and these protections closely track the minimum requirements of the POW Convention. In Part III, I identified four overlapping, alternative protective schemes generally applicable to unlawful combatants. The nature of the protections recognized in these schemes strongly suggests that the denial of POW status does not sharply curtail the rights of war detainees. Although the analysis in Parts II and III also makes clear that the scope and content of these alternative protective schemes are subject to important limitations, subsequent developments have further eroded the significance of POW status. In this Part, I review these limitations and draw out these developments.

In the end, the unique protective significance of POW status is combatant immunity. In other words, POWs, as lawful combatants, may not be punished for their very participation in the hostilities. Despite marked convergence in the protective schemes of Geneva law, unlawful combatants are not entitled to participate in the hostilities and consequently may be prosecuted and punished for doing so. This so-called "immunity" accorded to lawful combatants is, however, often misunderstood. Proper specification of its scope, content, and implications suggests that its significance is limited. Moreover, several developments—including the changing character of armed conflict and the general trajectory of humanitarian law, both substantive and procedural—have diminished the importance of the privilege.

---

tion, it seems highly improbable that the delegates, without any debate on the matter, concluded that the POW Convention should apply to a state's own nationals (even though the very suggestion that the Civilians Convention might so apply generated vigorous, and ultimately fatal, opposition). Finally, the drafting history of Common Article 3 provides good reason to think that states in general did not support the application of humanitarian rules to their own nationals. Debate surrounding this provision demonstrates that states struggled to make clear that the application of humanitarian law to internal matters would not, in any way, compromise the power of the state to quash rebellion and maintain public order. *See, e.g.*, 2A Diplomatic Conference, *supra* note 96, at 814–15.

303. Civilians Convention, *supra* note 1, art. 4 (emphasis added). Note that, because phrased in the negative, this language also seems to exclude dual (or poly-) nationals. That is, the requirement is that the would-be "protected person" must not be a national of the detaining state.

304. *See supra* Parts II.C, II.D.

305. *See supra* Part II.B.

A. *Persistent Gaps and Deficiencies in Geneva Law*

Geneva law provides substantial legal protection to all war detainees, including unlawful combatants. All persons detained by the enemy are entitled to the minimum protections of Common Article 3 and Article 75 of Additional Protocol I. Furthermore, by virtue of Articles 4 and 5 of the Civilians Convention, all enemy aliens are "protected persons" under the Conventions and are entitled, at a minimum, to humane treatment and fair trial rights. These provisions also make clear that unlawful combatants are presumptively covered by the full protections of the Civilians Convention—even if some of these protections may be suspended when (and so long as) necessary to protect state security. Moreover, all persons accused of "war crimes" are entitled to due process rights that mirror, in most important respects, the rights accorded POWs. As demonstrated in Parts II and III, these provisions establish a level of protection for unlawful combatants that closely approximates the protection accorded POWs.

As demonstrated in Part I, the POW Convention provides a detailed inventory of rights and privileges. In addition, the Convention also prescribes robust enforcement measures including criminalization of grave breaches of the treaty's rules. Nevertheless, the question remains whether there are any unique protective consequences of POW status. Although the analysis up to this point strongly suggests that there are no such consequences, each alternative protective scheme is arguably deficient in important respects. Of course, the Civilians Convention writ large accords protection that in most important respects mirrors that of the POW Convention. Although the Civilians Convention protects unlawful combatants, its field of application is limited to enemy nationals (who must also be nationals of a state party to the Convention). In addition, the derogation regime of Article 5 empowers states to deny unlawful combatants many of the rights recognized in the Convention if necessary to protect national security.

The other alternative protective schemes also exhibit potentially significant deficiencies. Common Article 3 protects all combatants no longer taking active part in hostilities, but the substantive rules of the provision are cast in abstract terms, the precise contours of which are unclear. In addition, the provision does not expressly include a right to release and repatriation at the close of hostilities. Moreover, no express provision is made in the Conventions for the enforcement of Common Article 3.[306] Recall that the persons protected by Common Article 3 are not, as a formal matter, "protected persons" within the meaning of the Conventions.[307] As a consequence, violations of Common Article 3 do not constitute "grave breaches" of the Conventions, and, at the time the Conventions were drafted, it was unclear whether violations of Common Article 3 might result in individual criminal

306. *See infra* Part IV.B.2 (discussing this issue).

307. *See supra* note 217 (noting the consensus view and evaluating the U.S. claim to the contrary).

liability at all.[308] Article 75 of Additional Protocol I gives rise to similar concerns. Although it protects all persons "in the power of" a belligerent state, Additional Protocol I does not prescribe an enforcement mechanism for this provision. That is, violations of Article 75, like those of Common Article 3, are not "grave breaches" of the Conventions, and it is unclear whether they give rise to individual criminal liability.[309] Moreover, the legal status of Additional Protocol I in many conflicts is itself somewhat ambiguous. The problem is that many states of geo-strategic significance—including India, Pakistan, Afghanistan, Iran, Iraq, Israel, and the United States—have not ratified Additional Protocol I.[310] As a consequence, its legal status for these states is unclear. Finally, the penal repression regime of the Conventions protects all persons subject to prosecution for violations of the laws of war, but these protections include only fair trial rights and fail to establish any protection outside that context. In short, some gaps arguably persist in the coverage of each of these protective schemes.

B. *The Progressive Convergence of Protective Schemes*

In recent years, however, the gaps in protection have been narrowed significantly. Specifically, two developments have clarified and, as a consequence, extended the legal protection accorded unlawful combatants: (1) abstract provisions have acquired a more concrete meaning through the elaboration of general humanitarian principles such as "humane treatment," "torture," and "essential judicial guarantees"; and (2) the conditions under which the identified alternative schemes apply have been broadened.

1. *Civilians Convention*

The Civilians Convention, when applicable in its entirety, provides a level of protection that closely approximates that of the POW Convention. Indeed, the drafters of the Geneva Conventions well understood that the two protective schemes were essentially identical in substance.[311] Given the broad language of Article 4, the Civilians Convention covers unlawful combatants so long as they satisfy the express nationality requirements.[312] Two features of the Civilians Convention potentially limit the protection of unlawful combatants: (1) the nationality requirements of Article 4, which may exclude many potential unlawful combatants; and (2) the derogation regime of Article 5, which may authorize denying unlawful combatants many impor-

---

308. *See, e.g.*, MOIR, *supra* note 186, at 52–58; Jinks, *September 11*, *supra* note 177, at 10–12.

309. *See* ADDITIONAL PROTOCOL I, *supra* note 10, art. 85 (noting that the "grave breaches" regime of Additional Protocol I does not include persons protected by Article 75); ICRC, COMMENTARY ON THE ADDITIONAL PROTOCOLS, *supra* note 109, at 992–93.

310. *See* ICRC, *States Party to the Geneva Conventions and their Additional Protocols*, *supra* note 42.

311. *See supra* note 54 (documenting this acknowledgement).

312. *See* CIVILIANS CONVENTION, *supra* note 1, art. 4.

tant protections. Subsequent developments, however, have considerably softened the impact of these limiting features.

First consider the nationality requirements of Article 4. Based on the "traditional state-centric, reciprocity-based approach,"[313] the Civilians Convention writ large applies only to persons who find themselves, in case of a conflict or occupation, "in the hands of a belligerent or occupying power of which they are not nationals."[314] In such cases, only nationals of a state that is bound by the Convention are protected.[315] Moreover, nationals of a neutral state who find themselves in the territory of a belligerent state and nationals of a co-belligerent state are not protected persons while their state of nationality maintains "normal diplomatic representation" in the state where they are found.[316]

As previously discussed, these rigid requirements exclude many persons, including unlawful combatants and peaceful civilians, from the protection of the Convention. Several important developments in humanitarian law, however, strongly suggest that the nationality requirements have been relaxed. For example, the literal interpretation of Article 4 has been rejected by international criminal tribunals in several cases, and its viability is now unclear. In the *Celebici* case, the ICTY concluded that Bosnian Serbs who had fallen into the hands of Bosnian authorities were "protected persons" under the Civilians Convention notwithstanding the apparent nationality bar.[317] The ICTY, eschewing formal conceptions of nationality, reasoned that "the nature of the international armed conflict in Bosnia and Herzegovina reflects the complexity of many modern conflicts and not, perhaps, the paradigm envisaged in 1949. In order to retain the relevance and effectiveness of the norms of the Geneva Conventions, it is necessary to adopt [a different] approach."[318] The Civilians Convention, the Tribunal held, protected the Serbs in question "as they were clearly regarded by the Bosnian authorities as belonging to the opposing party in an armed conflict and as posing a threat to the Bosnian State."[319] The ICTY Appeal Chamber elaborated the mature form of the view in the *Tadic* judgment:

> Article 4 . . . , if interpreted in the light of its object and purpose, is directed to the protection of civilians to the maximum extent possible . . . . Its primary purpose is to ensure the safeguards afforded by the Convention to those civilians who do not enjoy the diplomatic protec-

313. Meron, *supra* note 191, at 257.

314. CIVILIANS CONVENTION, *supra* note 1, art. 4.

315. It is important to note that this limitation is now irrelevant because all U.N. member states are parties to the Convention. *See* ICRC, *States Party to the Geneva Conventions and their Additional Protocols*, *supra* note 42.

316. CIVILIANS CONVENTION, *supra* note 1, art. 4.

317. Prosecutor v. Delalic, Case No. IT-96-21-T, Judgment, ¶ 245 (Nov. 16, 1998) [hereinafter Celebici].

318. *Id.* ¶ 263–66.

319. *Id.* ¶ 265.

> tion, and correlatively are not subject to the allegiance and control, of the State in whose hands they may find themselves . . . . Article 4 intends to look to the substance of relations, not to their legal characterisation as such.[320]

This redefinition (or relaxation) of the nationality requirements has now been upheld in several ICTY cases.[321] Moreover, the ICTY view finds implicit support in many national military regulations prescribing identical treatment to all civilian detainees without regard to nationality distinctions.[322] The ICC, which has concurrent jurisdiction over "grave breaches" of the 1949 Conventions, implicitly relaxes the nationality requirements of Article 4 along the same lines.[323] Finally, the consensus of commentators now endorses this ICTY interpretation of Article 4.[324]

Next consider the derogation regime of Article 5. As discussed in detail in Part II, Article 5 of the Convention conditions its protection of combatants.[325] As I demonstrated in Part II, the best reading of the provision is that it does not constitute a broad authorization to suspend the protections of the Convention. Nevertheless, Article 5 clearly limits, to some degree, the scope of protection the Convention accords unlawful combatants. Several developments in humanitarian and human rights law, however, have further eroded the significance of the provision: (1) the codification of prerequisites for lawful derogation from fundamental rights protections; and (2) the elabora-

320. Prosecutor v. Tadic, Case No. IT-94-1-A, Judgment, ¶ 168 (Appeals Chamber, ICTY, July 15, 1999) [hereinafter Tadic Judgment]. *See also* Guénaël Mettraux, *Crimes Against Humanity in the Jurisprudence of the International Criminal Tribunals for the Former Yugoslavia and for Rwanda*, 43 HARV. INT'L L.J. 237, 300 (2002) (arguing that the *Tadic* Appeals Chamber ruling gave the conventional reading of nationality requirement the "coup de grâce").

321. *See, e.g.*, Prosecutor v. Delalic, Case No. IT-96-21-A, ¶¶ 56–85 (Appeals Chamber, ICTY, Feb. 20, 2001); *id.* ¶ 83 (holding that Article 4 protects persons failing to satisfy its literal nationality requirements because "the victims may be 'assimilated' to the external State involved in the conflict, even if they formally have the same nationality as their captors"); Prosecutor v. Aleksovski, Case No. IT-95-14/1-A, Judgment, ¶ 151 (Appeals Chamber, ICTY, Mar. 24, 2000) ("Article 4 may be given a wider construction so that a person may be accorded protected status, notwithstanding the fact that he is of the same nationality as his captors."); Tadic Judgment, *supra* note 303, ¶ 169 (holding that "even if in the circumstances of the case the perpetrators and the victims were to be regarded as possessing the same nationality, Article 4 would still be applicable"); Celebici I, *supra* note 301, ¶ 263.

322. *See, e.g.*, U.S. ARMY, ENEMY PRISONERS OF WAR, RETAINED PERSONNEL, CIVILIAN INTERNEES AND OTHER DETAINEES, AR 190–8 (1997), at 2, 18–30, *available at* http://www.usapa.army.mil/pdffiles/r190_8.pdf (last visited Apr. 23, 2004).

323. The relevant mens rea element of the "grave breach" offense requires only that the perpetrator be aware that the person was fighting for the enemy—not that the perpetrator must know or have reason to know the nationality of the victim. *See* Preparatory Commission for the International Criminal Court, *Finalized Draft Text of the Elements of Crimes*, at 18, n.33, U.N. Doc. PCNICC/2000/INF/3/Add.2 (2000). These draft elements now have been adopted by the Assembly of States Parties. *See* Assembly of States Parties to the Rome Statute of the International Criminal Court, *First Session, New York, Sept. 3–10, 2002, Official Records*, ICC-ASP/1/3, ¶ 22. *See also id.* ¶ 10, 108 (Rules of Procedure and Evidence and Elements of Crimes).

324. *See, e.g.*, KRIANGSAK KITTICHAISAREE, INTERNATIONAL CRIMINAL LAW 139–41 (2001); Meron, *supra* note 191, at 260.

325. *See supra* Part II.A.2.

tion and concretization of non-derogable rights in both humanitarian and human rights law.

An extensive body of human rights law prescribes in some detail prerequisites for lawful derogation from fundamental rights. Much like the Civilians Convention, several widely ratified international human rights treaties expressly allow suspension of some rights in public emergencies, such as during times of war.[326] Article 4 of the ICCPR, for example, provides that in situations threatening the life of the nation, a government may issue a formal declaration suspending certain human rights guarantees provided that: (1) a state of emergency exists that threatens the life of the nation;[327] (2) the exigencies of the situation "strictly require" such a suspension;[328] (3) the suspension does not conflict with the nation's other international obligations;[329] (4) the emergency measures are applied in a non-discriminatory fashion;[330] and (5) the government notifies the U.N. Secretary-General immediately.[331] Although these requirements obviously do not apply formally to derogations under Article 5 of the Civilians Convention, they do suggest that broadly endorsed rules and principles have emerged which might limit the scope of legitimate derogations in Geneva law. Recall that the negotiating history

326. The derogation provisions of the major human rights treaties are remarkably similar. *See, e.g.*, ICCPR, *supra* note 227, art. 4(1); ACHR, *supra* note 227, art. 27(1), ECHR, *supra* note 227, art. 15(1). Note that the African Charter does not contain a provision authorizing States to derogate from their obligations under the treaty in times of public emergency. *See* Banjul Charter, *supra* note 227. For useful surveys of this area of law, see ANNA-LENA SVENSSON-MCCARTHY, THE INTERNATIONAL LAW OF HUMAN RIGHTS AND STATES OF EXCEPTION (1998); JOAN FITZPATRICK, HUMAN RIGHTS IN CRISIS: THE INTERNATIONAL SYSTEM FOR PROTECTING RIGHTS DURING STATES OF EMERGENCY (1994); JAIME ORAA, HUMAN RIGHTS IN STATES OF EMERGENCY IN INTERNATIONAL LAW (1992).

327. *See* Lawless Case (Ireland), 1961 Y.B. EUR. CONV. ON H.R. (Eur. Ct. H.R. 438, 472, 474) (holding that the ECHR's derogation clauses may be invoked only in "an exceptional situation of crisis or emergency which affects the whole population and constitutes a threat to the organized life of the community of which the State is composed"); SVENSSON-MCCARTHY, *supra* note 326, at 195–281; Fionnuala Ni Aolain, *The Emergence of Diversity: Differences in Human Rights Jurisprudence*, 19 FORDHAM INT'L L.J. 101, 103 (1995) (arguing that the concept of a "state of emergency refers to those exceptional circumstances resulting from temporary factors of a political nature, which, to varying degrees, involve extreme and imminent danger that threaten the organized existence of the state"). The concept of emergency does include circumstances other than armed conflict. For example, national disasters and extreme economic crises may constitute "public emergencies." *See* R. St. J. MacDonald, *Derogations Under Article 15 of the European Convention on Human Rights*, 36 COLUM. J. TRANSNAT'L L. 225, 235 (1997). Furthermore, the emergency must be temporary, imminent, and of such a character that it threatens the nation as a whole. *See, e.g.*, ORAA, *supra* note 326, at 11–33.

328. This provision incorporates the principle of proportionality into derogation regimes, thus requiring that the restrictive measures be proportional in duration, severity, and scope. Implicit in this requirement is that ordinary measures must be inadequate, and that the emergency measures must assist in the management of the crisis. *See, e.g.*, ORAA, *supra* note 326, at 143; MacDonald, *supra* note 327, at 233–35.

329. *See* SVENSSON-MCCARTHY, *supra* note 326, at 624–39.

330. *Id.* at 640–82.

331. *Id.* at 683–718; ICCPR, *supra* note 227, art. 4(3); ECHR, *supra* note 227, art. 15(3); ACHR, *supra* note 227, art. 27(3). The Human Rights Committee has emphasized the importance of notification for effective international supervision of derogations in states of emergency. *See* Report of the Human Rights Committee, U.N. GAOR, 36th Sess., Supp. No. 40, Annex VII, at 110, U.N. Doc A/36/40 (1981).

and ICRC Commentary IV suggest that the drafters of Article 5 sought only to authorize a narrow band of rights restrictions seen as absolutely necessary to the security of the state or the military security of the occupying power.[332] Indeed, the Commentary demonstrates that the conceptual structure of the provision mirrors that of human rights derogation regimes—and that this structure reflects the range of concerns of Geneva Conference delegates.[333] In this sense, the derogation regimes of human rights treaties provide a useful schematic for the systematic evaluation of the lawfulness of any exercise of Article 5 powers.

In addition, the list of so-called "non-derogable" rights has expanded. As discussed previously, the protections accorded by Article 75 of Additional Protocol I expressly augmented the scope and content of rights immune from Article 5 derogation.[334] Recall that these rights include robust due process protections and an implied right to repatriation.[335] Furthermore, developments in international human rights law bolstered considerably the fair trial rights recognized in Common Article 3 and, by implication, strengthened the Article 5 regime that makes non-derogable all fair trial rights "recognized in the present Convention," including those recognized in Common Article 3.[336]

2. *Common Article 3*

Common Article 3 establishes fundamental principles governing the treatment of all "war detainees"—a group that is, by definition, *hors de combat*. Despite this broad field of application, the provision, at the time of its drafting, exhibited several potentially important limitations. Take, for example, three oft-repeated criticisms of Common Article 3: (1) the conditions under which the provision applies are unclear;[337] (2) the rules outlined in the provision are too abstract to constrain state practice in any meaningful way;[338] and (3) the provision has not, until recently, benefited from the criminal enforcement regime of the Geneva Conventions.[339] These concerns, however, require substantial qualification in view of recent developments.

First, the scope of application of the provision has been clarified in at least one important respect. Although the lower threshold of applicability for Common Article 3 remains poorly defined,[340] there is now an emerging

332. *See supra* Part II.A.2.a (summarizing this drafting history).
333. ICRC, COMMENTARY IV, *supra* note 109, at 52–58.
334. ADDITIONAL PROTOCOL I, *supra* note 10, art. 75.
335. *Id.*
336. CIVILIANS CONVENTION, *supra* note 1, art. 5.
337. *See, e.g.*, MOIR, *supra* note 186; Jinks, *September 11*, *supra* note 177.
338. *See, e.g.*, Tom Farer, *Humanitarian Law and Armed Conflicts: Toward a Definition of "International Armed Conflict*," 71 COLUM. L. REV. 37 (1971).
339. *See infra* Part IV.B.2.
340. On the persistence of these problems, see Jinks, *September 11*, *supra* note 177; Jinks, Temporal Scope, *supra* note 177, at 2–8.

consensus on the upper threshold: Common Article 3 applies in both non-international and international armed conflict.[341] As such, all persons no longer taking active part in hostilities in any armed conflict must receive, at a minimum, humane treatment including the provision of fundamental judicial guarantees.

Second, the substantive rules of Common Article 3 have now acquired a more definite meaning. For example, Article 75 of Additional Protocol I (and Article 6 of Additional Protocol II) elaborate and clarify the meaning of Common Article 3 by specifying the minimum procedural guarantees for all persons subject to the authority of a belligerent. In addition, the vast reservoir of international human rights law discussed previously has clarified substantially the content of the seemingly abstract dictates of Common Article 3.[342] International human rights treaties and their supervisory organs have also made substantial progress in defining the scope of prohibitions on torture and cruel treatment.[343] Similarly, international fair trial rules have identified,[344] as a matter of positive law, those "judicial guarantees which are recognized as indispensable by civilized peoples."[345]

Third, the enforcement of Common Article 3 has improved markedly in recent years. Until recently, the prevailing view was that violations of Common Article 3 did not entail individual criminal responsibility.[346] However, recent developments in international criminal law make clear that violations of Common Article 3 are war crimes. For example, the ICC Statute, perhaps the most authoritative expression of the current state of humanitarian law, specifically criminalizes violations of Common Article 3.[347] The ICTR Statute also imposes individual criminal liability for serious violations of the provision.[348] Although the ICTY Statute does not expressly cover violations of Common Article 3,[349] the Tribunal held that the statute's provision con-

---

341. *See supra* Part II.C.1.

342. *See supra* Part II.C.3 (summarizing fair trial and humane treatment rights in human rights law and Additional Protocols).

343. *See generally* NIGEL RODLEY, THE TREATMENT OF PRISONERS UNDER INTERNATIONAL LAW (2d ed. 2001) (surveying these developments).

344. *See supra* Part II.C.3 (summarizing these rules).

345. Common Art. 3, *supra* note 59.

346. As recently as 1994, the U.N. Commission of Experts on Former Yugoslavia seemed to have held this view. *See Final Report of the Commission of Experts Established Pursuant to Security Council Resolution 780 (1992)*, ¶ 42, U.N. Doc. S/1994/674 (May 27, 1994) (stating that "in general . . . the only offences committed in internal armed conflict for which universal jurisdiction exists are 'crimes against humanity' and genocide, which apply irrespective of the conflicts' classification").

347. ICC STATUTE, *supra* note 51. Articles 8(2)(c) and 8(2)(e) of the ICC Statute cover Common Article 3 and Article 4 of Additional Protocol II, respectively. Article 8(2)(c) explicitly references Common Article 3 and its prohibitions, whereas Article 8(2)(e) addresses by implication the prohibitions of Article 4 in Additional Protocol II. All acts prohibited in Common Article 3(1) and Additional Protocol II, Articles 4(1) and 4(2), are prohibited by Articles 8(2)(c) and 8(2)(e), respectively, of the ICC Statute. *Id.*

348. STATUTE OF THE INTERNATIONAL CRIMINAL TRIBUNAL FOR RWANDA, art. 4, Nov. 8, 1994, 33 I.L.M. 1598, 1600 [hereinafter ICTR STATUTE].

349. STATUTE OF THE INTERNATIONAL CRIMINAL TRIBUNAL FOR THE FORMER YUGOSLAVIA, art. 3, May 25, 1993, 32 I.L.M. 1192 (1993) [hereinafter ICTY STATUTE].

cerning "violations of the laws and customs of war" necessarily included violations of Common Article 3.[350] Finally, the criminal law[351] and military manuals[352] of many countries, including the United States, recognize violations of Common Article 3 as war crimes.[353]

3. *Article 75 of Additional Protocol I*

Article 75 protects all persons who are "in the power of" a belligerent state, including unlawful combatants.[354] As discussed in Part II, Article 75 is modeled on Common Article 3, though it constitutes an important advancement over the protective scheme of that provision. Recall that Article 75 substantially clarifies the Common Article 3 scheme by specifying the content of due process protections and making clear the applicability of its rules in international armed conflicts. This provision also expressly revises two other protective schemes by (1) narrowing the class of derogable rights in Article 5 of the Civilians Convention, and (2) bolstering the minimum procedural rights accorded persons facing criminal charges under the laws of war.[355] In this sense, Article 75 of Additional Protocol I, drafted nearly thirty years after the 1949 Diplomatic Conference, is itself important evidence of the declining significance of POW status. In addition, the Article 75 protective scheme has, over the life of the provision, assumed an increasingly important position in Geneva law.

Two lingering problems potentially limit the utility of this protective scheme. First, as mentioned at the outset of this Part, whereas the 1949 Geneva Conventions now have universal participation, several important states are not party to Additional Protocol I. Second, violations of Article 75—like those of Common Article 3—are not expressly identified as war crimes in Geneva law. As such, the means and methods of enforcing this provision are not directly prescribed in or governed by Additional Protocol I.

---

350. *See* Tadic Appeal, *supra* note 200, ¶¶ 87–91 (interpreting Article 3 of the ICTY Statute).

351. *See* Thomas Graditsky, *Individual Criminal Responsibility for Violations of International Humanitarian Law Committed in Non-International Armed Conflicts*, 322 INT'L REV. RED CROSS 29 (1998) (collecting citations to penal codes).

352. *See id.* (collecting citations to military manuals).

353. The U.S. War Crimes Act was amended in 1997 to cover expressly all violations of Common Article 3. *See* Foreign Operations, Export Financing, and Related Programs Appropriations Act of 1998, Pub. L. No. 105-118, 111 Stat. 2386 (1997) (codified at 18 U.S.C. § 2441(c) (2000)) (amended in 1997 to replace the term "grave breaches" with "war crime" and to include violations of Common Article 3 within the definition of war crimes). Every U.S. court to consider the issue has classified violations of Common Article 3 as "serious violations of international law" and "war crimes." *See, e.g.*, Kadic v. Karadzic, 70 F.3d 232 (2d Cir. 1995); Linder v. Portocarrero, 963 F.2d 332, 336 (11th Cir. 1992) ("All of the authorities agree that torture and summary execution—the torture and killing of wounded non-combatant civilians—are acts that are viewed with universal abhorrence."); Doe v. Islamic Salvation Front, 993 F. Supp. 3 (D.D.C. 1998). This view is also clearly endorsed in U.S. military law and policy. *See, e.g.*, ARMY FM 27-10, *supra* note 44, ¶ 499; JUDGE ADVOCATE GENERAL, U.S. ARMY, LAW OF WAR WORKSHOP DESKBOOK, *supra* note 114, ch. 8 ("War Crimes").

354. ADDITIONAL PROTOCOL I, *supra* note 10, art. 75(1).

355. *See id.* art. 75(1)–(7).

The first of these concerns is diminishing in significance as the number of states party to Additional Protocol I rises (as does the number of states expressly incorporating Article 75, if not all of Additional Protocol I, into domestic law or policy). First, states party to Additional Protocol I are up. As of July 2003, 161 states are parties to Additional Protocol I including several major powers (e.g., China, Germany, North Korea, Russia, and the United Kingdom).[356] That is, most states have formally accepted Article 75 as the benchmark for the proper treatment of persons in the hands of a belligerent. Second, multinational and so-called coalition deployments typically utilize Additional Protocol I rules as the legal baseline governing hostilities.[357] Similarly, rules governing visiting forces—so-called Status of Forces Agreements (SOFAs)—also often define in terms of Article 75 the due process guarantees accorded persons arrested or detained by military forces.[358] Perhaps most importantly, many states not party to Additional Protocol I have nevertheless incorporated Article 75 into their law or policy.[359] Finally, many

356. *See* ICRC, *supra* note 42.

357. These include U.N. peacekeepers and other multinational forces. With respect to U.N. forces, see United Nations Secretariat, *Secretary-General's Bulletin, Observance by United Nations Forces of International Humanitarian Law*, U.N. Doc. ST/SGB/1999/13 (Aug. 6, 1999), *available at* http://www.un.org/peace/st_sgb_1999_13.pdf (last visited Apr. 23, 2004) (Annexes 1A, 4, 6).

With respect to multinational forces generally, see Michael N. Schmitt, *The Law of Armed Conflict as Soft Power*, *in* INTERNATIONAL LAW ACROSS THE SPECTRUM OF CONFLICT 454, 459 (Michael N. Schmitt ed., 2000) (stating, with specific reference to Protocol I, that typically the "greatest common normative denominator" will apply for multinational forces); JUDGE ADVOCATE GENERAL, U.S. ARMY, OPERATIONAL LAW HANDBOOK 70 (2003) (noting that combined rules of engagement (ROE) must be fashioned for multinational forces and that these rules may differ from U.S. ROE if coalition partners have different commitments under the law of war). Consider the example of NATO. There are no standing NATO ROE. Rather, NATO ROE are developed on a "mission specific" basis through a process of consensus. *See* CENTER FOR LAW AND MILITARY OPERATIONS, RULES OF ENGAGEMENT (ROE) HANDBOOK FOR JUDGE ADVOCATES 2-11 to 2-12 (2000), *available at* http://sja.hqmc.usmc.mil/JAO/sources/Files/ROEHB.pdf (last visited Apr. 24, 2004); W. Hays Parks, *International Humanitarian Law in Multinational Operations: How Do Multinational Forces Work Within Constraints Set by Differing Commitments of Individual States?*, Paper Presented to EAPC Workshop on International Humanitarian Law and Multinational Forces, London, Nov. 20–21, 2000, *available at* http://www.isn.ethz.ch/pfpdc/documents/2000/10-00_London/parks.htm (stating that NATO successfully incorporated Protocol I into its operational policy, notwithstanding the fact that the United States is not party to the treaty, through an extended consultation process in which troubling ambiguities in the treaty were clarified to the satisfaction of coalition members).

358. *See, e.g.*, Knut Ipsen, *Combatants and Non-Combatants*, *in* THE HANDBOOK OF THE LAW OF VISITING FORCES 65, 94 (Deiter Fleck ed., 1995).

359. Consider the example of the United States. According to Michael Matheson, then Legal Advisor to the U.S. Department of State, the United States views Articles 73–89 (concerning the treatment of persons in the power of a party to the conflict, women and children, and duties regarding implementation of Additional Protocol I) as either legally binding as customary international law or acceptable practice though not legally binding. *See* Michael J. Matheson, *The United States Position on the Relation of Customary International Law to the 1977 Protocols Additional to the 1949 Geneva Conventions*, 2 AM. U. J. INT'L L. & POL'Y 419, 420 (1987). This position is confirmed by U.S. military policy on the treatment of detainees and the due process rights recognized in the newly minted military commissions. *See* U.S. ARMY, AR 190-8, *supra* note 322, at 19–26; DEP'T OF DEF. MILITARY COMM'N ORDER NO. 1 (Mar. 21, 2002), *available at* http://www.defenselink.mil/news/Mar2002/d20020321ord.pdf (last visited Apr. 24, 2004) [hereinafter DOD ORDER].

commentators and some states now suggest that Additional Protocol I is "customary international law."[360]

The second of these concerns, however, persists. Of course, Additional Protocol I itself does not include violations of Article 75 in its "grave breach" regime. Neither violation of the provision is expressly identified as a war crime by the ICC, ICTY, or ICTR. Nevertheless, Article 75 is crucial to the proper interpretation of several provisions that do give rise to individual criminal liability, such as Common Article 3[361] and the "grave breach" regime of the Civilians Convention.[362]

4. *Penal Repression Regime Fair Trial Rights*

Two deficiencies have limited the significance of the enforcement provisions of the 1949 Conventions that specify the minimum fair trial rights applicable in war crimes prosecutions. Important recent developments, however, have substantially ameliorated these concerns.

First, the catalog of fair trial rights in these provisions—specifically Articles 105—108 of the POW Convention—is arguably limited. Of course, as already discussed, these protections have been augmented substantially—formally through Article 75 of Additional Protocol I[363] and, informally, through emerging international standards evidenced by the procedural rights regimes of international war crimes tribunals.[364] The important point is that there is no meaningful gap between the fair trial rights accorded POWs under the Third Convention and those accorded all persons facing prosecution for war crimes.

Second, the provisions often failed to accord any protection in the very circumstances in which their protection was most needed. That is, the persons most in need of these protections—persons arguably not entitled to greater due process protections in Geneva law—are often prosecuted under the municipal law of the detaining authority, rather than the laws of war. Or,

---

360. *See, e.g.*, LESLIE C. GREEN, ESSAYS ON THE MODERN LAW OF WAR 586 (2d ed. 1999); Dormann, *supra* note 80, at 67; Greenwood, *supra* note 109, at 45; Abella, *supra* note 202, ¶ 162; Paust, *supra* note 21, at 5. As I made clear in the introduction, the argument presented here does not rely on assertions that any particular norm is customary international law. Hence, I am not suggesting that Article 75 now applies of its own force because it has assumed the status of customary international law. Rather, I claim only that the general (and increasing) acceptance of Article 75 as binding law suggests that the importance of its ratification deficit is diminishing.

361. *See supra* Part IV.B.2 (outlining the progressive criminalization of violations of Common Article 3); *see also supra* Parts II.C.3, II.D.1 (arguing that fair trial protection in Common Article 3 must be interpreted in accord with Article 75).

362. *See* CIVILIANS CONVENTION, *supra* note 1, arts. 146–49. For example, denial of a protected civilian's fair trial rights is a "grave breach" of the Civilians Convention. *Id.* art. 146. As explained previously, Article 75 modifies the scope of derogable rights under Article 5 of the Civilians Convention; it establishes a floor for due process rights under the Civilians Convention. That is, denying a protected civilian (within the meaning of the Civilians Convention) the fair trial rights recognized in Article 75 would constitute a grave breach of the Civilians Convention.

363. ADDITIONAL PROTOCOL I, *supra* note 10, art. 75(6).

364. *See supra* Part II.D.1.

put differently, states could perhaps easily avoid the application of this regime by choosing to prosecute war criminals under domestic criminal law. This concern, despite its surface plausibility, is illusory on several levels. Consider that Article 75 of Additional Protocol I eliminates the problem by harmonizing the procedural rights regimes for all persons detained or punished in connection with an armed conflict at a level of protection that exceeds that of Articles 105–108 of the POW Convention. Of course, Common Article 3—interpreted in light of Additional Protocol I, human rights law, and the fair trial regimes of international criminal tribunals—also establishes a comparable if not more robust rights regime. Furthermore, it applies to criminal prosecutions irrespective of the governing substantive law. Moreover, substantial evidence suggests that states are now more willing (and able) to initiate prosecutions under the laws of war. The proliferation of international criminal tribunals, by increasing the salience and symbolic force of humanitarian law, has triggered a cascade of national war crimes legislation.[365] It is also important to note that state practice in the "war on terrorism" may signal greater willingness to invoke the laws of war when dealing with persons who may be fairly characterized as unlawful combatants.[366]

C. *Toward a Bottom Line: Assessing the Unique Protective Significance of POW Status*

Geneva law protects unlawful combatants, persons taking direct part in hostilities without satisfying the requirements for POW status, and these protections approximate those accorded POWs. In this Part, I have demonstrated that several developments in humanitarian law and policy have further narrowed the remaining protective inequalities. It is important, however, to address separately the unique protective consequences of POW status. Two potentially important protections merit extended consideration. These protections are derived from a curious feature of the POW Convention—that POWs must be "assimilated" into the armed forces of the detaining state.[367] This generates a cluster of rights that is, as a formal matter, unique to the POW Convention. Many of these rules concern only the right of captured military personnel to treatment honoring their status as military personnel.[368] These rules, as a consequence, have ambiguous protective consequences. For instance, the rule requiring that POWs be tried before military

365. *See* ICRC, International Humanitarian Law, National Implementation Database, *supra* note 43 (providing excerpts of humanitarian national legislation from over 50 countries); Coalition for the Int'l Criminal Court, National Legislation Database (providing full text of national war crimes legislation from over 35 states), *available at* http://www.iccnow.org/resourcestools/ratimptoolkit/nationalregionaltools/legislationdebates.html (last visited Mar. 13, 2004).

366. *See, e.g.*, Jinks, *supra* note 177, at 34 n.221; Fitzpatrick, *supra* note 22, at 353.

367. ICRC, COMMENTARY III, *supra* note 194, at 406–09 (discussing the "principle of assimilation").

368. *See, e.g.*, POW CONVENTION, *supra* note 1, art. 84 (requiring that POWs be tried by military—rather than civilian—courts).

courts will have adverse protective consequences in most circumstances. Two specific applications of the "principle of assimilation" are nevertheless important in the context of the war on terrorism. First, the POW Convention prohibits trial of POWs by special military courts (such as military commissions).[369] The Convention provides that POWs "can be validly sentenced only if the sentence has been pronounced by the same courts according to the same procedure as in the case of members of the armed forces of the Detaining Power . . . ."[370] Second, POWs enjoy a broad "combatant immunity" that precludes punishing them for their very participation in the hostilities.[371]

1. *Prohibition Against Ad Hoc "Military Commissions"*

One potentially important consequence of POW status is that it precludes the use of specialized criminal proceedings. As discussed above, the POW Convention requires that POWs be tried by the same courts in which the armed forces of the detaining power would be tried.[372] Therefore, POWs held by the United States, for example, must be tried in U.S. courts-martial. This rule, for which there is no direct analog in the Civilians Convention, seemingly suggests that ad hoc military commissions are a viable prosecutorial option only if the detainees are not POWs.

Given the express prohibition on specialized procedures in the POW Convention, this claim is certainly correct on one level: POWs may not be tried by special military commission. It does not necessarily follow, however, that unlawful combatants (war detainees denied POW status) may be tried by special military commission. The idea here is simple: even if unlawful combatants are not covered by the "principle of assimilation," they may be entitled to procedural rights which would effectively preclude the use of ad hoc commissions.

As described in detail in Parts II and III, unlawful combatants enjoy general criminal procedure rights that mirror the protections accorded POWs. If the policy value of military commissions derives from their summary procedures, then the protections afforded unlawful combatants would deprive the commissions of their value. That is, the rights of unlawful combatants would require procedural guarantees identical in all important respects to those of courts-martial. In addition, the Geneva Conventions arguably prohibit irregular "military commissions" irrespective of the procedural rights guaranteed in such proceedings. Recall that all persons facing criminal punishment are entitled to trial by "regular" courts.[373] Moreover, this POW

369. *See, e.g.*, Paust, *Courting Illegality*, *supra* note 21; Katyal & Tribe, *supra* note 21; Drumbl, *supra* note 11.

370. POW CONVENTION, *supra* note 1, art. 102.

371. *See supra* text accompanying note 38 (explaining concept and collecting citations).

372. *See* POW CONVENTION, *supra* note 1, art. 84.

373. *See* Common Art. 3, *supra* note 59; ADDITIONAL PROTOCOL I, *supra* note 10, art. 75.

"right" to trial by regular military court is, in many instances, a disability. It is well understood that trial procedures utilized by military courts often fall short of international due process standards, and typically fall short of the rights recognized in the parallel civilian system.[374] In other words, the "same procedures, same courts" right accorded POWs (derived from the principle of assimilation) has ambiguous protective consequences. Of course, the criminal procedural rights recognized in Geneva law establish a protective floor—no war detainee may be tried by procedures that fall short of the requirements outlined in the Conventions. The important point is that the procedures utilized in criminal proceedings must comport with the increasingly robust, increasingly precise body of international standards—irrespective of whether the tribunal is a "military court martial," "military commission," "national security court," or "federal district court."

The status of military commissions in U.S. law is, as a general matter, consistent with this analysis. That the U.S. Supreme Court has endorsed the use of military commissions to try unlawful combatants does not undermine the claims I advance here. In *Ex parte Quirin*, the Court held that Congress had authorized the President to try unlawful combatants by special military commission.[375] Specifically, the *Quirin* Court concluded that "Congress [in what is now 10 U.S.C. § 821] has explicitly provided, so far as it may constitutionally do so, that military tribunals shall have jurisdiction to try offenders or offenses against the law of war in appropriate cases,"[376] and that "Congress [in what is now § 821] has authorized trial of offenses against the law of war before such commissions."[377] *Quirin* was, at bottom, a statutory interpretation case. Moreover, the statutory scheme at issue in *Quirin* strongly suggests that military commissions are authorized only insofar as they are consistent with the law of war. Section 821 provides:

> The provisions of this chapter conferring jurisdiction upon courts-martial do not deprive military commissions, provost courts, or other military tribunals of concurrent jurisdiction with respect to offenders or offenses that by statute or by the law of war may be tried by military commissions, provost courts, or other military tribunals.[378]

The issue in *Quirin* was whether the predecessor of this provision authorized the use of commissions. And, of course, the Court concluded that it does (a strained reading of the provision, to be sure). Nevertheless, the language of the provision makes clear that the use of military commissions, even under

374. *See, e.g.*, U.N. Sub-Comm. on the Promotion and Protection of Human Rights, *Issue of the Administration of Justice Through Military Tribunals*, U.N. Doc. E/CN.4/Sub.2/2002/4 (July 9, 2002) (*prepared by* Louis Joinet) (summarizing poor human rights record of military courts).

375. *Ex parte* Quirin, 317 U.S. 1 (1942).

376. *Id.* at 28.

377. *Id.* at 29.

378. 10 U.S.C. § 821 (1994).

the *Quirin* court's reasoning, is authorized only insofar as they are consistent with the law of war.

Two further points on the *Quirin* case are in order here: (1) the Court substantially relied on the then-prevailing "laws of war" in reaching its conclusion—this is a crucial point given that the case was decided seven years before the drafting of the Geneva Conventions—and (2) the "laws of war" did not, prior to the Geneva Conventions of 1949, afford any protection to "unlawful combatants"—a matter that was expressly taken up at the 1949 Diplomatic Conference.[379] Even under the reasoning of the *Quirin* court, trial by military commissions must accord with the law of war, including, most importantly, the Geneva Conventions. Given the analysis offered at the beginning of this Part, "military commissions" are lawful only if the procedures utilized therein comport with the Geneva rules applicable to unlawful combatants. The upshot is that unlawful combatants may be tried by courts other than those in which members of the detaining state's armed forces are tried, but these courts must be "regular courts" affording the minimum due process guarantees established in the Conventions.

2. *Combatant Immunity*

Another potentially significant protective consequence of POW status is combatant immunity. Indeed, comparison of the schemes analyzed in Parts II and III makes clear that the one unique protective consequence of POW status is "combatant immunity." Indeed, the most significant consequence of POW status is that lawful combatants may not be punished for their otherwise lawful participation in the hostilities. This point of law, although firmly established, requires some qualification.

First, although POWs are entitled to engage in combat, they must comply with the laws of war.[380] Accordingly, a POW may be prosecuted for pre-capture offenses only if his actions (1) rise to the level of a "war crime"[381] or

379. *See supra* Part II.A.1 (discussing drafting history of Article 5 of the Civilians Convention).

380. For example, McDougal has stated that:

> [A]cts committed in war by enemy civilians and members of armed forces may be punished as crimes under a belligerent's municipal law only to the extent that such acts are violative of the international law on the conduct of hostilities. Clearly the rules of warfare would be pointless . . . if every single act of war may by unilateral municipal fiat be made a common crime and every prisoner of war executed as a murderer. International law delineates the outer limits of the liability of supposed war criminals; and conformity with that law affords a complete defense for the violent acts charged.

MYRES S. MCDOUGAL & FLORENTINO P. FELICIANO, THE INTERNATIONAL LAW OF WAR: TRANSNATIONAL COERCION AND WORLD PUBLIC ORDER 712 (1994) (citations omitted). *See also* DEP'T OF NAVY, ANNOTATED SUPPLEMENT TO THE COMMANDER'S HANDBOOK OF NAVAL OPERATIONS 490 n.47 (Naval War College, Int'l L. Studies vol. 73, A.R. Thomas & James C. Duncan eds., 1999) ("The [POW Convention]'s underlying philosophy is that POWs should not be punished merely for having engaged in armed conflict . . . ."); *id.* at 492 ("Prisoners of war may not be punished for hostile acts directed against opposing forces prior to capture, unless those acts constituted violations of the law of armed conflict.")

381. Even if convicted for pre-capture offenses, enemy combatants retain the benefits of the POW regime of the POW Convention according to Article 85 of that treaty: "Prisoners of war prosecuted under

"crime against humanity";[382] or (2) are unrelated to the state of hostilities (i.e., are common crimes).[383] Properly understood, the scope of combatant immunity therefore underscores its relative insignificance on the policy front. Consider that acts of terrorism in the context of an armed conflict are always war crimes,[384] as are all attacks directed against the civilian population as such.[385] In addition, violations of the rule of distinction are also war crimes,[386] as are acts of perfidy.[387] The point is that there are no protective consequences associated with POW status for persons who have engaged in terrorism, attacked civilians, or committed warlike acts without adequately distinguishing themselves from civilians.

Second, POWs, even if immune from criminal prosecution, may be deprived of their liberty because of their participation in the hostilities.[388] That is, *all* enemy combatants, even if POWs, may be detained without criminal charge for the duration of the hostilities.

Third, combatant status, in general, is also associated with an important disability: combatants, whether lawful or not, may be targeted, attacked, and killed by the enemy. That is, the laws of war expressly contemplate proportionate attacks aimed at overcoming the organized resistance of the opposition.

Up to this point, I have argued only that the policy and protective consequences of combatant immunity are minimal. Nevertheless, there is a nontrivial core of unlawful combatants for whom the rule has important protective consequences: unlawful combatants who have otherwise complied with the law of war. For these fighters, the combatant immunity issue is crucial

the laws of the Detaining Power for acts committed prior to capture shall retain, even if convicted, the benefits of the present Convention." POW CONVENTION, *supra* note 1, art. 85.

382. *See* ICRC, COMMENTARY III, *supra* note 194 (Commentary to Article 85 identifies "crimes against humanity" as crimes that pierce combatant immunity).

383. *See generally* ICRC, COMMENTARY III, *supra* note 194, at 413–23 (setting forth rule). *See, e.g.*, United States v. Noriega, 746 F. Supp. 1506, 1526 (S.D. Fla. 1990), *aff'd*, 117 F.3d 1206 (11th Cir. 1997), *cert. denied* 523 U.S. 1060 (1998) (prosecuting prisoner of war for drug trafficking). The immunity does not, therefore, shield from prosecution enemy combatants charged with pre-capture terrorist offenses not related to the conflict.

384. *See, e.g.*, Hans-Peter Gasser, *Acts of Terror, "Terrorism," and International Humanitarian Law*, 84 INT'L REV. RED CROSS 547 (2002) (cataloging various war crimes provisions implicated by acts of terrorism). Consider that such acts typically violate several provisions of Geneva law including: (1) the prohibition of attacks on civilians and civilian objects, ADDITIONAL PROTOCOL I, *supra* note 10, arts. 51, 52; (2) the prohibition on indiscriminate attacks, *Id.* art. 51; (3) the murder of persons no longer taking active part in hostilities, Common Art. 3, *supra* note 59; ADDITIONAL PROTOCOL I, *supra* note 10, art. 75; and (4) the murder of persons "protected" by the Conventions. *See, e.g.*, CIVILIANS CONVENTION, *supra* note 1, art. 146 ("grave breach" provision of Civilians Convention). Moreover, acts of terrorism are now expressly identified as "war crimes" in Additional Protocol I and the ICTR Statute. *See* ADDITIONAL PROTOCOL I, *supra* note 10, art. 51(2) ("Acts or threats of violence the primary purpose of which is to spread terror among the civilian population are prohibited."); ICTR Statute, *supra* note 348, art. 4(d) (criminalizing "acts of terrorism").

385. *See* ADDITIONAL PROTOCOL I, *supra* note 10, arts. 51(2), 52(1).

386. *See, e.g.*, ADDITIONAL PROTOCOL I, *supra* note 10, art. 45(1) (requiring combatants to distinguish themselves from the civilian population).

387. *See, e.g.*, ADDITIONAL PROTOCOL I, *supra* note 10, arts. 37–39.

388. POW CONVENTION, *supra* note 1, arts. 21–22.

because, if denied this protection, they may be prosecuted upon capture for their very participation in the hostilities (even if they otherwise scrupulously observed the rules of war). For this group, the denial of POW status means that they face the prospect of criminal prosecution and life imprisonment at the hands of the enemy (and perhaps the death penalty).

Fourth, there are, however, sound policy reasons to accord all captured combatants immunity for their otherwise lawful warlike acts. Combatant immunity, given its contours as just described, could and should be used as a tool to promote compliance with the rules of war.[389] If all captured combatants failing to satisfy the requirements for POW status are subject to prosecution for any warlike acts, the law provides irregular fighters with no incentive to comply with its dictates. Although their very failure to satisfy POW status requirements suggests some conduct contrary to the laws of war, this conduct, in many instances, may not reflect any individual culpability. Recall that many of the POW status requirements are collective, reflecting governmental or high command policies.[390] In addition, it is inapposite to characterize as "criminal" the otherwise lawful warlike acts of civilians who take up arms to defend their country against an enemy to whom they owe no allegiance (as a formal or sociological matter).

Critics of the view advanced here might defend the criminalization of unlawful belligerency on the grounds that (1) the irregularization of warfare resulting from such acts (irrespective of whether they exhibit a culpable mental state) poses a grave and generalized threat to civilians; and (2) the criminal sanction of it is necessary to deter such persons from taking up arms. Although plausible, this line of reasoning suffers from two structural defects. First, criminalization of belligerency creates perverse incentives for the unlawful combatants: because their very participation in the hostilities subjects them to criminal prosecution upon capture, they have no incentive to comply with the law of war. Protecting the victims of warfare, including civilians, might best be achieved by maximizing the incentives of combatants (those who are engaged in the fight) to comply with the law of war. As discussed above, the criminalization of belligerency eschews this type of incentive structure in favor of one that seeks to discourage would-be fighters from taking up arms in the first place.

Second, criminalization of belligerency does not substantially alter the incentive structure of civilians contemplating participation in hostilities. All would-be combatants have non-trivial reasons to refrain from any direct participation in the hostilities. Recall that "peaceful" civilians are immune from lawful attack; all combatants, on the other hand, may be made the object of attack. In addition, "peaceful" civilians may be detained only in a narrow range of circumstances, whereas all combatants, upon capture, may be detained for the duration of the hostilities. In short, the structure of Geneva

389. *See infra* Part V.

390. *See* POW CONVENTION, *supra* note 1, art. 4. See *infra* Part V for detailed examples.

law discourages civilian participation in armed conflict. This is not to say that civilians participate in hostilities at a low rate. The point is that would-be fighters take up arms only if they are willing to assume substantial risk to life and liberty. The pool of civilians otherwise willing to fight includes only those who value highly the benefits they expect to issue from participation in the fight. For these individuals, the criminalization of belligerency adds only a modest disincentive (if any) to join the fight.

To summarize: If combatants commit acts that constitute war crimes, they should be prosecuted (and they could be prosecuted regardless of whether they enjoy combatant immunity). Conversely, if combatants do not engage in such acts, they should not be punished for their very participation in the conduct of war. This protective logic helps explain why states sometimes choose to accord combatant immunity even in civil wars, as the United States did in the Civil War,[391] and why some inter-governmental forces now assign all captured combatants POW status.

D. *Illustration: POW Status and the "War on Terror"*

Returning to the current controversy surrounding the international legal status of detainees in the "war on terror," two points follow from the analysis offered here. First, the terms of debate in the current controversy are wrongly specified, which has obscured exactly what is at stake from a policy perspective. The conferral of POW status would not alter significantly the international legal duties owed the war detainees. Second, no pressing policy matters turn on the choice between the potentially applicable protective schemes. Consider the policy arguments advanced by the United States in the POW controversy. The United States suggests that POW status would impede the ongoing law enforcement investigation into the activities of Al Qaeda and other terrorist groups. However, the protection against coercive interrogation provided by the POW Convention is identical in all important respects to the protection accorded civilians under the Civilians Convention. Moreover, Common Article 3 and Additional Protocol I prohibit torture and other cruel treatment in all circumstances. The United States also argues that anti-terror efforts would be compromised by the obligation to release and repatriate POWs upon the cessation of active hostilities. However, civilians are entitled to the same protection under the Civilians Convention. The due process protections accorded by Common Article 3 and Additional Protocol I, coupled with widely recognized international human rights obligations, would also preclude detention without charge or trial of "war detainees" beyond the end of the conflict. The United States also maintains that POW status precludes the use of specialized criminal proceedings, such as the contemplated military commissions, but for reasons canvassed above, this claim has no

391. *See* JUDGE ADVOCATE GENERAL, U.S. ARMY, *Prisoners of War and Detainees*, *in* LAW OF WAR WORKSHOP DESKBOOK 69, 70–71 (2000).

merit. Finally, the United States might resist assigning POW status to the detainees on the grounds that these fighters should not enjoy combatant immunity for acts of international terrorism. But, as I argued in the previous Part, POWs are not entitled to combatant immunity with respect to terrorist acts (or any other acts that violate the laws of war). Moreover, there are sound policy rationales for prosecuting only those captured combatants who have committed acts that violate the law of war.

V. Conclusion: Toward Protective Parity

The Geneva Conventions protect unlawful combatants, and this protection very closely approximates that accorded POWs. As demonstrated in Part IV, several recent developments in law and policy suggest the emergence of "protective parity" across combatant status categories. At first glance, this outcome might seem normatively unattractive. After all, if POW status is irrelevant, then combatants and states arguably have no incentive to comply with the organizational requirements of the POW Convention. Such an incentive structure would erode (if not eviscerate) the "principle of distinction" which, in turn, would undermine the broader humanitarian ambitions of the law of war.

This "humanitarian" critique of protective parity assumes that protection is best understood as a carrot (and denial of protection, a stick) to induce law-abiding conduct in time of war.

Although a comprehensive normative defense of protective parity is beyond the scope of this Article, I want to highlight three points. First, this "denial of protection" approach is inconsistent with the structure of Geneva law. Indeed, the protective regimes of Geneva law expressly condition the authority of states to enforce its substantive rules. Consider that the penal repression regime of the 1949 Conventions and Article 75 of Additional Protocol I requires states to accord certain due process rights to all persons accused of violating the Conventions.[392] In addition, the POW Convention makes clear that POWs retain their protective status even if convicted of the most serious war crimes.[393]

392. *See supra* Parts II.C, II.D. Compare these robust procedural rights with the minimal procedural protections accorded in status determination proceedings. *See, e.g.*, POW Convention, *supra* note 1, art. 5 (requiring only that "in the case of doubt," status is determined by a "competent tribunal"). For a detailed analysis of Article 5, see Naqvi, *supra* note 25.

393. POW Convention, *supra* note 1, art. 85 ("Prisoners of war prosecuted under the laws of the Detaining Power for acts committed prior to capture shall retain, even if convicted, the benefits of the present Convention."). Although the provision references "the laws of the Detaining Power," which might be understood as distinct from the "laws of war," the drafting history, ICRC Commentary, and interpretation of leading military manuals make clear that the provision encompasses prosecution for "international" crimes. It is also important to note that the Civilians Convention does not have a direct analog to Article 85. However, this provision was considered necessary in the POW Convention because of the conduct elements embedded in the definition of POWs. *See id.* art. 4, ¶ A(2). No such provision is required in the Civilians Convention because: (1) its definition of "protected persons" does not include any conduct elements; and (2) the Article 5 derogation regime provides an exhaustive catalog of protec-

Second, protective schemes are conceptually distinct from enforcement schemes. Hence, protective parity can be paired with an effective enforcement strategy. Geneva law, as described above, provides for the criminal prosecution of persons committing war crimes. In this way, Geneva law provides actors with an incentive to comply with its substantive commitments, including the "principle of distinction." Geneva law, in this sense, exhibits a two-pronged strategy: (1) it protects *all persons* subject to the authority of a belligerent state (or armed opposition group) irrespective of their "status" (what I have called "protective parity"); and (2) it subjects *all persons* violating its substantive rules to criminal prosecution irrespective of their "status" (what I will call the "war crimes approach" to enforcement). The important point is that the scope and content of protective schemes are conceptually distinct from the scope and content of enforcement schemes. The former need not be inextricably connected to the latter. The upshot is that protective parity need not erode the rule of distinction—protection can coincide with the energetic suppression of war crimes.

Third, protective parity (coupled with a "war crimes approach" to enforcement) best promotes observance of the law of war, including the "principle of distinction." There are at least two ways to build into humanitarian regimes structural incentives to comply: (1) denial of humanitarian protection to bad actors (coupled perhaps with criminal prosecutions); and (2) crimi-nal prosecution of bad actors (all of whom nevertheless enjoy humanitarian protection). As discussed in Part IV, there are two structural problems with the first approach: (1) it creates perverse incentives for combatants; and (2) it targets for incentivization actors most resistant to the regime's influence.[394] In addition, the "denial of protection" approach might lengthen and intensify conflicts by providing a disincentive to surrender. Military planners and soldiers have long understood that poor treatment of captured enemy fighters often backfires because it encourages the enemy to fight to the death.[395] Indeed, many scholars suggest that the institutional design of the POW Convention is best explained in these terms—that is, protecting the enemy serves the interests of the detaining authority.[396] The important point here is that the same logic applies to the conduct of *all* combatants, regardless of whether they satisfy the requirements of POW status.

The second approach (protective parity coupled with the war crimes approach to enforcement), on the other hand, yields substantial benefits in that:

---

tive consequences issuing from conduct. *See* CIVILIANS CONVENTION, *supra* note 1, arts. 4, 5; *see also supra* Part II.A.

394. *See supra* Part IV.C.2 (discussing competing incentive structures in the context of combatant immunity).

395. *See, e.g.*, U.S. ARMY, *History of the Law of War*, *in* LAW OF WAR WORKSHOP DESKBOOK, *supra* note 391, at 3, 12; WILLIAM E.S. FLORY, PRISONERS OF WAR: A STUDY IN THE DEVELOPMENT OF INTERNATIONAL LAW 39–70 (1942) (documenting history).

396. *See, e.g.*, U.S. ARMY, *Prisoners of War and Detainees*, *supra* note 391, at 79–80; Eric Posner, *A Theory of the Laws of War*, 70 U. CHI. L. REV. 297 (2003); James D. Morrow, *The Institutional Features of the Prisoners of War Treaties*, 55 INT'L ORG. 971 (2001).

(1) it provides unlawful combatants with some incentive to comply with the law of war (even after they have decided to participate in the hostilities); and (2) it is more narrowly tailored to punish only bad actors—persons who, with a culpable mental state, have committed acts causing or risking grave consequences for protected persons.

* * *

What difference does POW status make? Contrary to conventional wisdom (and the prevailing policy debates in the current "war on terrorism"), I maintain that POW status carries *no significant, unique protective consequences.* As a descriptive matter, the unique protective significance of POW status is minimal and in sharp decline. The text, structure, and history of the 1949 Geneva Conventions and the 1977 Additional Protocols thereto strongly support this conclusion. As a normative matter, the move toward "protective parity" maximizes, within the bounds of military necessity, the humanitarian protection accorded combatants without exacerbating the dangers faced by non-combatant civilians.

[2]

PRISONERS OF WAR AND THE PROTECTING POWER

By Colonel Howard S. Levie, U.S.A.*

Legal Adviser, Headquarters, U. S. European Command

One of the more significant, but inadequately recognized, developments in the field of the law of war which has occurred during the past half-century is that with respect to the institution of the Protecting Power. Surprisingly little has been written, especially in English, either on the general subject of the Protecting Power or on the specific subject of the Protecting Power and its relationship to the prisoner-of-war problem.[1] This article will endeavor, to a necessarily limited extent, to fill that void, with the emphasis being placed on the gradual, but steady, expansion of the authority, responsibility, and functions of the Protecting Power in safeguarding the welfare of prisoners of war.

The term *Protecting Power* is comparatively simple of definition. It is a state which has accepted the responsibility of protecting the interests of another state in the territory of a third, with which, for some reason, such as war, the second state does not maintain diplomatic relations.[2] Because

* Formerly Chief, International Affairs Division, Office of The Judge Advocate General of the Army. The opinions expressed herein are those of the writer and are not necessarily those of The Judge Advocate General or of the Department of the Army.

1 A fairly complete contemporary bibliography of published items would consist of the following: Franklin, Protection of Foreign Interests (1946); Janner, La Puissance Protectrice en Droit International (1948; originally published in German); Siordet, The Geneva Conventions of 1949: The Question of Scrutiny (1953; originally published in French); and De la Pradelle, "Le Contrôle de l'Application des Conventions Humanitaires en cas de Conflit armé," in 2 Annuaire Français de Droit International 343 (1956). The subject is, of course, dealt with, but in a more limited fashion, in the various general treatises and articles on the 1949 Geneva Conventions such as De la Pradelle, La Conférence Diplomatique et les Nouvelles Conventions de Genève du 12 août 1949 (1951); Yingling and Ginnane, "The Geneva Conventions of 1949," in 46 A.J.I.L. 393 (1952); Kunz, "The Geneva Conventions of August 12, 1949," in Law and Politics in the World Community 279 (Lipsky, 1953); and Pictet, Commentary on the Geneva Convention Relative to the Treatment of Prisoners of War (hereinafter referred to as Commentary) (1960). Modern texts on international law do little more than paraphrase the provisions of the Geneva Conventions. See, for example, 2 Oppenheim (Lauterpacht), International Law 374–376 and 386 (7th ed., 1952), and Stone, Legal Controls of International Conflict 655, 658, 661, and 666 (1954). Many slightly older texts do not even include the term "Protecting Power" in their indices. See, for example, 2 Oppenheim (McNair), International Law (4th ed., 1926), and Wheaton (Phillipson), International Law (5th ed., 1916). It is to be hoped that this paucity of material does not indicate a continuation of the neglect of the law of war condemned by Kunz a decade ago. Kunz, "The Chaotic Status of the Laws of War and the Urgent Necessity for Their Revision," in 45 A.J.I.L. 37 (1951).

2 A state is frequently called upon to represent certain specified interests of another state in the territory of a third, even though normal, peaceful relations exist between

the protection is most frequently rendered to nationals of the protected state found in the third state, the former is often referred to as the *Power of Origin* and the latter as the *Power of Residence.* For obvious reasons, in the case of prisoners of war the state by which they are held is known as the *Detaining Power* rather than as the *Power of Residence.* And while the term *Power of Origin* may be a misnomer in the case of certain prisoners of war, as, for example, those who were captured while serving in the armed forces of a state other than their own, it will be used herein for lack of a more appropriate term.

I. Historical

The earliest indication of what we now term the Protecting Power probably appeared in the Capitulations of the Ottoman Empire of the sixteenth century.[3] Curiously enough, in those early days protection of non-nationals came about, not as a result of agreements reached with the Power of Residence by the Power of Origin, but as a result of agreements reached with the Power of Residence by the prospective Protecting Power itself, the latter having probably been primarily concerned with the resulting increase in its own prestige and influence in the territory in which it was acting and in the home territories of the protected persons. At that period the Protecting Power was, and in the three succeeding centuries it remained, completely a creature of custom and usage, with no conventional basis, definition, or functions. As a result, the extent of the activity of Protecting Powers varied in different countries and even, with respect to different Protecting Powers, within the same country. The passage of time resulted in the passing of the initiative for the designation of a Protecting Power in a particular case from the Protecting Power to the Power of Origin, where it more properly belonged. It also resulted in the concept of the Protecting Power as an international institution becoming more and more firmly intrenched in international law and practice. In its present form, however, the Protecting Power dates back less than one century—and its codified form is of even more recent vintage.

Most writers attribute the modern genesis of the Protecting Power to

the two latter. Thus, in 1955 the United States was, in varying degrees, representing some 25 states in some 80 other states (United States Foreign Service Manual, Vol. 2, Consular Affairs, pars. 923.31–923.32, July 13, 1955). This peacetime practice unquestionably played an important part in the historical development of the present-day wartime concept of the Protecting Power. The Protecting Power, which is the subject of this article, must not be confused with the protecting state exercising powers over a protectorate.

3 Isolated instances of this practice had occurred earlier. Thus, for example, we find that in the thirteenth century the Venetian Resident in Constantinople was charged with the protection of Armenians and Jews. The appearance of the Protecting Power has been attributed to a combination of three older institutions of international law: extraterritoriality; the employment of foreigners as diplomatic and consular agents; and the use of personal good offices. Franklin, *op. cit.* 7. It is doubtful that the concept of the Protecting Power as it first appeared in the Turkish Capitulations had any more direct progenitor.

developments which occurred during the Franco-Prussian War (1870–1871). In that conflict, probably for the first time, all of the belligerents were represented by Protecting Powers in the territory of the enemy. England was charged with the protection of the French in Germany; and the United States, Switzerland, and Russia acted as Protecting Powers in France for the various German States.[4] It may be said that the expansion of the functions of the Protecting Power during this conflict was, in large measure, due to two practices which originated during its course: that of expelling enemy consuls; and that of imposing stringent restrictions on enemy aliens.[5] Unquestionably, each of these practices could and did contribute to the need for the enlargement of the functions of the Protecting Power.

The precedents established during the Franco-Prussian War were adhered to in most subsequent international conflicts, many of which had, however, their own peculiar aspects. Thus, in the Sino-Japanese War (1894–1895) each side requested the United States to act as its Protecting Power and so we find the same state acting as the Protecting Power for each belligerent within the territory of the other. Similarly, Germany acted as the Protecting Power for both belligerents in the Italo-Turkish War (1911–1912) and in the Sino-Soviet War (1929). Going to the other extreme, in the Greco-Turkish War (1897), Germany acted as the Protecting Power for Turkey in Greece, while three other nations, England, France, and Russia, acted jointly for Greece in Turkey; in the Spanish-American War (1898), England acted as the Protecting Power for the United States, while France and Austria-Hungary acted jointly for Spain (it was during this conflict that, for the first time recorded, a belligerent, the United States, specifically requested neutral inspection of installations within which prisoners of war were being held);[6] and during the Balkan Wars (1912–1913) France and Russia acted jointly as the Protecting Power for Montenegro. This practice of using more than one friendly state as a Protecting Power has since almost disappeared, although at one time during World War II Spain was acting as the Protecting Power for Japan in the continental United States, while Sweden acted for her in Hawaii, and Switzerland in American Samoa.

The Boer War (1899–1902) may, perhaps, be considered to have been, at least to some extent, an exception to what was fast becoming a firmly established institution of international law. Early in that conflict the British requested the United States to represent their interests with the Boers. Apparently the consent of the Boers was not sought and they not only failed to designate a Protecting Power of their own, but, for all prac-

[4] Franklin, *op. cit.* 29 and 39; Eroglu, La Représentation Internationale en vue de Protéger les Intérêts des Belligérants 10–12 (unpublished thesis (1949) graciously furnished to the writer by the Dean of the Faculty of Law of the Université de Neuchâtel); detailed information concerning the designation of Protecting Powers in most of the conflicts mentioned herein may be found in this excellent study at pp. 10–29.

[5] Franklin, *op. cit.* 29.

[6] Flory, Prisoners of War 107–108 (1942).

tical purposes, at first refused to recognize the right of the United States consular representatives to act on behalf of the British. Subsequently the Boers did agree to permit the United States consuls in their territory to perform certain specific and limited functions with respect to British prisoners of war, upon the understanding that United States consuls in England would have similar privileges with respect to Boer prisoners of war held there.[7] Thus, to a limited degree, the institution of the Protecting Power was recognized even here.

The Russo-Japanese War (1904–1905) found the Protecting Powers once again exercising the full powers which it had become customary to allot to them. Perhaps as a result of the favorable experiences of the Sino-Japanese War, immediately upon the outbreak of hostilities Japan requested the United States to act on its behalf in Russia; while France was designated by Russia as its Protecting Power in Japan and Korea. And once again, but to an even greater extent than during the Spanish-American War, we find the representatives of the Protecting Powers concerning themselves with the welfare of prisoners of war.[8]

Thus it can readily be seen that when World War I burst upon Europe, the designation of Protecting Powers by belligerents was a firmly established international custom, although the Protecting Power as an institution had yet to be the subject of international legislation. During the course of that conflict four definite items of progress occurred: first, it was during World War I that public opinion in the belligerent countries achieved an understanding of how a friendly neutral could represent, at times vigorously, an enemy belligerent and its nationals;[9] second, the use of the Protecting Power as a means of safeguarding the welfare of prisoners of war, although at first somewhat restricted, was later greatly extended and received rather general acceptance;[10] third, the practice was adopted that

[7] Franklin, *op. cit.* 68.

[8] Eroglu, *op. cit.* 23–24; Franklin, *op. cit.* 78–79. The latter states that on one occasion when an American Vice Consul was inspecting a prisoner-of-war camp he was permitted to sample the meal which was then being given to the Japanese prisoners of war. In view of all these precedents, it is particularly difficult to comprehend why the 1899 and the 1907 Hague Conferences, both of which were sponsored by the Tsar of Russia, while codifying many customary rules concerning the treatment of prisoners of war, continued the silence of previous international conventions with respect to the institution of the Protecting Power.

[9] Siordet, *op. cit.* 7. World War I saw more men taken prisoner than in any previous conflict; and it likewise saw them held in captivity for a longer period of time. Both of these factors had the effect of focusing attention on prisoners of war. It was undoubtedly this situation which led to the more general public acceptance of the idea of a wider use of the Protecting Power in the interests of prisoners of war. Pictet, Commentary 93–94.

[10] Strangely enough, Germany, which had frequently acted as a Protecting Power, and the United States, which had not only frequently acted as a Protecting Power, but was probably the protagonist of the extension of the functions of the Protecting Power with respect to prisoners of war during the period prior to its own entry into World War I, were the two most important belligerents to resist the activities of Protecting Powers. At the beginning of the war Germany instituted rigid restrictions on visits by neutrals to its prisoner-of-war camps. By 1916 these restrictions had, due largely to the efforts

when a neutral which had been acting as a Protecting Power itself became embroiled in the conflict, a successor Protecting Power would be designated to fill the vacuum;[11] and finally, the Protecting Power received legal recognition in a number of international agreements entered into by various of the belligerents during the course of the hostilities in which, to a surprising extent, its functions were spelled out with some degree of definiteness.[12]

The precedents established during World War I were destined to bear fruit. A draft prisoner of war convention prepared in 1921 by the International Committee of the Red Cross (hereinafter referred to as the ICRC), while contemplating the use of Protecting Powers for certain limited purposes, would have assigned to the ICRC the responsibility for establishing mobile commissions composed of neutrals charged with assuring that the belligerents were complying with the convention. This proposal was probably due to two factors: first, the failure of the states which had acted as Protecting Powers during World War I adequately to report their activities; and second, the belief that the duties involved in the effective protection of the rights of prisoners of war would exceed the capacity of the diplomatic personnel of Protecting Powers.[13] However, when the Diplomatic Conference convened in Geneva in 1929 and drafted the convention which subsequently received the ratification of the vast majority of states, the ICRC proposal was not adopted and, instead, the basic principle of the Protecting Power received general acceptance, the former Protecting Powers taking the position that all that was needed to assure their activities was that their rôle "be distinctly set out, and their task clearly defined."[14] The Prisoner of War Convention drafted at that Conference[15] thus became

of the United States, for the most part disappeared. Yet when the United States became a belligerent in 1917, the then Secretary of War took the position that Germany had no right to designate the Swiss to inspect American prisoner-of-war camps unless under treaty law. His position was apparently overruled by President Wilson and members of the Swiss Foreign Service were permitted to make such inspections. Flory, *op. cit.* 108–109.

11 Eroglu, *op. cit.* 27–28.

12 For example, Art. VIII of the Final Act of the Conference of Copenhagen of Nov. 2, 1917 (photostatic copy on file in The Army Library, Washington, D.C.), to which Austria-Hungary, Germany, Rumania, and Russia were the belligerent parties, dealt with "Arrangements concerning the Admission of the Delegates of the Protecting Power . . . on the Basis of Reciprocity"; Art. XI of the Agreement between the British and Turkish Governments respecting Prisoners of War and Civilians, executed at Bern on Dec. 28, 1917 (111 Brit. and For. State Papers 557–568), dealt with the subject of visits to prisoner-of-war camps by "representatives of the Protecting Powers"; and the Agreement between the United States of America and Germany Concerning Prisoners of War, Sanitary Personnel, and Civilians, executed at Bern on Nov. 11, 1918 (13 A.J.I.L. Supp. 1 (1919); Foreign Relations of the United States, 1918, Supp. 2, p. 103), contains references to the Protecting Power in no less than 25 separate paragraphs.

13 Rasmussen, Code des Prisonniers de Guerre 56 (1931).

14 Siordet, *op. cit.* 12. Twenty years and one World War later, we again find them urging that the Protecting Power be given the benefit of "well-defined and precise provisions." Final Record of the Diplomatic Conference of Geneva of 1949 (hereinafter referred to as Final Record), Vol. II B, p. 19.

15 The 1929 Geneva Convention Relative to the Treatment of Prisoners of War (hereinafter referred to as the 1929 Convention), 47 Stat. 2021; Treaty Series, No. 846; 27

the first international agreement negotiated in time of peace to give official recognition to the institution of the Protecting Power.[16] However, it did not create a new international concept. It did not make the use of the Protecting Power by belligerents obligatory. It did not affect the relationships which had previously existed between the Power of Origin, the Protecting Power, and the Detaining Power. It did give the relationship a formal and agreed status which it had not previously had. It may well be considered that the provisions of the 1929 Convention relating to Protecting Powers constituted the most important advance contained in that convention over the provisions of the regulations relating to prisoners of war contained in the Annex to the Fourth Hague Convention of 1907.[17] The lessons learned during World War I had not been forgotten.

The advent of World War II provided, all too soon, an opportunity for the implementation and testing of this novel international legislation. Most of the belligerents were represented by Protecting Powers and, in general, these found the provisions of the 1929 Convention relating to their

---

A.J.I.L. Supp. 59 (1933). It is interesting to note that the companion convention drafted at the same Diplomatic Conference, The Geneva Convention for the Amelioration of the Condition of the Wounded and Sick of Armies in the Field (better known as the 1929 Geneva Red Cross Convention), 47 Stat. 2074; Treaty Series, No. 847; 27 A.J.I.L. Supp. 43 (1933), a direct descendant of the 1864 and 1906 Geneva Red Cross Conventions, continued to contain no reference to Protecting Powers, a situation which was only remedied 20 years later, after World War II.

16 Art. 86 of the 1929 Convention reads as follows:

"The High Contracting Parties recognize that the regular application of the present Convention will find a guaranty in the possibility of collaboration of the protecting Powers charged with safeguarding the interests of belligerents; in this respect, the protecting Powers may, besides their diplomatic personnel, appoint delegates from among their own nationals or from among the nationals of other neutral Powers. These delegates must be subject to the approval of the belligerent near which they exercise their mission.

"Representatives of the protecting Power or its accepted delegates shall be permitted to go any place, without exception, where prisoners of war are interned. They shall have access to all places occupied by prisoners and may interview them, as a general rule without witnesses, personally or through interpreters.

"Belligerents shall so far as possible facilitate the task of representatives or accepted delegates of the protecting Power. The military authorities shall be informed of their visit.

"Belligerents may come to an agreement to allow persons of the same nationality as the prisoners to be permitted to take part in inspection trips."

In addition, the Protecting Powers were specifically given such functions as: receiving complaints from prisoners of war (Art. 42); conferring with the representatives ("agents") of prisoners of war (Arts. 43 and 44); and assuring that prisoners of war who were subjected to judicial prosecutions were adequately protected (Arts. 60, 62, 65, and 66). Evidence that the drafters of the convention were attempting merely to formalize and perpetuate an existing status, and not to create a new one, is found in the use in relation to the exercise of its functions by the Protecting Power of such terms as "mediation" (Art. 31) and "good offices" (Art. 87).

17 Ch. 2 of the Annex to the 1907 Hague Convention (IV) Respecting the Laws and Customs of War on Land, 36 Stat. 2277; Treaty Series, No. 539; 2 A.J.I.L. Supp. 90 (1909).

activities extremely helpful. True, the designation and functioning of Protecting Powers on behalf of prisoners of war had previously become an almost universally accepted custom in international law. But it is necessary to bear in mind that, despite this, in the U.S.S.R. and Japan, neither of which nations was a party to the 1929 Convention, there was either complete or substantial failure in the functioning of the Protecting Powers.[18] In general, the fact that such a large number of countries were parties to the World War II hostilities had two distinct but related results. In the first place, not only did the absence of strong neutrals present a problem in the selection of Protecting Powers, but it also meant that there was no large neutral world public opinion to be affected by violations of the convention, and the power of neutral public opinion in forcing compliance with a humanitarian convention cannot be overestimated. And in the second place, because of the small number of neutrals available to act as Protecting Powers, it frequently occurred that the same neutral was designated to act as the Protecting Power for two opposing belligerents.

Once again wartime lessons were not forgotten and on August 12, 1949, just four years after the final termination of World War II, a new Prisoner of War Convention[19] was signed in which, as we shall see, the functions

18 The U.S.S.R. took the position that, as it was a party to the Fourth Hague Convention of 1907, the Annex to which, it asserted, covered "all the main questions of the regime of captivity" (but not, as has previously been pointed out in note 8 above, the question of the designation or functions of the Protecting Powers), there was no need for it to consider an Italian proposal to apply reciprocally the provisions of the 1929 Convention (Report of the International Committee of the Red Cross on its Activities during the Second World War (hereinafter referred to as ICRC Report), Vol. I, p. 412). While Japan stated its intention to "apply this Convention *mutatis mutandis*, to all prisoners of war" (*ibid.* 443), the Protecting Powers were never permitted to function in a manner even remotely resembling their manner of functioning in the territories of most of the other belligerents. As a result of the foregoing, and of the disappearance of many Powers of Origin during the course of hostilities, the ICRC estimates that during World War II approximately 70% of all prisoners of war were deprived of the services of a Protecting Power. De la Pradelle, *op. cit.* 226. Thus, Germany denied the status of states to Poland, Yugoslavia, France and Belgium (after the 1940 armistices), Free France, and Italy (after Mussolini's overthrow in 1943), and refused to permit the intervention of Protecting Powers on behalf of their captured personnel. Pictet, "La Croix-Rouge et les Conventions de Genève," in 76 Hague Academy Recueil des Cours 5, 87 (1950, I).

19 The 1949 Geneva Convention Relative to the Treatment of Prisoners of War (hereinafter referred to as the 1949 Convention), 6 U. S. Treaties 3316; 75 U.N. Treaty Series 135 (I: 972); 47 A.J.I.L. Supp. 119 (1953). There were signed, on the same day, three other conventions in which, for the first time in other than a prisoner-of-war convention, references were made to Protecting Powers: Art. 8 and others of the 1949 Geneva Convention for the Amelioration of the Condition of the Wounded and Sick in Armed Forces in the Field (the successor to the 1929 Red Cross Convention mentioned in note 15 above), 6 U. S. Treaties 3114; 75 U.N. Treaty Series 31 (I: 970); Art. 8 and others of the 1949 Geneva Convention for the Amelioration of the Condition of the Wounded, Sick and Shipwrecked Members of Armed Forces at Sea, 6 U. S. Treaties 3217; 75 U.N. Treaty Series 85 (I: 971); and Art. 9 and others of the 1949 Geneva Convention Relative to the Protection of Civilian Persons in Time of War, 6 U. S. Treaties 3516; 75 U.N. Treaty Series 287 (I: 973); 50 A.J.I.L. Supp. 724 (1956). This latter

of the Protecting Power are identified and defined with even greater particularity than had been the case in the 1929 Convention.[20] Since that time the hostilities in Korea have occurred. At the outbreak of those hostilities General Douglas MacArthur, as the commander of the United Nations Command, immediately announced that his forces would comply with the humanitarian principles of the 1949 Convention. In answer to a query made by the ICRC, the Foreign Minister of the so-called Democratic People's Republic of Korea sent a message to the Secretary General of the United Nations stating that its forces were "strictly abiding by principles of Geneva Conventions in respect to Prisoners of War." [21] Unfortunately, the provisions of the convention relating to the Protecting Power were evidently not among the principles with which they were "strictly abiding" so that, despite all efforts expended in this regard, those provisions were never implemented.[22]

From the foregoing brief historical survey it is apparent that prior to 1870 only the precursors of the modern Protecting Power existed, and not the latter itself; that during the period from 1870 to 1914 the concept of the Protecting Power began to take form, particularly with respect to its relationship to the problem of the prisoner of war; and that during the period subsequent to 1914 the form has become definite, the institution of the Protecting Power having become the subject of numerous bilateral and multilateral international agreements, culminating in the 1949 Geneva Conventions to which most of the nations of the world are parties.[23] It

---

convention will undoubtedly prove of major importance in extending the functions of the Protecting Power in any future international conflict.

[20] References to the Protecting Power are contained in 36 of its 132 substantive articles (4, 8, 10, 11, 12, 23, 56, 58, 60, 62, 63, 65, 66, 68, 69, 71, 72, 73, 75, 77, 78, 79, 81, 96, 98, 100, 101, 104, 105, 107, 108, 120, 121, 122, 126, and 128) as well as in two of its Annexes. The basic charter for the Protecting Power is contained in Art. 8, which reads:

"The present Convention shall be applied with the cooperation and under the scrutiny of the Protecting Powers whose duty it is to safeguard the interests of the Parties to the conflict. For this purpose, the Protecting Powers may appoint, apart from their diplomatic or consular staff, delegates from amongst their own nationals or the nationals of other neutral Powers. The said delegates shall be subject to the approval of the Power with which they are to carry out their duties.

"The Parties to the conflict shall facilitate to the greatest extent possible the task of the representatives or delegates of the Protecting Powers.

"The representatives or delegates of the Protecting Powers shall not in any case exceed their mission under the present Convention. They shall, in particular, take account of the imperative necessities of security of the State wherein they carry out their duties."

[21] Le Comité International de la Croix-Rouge et le Conflit de Corée: Recueil de Documents, Vol. I, p. 16 (1952).

[22] The U.N. Command permitted the ICRC to perform its usual functions with respect to the Communist prisoners of war held by the UNC. Pictet, Commentary 546. As we shall see (p. 395 below), many of these functions parallel, or may be substituted for, those of a Protecting Power. Unfortunately, all efforts of the ICRC to act north of the battle line were repulsed by the Communists. Treatment of British Prisoners of War in Korea 33-34 (British Ministry of Defence, 1955).

[23] Up to the end of 1959 there had been 77 ratifications of, and accessions to, these conventions. International Committee of the Red Cross, Annual Report, 1959, at p. 45

now becomes appropriate to analyze the form and the character which the Protecting Power received during this evolutionary process.[24]

II. The Modern Concept of the Protecting Power

A. Designation

As will have been noted, Article 86 of the 1929 Convention was, to say the least, somewhat vaguely worded:

> The High Contracting Parties *recognize* that the regular application of the present Convention will find a guaranty in the *possibility* of collaboration of the protecting Powers charged with safeguarding the interests of belligerents . . . (Italics added.)

There is nothing mandatory here. There is no requirement here that a Protecting Power actually be designated or that, if designated, it be permitted to function as such by the Detaining Power. The comparable provision of the 1949 Convention reads quite differently. Article 8 of this latter convention provides:

> The present Convention *shall be applied with the cooperation and under the scrutiny* of the Protecting Powers *whose duty* it is to safeguard the interests of the Parties to the conflict. . . . (Italics added.)

It would appear that the designation of Protecting Powers has now become at least a moral obligation of the belligerent; and that, once designated, a Protecting Power has a duty not only to the Power of Origin,[25] but also to

(1959). These include all of the more important Powers except Canada and the Republic of China. The use of the institution of the Protecting Power has since been resorted to in the Convention for the Protection of Cultural Property in the Event of Armed Conflict, signed at The Hague on May 14, 1954 (249 U.N. Treaty Series 215 (I: 3511)), where it is adopted as a means of overseeing the protection of inanimate objects—which is, actually, merely a variation of the protection furnished historically by the Protecting Power, a very large part of its energies having once been directed towards the protection of the embassy buildings and diplomatic archives of the Protected Power.

24 As was aptly stated by one author: "What happened was that an existing usage was taken, and transformed into a regulation. It was the organ which created the function." Siordet, *op. cit.* 3.

25 It must at all times be borne in mind that the Protecting Power is *not* a general agent of the Power of Origin. In his book, The Present Law of War and Neutrality (1954), Castrén defines the over-all relationship between these two Powers as follows (at p. 92):

"The protecting Power does not act in its own name but rather as a kind of caretaker or *intermediary*. Nevertheless, it acts *independently* in so far as the State whose interests it protects cannot demand, but only request, it to perform certain services, and the protecting Power itself decides the way in which it discharges its mission. Nor may a belligerent give instructions to those organs of the protecting Power which carry out this mission. Instead, requests to the protecting Power have to be made through *diplomatic channels*. The protecting Power may refuse to act when compliance with a request would be contrary to its own interests or infringe the lawful right of the enemy State."

the other parties to the conflict, to perform the functions which have been assigned to it by the 1949 Convention.[26]

What are the qualifications required of a state before it may be designated as a Protecting Power? It must, first of all, be a state within the meaning of that term in international law. It must also, of course, be a *neutral* state—and it is advisable that it be one which can reasonably be expected to remain neutral, although this latter qualification has become more and more difficult to assure. And, finally, it must be a state which maintains diplomatic relations with both the requesting state (the Power of Origin) and the state in which it is being requested to operate (the Detaining Power).

How does a state actually become a Protecting Power? The belligerent state desiring the services of a Protecting Power requests a neutral state which has the qualifications listed above to act on its behalf. If the latter is willing to assume the functions of a Protecting Power, it so notifies the requesting state. It must then obtain from the Detaining Power permission to function as the Protecting Power for the requesting state vis-à-vis and within the territory of the Detaining Power.[27] In other words, the actual designation of the Protecting Power is based upon the request of the Power of Origin and the consent of both the proposed Protecting Power and the Detaining Power.[28]

As we have seen, it has frequently occurred in the past that more than one state has been designated as the Protecting Power for a belligerent, and there is nothing in the 1949 Convention, nor in general international law, to preclude this practice. However, the advantages of the other extreme—one and the same Protecting Power for both belligerents—are many. Even a small nation, when acting as the Protecting Power for both sides, is in a unique position to obtain a general observance of the law of war by each belligerent on the basis of reciprocity. This was made

26 Siordet states that the designation of a Protecting Power is no longer optional but is now "quasi obligatoire" ("De l'Application et du Contrôle des Conventions de Genève de 1949," in 1956 Revue Internationale de la Croix-Rouge 464, 468); that it is now put in the "imperative form" (The Geneva Conventions of 1949: The Question of Scrutiny 36); and that in performing its mission the Protecting Power is no longer the special representative of one of the parties, but is "the representative of all the Contracting Parties to the Convention" (*ibid.*).

27 This is the step which the United States apparently failed to take when it was requested to perform the functions of the Protecting Power for Great Britain during the Boer War. See page 376 above.

28 The 1949 Convention contains no provisions with respect to the qualifications of a Protecting Power, the method of designation, etc., leaving these problems for settlement under general international law. Heckenroth, Les Puissances Protectrices et les Conventions de Genève 62 and 224 (unpublished thesis, Université d'Aix-Marseille, 1951). This solution will work until one belligerent arbitrarily elects to deny its consent to every neutral nominated by its enemy. In the light of the adamant refusal of the U.S.S.R. to permit any type of inspection to take place on its territory during peacetime, it seems unlikely that such activity would be permitted in time of war, even though the U.S.S.R. participated actively in the drafting of the 1949 Geneva Conventions and has ratified them, as have all of its satellites, without any reservations as to Art. 8.

quite apparent during World War II, when Switzerland acted as the Protecting Power for many of the belligerents on both sides of the conflict. Some of the advantages of this situation are summed up as follows:

> For uniformity and simplicity of administration it is obviously desirable for the protected power to entrust its interests in another country to only one protecting power, and in instances involving the protection of belligerent interests there are advantages to all concerned if both belligerents entrust their interests in the other's territory to the same protecting power. . . . The experience of World War II indicates that a more uniform administration and a higher standard of treatment of enemy interests by both belligerents result from a reciprocal protection of the interests of those belligerents by the same protecting power throughout the territories under the control of each belligerent.[29]

The limited number of states which would be available and competent to act as Protecting Powers in any future world conflagration would, in all probability, almost automatically bring about this result, just as it did during World War II.

The delegates at the Diplomatic Conference which drafted the 1949 Convention foresaw the possibility of numerous situations in which there would be no Protecting Power.[30] They attempted to solve this problem by providing in Article 10 of the convention for the designation of "substitutes" for Protecting Powers.[31] It must, however, be emphasized that the provisions of this article should not be considered as affecting the basic method of selecting either Protecting Power or successor Protecting Powers as long as the Power of Origin continues to exist. A successor Protecting Power, necessitated, perhaps, because the original Protecting Power has become

[29] Franklin, *op. cit.* 164–165. A similar conclusion is reached in Pictet, Commentary 95–96, wherein this statement appears:

"It became more and more common for these neutral Powers to find themselves responsible for representing the respective interests of two opposing Parties at one and the same time. This gave them additional authority, and incidentally altered their role; for once a Power represented the interests of two opposing belligerents, it became not so much the special representative of each of them, as the common agent of both, or a kind of umpire. This enabled it to bring directly into play that powerful instrument, the argument of reciprocity, to obtain the improvements desired."

In 1945 Switzerland alone represented 34 belligerents, and in many cases it represented opposing belligerents in the territory of each other. Eroglu, *op. cit.* 144–148.

[30] For some of these possible situations see Siordet, *op. cit.* 49–53; and Heckenroth, *op. cit.* 229–236.

[31] The French Delegation strongly urged that a provision be included in the 1949 Convention setting up an international body to perform the functions of Protecting Powers in the absence of the latter (Final Record, Vol. II B, p. 27; *ibid.*, Vol. III, pp. 30–31). The substance of this proposal was included in Resolution 2 adopted by the Diplomatic Conference (*ibid.*, Vol. I, p. 361), but, as far as the writer has been able to ascertain, no steps have been taken, or are contemplated, to implement the resolution. The U.S.S.R. opposed both the original French proposal and the adoption of the resolution, stating as to the latter that it "sees no need to consider this question or to create such a body, since the problem of the Protecting Powers has been satisfactorily solved by the Conventions established in the present Conference." Declaration made by the Delegation of the U.S.S.R. at the time of the signing of the conventions. *Ibid.*, Vol. I, p. 201.

a belligerent, is not a "substitute" for a Protecting Power within the meaning of Article 10, and its designation is governed by the same rules of international law as those which govern the designation of the original Protecting Power.[32] It must also be emphasized that a state or organization designated under the provisions of Article 10 is not a Protecting Power as that term is used generally in international law and as it is used specifically elsewhere in the 1949 Convention, but is merely a state or organization performing some or many of the functions allocated to Protecting Powers by the convention.

B. Personnel

Article 8 of the 1949 Convention provides that

> . . . the Protecting Powers may appoint, apart from their diplomatic and consular staff, delegates from amongst their own nationals or the nationals of other neutral Powers. The said delegates shall be subject to the approval of the Power with which they are to carry out their duties.

It is obvious that the convention has accorded to the Protecting Power two sources of personnel for the execution of its functions: its diplomatic and consular officers stationed within the territory of the Detaining Power;[33] and others of its nationals and other neutral nationals specifically appointed for the purpose. We shall discuss each of these sources in turn.

The normal and natural source of personnel for the execution of the functions of the Protecting Power is, of course, the diplomatic and consular personnel already assigned to and stationed in the territory of the Detaining Power. These officials, working under the ambassador, are ex-

[32] Pictet, Commentary 117–118. All of the Communist countries (and Portugal) made reservations to Art. 10 to the effect that they would not recognize as legal "requests by the Detaining Power to a neutral State or to a humanitarian organization, to undertake the functions performed by a Protecting Power, unless the consent of the Government of the country of which the prisoners of war are nationals is obtained." While there is a not unnatural tendency to view with suspicion this position taken almost uniquely by the U.S.S.R. and its satellites (see, for example, Brockhaus, "Sowjetunion und Genfer Kriegsgefangenen-Konvention von 1949," 2 Ost-Europa Recht 286, 291 (1956)), it appears to have a valid basis. If there is an existing Power of Origin, not only is its consent to the designation of a Protecting Power to act on its behalf essential, but it has the right to make the selection itself in the first place! And the statements made at the Diplomatic Conference by Soviet representatives Morosov (Final Record, Vol. II B, pp. 29 and 351) and Sokirkin (*ibid.*, p. 347) make it clear that they merely desired to limit specifically the right of the Detaining Power to select a substitute for the Protecting Power to those cases where there is no existing Power of Origin—a limitation as to which there should have been no dispute. It is to be hoped that by overruling the Soviet thesis the Diplomatic Conference did not establish the proposition that a Detaining Power may, on its own, select and designate a substitute for a Protecting Power even though there is a Power of Origin in being.

[33] Neither the 1929 Convention nor the working (Stockholm) draft used at the Diplomatic Conference includes the term "consular" in specifying the authorized representatives of the Protecting Power. The authorization for the Protecting Power to use this category of personnel as representatives was proposed by Australia and was unanimously approved. Final Record, Vol. II B, p. 58.

perienced, they are known to the local officials, and, perhaps most important, they are already present within the area of operations. It is, of course, true that they already have their usual functions to perform; but many of these functions disappear or are seriously curtailed upon the advent of war (commercial, immigration, tourists, etc.). While any large-scale war of lengthy duration will undoubtedly make it necessary for the Protecting Power to supplement its regular diplomatic and consular staff within the territory of the Detaining Power, there will be numerous instances in which the Protecting Power will be able to perform its functions with only its normal complement of officials, at least for some considerable period of time and until the number of prisoners of war held by the Detaining Power makes a build-up of personnel essential. Of course, the term "diplomatic and consular staff" includes not only those officials of the Protecting Power who were already stationed within the territory of the Detaining Power at the time of the designation of the Protecting Power, but also any of its other diplomatic and consular personnel who may be sent to replace or supplement them.

With the heavy commitments which Switzerland had during World War II, it would obviously have been impossible for it to have made even a pretense of performing its far-flung responsibilities as a Protecting Power without a considerable increase in its staffs in the territories of the many Detaining Powers where it had consented to function. To accomplish this purpose the Swiss Government recruited in Switzerland and sent to its various affected embassies and legations "camp inspectors," who had the function of periodically visiting prisoner-of-war camps and work areas to assure that there was compliance by the Detaining Power with the provisions of the 1929 Convention.[34] This is typical of the second source of personnel the use of which is authorized by Article 8 of the 1949 Convention—the non-career national who is selected by the government of the Protecting Power solely for the purpose of assisting it in performing its functions. He may also be the national of another neutral, but normally the Protecting Power would resort to this type of selection only when it has exhausted its own manpower potential. Of course, a major source of non-career personnel is to be found among the nationals of the Protecting Power and of other neutral Powers who are residing within the territory of the Detaining Power when the use of additional personnel becomes necessary. The Protecting Power may sometimes find it more convenient, when it has exhausted the list of its own nationals residing in the territory of the Detaining Power, to use neutral nationals falling within this category before resorting to the policy of recruiting its own nationals in its own territory and sending them to the territory of the Detaining Power.

It will have been noted that these non-career, or auxiliary, personnel are subject to the approval of the Detaining Power. This has occasioned considerable discussion, both at and since the Diplomatic Conference. No objection can be perceived to this procedure. The diplomatic and consular

[34] Janner, *op. cit.* 52.

personnel of the Protecting Power stationed within the territory of the Detaining Power must have the normal approval of the state to which they are accredited (*agrément, exequatur*), required for all such personnel, and any one of them may, at any time, be declared *persona non grata* by that state, the Detaining Power. The writer finds himself in complete accord with the statement that

> . . . it appeared to be incompatible with international usage that the occasional, auxiliary and temporary staff recruited by the Protecting Power should enjoy a more favorable status than the usual diplomatic or consular staff.[35]

The fear has been expressed that a Detaining Power might arbitrarily refuse to approve any of the auxiliary personnel nominated by the Protecting Power and thereby make it impossible for the latter properly to perform its functions. But a Detaining Power so minded could also, and with equal ease, arbitrarily decline to grant the necessary *agrément* or *exequatur* to replacement or supplementary diplomatic or consular personnel of the Protecting Power. Either of these acts would constitute a violation of the spirit, if not the letter, of the convention. Until the contrary is affirmatively established, it must be assumed that states parties to the convention will carry out their obligations in good faith.

The restriction which we have just been discussing is logical from another standpoint. The individuals concerned will, in the performance of their functions, be required to do considerable traveling within a country at war. Any country at war must institute controls on the right to enter into and to travel within its territory. To tell it that it must accept anyone selected by the Protecting Power, even though it has good reason not to trust the particular individual, is to close one's eyes to the facts of life. And for this same reason, the Detaining Power must retain the right to declare members of the staff of the Protecting Power *persona non grata,* whether the individual concerned has diplomatic, consular, or auxiliary status.

It has been stated that the representatives of the Protecting Power engaged in performing its functions in the territory of the Detaining Power have a triple responsibility: to their own government; to the government of the Power of Origin; and to the government of the Detaining Power.[36] If this is another way of saying that these individuals must be completely neutral and unbiased, it is correct. It would, however, be less controversial to state, as did William Jennings Bryan, that they are "representatives

35 Siordet, *op. cit.* 27. A provision of the working (Stockholm) draft used at the Diplomatic Conference would have required the Detaining Power to give "serious grounds" for any refusal to approve the nomination of a non-career individual by the Protecting Power. Final Record, Vol. I, p. 73. This proposal was equally lacking in logic, since a state need give no reasons for refusing to agree to the assignment to a post in its territory of a member of the diplomatic or consular service of the Protecting Power or for declaring such an individual *persona non grata.* The provision was deleted at Geneva. *Ibid.*, Vol. II B, pp. 58 and 110.

36 De la Pradelle, "Le Contrôle de l'Application des Conventions Humanitaires en cas de Conflit armé," in 2 Annuaire Français de Droit International 343, 344 (1956).

of a neutral power whose attitude toward the parties to the conflict is one of impartial amity.''[37]

C. *Functions*

Unfortunately, with only a very few exceptions, the drafters of the 1949 Convention apparently found it necessary to avoid any attempt to specify in detail the functions of the Protecting Power. Most frequently these functions are expressed either in the form of duties of the Detaining Power or rights of the prisoners of war. Where a precedent had previously been established, it is set forth in appropriate detail. Where no precedent had previously been established, the problem is normally left to *ad hoc* decision. It was probably anticipated that such problems would be solved by the Protecting Power through the exercise by it of the basic power guaranteed to it, that of surveillance to insure that there is, at all times, full compliance with the provisions of the convention. Should the Protecting Power ascertain that there is a default in the performance of some particular provision, it is apparently assumed that it will find a means of procuring a correction of the situation, even though such means is not specified.[38]

Nevertheless, the convention does contain repeated references to the Protecting Power and a function may usually be implied in a particular instance merely from such a reference. It is difficult, indeed, to categorize these varied references to the Protecting Power. Extremely broad categories are required, and even then not every function will fall within them. Several not wholly successful efforts have been made to list these references on a functional basis.[39] For the purposes of this discussion they will be considered under three general categories: powers and duties; liaison functions; and miscellaneous functions (the functions listed in each category do not purport to be all-inclusive).

(1) *Powers and Duties:*

The basic and overriding power granted to the Protecting Power by the 1949 Convention is, of course, that contained in Article 8, the very first sentence of which states that the convention

[37] Letter of Instructions of Secretary of State William Jennings Bryan, dated Aug. 17, 1914 (9 A.J.I.L. Supp. 118 (1915)). See also, Franklin, *op. cit.* 114; United States Foreign Service Manual, Vol. 2, Consular Affairs, pars. 924.1 and 931.

[38] ''It is not the function of the Protecting Power to command or to overrule; it is its function to observe, to comment, to make representations, and to send reports to the outside world. If we are faced with an unscrupulous belligerent, the presence of the Protecting Power and the ability of the Protecting Power to examine what is going on and to observe is the only preventive measure which we have.'' Statement of Quentin-Baxter, representative of New Zealand, at the 1949 Diplomatic Conference, Final Record, Vol. II B, p. 344.

[39] Thus, Heckenroth, *op. cit.* 135, and Janner, *op. cit.* 52, have each listed seven separate categories of functions of the Protecting Power, but the lists coincide with respect to only four functions! Still a third functional listing appears in Pictet, Commentary 98–99.

> . . . shall be applied with the cooperation and under the scrutiny of the Protecting Powers whose duty it is to safeguard the interests of the Parties to the conflict.

This provision has been termed, and rightly so, "the keystone of the conventions."[40]

Strangely enough, the only extended debate on this extremely crucial article which took place at the Diplomatic Conference concerned the selection of the proper word to characterize the activities of the Protecting Power, and that debate occurred primarily as a result of difficulties of translation. The delegates at the Diplomatic Conference were agreed that the Protecting Power could not give orders or directives to the Detaining Power. The idea which it was desired to convey was that the authority of the Protecting Power would entitle it to verify whether the convention was being properly applied and, if necessary, to suggest measures on behalf of prisoners of war.[41] In the draft text the words "under the supervision of the Protecting Power" were used in the English version and the words "*sous le contrôle des Puissances protectrices*" in the French. This was acceptable to the French-speaking delegates but was opposed by those who were English-speaking. It eventually became apparent that the two groups were actually in agreement and that the seeming dispute had arisen because the word "*contrôle*" in French is much weaker than either "control" or "supervision" in English. The English-speaking delegations were given a choice of a number of words to be used as a counterpart for the French word "*contrôle*" and unanimous agreement was ultimately reached on the word "scrutiny."[42]

The importance of Article 8 may, perhaps, be found to lie in the very generality of its phrasing. The fact that the entire convention is to be "applied with the cooperation" of the Protecting Power undoubtedly empowers the latter to make suggestions to the Detaining Power with a view to the improvement of the lot of the prisoner of war even with respect to areas in which no specific reference is made to the Protecting Power. Thus, a Protecting Power might suggest to, and seek to obtain the agreement of, the Detaining Power that certain specified types of offenses committed by prisoners of war be punished by disciplinary rather than judicial measures, even though Article 83 contains no reference to the Protecting Power. Similarly, the fact that the convention is to be applied "under the scrutiny" of the Protecting Power undoubtedly empowers it to investigate and to request reports from the Detaining Power in unspecified areas. Thus, a Protecting Power might seek from the Detaining Power a complete report as to the reasons for delays in the delivery or dispatching of mail or for the prohibition of correspondence, even though Article 76, dealing with

[40] Yingling and Ginnane, *loc. cit.* 397. In the British Army Manual of Military Law (Part III, The Law of War on Land, 1958) 92, the Protecting Power is termed "the principal organ, apart from the Contracting Parties themselves, for ensuring the observance of the Convention." Part III of the Manual was largely the work of the late Sir Hersch Lauterpacht.

[41] Final Record, Vol. II B, p. 110.

[42] *Ibid.;* Siordet, *op. cit.* 24–25.

these subjects, contains no mention of the Protecting Power; again, it might seek a report from the Detaining Power as to the action taken with respect to a complaint made by a prisoner of war, through the Protecting Power, regarding the conditions of his captivity, even though Article 78, which authorizes such complaints, does not specifically provide for such a report.

Perhaps on only a slightly lower level of importance than Article 8 is Article 126 which empowers the representatives of the Protecting Power to visit all places where prisoners of war may be, themselves selecting the places they will visit and determining the frequency of the visits; to have access to all premises where prisoners are confined; to go to the place of departure, passage, and arrival of prisoners who are being transferred; and to interview prisoners and prisoners' representatives without witnesses.[43] The significant nature of these provisions is so patent as to make any discussion superfluous.

Other powers and duties of the Protecting Power are, indeed, varied. For example, it is directed to lend its good offices to assist in settling disputes with respect to the application and interpretation of the convention (Article 11); it is authorized to inspect the financial records of individual prisoners of war (Article 65); it may, in the interests of the prisoners, permit the Detaining Power to reduce below the specified minimum the number of communications which may be sent out each month by each prisoner (Article 71); it may, in the interests of the prisoners, propose a limit on the number of packages which a prisoner may receive (Article 72); it may itself take over the transport of capture cards, mail, packages, and legal documents, should military operations prevent the Detaining Power from fulfilling its obligations in this respect (Article 75); it has an unrestricted right to receive complaints from individual prisoners and from prisoners' representatives (Article 78); it has the right to inspect the record of disciplinary punishments (Article 96); and it has the duty to find counsel for a prisoner against whom judicial proceedings have been instituted, and the right to attend the trial (Article 105).

(2) *Liaison Functions:*

In its liaison capacity the Protecting Power is actually little more than a conduit. It serves merely as the means of relaying necessary communications between the Detaining Power and the Power of Origin. Protecting Powers are, not infrequently, the sole means readily available for the transmittal of messages between the two belligerents. And, of course, while a great many liaison functions are specifically set forth in the 1949 Convention, this is one area in which the Protecting Power may safely operate, even where the particular liaison mission which it undertakes is not among those enumerated in the convention.

The Detaining Power is required to give to the Protecting Power for relay to the Power of Origin the geographical location of all prisoner-of-

[43] The right of visitation granted by Art. 126 is reiterated in Arts. 56 (labor detachments), 98 (prisoners undergoing disciplinary punishment), and 108 (prisoners undergoing judicial punishment).

war camps so that the prisoners will not, as has happened, accidentally become the target of their own compatriots (Article 23). The reasons for any limitations placed by the Detaining Power on the amount of funds made available to a prisoner of war from advances of pay must be conveyed to the Protecting Power, presumably for transmittal to the Power of Origin (Article 60). The Detaining Power must advise the Protecting Power, for relay to the Power of Origin, of the rate of daily working pay which it has fixed (Article 62). Transmittals of payments by prisoners of war to their own country are made by notification from the Detaining Power to the Power of Origin through the medium of the Protecting Power (Article 63). Notifications with respect to the status of the accounts of prisoners of war (Article 65) and of prisoners whose captivity has, for some reason, such as escape, death, or other means, terminated (Article 66), are also sent by the Detaining Power to the Power of Origin through the medium of the Protecting Power. Claims of prisoners for injury or disease arising out of assigned work are similarly transmitted (Article 68). Information with respect to the measures taken by the Detaining Power to enable prisoners to communicate with the exterior must be transmitted to the Power of Origin through the Protecting Power (Article 69). And the Protecting Power must be informed, presumably for the information of the Power of Origin, as well as for its own, of all offenses punishable by death under the laws of the Detaining Power (Article 100).

In several instances the convention provides for the exchange of information between the belligerents without specifying how this is to be accomplished. Unquestionably, these are areas in which, as noted above, the Protecting Power would feel qualified to intervene, even though it has no specific mandate. For example, Article 21 provides for an exchange of information between belligerents as to their respective laws and regulations on the subject of parole, and Article 43 provides for an exchange of information with respect to military titles and ranks, but neither of these articles states how the exchange is to be made. The Protecting Powers are available and competent to perform this liaison function; and it may be assumed that either the Detaining Powers would request their services for this purpose or the Protecting Powers would, themselves, offer their services for the transmittal of the required information.

(3) *Miscellaneous Functions:*

There are a number of references to the Protecting Power in the 1949 Convention which cannot rightly be designated as powers or duties but which are likewise not precisely liaison functions. For lack of a more descriptive term, and because, for the most part, they bear little or no relationship to each other, they are here considered as miscellaneous functions.

Thus, Article 12 provides that if a Detaining Power, to whom prisoners of war have been transferred by the original Detaining Power, fails to carry out the provisions of the convention, the original Detaining Power will, upon being notified to that effect by the Protecting Power, either take measures to correct the situation or request the return of the prisoners concerned. And Article 58 indicates, without specifically so providing, that some time after the outbreak of hostilities the Detaining Power and the Protecting Power will enter into an arrangement relating to the possession of money by prisoners of war.

Again, Article 79 requires the Detaining Power to inform the Protecting Power of its reasons therefor whenever it refuses to approve a duly elected prisoners' representative; and Article 81 requires the Detaining Power to inform the Protecting Power of its reasons for dismissing a prisoners' representative. In neither of these articles is there any indication of the action it is contemplated that the Protecting Power will take when the required information is given to it. While the information might, in the exercise of the Protecting Power's liaison function and as a matter of routine, be passed to the Power of Origin, this action alone would have little significance. Under its right to scrutinize the application of the convention, the Protecting Power would probably, in an appropriate case, take issue with the Detaining Power's action with respect to the non-approval or the dismissal of a prisoners' representative.

Further, Article 121 provides that the Detaining Power shall investigate and make a full report to the Protecting Power of every death or serious injury of a prisoner of war caused or suspected to have been caused by a sentry, another prisoner of war, or any other person, or where the cause of death is unknown; and that if guilt is indicated, the Detaining Power will prosecute the responsible persons. Certainly it is to be expected that the Protecting Power will forward the report of the incident to the Power of Origin; but it is equally certain that the Protecting Power would, on its own initiative, make *démarches* to the Detaining Power, if it felt that the investigation had been inadequate or that a prosecution indicated by the investigation had not taken place.[44]

It is believed that the foregoing short presentation of only a few types of provisions adequately establishes that the Protecting Power has certain functions which cannot exactly be fitted into either the category of powers or duties or the category of liaison functions, and that these miscellaneous functions can probably become whatever the particular Protecting Power desires them to be.

(4) *Limitations:*

Each of the four conventions drafted at the 1949 Diplomatic Conference contains an article similar to Article 8 of the Prisoner of War Convention.[45] However, in the Third and Fourth Conventions (Prisoner of War and Civilian Conventions, respectively) the Protecting Powers are merely admonished to "take account of the imperative necessities of security of the State wherein they carry out their duties," while in the First and Second (Wounded and Sick of Armed Forces in the Field—the "Red Cross Convention"—and Wounded, Sick and Shipwrecked at Sea, respectively), not only are they so admonished, but they are told in an oblique fashion that

[44] Pictet, Commentary 571.

[45] See note 19 above.

their activities *may be* restricted "as an exceptional and temporary measure when this is rendered necessary by imperative military necessities."[46] The importance of the distinction drawn between the two pairs of conventions was fully appreciated at the time of the drafting of the conventions and was the occasion for some spirited debate. While on its face the solution reached by the convention is plainly a victory for those who sought to exclude the possibility of any shackles being placed on the Protecting Power in the performance of its functions with respect to prisoners of war, it remains to be seen whether this result was actually attained.[47]

Assuming that the Detaining Power desires to impose the "exceptional and temporary" restrictions on visits of the Protecting Power which are authorized in Article 126 of the 1949 Convention, or the right to the even more extensive restrictions on the activities of the Protecting Power which is asserted by some states to exist, whether or not specified in the convention, how and by whom is the decision to be made as to whether "imperative military necessities" do, in fact, exist? There is one school of thought which takes the position that it would be illogical to permit the determination to be made by the Detaining Power itself, as it would be judging its own case, and which insists that only the Protecting Power can validly make such a determination.[48] While, from a strictly humanitarian point of view, there is much to be said in favor of this position, it cannot, as a practical matter, be justified. If, for example, the Detaining Power deems it essential to keep representatives of the Protecting Power temporarily out of an area, lest military movements noted therein inad-

46 A similar restriction is contained in Art. 126 of the 1949 Convention with respect to visits to places where prisoners of war may be. This is the only area in which the 1949 Convention specifically permits the activities of the Protecting Power to be restricted by the Detaining Power. While it is, of course, a very important one, it is not believed that a Detaining Power could really justify the imposition of such a restriction except in very rare cases, such as prohibiting visits to extremely forward collecting points during the actual course of an attack.

47 The proponents of the distinction between the two pairs of conventions argued that it was "obvious and reasonable that the activities of a Protecting Power in sea warfare and on the field of battle must be restricted," but that as to the Prisoner of War and Civilian Conventions "the vital force which animates those rules and gives them effect is the presence of the Protecting Power." Final Record, Vol. II B, p. 344. The pessimism which may be apparent in the text is occasioned by the fact that the U.S.S.R. took the position that, even without such a restrictive limitation in the convention, it would exist in fact. *Ibid.* 345.

48 Pictet, Commentary on the Geneva Convention for the Amelioration of the Condition of the Wounded and Sick of Armed Forces in the Field 101 (1952). Even there it is admitted that "this is precisely what it [the Protecting Power] would, in such a case, be debarred from doing. It will only be possible to show after the event whether or not the restriction was justified." In Pictet, Commentary, published 8 years later, a much more realistic approach is taken (at p. 611):

"If they are to justify the prohibition of visits, military necessities must be imperative. Whether they are or not is a matter for the Detaining Power alone to decide and the right of supervision of the Protecting Powers is restricted by this exercise of sovereignty. Such a decision must not be lightly taken, however, and any prohibition of visits must be an exceptional measure."

vertently lead to the disclosure of important impending military actions, there would be little logic in compelling it to advise the Protecting Power what and why it was so doing in order to permit the latter to determine whether imperative military necessities actually existed and whether the restriction was really justified. This is unquestionably a matter which will, in the course of events and through reciprocal actions of the belligerents, adjust itself inasmuch as time and experience will very quickly result in an informal mutual appreciation as to where the line is to be drawn.[49]

D. Relationship to the ICRC

The multifold operations of the ICRC are obviously not within the scope of this article. However, inasmuch as the functions of the Protecting Power and those of the ICRC often overlap insofar as prisoners of war are concerned, it appears appropriate to mention, at least briefly, some of the overlapping areas.[50]

The basic safeguard to the activities of the ICRC is contained in Article 9 of the 1949 Convention, which specifies:

> The provisions of the present Convention constitute no obstacle to the humanitarian activities which the International Committee of the Red Cross or any other impartial humanitarian organization may, subject to the consent of the Parties to the conflict concerned, undertake for the protection of prisoners of war and for their relief.

Despite a substantially similar provision in Article 88 of the 1929 Convention, the ICRC found, during World War II, that it was, at times, necessary to overcome the feeling of some belligerents that it was attempting to duplicate the functions of the Protecting Powers. Apparently it succeeded in convincing them that such was not the case.[51]

It has already been pointed out that Article 10 of the 1949 Convention contains provisions for the designation of "substitutes" for Protecting Powers under certain circumstances. The third paragraph of Article 10

49 In Pictet, Commentary, *loc. cit.*, the following remedial procedure is suggested: "The Protecting Powers and the International Committee will have the right to bring the temporary nature of the prohibition to the notice of the Detaining Power and, after a certain length of time, to request it to raise all restrictions. Moreover, the Protecting Power will be able to check afterwards whether the prohibition of visits has been used by the Detaining Power to violate the Convention. In any case, it is not in the interests of the Detaining Power to misuse this reservation, because it would very soon be suspected of deliberately violating the Convention by evading supervision by qualified witnesses."

50 As stated in the ICRC Report, Vol. I, p. 39: "Despite partial overlapping, the functions of the Protecting Power are fundamentally dissimilar in kind and extent [from those of the ICRC]. The Protecting Power is the mandatory of one or both belligerents, with competency to protect the rights and interests of the States from which it derives authority. The Committee is concerned exclusively with humanitarian tasks; its functions are not limited to those which are guaranteed by law, but embrace such enterprises in the interests of humanity as appear essential, or which are justified through a request made by a belligerent."

51 *Ibid.*

provides that, failing such a "substitute," the Detaining Power shall request or accept

> . . . the offer of the services of a humanitarian organization, such as the International Committee of the Red Cross, to assume the humanitarian functions performed by Protecting Powers under the present Convention.

It must be emphasized that when the ICRC is thus called upon to serve, it does so as a humanitarian organization and *not* as a Protecting Power which, by definition, it cannot be, inasmuch as it is not a state.[52]

In a number of areas the convention places the ICRC on the same plane as the Protecting Power. As we have seen, Article 126 is of major importance in its grant of authority to the Protecting Power to go wherever prisoners of war are located.[53] That article also specifies that "The delegates of the International Committee of the Red Cross shall enjoy the same prerogatives." A similar parallel is to be found in Article 56 dealing with the locations of, and visits to, labor detachments. And it is not surprising that we find the ICRC referred to along with the Protecting Power in Articles 72 and 75, for these two articles are among those relating to individual and collective relief shipments, a subject of particular interest to the ICRC and one with respect to which it has developed an unchallengeable *expertise* as a result of experience gained in innumerable conflicts. Most Protecting Powers would probably be more than willing to permit the ICRC to pre-empt the handling of this difficult and complicated function.

Articles 79 and 81 authorize the prisoners' representatives to communicate with the ICRC as well as the Protecting Power. Here, however, it is believed that the purpose of each such authorization to communicate is fundamentally different. The creation of the position of prisoners' representative was first suggested during the Franco-Prussian War (1870–1871) and became a reality during World War I.[54] The function for which it was originally created was to receive and distribute relief packages. However, over the course of time, the functions of the prisoners' representatives have been greatly expanded, and during World War II it was not unusual to find them involved in practically all of the problems of a prisoner-of-war camp. Thus, they were frequently used by the prisoners as the channel for the transmittal of complaints both to the Detaining Power and to the Protecting Power. The drafters of the 1949 Convention were fully aware

52 In Pictet, Commentary 119, the following statement appears:

"The Convention in this case [paragraph 3 of Article 10] no longer uses the words 'undertake the functions performed by a Protecting Power,' but speaks only of 'humanitarian functions.' The distinction is logical. There is no longer any question of a real substitute, and a humanitarian organization cannot be expected to fulfil *all* the functions incumbent on a Protecting Power by virtue of the Conventions."

See also Final Record, Vol. II B, pp. 61 and 63.

53 See page 390 above.

54 ICRC Report, Vol. I, pp. 342–343. At that time a prisoners' representative was known as a "man of confidence." In the 1929 Convention they were called "agents."

of this development,[55] and it appears that the steps which they took were intended to insure that the privileges accorded to the prisoners' representative would permit him to communicate with the delegates of the ICRC on problems relating to relief shipments and with the Protecting Power on this subject as well as on the myriad of other problems into which the prisoners' representative is now projected.

It is probably safe to state that, while the allocation of functions by the 1949 Convention between the Protecting Power and the ICRC is not always as clearly stated as it might have been, the fundamental differences between the two and between their methods of operation are such that conflicts between them would be extremely rare.[56]

III. Conclusion

The past century has seen tremendous advances made in the concept of the Protecting Power as an instrument of international law, both in the rôle which it is called upon to play and in the prestige which it enjoys and which goes far in assisting it to perform the numerous functions which have now been assigned to it. It appears unquestionable that:

> The presence of the Protecting Powers today remains the sole means of putting a brake on the excesses of Detaining Powers, the sole element of moderation and of morality in the treatment of enemy persons, their belongings, and their interests: this was noted and affirmed many times at Geneva.[57]

[55] See, for example, Art. 78, wherein specific provision is now contained permitting individual complaints to be transmitted to the Protecting Power either directly, as had been provided in Art. 42 of the 1929 Convention, or through the medium of the prisoners' representative. Although Art. 42 of the 1929 Convention, the predecessor of Art. 78 of the 1949 Convention, made no mention of the ICRC as an authorized recipient of complaints from prisoners of war, the ICRC took the position that "it is, according to the spirit of the [1929] Convention, undoubtedly meant to be placed, in this respect, on the same footing as the Protecting Powers." ICRC Report, Vol. I, p. 341. This conclusion is subject to dispute and, in view of the fact that Art. 78 of the 1949 Convention again omits all reference to the ICRC, it would, in interpreting that article, now be even more difficult to accept the ICRC position. Certainly, if such had been the intention of the drafters, they could easily have attained their objective by merely including the ICRC in the article, along with the Protecting Power, as they did in a number of other articles. Their failure to do so in the light of the announced ICRC position strongly militates against the ICRC interpretation.

[56] Castrén, *op. cit.* 95; Pictet, Le Droit International et l'Activité du Comité International de la Croix-Rouge en temps de Guerre 25 (1943). It is more probable that, as in World War II, it will be the Detaining Power which will object where activities of the ICRC appear to duplicate those being performed by the Protecting Power. That the ICRC does not consider the Protecting Power to be a rival, but rather another means of making the life of a prisoner of war a little less miserable, is apparent from the communication sent by its President early in the Korean conflict in which he said: "The International Committee views, in the activities of the 'Protecting Powers,' a forceful instrument for insuring full implementation of the Geneva Conventions and an always desirable corollary to the activities which the Committee itself undertakes." Le Comité International de la Croix-Rouge et le Conflit de Corée: Recueil de Documents, Vol. I, p. 32.

[57] Heckenroth, *op. cit.* 229.

The results of the 1949 Diplomatic Conference reveal clearly that the nations of the world were generally prepared to accept a solid basis for the activities of the Protecting Power. It was conceded a mission of close observation of the application of the provisions of the Prisoner of War Convention drafted at that Conference, a mission which necessarily incorporates within it a right to call to the attention of the Detaining Power any failure of performance which it finds and to report any such failure of performance to the Power of Origin; a sizeable expansion was made in its functions and, correlatively, in its power and authority; provision was made for substitutes for Protecting Powers in order to insure that prisoners of war would at all times benefit from the exercise of the functions of the Protecting Power, thus correcting the situation which had arisen all too frequently during World War II; and the use of the institution of the Protecting Power was extended not only to the Red Cross Convention (Wounded and Sick of Armed Forces in the Field), but also to the convention which adapts the Red Cross Convention to maritime warfare (Wounded, Sick and Shipwrecked at Sea), and to the completely new Civilian Convention.[58] These few examples alone demonstrate the great distance which has been traversed since 1907, when the prisoner-of-war provisions of the Regulations Respecting the Laws and Customs of War on Land were drafted at The Hague and contained no reference whatsoever to the Protecting Power.

In many respects the provisions of the 1949 Geneva Conventions relating to the Protecting Power represent compromises. Positions reached solely in order to bring about agreement between opposing viewpoints can rarely be considered perfect and the present case is no exception. However, these provisions unquestionably represent a great step forward in the evolution of international law and would undoubtedly be viewed with amazement by those who drafted the first Red Cross Convention in 1864 or even by those who acted on behalf of the Protecting Powers as recently as in 1914, at the beginning of World War I.[59]

The Protecting Power is now a generally accepted institution of international law. It is the subject of international agreements to which most of the states of the world are parties. There are clear indications that it has been weighed in the balance and not been found wanting, with the result that it has been, and in the future will continue to be, requested to assume numerous new functions on behalf of states at war.

[58] *Ibid.* 222.

[59] In Pictet, Wounded and Sick Commentary 101–102, the following statement appears: "As it stands, Article 8 is not perfect, far from it. But we have to consider the huge advance which it represents in international humanitarian law. We have to realize that, to achieve this much, the diplomats assembled in Geneva had to cope with divergent opinions; they had to reconcile the claims of the sovereignty of their respective countries with the claims of humanity; and they had to harmonize two opposed conceptions of the role of the Protecting Power, viewed by some as their agent (of whom one demands the maximum), by others as the agent of the enemy (to whom one accords the minimum)."

[3]

International Law Aspects of Repatriation of Prisoners of War during Hostilities

By Richard A. Falk *

I

On September 2, 1972, the North Vietnamese Foreign Ministry issued a statement announcing the release of three American pilots who were being held in detention since their capture by North Vietnam. The statement gave no particular reason for the release except to affirm North Vietnam's "lenient policy" and to indicate that the release was being made "on the occasion" of an annual independence day holiday called National Day. It was subsequently learned that the release was part of a wider amnesty, which included Vietnamese citizens who had been sent to jail for ordinary criminal activity.

The North Vietnamese statement also indicated that the pilots would be released "to a U.S. social organization animated with good will and a desire to bring about an early end to the U.S. war in Viet Nam and to help those released not to be used in activities against the Vietnamese people and the Government of the Democratic Republic of Vietnam." Through contact with the North Vietnamese delegation negotiating in Paris, it was learned that the Committee of Liaison with Families of Servicemen Detained in North Vietnam had been designated as "the social organization" entrusted with the task of escorting the released Americans back to the United States.[1] In addition, each family of a released man was invited to send a relative to Hanoi and to join in the repatriation process. Minnie Lee Gartley, mother of Navy Lt. JG Markham Gartley, and Olga Charles, wife of Navy Lt. JG Norris Alphonzo Charles, accepted the invitation. No relative of the third released pilot, Air Force Major Edward K. Elias, responded positively to the invitation. Initially, Major Elias' father accepted but later withdrew on advice from Pentagon officials.

In the release statement reference was made to earlier repatriations of a comparable kind that had taken place in 1968 and 1969. Three earlier releases had occurred, each involving three pilots and each involving an escort group comprised of well-known Americans who were actively

* Of the Board of Editors.

[1] A second anti-war organization in the United States—People's Coalition for Peace and Justice—was also designated by the North Vietnamese to receive the three pilots, but the planning and execution of the undertaking was carried out virtually exclusively under the auspices of the Committee of Liaison. The escort group consisted of the two co-chairmen of the Committee of Liaison, Cora Weiss and David Dellinger and of the Rev. William Sloan Coffin, Jr., the chaplain of Yale University, and the author of this article. Peter Arnett of Associated Press also traveled as a member of the escort group, but made the trip solely for journalistic purposes.

opposed to the Vietnam War and later became charter members of the Committee of Liaison. The statement issued in Hanoi charged that:

> In 1969 the U.S. Government compelled the U.S. pilots released in July that year to put forward distortion [*sic*] about the humane treatment policy of the government of the DRV. At complete variance with their previous statements the U.S. Government has also used those released pilots in war activities against the Vietnamese people and other peoples of Indochina. It is for this reason that such releases have been temporarily suspended. . . .

The point was reiterated with reference to this news release as follows:

> The government of the DRV draws particular attention of the U.S. government to this: in the interests of the families of the U.S. pilots captured in North Vietnam stop using the released pilots to slander the DRV and further the U.S. policy of aggression in North Vietnam.

In Hanoi officials of the North Vietnamese Government made it clear, furthermore, that the prospects for additional releases of this type would be diminished if there was any interference by the U.S. Government prior to entry into the territorial limits of the United States. And, indeed, there were no releases for three years after the 1969 experience. To make the prospect of such interference less likely the return trip was arranged via Peking, Moscow, and Copenhagen rather than by way of the normal and more direct route of Vientiane, Laos, and Bangkok.

The escort group together with Mrs. Gartley and Mrs. Charles arrived in Hanoi on September 16, 1973 and the three pilots were formally released to the custody of the escort group on the evening of September 17. The release ceremony consisted of a transfer of control from the North Vietnamese Army to a spokesman of an organization called The Committee of Solidarity, who in turn, transferred custody to the Committee of Liaison, the acceptance of which was effected by Cora Weiss on behalf of the escort group.

Between September 17 and 24 the three released pilots lived in the Hoa Binh Hotel in Hanoi with their relatives and the four escorts. An informal atmosphere prevailed and there were no guards present. The pilots were as free as the other American visitors to move about. Some social activities and visits to heavily bombed areas were organized by the Solidarity Committee during the week, but there was no obligation on the part of the pilots or others to take part.

Neither the relatives nor the pilots participated with the escort group in their various meetings with North Vietnamese high officials (including Pham Van Dong, the Prime Minister), or in discussions about conditions in the prison camps, or in a meeting on September 25 with seven other captured American pilots.

While in Hanoi the entire group discussed on several occasions the appropriate procedure for returning to the United States. The escort group did suggest that it had a series of responsibilities: to encourage civilian return for the sake of remaining pilots and their families and to secure as humane and orderly a process of return as possible for the sake of the three pilots and their accompanying relatives. Accordingly, on September 22, 1972 the following cablegram was sent to President Nixon from Hanoi by the escort group:

> We are happy to report that Navy Lt. Markham Gartley, Air Force Major Edward Elias, and Navy Lt. jg Norris Charles have been released to our custody so that we may escort them home to the United States.
>
> In accordance with the expressed expectations of the North Vietnamese Government, and in order not to jeopardize the possibility of future releases, we believe the repatriation of these men should be carried out in the following manner:
>
> (1) The men shall proceed home with us and representatives of their families in civilan aircraft.
>
> (2) The men, if they wish, shall be granted a 30 day furlough.
>
> (3) The men shall receive a complete medical checkup at the hospital of their choice, civilian or military.
>
> (4). The men shall do nothing further to promote the American war effort in Indochina.
>
> We believe that these terms are reasonable and humane and in the best interests of the remaining pilots and their families.

No response or acknowledgment was received directly or indirectly from the U.S. Government.

On the same day the pilots, on their own initiative, sent a second cablegram to President Nixon:

> In the best interests of all parties concerned we think we should be allowed to return to New York with the escort delegation and be allowed to spend a few days with our families, if so desired.

None of the cables sent by the released prisoners or the escort group elicited any official response. All of these cables were made available to the press at the time they were sent.

On September 25 in the late afternoon the group departed by plane from Hanoi and proceeded to Peking. On the morning of September 27 the group boarded the regularly scheduled flight to Moscow.

On arrival in Moscow the plane was met by several representatives of the United States Embassy, led by Mr. Adolph Dubs, the Chargé d'Affaires. The escort group explained to Mr. Dubs that it had no objection to his meeting with the pilots, but that it felt an obligation to provide them with civilian escort back to the United States and that any official attempt to order them to leave our escort might jeopardize the prospects for future releases. It was also made clear to Mr. Dubs that the escort believed that he had no authority to give orders of any kind to the men while outside Embassy premises in Moscow. Mr. Dubs "warmly recommended" that the pilots consider returning to the United States by means of a U.S. Medevac plane that could take them directly home from Moscow. The pilots thanked Mr. Dubs for his offer but indicated their preference, "for the sake of all concerned," to continue back to the United States under our escort. They affirmed their good health. Mr. Dubs ofiered the pilots and their relatives Embassy hospitality, including a place to sleep, food and drink, and phone calls to the United States. These offers were also declined.

The group left Moscow on the morning of September 27 and deplaned for a stopover and change of planes at Copenhagen. Once again the plane was met by Embassy representatives who once again offered the possibility of return by Medevac plane, which on this occasion was standing by the runway at the Copenhagen Airport. As in Moscow, the pilots declined all offers including offers of Embassy hospitality.

From Moscow onwards two members of the U.S. Embassy staff were on the plane. The three pilots accepted the suggestion of the Embassy officials that they change into military uniform shortly before deplaning in the United States.

On arrival at Kennedy Airport in New York early in the evening of September 28 the plane was cleared of passengers other than our group (4 escorts, 2 press, 2 relatives, and 3 pilots). U.S. Government representatives came on board, and the pilots were told that they would immediately be flown to the military hospital closest to their area of residence. Such an arrangement was acceptable to Major Elias, but it was not satisfactory to either Lt. Gartley or Lt. Charles who wanted to be with their families for several days before reporting for a checkup and debriefing at a military hospital. Both pilots had also hoped to meet with the press and to attend a private reception in the airport vicinity that had been planned by the Committee of Liaison for their relatives and for relatives of other POWs. There was considerable personal distress on the part of the two families when it was learned that all of the pilots were expected to depart immediately by plane for a military hospital. It is not altogether clear whether the pilots were given any orders to this effect or whether only a more informal kind of insistence was relied upon by government officials.

After returning to the United States the men were given medical checkups and debriefings at the three hospitals. All three of the pilots have been allowed to be with their families and to talk with the public, although the specific arrangements have varied to a certain degree. Finally, a representative of the Department of Defense gave assurances to the House Armed Forces Committee that none of these men would be reassigned to duty that related in any way to the Indochina War.[2]

II

Several legal issues are presented by these facts. First of all, there is some question as to the relevance of the Geneva Convention relative to the Treatment of Prisoners of War. As has been discussed in the literature, North Vietnam claims that the Geneva Conventions do not apply because

[2] *See* New York Times, Oct. 11, 1972, at 9.

these captured men are "war criminals" under their reservation to Article 85 that was included, in common with other Socialist bloc countries, in their instrument of ratification.[3] The United States has rejected this invocation of the Article 85 reservation, but even accepting this rejection, it remains unclear whether North Vietnam would be bound to treat the armed conflict as one of international character bringing the whole of the Convention into play or would be bound only to uphold the more general and limited mandate of Article 3. North Vietnam on its side claims the right to determine treatment standards and provides only the assurance that it is pursuing a lenient policy that protects the humanitarian interests of the individuals concerned.[4]

Since the capture of the first American pilot by North Vietnam in August 1964, the U.S. Government has made a consistent demand that North Vietnam apply the Geneva Conventions, has asserted that the terms of the Convention are fully applicable to this war, and, by implication has indicated an acceptance of corresponding obligations toward enemy personnel. No American official has claimed a right to disregard the Geneva Conventions because of North Vietnam's refusal to be bound in any strict sense. It should be noted, of course, that the *formal* acceptance of the Geneva system does not assure *better* treatment of prisoners as a matter of actual fact.[5] The escort group regarded the Geneva Prisoners of War

[3] For an intelligent appreciation of this issue *see* Note, *The Geneva Convention and the Treatment of Prisoners of War in Vietnam,"* 80 HARVARD L. REV. 851 (1967), reprinted in 2 FALK, ed., THE VIETNAM WAR AND INTERNATIONAL LAW, 397–415, at 405–15 (1969).

[4] There are a number of distinct treatment issues including frequency and transmittal of mail and packages, release of sick and wounded prisoners for treatment and confinement in a neutral country, failure of North Vietnam to provide all information at its disposal about men held captive, and allegations of various sorts of abuse. *See. Hanoi Refuses to Comply with the Terms of the Geneva Convention of 1949*, Dept. of State, Public Information Series, Oct. 5, 1972. In addition to denying any wrongdoing, the North Vietnamese charge the U.S. Government with spreading false propaganda about prison conditions and with seeking to disrupt prison camp discipline by abusing mail privileges through the infiltration of forbidden items, especially to facilitate covert communication between prisoners and the Department of Defense. Also, the Son Tay raid of Nov. 21, 1970 manifested a willingness by American military forces to disrupt normal security arrangements for POWs in North Vietnam. Although the Son Tay camp was abandoned, Administration officials threatened to repeat such rescue efforts. In view of this threat directed at North Vietnamese prison security it is not surprising that POWs were thereafter kept under greater confinement. This tightening of prison discipline was confirmed by conversations with several present prisoners.

[5] Throughout the war there have been numerous reports of abuse of North Vietnamese and National Liberation Front prisoners by the United States and by the South Vietnamese Government, despite their acceptance of the Geneva system. Perhaps the most serious kind of abuse was the widespread practice in certain theaters of ground combat of inflating "body count" totals by killing prisoners. The most well-known disclosures surrounded the court martial proceedings of Lt. James Duffy. Some material on this case, including Lt. Duffy's own statement, is found in FALK, KOLKO, and LIFTON, eds., CRIMES OF WAR 239–54 (1971). There have also been numerous reports of battlefield reliance on "water torture" to secure information from captured enemy personnel or suspects. In addition, the reliance by Saigon authorities on

Convention as a source of authoritative guidelines to the extent relevant to this type of repatriation.

The principal point of difficulty with this approach arises because repatriation to a belligerent power while hostilities are in progress is not covered in explicit terms by the Geneva Prisoners of War Convention. Part IV of the Convention, which deals with Termination of Captivity, is divided into three sections:

> Section I: Direct Repatriation and Accommodation in Neutral Countries [Articles 109–117]
>
> Section II: Release and Repatriation of Prisoners of War at the Close of Hostilities [Articles 118–119]
>
> Section III: Death of Prisoners of War [Articles 120–121]

It is readily apparent that Section I does not apply because these pilots were not sick or wounded, nor were they repatriated to a neutral country; that Section II does not apply because hostilities were continuing; and that Section III does not apply because the men were alive.

At the same time, the Geneva provisions on repatriation of the sick and wounded provide some guidelines that seem relevant to this situation. Article 117 is the most direct instance:

> No repatriated person may be employed on active military service.

Certainly, if such a restriction is applicable to sick or wounded men repatriated to a neutral country, then it is even more strongly relevant to repatriations that send healthy combat personnel back to a belligerent power while the war continues. The U.S. Government seems also to accept the relevance of Article 117, at least as it applies to this repatriation.[6] It is not clear whether activity by a repatriated prisoner to arouse public support for the war would violate Article 117. The fourth guideline in the escort cable to President Nixon on September 22 proposed that "the men shall do nothing further to promote the American war effort in Indochina," which was intended to be wider than Article 117 and to take account of the past use of previously repatriated men from North Vietnam to engage in official or semiofficial pro-war propaganda.[7] The rationale for this wider prohibition is that it is inconsistent with the spirit of the release, as Hanoi made clear in its statement of September 2, for repatriated men to take even an indirect public role in relation to the war effort. The escort group believed that North Vietnam's position was reasonable on this point

torture in their prison system seems documented beyond reasonable doubt. One famous incident involved "the tiger cages" at Con Son prison which were unintentionally exposed to United States congressional visitors in July 1970. *See* "Statement on Con Son Prison" of Cong. Augustus F. Hawkins reprinted in same volume, at 258–60; *see also* Drinan, at 255–57 on American involvement.

[6] *See supra* note 2.

[7] *See, e.g., Hearings on American Prisoners of War in Southeast Asia, 1971, Before the Subcommittee on National Security Policy and Scientific Developments of House Committee on Foreign Affairs,* March 23–25, 30–31; April 1, 6, 20, 1971 (*Cf.* statements of Barnet, Meacham, and Weiss with those of Overly and Stockstill, at 2–24, 215–240, 359–406).

and that such propaganda activity would definitely discourage future releases.

Aside from Article 117, the Geneva Prisoners of War Convention does not give much guidance as to reasonable terms of repatriation. The September 22 escort cable sought to fill this vacuum by providing additional guidelines, formulated with a view to promoting the best interests of the three released men and of the remaining pilots and their families, in response to experience with earlier repatriations during the Vietnam War.

Guideline 1 affirmed the importance of a civilian escort back to the United States. Although the release was unconditional, the North Vietnamese officially indicated its preference for civilian return and declared that any interference would jeopardize further releases. The Defense Department, including the Secretary of Defense, advised the media that the pilots should present themselves to U.S. military jurisdiction at the earliest possible opportunity and intimated that they could be found absent without leave (AWOL) for their failure to do so. In this situation the pilots were caught in a crossfire between official directives by the United States and their sense of obligation to the remaining prisoners and their families. By rejecting U.S. Government initiatives in Moscow and Copenhagen, the pilots accepted the primacy of Guideline 1, and the government by its failure to issue orders while en route or to threaten any disciplinary action since return can be said to have substantially acquiesced, although Secretary Laird made some public statements about possible disciplinary actions that seemed calculated to have an intimidating impact.[8] Indeed, the U.S. Government representations in Moscow and Copenhagen can be regarded as nothing more than an effort to establish by independent means whether the released men did indeed wish to accept civilian escort back to the United States. Washington was clearly prepared to have the pilots leave civilian escort, "warmly recommending" that they do so, even though such a result could have jeopardized the prospect for future releases.

Guideline 2 involving a post-return option of a thirty-day furlough was designed to provide as humane a reentry into American life as possible and to take issue with the assumption of the Department of Defense that all repatriated prisoners of war would require prolonged medical detention. Warren G. Nutter, Assistant Secretary of Defense, had testified before a congressional committee as follows on May 11, 1972:

> We assume that all returnees will require medical attention, some much more than others. Certainly, all will require rest and time to readjust. Therefore, our policies require that all returnees be placed immediately under medical auspices for complete medical checkups.[9]

After being with these men and their relatives for a week after their release, it was clear to the escort group, as well as to the released pilots and their relatives, that there was no immediate need for medical sur-

[8] *See* N.Y. Times, Sept. 30, 1972, at 11 for indication of this shift in official policy as a consequence of a White House decision.

[9] *Hearings on American Prisoners of War in Southeast Asia, 1972*, same subcommittee at note 7, *supra.* Part 3, Feb. 3, March 16, 1972 (Mr. Nutter's statement begins at 25, the quoted passage appears at 31).

veillance. A discretionary period of leave seemed like a desirable option to include in this kind of repatriation. As a matter of formal position the government has not granted the returnees an option of immediate leave, but, in fact, the medical confinement has been so "open," at least as compared to what happened after prior repatriations, that a relaxed period of reunion with families has been possible. It may be that a preliminary medical examination, perhaps under neutral auspices if the returnee so wishes, could determine whether it is appropriate to grant a thirty-day furlough before checkup and debriefing.

Guideline 3 recognizes that a medical checkup is desirable but grants the repatriated man the option of choosing either a civilian or military hospital. This guideline was formulated on the basis of reported abuses in relation to prior treatment in military hospitals and to the government's professed intention to provide a returnee with "proper balance" on the war during the period of detention and debriefing.[10] It seemed objectionable to compel a prisoner released during a controversial war to undergo a process that would include his political reeducation, perhaps under circumstances that might be intimidating or even threatening.[11] In particular, the escort group was sentitive to recent disclosures that reveal Soviet reliance on medical and psychiatric detention to remove clinically normal, but politically dissident, voices from society.

In fact, the three pilots preferred, or at least were unwilling to contest, the government's insistence on a medical checkup under military auspices. To date, however, there have been no complaints or evidence of political pressures and reeducation such as accompanied prior releases, and therefore the publicity associated with the formulation of this guideline may have served a constructive purpose.

Perhaps, the guidelines set forth in the September 24 cable are drawn too specifically with the particular situation of this war and these men in mind to serve as a general precedent, but it does seem desirable for the International Committee of the Red Cross and others concerned with repatriation to a belligerent power during hostilities to consider proposing a new section in Part IV of the 1949 Convention. The United States Government has been reluctant to deal with or confer status upon the Committee of Liaison with Families of Servicemen Detained in North Vietnam. Since its inception in 1969 the Committee has attempted to facilitate the transmission of information and mail between the prison camps and prisoner families. Until the Paris accords of 1973, the North Vietnamese Government had refused to deal with the U.S. Government on prisoner issues; it was willing to deal with the Committee of Liaison.

No attempt has been made to account for the existence and role of the Committee of Liaison by reference to the Geneva Prisoners of War Convention, but it seems clearly possible to do so.

[10] *See* article by Everett R. Hollis, "U.S. Planned More Gradual Homecoming for P.O.W.'s," N.Y. Times, Sept. 30, 1972, at 10.

[11] On this *see* SMITH, P.O.W.: TWO YEARS WITH THE VIETCONG (1971), esp. epilogue by Donald Duncan on George Smith's treatment by U.S. medical authorities after his release from National Liberation Front captivity, at 285–94.

Article 9 of the Convention is as follows:

> The provisions of the present Convention constitute no obstacle to the humanitarian activities which the International Committee of the Red Cross or *any other impartial humanitarian organization* may, subject to the consent of the Parties to the conflict concerned, undertake for the protection of prisoners of war and for their relief.

Article 10 reads:

> The High Contracting Parties may at any time agree to entrust to an organization which offers all guarantees of impartiality and efficacy the duties incumbent on the Protecting Parties by virtue of the present Convention.
>
> When prisoners of war do not benefit or cease to benefit, no matter for what reason, by the activities of a Protecting Power or of an organization provided for in the first paragraph above, the Detaining Power shall request a neutral State, or such an organization, to undertake the functions performed under the present Convention by a Protecting Power designated by the Parties to a conflict.
>
> If protection cannot be arranged accordingly, *the Detaining Power shall request or shall accept, subject to the provisions of this Article, the offer of the services of a humanitarian organization, such as the International Committee of the Red Cross, to assume the humanitarian functions performed by Protecting Powers under the present Convention.*
>
> Any neutral Power or any organization invited by the Power concerned or offering itself for these purposes, shall be required to act with a sense of responsibility towards the Party to the conflict on which persons protected by the present Convention depend, and shall be required to furnish sufficient assurances that it is in a position to undertake the appropriate functions and to discharge them impartially.
>
> No derogation from the preceding provisions shall be made by special agreements between Powers one of which is restricted, even temporarily, in its freedom to negotiate with the other Power or its allies by reason of military events, more particularly where the whole, or a substantial part, of the territory of the said Power is occupied.
>
> Whenever in the present Convention mention is made of a Protecting Power, such mention applies to substitute organizations in the sense of the present Article.[12]

There are several problems with conferring a formal status on the Committee of Liaison. First, was it designated by the Detaining Power? There was no formal designation, as such, but a series of dealings on prisoner matters between the North Vietnamese Government and the Committee amounted to such a designation. Clearly the Committee of Liaison by aiding the exchange of mail and information and by facilitating interim repatriation contributed toward the realization of the humanitarian objectives of the Convention.

Secondly, does the Committee of Liaison qualify as an "impartial" humanitarian organization? The Committee is exclusively composed of American citizens who have taken a public position against the U.S. role in Indochina. On the other hand, these individuals are American citizens con-

[12] 6 UST 3316; TIAS 3364; 75 UNTS 135; 47 AJIL SUPP. 119 (1953). Emphasis added.

cerned with the welfare of their fellow American prisoners detained in North Vietnam. The Committee did not seek to do more in relation to prisoner issues than to serve its humanitarian purposes and to disseminate its views on the condition of camps and on how to secure the repatriation of other prisoners. Such views were at variance with the Administration position on these matters and with other private and nongovernmental groups that also proclaim their humanitarian purposes, despite their commitment to President Nixon's war policies.[13] As President Nixon and Secretary Laird have frequently observed "this is strictly a humanitarian issue." That is, Americans might disagree about the war, but no American questioned the propriety of helping the American prisoners secure better conditions and quicker release. In the circumstances of the war, the Committee of Liaison, precisely because its members opposed the war, were uniquely able to produce tangible benefits for the prisoners of war and their families.[14] Such tangible benefits seem to be just those humanitarian contributions that Articles 9 and 10 of the Geneva Convention have in mind.

Thirdly, does the Committee of Liaison require the consent of the U.S. Government before it can perform these humanitarian functions? The situation here is quite ambiguous. Although government officals have been critical of the Committee of Liaison, there was no effort to interfere with its activities. The government, indeed, did not oppose granting Mr. David Dellinger, who was at the time subject to court-imposed travel restrictions, permission to leave the United States on the escort mission even though the trip would involve travel to countries with whom there were no extradition arrangements and even though his alleged crimes could readily be viewed as nonextradictable "political" offenses. The point is that the government might have relied on a technical objection to Mr. Dellinger's inclusion in the escort group, but refrained from doing so.

The language of Articles 9 and 10 is also ambiguous with regard to whether the belligerent must agree to the designation of a humanitarian organization. I think it most reasonable, both in relation to treaty interpretation and policy rationale, to view the second paragraph of Article 10 as giving the Detaining Power, North Vietnam, the capacity to deal with an organization, like the Committee of Liaison for purposes of carrying out the basic substantive mandate of the Convention to promote the interests of prisoners of war.

There is also some support for this view derived from hearings before the Senate Foreign Relations Committee. The Department of State submitted a statement clarifying certain points on the Geneva Conventions which included a significant reference to the meaning of Article 10:

> Common Article 10 (Article 11 of the Civilian Convention) provides for substitutes for protecting powers when protected persons for any

[13] *E.g.*, the initiatives associated with Ross Perot, the Texas millionaire, or the activities of the National League of Families of American Prisoners and Missing in Southeast Asia.

[14] As of November 1972 the Committee of Liaison has delivered 14,000 letters from and to prisoners detained in Vietnam and has also provided informational services for relatives of detained men.

> reason do not benefit by the activities of such a power. In such an event, the detaining power is requied unilaterally to undertake the functions performed by a protecting power. If such protection cannot be arranged, the detaining power is obligated to request or accept the offer of the services of a humanitarian organization, such as the International Committee of the Red Cross, to assume the humanitarian functions performed by protecting powers.[15]

The statement notes its opposition to a Soviet bloc reservation to Article 10 because its effect is to "diminish the belligerent rights of the state on which the protected persons depend." These states made a reservation that they would not accept a designation "unless the consent of the government of the state of which the protected persons are nationals has been obtained."[16] Such a statement seems to confirm the United States view that the Detaining Power had the capacity, even the duty, to designate an impartial humanitarian organization and that such designation would be determinative at least in the absence of objection from the country whose men are detained that the organization is not "impartial" or not "humanitarian."[17]

It would seem clear, then, that the Committe of Liaison could be designated by North Vietnam to carry out humanitarian functions, including repatriation in accordance with Article 10. The failure of the U.S. Government to make an objection either to the Committee or to the repatriation procedures is a further indication of this propriety. Given such an Article 10 role, then it seems reasonable for the Committee of Liaison to have some authority to specify guidelines that cover the discharge of a humanitarian mission not dealt with in the Convention and hence unreasonable for the U.S. Government not to respond either by way of acceptance, reasoned rejection, or through the proffer of an alternative set of guidelines.

It should be reiterated here that the discussion of Article 10 does not imply a formal application of its procedure to this repatriation. Article 10 does cast rather authoritative light, however, on what the treaty-drafting governments, and particularly the U.S. Government, regarded as *reasonable*

[15] *Hearings on the Geneva Conventions for the Protection of War Victims, Before the Senate Foreign Relations Committee*, June 3, 1955, at 62.

[16] *Id.* North Vietnam has made a reservation to its adherence exempting itself from Article 10.

[17] *See also Hearings, supra* note 15 at 62, for a covering letter from John Foster Dulles, as Secretary of State, to Senator Walter F. George, Chairman of the Committee:

> It is particularly recommended that this Government should not accept these reservations. The United States, should, however, express its intention to enter into treaty relations with the reserving states so that they will be bound toward the United States to carry out all the provisions of the conventions on which no reservations were specifically made. It should be clear that we hope that the reserving states will at some time elect to withdraw their reservations and if in the event of conflict reserving states seek to use their reservation in an unwarranted fashion so as to defeat the broad humanitarian purposes of the conventions, the United States would, of course, be in a position to consider that it was not required further to apply the conventions vis-à-vis such defaulting states.

By acting as it has in relation to this September 1972 repatriation North Vietnam has, it would seem, made a proper use of Article 10 so as to promote the underlying objectives of the Prisoner of War Convention.

in a situation in which no governmental actor was available to carry out the humanitarian mandate of the Convention. Actions in this situation, then, can be assessed in terms of such standards of reasonableness.

Fourth, does not the U.S. Government have some protection against the use of the process of repatriation to disseminate hostile propaganda? Why should North Vietnam not be expected to deal with a "genuinely" neutral organization? Such issues are difficult to resolve. There is a deep disagreement as to what constitutes neutrality in the POW context. If the North Vietnamese Government can be faulted for its attitude of hostility toward the International Committee of the Red Cross, then the U.S. Government can be criticized on purely humanitarian grounds for its reliance on various pro-war groups interested in the POW issue. In such circumstances, the Detaining Power has to be able to make the designation in the first instance, and the impropriety of its action has to be assessed by reference to whether or not there has been substantial fulfillment of the humanitarian purposes underlying the Geneva Convention. In this instance there has been no indication or allegation that the Committee of Liaison did more than provide escort facilities under as pleasant conditions as possible and with due regard for the welfare of the returning men and the remaining pilots.

While in Hanoi the Committee of Liaison also delivered and received mail, forwarded specific inquiries regarding health of detained men, examined complaints about camp conditions, received evidence from North Vietnam as to American abuse of mail privileges by including improper materials in packages designed to aid clandestine communication and possible rescue operations, and met with seven additional POWs in a free exchange of views. The Committee of Liaison escorts also expressed their views on the civilian damage being done by the air war and on the proper way to end the war and bring home the other American POWs, but this was done in their individual capacity. No effort was made to associate the three released men with views. The men were allowed, at most, to have a forum for the expression of their views, an opportunity that was used only very sparingly. The situation would have been different, it seems, if these men had been "brainwashed" and were then given a wide public forum to denounce the war under the cover of their repatriation, but no one has made such charges. In their absence, these released men are citizens with constitutional rights of freedom of speech; as such, they are entitled to oppose (or favor) the war, as they may have before being shot down, and they are certainly not precluded from saying that they saw (or didn't see) hospitals and churches that had been destroyed by bombs. The range of reactions exhibited by these three men toward the war confirms the view that they were not brainwashed and that they were not released because it was expected that they would denounce the war or join the peace movement.[18]

[18] These three men were released without conditions and without any explanation of the basis on which they were chosen. Their behavior since the moment of release exhibits a sense of independence on the part of the three men.

In conclusion, then, the Committee of Liaison appears to have been an appropriate organization for North Vietnam to designate to carry out the humanitarian objectives of the Geneva Conventions under the special circumstances of this war. Furthermore, there is nothing in the Convention nor in the Committee's record of performance to indicate its unsuitability for such a role. And, finally, the U.S. Government itself has done nothing to repudiate this designation, and it is not clear that such a repudiation could be justified in relation to the facts or to the guidelines embodied in the Convention.

III

It seems appropriate to make some wider observations about this minor event:

(1) The humanitarian objectives of the Convention may have to be realized in a flexible manner that is responsive to the characteristics of a particular armed conflict;

(2) A private organization of nationals of the "enemy" state may be more acceptable to the Detaining Power in certain situations than either the International Committee of the Red Cross or a neutral or even a friendly third power government;

(3) The Geneva system is comprehensive enough to provide general guidelines of relevance even in relation to a form of repatriation not specifically covered by the existing treaty;

(4) Treaty revision efforts should take explicit account of the possibility of repatriation of healthy prisoners to the enemy belligerent during the period of active hostilities;

(5) Repatriated prisoners should also be entitled to humanitarian protection once returned to their country of nationality and should be removed from any further relationship, direct or indirect, to an armed conflict in progress.

IV

We are left, then, with the underlying policy issue: How do we interpret the release and repatriation of three prisoners out of a prisoner population in North Vietnam of several hundred? Why only three? Why these three? There is no way to resolve altogether this underlying set of doubts. We can, however, make an analysis of whether this release seemed generally reasonable in method and effect and therefore deserved implementation.

First of all, it was a consensual process. The North Vietnamese initiative was not repudiated, as such, by the U.S. Government or by the three men selected for release.

Secondly, there was some humanitarian benefit for the three families concerned and some degree of reassurance more generally felt, given their good health and positive reports of general camp conditions and morale.

Thirdly, there were no negative consequences to legitimate prisoner interests.

It can be argued, of course, that North Vietnam was motivated by a desire to make hostile propaganda in connection with the release. Why else did they release the men into the custody of anti-war leaders? Why else did they provide tours of the bombed areas and entertainment for the released men and their relatives? Why was it insisted that the released men be returned to the American people rather than the American Government? Why was a return route arranged that was indirect and proceeded as far as possible by way of countries opposed to American policy in Vietnam? Why was the release timed to coincide with a pre-election period in which the Administration's war and prisoner policy was under attack by the opposition candidate? On one level, North Vietnamese motivations are of no account. Their behavior seemed correct, their initiative promoted a humanitarian end, and no effort was made to impose conditions on the terms of release.

In retrospect, it seems important to understand several features of the context. First of all, a humane experience of repatriation was aided by the presence of an accompanying relative and that some unnecessary trauma was generated by the efforts of the government to obtain jurisdiction over the men prior to and immediately upon their return to the United States. Secondly, the situation as to the Vietnamese prisoners does not resemble the situation of the Korean prisoners and expectations about repatriation should be adjusted accordingly. Thirdly, a long war in which reasonable and loyal citizens reach opposite conclusions about the best interests of the country places particular burdens on combat personnel who are captured under these circumstances, especially in relation to compliance with the Code of Conduct.[19] Fourthly, in these circumstances humanitarian purposes in accordance with the Geneva system may be and have been, in fact, served by a link between the enemy government and a prisoner of war organization constituted by anti-war nationals.

It seems reasonable, on this basis, to regard the North Vietnamese National Day Release as creating a precedent with international law relevance. At least, in the absence of revision of the Geneva Prisoner of War Convention, this release provides guidelines and experience as to repatriation during hostilities to a belligerent power, and affirms the capacity of a nongovernmental organization of private citizens to play a direct role in this process.

[19] For a sensitive treatment of the dilemma confronting a prisoner of war *see* Michael Waltzer's essay *Prisoners of War: Does the Fight Continue After the Battle?* in WALZER, OBLIGATIONS: ESSAYS ON DISOBEDIENCE, WAR, AND CITIZENSHIP 146–166 (1970). The problems posed for a conscripted citizen-soldier of a democratic society who opposes a war policy before his capture is particularly acute. Government writing does not exhibit an awareness of these issues. *See* "POW—The Fight Continues After the Battle," Report of the Secretary of Defense's Advisory Committee on Prisoners of War, Aug. 1955, which heavily reflects an effort to establish POW guidelines that would be resistant to brainwashing tactics used so successfully by North Korea in the Korean War. *See also* Prugh, *The Code of Conduct for the Armed Forces,* 56 COLUMBIA L. REV. 678 (1956); Note, *Misconduct in the Prison Camp: A Survey of the Law and an Analysis of the Korean Cases, ibid.,* 709.

[4]

Procedural principles and safeguards for internment/administrative detention in armed conflict and other situations of violence

Jelena Pejic*

Jelena Pejic is Legal Advisor at the International Committee of the Red Cross and Head of the ICRC Project on the Reaffirmation and Development of International Humanitarian Law

Abstract

Deprivation of liberty for security reasons is an exceptional measure of control that may be taken in armed conflict, whether international or non-international. Administrative detention of persons believed to represent a threat to State security is also being more and more widely practised outside of armed conflict situations. This paper argues that both internment and administrative detention are insufficiently elaborated from the point of the view of the protection of the rights of the persons affected. Drawing on international humanitarian law and on human rights law and standards, the paper proposes a set of procedural principles and safeguards that should — as a matter of law and policy — be applied as a minimum to all cases of deprivation of liberty for security reasons.

: : : : : : :

Internment or administrative detention is defined as the deprivation of liberty of a person that has been initiated/ordered by the executive branch — not the judiciary — without criminal charges being brought against the internee/administrative

* The views expressed in this article reflect the author's opinions and not necessarily those of the ICRC.

detainee.[1] Internment is an exceptional measure of control that may be ordered for security reasons in armed conflict, or for the purpose of protecting State security or public order in non-conflict situations provided the requisite criteria have been met.[2] The purpose of this text is to outline procedural principles and safeguards that govern internment/administrative detention in armed conflict and in other situations of violence as a matter both of law and of policy.[3]

In the text, the terms "internment" and "administrative detention" are interchangeably used.[4] The definition of internment therefore does not include the lawful pre-trial detention of a person held on criminal charges, whether in or outside armed conflict. Also, for the purposes of this text, it does not include the internment of prisoners of war (POWs) in international armed conflicts, which is a specific and separate regime of deprivation of liberty.

Insofar as armed groups involved in non-international armed conflicts deprive persons of liberty in practice — regardless of the lawfulness of such conduct — they are bound by the applicable treaty-based and customary rules of international humanitarian law governing non-international armed conflicts summarized in this text. Where practically feasible, the other principles and safeguards set forth below should also be applied as a means of ensuring the protection of persons deprived of their liberty.[5]

The reason for outlining the procedural principles and safeguards that govern internment/administrative detention is that although this type of deprivation of liberty is often practised in both international and non-international armed conflicts and other situations of violence, the protection of the rights of the persons affected by it is insufficiently elaborated.[6]

Furthermore, it is fairly common that in practice people interned or held in administrative detention are not or are only vaguely informed of the reasons for their deprivation of liberty. There is often no mechanism in place to review, initially and periodically, the lawfulness of internment/administrative detention or, if there is one, its lack of independence prevents it from effectively examining cases. The question of legal assistance to internees/administrative detainees in challenging the lawfulness of their internment/administrative detention remains contentious, as do other issues, such as contact for internees/administrative detainees with their families, family visits to them, etc.

1 See *Commentary on the Additional Protocols of 8 June 1977 to the Geneva Conventions of 12 August 1949*, ICRC/Martinus Nijhoff Publishers, Geneva, 1987, "Commentary on Protocol I relative to international armed conflicts", Art. 75 (3), para. 3063.

2 The relevant criteria, which are explained in greater detail below, are laid down in Article 4 of the International Covenant on Civil and Political Rights (ICCPR).

3 The term "other situations of violence" refers to situations below the threshold of armed conflict and includes situations of "internal disturbances or tensions" as specified in Article 1 (2) of Additional Protocol II.

4 The term "internment" is also intended to cover the notion of "assigned residence," to which identical provisions of the Fourth Geneva Convention apply.

5 This should in no way be read as referring to (or legitimizing) the practice of hostage-taking, which is strictly prohibited by international humanitarian law. The ICRC's position is that hostages must be immediately and unconditionally released.

6 For differences in the legal regulation of internment in international and non-international armed conflicts and in other situations of violence see section I, "Legal sources," below.

Volume 87 Number 858 June 2005 REVIEW of the Red Cross

Legal sources

The legal sources on which the present standards are based are the Fourth Geneva Convention; Article 75 of Additional Protocol I to the Geneva Conventions, which is considered to reflect customary international law; Article 3 common to the Geneva Conventions; Additional Protocol II thereto; and customary rules of international humanitarian law.

Even though internment in international armed conflicts is regulated by the Fourth Geneva Convention and Additional Protocol I,[7] these treaties do not sufficiently elaborate on the procedural rights of internees, nor do they specify the details of the legal framework that a detaining authority must implement. In non-international armed conflicts there is even less clarity as to how administrative detention is to be organized. Article 3 common to the Geneva Conventions, which is applicable as a minimum standard to all non-international armed conflicts, contains no provisions regulating internment, i.e. administrative detention for security reasons, apart from the requirement of humane treatment. Internment is, however, clearly a measure that can be taken in non-international armed conflict, as evidenced by the language of Additional Protocol II, which mentions internment in Articles 5 and 6 respectively, but likewise does not give details of how it is to be organized. Bearing in mind the principles of humanity and the dictates of public conscience (the Martens clause),[8] the principles and rules of the Fourth Geneva Convention may, in practice, serve as guidance in non-international armed conflicts in resolving some of the procedural issues mentioned in this text.

In addition to humanitarian law, the present analysis draws on human rights law, of both a binding and a non-binding nature ("soft law"), as a complementary source of law in situations of armed conflict or as an autonomous source of law outside of armed conflict. The complementary relationship between humanitarian and human rights law has most recently been confirmed by the International Court of Justice, the UN's principal legal body. In a July 2004 Advisory Opinion, the Court stated that humanitarian and human rights law are by no means mutually exclusive. According to the Court, some rights are protected only by human rights law, some are protected only by humanitarian law, and "yet others may be matters of both these branches of international law."[9]

The rights of persons interned for security reasons in armed conflict — whether international or non-international — may be said to fall into the category of rights that, in the ICJ's wording, are "matters" of both branches

7 GC IV, Arts. 43 and 78; AP I, Art. 75 (3).

8 The Martens clause is, *inter alia*, included in Article 1 (2) of Additional Protocol I which reads: "In cases not covered by this Protocol or by other international instruments, civilians and combatants remain under the protection and authority of the principles of international law derived from established custom, from the principles of humanity and from the dictates of public conscience."

9 ICJ Advisory Opinion on the Legal Consequences of the Construction of a Wall in the Occupied Palestinian Territory, 9 July 2004, para. 106.

of law. Given the aforesaid absence of rules for the internment of individuals in non-international armed conflicts, it is necessary to draw on human rights law in devising a list of procedural principles and safeguards to govern internment in such conflicts. To a large extent the same may be said with regard to any effort to clarify the rights, and therefore the legal protection, that should be accorded to persons covered by the Fourth Geneva Convention or Additional Protocol I in international armed conflicts.

Recourse to human rights law as a legal regime complementary to humanitarian law is expressly recognized in both Additional Protocols to the Geneva Conventions.

According to Article 72 of Additional Protocol I: "The provisions of this Section ["Treatment of persons in the power of a party to the conflict"] are additional to the rules concerning humanitarian protection of civilians and civilian objects in the power of a Party to the conflict contained in the Fourth Convention, particularly Parts I and III thereof, *as well as to other applicable rules of international law relating to the protection of fundamental human rights during international armed conflict*" (emphasis added). This article allows recourse to human rights law as an additional frame of reference in regulating the rights of internees, who belong to "persons in the power of a party to the conflict."[10]

There are two further indications — in Article 75 of Additional Protocol I, which is considered to reflect customary law — that human rights law may be drawn on to fill the gaps. First, and this must be stressed, Article 75 (1) states that persons falling within its scope shall enjoy the protection provided for by this article "*as a minimum*" (emphasis added). Given that Article 75 is a "safety net" meant to cover all persons who do not enjoy more favourable treatment under the Geneva Conventions or Protocol I, and when it is read in conjunction with Article 72, it necessarily follows that the "minimum" mentioned is supplemented by other provisions of humanitarian and human rights law.

Secondly, any possible doubt that Article 75 constitutes a minimum benchmark of protection is dispelled by the final clause thereof: "No provision of this Article may be construed as limiting or infringing any other more favourable provision granting greater protection, under any applicable rules of international law, to persons covered by paragraph 1."[11] The applicable rules of international law include human rights law.

In non-international armed conflicts the provisions of Common Article 3 and of Additional Protocol II articulate minimum standards that must be applied in internment. Where the parties to a non-international armed conflict bring into force, by means of special agreements, all or part of the provisions of the Fourth Geneva Convention, the provisions of such an agreement prevail.[12] It must be noted that preambular paragraph 2 of Additional Protocol II

10 See "Commentary on AP I", *op. cit.* (note 1), paras. 2927– 2935.

11 AP I, Art. 75 (8).

12 See Article 3 common to the Geneva Conventions, which also specifies that the conclusion of a special agreement "shall not affect the legal status of Parties to the conflict." Special agreements can be effective particularly in high-intensity non-international armed conflicts which resemble inter-State armed conflict.

Volume 87 Number 858 June 2005 REVIEW of the Red Cross

establishes the link between the Protocol and human rights law by stating that "international instruments relating to human rights offer a basic protection to the human person." The Commentary on that Protocol specifies that the reference to international instruments includes treaties adopted by the UN, such as the International Covenant on Civil and Political Rights (ICCPR) and the Convention against Torture, as well as the regional human rights treaties.[13]

The right to liberty of person, which is the primary focus of this text, is *inter alia* provided for in Article 9 (1) of the ICCPR. A State Party may derogate from (suspend) its obligations under that treaty under very strict conditions, one of which is the existence of a public emergency threatening the life of the nation.[14] Non-international armed conflict is an example of a public emergency in which measures of derogation — necessary for enabling internment — would be lawful under the Covenant provided the other requisite conditions have been met. In non-conflict situations States Parties to the ICCPR must likewise comply with the derogation clauses of the Covenant in order to institute measures affecting the right to liberty of person, such as administrative detention. The present analysis is based on the assumption that internment in non-international armed conflict and administrative detention implemented in non-conflict situations comply with the derogation criteria specified in the ICCPR.[15]

However, even in emergency situations the so-called "hard core" of human rights, which includes the right to life and the prohibition of torture and other cruel, inhuman or degrading treatment or punishment, cannot be derogated from under any circumstances.[16] The jurisprudence of international and regional human rights bodies has determined which other human rights, apart from those expressly listed in the treaties, should also be considered non-derogable. Among them is the right of a person deprived of liberty to challenge the lawfulness of his or her detention (habeas corpus), which is an essential element of the right to liberty of person.[17]

Human rights soft law instruments and jurisprudence provide further standards that, it is submitted, should as a matter of policy and good practice be applied with respect to internment/administrative detention.

13 "Commentary on P II", *op. cit.* (note 1), paras. 4428 – 4430.

14 The full text of Article 4 of the ICCPR reads: "1. In time of public emergency which threatens the life of the nation and the existence of which is officially proclaimed, the States Parties to the present Covenant may take measures derogating from their obligations under the present Covenant to the extent strictly required by the exigencies of the situation, provided that such measures are not inconsistent with their other obligations under international law and do not involve discrimination solely on the ground of race, colour, sex, language, religion or social origin. 2. No derogation from articles 6, 7, 8 (paras. 1 and 2), 11, 15, 16 and 18 may be made under this provision. 3. Any State Party to the present Covenant availing itself of the right of derogation shall immediately inform the other States Parties to the present Covenant, through the intermediary of the Secretary-General of the United Nations, of the provisions from which it has derogated and of the reasons by which it was actuated. A further communication shall be made, through the same intermediary, on the date on which it terminates such derogation."

15 In cases where a State is not a party to the ICCPR or similar regional human rights treaties, it is submitted that the procedural principles and safeguards listed below should be followed as a matter of policy.

16 ICCPR, Art. 4 (2).

17 ICCPR, Art. 9 (4).

The commentary to the procedural principles and safeguards outlined in this text mentions the different legal sources governing deprivation of liberty for security reasons in international armed conflicts, non-international armed conflicts and other situations of violence. It is precisely the similarity in content of the various legal sources reviewed that guided the specific formulation of the procedural principles and safeguards listed, and which allows the conclusion that they can be considered a minimum applicable in all cases of deprivation of liberty for security reasons.[18]

General principles applicable to internment/administrative detention

Internment/administrative detention is an exceptional measure

The Fourth Geneva Convention makes it explicitly clear that internment (and assigned residence) are the most severe measures of control that a detaining authority or Occupying Power may take with respect to protected persons against whom no criminal proceedings have been initiated. In both cases it is stipulated that recourse to these measures may be had only if the security of the State makes it "absolutely necessary" (GC IV, Article 42) or for "imperative reasons of security" (GC IV, Article 78). The exceptional nature of internment lies in the fact that it allows the detaining authority to deprive persons of liberty who are not subject to criminal process, but are nevertheless considered to represent a real threat to its security in the present or in the future. As the Commentary on the Fourth Geneva Convention explains, "It did not seem possible to define the expression 'security of the State' in a more concrete fashion. It is thus left very largely to Governments to decide the measure of activity prejudicial to the internal or external security of the State which justifies internment or assigned residence."[19] While this may be the case it is clear, for example, that internment or administrative detention for the sole purpose of intelligence gathering, without the person involved otherwise presenting a real threat to State security, cannot be justified.[20]

That internment is an exceptional measure is also true in non-international armed conflicts and other situations of violence, based on the general principle that personal liberty is the rule, and on the assumption that the criminal justice system is able to deal with persons suspected of representing a danger to State security.

18 It should again be noted that this text does not deal with the internment of prisoners of war in international armed conflicts, which is governed by the Third Geneva Convention. As already mentioned, it is assumed that the right to liberty of person has been derogated from in keeping with Article 4 of the ICCPR.

19 See *Commentary on the Geneva Conventions of 12 August 1949*, Vol. IV, *Geneva Convention relative to the Protection of Civilian Persons in Time of War*, Art. 42, p. 257. See also the Commentary on Article 78, at page 368, which reiterates that: "In any case such measures can only be ordered for real and imperative reasons of security; their exceptional character must be preserved."

20 Similarly, interning or administratively detaining persons for the purpose of using them as "bargaining chips" is also not justifiable as a reason for internment. Such deprivation of liberty would in fact amount to hostage-taking, which is prohibited.

Volume 87 Number 858 June 2005 REVIEW of the Red Cross

Internment/administrative detention is not an alternative to criminal proceedings

Internment/administrative detention is a measure of control aimed at dealing with persons who pose a real threat to State security, currently or in the future, in situations of armed conflict, or to State security or public order in non-conflict situations; it is not a measure that is meant to replace criminal proceedings. A person who is suspected of having committed a criminal offence, whether in armed conflict or other situations of violence, has the right to benefit from the additional stringent judicial guarantees provided for in humanitarian and/or human rights law for criminal suspects, which include the right to be tried by a regularly constituted, independent and impartial court. Unless internment/administrative detention and penal repression are organized as strictly separate regimes there is a danger that internment might be used as a substandard system of penal repression in the hands of the executive power, bypassing the one sanctioned by a country's legislature and courts. The rights of criminal suspects would thus be gravely undermined.[21]

Internment/administrative detention can only be ordered on an individual case-by-case basis, without discrimination of any kind

A civilian can be interned in international armed conflict only on the basis of an individual decision taken in every specific case. The notion that internment cannot be a collective measure is established under the Fourth Geneva Convention in situations of occupation.[22] *En bloc* internment of enemy nationals in a State's own territory is also prohibited, as it would amount to, and violate the general prohibition of, "collective punishments" under Article 75 (2) (d) of Additional Protocol I. This does not mean that a detaining authority cannot intern a large number of persons, but that both the initial decision on internment and any subsequent decision to maintain it, including the reasons for internment, must be taken with respect to each individual involved.

In non-international armed conflicts — in which collective punishments are also prohibited[23] — and in other situations of violence, both the initial

21 The argument that administrative and criminal detention are two distinct regimes is — at first glance — undermined by Article 68 of the Fourth Geneva Convention which deals with petty offences committed by protected persons in occupied territory. The Commentary on Article 68, however, rectifies any possible perception of overlap between the regimes of administrative and criminal detention that the wording of the provision suggests. It reads: "Internment is a preventive administrative measure and cannot be considered a penal sanction. It is nevertheless mentioned here under the same head[ing] as simple imprisonment, because the authors of the Convention wished to make it possible for the military courts of the Occupying Power to give persons guilty of minor offences the *benefit of conditions of internment* (emphasis added) provided for in Article 79 *et seq*. The provision was a humane one and was intended to draw a distinction between such offenders and common criminals." *Commentary* on GC IV, *op. cit.* (note 19), pp. 343–344.

22 *Ibid.*, Art. 78, p. 367.

23 AP II, Art. 4 (2) (b).

decision on internment/administrative detention and any subsequent decision to maintain it must be taken on an individual basis. Even though humanitarian law governing non-international armed conflicts is silent as to the procedural rights of internees, under human rights law any measure derogating from the right to liberty of person must be "strictly required by the exigencies of the situation" of public emergency necessitating the derogation;[24] it may be taken only to the extent required thereby, and must thus be in accordance with the principle of proportionality.

A State's *en bloc*, non-individual detention of a whole category of persons could in no way be considered a proportional response, regardless of what the circumstances of the emergency concerned might be. The idea of collective measures of any kind is antithetical to the rules, spirit and purpose of human rights law.

Decisions on internment/administrative detention must also not be taken on a discriminatory basis. The principle of non-discrimination is a basic tenet of both humanitarian and human rights law.

Internment/administrative detention must cease as soon as the reasons for it cease to exist

One of the most important principles governing internment/administrative detention is that this form of deprivation of liberty must cease as soon as the individual ceases to pose a real threat to State security, meaning that deprivation of liberty on such grounds cannot be indefinite. In view of the rapid progression of events in armed conflict, a person considered to be a threat today might not pose the same threat after a change of circumstances on the ground. In other words, the longer internment lasts, the greater the onus on a detaining authority to prove that the reasons for it remain valid. The rationale of the principle is thus to facilitate the release of a person as soon as the reasons justifying the curtailment of liberty no longer exist. The principle that internment must cease as soon as the reasons for it cease to exist is clearly enunciated in the Fourth Geneva Convention (Article 132) and in Article 75 (3) of Additional Protocol I, which is considered to reflect customary international law in international armed conflicts.

In non-international armed conflicts and other situations of violence this principle must, if anything, be even more stringently observed, particularly as human rights jurisprudence rejects the notion of indefinite detention.[25] In order to ensure that a deprivation of liberty is not arbitrary, which would be the case if the reasons for it do not or no longer exist, the ICCPR (Article 9 (4)) pro-

24 ICCPR, Art. 4 (1).

25 See e.g. Report of the Working Group on Arbitrary Detention, UN Doc. E/CN. 4/2004/3, 15 December 2003, para. 60 ("in no event may an arrest based on emergency legislation last indefinitely"), and Inter-American Commission on Human Rights — Annual Report, 1976, OAS Doc. OEA/Ser.L/V/II.40, Doc. 5 corr. 1 of 7 June 1977, Section II, Part I ("the declaration of a state of emergency or a state of siege cannot serve as a pretext for the indefinite detention of individuals, without any charge whatever. It is obvious that when these security measures are extended beyond a reasonable time they become true and serious violations of the right to freedom").

Volume 87 Number 858 June 2005 REVIEW of the Red Cross

vides that anyone deprived of liberty has the right to challenge the lawfulness of his or her detention — file a petition for habeas corpus or the equivalent — in order that a court may decide "without delay" whether he or she is being held lawfully or not. While the right to liberty is not among the non-derogable rights listed in the ICCPR,[26] the jurisprudence of both universal and regional human rights bodies has confirmed that the right to habeas corpus must in fact be considered non-derogable.

Internment/administrative detention must conform to the principle of legality

In the context of internment/administrative detention, the principle of legality means that a person may be deprived of liberty only for reasons (substantive aspect) and in accordance with procedures (procedural aspect) that are provided for by domestic and international law.

The Geneva Conventions and their Additional Protocols, as well as human rights law, provide the international legal standards that are to be applied to internment/administrative detention in armed conflict and other situations of violence. In terms of reasons for internment, the Fourth Convention specifies that a protected person may be interned or placed in assigned residence only if "the security of the Detaining Power makes it absolutely necessary" (Article 42) or, in occupied territory, for "imperative reasons of security" (Article 78). In addition to specifying the reasons for internment, the Fourth Convention lays down certain procedures that must be followed for internment to be lawful both in the territory of a party to conflict and in occupied territory. In the latter case, for example, Article 78 of the Fourth Convention stipulates that decisions regarding assigned residence or internment "shall be made according to a regular procedure to be prescribed by the Occupying Power in accordance with the provisions of the present Convention." Deprivation of liberty that is not in conformity with the various rules provided for in the Convention may constitute "unlawful confinement."[27]

Human rights standards applicable in non-international armed conflicts and other situations of violence provide even more detailed provisions aimed at ensuring respect for the principle of legality. Under the ICCPR (Article 9 (1)), for example, persons may not be deprived of their liberty "except on such grounds and in accordance with such procedure as are established by law." Where a State decides to derogate from the right to liberty, such a decision must, *inter alia*, be officially proclaimed[28] so as to enable the affected population to know the exact material, territorial and temporal scope of application of that emergency measure.

26 ICCPR, Art. 4 (2).
27 GC IV, Art. 147.
28 ICCPR, Art. 4 (1).

Procedural safeguards

Right to information about the reasons for internment/administrative detention

Any person interned/administratively detained must be informed promptly, in a language he or she understands, of the reasons why that measure has been taken so as to enable the person concerned to challenge the lawfulness of his or her detention. The right of a person to know why he or she has been deprived of liberty may be said to constitute an element of the obligation of human treatment, as a person's uncertainty about the reasons for his or her detention is known in practice to constitute a source of acute psychological stress.

Neither the Fourth Geneva Convention nor humanitarian law applicable in non-international armed conflicts contain explicit provisions on the duty to provide information about the reasons for which a person has been deprived of liberty. The foregoing procedural safeguard is, however, one of the "Fundamental Guarantees" laid down in Article 75 (3) of Additional Protocol I. It is moreover provided for in most of the relevant human rights treaties and is spelt out in soft law instruments as well.[29]

The information given must also be sufficiently detailed for the detained person to take immediate steps to challenge, and request a decision, on the lawfulness of the internment/administrative detention (see below). Information on the reasons for internment/administrative detention must be conveyed promptly,[30] so as to enable the person in question to also promptly request a decision on the lawfulness of detention, and must be conveyed in a language he or she understands. Where an initial decision on detention is maintained on review, the reasons for continued detention must be provided as well.

Right to be registered and held in a recognized place of internment/administrative detention

Any person interned/administratively detained must be registered and held in an officially recognized place of internment/administrative detention. Information that a person has been taken into such custody and on any transfers between places of detention must be available to that person's family within a reasonable time,[31] unless he or she has expressed a wish to the contrary; the family should also be notified of the place of custody. The same information must be supplied to the ICRC when humanitarian law or specific agreements so require.

Humanitarian law applicable to international armed conflicts contains numerous provisions and extensive requirements concerning the registration

29 ICCPR, Art. 9 (2); Body of Principles for the Protection of All Persons under Any Form of Detention or Imprisonment, Principles 10; 11 (2); 12 (1) (a) and (2); 14; UN General Assembly resolution 43/173 of 9 December 1988 (hereinafter "Body of Principles").

30 AP I, Art. 75 (3), Body of Principles, Principle 14.

31 GC IV, Arts. 106 and 138.

Volume 87 Number 858 June 2005 REVIEW of the Red Cross

of protected persons deprived of their liberty and notification of their own country's authorities,[32] visits to places of detention[33] and the transmission of information about such persons to their next of kin, among others.[34] The entire system of detention laid down by the Conventions, and in which the ICRC plays a supervisory role, is based on the idea that detainees must be registered and held in officially recognized places of detention accessible, in particular, to the ICRC. Human rights jurisprudence and soft law instruments contain similar explicit provisions on the obligation to register detainees and the prohibition of unacknowledged detention[35] which are relevant in non-international armed conflicts and other situations of violence.[36]

Foreign nationals in internment/administrative detention

The national authorities of a person interned/administratively detained must be informed thereof unless a wish to the contrary has been expressed by the person concerned. The relevant diplomatic or consular authorities — provided diplomatic or consular relations exist — must be allowed to communicate with and visit their nationals. This is a rule of public international law that remains applicable in armed conflicts and other situations of violence.[37]

A person subject to internment/administrative detention has the right to challenge, with the least possible delay, the lawfulness of his or her detention

With regard to international armed conflicts the Fourth Geneva Convention, in Article 43 applicable to the internment of persons in the territory of a party to the conflict, stipulates that any protected person interned or placed in assigned residence is "entitled to have such action reconsidered as soon as possible by an appropriate court or administrative board designated by the Detaining Power for that purpose." Under Article 78 of the Fourth Convention, applicable to the internment of persons in occupied territory, decisions regarding assigned residence or internment "shall be made according to a regular procedure to be prescribed by the Occupying Power in accordance with the provisions of the present Convention. This procedure shall include the right of appeal for the parties concerned. Appeals shall be decided with the least possible delay."

32 *Ibid.*, Art. 136.
33 *Ibid.*, Art. 143.
34 *Ibid.*, Arts. 106, 107, 137 and 138.
35 Body of Principles, *op. cit.* (note 29), Principles 12 and 16 (1).
36 See also UN Declaration on the Protection of All Persons from Enforced Disappearance, Art. 10 (1), and Principles on the Effective Prevention and Investigation of Extra-legal, Arbitrary and Summary Executions, recommended by UN Economic and Social Council, Principle 6.
37 See Art. 36 of the Vienna Convention on Consular Relations. In international armed conflicts, the official Information Bureaux and the Central Tracing Agency are mechanisms through which the adverse party is informed of the internment of its nationals (GC IV, Arts. 136–141). In non-international armed conflicts the ICRC is also available to facilitate contact between a person deprived of liberty and the State of which he or she is a national, provided that person consents to such notification.

While the Convention does not specifically speak of these actions as challenges to the lawfulness of detention, that is what they essentially are. The purpose of the "reconsideration" or "appeal" is to enable the competent body to determine whether the person was deprived of liberty for valid reasons and to order his or her release if that was not the case. The authority that initially deprived a person of liberty and the body authorized to conduct the review on appeal must not be the same if the right of petition is to be effective. The characteristics of the latter body and the existence of other procedural safeguards, mentioned below, are the crucial factor.

The right of a person to challenge the lawfulness of his or her detention in non-international armed conflicts and in other situations of violence is a key component of the right to liberty of person under human rights law. Even though the right to liberty may be derogated from in situations of emergency, human rights soft law and jurisprudence have established that the right to challenge the lawfulness of one's detention before a judicial body must be preserved in all circumstances.[38] It may in particular not be diminished where the challenge to lawfulness of detention serves, *inter alia*, to protect non-derogable rights, such as the right to life or freedom from torture and other cruel, inhuman or degrading treatment or punishment.[39]

As may be concluded from the sources above, a review of the lawfulness of internment/administrative detention within a short time is required by both humanitarian and human rights law.

Review of the lawfulness of internment/administrative detention must be carried out by an independent and impartial body

Article 43 of the Fourth Geneva Convention stipulates that an "appropriate court or administrative board" shall be charged with reconsidering the initial decision on the internment of a civilian in the territory of a party to the conflict. According to Article 78 applicable in occupied territory, a decision on internment must be made pursuant to a "regular procedure" prescribed by the Occupying Power in accordance with the Convention. Article 78 adds that the periodic review envisaged must be undertaken by a "competent body set up" by the Occupying Power. Despite the difference in language — "court or administrative board" in Article 43 versus "regular procedure" in Article 78 — the commentary on the latter article states that the Occupying Power "must observe the stipulations in Article 43" and that it is up to the Occupying Power "to entrust the consideration of appeals either to a 'court' or a 'board'."[40]

A State's freedom to choose between a "court or administrative board" as provided for in Article 43 (and Article 78 by analogy) is explained in the

38 Body of Principles, *op. cit.* (note 29), Principle 32. See also Human Rights Committee, General Comment No. 29, para. 11.

39 Human Rights Committee, *ibid.*, para. 15.

40 *Commentary* on GC IV, *op. cit.* (note 19), Art. 78, pp. 368–369.

Volume 87 Number 858 June 2005 REVIEW of the Red Cross

Commentary as allowing "sufficient flexibility to take into account the usage in different States." The Commentary adds that "where the decision is an administrative one, it must not be made by one official but by an administrative board offering the necessary guarantees of independence and impartiality."[41] It may be presumed that judicial supervision of internment would more likely comply with the requirements of independence and impartiality. It is therefore submitted that judicial supervision would be preferable to an administrative board and should be organized whenever possible. The reviewing body must at the very least, as stated in the Commentary, be constituted and function in a way that allows it to be independent and impartial. An element of the required independence of such a body is that it must have the authority to render final decisions on internment or release.

While the Fourth Geneva Convention allows the State to choose between a court and an administrative board in international armed conflicts, human rights law and jurisprudence applicable to situations of non-international armed conflict or other situations of violence unequivocally require that challenges to the lawfulness of internment/administrative detention be heard by a court. Under the ICCPR, anyone deprived of liberty is entitled to "take proceedings before a court, in order that that court may decide without delay on the lawfulness of his detention and order his release if the detention is not lawful."[42]

As has already been stressed above, even though the right to liberty of person may be derogated from in situations of emergency, such as non-international armed conflict, human rights soft law and jurisprudence have established that the right to challenge the lawfulness of one's detention before a judicial body must be preserved in all circumstances.[43] It may in particular not be diminished where the challenge to lawfulness of detention serves, *inter alia*, to protect non-derogable rights, such as the right to life or freedom from torture and other cruel, inhuman or degrading treatment or punishment.[44]

It should be reiterated that the reason for challenges to the lawfulness of internment/administrative detention is to put an end to the deprivation of liberty if it is not justified. This means that an internee must be informed without delay of any decision taken on appeal and be immediately released if the petition is upheld. Even though the obligation of speedy information and release is not explicitly mentioned in either humanitarian or human rights law, any deprivation of liberty without a legal basis is considered to be a violation of the general legal principle prohibiting arbitrary detention. If a person is kept in internment/administrative detention despite a final release order, that is a clear case of arbitrary detention.

41 *Ibid.*, Art. 43, p. 260.
42 ICCPR, Art. 9 (4).
43 Body of Principles, *op. cit.* (note 29), Principle 32. See also Human Rights Committee, General Comment No. 29, para. 11.
44 Human Rights Committee, *ibid.*, para. 15.

An internee/administrative detainee should be allowed to have legal assistance

Neither humanitarian nor human rights treaty law explicitly provide for the right to legal assistance for persons interned or administratively detained (that right is guaranteed to persons subject to criminal charges).

It must be noted, however, that legal assistance to internees in international armed conflicts is not prohibited. The Commentary on Article 43 of the Fourth Geneva Convention in fact states that the "procedure provided for in the Convention is a minimum"[45] and that "it will be an advantage, therefore, if States Parties to the Convention afford better safeguards."[46] It may be said that nowadays the right to effective legal assistance is not just an "advantage", but a basic procedural safeguard.

Human rights soft law and the jurisprudence of human rights bodies provide extensive standards that fill the gaps in treaty law applicable in non-international armed conflicts and other situations of violence.[47] The right to effective legal assistance is thus considered to be an essential component of the right to liberty of person. The relevant soft law standards provide for the right of persons in custody to legal counsel regardless of the type of detention involved. They also contain provisions on the modalities of communication with a lawyer.[48]

Where necessary, reasonable security arrangements may be made, such as requiring security clearance for an internee's/administrative detainee's legal counsel.

An internee/administrative detainee has the right to periodical review of the lawfulness of continued detention

Periodical review of administrative detention if the initial decision on detention is confirmed after "reconsideration" (Article 43), or on "appeal" (Article 78), is a basic component of the procedure laid down in the Fourth Geneva Convention. Article 43 specifies that periodical review shall take place "at least twice yearly," while Article 78 provides that such review shall take place "if possible every six months."

The purpose of the periodical review is to ascertain whether the detainee continues to pose a real threat to the security of the detaining power and to order release if that is not the case. All the safeguards that apply to the initial review must apply to the periodical review(s) as well, which, among other things, means that the review has to be effective and must be conducted by an independent and impartial body.

45 *Commentary* on GC IV, *op. cit.* (note 19), p. 261.
46 *Ibid.*
47 See, *inter alia*, Body of Principles, *op. cit.* (note 29), Principles 17 and 18.
48 *Ibid.*, Principle 18.

Volume 87 Number 858 June 2005 REVIEW of the Red Cross

There is no specified periodicity of review available to persons detained in non-international armed conflicts or other situations of violence, because human rights law does not limit the frequency of challenges that may be submitted by an interned/administratively detained person to the lawfulness of detention (habeas corpus petitions).[49] Internment/administrative detention will in practice be regulated by the domestic law of the State involved in a non-international armed conflict or other situation of violence, meaning that a person's ability to challenge the lawfulness of his or her internment/administrative detention will be regulated by those norms.

If the relevant domestic law makes no such provision, it is submitted that at least six-monthly reviews of internment/administrative detention should be provided for, similar to the rules applicable in international armed conflicts.

An internee/administrative detainee and his or her legal representative should be able to attend the proceedings in person

An internee/administrative detainee and his or her legal representative should, as a general rule, be able to be present at the initial review of the lawfulness of internment, as well as at periodical reviews, in order to be able to present the internee's/administrative detainee's position and contest the claims made against him or her. Where necessary, reasonable arrangements for the preservation of classified information may be made, such as requiring security clearance for the internee's/administrative detainee's legal representative.

While neither humanitarian nor human rights treaty law expressly mention the right of internees/administrative detainees and of their legal representative to be present at proceedings related to internment/administrative detention, it has been observed in practice that their absence often leads to hearings in which their case is given inadequate attention. Because such proceedings result in decisions on the continuation of internment/administrative detention, it is submitted that the internee/administrative detainee and his or her legal representative should be allowed to be present at the proceedings. If they do not understand the language of the court, they will need to be provided with an interpreter.

An internee/administrative detainee must be allowed to have contacts with — to correspond with and be visited by — members of his or her family

The preservation of family life and contacts is one of the basic aims of international humanitarian law and may be said to constitute an element of the broader obligation that persons deprived of their liberty in both international and non-international armed conflicts must be treated humanely. This safeguard, as well as the two listed immediately below, belong to those aimed at ensuring proper conditions and treatment in detention, which is not the

49 *Ibid.*, Principle 32.

subject of this text. They have been included here because of their importance for enabling the other procedural safeguards dealt with in this text to be implemented.

The Fourth Geneva Convention contains provisions facilitating contact between internees and their families that are too numerous to repeat here. In brief, the general presumption is that family contacts — correspondence and visits — must be allowed within a reasonable time frame[50] in all but very exceptional circumstances.[51] In no case may a detainee's contact with his or her family be made dependent on his or her "cooperativeness" with the detaining authority or be used as a form of incentive or reward for other behaviour.

Additional Protocol II also contains provisions designed to maintain family contacts[52] and numerous non-treaty human rights standards have the same aim.[53]

An internee/administrative detainee has the right to the medical care and attention required by his or her condition

The right to medical care and attention is a component of the essential obligation that all persons deprived of their liberty must be treated humanely. Medical care and attention serve among other things to prevent ill-treatment and also to refute the admissibility of evidence against a person that has been obtained by torture or other forms of ill-treatment. They are mentioned in this context because a person's health is obviously a prerequisite for his or her ability to claim most of the procedural rights outlined in this text.

The general rule laid down in the Fourth Geneva Convention (Article 81) stipulates that: "Parties to the conflict who intern protected persons shall be bound to provide free of charge for their maintenance, and to grant them also the medical attention required by their state of health." More specific rules on hygiene and medical attention are contained in Articles 91 and 92.

In non-international armed conflicts, Article 5 (1) (b) of Additional Protocol II stipulates that internees "shall, to the same extent as the local civilian population, be provided with food and drinking water and be afforded safeguards as regards health and hygiene and protection against the rigours of the climate and the dangers of the armed conflict." Provisions on access to a doctor and medical attention are also contained in the relevant human rights non-treaty instruments (Body of Principles, Principles 24 and 26).

It must be stressed that access to medical care that might be required by a person's condition cannot in any circumstances be made dependent on his or her "cooperativeness" with the detaining authority or be used as a form of incentive or reward for other behaviour.

50 See, *inter alia*, GC IV, Arts. 106, 107 and 116.

51 See GC IV, Art. 5, and *Commentary* on GC IV, *op. cit.* (note 19), p. 56.

52 AP II, Art. 5 (2) (b).

53 Body of Principles, *op. cit.* (note 29), Principle 19.

Volume 87 Number 858 June 2005 REVIEW of the Red Cross

An internee/administrative detainee must be allowed to make submissions relating to his or her treatment and conditions of detention

Both international humanitarian law (Article 101 of the Fourth Convention)[54] and human rights soft law stipulate that internees/persons subject to administrative detention have the right to make submissions to the detaining authority regarding their treatment and conditions of detention.[55] The purpose of this safeguard is to enable the detaining authority to prevent and stop possible violations of the law. The authorities are thus obliged to put in place a procedure that allows the submission and speedy as well as effective examination of petitions or complaints. The submission of such representations must not have any adverse consequences for the petitioner.

Access to persons interned/administratively detained

ICRC access to persons interned in international armed conflicts is provided for in the Fourth Geneva Convention (Article 143), which also lays down the conditions and procedure for ICRC visits and establishes the duty of a detaining authority to grant access and to respect the said conditions and procedure.

In non-international armed conflicts[56] and in other situations of violence[57], the ICRC may offer its services and conclude agreements with the detaining authority on visits to persons deprived of their liberty for security reasons, and to other persons. The ICRC's right of access in these situations is widely recognized.

By means of visits to persons deprived of their liberty the ICRC, which is an independent, impartial and neutral humanitarian organization, seeks to ensure that they are treated humanely in all circumstances and that their fundamental rights are respected. It is thus concerned essentially with their conditions of detention and their treatment, including respect for fundamental procedural guarantees at all stages of detention.

Certain international and regional human rights treaties, too, provide for on-site visits to such persons by visiting mechanisms established under those treaties.[58] There are likewise a number of non-treaty mechanisms created under the auspices of the UN Commission on Human Rights that may carry out visits to places of detention.[59]

54 Under Art. 102 of the Fourth Geneva Convention, Internee Committees also have the right to make representations to, *inter alia*, the ICRC.

55 It should be noted that under human rights soft law the legal counsel, a family member or another person who has knowledge of the case may also make submissions regarding the treatment of a person in administrative detention. See Body of Principles, *op. cit.* (note 29), Principle 33 (1) and (2).

56 See Art. 3 common to the four Geneva Conventions.

57 See Art. 5 (3) of the Statutes of the International Red Cross and Red Crescent Movement (1986).

58 E.g. the European Committee for the Prevention of Torture and Inhuman or Degrading Treatment or Punishment set up by the European Convention for the Prevention of Torture and Inhuman or Degrading Treatment or Punishment.

59 E.g. the UN Commission on Human Rights Working Group on Arbitrary Detention.

[5]

Evolving Geneva Convention Paradigms in the "War on Terrorism": Applying the Core Rules to the Release of Persons Deemed "Unprivileged Combatants"

Sean D. Murphy*

Introduction

The purpose of this Article is to take stock of the current application of the Geneva Conventions in the global "war on terrorism," including interpretations recently taken by the U.S. Supreme Court in *Hamdan v. Rumsfeld*.[1] As will be evident in the discussion that follows, both the Geneva Conventions and the laws of war more generally comprise a sophisticated regulatory regime whose rules can and should be closely analyzed by lawyers. Yet, like all law, the inevitable imprecision in the rules presents opportunities for governments to exploit gray areas so as to augment governmental authority and to avoid sensible interpretations that will protect individuals from overreaching governmental power. Such exploitation, however, invariably severs the rules from their ethical foundation and loses sight of their underlying object and purpose.

The events of 9/11 and their aftermath revealed complicated scenarios that do not fit easily into the traditional paradigms of the laws of war, including the 1949 Geneva Conventions.[2] Highly knowledgeable persons in the field have reached diametrically opposite conclu-

---

* Professor of Law, The George Washington University. The author wishes to thank John Crook, Ashley Deeks, Monica Hakimi, and Mike Matheson for very helpful comments on an earlier draft, and Kevin Futch ('08) and Kelly Dunn ('09) for excellent research assistance.

1 Hamdan v. Rumsfeld, 126 S. Ct. 2749 (2006).

2 Geneva Convention Relative to the Amelioration of the Condition of the Wounded and Sick in Armed Forces in the Field, Aug. 12, 1949, 6 U.S.T. 3114, 75 U.N.T.S. 31 [hereinafter Geneva Convention I]; Geneva Convention Relative to the Amelioration of the Condition of Wounded, Sick and Shipwrecked Members of Armed Forces at Sea, Aug. 12, 1949, 6 U.S.T. 3217, 75 U.N.T.S. 85 [hereinafter Geneva Convention II]; Geneva Convention Relative to the Treatment of Prisoners of War art. 4(A)(2), Aug. 12, 1949, 6 U.S.T. 3316, 75 U.N.T.S. 135 [hereinafter Geneva Convention III]; Geneva Convention Relative to the Protection of Civilian Persons in Time of War, Aug. 12, 1949, 6 U.S.T. 3516, 75 U.N.T.S. 287 [hereinafter Geneva Convention IV]. As of 2007, 194 states have adhered to the 1949 Geneva Conventions. *See* INT'L COMM. OF THE RED CROSS, STATE PARTIES TO THE FOLLOWING INTERNATIONAL HUMANITARIAN LAW AND OTHER TREATIES, http://www.icrc.org/IHL.nsf/(SPF)/party_main_treaties/$File/IHL_and_other_related_Treaties.pdf (last visited June 27, 2007) [hereinafter ICRC, STATE PARTIES].

sions about certain fundamental issues, such as whether the conflict with al Qaeda constitutes an "armed conflict" within the meaning of the laws of war, whether it matters if the Taliban wore regular uniforms or operated within a regular command structure, and whether a person who fails to qualify as a prisoner of war under one convention must invariably then qualify as a protected civilian under another. Many of these controversies arise because the two dominant paradigms that operate within the Geneva Conventions—one concerning "international" armed conflict (i.e., conflict between two or more states) and the other concerning "noninternational" armed conflict between a state and nonstate actors (typically understood as conflict internal to a single state)—do not fit the phenomenon of global terrorism, where the dominant paradigm concerns transnational armed conflict between state and nonstate actors.

Yet from their earliest formation, the laws of war have recognized the problem of dealing with irregular forces and the problem of adapting the law to circumstances that change over time. For that reason, built into the 1949 Geneva Conventions and their Additional Protocols are the means for taking account of areas that are not addressed explicitly or in detail. Rather than trying to exploit such gray areas in the law, lawyers should seek to inject the dictates of humanity into them in a manner that best reconciles the competing interests during armed conflict of both governments and persons who are at risk.

Part I of this Article recounts some of the history concerning the formation of contemporary laws of war, with a particular focus on the writings of Francis Lieber. This Part sets forth how the problem of the "guerrilla" (or "brigand" or "outlaw") is not unique to our post–9/11 era; it is a problem that has bedeviled the law of war for quite some time. Lieber saw it as desirable to try to draw distinctions among different types of guerrillas and to contemplate according varying levels of protection to each type. Thereafter, the laws of war began evolving to try to take account of certain kinds of guerrillas—such as civilians rising as part of a *levee en masse*, organized partisans operating in coordination with a belligerent, and peoples fighting against colonial domination or racist regimes—by according to them protections despite not being members of a state's regular armed forces. Even so, this evolution stopped short of seeking to accord protections under the laws of war to organizations engaged in terrorist activity.

Part II briefly recounts the two central paradigms that emerged for rules on protections of persons caught up in armed conflict in the post-Lieber era. Now reflected in the 1949 Geneva Conventions and their additional protocols, the two paradigms speak to rules that apply to "international" conflicts and rules that apply to "noninternational" armed conflicts. Here, too, the laws of war evolved in a manner that largely did not, at least expressly, address the phenomenon of a state-versus-non-state-actor conflict that was transnational in scope.

Part III recounts how these deficiencies played out in the aftermath of the terrorist attacks of 9/11. The central paradigms of the Geneva Conventions were strictly construed by the U.S. government, resulting in a classification of alleged Taliban and al Qaeda detainees as "combatants" who could be detained until the "cessation of hostilities," but as "unlawful" (or unprivileged) combatants who had no ability to take advantage of the protections normally accorded prisoners of war or civilian internees under the laws of war. Indeed, these two central paradigms proved inadequate for dealing with three different types of armed conflict that emerged in the post–9/11 period. Even so, a set of fundamental humanitarian principles—principles that are widely regarded as the hallmark of an advancing civilization—ultimately became recognized as relevant for regulating each of these conflicts. Article 3 common to the four Geneva Conventions came to be seen as a set of basic default rules that should be applied even in the unusual context of a conflict between a country and a global terrorist movement, al Qaeda.

Part IV explains why a parsimonious construction of the Geneva Conventions is neither helpful nor appropriate. Within the broader field of the laws of war exist concepts that allow the law to adapt to the changed circumstances that global terrorism presents. Although the immediate source of law relevant to the protection of persons in times of war is the 1949 Geneva Conventions, those conventions are embedded in a broader field (traditionally referred to as the *jus in bello*) that contains relevant, fundamental principles that transcend issue areas. Indeed, the manner in which events unfolded after 9/11 suggests that states moved ultimately to a position of applying fundamental principles of international humanitarian law to the unusual circumstances that unfolded. As an example of how one might allow the Geneva Conventions to evolve in a sensible fashion, Part IV discusses the rules that should be applied with respect to the termination of the captivity of unprivileged combatants, such as those held at Guantanamo Bay. Though the environment for handling such detainees remains fluid and the norms expressed by the laws of war on these points are far from certain, this Article suggests answers that are legally plausible and that appear consistent with sound policy choices.

Similar efforts to fill in the gray areas for other aspects of the law of war as it relates to global terrorism should also be pursued.

I. Of Guerrillas and Brigands: The Ghost of Francis Lieber

The problem of the unprivileged or irregular combatant in a time of armed conflict is not new to the laws of war.[3] From the start, efforts to codify the laws of war have grappled with whether and how to accommodate the phenomenon of persons fighting outside regular military units. By recounting some of the early history of these codification efforts, this Part seeks to demonstrate that this is an old problem, and that the laws of war have emerged cognizant of its existence.

Contemporary laws of war often are traced back to the writings of Francis Lieber during the course of the American Civil War. Lieber is best known as the author of one of the first codifications of the laws of land warfare—the 1863 *Instructions for the Government of Armies of the United States in the Field*[4]—which thereafter influenced the development of national manuals on warfare by many countries, and helped pave the way for the 1899 and 1907 Hague conventions on the laws of war.[5] Less known is his work on the problem of "guerrillas" during wartime.[6] After the outbreak of the Civil War, the Union Army found itself confronted not just by the Confederate Armies operating largely as armies do (i.e., under a centralized command, with regular and open movements, etc.), but by a wide range of irregular forces that were loosely referred to as "guerrillas." General Henry Halleck, the General-in-Chief of the Union Armies, and also an acclaimed expert in the field of international law,[7] asked Lieber for his

[3] *See* Edward Kossoy, Living with Guerrilla 47–58 (1976) (tracing the history of guerrilla warfare to antiquity).

[4] The instructions were part of the U.S. War Department's General Orders No. 100, which is reprinted in Richard Shelly Hartigan, Lieber's Code and the Law of War 45 (1983).

[5] *See* Theodor Meron, *Francis Lieber's Code and Principles of Humanity*, 36 Colum. J. Transnat'l L. 269, 278–79 (1997) ("Both the Code's high quality and its timing, written when no other significant compilations of laws and customs of war were available, can explain its tremendous impact on the codification of international humanitarian law.").

[6] Even less known is that Lieber had sons who fought on both sides of the American Civil War (one of whom died), *see* Hartigan, *supra* note 4, at 6–7, which no doubt animated his interest in promoting humanity in warfare.

[7] *See* H.W. Halleck, International Law; Or, Rules Regarding the Intercourse of States in Peace or War (1861).

views on how to treat such guerrillas: were they to be treated simply as criminals or as something else?[8]

Lieber's essay responding to Halleck, entitled *Guerrilla Parties Considered with Reference to the Laws and Usages of War*,[9] helped clarify that there were differing types of guerrillas who were entitled to differing levels of protection.[10] After noting the origins of the term "guerrilla"—"the diminutive of the Spanish word guerra," thus meaning "petty war"[11]—Lieber stated: "it is universally understood in this country at the present time that a guerrilla party means an irregular band of armed men, carrying on an irregular war, not being able, according to their character as a guerrilla party, to carry on what the law terms a regular war."[12] That understanding speaks volumes to us today as we consider the threat of a terrorist organization such as al Qaeda, which cannot operate in the manner of a regular army and yet can carry on acts that in their violence and intensity can approximate that of a military attack.

For Lieber, this broad understanding of "guerrillas" was not good enough; one needed to dig deeper and to be more discriminating. He considered multiple "ideas" that could be associated with multiple types of guerrillas. One idea of the guerrilla is simply an irregular force that is self-constituted and not a part of the normal process of conscription or volunteering for the regular army.[13] Such a guerrilla force might be fighting for the same cause as an army, and it might operate in close coordination with the army, but it is not associated with the system of army "pay, provision, and movements."[14] Because the guerrilla force is not self-sustaining, Lieber noted that such guerrilla's might be engaged in pillaging of the countryside, an act that imposed hardships on the civilian population, but that to a certain extent is an understandable necessity for such a force.[15]

Yet Lieber identified far more pernicious ideas of the guerilla that might arise. For example, a guerrilla group might be motivated by an "idea of intentional destruction for the sake of destruction, because the guerrilla chief cannot aim at any strategic advantages or any

---

8 *See* HARTIGAN, *supra* note 4, at 2.

9 FRANCIS LIEBER, GUERRILLA PARTIES CONSIDERED WITH REFERENCE TO THE LAWS AND USAGES OF WAR (1861), *reprinted in* HARTIGAN, *supra* note 4, at 31.

10 *See id.* at 33–34.

11 *Id.* at 31.

12 *Id.* at 33.

13 *See id.*

14 *See id.*

15 *See id.*

regular fruits of victory."[16] Similarly pernicious is the idea of guerrillas engaging in "necessitated murder, because guerrilla bands cannot encumber themselves with prisoners of war; they have, therefore, frequently, perhaps generally, killed their prisoners . . . thus introducing a system of barbarity which becomes intenser in its demoralization as it spreads and is prolonged."[17] Indeed, since the organization of some guerrillas

> being but slight and the leader utterly dependent upon the band, little discipline can be enforced, and where no discipline is enforced in war a state of things results which resembles far more the wars recorded in Froissart, or Comines, or the thirty-years' war, and the religious war in France, than the regular wars of modern times.[18]

These more pernicious ideas resonate with the contemporary sense of the terrorist threat and with some of the sentiments felt by those responding to that threat.

Hence, Lieber thought it useful to classify various types of persons who fall within the general rubric of "guerrilla," to wit: "The freebooter, the marauder, the brigand, the partisan, the free corps, the spy, the rebel, the conspirator, the robber, and especially the highway robber, the rising en masse, or the 'arming of peasants.'"[19] Some of these types of persons might be allied closely with a regular army; Lieber viewed "partisans" as a corps operating separately from a main army but that is nevertheless "part and parcel of the army."[20] Such persons are not inherently lawless and may be entitled to the benefits of the laws of war.[21] Other types of persons may not be allied with a regular army but are still entitled to protection, such as the rising *en masse* of peasants to resist an invasion.[22] Yet there are those who fall outside any protection. Lieber wrote:

> It is different if we understand by guerrilla parties, self-constituted sets of armed men in times of war, who form no integrant part of the organized army, do not stand on the regular pay-roll of the army, or are not paid at all, take up arms and lay them down at intervals, and carry on petty war (guerrilla) chiefly by raids, extortion, destruction, and massa-

16 *Id.*

17 *Id.*

18 *Id.* at 33–34.

19 *Id.* at 34.

20 *Id.* at 35.

21 *See id.* at 35–36.

22 *See id.* at 38–39.

> cre, and who cannot encumber themselves with many prisoners, and who will therefore generally give no quarter.
>
> They are peculiarly dangerous because they easily evade pursuit, and by laying down their arms become insidious enemies; because they cannot otherwise subsist than by rapine, and almost always degenerate into simply robbers or brigands.[23]

Although such persons might be granted certain protections if captured in the midst of a "fair fight and open warfare,"[24] as a general matter such persons are to be treated as "brigand[s]," who are "subject to the infliction of death if captured."[25] Lieber concludes his essay with the admonition that "no army, no society engaged in war, any more than a society at peace, can allow unpunished assassination, robbery, and devastation without the deepest injury to itself and disastrous conseq[u]ences which might change the very issue of war."[26]

Thus, although Lieber is credited with helping launch the formation of our contemporary international humanitarian law,[27] he regarded a certain category of brigands as being fully outside the scope of that law and viewed such persons as a unique threat to society that could not be tolerated. Though Lieber did not identify specific persons or groups during the Civil War that would fall into differing categories of guerrillas, one can imagine what he had in mind.[28] For example, one of the main guerrilla groups operating outside the Confederate command system, comprising in total up to 800 men, was under the command of John Singleton Mosby in Western Virginia. Small squads of "Mosby's Rangers" would attack Union outposts and wagon trains with such vigor that the area became know as "Mosby's Confederacy."[29] One imagines that these forces, preying solely upon the Union military, were viewed by Lieber as a somewhat more acceptable form of guerrilla: Confederate partisans who shared the objectives and targets of an established belligerent.

By contrast, a very different form of guerrilla was epitomized by William Clarke Quantrill, whose raiders in Kansas and Missouri sim-

---

23 *Id.* at 41.

24 *Id.* at 42.

25 *Id.*

26 *Id.* at 44.

27 *See generally* Meron, *supra* note 5 (discussing how "Lieber left an indelible imprint on humanitarian law").

28 HARTIGAN, *supra* note 4, at 11.

29 *See* JAMES M. MCPHERSON, BATTLE CRY OF FREEDOM: THE CIVIL WAR ERA 737–38 (1988).

ply slaughtered unarmed soldiers and civilians, including an infamous massacre at Lawrence, Kansas in 1863.[30] As James McPherson has put it, "[t]he guerrilla fighting in Missouri produced a form of terrorism that exceeded anything else in the war. Jayhawking Kansans and bushwhacking Missourians took no prisoners, killed in cold blood, plundered and pillaged and burned (but almost never raped) without stint."[31] Lieber no doubt viewed such raiders as the "peculiarly dangerous" brigands that society simply cannot tolerate and that the laws of war do not protect.[32]

The contemporary terrorist threat posed by a group such as al Qaeda is largely viewed in the United States as comparable to Lieber's guerrilla brigands. The terrorist may have some generalized strategic objective, but he operates in a free-wheeling manner unmoored from the constraints of being a sovereign entity and engages in attacks that fail to discriminate between military and nonmilitary targets. To the extent that the United States regards members of al Qaeda as contemporary brigands who are qualitatively different from those the laws of war were intended to protect, it appears that Lieber's ghost is still with us.

Lieber was concerned with the "guerrilla" principally as a feature of a civil war, of course—not as a stand-alone phenomenon—and that has been the case since his time as well. The normal guerrilla model is one of indigenous bands fighting against a colonial oppressor (e.g., French partisans fighting the German Army in occupied France during World War II or the Algerian Front de Libération Nationale fighting the French Army in Algeria in 1954–1962) or fighting against an indigenous government (e.g., Fidel Castro's rise to power in Cuba in 1956–1959). Though operating with many of the same tactics and objectives as guerrillas of the past, a terrorist group such as al Qaeda is far more transnational in nature, and it operates without any connection to a sustained contestation with a standing army.

Since Lieber's time, the laws of war have evolved in ways that accommodate some aspects of the phenomenon of the guerrilla. The 1899 and 1907 Hague Peace Conferences accorded combatant status to "militia" and "volunteer corps" who fulfilled certain conditions and to persons engaged in a *levée en masse*, whereby civilians spontaneously take up arms to resist an invading force in unoccupied terri-

30 *Id.* at 784–86.

31 *Id.* at 784.

32 *Cf.* HARTIGAN, *supra* note 4, at 11.

tory.[33] The latter persons, though civilians, can become protected POWs so long as they carry their arms openly and obey the laws and customs of war.[34] After World War II, combatant status was further expanded to include "organized resistance movements,"[35] such as the French forces who fought within France during the Nazi occupation.

With the advent of global terrorist movements, such as al Qaeda, it has become necessary to consider whether and how the laws of war apply to such movements. On the one hand, persons associated with al Qaeda may be seen as modern outlaws or brigands, entitled to no protection as "unprivileged" combatants. On the other hand, the magnitude of the threat posed by such a movement has prompted the United States to view its response as a "war on terrorism," to invoke legal doctrines associated with wartime action, and to deploy vast military forces to combat the threat. The next Part discusses how the central paradigms that exist under contemporary laws of war do not easily address the phenomenon of global terrorism.

II. The Central Paradigms in the 1949 Geneva Conventions

The 1949 Geneva Conventions are principally concerned with *international* armed conflicts, by which is meant armed conflicts that arise between two or more states. Though it does not matter whether either of the states formally recognizes the existence of a "war," nor whether they recognize the legitimacy of each other, the Conventions' several hundred articles are built around the paradigm of two opposing states, operating normally through the use of their regular armies, though perhaps assisted by militias or volunteer corps. Thus, Geneva Convention III on the treatment of prisoners of war ("POWs") anticipates that the well-functioning government of each belligerent will be in a position to detain prisoners at organized camps, where a variety of rights can be accorded to the prisoners and where a protecting power may monitor the prisoner's well-being. A modern application

---

33 *See* Regulations Respecting the Laws and Customs of War on Land arts. 1–2 [hereinafter Hague Regulations], *annexed to* Convention Respecting the Laws and Customs of War on Land, Oct. 18, 1907, 36 Stat. 2277, 187 Consol. T.S. 227 [hereinafter Hague Convention]; *see also* KOSSOY, *supra* note 3, at 73–105 (examining the text, historical origins, interpretation, and application of articles 1 and 2 of the Hague Regulations).

34 *See* Hague Regulations, *supra* note 33, art. 2.

35 *See* Geneva Convention III, *supra* note 2, art. 4(A)(2); KOSSOY, *supra* note 3, at 106–12 (tracing the development of Geneva Convention III). *See generally* Theodore Draper, *The Status of Combatants and the Question of Guerrilla Warfare*, 45 BRIT. Y.B. INT'L L. 173 (1971) (tracing the development of guerrilla warfare and examining the legal status of combatants under the Hague Regulations and Geneva Convention III).

of Geneva Convention III may be seen in Ethiopia's treatment of Eritrean prisoners during the 1998–2000 Ethiopia-Eritrea War. Though Ethiopia viewed Eritrea as having initiated the war by its May 1998 invasion,[36] nevertheless Ethiopia, as a party to the 1949 Geneva Conventions, operated its prison camps largely in accordance with Geneva Convention III, and allowed access by the International Committee of the Red Cross ("ICRC") throughout the conflict.[37]

This paradigm of two opposing states engaged in an interstate armed conflict is also apparent with respect to the protections accorded to civilians. Geneva Convention IV largely contemplates two particular categories of civilians who need protection in the course of a conventional armed conflict between two states: (1) civilians of one belligerent who happen to be in the other belligerent's territory, such as might occur at the outbreak of the armed conflict; and (2) civilians who are in their own country but fall under the occupation of the enemy belligerent.[38] Thus, the Convention is closely tied into the notion of geography; it assumes that both of the belligerents will be exercising sovereign control over territory and thus will have obligations with respect to enemy aliens located within that territory.[39]

---

36 *Jus Ad Bellum* (Eth. v. Eri.), Ethiopia's Claims Nos. 1–8, Partial Award, paras. 6 & 8 (Eritrea Ethiopia Claims Comm'n Dec. 19, 2005), 45 I.L.M. 430 (2006). The author served as counsel to Ethiopia for the Eritrea-Ethiopia claims referenced in this Article.

37 Prisoners of War (Eth. v. Eri.), Ethiopia's Claim No. 4, Partial Award paras. 45, 55 (Eritrea Ethiopia Claims Comm'n July 1, 2003), 42 I.L.M. 1056, 1064 (2003).

38 *See* Geneva Convention IV, *supra* note 2, at pt. III, § II (provisions on aliens in the territory of a party to the conflict) and pt. III, § III (provisions on persons in occupied territory).

39 Here, too, the recent Ethiopia-Eritrea War demonstrates the paradigm. The Eritrea Ethiopia Claims Commission determined that, under Geneva Convention IV, Eritrea was bound to various obligations as an occupying power in Ethiopia over the course of two years, and further had obligations with respect to Ethiopians that found themselves in Eritrea at the outbreak of the war. Ethiopia had the same obligations with respect to its brief occupation of Eritrean territory in 2000 and with respect to Eritreans who were in Ethiopia at the outbreak of the war. *See* Civilians' Claims (Eth. v. Eri.), Eritrea's Claims Nos. 15, 16, 23, & 27–32 (Eritrea Ethiopia Claims Comm'n Dec. 17, 2004), 44 I.L.M. 601 (2005); Civilians' Claims (Eth. v. Eri.), Ethiopia's Claim No. 5 (Eritrea Ethiopia Claims Comm'n Dec. 17, 2004), 44 I.L.M. 630 (2005).

In the context of a discussion about "asymmetric warfare," it is interesting to note that Eritrea only acceded to the 1949 Geneva Conventions in August 2000 and thus was not—as a matter of treaty law—bound to them for most of the armed conflict. Nevertheless, Ethiopia determined that it would act in accordance with the Conventions in its treatment of victims of the conflict, and called upon Eritrea to do the same. After the conflict was over, the Claims Commission found that contemporary customary international humanitarian law was "exemplified by the relevant parts of the four Geneva Conventions of 1949." The Commission noted: (1) the widespread acceptance by states of the conventions over the course of their fifty-year existence; (2) that law of war treaties "build upon the foundation laid by earlier treaties and by customary international law"; and (3) that "rules that commend themselves to the international community in general . . . can more quickly become part of customary international law than

The 1949 Geneva Conventions do contemplate an alternative paradigm, in the form of armed conflict that is *not* international in nature. Article 3 common to all four conventions ("Common Article 3") briefly sets forth certain minimum standards that are to be applied "[i]n the case of armed conflict not of an international character occurring in the territory of one of the High Contracting Parties."[40] Those standards provide that persons no longer taking active part in such hostilities "shall in all circumstances be treated humanely" and, to that end, certain acts against them are prohibited:

> (a) violence to life and person, in particular murder of all kinds, mutilation, cruel treatment and torture;
> (b) taking of hostages;
> (c) outrages upon personal dignity, in particular, humiliating and degrading treatment;
> (d) the passing of sentences and carrying out of executions without previous judgment pronounced by a regularly constituted court affording all the judicial guarantees which are recognized as indispensable by civilized peoples.[41]

Further, the parties to such a conflict should "endeavour to bring into force, by means of special agreements, all or part of the other provisions of [the Geneva Conventions]."[42]

A fair reading of the negotiating history suggests that this Common Article 3 paradigm was principally designed to address the situation of an armed conflict *internal* to a single state.[43] One of the parties

---

other types of rules found in treaties." Partial Award on Prisoners of War, *supra* note 37, paras. 30–31. Consequently, the Commission found that Ethiopia and Eritrea were bound throughout their conflict to rules of customary international law as reflected in the 1949 Geneva Conventions.

40 Geneva Conventions I–IV, *supra* note 2, art. 3.

41 *Id.* art. 3(1).

42 *Id.*

43 *See, e.g.*, GEOFFREY BEST, WAR AND LAW SINCE 1945, at 169 (1994) ("The Red Cross movement . . . , as after the war it focused on the question of revising and improving the Geneva Conventions, had their extension to civil wars in the centre of its sights."); Richard R. Baxter, *Ius in Bello Interno: The Present and Future Law*, *in* LAW AND CIVIL WAR IN THE MODERN WORLD 518, 519 (John Norton Moore ed., 1974) ("The [1949 Diplomatic Conference held in Geneva] ultimately came around to the view that the most that states could be expected to accept would be a short statement of the basic humanitarian principles that should be given effect in civil conflicts. The result was Article 3 . . . ."); Derek Jinks, *September 11 and the Laws of War*, 28 YALE J. INT'L L. 1, 39–40 (2003); *see also* U.S. DEP'T OF THE ARMY, FIELD MANUAL NO. 27-10: THE LAW OF LAND WARFARE 9 (1956) (quoting Common Article 3 in discussing the law applicable to "civil war"); U.K. MINISTRY OF DEF., THE MANUAL OF THE LAW OF ARMED CONFLICT 384–86 (2004) (discussing Common Article 3 as applying to "internal armed conflict"). The same thinking carried over to the initial negotiations of the additional protocols. *See* MICHAEL

to that armed conflict would normally be the government of the state; the other party would be a major insurgent group seeking to obtain control of the country. Thus, Common Article 3 contemplates an armed conflict between a state and nonstate actor, but does so largely in the context of the classic civil war. For such a conflict, the Geneva Conventions do not accord any "prisoner of war" or "protected civilian" status to detainees. Moreover, detainees may be prosecuted under the criminal laws of the state for having engaged in violent acts; there is no privileging of their conduct under the laws of war. Yet certain minimum standards of Common Article 3 do apply: persons who are no longer taking an active part in the hostilities must be treated humanely and cannot be exposed to violence, outrages upon personal dignity, or the passing of sentence or execution without a judgment pronounced by a regularly-constituted court.

The paradigms of the 1949 Geneva Conventions were largely followed and extended by two 1977 protocols, generally referred to as "Protocol I"[44] and "Protocol II."[45] Protocol I focuses on codifying and developing the law relating to the first paradigm—international armed conflict—by clarifying and advancing the law both on protection of victims and on means and methods of war.[46] With respect to the protection of victims, Protocol I revisits, clarifies, and expands on the various protections addressed in the earlier 1907 Hague Regulations and the 1949 Geneva Conventions.[47] In particular, as discussed further below, article 75 of Protocol I lays down a series of fundamental protec-

---

BOTHE, KARL JOSEF PARTSCH & WALDEMAR A. SOLF, NEW RULES FOR VICTIMS OF ARMED CONFLICTS: COMMENTARY ON THE TWO 1977 PROTOCOLS ADDITIONAL TO THE GENEVA CONVENTIONS OF 1949, at 39 (1982) [hereinafter NEW RULES] ("The *pre-conference work* . . . was based on the following concept: The distinction between international and national conflicts, which is made on the factual and objective basis of whether a conflict takes place in the territory of different States or inside one particular State . . . , should be maintained.").

44 Protocol Additional to the Geneva Conventions of 12 August 1949, and Relating to the Protection of Victims of International Armed Conflicts, June 8, 1977, 1125 U.N.T.S. 3 [hereinafter Protocol I].

45 Protocol Additional to the Geneva Conventions of 12 August 1949, and Relating to the Protection of Victims of Non-International Armed Conflicts, June 8, 1977, 1125 U.N.T.S. 609 [hereinafter Protocol II]. In December 2005, a third additional protocol was adopted to create an additional emblem alongside the Red Cross and Red Crescent, *see* Protocol Additional to the Geneva Conventions of 12 August 1949, and Relating to the Adoption of an Additional Distinctive Emblem, Dec. 8, 2005, 45 I.L.M. 558 (Protocol III), *available at* http://www.icrc.org/ihl.nsf/FULL/615, known as the red crystal, *see* Int'l Comm. of the Red Cross, Additional Emblem: Questions and Answers (Dec. 6, 2005), http://www.icrc.org/web/Eng/siteeng0.nsf/html/emblem-questions-answers-281005.

46 *See* Protocol I, *supra* note 44, arts. 10, 11, 35.

47 For the authoritative ICRC commentary on the meaning of Protocols I and II and their relationship to earlier treaties, see INT'L COMM. OF THE RED CROSS, COMMENTARY ON THE

tions to which all persons "in the power of a Party to the conflict" are entitled without discrimination.[48] As of 2007, 167 states have adhered to Protocol I, not including the United States.[49]

Protocol II focuses on the law relating to the second paradigm, stating that it "develops and supplements Article 3 common to the Geneva Conventions."[50] In so doing, Protocol II expressly states that it covers conflicts "which take place . . . between [a High Contracting Party's] armed forces and dissident armed forces or other organized armed groups which, under responsible command, exercise such control over a part of its territory as to enable them to carry out sustained and concerted military operations and to implement this Protocol."[51] Such language confirms the general understanding that Common Article 3 is focused on internal armed conflicts or civil wars. Protocol II then lays down a series of fundamental protections to which all persons involved in internal conflicts are entitled without discrimination.[52] As of 2007, 163 states had adhered to the protocol, not including the United States.[53]

The problem of the "guerrilla" was partially addressed as a part of Protocol I. Article 1(4) of Protocol I extended "international armed conflict" to cover armed conflicts involving peoples "fighting against colonial domination and alien occupation and against racist regimes in the exercise of their right of self-determination."[54] Thus, just as Lieber grappled with making distinctions among different kinds of guerrillas, deeming some kinds entitled to full protection,[55] a particular type of modern-day guerrilla—the nonstate actor fighting against a colonial or racist regime—is allowed to enter into the full realm of the 1949 Geneva Conventions (not just the realm of Common Article 3). Such guerrillas are expected to conduct themselves in a manner that approximates the conduct expected of a regular army; thus they can receive POW status if captured so long as they take certain limited steps to distinguish themselves from the civilian population at the time

---

ADDITIONAL PROTOCOLS OF 8 JUNE 1977 TO THE GENEVA CONVENTIONS OF 12 AUGUST 1949 (Yves Sandoz et al. eds., 1987) [hereinafter SANDOZ COMMENTARY].

48 Protocol I, *supra* note 44, art. 75.

49 *See* ICRC, STATE PARTIES, *supra* note 2.

50 Protocol II, *supra* note 45, art. 1.

51 *Id.*

52 *Id.* arts. 2, 4.

53 *See* ICRC, STATE PARTIES, *supra* note 2.

54 Protocol I, *supra* note 44, art. 1(4).

55 *See supra* notes 9–26 and accompanying text.

of their attacks.[56] If they fail to so conduct themselves, they are still granted protections "equivalent in all respects to those accorded" to POWs under Geneva Convention III and Protocol I,[57] including judicial safeguards, but the conduct constitutes a violation of international law for which the guerrilla may be prosecuted.[58] There is no requirement that the nonstate actor control a portion of territory, and therefore it may operate entirely from bases located in adjacent countries.[59]

The United States opposed this expansive approach of Protocol I, claiming that it accords far too much protection and legitimacy to nonstate groups, potentially including terrorist organizations.[60] Even if the United States had ratified Protocol I, characterizing the Taliban or al Qaeda as engaged in conflict with the United States as a fight "against colonial domination and alien occupation" or against a "racist" regime, is a considerable stretch; for all its missteps, the United States never colonized Afghanistan, nor engaged in racist oppression of the kind seen in South Africa or Rhodesia. Further, al Qaeda has never made the necessary unilateral declaration seeking status, and assuming rights and obligations, under Protocol I.[61] In short, although Protocol I may be seen as extending the full panoply of laws-of-war protections to certain contemporary guerrillas, it does not do so with respect to the entire range of nonstate actors. In any event, the United States rejected Protocol I principally because of the expansion of the traditional laws of war it embodies.

Hence, as originally designed, the 1949 Geneva Conventions left something of a gray area. Conflicts between two states were regulated

---

56 Protocol I, *supra* note 44, art. 44(3). They may dress in civilian clothing and carry their arms secretly, but they must carry their arms openly just before and during their attack. *See id.*

57 *Id.* art. 44(4).

58 *See* New Rules, *supra* note 43, at 255.

59 *See* Leslie C. Green, The Contemporary Law of Armed Conflict 321 (2d ed. 2000). By contrast, Protocol II requires that the nonstate actor control part of the national territory, making its application to guerrillas problematic. According to Green:

> If the dissident forces are constantly on the move and lack any fixed location from which to exercise control the Protocol [II] will not operate. Guerrilla or partisan activities against the administration, however effective, would therefore not be protected by the Protocol, though they would be covered by Common Article 3.

Id.

60 For a discussion of the U.S. rejection of Protocol I, see generally Hans-Peter Gasser, *Agora: The U.S. Decision Not to Ratify Protocol I to the Geneva Conventions on the Protection of War Victims*, 81 Am. J. Int'l L. 910 (1987); Abraham D. Sofaer, *Agora: The U.S. Decision Not to Ratify Protocol I to the Geneva Conventions on the Protection of War Victims (Cont'd)*, 82 Am. J. Int'l L. 784 (1988); *see also* Theodor Meron, *The Time Has Come for the United States to Ratify Geneva Protocol I*, 88 Am. J. Int'l L. 678 (1994).

61 Protocol I, *supra* note 44, art. 96(3).

and conflicts between a state and an insurgency were regulated, but (with the one exception in Protocol I discussed above) nothing specifically addressed a transnational conflict between a state and a nonstate actor. In the aftermath of 9/11, the Bush administration sought to exploit that gray area as one means for denying to al Qaeda detainees any of the protections accorded under the 1949 Geneva Conventions, including Common Article 3. On the one hand, the Bush administration argued that there was no interstate conflict between the United States and al Qaeda, as al Qaeda was not a state; on the other hand, members of al Qaeda fell outside Common Article 3 because al Qaeda was not an insurgency against the U.S. government within U.S. territory.

Views have differed over whether the administration's position with respect to al Qaeda was correct, but few would disagree that the intervention in Afghanistan introduced an array of problems in applying the Geneva Convention paradigms and exposed the paradigms' weaknesses and limits. The circumstances that unfolded in Afghanistan ultimately may prove to be *sui generis*, but the ability of terrorist groups to thrive in countries where there is a poorly functioning government (at present, countries such as Somalia and Sudan come to mind) suggests that history in this context may well repeat itself. The next Part briefly recounts that history.

III. The Paradigms Applied Post–9/11

The events that followed 9/11, especially but not exclusively as they relate to al Qaeda, do not fit neatly into 1949 Geneva Conventions' paradigms. Most observers would likely accept that there were three types of conflicts that came into play: (1) an internal armed conflict between the Northern Alliance and the Taliban, a conflict that predated 9/11; (2) an international armed conflict between a U.S.-led coalition of states and Afghanistan; and (3) a particularly-hard-to-analyze conflict between the United States and a nonstate organization, al Qaeda. By considering each of these conflicts in turn, it becomes apparent why many roads in contemporary armed conflict can lead to application of the minimum standards of Common Article 3, rather than the full range of protections contained in the 1949 Geneva Conventions as a whole.

A. *De Jure Afghan Government/Northern Alliance versus De Facto Afghan Government (Taliban).*

The post–9/11 period saw an armed conflict between members of the Northern Alliance and the Taliban, but that conflict predated 9/11. Two principal actors were engaged in that armed conflict: a de jure government of Afghanistan that politically headed military forces in the form of the Northern Alliance and a de facto government of Afghanistan in the form of the Taliban.

Burhanuddin Rabbani headed the government of Afghanistan at the time of the rise of the Taliban. Rabbani had previously served as a leader of the mujahideen in their fight against Soviet rule in Afghanistan. Rabbani's forces were the first mujahideen group to enter Kabul in 1992 when the puppet communist government was overthrown. Rabbani then served as President of Afghanistan from 1992 to 1996 until he was forced to leave Kabul because of the Taliban takeover of the city.

As discussed in somewhat more detail below, the Taliban was originally a religious movement that, in 1994, began military operations to seize control of Afghanistan.[62] From 1994 to 2001, it was in relatively constant armed conflict with the existing Afghan warlords and their militias, who ultimately banded together in 1996–1997 to form the Afghan Northern Alliance, formally known as the "United Islamic Front for the Salvation of Afghanistan." By 2001, the Taliban had gained control of ninety percent of the territory of Afghanistan. Thus, as of 9/11, the de facto government of Afghanistan was the Taliban.

Though ousted from control of Afghanistan, Rabbani maintained that he was the head of the Afghan government and continued to control most of Afghanistan's embassies abroad. Further, his representatives retained Afghanistan's seat at the United Nations. Meanwhile, the U.N. General Assembly repeatedly deferred consideration of the Taliban representative's credentials. Rabbani was regarded as the political head of the Northern Alliance and his military commander, Ahmed Shah Massoud (and later Mohammed Fahim after Massoud's assassination), maintained control of the ten percent of Afghanistan (in the northeast) not under Taliban control. It was Rabbani who formally handed over power to an interim government headed by Hamid Karzai on December 22, 2001.

62 *See generally* PETER MARSDEN, THE TALIBAN: WAR, RELIGION AND THE NEW ORDER IN AFGHANISTAN (1998).

One might regard this Northern Alliance–Taliban conflict as fitting the paradigm of a noninternational armed conflict, because it has the characteristics of an internal armed conflict (or civil war). If so, then Common Article 3 would set forth the governing norms from the 1949 Geneva Conventions, because Afghanistan ratified the conventions in 1956. As Afghanistan has not yet ratified Protocol II,[63] both sides in this conflict would be obligated to adhere to the minimum standards set forth in Common Article 3, but not the more detailed standards of the remainder of the Geneva Conventions or of Protocol II.

Afghan politics, however, are anything but simple. Even in 1996 the Security Council was calling on foreign countries to stop sending arms, ammunition, and personnel in support of the Afghan parties, and declaring that continuation of the conflict provided "fertile ground for terrorism and drug trafficking which destabilize the region and beyond . . . ."[64] The perception that the conflict had international dimensions was reinforced in 1998 when the Security Council directly addressed the application of the laws of war to Afghanistan. Expressing concern that the conflict was "causing a serious and growing threat to regional and international peace and security"[65] and that there had been "foreign interference in Afghanistan, including the involvement of foreign military personnel and the supply of arms and ammunition to all parties in the conflict,"[66] the Security Council expressly and unanimously reaffirmed

> that all parties to the conflict are bound to comply with their obligations under international humanitarian law and in particular the Geneva Conventions of 12 August 1949, and that persons who commit or order the commission of grave breaches of the Conventions are individually responsible in respect of such breaches.[67]

The reference to "grave breaches" of the Convention appears to signal a belief by the members of the Security Council that the entirety of the 1949 Geneva Conventions (not just Common Article 3) applied to the Afghan civil war,[68] as the grave breaches provisions relate to various obligations under the conventions other than Common

---

63 *See* ICRC, STATE PARTIES, *supra* note 2.

64 S.C. Res. 1076, pmbl. & ¶¶ 3–5, U.N. DOC. S/RES/1076 (Oct. 22, 1996).

65 S.C. Res. 1193, pmbl., U.N. DOC. S/RES/1193 (Aug. 28, 1998).

66 *Id.*

67 *Id.* para. 12.

68 *See* Adam Roberts, *The Laws of War in the War on Terror*, *in* INTERNATIONAL LAW AND THE WAR ON TERROR 175, 193 (Fred L. Borch & Paul S. Wilson eds., 2003).

Article 3, such as unlawful deportation or transfer.[69] This has prompted some scholars to refer to the Afghan conflict—even prior to the events of 2001—as an "internationalized civil war"[70] or "internationalized non-international armed conflict."[71] Similar phenomena of largely civil wars that attract foreign involvement may be seen in prior conflicts in Vietnam, Cambodia, and Lebanon,[72] and also in situations where a unitary state in the midst of civil war fragments into several new states, as occurred in the former Yugoslavia.[73] In such cases, one might take the position that "the whole of the law of armed conflict would apply,"[74] or might more cautiously maintain that "the rules pertaining to both international and civil wars may be applicable in different aspects and phases of the conflict."[75] After the intervention in the Afghan conflict by the U.S.-led coalition in October 2001, whereby coalition forces joined the Northern Alliance in largely ousting the Taliban from their control of Afghanistan, it seems plausible to maintain that, whatever might have been the situation before, the Afghan conflict either:

- had been transformed into an international armed conflict, thus binding all parties (foreign and Afghan) to the full panoply of obligations of the Geneva Conventions; or
- now consisted of two armed conflicts, one that was internal between the Northern Alliance and the Taliban (governed by Common Article 3), and another that was international between the Coalition and the Taliban (governed by the full Geneva Conventions).[76]

The first scenario is not very compelling, in that no matter what facts may develop on the ground, the 1949 Geneva Conventions were not designed to impose obligations (other than those contained in Common Article 3) on nonstate actors. The second scenario is also

69 *See* Geneva Convention IV, *supra* note 2, arts. 146–47.

70 *Id.*

71 Hans-Peter Gasser, *Internationalized Non-International Armed Conflicts: Case Studies of Afghanistan, Kampuchea and Lebanon*, 33 Am. U. L. Rev. 145, 145, 150–51 (1983).

72 *See* Baxter, *supra* note 43, at 523–24 (discussing Vietnam); Gasser, *supra* note 71, at 152–57 (discussing Cambodia and Lebanon); *see also* Hilaire McCoubrey & Nigel D. White, International Organizations and Civil Wars 63–65 (1995) (discussing implications of an "internationalized" civil war). *See generally* The International Law of Civil War (Richard A. Falk ed., 1971).

73 *See* A.P.V. Rogers, Law on the Battlefield 220 (2d ed. 2004).

74 *Id.* at 219.

75 Roberts, *supra* note 68, at 193.

76 *Cf.* George H. Aldrich, *The Taliban, al Qaeda, and the Determination of Illegal Combatants*, 96 Am. J. Int'l L. 891, 893 (2002).

problematic, because it envisages two completely separate sets of rules governing allied armed forces that may be fighting side-by-side, perhaps even inviting the more-regulated force to shift certain responsibilities to the less-regulated force so as to avoid significant laws-of-war obligations. Further confusion arises in determining whether either scenario continued after the Taliban had been severely decimated and driven to the southern part of the country, and particularly after the Afghan Interim Authority assumed power in December 2001, followed in June 2002 by creation of the Afghan Transitional Government. According to the ICRC, after June 2002 there was no longer any international armed conflict in Afghanistan, only an internal armed conflict.[77] That conclusion may seem odd given that, as of late 2006, there remained about 20,000 U.S. troops in Afghanistan engaged in active fighting against the Taliban.[78] Yet the theory is that, by June 2002, there were two states—the United States (and its allies of course) and Afghanistan—that were no longer engaged in an armed conflict with each other. The conflict was between the new, internationally recognized and internationally supported Afghan government and a largely indigenous insurgent group, the Taliban. As such, the conflict was noninternational in nature and was principally governed by Common Article 3 of the Geneva Conventions.

B. U.S.-Led Coalition of States versus Afghanistan

In light of the above, it seems clear that there was an international armed conflict between the states of the U.S.-led coalition and Afghanistan that commenced on October 7, 2001, with the coalition bombing campaign against targets in Afghanistan. All four of the 1949 Geneva Conventions came into play at that time with respect to actions between the belligerents. That campaign was directed against both the de facto government of the Taliban and against the terrorist organization al Qaeda, but this particular conflict is best analyzed as only encompassing the Taliban and those members of al Qaeda who were integrated into Taliban fighting units and who fought alongside the Taliban in Afghanistan.

The United States took the view that members of the armed forces of the de facto government of Afghanistan, the Taliban, would not be accorded POW status under Geneva Convention III.[79] At the

77 *See* Roberts, *supra* note 68, at 196.

78 *See* Ann Scott Tyson, *Taliban's Gains Forestall U.S. Troop Reductions in Afghanistan*, WASH. POST, Sept. 22, 2006, at A13.

79 *See* OFFICE OF THE PRESS SEC'Y, THE WHITE HOUSE, FACT SHEET: STATUS OF DETAIN-

time of the outbreak of the conflict, the Taliban was not recognized by the United States (or by the vast majority of countries) as the lawful government of Afghanistan. Nevertheless, this alone was not a basis for denying the Taliban POW status, because article 4(A)(3) of Geneva Convention III requires the detaining power to regard as POWs persons who are "[m]embers of regular armed forces who profess allegiance to a government or an authority not recognized by the Detaining Power."[80]

According to the United States, article 4(A)(3) implicitly requires that members of "regular armed forces" of a party meet four criteria found in article 4(A)(2): they must operate within a command structure, dress in a manner whereby they are recognizable at a distance as being military forces, carry arms openly, and conduct their operations in accordance with the laws of war.[81] Although the Taliban could have qualified for POW status under article 4(A)(3), the U.S. government decided that it failed to do so because it did not operate in a command structure whereby military commanders took responsibility for subordinates, did not wear distinctive uniforms or other insignias, and did not act in accordance with the laws of war.[82] U.S. courts, to the extent

---

EES AT GUANTÁNAMO (Feb. 7, 2002), http://www.whitehouse.gov/news/releases/2002/02/20020207-13.html [hereinafter GUANTÁNAMO FACT SHEET].

80 Geneva Convention III, *supra* note 2, art. 4(A)(3). Commentary on this issue tends to focus on Geneva Convention III article 4(A)(1), which says that members of the "armed forces" of a party, as well as members of militias or volunteer corps forming a part of such armed forces, are to be treated as POWs, without any reference to these four criteria. This provision is then contrasted with article 4(A)(2), which says that members of other militias or volunteers corps (i.e., those not forming part of the regular armed forces) must meet the criteria to qualify as POWs. The relevant provision for the Taliban armed forces, however, is article 4(A)(3), because the United States did not recognize the Taliban government at the outbreak of the conflict.

81 Memorandum from Jay S. Bybee, Assistant Att'y Gen., Office of Legal Counsel, to Alberto Gonzales, Counsel to the President, Status of Taliban Forces under Article 4 of the Third Geneva Convention of 1949 (Feb. 7, 2002) [hereinafter OLC Memo], *in* THE TORTURE PAPERS: THE ROAD TO ABU GHRAIB 136, 137–39 (Karen J. Greenberg & Joshua L. Dratel eds., 2005) [hereinafter THE TORTURE PAPERS].

82 *See id.*; GUANTÁNAMO FACT SHEET, *supra* note 79; *see also* John Mintz & Mike Allen, *Bush Shifts Position on Detainees*, WASH. POST, Feb. 8, 2002, at A1; Katherine Q. Seelye, *In Shift, Bush Says Geneva Rules Fit Taliban Captives*, N.Y. TIMES, Feb. 8, 2002, at A1.

Secretary of Defense Rumsfeld stated:

> [T]he Taliban . . . did not wear uniforms, they did not have insignia, they did not carry their weapons openly, and they were tied tightly at the waist to al Qaeda. They behaved like them, they worked like them, they functioned with them, they cooperated with respect to communications, they cooperated with respect to supplies and ammunition, and there isn't any question in my mind . . . that they are not, they would not rise to the standard of a prisoner of war.

U.S. Dep't of Def. News Transcript, Secretary Rumsfeld Media Availability En Route to Camp X-Ray (Jan. 27, 2002), http://www.defenselink.mil/Transcripts/Transcript.aspx?transcriptID=

they have reached this issue, have concurred.[83]

Knowledgeable laws-of-war experts have divided over whether the Taliban was required meet these criteria.[84] There are at least three issues operating here. The first issue is whether there are criteria that the detaining country may apply in determining whether certain persons should be regarded as "[m]embers of regular armed forces"[85] of an unrecognized belligerent. Although it is clear that Geneva Convention III article 4(A)(3) does not expressly apply the four criteria to "regular armed forces," the real question is what is meant by that phrase. Presumably it is not enough that a government merely declare that certain persons are a part of its regular armed forces. If that were the case, then any government could designate any persons—whether militias, mercenaries, volunteers, guerrillas, brigands, or pirates—that are willing to attack its enemy as part of its "regular armed forces," thereby extending to them a status that the laws of war clearly do not contemplate.

The better view is that it is implicit in the idea of establishing "regular armed forces" that the government must be responsible for organizing, training, and using its recruits so that they can operate in the manner anticipated under the 1949 Geneva Conventions and other laws of war.[86] Seen in that light, the four criteria are simply a

2338; *see also* Pierre-Richard Prosper, Ambassador-at-Large for War Crimes Issues, Status and Treatment of Taliban and al-Qaida Detainees, Remarks at Chatham House, London, United Kingdom (Feb. 20, 2002), http://www.state.gov/s/wci/us_releases/rm/2002/8491.htm.

83 *See, e.g.*, Hamdan v. Rumsfeld, 415 F.3d 33, 40 (D.C. Cir. 2005), *rev'd on other grounds*, 126 S. Ct. 1749 (2006) (holding that Hamdan did not fall within article 4's definition of "prisoner of war" because he "did not purport to be a member of a group who displayed a fixed distinctive sign recognizable at a distance and who conducted their operations in accordance with the laws and customs of war"); United States v. Lindh, 212 F. Supp. 2d 541, 558 (E.D. Va. 2002) (concluding that Taliban was not entitled to article 4(A)(2)'s protections because it lacked a command structure, wore no uniforms or insignia, did not observe the laws and customs of war, but finding Lindh did carry their arms openly).

84 *Compare* Aldrich, *supra* note 76, at 894–98 (arguing that whether the four criteria apply to members of the "armed forces" of a party is "debatable"), *with* Yoram Dinstein, *Unlawful Combatancy*, *in* INTERNATIONAL LAW AND THE WAR ON TERROR, *supra* note 68, at 151 (finding that the criteria express a general standard for lawful combatancy and, although there may be a presumption that regular armed forces meet the criteria, the presumption may be rebutted).

85 Geneva Convention III, *supra* note 2, art. 4(A)(3).

86 As Bothe, Partsch, and Solf observed:

> It is generally assumed that these conditions were deemed, by the 1874 Brussels Conference and the 1899 and 1907 Hague Peace Conferences, to be inherent in the regular armed forces of States. Accordingly, it was considered to be unnecessary and redundant to spell them out in the Conventions. It seems to be clear that regular armed forces are inherently organized, that they are commanded by a per-

surrogate for determining whether a particular group of persons fall within the meaning of "[m]embers of the regular armed forces of a Party." Thus, a government that does not exercise command and control over the group of persons cannot expect other state-parties to view those persons as part of the government's "regular armed forces." Similarly, a government that organizes the group of persons in a manner that prevents operation of a cardinal principle of the laws of war—i.e., the obligation to distinguish combatants from noncombatants—and that fails to inculcate in them awareness of and fidelity to the laws of war, cannot expect other states to view those persons as part of the government's "regular armed forces." The official ICRC commentary supports that position, asserting that the "regular armed forces" referred to in article 4(A)(3)

> have all the material characteristics and all the attributes of armed forces in the sense of subparagraph (1): they wear uniform[s], they have an organized hierarchy and they know and respect the laws and customs of war. The delegates to the 1949 Diplomatic Conference were therefore fully justified in considering that there was no need to specify for such armed forces the requirements stated in sub-paragraph 2(a), (b), (c) and (d).[87]

The second issue is whether Taliban personnel were in fact operating as the "regular armed forces" of Afghanistan. Here, neither the U.S. government nor most legal commentators parsing the Geneva Conventions have done much to advance our understanding of the nature of the Taliban as a military force. One of the more detailed U.S. government analyses that is publicly available is a February 2002 memorandum by the Department of Justice Office of the Legal Counsel, which was based on information about the Taliban provided by the Department of Defense.[88] Much of the memorandum, however is conclusory in nature and could have been strengthened by a more robust and nuanced analysis.

> son responsible for his subordinates, and that they are obliged under international law to conduct their operations in accordance with the laws and customs of war.

New Rules, *supra* note 43, at 234–35. Because the Geneva Conventions obligate a party to train its military authorities regarding their obligations under the Conventions, *see, e.g.*, Geneva Convention III, *supra* note 2, art. 127, it is reasonable to expect the armed forces to conduct their operations in accordance with the laws and customs of war.

87 3 Int'l Comm. of the Red Cross, The Geneva Conventions of 12 August 1949: Commentary 63 (Jean S. Pictet ed., 1952) [hereinafter Pictet Commentary].

88 OLC Memo, *supra* note 81.

When the Soviet Union withdrew its military forces from Afghanistan in 1989, the Afghan militias that were previously allied against the Soviets turned on one another, causing significant disorder and civil strife. In 1994, the Taliban—which was a Pashtun-dominated, ultra-conservative Islamic group—began seizing Afghan territory, starting at its home base of Kandahar province and ultimately reaching the capital of Kabul in 1996. The Taliban succeeded in quelling the strife unleashed by the warring militias, seizing ninety percent of Afghanistan's territory, and imposing a strict form of Islam throughout most of the country.[89] Thus, the Taliban was not an organization initially formed to constitute the regular army of a government; the Taliban was a religious and a military movement that ultimately swept across Afghanistan. As one commentator has noted: "Ironically, the Taliban were a direct throwback to the military religious orders that arose in Christendom during the Crusades to fight Islam—disciplined, motivated and ruthless in attaining their aims."[90]

After seizing power, did the Taliban have a command-and-control system characteristic of "regular armed forces?" Much of its organization remained secretive, in part because the Taliban issued no press releases or policy statements and held no press conferences, and in part because its ban on photography and television made identification of its leaders difficult. Yet the Taliban did have a military structure of sorts. It was headed at the top by Mullah Muhammed Omar, followed by the Chief of the General Staff, who reported to Omar and who in turn directed the Chief of the Army and the Chief of the Air Force.[91] Omar would communicate orders to military commanders, such as allowing them to make an attack, either in person or by wireless radio. Further, the Taliban had at least four army divisions and an armored division.[92] A military *Shura* helped plan strategy, but apparently had no strategic decisionmaking power.[93] At the lower level, however, the idea of the Taliban as a regular armed force begins to break down. The Taliban fighters (numbering some 25,000 to 30,000 men) were structured less like a normal army and more like a traditional tribal militia (or *lashkar*), in which personnel were constantly being shifted between the front lines and their villages.[94] As such,

89 *See generally* MARSDEN, *supra* note 62; AHMED RASHID, TALIBAN: MILITANT ISLAM, OIL AND FUNDAMENTALISM IN CENTRAL ASIA (2001).

90 RASHID, *supra* note 89, at 33.

91 *See id.* at 99.

92 *Id.*

93 *Id.* at 98.

94 *Id.* at 100.

"there [was] no clear military structure with a hierarchy of officers and commanders, while unit commanders [were] constantly being shifted around."[95]

As for whether Taliban fighters were identifiable as part of an armed force and could be distinguished from civilians, here, too, the factual analyses by the U.S. government and legal commentators have been rather thin. Some assert that the Taliban "did not wear uniforms nor did they display any other fixed distinctive emblem,"[96] while others opine that "various Taliban units . . . may have been wearing a distinctive insignia as they wore a black head-covering of a similar type."[97] In any event, it seems to be the case that the vast majority of Taliban fighters were not wearing any particular uniform, nor had any of the normal insignia that one normally associates with regular armed forces (patches, berets, etc.), even in the developing world. The lack of such identification tends to reinforce the idea that most Taliban fighters were not part of a regular armed force. Yet it also seems that Northern Alliance fighters were not wearing any normal uniform or insignia, but they apparently were regarded by the United States as wearing "nonstandard" uniforms by donning a certain style of cap and scarf; indeed, U.S. special operations forces who dressed similarly were viewed as not dressing like a civilian.[98] Why the Taliban was considered out-of-uniform while the Northern Alliance was not was never made clear by the U.S. government. Further, even if the Taliban was largely out-of-uniform, it still leaves room for the possibility that some units were distinctive, such as personnel associated with an armored division. Perhaps the United States engaged in a systematic assessment of whether any such units existed and concluded that

---

95 *Id.* at 99. Globalsecurity.org maintains:

> The Taliban-led "Islamic Emirate of Afghanistan" lacked the administrative efficiency of a state. The military did not exist on a national basis. Some elements of the former Army, Air and Air Defense Forces, National Guard, Border Guard Forces, National Police Force (*Sarandoi*), and tribal militias existed, but were factionalized among various groups. The Taliban's "army" was a coalition of militia formations composed of assorted armed groups with varying degrees of loyalty, commitment, skill, and organizational coherence. Many had a history of switching sides and shifting loyalties prior to coming under the nominal command of the Taliban.

GlobalSecurity.org, Taliban Militia, http://www.globalsecurity.org/military/world/afghanistan/militia-taliban.htm (last visited June 27, 2007).

96 Dinstein, *supra* note 84, at 171.

97 Leslie Green, *Commentary: Jus in Bello*, *in* INTERNATIONAL LAW AND THE WAR ON TERROR, *supra* note 71, 235–40.

98 *See* W. Hays Parks, *Special Forces' Wear of Non-Standard Uniforms*, 4 CHI. J. INT'L L. 493, 498 (2003).

they did not, but public information to date has not revealed such an effort.

Finally, in terms of whether the Taliban adhered to the laws of war, the position taken by the United States on this issue was somewhat risky. Allegations by one side that another side has engaged in war crimes have been a recurrent feature of armed conflict; linking POW status to such allegations creates significant opportunities for summary denial of protections to U.S. and allied forces for spurious reasons.[99] At the same time, no one has suggested that the Taliban ever trained its forces in the laws of war or viewed itself as bound by such rules. In the course of the Taliban's conflict with the Northern Alliance, both sides committed horrific atrocities, with the Taliban carrying out summary executions of noncombatants, including women and children, arbitrarily detaining persons, forcibly relocating the civilian population, burning homes and crops, and using forced labor.[100] Perhaps the more notorious atrocity was the torture and execution of former Afghanistan President Najibullah after the Taliban entered Kabul.[101] Although members of regular armed forces do commit atrocities on occasion, and although that alone does not result in the violator losing his status as a POW—let alone stripping an entire army of its entitlement to POW status—the systematic violation of basic human rights by the Taliban suggests the existence of something other than a regular armed force.

All things considered, and though opinions clearly differ, there seems to be a reasonable basis for the U.S. government to have concluded that the vast majority of Taliban fighters were not "[m]embers of regular armed forces." At the same time, it seems less reasonable to regard the higher levels of Taliban military authorities—as well as discrete units, such as its armored division—as *ipso facto* failing to constitute a regular armed force. For the United States to credibly maintain that position, it should have explained with greater detail and nuance why the Taliban *in toto* fell outside the scope of article 4(A)(3). The failure to do so invites a similar lack of discrimination by other countries in future conflicts in situations where some U.S. forces (e.g., special operations forces) are found not have fulfilled the

99 *See* New Rules, *supra* note 43, at 250.

100 *See, e.g.*, Bureau of Democracy, Human Rights, and Labor, U.S. Dep't of State, 1999 Country Reports on Human Rights Practices: Afghanistan (Feb. 25, 2000), http://www.state.gov/www/global/human_rights/1999_hrp_report/afghanis.html.

101 Rashid, *supra* note 89, at 49–50.

four criteria, leading to a denial of POW status to U.S. forces as a whole.

The third issue is whether there was "doubt" about the status of the Taliban sufficient to trigger the requirements of Geneva Convention III article 5, which states that "should any doubt arise" as to whether certain detainees fall within article 4, the detainees "shall enjoy the protection of the present Convention until such time as their status has been determined by a competent tribunal."[102] Here, much turns on what it means to have "doubts" and who is supposed to have them. Though there appears to have been some internal dissent, the leadership of the U.S. executive branch appears to have had no doubt, from the early stages of the conflict, that all Taliban fighters as a group failed to fall within the scope of article 4.[103] To the extent that the issue is whether the detaining power is uncertain, then article 5 does not seem to be engaged. To the extent, however, that article 5 is speaking to a broader viewpoint, doubts were certainly expressed by others, be it the ICRC[104] or legal commentators.[105]

In my view, article 5 is written essentially as a guide to governments as to how they should act in a time of war. When article 5 notes "should any doubt arise," it appears to be directed at doubts by the government who has taken custody of the detainee, and appears to be telling the government to resolve those doubts in a particular manner. There is no sense of any other entity, including a protecting power or the ICRC, being involved in determining whether the doubt exists or whether it has been resolved. At the same time, it is implicit in article 5 that the detaining power is responsible for undertaking a serious and careful analysis as to whether persons who are detained are entitled to status as POWs. Further, in my view, the spirit of the Convention suggests that such an analysis should be communicated to any state or body that would otherwise serve as the protecting power for such per-

102 Geneva Convention III, *supra* note 2, art. 5.

103 In early 2002, the State Department argued forcefully that the 1949 Geneva Conventions should be regarded as applying to the conflict in Afghanistan, but it accepted that members of al Qaeda and the Taliban may not be entitled to POW status under Geneva Convention III. *See* Memorandum from William H. Taft IV, Legal Adviser, U.S. Dep't of State, to Alberto R. Gonzales, Counsel to the President, Comments on Your Paper on the Geneva Convention (Feb. 2, 2002), *in* THE TORTURE PAPERS, *supra* note 81, at 129.

104 *See* Press Release, Int'l Comm. of the Red Cross, Geneva Convention on Prisoners of War (Feb. 9, 2002), http://www.icrc.org/web/eng/siteeng0.nsf/htmlall/57jrm3?opendocument ("There are divergent views between the United States and the ICRC on the procedures which apply on how to determine that the persons detained are not entitled to prisoner of war status.").

105 *See, e.g.*, Aldrich, *supra* note 76, at 897–98.

sons were they to be accorded POW status, so that the status of the persons and the reasons for that status are clearly understood.

Less clear is whether the decision that "no doubt exists" can occur on a group basis or must be resolved on a person-by-person basis. The text of article 5 certainly suggests that group determinations are permissible, in that it uses the word "persons" rather than "a person."[106] Further, past state practice reveals that classification by groups of persons has been undertaken when considering POW status, such as the distinctions made between regular North Vietnamese army troops, the Viet Cong main force, and the Viet Cong local force during the Vietnam War. In short, the U.S. government probably did have the leeway to determine that all the persons in its custody who were Taliban fighters captured on the battlefield in Afghanistan fell outside the scope of Geneva Convention III, though in doing so there may well have been some overbreadth. The error by the United States was not so much in making that determination as it was in making sure that the persons in its custody *were in fact part of the Taliban (or al Qaeda)*, rather than a wayward tourist or relief worker. We now know that there were persons detained by the United States who had nothing to do with either the Taliban or al Qaeda; they were just in the wrong place at the wrong time.[107] Article 5 does not appear to encompass the process by which a state determines whether an individual has committed a belligerent act against the detaining power; it assumes that such an act has occurred and then addresses what is to be done if there is doubt about the person's status as a POW. Yet, again, it seems within the spirit of article 5 to see the detaining power as having a responsibility to review carefully and expeditiously whether persons detained are in fact combatants at all. Such a review seems especially merited in situations where persons are captured on a chaotic battlefield, where combatants and noncombatants by their dress are easily confused, or have been handed over by indigenous groups who are paid a bounty for doing so, as was the case in Afghanistan. As discussed in more detail below, the United States, in 2004, created "combatant status review tribunals" ("CSRT") to determine whether each detainee at Guantanamo Bay was properly classified as a com-

---

106 Geneva Convention III, *supra* note 2, art. 5.

107 *See, e.g.*, Josh White, *Suspect Is Freed from Guantánamo; Release Is First Under Tribunals*, Wash. Post, Sept. 9, 2004, at A3 (recounting the release of a detainee picked up on the battlefield in Afghanistan whom the United States determined, after three years at Guantanamo, not to be an enemy combatant).

batant and to release those who were not.[108] The United States can and should be criticized for not doing more, and sooner, to ensure that such mistakes were not made.

If the Taliban detainees are not entitled to POW status, that does not mean they lack any status under the laws of war. One possibility is that they should be accorded protections as civilians in accordance with Geneva Convention IV, on a theory that the conventions were designed to ensure that all persons would fall into some category of protection. Support for that position may be found in article 4 of Geneva Convention IV, which states in rather broad terms that the Convention protects persons who, "in any manner whatsoever, find themselves . . . in the hands of a Party to the conflict . . . of which they are not nationals."[109]

On the other hand, the whole structure of Geneva Convention IV is oriented toward protection of civilians detained either in occupied territory or in the detaining power's own territory; there is little to suggest regulation of the civilian bearing arms on the battlefield.[110] Moreover, article 4 itself makes clear that certain persons in the hands of a belligerent are *not* protected by Geneva Convention IV. Nationals of the detaining power itself are not protected. Neither "[n]ationals of a neutral state who find themselves in the territory of a belligerent state" nor "nationals of a co-belligerent state" are protected so long as their states have diplomatic relations with the detaining state.[111] As such, detainees at Guantanamo Bay who are nationals of a co-belligerent in the conflict against either the Taliban or al Qaeda (e.g., Australia or the United Kingdom) clearly are not covered by the Geneva Convention IV.[112] Nationals of "neutral states," which

108 *See infra* notes 218–19 and accompanying text.

109 Geneva Convention IV, *supra* note 2, art. 4.

110 The Pictet commentary is also a bit conflicted on the issue, asserting on the one hand that "[e]very person in enemy hands must have some status" under the four conventions, 4 Pictet Commentary, *supra* note 87, at 51, but on the other hand stating that Geneva Convention IV basically concerns civilians living in the enemy belligerent's territory or in territory occupied by the enemy belligerent (which seems to exclude a civilian combatant who is taken into custody on the battlefield), *id.* at 45.

111 Geneva Convention IV, *supra* note 2, art. 4. Nationals of a state that has not ratified the Conventions are also not protected, *see id.*, but because all states admitted to the United Nations have ratified or acceded to the 1949 Geneva Conventions, *see* ICRC, State Parties, *supra* note 2, this carve-out would not apply.

112 "Co-belligerents" are generally regarded as states "engaged in a conflict with a common enemy, whether in alliance with each other or not." Parry & Grant Encyclopaedic Dictionary of International Law 84 (John P. Grant & J. Craig Barker eds., 2d ed. 2004). With respect to the U.S. intervention in Afghanistan, "co-belligerent" might be defined as the wide range of states that provided support for "Operation Enduring Freedom," in the form of military

might be defined as states other than Afghanistan that did not provide support for Operation Enduring Freedom, are not protected by Geneva Convention IV if they "find themselves" in U.S. territory.[113]

Further evidence that persons caught up in armed conflict regulated by the Geneva Conventions are not necessarily protected, at the minimum, by the full range of Geneva Convention IV may be seen in Geneva Convention IV article 5, which sets forth circumstances where a civilian loses most of the protections under the Convention. These circumstances include when the person is a spy or saboteur or is suspected of engaging in activities hostile to the security of the detaining state.[114] Likewise, Common Article 3 protects a certain category of persons but without providing them the full status enjoyed by either POWs or protected civilians under the Geneva Convention.[115] Perhaps most importantly, Protocol I—which is viewed as clarifying and supplementing the 1949 Geneva Conventions—explicitly envisages a situation where a person who takes part in hostilities and is then detained may be found not entitled to either POW status or protected civilian status.[116] In other words, Protocol I expressly states that the failure to qualify under Geneva Convention III does not *ipso facto* result in protection under Geneva Convention IV. Thus, the 1949 Geneva Conventions do not, by their terms, create a seamless system of full protection of all individuals, whereby if you do not qualify under the comprehensive protections of one convention, you automatically fall under the full protections of another.

The further question, however, is whether Taliban personnel who fail to qualify as POWs should be considered protected civilians under

---

assistance, financial assistance, intelligence, overflight and landing rights, or political support. *See, e.g.*, U.S. DEP'T OF STATE, FACT SHEET: OPERATION ENDURING FREEDOM OVERVIEW (Oct. 1, 2001), http://www.state.gov/s/ct/rls/fs/2001/5194.htm (listing examples of countries providing to the United States in Operation Enduring Freedom).

113 Ironically, this is apparently one area where detaining persons outside U.S. territory may give them greater rights than detaining them within.

114 *See* Geneva Convention IV, *supra* note 2, art. 5.

115 *See* Geneva Conventions I–IV, *supra* note 2, art. 3.

116 *See* Protocol I, *supra* note 44, art. 45(3) ("Any person who has taken part in hostilities, who is not entitled to prisoner-of-war status and who does not benefit from more favorable treatment in accordance with the Fourth Convention shall have the right at all times to the protection of Article 75 of this Protocol."); *see also id.* art. 75(7)(b) (referring to persons who do not benefit from the general protections of the 1949 Geneva Conventions or Protocol I). The official ICRC commentary on the protocol states that article 45 "covers persons who not only cannot claim prisoner-of-war status, but are also not protected persons under the Fourth Convention." SANDOZ COMMENTARY, *supra* note 47, at 870. The ICRC originally proposed article 75 so as to protect "any person who was, for one reason or another, unable to claim a particular status, such as that of prisoner of war or civilian internee." *Id.* at 864.

Geneva Convention IV. Certainly they are not persons who simply happened to be present in the United States (or one of its allies) at the outbreak of the conflict, nor persons who just happened to be living in an area of Afghanistan placed under occupation by the U.S.-led coalition. Thus, they do not squarely fit within the dominant paradigm of Geneva Convention IV. Moreover, they are not persons who were normally civilians but happened to take part in the hostilities in the course of unusual or extraordinary circumstances, which would seem the most likely scenario by which a combatant who fails to qualify for POW status might be placed in protected civilian status. Rather, the Taliban personnel were trained to engage in, and did engage in, armed hostilities on a rather sustained basis, albeit in a capacity different from that of a regular army. Although as a policy matter it might have been desirable for the United States to treat Taliban fighters in accordance with Geneva Convention III or IV, as a legal matter neither status was compelled. Indeed, a key reason not to accord the Taliban fighters status as protected civilians is to avoid blurring the distinction between combatants and noncombatants, which, of course, is a central organizing tenet of the 1949 Geneva Conventions.[117] Regarding persons engaged in active hostilities as protected civilians may provide greater protections to such combatants, but it concomitantly invites belligerents to treat noncombatant civilians as hostile threats, thereby diminishing the protections for such civilians.

Assuming that the Taliban detainees are not entitled to either POW or protected civilian status under the Conventions, what is left for them appears to be the core standards advanced in Common Article 3. For though Common Article 3 was designed to deal with "armed conflict not of an international character,"[118] over time it has come to be regarded as setting minimum standards of humanity applicable in *all* armed conflicts, including international armed conflicts. A key source often cited for confirming this proposition is the statement by the International Court of Justice ("ICJ") in the 1986 *Nicaragua v. United States* case regarding the status of Common Article 3.[119] In commenting on Common Article 3's rules, the Court stated:

> There is no doubt that, in the event of international armed conflicts, these rules also constitute a minimum yardstick, in addition to the more elaborate rules which are also to apply

117 *See* Legality of the Threat or Use of Nuclear Weapons, Advisory Opinion, 1996 I.C.J. 226, 257 (July 8).

118 Geneva Conventions I–IV, *supra* note 2, art. 3.

119 Military and Paramilitary Activities (Nicar. v. U.S.), 1986 I.C.J. 14 (June 27).

> to international conflicts; and they are rules which, in the Court's opinion, reflect what the Court in 1949 called "elementary considerations of humanity."[120]

In other words, Common Article 3 establishes rules "with legs," capable of operating outside the confines of the paradigm of conflicts "not of an international character." As such, like the case of the Northern Alliance-versus-Taliban conflict discussed above, the regulatory road with respect to the U.S.-led coalition-versus-Taliban international armed conflict leads ultimately to Common Article 3.

C. United States-Led Coalition versus al Qaeda as a Non-Afghan Movement

Problems with applying the Geneva Conventions to the two prior conflicts pale in comparison to their application to the conflict between the U.S.-led coalition and al Qaeda as a non-Afghan movement. One might first try to view this conflict as a "state-versus-state" conflict. Yet the attacks of 9/11, orchestrated and funded by al Qaeda, were the product of a global terrorist movement; they were not directed by the de facto government of Afghanistan, although that government did tolerate and benefit from the presence of al Qaeda in Afghanistan.[121] At its essence, al Qaeda is an armed Sunni Islamist organization that is seeking to eliminate foreign influence in Muslim countries.[122] Though its exact organization is shrouded in secrecy, most analysts describe it as comprising numerous independent and collaborative cells operating across multiple countries.[123] As such, al Qaeda is not an entity temporally or geographically tied to the prior de facto government of Afghanistan, but rather an independent force engaged in a private war.[124]

Alternatively, one might try to view this conflict as a "state versus nonstate actor" internal conflict. Yet that, too, is a poor fit for the

---

120 *Id.* at 114 (quoting Corfu Channel (U.K. v. Alb.), 1949 I.C.J. 4, 22 (Apr. 9)).

121 *See, e.g.*, LAWRENCE WRIGHT, THE LOOMING TOWER: AL-QAEDA AND THE ROAD TO 9/11, at 245 (2006).

122 *See id.* at 247.

123 *See, e.g.*, *The Global Reach of Al-Qaeda: Hearing Before the Subcomm. on Int'l Operations and Terrorism of the S. Comm. on Foreign Relations*, 107th Cong. 7 (2001) (statement of Thomas Wilshere, Deputy Section Chief, International Terrorism Operational Section, Federal Bureau of Investigation); *id.* at 21 (statement of Michele Flournoy, Senior Advisor, International Security Program, Center for Strategic and International Studies) (describing al Qaeda as a "multiheaded hydra").

124 *See generally* JANE CORBIN, AL-QAEDA: IN SEARCH OF THE TERROR NETWORK THAT THREATENS THE WORLD (2003); AL QAEDA NOW: UNDERSTANDING TODAY'S TERRORISTS (Karen J. Greenberg ed., 2005); WRIGHT, *supra* note 121.

Geneva Conventions paradigm, given that the conflict is transnational in scale. Al Qaeda as an organization has a presence in numerous countries; it is not limited in its operations to Afghanistan or even countries adjacent to Afghanistan.[125]

Thus, it is of no surprise that the ICRC and various scholars,[126] as well as leading nongovernmental organizations,[127] see no basis for viewing the U.S. "global war" on al Qaeda as an "armed conflict" within the meaning of the 1949 Geneva Conventions. For these observers, although the phrase "war on terrorism" is a catchy rhetorical device expressing a general policy of taking seriously a particular problem (not unlike the "war on poverty" under the Johnson Administration or the "war on drugs" in recent years), this conflict is not really a "war" in the traditional sense, nor is there a discrete enemy called "terrorism."[128] Consequently, they argue that—leaving aside those collected on the battlefield in Afghanistan—the pursuit of al Qaeda suspects should be undertaken in accordance with the norms that operate with respect to any pursuit of persons believe to have violated criminal laws, and not on the basis of the laws of war.[129]

If, as some scholars have done,[130] one were to make the case for why this "state-versus-nonstate actor transnational conflict" should fall within the scope of the laws of war, it would be along the following lines. First, Common Article 3 does not expressly limit its scope to "internal" armed conflicts (or "civil wars"). The Article does not, for example, refer to "armed conflict between the government of a High Contracting Party and an opposing resistance movement within its ter-

125 *See supra* note 123.

126 *See, e.g.*, Mary Ellen O'Connell, *When Is a War Not a War? The Myth of the Global War on Terror*, 12 ILSA J. INT'L & COMP. L. 535, 538 (2005) ("Outside the real wars of Afghanistan and Iraq, al Qaeda's actions and our responses have been too sporadic and low-intensity to qualify as armed conflict."); Jordan J. Paust, *Post–9/11 Overreaction and Fallacies Regarding War and Defense, Guantánamo, the Status of Persons, Treatment, Judicial Review of Detention, and Due Process in Military Commissions*, 79 NOTRE DAME L. REV. 1335, 1342 (2004) ("[A]ny conflict between the United States and al Qaeda as such cannot amount to war or trigger application of the laws of war.").

127 *See, e.g.*, Kenneth Roth, *The Law of War in the War on Terror*, FOREIGN AFF., Jan.–Feb. 2004, at 2, 7 (argument by the director of Human Rights Watch that the laws of war are not applicable to the non-battlefield campaign against al Qaeda); INT'L COMM. OF THE RED CROSS, THE RELEVANCE OF IHL IN THE CONTEXT OF TERRORISM (Jul. 21, 2005), http://www.icrc.org/Web/eng/siteeng0.nsf/html/terrorism-ihl-210705.

128 *See, e.g.*, Roth, *supra* note 127, at 2.

129 *See id.* at 2–3.

130 *See, e.g*, Jinks, *supra* note 43, at 38 ("[T]he September 11 attacks constituted the initiation of an 'armed conflict' within the meaning of . . . the Geneva Conventions."); John C. Yoo & James C. Ho, *The Status of Terrorists*, 44 VA. J. INT'L L. 207, 211 (2003).

ritory" or some such thing, as was later done in Protocol II.[131] Rather, the language speaks of "armed conflict not of an international character occurring in the territory of one of the High Contracting Parties."[132] Although that language might be viewed as solely directed at civil war, the language is susceptible to a broader interpretation. In short, "not of an international character" is capable of meaning "between any state and a nonstate actor," rather than meaning "internal armed conflict."

Second, "in the territory of one of the High Contracting Parties" can be interpreted as reference to conduct rising to the level of armed conflict between those two types of participants in any territory of a party to the Geneva Conventions. Though it might normally be the case that a particular nonstate actor is operating solely in the territory of a single state, if the nonstate actor is operating in multiple territories against a state actor, then the conflict remains governed by Common Article 3, except in states that have not joined the Geneva Conventions. Because all states of the world are now parties to the Geneva Conventions, this latter limitation has fallen into desuetude.

Third, application of Common Article 3 to a state-versus-nonstate actor transnational conflict appears consistent with the thinking that emerged from the negotiations of the additional protocols. As discussed above, Protocol I article 1(4) extended the reach of protections associated with "international armed conflicts" to certain situations where a state is in armed conflict with a nonstate actor (struggles against colonial domination, alien occupation, and racist regimes).[133] There is no inherent reason why the protections associated with "noninternational armed conflicts" might not be extended to other situations where a state is in armed conflict with a nonstate actor. Indeed, Bothe, Partsch, and Solf—who participated in the Protocol negotiations—have maintained that an independent force engaged in a private war has a status akin to insurgents in a noninternational

---

131 *See* Protocol II, *supra* note 45, art. 1 ("This Protocol, which develops and supplements Article 3 common to the Geneva Conventions of 12 August 1949 without modifying its existing conditions of application, shall apply to all armed conflicts which are not covered by Article 1 of [Protocol I] and which take place *in the territory of a High Contracting Party between its armed forces and dissident armed forces or other organized armed groups* which, under responsible command, *exercise such control over a part of its territory* as to enable them to carry out sustained and concerted military operations and to implement this Protocol." (emphasis added)).

132 *See* Geneva Conventions I–IV, *supra* note 2, art. 3.

133 *See supra* notes 46–49, 54–59 and accompanying text.

armed conflict,[134] which suggests that the operative standards applicable to that war should be found in Common Article 3.

Such points help explain the position taken by the Supreme Court in *Hamdan v. Rumsfeld.*[135] There, the Court found that even if Hamdan was not a part of the state-versus-state (i.e., coalition-versus-Taliban) conflict, he was part of an "armed conflict not of an international character" between the United States and a nonstate actor (al Qaeda) that occurred in the territory of a party to the Geneva Conventions.[136] According to the Court, the phrase "conflict not of an international character" in Common Article 3 is broad enough to encompass a conflict between a state and any individuals not associated with a state who are involved in a conflict in the territory of a state party.[137] The Court relied in part on the negotiating history of Common Article 3:

> Although the official commentaries accompanying Common Article 3 indicate that an important purpose of the provision was to furnish minimal protection to rebels involved in one kind of "conflict not of an international character," i.e., a civil war, the commentaries also make clear "that the scope of the Article must be as wide as possible." In fact, limiting language that would have rendered Common Article 3 applicable "especially [to] cases of civil war, colonial conflicts, or wars of religion," was omitted from the final version of the Article, which coupled broader scope of application with a narrower range of rights than did earlier proposed iterations.[138]

134 Bothe, Partsch, and Solf write:

> A question under the Hague Regulations and the Third Convention involves the status of an independent force which has no factual link to a party to an international armed conflict. In general, it may be said that such a force would probably be viewed as waging a private war. In any event, it would have no status better than that of insurgents in a non-international armed conflict, unless the movement they represent has such *de facto* objective characteristics of a belligerency that the movement itself could be recognized as a Party to an international armed conflict.

New Rules, *supra* note 43, at 235. They later note that "gangs of terrorists acting on their own behalf and not linked to an entity subject to international law are excluded" from the armed forces "of a party to the Conflict" under article 43 of Protocol I. *Id.* at 237.

135 Hamdan v. Rumsfeld, 126 S. Ct. 2749 (2006).

136 *Id.* at 2795.

137 *See id.* at 2795–96.

138 *Id.* at 2796 (quoting Pictet Commentary, *supra* note 87, at 36–37) (other citation and footnote omitted). In its footnote, *see id.* at 2796 n.63, the Court cited to the ICJ's decision in Military and Paramilitary Activities (Nicar. v. U.S.), 1986 I.C.J. 14, 114 (June 27).

On the facts, the Court had before it a person who was detained on the battlefield in Afghanistan at the time of the armed conflict between the United States and the Taliban. Therefore, it is possible that the Court's reasoning about the "armed conflict" is limited to the situation of al Qaeda persons detained in Afghanistan in the 2001–2002 time frame.[139] The Court did not speak to whether *any* persons associated with al Qaeda who are detained *anywhere* around the world fall within the scope of Common Article 3, which may be an important issue given that several of the persons currently detained at Guantanamo Bay were not apprehended on the battlefield in Afghanistan.[140] At the same time, the Court did not expressly limit its holding to persons detained in Afghanistan, and the language quoted above can be read to speak to military actions worldwide by the United States against al Qaeda. In the aftermath of the *Hamdan* decision, the Department of Defense issued a directive stating that it is Department of Defense policy that all U.S. forces "shall apply, without regard to a detainee's legal status, at a minimum the standards articulated in Common Article 3 to the Geneva Conventions of 1949," for "all armed conflicts, however such conflicts are characterized, and in all other military operations."[141] The Directive makes no distinction be-

139 The D.C. Circuit Court of Appeals found, in the alternative, that the Geneva Conventions did not apply to Hamdan because he was captured as part of a global U.S. war with al Qaeda—one that was separate from the war with the Taliban occurring in Afghanistan. *See* Hamdan v. Rumsfeld, 415 F.3d 33, 41–42 (D.C. Cir. 2005), *rev'd on other grounds*, 126 S. Ct. 2749 (2006) ("Hamdan was captured in Afghanistan in November 2001, but the conflict with al Qaeda arose before then, in other regions, including this country on September 11, 2001."). In so holding, the D.C. Circuit disagreed with the district court, which had found that the conflict with al Qaeda was not distinct from the conflict with the Taliban. *See* Hamdan v. Rumsfeld, 344 F. Supp. 2d 152, 161 (D.D.C. 2004). The Supreme Court, per Justice Stevens, did not expressly accept that there was a global conflict with al Qaeda distinct from the conflict in Afghanistan with the Taliban. Instead, the Court found that even if a separate conflict existed with al Qaeda, and even if Hamdan was detained as part of that conflict, he would still be protected by Common Article 3. *See Hamdan*, 126 S. Ct. 2749, 2795–96 (2006). The Court left open the possibility that Hamdan might be protected by the full range of the Geneva Conventions, but it also appeared to leave open the possibility that the Geneva Conventions may not apply at all to persons detained outside Afghanistan.

140 For example, Bosnian Federation police in January 2002 transferred six Bosnian residents of Algerian origin from a Sarajevo prison to U.S. custody. The men were transported to Guantanamo Bay for detention. The detainees were said to be suspects in an alleged plot to attack the U.S. and U.K. embassies in Sarajevo. *See* Press Release, European Parliament, MEPs Examine the Case of Six Prisoners Taken from Bosnia to Guantánamo (Apr. 26, 2006), http://www.europarl.europa.eu/news/expert/infopress_page/017-7559-115-04-17-902-20060424IPR07546-25-04-2006-2006-false/default_en.htm.

141 U.S. Dep't of Def., Directive No. 2310.01E, paras. 2.2, 4.2 (Sept. 5, 2006), *available at* http://www.defenselink.mil/pubs/pdfs/Detainee_Prgm_Dir_2310_9-5-06.pdf.

tween persons detained in Afghanistan or abroad, nor limits its scope to persons associated with al Qaeda.[142]

Thus, as was the case with the other types of conflicts, Common Article 3 emerges as an important set of default rules when considering post–9/11 armed conflict. Yet the *Hamdan* analysis will not be the last word on this subject. There remain proponents for the proposition that al Qaeda detainees should be accorded greater protections than just those contained in Common Article 3—as POWs under Geneva Convention III, as protected civilians under Geneva Convention IV, or simply as humans under otherwise applicable human rights law. Conversely, despite the *Hamdan* decision, there will no doubt remain some skeptics as to whether even Common Article 3 should apply to al Qaeda detainees, especially those who were not battlefield detainees in Afghanistan.

IV. Adapting the Geneva Conventions to the New Landscape of Warfare

As demonstrated by the events following 9/11, contemporary rules on the laws of war were not designed to take account of irregular forces or guerrillas, and certainly not to take care of persons who conducted themselves as brigands or outlaws. One can formulate various arguments for why members of irregular forces, whether they be Taliban or al Qaeda, should be accorded a full range of protections under the Geneva Conventions, but historically the fit is not a good one. Moreover, the resistance of the United States to fitting the square peg of the Geneva Conventions to the round hole of the conflict with al Qaeda is not particularly surprising, especially in light of its vigorous rejection of the efforts in Protocol I to extend traditional protections to nonstate actors fighting oppressive regimes.

Nevertheless, although the full panoply of Geneva Convention protections may not be available, this Part argues (in Subsection A) that the historical trend is one that has favored development of certain core protections for all persons engaged in armed conflict, in fulfillment of the "dictates of public conscience." The broad scope of international law, whether relating to treatment of persons in times of war or peace, has evolved to provide considerable protections even for those who have committed the most heinous of acts. Relatively clear, core protections for any individuals detained in time of war may now be found in customary international law and should be applied in situ-

142 *See generally id.*

ations where the status of persons is uncertain or contested. To demonstrate how such core protections should be applied, this Part (in Subsection B) addresses the specific problem of the termination of captivity of persons currently detained at the U.S. naval base at Guantanomo Bay, Cuba. The core protections establish specific rules concerning termination of captivity, imply a process for determining whether continued detention is merited, and suggest outcomes for different categories of detainees. Such application of the core protections is legally compelled, is consistent with sound policy choices, and suggests possibilities for similar application of the core protections to other aspects of the "war on terrorism."

A. The Dictates of Public Conscience

Despite the failure to apply the full panoply of Geneva Convention protections to irregular forces, there can be little doubt that the world has changed since Lieber's time. The idea of simply subjecting a brigand to death upon capture is today unacceptable. One can point to many developments in international law that have fostered protections even for persons who are responsible for the most heinous of acts. Though senior leaders in the government of Nazi Germany had committed horrific atrocities, it was ultimately accepted by the Allied Powers that those leaders would be punished only after a public prosecution before a tribunal at Nuremberg, at which they would be represented by counsel and able to challenge the evidence against them (some were in fact acquitted). The past dozen years have seen a flourishing of such international criminal tribunals, from the Hague to Tanzania and from Sierra Leone to Cambodia and East Timor. The relative successes and failures of those tribunals is less relevant than the fact that our contemporary global society regards even individuals who appear to have committed genocide, crimes against humanity, and grave war crimes to be entitled to certain core standards of treatment.

The parallel development of human rights law since World War II reinforces the idea of core protections even for persons allegedly responsible for heinous acts. Modern human rights law centers on important treaties and institutions that have had a significant, if not systematic, influence on the constitutions, laws, judicial decisions, and policies of states worldwide.[143] A key fount for human rights law, the

143 *See generally* CHRISTOF HEYNS & FRANS VILJOEN, THE IMPACT OF THE UNITED NATIONS HUMAN RIGHTS TREATIES ON THE DOMESTIC LEVEL (2002). Some empirical findings call into doubt the connection between ratification of human rights treaties and improvements in

1948 Universal Declaration of Human Rights ("Universal Declaration"),[144] heralded a series of important rights possessed by individuals as against government power: all persons "are born free and equal in dignity and rights";[145] all persons have the right to life, liberty, and security;[146] no one shall be held in slavery or tortured;[147] all persons are entitled to equal protection under the law;[148] there shall be no arbitrary arrest, detention, or exile;[149] all persons have the right to a fair trial;[150] and each person is entitled to an "effective remedy by the competent national tribunals" to vindicate these rights.[151] The 1966 International Covenant on Civil and Political Rights ("ICCPR") embellishes on such core standards,[152] and it further sets forth certain fundamental rights that cannot be derogated from even in time of national emergency,[153] including the right not to be arbitrarily deprived of life,[154] the right not to be tortured,[155] the right not to be held in slavery,[156] the right not to be found guilty of an offense made criminal ex post facto,[157] and the right to recognition as a person before the law.[158] As of 2006, the ICCPR has 154 parties, including the United States.[159]

The application of such instruments as a matter of law to particular detained persons raises special issues, given that the Universal Declaration is not a binding treaty and the ICCPR is interpreted by

---

domestic practice. *See, e.g.*, Oona A. Hathaway, *Do Human Rights Treaties Make a Difference?*, 111 YALE L.J. 1935, 1940 (2002) (finding no significant correlation between treaty ratification and better human rights practices); Oona A. Hathaway, *Testing Conventional Wisdom*, 14 EUR. J. INT'L L. 185, 185–86 (2003) (same, and responding to methodological critiques). *But see* Ryan Goodman & Derek Jinks, *Measuring the Effects of Human Rights Treaties*, 14 EUR. J. INT'L L. 171, 173, 178, 183 (2003) (criticizing Hathaway's research design and empirical conclusions).

144 Universal Declaration of Human Rights, G.A. Res. 217A (III), at 71, U.N. Doc. A/810 (Dec. 10, 1948).

145 *Id.* at 72, art. 1.

146 *Id.* at 72–73, art. 3.

147 *Id.* at 73, arts. 4–5.

148 *Id.* arts. 6–7.

149 *Id.* art. 9.

150 *Id.* arts. 10–11.

151 *Id.* art. 8.

152 International Covenant on Civil and Political Rights, Dec. 19, 1966, S. TREATY DOC. NO. 95-2 (1978), 999 U.N.T.S. 171 [hereinafter ICCPR].

153 *Id.* art. 4(2).

154 *Id.* art. 6(1).

155 *Id.* art. 7.

156 *Id.* art. 8(1).

157 *Id.* art. 15(1).

158 *Id.* art. 16.

159 *See* ICRC, STATE PARTIES, *supra* note 2.

the United States as not applying to U.S. conduct outside U.S. territory.[160] Yet regardless of such technical arguments, the historical arc of such human rights law helps explain why Common Article 3 has emerged as a common denominator for all persons captured in the course of armed conflict. Though the full range of Geneva Convention protections are not easily grafted onto the contemporary threat of global terrorism, Common Article 3 expresses those "elementary considerations of humanity" that the global community has come to embrace.[161]

Adapting the laws of war to address new circumstances is a notion readily accepted within such laws. An enduring element of the 1899 and 1907 Hague conferences is the recognition that codes of conduct cannot address all conceivable actions that may occur, especially as new technological developments arise. Consequently, the drafters of the 1907 Hague Convention on land warfare inserted a clause providing that even if a law-of-war code did not expressly apply to a specific situation, states were still bound to certain dictates of humanity:

> Until a more complete code of the laws of war has been issued, the High Contracting Parties deem it expedient to declare that, in cases not included in the Regulations adopted by them, the inhabitants and the belligerents remain under the protection and the rule of the principles of the law of nations, as they result from the usages established among civilized peoples, from the laws of humanity, and the dictates of the public conscience.[162]

This clause—known as the Martens Clause, after the Russian diplomat who called for its insertion—is binding treaty law on states, including the United States. The clause was maintained in the 1949 Geneva Conventions,[163] and it was adopted in a somewhat more mod-

---

160 *See* Michael J. Dennis, *Application of Human Rights Treaties Extraterritorially in Times of Armed Conflict and Military Occupation*, 99 Am. J. Int'l L. 119, 122–27 (2005) (recounting the U.S. position when the ICCPR was negotiated and finding that extraterritorial application "is at odds with the plain meaning of [the ICCPR], the practice of states that have ratified the Covenant, and the original intent of the negotiators"). *But see* Theodor Meron, *Extraterritoriality of Human Rights Treaties*, 89 Am. J. Int'l L. 78, 79 (1995) (stating that the extraterritorial application of the ICCPR has "almost never been questioned and has long ceased to be the preserve of scholars; it has obtained the imprimatur of the Human Rights Committee and UN rapporteurs").

161 *Cf.* Military and Paramilitary Activities (Nicar. v. U.S.), 1986 I.C.J. 14, 22 (June 27).

162 Hague Convention, *supra* note 33, pmbl.

163 The "denunciation clause" common to all four Geneva Conventions provides that a denunciation "shall in no way impair the obligations which the Parties to the conflict shall remain bound to fulfil by virtue of the principles of the law of nations, as they result from the usages established among civilized peoples, from the laws of humanity and the dictates of public

ern form in Protocol I without any controversy.[164] Though it has not figured in the U.S. government's discussions of the application of the Geneva Conventions in the "war on terror," the Martens Clause is an important means for clarifying law-of-war instruments where they fall short. Thus, in the 1996 advisory opinion of the ICJ on the legality of nuclear weapons, the Court found no treaty provision or customary international law norm specifically prohibiting the use of nuclear weapons.[165] However, the Court relied on the enduring significance of the Martens Clause to find that certain cardinal principles contained in law-of-war treaties (the need to distinguish combatants from non-combatants and the need to avoid unnecessary suffering to combatants) must be applied to new forms of military technology.[166] As such, the Court found that the use of nuclear weapons was generally prohibited.[167]

This confluence of events—the receptivity to change as reflected in the Martens Clause, the rise of human rights protections, and the belief that even those thought to have committed atrocities are entitled to certain rights—helps explain why Common Article 3 has gained such traction in the post–9/11 era; that is, why all roads lead to it. Yet there are also less altruistic explanations. International humanitarian law is built, to a certain extent, on a belief by countries that they can maintain better discipline among their armed forces if they operate in accordance with certain standards of decency; the path to anarchy is too well-trod when no standards exist. Further, there is a deep-seated belief (or at least hope) that by one side promoting such standards, there is a greater likelihood that the other side will apply them as well, at least in some measure. With a terrorist organization such as al Qaeda, or a government such as the Taliban, placing such faith in minimum standards of protection may be misplaced. But even the most heinous of actors have been known to show mercy, and efforts to promote such compassion, all things being equal, are rational and understandable.

conscience." Geneva Convention I, *supra* note 2, art. 63; Geneva Convention II, *supra* note 2, art. 62; Geneva Convention III, *supra* note 2, art. 142; Geneva Convention IV, *supra* note 2, art. 158.

164 Protocol I, *supra* note 44, art. 1(2) ("In cases not covered by this Protocol or by other international agreements, civilians and combatants remain under the protection and authority of the principles of international law derived from established custom, from the principles of humanity and from the dictates of public conscience."); *see* New Rules, *supra* note 43, at 37–38.

165 Legality of the Threat or Use of Nuclear Weapons, Advisory Opinion, 1996 I.C.J. 226, 266 (July 8).

166 *See id.* at 257.

167 *See id.* at 266.

Yet our understanding of the core protections of Common Article 3 should not stop with its language, for Common Article 3 also has experienced refinement since 1949. When Protocol I was adopted in 1977, it contained in article 75 on *Fundamental Guarantees* a series of provisions that track the core protections of Common Article 3 and deepen our understanding of them. Thus, whereas Common Article 3 includes a prohibition on "outrages upon personal dignity, in particular, humiliating and degrading treatment,"[168] article 75 of Protocol I embellishes by reference to "outrages upon personal dignity, in particular humiliating and degrading treatment, enforced prostitution and any form of indecent assault."[169] Similarly, whereas Common Article 3 briefly speaks to the right of detainees to be tried only by "a regularly constituted court, affording all judicial guarantees which are recognized as indispensable by civilized peoples,"[170] article 75 describes over the course of several paragraphs what constitutes "principles of regular judicial procedure," including the right to conduct one's defense and be present at one's trial, the presumption of innocence, the right to remain silent, the right to cross-examine witnesses, and protection against double jeopardy.[171]

Article 75 is directed at persons who are "affected" by the conflict, are in the hands of a party, and who do not already benefit from more favorable treatment outside article 75's protections.[172] As such, the "main function of the article is *to fill gaps* in treaty law by providing protection for categories of persons not already protected by such law,"[173] such as captured persons who engaged in hostilities but are not entitled to POW status.[174] Article 75 thus is an appropriate touchstone for determining the rights of nonstate actors, such as alleged members of a terrorist organization, engaged in armed conflict against a state. At the same time, article 75 provides that it does not limit or infringe upon other applicable international law; it is not a *lex specialis* that displaces other human rights protections.[175]

Because the United States is not a party to Protocol I (nor is Afghanistan for that matter),[176] article 75's terms are not binding as a

168 *See* Geneva Conventions I–IV, *supra* note 2, art. 3(1)(c).

169 Protocol I, *supra* note 44, art. 75(2)(b).

170 Geneva Conventions I–IV, *supra* note 2, art. 3(1)(d).

171 *See* Protocol I, *supra* note 44, art. 75(4).

172 *See id.* art. 75.

173 New Rules, *supra* note 43, at 457.

174 *See* Protocol I, *supra* note 44, art. 45(3); New Rules, *supra* note 43, at 457.

175 Protocol I, *supra* note 44, art. 75(8).

176 *See* ICRC, State Parties, *supra* note 2.

matter of treaty law with respect to the conflicts discussed above. Nevertheless, there is strong evidence that article 75 has passed into customary international law. More than 160 states have adhered to Protocol I, including article 75,[177] and no state has announced that article 75 does not reflect customary international law. The ICRC views these fundamental guarantees as having passed into customary international law.[178] Most scholars in the field[179]—as well as international tribunals that have addressed the issue, such as the Eritrea Ethiopia Claims Commission—have maintained that article 75 reflects customary international law. The Eritrea Ethiopia Claims Commission has stated:

> 30. The Commission views Article 75 of Protocol I as reflecting particularly important customary principles. . . . These guarantees distill basic human rights most important in wartime. Given their fundamental humanitarian nature and their correspondence with generally accepted human rights principles, the Commission views these rules as part of customary international law.
>
> 31. Article 75 of Protocol I "acts as a 'legal safety net' guaranteeing a minimum standard of human rights for all persons who do not have protection on other grounds."[180]

Although the United States did not ratify Protocol I, it also has not objected to article 75 as constituting a part of customary international law, and thus it has not placed itself in the position of being a persistent objector to such a rule. Indeed, the United States has publicly embraced article 75: after the adoption of Protocols I and II, the U.S. government "completed an extensive review of the Additional Protocols, both from the viewpoint of military considerations and from the viewpoint of national policy."[181] In 1986, that internal review

---

177 *See id.*

178 *See generally* 1 CUSTOMARY INTERNATIONAL HUMANITARIAN LAW 299–383 (Jean Marie-Henckaerts & Louise Doswald-Beck eds., 2005).

179 *See, e.g.*, Hans-Peter Gasser, *Protection of the Civilian Population*, *in* THE HANDBOOK OF HUMANITARIAN LAW IN ARMED CONFLICTS 209, 233 (Dieter Fleck ed., 2005) [hereinafter THE HANDBOOK OF HUMANITARIAN LAW].

180 *See* Civilians' Claims (Eth. v. Eri.), Eritrea's Claims Nos. 15, 16, 23, 27–32 (Eritrea Ethiopia Claims Comm'n Dec. 17, 2004), 44 I.L.M. 601 (2005) (quoting Gasser, *supra* note 179, at 233).

181 *See* Michael J. Matheson, *The United States Position on the Relation of Customary International Law to the 1977 Protocols Additional to the 1949 Geneva Conventions*, 2 AM. U. J. INT'L L. & POL'Y 419, 419 (1987) (statement by the U.S. Department of State Deputy Legal Adviser). Matheson recently reiterated that the Reagan Administration

> accepted as customary law . . . Article 75 of Additional Protocol I, which set forth a

concluded that the United States should not submit Protocol I to the Senate, but it also determined that "the United States will consider itself legally bound by the rules contained in Protocol I . . . to the extent that they reflect customary international law, either now or as it may develop in the future."[182] According to a Department of Defense memorandum, among the rules found in Protocol I that were already customary international law were the fundamental guarantees of article 75.[183] Describing publicly the outcome of the review, the U.S. Department of State Deputy Legal Adviser stated in 1987:

> We support in particular the fundamental guarantees contained in article 75, such as the principle that all persons who are in the power of a party to a conflict and who do not benefit from more favorable treatment under the Conventions be treated humanely in all circumstances and enjoy, at a minimum, the protections specified in the Conventions without any adverse distinction based upon race, sex, language, religion or belief, political or other opinion, national or social origin, or any similar criteria. We support the principle that these persons not be subjected to violence to life, health, or physical or mental well-being, outrages upon personal dignity, the taking of hostages, or collective punishments, and that no sentence be passed and no penalty executed except pursuant to conviction pronounced by an impartial and regularly constituted court respecting the generally recognized principles of regular judicial procedure.[184]

Thus, as of 1986, the U.S. government regarded article 75 as reflecting customary international law.

Today, twenty years later, there can be little doubt that article 75 is well-settled customary international law. Indeed, the Department of State Legal Adviser in 2003 asserted that "the United States . . . does regard the provisions of article 75 as an articulation of safeguards to which all persons in the hands of an enemy are enti-

---

> series of fundamental guarantees that would apply to all persons in the hands of a party to a conflict, even if they did not qualify for POW treatment. This provision was of course designed to fill the gaps in the 1949 Conventions to some degree.

Michael J. Matheson, *Continuity and Change in the Law of War: 1975 to 2005: Detainees and POWs*, 38 GEO. WASH. INT'L L. REV. 543, 546–47 (2006).

182 Matheson, *The United States Position*, *supra* note 181, at 420.

183 *See* Memorandum of the Dep't of Def. Law of War Working Group (May 9, 1986) ("We view the following provisions as already part of customary international law: . . . Fundamental guarantees: Article 75 . . . .") (cited in Matheson, *Continuity and Change*, *supra* note 181, at 547 n.9).

184 Matheson, *The United States Position*, *supra* note 181, at 427 (footnote omitted).

tled."[185] In *Hamdan*, the plurality opinion cited to that statement when finding that the provisions of article 75 relating to trial protections are "indisputably part of . . . customary international law."[186] The four justices in the plurality had no difficulty in using the more detailed provisions of article 75 as a means of illuminating the more general obligations set forth in Common Article 3.[187] In short, the "dictates of public conscience" are aptly captured in Common Article 3 of the 1949 Geneva Conventions and are further elaborated in article 75 of Protocol I, both of which are legally binding on the United States.

Assuming that article 75 and Common Article 3 are the principal sources of international humanitarian law with respect to the treatment of persons in armed conflict with terrorist organizations, do they help answer some of the key questions that will arise in years to come? Considerable attention has already been paid to whether the conditions of captivity accorded to detainees in the "war on terrorism" are compatible with international humanitarian law, including the methods employed by the United States in interrogating detainees and the rendition of detainees to countries where they are tortured and abused. One issue that has not received sufficient attention in legal commentary to date, however, concerns the duration of detention of unprivileged combatants and the conditions under which their captivity should be terminated. The next Part briefly addresses that issue.

B. Termination of Captivity

One of the most important issues at present in the "war on terror" is whether terrorist suspects initially classified as unlawful combatants may be detained virtually indefinitely by the United States without trial. In the aftermath of 9/11, the United States took into custody in Afghanistan, eastern Pakistan, and elsewhere about 775 persons who were transferred to detention facilities at the U.S. naval base at Guantanamo. As of mid-2007, the Department of Defense reported that about 395 of those detainees had been released or transferred to the custody of their home country. Of the 380 detainees still remaining at Guantanamo, approximately 80 had been designated for release. The remaining approximately 300 persons faced indefinite

185 William H. Taft IV, *The Law of Armed Conflict After 9/11: Some Salient Features*, 29 YALE J. INT'L L. 319, 322 (2003).

186 Hamdan v. Rumsfeld, 126 S. Ct. 2749, 2798 (2006).

187 *See id.* at 2797–98.

detention, without any expectation of either being released or prosecuted. Reportedly, some seventy to seventy-five persons might be placed before military commissions for trial, though only four persons had been indicted as a part of the current military commission process.[188]

Of the 380 detainees that remained at Guantanamo Bay most had been in U.S. custody for five years, longer than the duration of U.S. involvement in World War II. Detaining individuals without trial, even in time of war, is an extraordinary measure that imposes significant physical and mental burdens on the detainee. In June 2006, three of the detainees committed suicide. Consequently, the obligations of humane treatment both during the detention and in repatriation should be taken quite seriously.

1. Applicable Law

To the extent that the issue of termination of captivity has been addressed by the U.S. government, the standard assertion has been that the detainees may be held for "the duration of the hostilities," after which they must be repatriated to their country of nationality.[189] In *Hamdi v. Rumsfeld*,[190] the Supreme Court appeared to adopt that view as well, at least in the context of considering Hamdi's objection that Congress, by enacting the 2001 Authorization to Use Military Force ("AUMF") statute,[191] had not authorized indefinite detention.[192] The Court stated that "[i]t is a clearly established principle of the law of war that detention may last no longer than active hostilities."[193]

The general assertion that all detainees at Guantanamo Bay may be detained for the "duration of hostilities" is doubtful. First, that assertion may be overbroad in covering all persons detained worldwide in the "war on terrorism." Although detention of persons on the battlefield in Afghanistan—whether the person is associated with the Taliban or with al Qaeda—seems fairly to fall within the scope of the

188 These numbers have gradually changed over time as more detainees are released or transferred. The Department of Defense website that tracks this issue is http://www.defenselink.mil/news/nrdgb.html.

189 *See, e.g.*, Press Release, U.S. Dep't of State, Remarks upon Her Departure for Europe: Secretary Condoleezza Rice (Dec. 5, 2005), http://www.state.gov/secretary/rm/2005/57602.htm (statement by Secretary of State Condoleezza Rice, asserting that "[i]nternational law allows a state to detain enemy combatants for the duration of hostilities").

190 Hamdi v. Rumsfeld, 542 U.S. 507 (2004).

191 Authorization to Use Military Force, Pub. L. No. 107-40, 115 Stat. 224 (2001).

192 *Hamdi*, 542 U.S. at 520–21.

193 *Id.* at 520.

evolving laws of war, the detention of persons outside Afghanistan who are suspected of connections to global terrorism is more problematic. The laws of war operate within temporal and geographic realms; considerable attention is given to when it can be said that an "armed conflict" has arisen and ended, and also to where it is that protected persons are located (e.g., in enemy territory, in occupied territory, in neutral territory, etc.). These rules do not fit well the new paradigm of an armed conflict between a state and a nonstate actor that is transnational in nature, especially when that nonstate actor is not a centralized organization. Links to al Qaeda may be found in numerous countries—not because the indigenous factions there are actively engaged in a coordinated fight against the United States, but because al Qaeda attracts movements that seek to reduce Western influence in their own countries (or regions), be it Somalia, Algeria, or elsewhere.[194] A principal architect of the radical thinking that came to characterize al Qaeda, Abu Musab al-Suri, has written that "al Qaeda is not an organization, it is not a group, nor do we want it to be. . . . It is a call, a reference, a methodology."[195] If that is correct, it becomes very strained to view all persons suspected of ties to al Qaeda as unlawful combatants engaged in an armed conflict with the United States. It would be as if, during the Cold War, the United States decided to treat all persons suspected of being communists as combatants solely because communist groups were fighting the United States in places like Vietnam or Korea.

Although it may be true that al Qaeda-affiliated persons detained outside Afghanistan fall within the same rules as those detained on the battlefield, it may also be the case that the rules are different. Perhaps in recognition of this fact, the Supreme Court in *Hamdi*, after stating the general principle of the law of war that detention may last no longer than active hostilities, went on to note that "[i]f the practical circumstances of a given conflict are entirely unlike those of the conflicts that informed the development of the law of war, that understanding may unravel."[196] Indeed, the Court appears to have been influenced by the fact that Hamdi's case bore a strong resemblance to the conventional paradigm: Hamdi allegedly took up arms with the

194 *See* Editorial, *Somalia Simmers*, WASH. POST, Oct. 18, 2006, at A20 (recounting the Islamic fundamentalist movement in Somalia and its willingness to shelter al Qaeda members); Craig Whitlock, *Al-Qaeda's Far Reaching Partner*, WASH. POST, Oct. 5, 2006, at A1 (recounting an Algerian underground network's decision to partner with al Qaeda).

195 Lawrence Wright, *The Master Plan*, NEW YORKER, Sept. 11, 2006, at 48, 50.

196 *Hamdi*, 542 U.S. at 521.

Taliban and that active fighting against Taliban forces remained ongoing in Afghanistan.[197] By contrast, if al Qaeda suspects picked up in places other than the battlefield in Afghanistan are not regarded as combatants under the laws of war, then they would fall under the same rules that apply to any transnational criminal. They could be arrested and tried in regular courts for transnational crime, or they could be closely monitored by law enforcement authorities. They could not, however, simply be detained without trial indefinitely.

Second, even if one assumes that all the detainees at Guantanamo Bay should be treated alike, the general assertion that they may be detained for the "duration of hostilities" is not correct. That general assertion appears based on article 118 of Geneva Convention III which speaks in terms of repatriation after the "cessation of hostilities,"[198] and perhaps on the analogous article 133 of Geneva Convention IV which speaks of cessation of internment after the "close of hostilities."[199] Persons who have been prosecuted in accordance with the Conventions, of course, may be held even after the cessation or close of hostilities, but they remain under the protections of the Conventions until the completion of their sentences and their release.

The sentiment expressed by the 1949 Geneva Convention provisions in favor of expeditious release after the cessation or close of hostilities was animated by the problems that were experienced prior to 1949. The 1907 Hague Regulations[200] and the 1929 Geneva Conventions on Prisoners of War[201] were interpreted as allowing a detaining power not to repatriate until either the conclusion of an armistice agreement or even a final peace agreement. Because those agreements might take months or even years after the cessation of active hostilities, the repatriation of millions of prisoners of war in both the world wars were considerably delayed.[202] Consequently, the 1949 Geneva Conventions (and Protocol I) sought to detach the issue of repatriation from the conclusion of a formal agreement, and instead to tie

---

197 *See id.* at 510, 521.

198 *Cf.* Geneva Convention III, *supra* note 2, art. 118 ("Prisoners of war shall be released and repatriated without delay after the cessation of active hostilities.").

199 *Cf.* Geneva Convention IV, *supra* note 2, art. 133 (providing that any internment of civilians "shall cease as soon as possible after the close of hostilities").

200 Article 20 of the 1907 Hague Regulations provides that "[a]fter the conclusion of peace, the repatriation of prisoners of war shall be carried out as quickly as possible." Hague Regulations, *supra* note 33, art. 20.

201 Convention Relative to the Treatment of Prisoners of War art. 75, July 27, 1929, 47 Stat. 2021, 118 U.N.T.S. 343 ("When belligerents conclude a convention of armistice, they must, in principle have appear therein stipulations regarding the repatriation of prisoners of war.").

202 *See* 3 PICTET COMMENTARY, *supra* note 87, at 541.

the matter to the core justification for detention—i.e., whether the individual would pose a threat to the detaining power after release. In this sense, the obligation became a unilateral one imposed on the detaining power, and not one contingent on some form of consent from the opposing belligerent. For the 1949 Geneva Conventions, the threat no longer existed once the hostilities were over.

Yet, regardless of the duration of the conflict, Geneva Conventions III and IV are oriented toward an individualized assessment of the circumstances arising with respect to individual POWs and civilian internees. Under Geneva Convention III, a detaining power may release a particular POW on "parole or promise,"[203] and it may also "conclude agreements with a view to the direct repatriation or internment in a neutral country of able-bodied prisoners of war who have undergone a long period of captivity."[204] Likewise, the standard set forth in Geneva Convention IV for release of civilian internees is not solely tied to the close of hostilities; it provides that civilian internees "shall be released by the Detaining Power as soon as the reasons which necessitated his internment no longer exist."[205]

Moreover, as previously noted, the most relevant standards for the detainees in Guantanamo are not those relating to POWs or civilian internees, as the Guantanamo detainees have not been classified as such. The more relevant standards arise under Common Article 3 and Protocol I article 75. Common Article 3 is silent about termination of captivity. Article 75(3) of Protocol I, however, does address the matter, stating:

> Any person arrested, detained or interned for actions related to the armed conflict shall be informed promptly, in a language he understands, of the reasons why these measures have been taken. Except in cases of arrest or detention for penal offenses, such persons *shall be released with the minimum delay possible and in any event as soon as the circumstances justifying the arrest, detention or internment have ceased to exist.*[206]

The first sentence tracks the language of article 9(2) of the ICCPR,[207] a treaty that had been adopted before the Protocol I negotiations and that the Supreme Court plurality in *Hamdan* used to inform its under-

203 Geneva Convention III, *supra* note 2, art. 21.

204 *Id.* art. 109.

205 Geneva Convention IV, *supra* note 2, art. 132.

206 Protocol I, *supra* note 44, art. 75(3) (emphasis added).

207 ICCPR, *supra* note 152, art. 9(2).

standing of Protocol I article 75.[208] The second sentence indicates that unless the person is arrested or detained for a penal offense, they are to be released with "minimum delay" and as soon as the circumstances justifying the detention cease to exist. There is no linkage here to the conclusion of a peace agreement, as is the case for POWs under the 1907 Hague Regulations.[209] Yet neither is there any linkage to release only after cessation of active hostilities, as is the case generally for POWs under the 1949 Geneva Convention III.[210] Rather, the standard is closer to that of Geneva Convention IV, whereby regardless of the duration of the conflict, the individual is to be released once the reasons necessitating the detention no longer exist.

The official ICRC commentary on the Protocol maintains that there is an important link between these two sentences of Protocol I article 75(1). The first sentence speaks to a particular temporal period: the period between the time that the person is detained and the time that they are informed of the reasons for the detention. According to the ICRC, this period should last no more than ten days.[211] Turning to the second sentence, the ICRC commentary states that

> it seems clear that detainees not charged with a criminal offence within the period mentioned must be released; this is laid down in all national legislation. However, in time of armed conflict States often assume the right to take security measures with regard to certain persons who are considered dangerous.[212]

The implication of this commentary is that the decision whether to charge a detainee must be taken within ten days after capture; if the decision is not to charge, then the person should be released. If the person is considered dangerous, then the detention can continue, but it must end once the person is no longer viewed as dangerous. If this analysis is correct, then the standards applicable to persons detained by the United States in the "war" against al Qaeda require that the

208 Hamdan v. Rumsfeld, 126 S. Ct. 2749, 2797 (2006).

209 *See supra* note 198 and accompanying text.

210 *See supra* notes 199, 205 and accompanying text.

211 Sandoz Commentary, *supra* note 47, at 876–77 ("Legal practice in most countries recognizes preventive custody, i.e., a period during which the police or public prosecutor can detain a person in custody without having to charge him with a specific accusation; in peacetime this period is no more than two or three days, but sometimes it is longer for particular offences (acts of terrorism) and in time of armed conflict it is often prolonged. Useful indications can be found in national legislation. In any case, even in time of armed conflict, detaining a person for longer than, say, ten days without informing the detainee of the reasons for his detention would be contrary to this paragraph.").

212 *Id.* at 877.

United States release such detainees immediately upon determination that they no longer represent a threat to the United States or its allies, not upon the cessation of hostilities. The process that has now unfolded for the release of detainees, as discussed in the next Part, supports this conclusion, in that the United States is releasing detainees upon determining that they no longer constitute a threat to the United States and its allies.

2. *Process for Determining if Continued Detention Is Merited*

Neither Common Article 3 nor Protocol I article 75 addresses the method by which a detaining power should determine whether a detainee is considered dangerous. However, Protocol I article 75(3) was "based on Articles 43 and 132 of the Fourth [Geneva] Convention, which are concerned with periodic review of internment decisions."[213] The standards set forth in those articles call for: (1) review of the internment by an appropriate court or administrative board;[214] (2) periodic reviews conducted at least twice a year;[215] (3) communication to a protecting power, which could be the ICRC, of the names of the detainees and the decisions of the court or board;[216] and (4) release "as soon as the reasons which necessitated his internment no longer exist."[217] These standards appear to be appropriate ones to apply in considering the process for a detaining power's compliance with article 75(3).

In March 2004, the United States initiated two types of review processes concerning the detainees. First, it established a system of CSRTs, which were instituted to determine whether the detainee was properly classified as a "combatant."[218] The sole purpose of this process was to determine whether each detainee at Guantanamo Bay was properly determined to be a "combatant," not to determine whether each was a "prisoner of war" because that determination had previously been made by the President on a generalized basis. Thus, the

---

213 *Id.*

214 *See* Geneva Convention IV, *supra* note 2, art. 43.

215 *See id.*

216 *See id.*

217 *Id.*

218 *See* Memorandum from Paul Wolfowitz, Deputy Sec'y of Def., to the Sec'y of the Navy, Order Establishing Combatant Status Review Tribunal 1 (July 7, 2004), *available at* http://www.defenselink.mil/news/Jul2004/d20040707review.pdf. *See generally* John Mintz, *Pentagon Sets Hearings for 595 Detainees*, Wash. Post, July 8, 2004, at A1; Memorandum from the Sec'y of the Navy, Implementation of Combatant Status Review Tribunal Procedures for Enemy Combatants Detained at Guantánamo Bay Naval Base, Cuba (July 29, 2004), *available at* http://www.defenselink.mil/news/Jul2004/d20040730comb.pdf.

CRST process helped determine if an innocent tourist or relief worker was captured in the mistaken belief that he was a combatant. As a part of this process, the detainees were not assigned lawyers, but they were assigned U.S. military personnel to assist them in representing their views to the tribunal. By March 2005, 558 proceedings had been held, resulting in a determination that 520 persons were combatants and 38 persons were noncombatants.[219]

Second, the United States initiated an annual review process in which each detainee would be assessed to determine whether the individual continued to pose a threat to the United States or its allies, or whether he should be released.[220] Final review procedures were adopted in May 2004,[221] and an implementation directive was issued in September 2004.[222] Under this review process, an administrative review board ("ARB"), composed of three military officers with relevant training, assesses each detainee and recommends whether the individual should continue to be detained.[223] The final decision, however, rests with a Department of Defense civilian, appointed by the President with the advice and consent of the Senate.[224] "To the extent consistent with security," the government of the detainee's nationality may submit to the review board written information "of any nature, including information related to the threat posed by the enemy combatant to the United States and its allies."[225] A designated military officer presents to the board the reasons and evidence for and against

219 For the dates and results of the CSRT proceedings, see U.S. DEP'T OF DEF., COMBATANT STATUS REVIEW TRIBUNAL SUMMARY, http://www.defenselink.mil/news/Mar2005/d20050329csrt.pdf (last visited June 27, 2007).

220 *See* Memorandum from U.S. Dep't of Def. on Administrative Review Procedures for Enemy Combatants in the Custody of the Department of Defense at Guantánamo Bay Naval Base, Cuba (Draft Memorandum) 1 (Mar. 2, 2004), *available at* http://www.dod.mil/news/mar2004/d20040303ar.pdf.

221 *See* Paul Wolfowitz, Deputy Sec'y of Def., Order, Administrative Review Procedures for Enemy Combatants in the Control of the Department of Defense at Guantánamo Bay Naval Base, Cuba 1 (May 11, 2004) [hereinafter Order on Administrative Review Procedures], *available at* http://www.defenselink.mil/news/May2004/d20040518gtmoreview.pdf.

222 *See* Memorandum from U.S. Dep't of Def. on Implementation of Administrative Review Procedures for Enemy Combatants Detained at U.S. Naval Base Guantánamo Bay, Cuba (Sept. 14, 2004), *available at* http://www.defenselink.mil/news/Sep2004/d20040914adminreview.pdf.

223 *See* Order on Administrative Review Procedures, *supra* note 221, at 3, 7–8.

224 *See id.* at 3, 8. The Secretary of the Navy was so designated for this task. *See* News Release, U.S. Dep't of Def., Defense Department Conducts First Administrative Review Board, No. 1292-04 (Dec. 14, 2004), *available at* http://www.defenselink.mil/releases/release.aspx?releaseid=8068.

225 *See* Order on Administrative Review Procedures, *supra* note 221, at 4.

continued detention.[226] The detainee may present information to the board at a hearing and is supposed to have access to the presentations of his home government and the military officer "to the extent it is both necessary to his presentation . . . and consistent with national security."[227] The detainee is assisted by a military officer, who may also serve as his spokesman at the board hearing.[228] In December 2004, the Department of Defense began conducting these administrative review hearings.[229] By December 2005, a first round of 464 ARB proceedings had been held, resulting in decisions to continue to detain at Guantanamo 330 persons, to transfer to other countries 119 persons, and to release 14 persons.[230] By the end of 2006, a second round of ARB proceedings had been completed,[231] and these reviews will continue on an annual basis.

The Detainee Treatment Act of 2005,[232] which was issued in part as a reaction to the Supreme Court's decision in *Rasul v. Bush*,[233] imposes certain requirements on the CSRT and ARB processes, and it limits the remedies available to detainees who seek to challenge their status.[234] The Secretary of Defense is required to report to the Senate and House Armed Services Committees regarding the CSRT and ARB procedures, as well as the procedures in operation for status determinations regarding detainees in Iraq and Afghanistan.[235] The statute also sets forth the rules of evidence to be used regarding admissibility of coerced statements, the characteristics of the reviewing authority, and certain other procedural issues. Finally, it precludes federal court review of ARB determinations and grants the D.C. Circuit Court of Appeals exclusive and limited jurisdiction to hear appeals of the final decisions of the CSRT.[236]

---

226 *See id.* at 5.

227 *See id.* at 4–6.

228 *See id.* at 6.

229 *See* News Release, U.S. Dep't of Def., *supra* note 224.

230 For the dates and results of the CSRT proceedings, see U.S. DEP'T OF DEF., ADMINISTRATIVE REVIEW BOARD SUMMARY, http://www.defenselink.mil/news/Jan2006/d20060130arb.pdf (last visited May 4, 2007).

231 *See* U.S. DEP'T OF DEF., ADMINISTRATIVE REVIEW BOARD SUMMARY: ARB-2, http://www.defenselink.mil/news/arb2.pdf (last visited May 4, 2007).

232 Detainee Treatment Act of 2005, Pub. L. No. 109-148, § 1005, 119 Stat. 2739 (2005).

233 Rasul v. Bush, 542 U.S. 466 (2004).

234 Detainee Treatment Act, § 1005(a)(1).

235 *Id.* § 1005(a)(3), (b)–(d).

236 The D.C. Circuit Court of Appeals is limited to considering:

> (i) whether the status determination of the [CSRT] with regard to such alien was consistent with the standards and procedures specified by the Secretary of Defense for [CSRTs] (including the requirement that the conclusion of the Tribunal be sup-

There would appear to be no basis for arguing that the CSRT and ARB processes on their face run afoul of the customary international law obligation regarding release of unprivileged combatants, as expressed in Protocol I article 75 and read in light of Geneva Convention IV articles 43 and 132. The need for continued detention is periodically considered by an administrative board composed of persons competent to make such decisions, after receiving relevant information from the detainee, and it is then reviewed at a more senior level. Those decisions are likely communicated to the ICRC, which has been granted access to the Guantanamo detainees since their arrival in Guantanamo in early 2002. Further transparency exists in the reports provided to Congress regarding those determinations and the public release of associated of documents, transcripts, and decisions from the proceedings.[237] Whether those procedures are being conducted in a manner that is truly meaningful is outside the scope of this Article and will no doubt be the subject of scrutiny as more information becomes available.

3. *Application of the Relevant Law to Categories of Detainees*

Persons Transferred to Other Countries. Most of the detainees were found by the CRST proceedings to be combatants and were found by the ARB proceedings to constitute continuing threats to the United States and its allies. For many of these detainees, however, the ARB proceedings determined that they could be transferred to other countries, which could then take responsibility for monitoring, detaining, or prosecuting them despite the continuing threat. From 2002 to 2006, approximately 345 detainees at Guantanamo were transferred to the custody of other countries.[238] As of November 2006, it appeared

> ported by a preponderance of the evidence and allowing a rebuttable presumption in favor of the Government's evidence); and
>
> (ii) to the extent the Constitution and laws of the United States are applicable, whether the use of such standards and procedures to make the determination is consistent with [them].

Id. § 1005(e)(2)(C).

237 *See, e.g.*, U.S. Dep't of Def., Combatant Status Review Tribunal (CSRT) and Administrative Review Board (ARB) Documents Released March 3, April 3, and April 19, 2006: Testimony of Detainees Before the Combatant Status Review Tribunal, http://www.dod.mil/pubs/foi/detainees/csrt/index.html (last visited June 27, 2007).

238 *See* Press Release, U.S. Dep't of Def., Detainee Release Announced (Nov. 17, 2006), *available at* http://www.defenselink.mil/Releases/Release.aspx?ReleaseID=10204 (reporting that detainees had been transferred to Albania, Afghanistan, Australia, Bahrain, Belgium, Denmark, Egypt, France, Germany, Iran, Iraq, Jordan, Kuwait, Maldives, Morocco, Pakistan, Russia, Saudi Arabia, Spain, Sweden, Sudan, Tajikistan, Turkey, Uganda, United Kingdom, and Yemen).

that the United States planned to transfer approximately another 110 detainees.[239]

Where a detainee has been transferred to his country of nationality, any U.S. obligations arising under the Geneva Conventions would appear to end. If a detainee has not been transferred to his country of nationality, however, it seems appropriate to regard the United States as having a continuing obligation to ensure that the country of transfer abides by the standards of Common Article 3 and Protocol I article 75 in its treatment of the transferee, as is the case with respect to transfers of POWs under Geneva Convention III.[240]

Persons Deemed Eligible for Release. Between September 2004 and March 2005, the CSRT proceedings determined that 38 persons detained at Guantanamo—about five percent of the persons who spent time there—were not combatants.[241] The first round of ARB proceedings ending in 2005 determined that fourteen detainees were no longer a threat to the United States or its allies and could be released.[242] By mid-2007, some eighty-two persons were found either not to be combatants or to no longer pose a security risk.[243] Given such findings, the United States was under an obligation to release the individuals immediately; there was no basis for stating that the detention remained permissible due to ongoing hostilities against the Taliban in Afghanistan or against al Qaeda worldwide.

These persons, however, have not been released immediately. The U.S. Department of State sought to coordinate the return of the initial thirty-eight individuals deemed to be noncombatants to their countries of nationality,[244] but it experienced difficulties in doing so.[245]

---

239 *See id.*

240 *See* Geneva Convention III, *supra* note 2, art. 12.

241 *See* U.S. Dep't of Def., Combatant Status Review Tribunal Summary, *supra* note 219; *see also* News Release, U.S. Dep't of Def., Defense Department Special Briefing on Combatant Status Review Tribunals (Mar. 29, 2005), http://www.defenselink.mil/transcripts/2005/tr20050329-2382.html (statement by Secretary of the Navy that of the "558 CSRT hearings conducted, the enemy combatant status of 520 detainees was confirmed. The tribunals also concluded that 38 detainees were found to no longer meet the criteria to be designated as enemy combatants. So 520 enemy combatants, 38 non-enemy-combatants."). These persons have been referred to at times as "No Longer Enemy Combatants" or "NLEC." *See Guantánamo Bay Detainees Classified as "No Longer Enemy Combatants,"* Wash. Post, http://projects.washingtonpost.com/guantanamo/nlec (last visited June 27, 2007).

242 *See* U.S. Dep't of Def., Administrative Review Board Summary, *supra* note 230.

243 *See* Craig Whitlock, *82 Inmates Cleared But Still Held at Guantanamo*, Wash. Post, Apr. 29, 2007, at A1 (reporting information obtained from U.S. government officials and lawyers for the detainees).

244 These persons were nationals of various countries: Afghanistan; Algeria; China; Egypt; France; Jordan; Maldives; Russia; Saudi Arabia; Sudan; Turkey; and Yemen. *See Guantánamo*

The first five were released by March 2005,[246] yet it took until November 2006 before all thirty-eight detainees were released.[247] The speed with which persons are released who are no longer deemed a threat under the ARB process is unclear; the Department of Defense seems to lump such persons together in its data on persons awaiting transfer to other countries. The reasons for the continued delay in releasing persons who have been found either not to be combatants or not to pose any further threat appear to fall into three categories: detainees who could not be returned to their country of origin out of a fear they would be mistreated; detainees whose country of origin would not allow their return; and detainees who were either stateless or whose apparent country of origin challenged their nationality.

With respect to the first category, article 75 does not provide for an exception where the detainee does not wish to return to his country of origin for fear of mistreatment. Although that issue was discussed in the course of negotiations of both Geneva Convention III and Protocol I regarding repatriation, exceptions were not adopted out of a concern that prisoners might not be able to make a free choice while still in captivity.[248] Nevertheless, contemporary human rights must be viewed as now informing this obligation to repatriate, especially in light of article 75(8). For example, article 3 of the Convention against Torture prohibits the return of an individual to a country where a person would likely be tortured.[249] The United States implements this obligation through a statute that declares that it

> shall be the policy of the United States not to expel, extradite or otherwise effect the involuntary return of any person to a country in which there are substantial grounds for believing the persons would be in danger of being subjected to torture,

---

Bay Detainees Classified as "No Longer Enemy Combatants," supra note 241 (listing the detainees, their nationality, and providing links to transcripts of their CRST proceeding).

245 *See* Craig Whitlock, *U.S. Faces Obstacles to Freeing Detainees*, WASH. POST, Oct. 17, 2006, at A1.

246 *See* News Release, U.S. Dep't of Def., Defense Department Special Briefing on Combatant Status Review Tribunals, *supra* note 241.

247 *See* Press Release, U.S. Dep't of State, Release of Three No Longer Enemy Combatant (NLEC) Detainees from Guantánamo (Nov. 17, 2006), *available at* http://www.state.gov/r/pa/prs/ps/2006/76275.htm.

248 *See* 3 PICTET COMMENTARY, *supra* note 87, at 543.

249 Convention Against Torture and Other Cruel, Inhuman or Degrading Treatment or Punishment art. 3, Dec. 10, 1984, S. TREATY DOC. NO. 100-20 (1988), 1465 U.N.T.S. 85. The Convention entered into force for the United States in 1994.

> *regardless of whether the person is physically present in the United States.*[250]

With respect to the second and third categories, the United States presumably has impressed on the detainee's country of origin that it is a violation of international law to render a person stateless.

Yet for all three categories, the United States was under an obligation to release the detainees with the minimum delay possible, and that release is *not* contingent on an ability to return the detainee to a particular country. Consequently, in my view, the United States was obligated, at a minimum, to parole such individuals into the United States pending a final resolution of their status. Our immigration laws are fully capable of handling persons in nonimmigrant status who are paroled in the United States pending proceedings for their removal to another country. The only reason not to do so is a political one: the embarrassment of bringing into the United States and allowing free movement to persons previously declared to be terrorists or unlawful combatants. Yet it was the choice of the United States, for its own benefit, to bring these individuals to Guantanamo from the places they had been abroad. To the extent that the United States experienced difficulty in returning those persons, it, and not the individuals, should bear the burden of that difficulty.

By way of example, the United States captured in Afghanistan and brought to Guantanamo Chinese nationals who were ethnic Uighur Muslims.[251] In 2004—even before initiation of the CSRT and ARB proceedings—the U.S. government determined that these individuals were either not enemy combatants or posed no risk to the United States and its allies, and therefore they could be released. Be-

250 8 U.S.C. § 1231 note (2000). For the Immigration and Naturalization Service implementing regulations, see 8 C.F.R. §§ 208.16(c), 208.18 (2005). For the Department of State implementing regulations, see 22 C.F.R. § 95.2–.4 (2005). Taking account of such concerns is consistent with the practical implementation of the laws of war. As far back as the aftermath of the Korean War, it has been accepted that in exceptional cases prisoners need not be forced to return to their homeland against their will, and that the obligation to treat them humanely includes taking into account the conditions that they might face upon repatriation. *See* G.A. Res. 610, ¶ 2, UN GAOR, 7th Sess., Supp. No. 20, UN Doc. A/2361 (Dec. 3, 1952) (affirming that force shall not be used against POWs either to prevent or to effect their repatriation and that they shall at all times be treated humanely); *see also* 3 PICTET COMMENTARY, *supra* note 87, at 547–48; R.R. Baxter, *Asylum to Prisoners of War*, 30 BRIT. Y.B. INT'L L. 489, 489 (1953); Jaro Mayda, *The Korean Repatriation Problem and International Law*, 47 AM. J. INT'L L. 414, 414 (1953). Having said that, the soundest course of action in the event that detainees are not to be repatriated is to have their consent verified by an entity other than the detaining power, such as the ICRC.

251 *See* John R. Crook, *Contemporary Practice of the United States Relating to International Law*, 100 AM. J. INT'L L. 690, 710–11 (2006).

cause many Chinese Uighurs oppose the government of China, these individuals feared that they would be imprisoned, persecuted, or tortured if returned to China. The United States apparently agreed and engaged in an extensive effort to find a country willing to accept the Uighurs.[252] Ultimately it succeeded for a few of them, but as of mid-2007 seventeen of them remain at Guantanamo.[253] Such lengthy detention of innocent persons is unconscionable and a violation of U.S. obligations under Common Article 3 and Protocol I article 75.

Persons Neither Transferred Nor Released. As of mid-2007, there remained about 300 persons detained at Guantanamo who are regarded as threats to U.S. security. Perhaps some sixty to eighty of those persons will be tried before the U.S. system of military commissions that will now operate under the Military Commissions Act of 2006.[254] Although the United States is still engaged in an aggressive effort to transfer many of these individuals to other countries, it has encountered considerable resistance to these transfers, including from close allies such as the United Kingdom. These detainees present the most difficult scenario for balancing the needs of the security of the detaining power against the rights of protected persons to humane treatment.

With respect to the Taliban detainees, the United States, its allies, and the government of Afghanistan should be permitted to continue the detentions so long as the individuals remain a threat, which may be the case as long as the Taliban remains involved in active hostilities against the government of Afghanistan.[255] If those hostilities conclude, the detainees should be repatriated as soon as possible to their country of origin. Such repatriation should not be delayed based on the lack of a formal agreement concerning the cessation of hostilities,

252 *See* Robin Wright, *Chinese Detainees Are Men Without a Country*, WASH. POST, Aug. 24, 2005, at A1. Two of the men filed suit in U.S. court seeking habeas relief but were unsuccessful before the district court. *See* Qassim v. Bush, 407 F. Supp. 2d 198, 203 (D.D.C. 2005), *appeal dismissed*, 466 F.3d 1073 (D.C. Cir. 2006).

253 *See* Associated Press, *3 Detainees at Guantánamo Are Released to Albania*, WASH. POST, Nov. 18, 2006, at A13; Whitlock, *supra* note 245.

254 Military Commissions Act of 2006, Pub. L. No. 109-366, 120 Stat 2600 (2006).

255 *See* Hamdi v. Rumsfeld, 542 U.S. 507, 517 (2004) ("There can be no doubt that individuals who fought against the United States in Afghanistan as part of the Taliban, an organization known to have supported the al Qaeda terrorist network responsible for [the 9/11] attacks, are individuals Congress sought to target in passing the AUMF. We conclude that detention of individuals falling into the limited category we are considering, *for the duration of the particular conflict in which they were captured*, is so fundamental and accepted an incident to war as to be an exercise of the 'necessary and appropriate force' Congress has authorized the President to use." (emphasis added)).

the integration of the Taliban into the Afghan government, amnesty, or any related matter. If it is more likely than not that the detainee will be subject to human rights abuses, such as torture, upon his repatriation, then the repatriation should not go forward, and an alternative means of release should be developed until circumstances change. In the event that the United States withdraws its forces from Afghanistan prior to the cessation of those hostilities, the United States would be withdrawing from the conflict and would no longer have a basis under the laws of war for detaining Taliban personnel.

With respect to al Qaeda detainees, the United States must continue to engage in periodic reviews of the threat posed by each individual detainee. Obviously, that threat can diminish over time, in light of the age, health, and psychological condition of the detainee. Moreover, the process for review must take account of the exact relationship of the detainee to al Qaeda. As indicated before, al Qaeda is a network of groups or cells, some of which are rather peripheral to its strategic activities. Splinter groups in Iraq, Somalia, and elsewhere may fall under the rubric of al Qaeda, but their fortunes may change dramatically over time in terms of their vitality and significance. As such, if a detainee is connected to a group that, for whatever reason, has been thoroughly routed, and if it is probable that the detainee would return to his homeland without re-engaging with his al Qaeda faction, then that fact should be taken into account in any threat assessment. In other words, al Qaeda should not be viewed as a monolithic entity; the threat of the detainee should be gauged based on the part of al Qaeda to which he relates, rather than the overall threat of the existence of al Qaeda.

Wounded or Sick in Detention. The longer the United States holds detainees, the more likely significant issues will arise with respect to their health and well-being. Already, difficult issues have arisen, such as whether a detainee should be transferred to the United States (or another country) for heart surgery, or whether it should be performed at Guantanamo Bay.[256] Ultimately, questions must be addressed about whether certain detainees should be released for health reasons.

The standards set forth in Common Article 3 and in Protocol I article 75 do not address the issue of repatriating detainees who are sick or severely injured. Yet given the requirement for humane treatment in both Common Article 3 and article 75, there are compelling

256 *Detainee Wants to Be Relocated for Surgery*, WASH. POST, Nov. 19, 2006, at A10.

reasons to view the standards set forth in Geneva Convention III article 110 as establishing general benchmarks for humane treatment on this issue. Article 110 provides that the following POWs should be repatriated even during the course of the conflict:

> (1) Incurably wounded and sick whose mental or physical fitness seems to have been gravely diminished.
>
> (2) Wounded and sick who, according to medical opinion, are not likely to recover within one year, whose condition requires treatment and whose mental or physical fitness seems to have been gravely diminished.
>
> (3) Wounded and sick who have recovered, but whose mental or physical fitness seems to have been gravely and permanently diminished.[257]

To the extent that any of the detainees at present or in the future reach such stages of mental or physical fitness, the obligation of humane treatment imposed on the United States requires termination of their captivity.

VI. Conclusion

The dominant paradigms of the 1949 Geneva Conventions, which concern either interstate or internal armed conflict, do not sit well with the new face of armed conflict presented by al Qaeda. The non-state actor who engages in heinous conduct has been an outcast to the laws of war, whether one looks at the terrorism of William Quantrill in the 1860s or the terrorism of al Qaeda today. For that reason, it is understandable that the full protections envisaged by those Conventions were not applied in the types of conflicts that emerged after 9/11. Nevertheless, influenced by developments in the fields of human rights and international criminal law, the laws of war have now evolved to a point where the "dictates of public conscience" compel the application of core protections even for the outcast. Those protections are reflected in both conventional and customary international law, and they may be seen in Common Article 3 of the 1949 Geneva Conventions and in article 75 of their Additional Protocol I. If the United States wishes to act in accordance with international law, such standards should guide the United States in the conditions of the detention and the mechanisms by which detainees are prosecuted for crimes.

---

257 Geneva Convention III, *supra* note 2, art. 110.

For example, those standards should guide the United States in its decisionmaking on the release of detainees. Detainees in the "war on terror" may *not* be held until the "cessation of hostilities." They may only be held so long as the particular detainee at issue represents a danger or threat to the detaining power. The detaining power is obligated to undertake periodic reviews, by an appropriate court or administrative board, of whether that threat continues to exist. Once the detainee is determined not to be a threat, or their mental or physical fitness has been gravely diminished, the detainee must be released immediately. If the detainee will likely be exposed to abuse by being sent back to his country of origin, he may not be returned. In that case, or in the case of a detainee whose country of origin will not accept his return or recognize his nationality, the United States is obligated to release the detainee in the United States until an appropriate alternative place for relocation can be resolved. Continued detention of persons deemed not to be a threat is unlawful and unconscionable.

Part II
Occupation

[6]

The Origins of the Concept of Belligerent Occupation

EYAL BENVENISTI

The contemporary international law of occupation, which regulates the conduct of occupying forces during wartime, was framed over the course of deliberations among European governments during the second half of the nineteenth century. The debates between representatives of strong and weak powers on this matter dominated the conferences in Brussels (1874) and The Hague (1899), whose goal was to formulate the laws of war through an international agreement. The outcome, enshrined in what is known as the Hague Regulations of 1899,[1] represented a delicate balance that both provided protection for a civilian population brought under the control of an occupant and safeguarded the interests of the ousted government for the duration of the occupation. Occupation was conceived of as a temporary regime existing until the conclusion of a peace agreement between the enemy sides (unless the defeated party ceased to exist as a result of

1. Convention (II) with Respect to the Laws and Customs of War on Land and its Annex: Regulations concerning the Laws and Customs of War on Land. The Hague, 29 July 1899 (http://www.icrc.org/ihl.nsf/FULL/150?OpenDocument). The text concerning occupation is repeated in the 1907 Regulations: Convention (IV) respecting the Laws and Customs of War on Land and its annex: Regulations concerning the Laws and Customs of War on Land. The Hague, 18 October 1907 (http://www.icrc.org/ihl.nsf/FULL/195?OpenDocument).

Eyal Benvenisti is Professor of Law, Tel Aviv University <ebenve@post.tau.ac.il>.
He is grateful to Maria Smolka-Day, Associate Director of the University of Pennsylvania School of Law library, for her resourcefulness and dedication, and to Shay Gurion and Mary Ellen Payne for their excellent research assistance. He also thanks the Institute for International Law at the University of Munich, where much of the research for this article was conducted. Earlier versions were presented at the Center for International History at Columbia University (2005), the University of Glasgow (2006), and the University of California, Berkeley (2007). He thanks the participants at these conferences and a referee from this journal for their helpful comments on those versions.

the war, a situation referred to as *debellatio*).[2] The evolution of the law of occupation in the nineteenth century was a gradual process, shaped by changing conceptions about war and sovereignty,[3] as well as by the balance of power emerging in Europe.[4]

The law of belligerent occupation as ultimately expressed in the 1899 Hague Regulations imposes two types of obligations on an army that seizes control of enemy land during war: the obligation to protect the life and property of the inhabitants and the obligation to respect the sovereign rights of the ousted government. These two prongs are not necessarily related to one another and, in fact, derive from different normative backgrounds and are subject to different political constraints. This essay tracks the evolution of the two obligations culminating in their merger in the text of the Regulations. The first principle, protecting individuals and their property, evolved from an earlier distinction between combatants and non-combatants and the duty to spare the latter from the scourges of war. The extension of this principle to encompass the property of non-combatants was first noted by Vattel and Rousseau in the second half of the eighteenth century. The obligation to respect the sovereign rights of the ousted government, the second principle, reflects the final stages of the crystallization of the concept of sovereignty as a nation's claim for exclusive control over its territory and nationals.

2. See, in general, Eyal Benvenisti, *The International Law of Occupation* (Princeton: Princeton University Press, 1993); Adam Roberts, "What Is a Military Occupation?" *1984 British Year Book of International Law* 55 (1985): 249.

3. The concept of occupation was applied in the context of both just and unjust wars. As pointed out by Vattel, the unjust enemy "can absolutely have no right whatever: every act of hostility that he commits is an act of injustice." Emerich de Vattel, *The Law of Nations*, ed. and trans. Joseph Chitty (1758; Philadelphia, 1852), vol. 2, bk. 3, chap. 13, para. 183, see also para. 187). But the law between nations could not be based on such a principle, which would require one sovereign to judge another (para. 188). Both for reasons of principle ("[e]very free and sovereign state has a right to determine, according to the dictates of her own conscience, what her duties require of her, and what she can or cannot do with justice") as well as for pragmatic reasons (para. 188), the law of war must accept reciprocal rights between enemy parties. As a result, "[e]very acquisition [. . .] which has been made in regular warfare, is valid according to the voluntary law of nations, independently of the justice of the cause and the reasons which may have induced the conqueror to assume the property of what he has taken. Accordingly, nations have ever esteemed conquest a lawful title; and that title has seldom been disputed, unless where it was derived from a war not only unjust in itself, but even destitute of any plausible pretext" (para. 195).

4. As Oppenheim wrote in 1905, "The distinction between mere temporary military occupation of territory, on the one hand, and, on the other, real acquisition of territory though conquest and subjugation, became more and more apparent, since Vattel had drawn attention to it. However, it was not till long after the Napoleonic wars in the nineteenth century that the consequences of this distinctions were carried out to their full extent by the theory and practice of International Law." Lassa Oppenheim, *International Law: A Treatise,* 1st ed. (London: Longmans, Green, 1905), 2:168.

This obligation emerged in Europe during the second half of the nineteenth century, a manifestation of the evolution of national identities in Europe.

The nineteenth-century notion of occupation as a temporary regime that does not confer sovereign authority can be understood as the culmination of a long process in which the concept of sovereignty was refined.[5] Indeed, the evolution of the concept of occupation can be seen as the mirror-image of the development of the concept of sovereignty. These parallel and interrelated processes were to continue in the twentieth century. The new principles of self-determination, democracy, and human rights that pierced the veil of national sovereignty and limited the sovereign affected also the law of occupation by modifying the restrictions on the occupant's exercise of authority. By the end of the twentieth century, the occupant would, for example, be required to respect the human rights of indigenous populations, who, in turn, would be entitled to promote their collective interests against the oppressive sovereign.[6] Indeed, the law of occupation can be seen as indirectly defining the concept of sovereignty just as tort law defined the Common Law private right to property by providing causes of action for its violation.

Given the evolution of the notion of belligerent occupation throughout the nineteenth century and due to the different political realities in different parts of the world, a variety of contemporaneous understandings of this notion arose. The development of the concept was principally a European project in the nineteenth century. At the same time, the term "occupation" was used quite differently in other parts of the world. The colonial powers operating outside Europe maintained the older doctrine of "occupation," which does not distinguish between conquest and occupation and therefore enabled the unilateral assumption of sovereignty over lands inhabited by what they deemed to be uncivilized peoples. The United States applied the concept of occupation with respect to its adjacent territories to denote an area that had been conquered by the U.S. and thereby became American vis-à-vis other states but did not enter the Union until Congress decided to incorporate it. The two-pronged European concept of occupation only became part of general international law in the early twentieth century, by which time the U.S. and the European colonial powers had already consolidated their territorial gains.[7]

5. Scholars like to portray the Peace of Westphalia (1648) as the birth of the idea of sovereignty. But as Derek Croxton shows, the concept of sovereignty remained vague and contested for centuries, reflecting the evolving balance of power in Europe. See Derek Croxton, "The Peace of Westphalia of 1648 and the Origins of Sovereignty," *International History Review* 21 (1999): 569.

6. Benvenisti, *Occupation*, chap. 6.

7. On the further evolution of the law of occupation during the twentieth century, see Benvenisti, *Occupation*.

The diverging understandings of the same term created some confusion in the literature on the evolution of the concept of military occupation. In this essay, I attempt to distinguish between these different meanings and trace their distinct lineages. Part I outlines the intellectual roots of the European doctrine on occupation and examines their link with the evolving social and political conditions in Europe. Part II describes the meandering process of translating the doctrine from an idea into a legally binding norm of international law. Part III presents my conclusions.

I. The Intellectual Roots of an Emerging European Concept

Part I considers the different theoretical approaches that led to the consolidation of the European concept of belligerent occupation by the mid-nineteenth century. Two lines of thought shape this concept: the principle of humanity, which entails a distinction between combatants and civilians as legitimate targets of warfare (discussed in Section A), and the principle of nationality, inspired by the French Revolution (Section B).

A. The Principle of Humanity: The Obligation to Protect the Property of Enemy Civilians

The personal aspect of the law of belligerent occupation is derived from the fundamental distinction in the law of war between combatants and non-combatants. There is a long tradition of a duty to spare non-combatants, going back, Grotius suggested, to Biblical times.[8] But it was in 1758 that Vattel first proposed extending the personal immunity granted to civilians beyond their bodily integrity to include also their property.[9] Vattel explained that this would improve on ancient tradition (the latter acknowledged by Grotius as "a departure from the principles of humanity"),[10] stating,

8. Hugo Grotius, *De Jure Belli ac Pacis* (The Rights of War and Peace) (1625), bk. 3, chap. 11, paras. 9, 10.

9. Vattel, *The Law of Nations*, at para. 200. On the emerging distinction during that period between the conqueror's rights vis-à-vis the former ruler and its more limited authority over the indigenous population, see also Sharon Korman, *The Right of Conquest* (New York: Clarendon Press, 1996): 29–40.

10. According to Grotius, *Jure Belli*, chap. 15, paras. 1–3, the property of enemy subjects may be taken in a just war to recover the debt that the enemy has incurred or by way of reprisal in return for other goods taken by the enemy. In paragraph 4, Grotius explained the logic of his assertion but admitted that "it is in some measure a departure from the principles of humanity."

> In the conquests of ancient times, even individuals lost their lands. Nor is it a matter of surprise that in the first ages of Rome such a custom should have prevailed. The wars of that era were carried on between popular republics and communities. The state possessed very little, and the quarrel was in reality the common cause of all the citizens. But at present war is less dreadful in its consequences to the subject: matters are conducted with more humanity: one sovereign makes war against another sovereign, and not against the unarmed citizens. The conqueror seizes on the possessions of the state, the public property, while private individuals are permitted to retain theirs. They suffer but indirectly by the war; and the conquest only subjects them to a new master.[11]

Note that this proposition is devoted solely to the principle of personal protection and says nothing about the public aspect of belligerent occupation, namely, the ousted prince's retention of sovereignty. Vattel assumed that the occupant replaces the prince and gains valid title over his property. In other words, according to Vattel, there is no distinction between an occupant and a conqueror who may treat the territory gained as under its sovereignty: "If the conquered town or province fully and perfectly constituted a part of the domain of a nation or sovereign, it passes on the same footing into the power of the conqueror. Thenceforward united with the new state to which it belongs."[12]

Similarly, under Vattel's notion, the conqueror acquires other rights of the enemy, such as his right to any "city or a country which is not simply an integrant part of a nation, or which does not fully belong to a sovereign, but over which that nation or that sovereign has certain rights"[13] and title to the ousted sovereign's property.[14]

In the *The Social Contract* (1762), Jean-Jacques Rousseau likewise elaborated on the concept of war as a conflict that takes place only between governments.[15] He attributed the necessary implications of this concept

11. Vattel, *The Law of Nations*, at para. 195 (note that civilians who do take arms against the conqueror may lose their property [para. 19]).

12. Ibid., para. 195.

13. Ibid., para. 199.

14. Ibid., para. 197. However, the conqueror's right to transfer title to a third party must await a peace treaty: "Immovable possessions, lands, towns, provinces, &c., become the property of the enemy who makes himself master of them: but it is only by the treaty of peace, or the entire submission and extinction of the state to which those towns and provinces belonged, that the acquisition is completed, and the property becomes stable and perfect. [. . .] Thus, a third party cannot safely purchase a conquered town or province, till the sovereign from whom it was taken has renounced it by a treaty of peace, or has been irretrievably subdued, and has lost his sovereignty." Ibid., paras. 197, 198.

15. Jean-Jacques Rousseau, *The Social Contract*, trans. G. D. H. Cole (1762), bk. 14 ("War then is a relation, not between man and man, but between State and State, and individuals are enemies only accidentally, not as men, nor even as citizens, but as soldiers; not as members of their country, but as its defenders").

to the rights of governed peoples, recognizing the distinction between public and private property and the consequent immunity of private property: "Even in real war, a just prince, while laying hands, in the enemy's country, on all that belongs to the public, respects the lives and goods of individuals: he respects rights on which his own are founded."[16]

During the first half of the nineteenth century, this statement by Rousseau gained little notice.[17] Better known were pronouncements made by the French jurist Jean-Étienne-Marie Portalis and by Talleyrand, which were later described as heavily influenced by the ideas underpinning the French Revolution, human rights and self-determination.[18] In his inauguration speech at the *Conseil des prises,* on 14 floréal year VIII, Portalis declared, "It is a relationship between objects, not between individuals, which constitutes war; it is the relations between states, not between individuals."[19] Talleyrand was apparently the first to turn this distinction into legal doctrine. Writing to Napoleon on November 20, 1806, he stated: "D'après la maxime que la guerre n'est point une relation d'homme à homme, mais un relation d'État à État, dans laquelle les particuliers ne sont enemis qu'accidentellement . . . le droit de gens ne permet pas que le droit de guerre et le droit de conquêste qui en derive, s'éntendent aux citoyens paisibles et sans armes . . . ."[20]

This view evolved into a general theory of war in the nineteenth century, to be known later as the Rousseau-Portalis doctrine, based on the principle of humanity. Harming non-combatants was deemed excessive under this theory. As Talleyrand suggested, the law of war rested on the principle that nations in war must wreak the least possible harm.[21] As long as civilians keep themselves outside the war, it is not necessary to harm them.[22] This

16. Ibid.

17. As mentioned below, notes 18–22, the German scholars Heffter and Bluntschli who elaborate on this idea do not mention Rousseau in this context.

18. J. C. Bluntschli, *Das Beuterecht im Krieg und das Seebeuterecht Inbesondere: Eine Völkerrechtliche Untersuchung* (Nördlingen: C. H. Beck,1878), 60.

19. "C'est le rapport des choses et non des personnes, qui constitue la guerre; elle est une relation d'État à État, et non d'individu à individu." Cited by August Wilhelm Heffter, *Das Europäische Völkerrecht der Gegenwart* (Berlin: E. H. Schroeder, 1844), at para. 119, n. 3.

20. "On the basis of the principle that war is not a relationship between men but a relationship between states, in which individuals are enemies only by coincidence . . . the law of nations does not permit the right of war and the right of conquest that is derived from it, to affect peaceful and unarmed [enemy] citizens." Cited by Heffter, *Das Europäische Völkerrecht,* at para. 119, n. 3. Note that Talleyrand does not restrict the right of conquest. This message found succinct expression in the famous statement of King William of Prussia on August 11, 1870, as the Prussian Army invaded France: "I conduct war with the French soldiers, not with the French citizens."

21. Cited by Heffter, *Das Europäische Völkerrecht,* at para. 119, n. 3.

22. Ibid., para. 119; Bluntschli, *Das Beuterecht,* at 60–70.

approach was reflected in military manuals[23] and, thereafter, in international conventions.[24] In the specific context of the international law of war, this distinction produced rules protecting against the taking of private property in conquered areas.

B. Enter National Self-Determination: "Occupation" Becomes Distinct from "Conquest"

The principle of humanity did not prevent invading armies from annexing or otherwise imposing their governmental structures on the occupied population while, simultaneously, respecting private property. The principle could not explain why such annexations should be illegal under the law. With the French Revolution, however, a new concept emerged—national self-determination—which would ultimately restrict the authority of the occupant. Under this concept, among other things, the territory of the state belongs to its people, not to the king. The ramifications were apparent: The first French Constitution of 1791 proclaimed that "the kingdom is one and indivisible"[25] and no prince may cede it to foreigners. It gave the principle Europe-wide validity:[26] The Constitution recognized further "the liberty of any people" and declared that France would never use its might to conquer other peoples.[27] This marked the beginning of an era in which individuals identified themselves more and more with their governments. Wars were no longer duels between princes. In a war between nations, citizens were expected to sacrifice their lives to repel the invader and resist the occupier. That citizens were interested in far more than the protection of their private property became eminently clear already in

23. Bluntschli, *Das Beuterecht,* at 64–69, described the French military criminal codes of 1793 and 1796, which prohibited pillage and other takings of private property, the 1845 Prussian criminal statute, which prohibited unauthorized acts against enemy combatants and civilians, and the German military criminal statute of 1872, which prohibited "unauthorized" pillage and plunder; and, of course, there was the so-called Lieber Code of 1863 (see below note 95 and accompanying text).

24. The Rousseau-Portalis Doctrine was considered to be reflected in the Hague Regulations of 1899 and 1907. See Raphael Lemkin, *Axis Rule in Occupied Europe* (Washington: Carnegie Endowment for International Peace, 1944), 79.

25. The Constitution of 3 September 1791, Title II ("Of the Division of the Kingdom and of the Status of Citizens").

26. The Miscellaneous Provisions of the Constitution note that "the French colonies and possessions in Asia, Africa, and America, although constituting part of the French dominion, are not included in the present Constitution."

27. The Constitution of 3 September 1791, Title VI ("Of the Relations of the French Nation with Foreign Nations"): "The French nation renounces the undertaking of any war with a view of making conquests, and it will never use its forces against the liberty of any people."

1808, with the eruption of guerrilla warfare in Spain against the occupying French Army.[28] It thus became increasingly difficult to assert that citizens' allegiance to their nation could be cut simply through military defeat. In fact, by the mid-nineteenth century and, in particular, subsequent to the Franco-Prussian War, the prevalence of irregular fighters in occupied territories threatened to entirely jeopardize the effort to regulate the law of occupation. The failure of the 1874 Brussels Conference was undoubtedly attributable to a lack of accord over the right of citizens to use force against an occupant.[29] The idea of national self-determination and its corollary in the context of war and occupation contributed to the balance of power that emerged in Europe following the Napoleonic Wars. The prohibition on unilateral annexation further bolstered the territorial stability enshrined in the Congress of Vienna in 1815.

Thus, the emerging European order of nation-states and the notion of *national* sovereignty necessitated a new theory that would delineate and provide the rationale for more stringent limits on the occupant's powers. This new theory distinguished "occupation" from "conquest" and was developed in two steps. The first theoretical step was the recognition of the principle of the inalienability of sovereignty through sheer force. Occupation as such does not confer sovereignty over enemy territory. The second step was the recognition of what Gregory Fox has termed "the conservationist principle,"[30] which seeks to protect the bases of power of the ousted government and, hence, imposes limitations on the occupant's authority to manage public property and modify existing legislation.

French practice and law seem to have been the impetus for recognizing the principle of inalienability of sovereignty. In adherence with the 1791 Constitution, invading French armies would refrain from unilateral annexation of territories and would not seek treaties of cession with defeated enemies to legitimate new French holdings. The principle of national self-determination, as applied outside of France, meant that invaded populations were, at least in French eyes, entitled to determine their preferred form of government.[31] A decision to "reunite" with France could be made only by

28. On the evolution of guerrilla warfare in Europe in the early nineteenth century and its legal implications, see Francis Lieber, *Guerrilla Parties* (New York: Nostrand,1862).

29. See below, notes 35–43 and accompanying text.

30. Gregory H. Fox, "The Occupation of Iraq," *Georgetown Journal of International Law* 36 (2005): 195–297, 199.

31. J. H. W. Verzijl, in his *International Law in Historical Perspective* (Leyden: Sijthoff, 1978), 9–A: 152, reproduces the French Decree of 15/17 December 1792, which promised to export the French ideas of liberty, equality, and fraternity to occupied countries, which, in turn, would thereby achieve sovereignty and self-determination.

local assemblies in the occupied territories.[32] "Les Pays Réunis" would then become part of the French nation.[33]

The French Cour de cassation, despite its initial hesitation,[34] for the most part followed the same line of thought when deciding that occupation of enemy territory does not transform into sovereignty, nor does it otherwise alter the status of that territory or subject it to the laws of the occupant. Challine reported that the Cour de cassation began to apply this doctrine in 1812, when it ruled that the French occupation authorities in the Papal States need not respect laws promulgated by the King of Naples, the previous occupant of the same area, due to his lack of sovereignty over the territories; the court asserted that recognition of the laws of the previous occupant would violate the rights of the sovereign, the Pope.[35] In another decision, from January 22, 1818, which later caught the attention of legal scholars and was even cited by the U.S. Supreme Court,[36] the Cour de cassation determined that the French occupation "had not communicated to the inhabitants of Catalonia the title of Frenchman, nor to their territory the quality of French territory; this communication could result only from an act of union emanating from the public authority, which never existed."[37] The same court subsequently found, in 1837, that the temporary occupation of Martinique by Britain in 1813 could not effect any change to the status of the island as French nor to the laws there. "The temporary

32. See Nehal Bhuta, "The Antinomies of Transformative Occupation," *European Journal of International Law* 16 (2005): 733 ("The revolutionary government in France renounced the right of conquest, and offered instead 'fraternity' with peoples who rejected the dynastic principle of legitimacy in favour of popular sovereignty"); Thomas Baty, "The Relations of Invaders to Insurgents," *Yale Law Journal* 36 (1927): 974–77 ("When the French in 1792 invaded Italy, they had no scruple in summoning the invaded populations to repudiate all allegiance to their sovereigns. . . . Nys may tell us that the French generals 'limited themselves' to breaking the ties between invaded peoples and their princes and to convoking assemblies to determine the form of government").

33. Paul Challine, *Le droit international public dans la jurisprudence française de 1789 à 1848* (Paris: Domat-Montchrestien, 1934): 116. Challine also noted the Decree of 15/17 December 1792 (see above, note 31), which provided, inter alia, that it was not necessary to sign a treaty of cession to effect sovereignty change when the people situated in the occupied area, being the sovereign there, had manifested their wish to be reunited with France.

34. Edgar Löning reported on an early decision of the Paris Cour de cassation from 23 Frimaire year V, which determined that a French area occupied by an enemy was no longer to be considered part of France. Edgar Löning, *Die Verwaltung des General-Gouvernements im Elsaß* (Strassburg: K. J. Trübner, 1874), 27, n. 1.

35. Challine, *Le droit international public* at 116–19.

36. Ibid., 119. This was later discussed by Heffter, *Das Europäische Völkerrecht,* at para 186, 350; Henry W. Halleck, *International Law* (New York: D. Van Nostrand,1861), 775 and following.

37. Halleck, *International Law,* 782 (quoting Ortolan's *Diplomatie de la Mer*).

suspension of possession as a consequence of the conquest did not end the area's subjection to French law."[38] Moreover, Challine described a Cour de cassation 1841 ruling that occupation cannot abrogate the laws in force in the occupied territory,[39] as well as an 1843 decision that concluded that regulations promulgated by an occupant imposing limits on interest rates were no longer in force from the moment the occupation had ended.[40] The doctrine was far from clear at the time, however. Challine pointed also to several decisions that seem to contradict the new theory, such as the Cour de cassation's reference to events occurring in French territory occupied by Spain as taking place in enemy territory.[41]

But the Cour de cassation's assertions were pronounced only in the context of civil or criminal litigation and were not conceptualized as a general doctrine of the laws of war. Instead, such a conceptualization was to be the achievement of the German scholar August Wilhelm Heffter, a University of Berlin professor of law.[42] In his influential 1844 treatise on European international law,[43] he suggested that, except in situations of complete subjugation (*debellatio*), occupation should be regarded as temporary control that does not amount to the acquisition of sovereignty: "By the mere occupation of the other side's territory or part thereof, the invading enemy does not immediately replace the former state authority, for as long as the invader continues the war, when it is still possible that the fortunes of the war will change. . . . From a legal perspective, the defeat of the enemy does not immediately bring about the complete subjugation of the enemy's state authority."[44]

38. "L'occupation temporaire de cette colonie par la Puissance anglaise n'a pu porter aucune attainte aux droits de la France ni changer le caractére de sa possession sur la Martinique, possession momenanément suspendue par l'effet de la conquête, mais qui n'a pas cessé quant au droit d'être régie par la loi française." Charles Rousseau, *Le droit des conflits armés* (Paris: Pedone, 1983), 136–37 (citing the French Cour de cassation decision of February 1, 1837, *Magill v. Héritiers Monnel-Gonnier*).

39. Challine, *Le droit international public* at 122–24.

40. Ibid., 124–25.

41. Ibid., 119–22.

42. According to Schulze, "notice nécrologique," *Annuaire de l'institut de droit international* 5 (1882): 25–40, Heffter (1796–1880) was influenced by French law and culture while serving as a young professor in Bonn. When he later moved to Berlin, he came to be influenced by his friend Eduard Gans, who had been Hegel's student. In fact it was Gans who suggested to Heffter that he write the 1844 book. Heffter also served as a consultant to governments and as a high-ranking judge. According to one commentator, his dual role kept him from pushing his ideas forward and from seeing through the chrysalis of the modern state (ibid., 38).

43. His 1844 book is the first attempt of a "real" lawyer to tackle international law. This is probably the reason for some of his normative refinements and the book's impact within the German and international academia (ibid.).

44. Heffter, *Das Europäische Völkerrecht,* 220–21: "Der eindringende Feind tritt nicht

Heffter noted that his thesis diverged from the vast literature on the subject, which had failed to distinguish between occupation and conquest.[45] His theory was formulated as a logical inference ("*unmittelbar folgerung*")[46] from what he referred to as "the new principle of war" ("*neuere Kriegsprincip*"), namely, the principle that war among civilized nations is not a war of mutual annihilation but one of limited duration that never loses sight of the goal of reestablishing peace. This principle rested on the two basic tenets of the society of states in Europe, sovereign equality[47] and minimum harm,[48] which, together, yielded a new theory on limited warfare.[49]

But not only was Heffter a thinker, he was also a realistic lawyer attuned to state practice and power relations.[50] Despite his reliance on Portalis and Talleyrand and his vision of a society of sovereign and equal European states as the basis for the modern law of nations, he stopped short of requiring the occupant, when acting as an administrator of the occupied territory, to respect the bases of power of the ousted government under the principle of minimum harm. He also did not subscribe to the French understanding of the consequences of the principle of national self-determination, that treaties of cession are not a legitimate way of ending wars. Quite to the contrary, he believed that occupants have a legitimate expectation of acquiring sovereignty after a successful military campaign. This expectation,

---

sofort durch die bloße Besitzgreifung des anderseitigen Gebietes oder eines Theiles desselben an die Stelle der bisherigen Staatsgewalt, so lange der letztern noch eine Fortsetzung des Krieges, mithin auch eine Umkehr des Kriegsglückes ist. . . . eine vollkommene Subjugation des eingedrungenen Feindes in die Staatsgewalt des Andern, vermag juristisch nicht sofort gefolgert zu werden."

45. Ibid., 221, n. 1. He did single out one commentator, Cocceji, in his book "de iure victoriae" and his commentary on Grotius, who had been, according to Heffter, "on the right track."

46. Ibid., 221.

47. Heffter understood sovereign equality and independence as implying "complete equality" among states under international law (ibid., para. 27). States, just like individuals, have the fundamental right to exist and to develop themselves physically and morally (para. 29). Moreover, states are entitled to respect for their physical personalities as members of human society (para. 31) ("Achtung des fremden Staates in seiner physischen Persönlichkeit, als eines Theiles des Menschengeschlechtes").

48. Heffter's principle of necessity, articulated as a "fundamental maxim": "Do not cause more harm to your enemy, even during the war, beyond what is necessary for accomplishing the goal." ("[F]üge Deinen Feinden auch im kriege nicht mehr Uebel zu, als es für die Durchsetzung des Zweckes unvermeidlich ist.") Ibid., para. 119.

49. Ibid., para. 130.

50. Immediately following the "fundamental maxim" of necessity (see above, note 48) Heffter recognizes the doctrine of the "reason of war" ("Kriegsräson"), which accepts that, in situations of extreme danger or in the face of a need to reestablish equality in combat, one is released from the principle of necessity.

based on state practice, entitles the occupant to administer the territory under its control like the sovereign. In his discussion of how war ends, Heffter relied on state practice, rather than moral principles, to explore the limits of the occupant's authority. According to Heffter, European state practice revealed that peace agreements usually assign sovereignty to occupants over territory they gained during war. Therefore, an occupant that seeks to acquire sovereignty in a peace treaty can be regarded as having "definitive possession." Its expected sovereignty authorizes the occupant to exercise provisional authority over the territory also during the interim period between the end of hostilities and commencement of peace. While the occupant is required to respect both general human rights as well as the private rights of citizens, it is not otherwise bound by the laws of the former sovereign.[51] Only when the occupant has no intention of keeping the occupied area under its sovereignty, must it be more circumspect, upholding the ousted sovereign's laws and institutions and generally acting like a creditor handling his debtor's goods.[52]

The second theoretical step in the evolution of the law of belligerent occupation, namely, recognition of the conservationist principle, was developed by the Italian jurist Pasquale Fiore.[53] Writing in 1865, this young international lawyer provided the missing theoretical basis for the conservationist principle by founding the system of international law on the idea of the *nation,* as proclaimed by the French Revolution, rather than the *state.* In Fiore's view, under prevailing international law, all nations must be considered equal and autonomous. Their equal right to sovereignty in their territories implies that their title cannot be taken away by force: "According to our principles, all nations are equal and autonomous and have equal right to sovereignty in their territories, [they] do not succumb to the law of force, and their territories do not pass to the dominion of the victorious power if it arbitrarily and violently occupies them."[54]

51. Heffter, *Das Europäische Völkerrecht,* paras. 181–86. At para. 185, he states, "Der Eroberer ist dabei auch keinesweges, wie Manche behaupten, an die Regel des früheren Staates gebunden. Er hat nur die allgemeinen Menschenrechte, so wie die demgemäß erworbenen speciellen Privatrechte der Unterthanen zu beachten; aber die Form des öffentlichen Verhältinsses hat er allein als freier Inhaber der Staatsgewalt zu bestimmen. Das Staatsgut steht unter seiner Disposition."

52. Ibid., 186.

53. On Fiore's (1837–1914) humanitarian-liberal philosophy and his approach to the study of international law, see Martti Koskenniemi, *The Gentle Civilizer of Nations* (Cambridge: Cambridge University Press, 2001): 54–57.

54. Pasquale Fiore, *Nuovo dritto internazionale pubblico* (Milan: Casa Ed. e Tip. degli autori-ed,1865), 177 ("[S]econdo I nostri principii essendo le nazioni tutte eguali ed autonome, ed avendo l'egual dritto di sovranità nel loro territorio, non possono soggiacere al dritto della forza, nè le loro terre possono passare nel domino del vincitore se questo arbitrariamente e violentemente le avesse occupate").

From this premise, Fiore deduced the limitations on the occupant's authority. Just as it is restricted from interfering with the property of individuals, an occupant is precluded from interfering with the property of the nation: "The law of postliminium, which, according to our doctrine, is founded on the principle that the fact of war is not sufficient to destroy legitimate rights and that these rights may not be lost without the consent of the individuals to whom they belong, applies to private relations as well as to public relations."[55] For this reason, Fiore asserted that laws promulgated by the occupant that seek to change the preexisting public legal order expire with the termination of the occupation, unless the nation has consented to those laws.[56]

In the 1885 French edition of Fiore's book,[57] the restrictions on the occupant's authority are more elaborate and clear. The occupant is obligated to exercise only the authority necessary for meeting the immediate needs of the occupation. This, according to Fiore, is the product of the consolidation of three principles: all communities' need for a governing body, the need to enable the entity with authority to exercise sovereign functions, and the principle that the entity that exercises sovereign rights in an occupied territory must do so without dispossessing the actual sovereign completely and definitively. The occupant must exercise its power under the constraints of necessity and the immediate goals of the occupation[58] and in accordance

55. Ibid., 443: "Il dritto di postliminio, che secondo la nostra dottrina si fonda sul principio che il fatto della Guerra non è sufficiente a distruggere I dritti legittimi, e che questi non posson perdre senza il consenso degli individui a cui appartengono, si applica ai rapporti privati ed ai rapporti pubblici."

56. Ibid., 444: "[T]utti gli atti amministrazione fatti per ordine del sovrano invasore cessano di aver vigore, tutte le modificazioni fatte alla costituzione dello Stato e alle relazioni politiche dei citadini, cessano egualmente, a menochè non siamo volute e consentite dalla nazione. . . . per quello che si riferisce ai giudizii compiuti, questi sono validi a meno che non contraddicano il dritto pubblico costituzionale voluto e consentito dalla nazione." ("When the occupation ends, all administrative acts made by the invading sovereign expire, all amendments made to the constitution of the State and to the political relations of the citizens cease equally, unless the nation sought and consented to them. . . . With respect to final judgments, these shall be valid as long as they do not contradict the public constitutional law sought and consented to by the nation.") See also Charles Calvo, *Le droit international théorique et pratique,* 4th ed. (Paris: Guillaumin,1888), vol. 4, para. 2181 (p. 220): "Le droit international ne reconnaît pas à l'occupant la faculté de changer les lois civiles et criminelles des territories sur lesquels se trouvent ses troupes, ni d'y faire administrer la justice en son nom. . . . Cependant, si des necessities militaries l'y contraignent, l'occupant peut empêcher l'application de certaines lois et substituer le pouvoir militaire à l'autorité legal du pays, mais uniquement dans la mesure où cette authorité constitue une force pour l'ennemi et par consequent un danger pour l'armée d'occupation." (Calvo, an envoy for Argentina, was a founding member of the *Institute de droit international.*)

57. Pasquale Fiore, *Nouveau droit international public,* trans. Charles Antoine, 2nd ed., (Paris: Durand, 1885), vol. 3.

58. Ibid., 317–18.

with the laws of humanity and justice and honor, as well as with the laws and functions of the sovereign and laws and customs recognized by civilized peoples.[59] Calvo took the same approach.[60]

The theoretical basis for the law of belligerent occupation is derived from the idea of equal sovereignty, which implies the inalienability of sovereign title without the consent of the sovereign. Under this theory, sovereignty, just like private property, is protected from unilateral alienation from its rightful owner. Therefore, the mere exercise of control over enemy territory does not confer sovereignty on the occupant, whose authority is temporary and limited. As a result—a step Heffter hesitated to make, but Fiore took—the occupant must take into account not only the rights and interests of the local inhabitants, but also those of the nation as represented by the ousted government. This vision of the regime of occupation yields restrictions on the occupant's powers that are aimed, among other things, at ensuring the preservation of the ousted government's bases of power until its return to power.

No doubt, these two scholars, Heffter and Fiore, managed to capture and translate into a legal concept both the evolving perceptions as well as the political realities of their period. Factors that contributed to the evolution of these two dimensions of the legal doctrine included the French Revolution, with its notions of human rights and national self-determination, the subsequent Napoleonic Wars and the ensuing rise of national identities, the Congress of Vienna and the balance of power it successfully established, and, lastly, the actions of private entrepreneurs that stirred public outcry against the scourges of war. This new doctrine accommodated well the emerging political order in Europe, an order of nation-states, not of princes fighting private duels. These nation-states sought two principal goals. On the one hand, they were committed to their nationals and, hence, wanted to guarantee the lives of their citizens once subject to enemy control. Yet, on the other hand, they were also apprehensive of their citizens and sought, at the same time, to ensure that their citizens did not seize the moment to secede or unite with the enemy. Hence the rules protecting private individuals and their property; hence the rules authorizing the occupant to apply but also to protect—against indigenous challenges as well—the ousted sovereign's laws and property during the occupation. These common European concerns explain why the European version of the doctrine on occupation was accepted as law within a relatively short period of time.[61] The shared understanding of the concept of occupation did not mean that everyone saw all aspects

59. Ibid., 323.

60. Calvo, *Le droit international,* vol. 4, para. 2181 (p. 220). See above, note 56.

61. On the codification efforts, see below, Part II (B).

of the law in the same light. Quite the contrary: the views of potential occupants diverged significantly from those of the potentially occupied. But both sides were prepared to obscure these differences—with the aid of able drafters—because both had much to gain from an agreement.

II. The Transformation of the Concept of Occupation into European and International Law

The transformation of the doctrine on belligerent occupation from an idea into a binding legal norm was a meandering process with many participants. This Part outlines the different shapes and forms the idea took until it was ultimately included in the 1899 Regulations of the First Peace Conference at The Hague. As pointed out below, the inclusion of the doctrine of belligerent occupation in these Regulations did not endow it with global applicability. Rather, it was understood, at the time, as applying only among the signatories, which were mostly European states.[62] The last Section of this Part describes the territorial scope of the doctrine as things stood in 1899.

A. The Doctrine on Belligerent Occupation Arrives in America

The evolving doctrine on occupation reached the United States of America as part of a process of territorial expansion through war. As could be expected, this doctrine took on an idiosyncratic meaning, or even a number of meanings, once it crossed the Atlantic, which reflected the constraints of a nation engaged in wars of expansion as well as civil war. The American doctrine on occupation was shaped by two conflicting approaches. On the one hand, the evolving European doctrine had a significant influence; on the other hand, the Americans were intimately and acutely aware of the British position, which did not distinguish between occupation and conquest[63] and

62. This should not be surprising, given the European view at the time that international law encompassed relations only among "civilized nations." See Oppenheim, *International Law,* 1:31 (the family of civilized nations has the discretion to consent to the entry of a new member based on the family's assessment of the new entrant's being a "civilized State which [wa]s in constant intercourse with members of the Family of Nations"). On the law of occupation as a European project, see also Bhuta, "The Antinomies of Transformative Occupation."

63. This was made clear in the case of *The Foltina,* 1 Dodson 450, 451 (1814), 165 Eng. Rep. 1374, 1375 (1752–1865). ("No point is more clearly settled in the Courts of Common Law than that a conquered territory forms immediately part of the King's dominions.") Despite the asserted "clarity" of the law, the High Court of Admiralty was breaking ground in this decision. The case it cited as authority for its decision, *Campbell v. Hall,* 98 ER 1045,

whereby mere occupation was an effective way of expanding its dominion to occupied territories and their inhabitants.[64] Indeed, as late as 1914 and despite ratifying the 1899 and 1907 Hague Regulations, Britain asserted sovereignty over Egypt and Cyprus through occupation.[65]

The British influence is reflected in the jurisprudence of the U.S. Supreme Court throughout the nineteenth century. In the case of *U.S. v. Rice,* for example, which discussed the legal status of a port captured by the British during the War of 1812, Justice Story recognized that "[b]y the conquest and military occupation of [the U.S. territory of] Castine, the [British] enemy acquired that firm possession which enabled him to exercise the fullest rights of sovereignty over that place."[66] The occupant was not subject to any restrictions imposed by international law: "By the surrender the inhabitants passed under a temporary allegiance to the British government, and were bound by such laws, and such only, as it chose to recognise and impose."[67] In a case from 1850, this time dealing with

---

1047 (1774), referred to a territory (Grenada) that had been formally ceded by France to Britain in a peace treaty. But Heligoland, where the *Foltina* had been seized, had not been ceded (by Denmark) to Britain at the time of seizure. In *The Foltina,* the court acknowledged as "somewhat extraordinary, that, in the course of the numerous and long wars in which this country has been engaged, no case should have been determined which might serve as a guide to the Court in the decision of the present question." Ibid. The claimant was probably relying on the distinction made by Vattel between title based on possession, which becomes complete upon a treaty, and title based on right (see above note 12 and accompanying text); the court, however, rejected this distinction as "more formal than real and substantial" (ibid., 452, 1375).

64. Halleck, *International Law,* 784: "[F]oreign territory becomes a dominion, and its inhabitants the subjects of the king, ipso facto, by the conquest made by the British arms, without any action of the legislature."

65. For a critical assessment of these occupations, see Baty, "The Relations of Invaders to Insurgents," 974–77; Bhuta, "The Antinomies of Transformative Occupation," 729. It would not be surprising to learn that the British government was, in principle, not very enthusiastic about the European efforts to codify the laws of war on land during the nineteenth century. It opposed the Russian idea of convening the conference in Brussels, initially rejecting the invitation to participate. Later, after receiving proper assurances, the British government instructed its delegate to monitor the negotiations without taking an active part. See Fedor F. de Martens, *La paix et la guerre,* trans. N. de Sancé (Paris: A. Rousseau, 1901), 106–9.

66. *United States v. Rice,* 4 Wheat. 246, 17 U.S. 246, 254, 4 L.Ed. 562 (1819). Justice Taney further noted, "The sovereignty of the United States over the territory was, of course, suspended, and the laws of the United States could no longer be rightfully enforced there, or be obligatory upon the inhabitants who remained and submitted to the conquerors. By the surrender the inhabitants passed under a temporary allegiance to the British government, and were bound by such laws, and such only, as it chose to Recognise and impose. . . . Castine was, therefore, during this period, so far as respected our revenue laws, to be deemed a foreign port; and goods imported into it by the inhabitants, were subject to such duties only as the British government chose to require." Ibid., 254.

67. Ibid.

the U.S. occupation of Mexico, Chief Justice Taney reaffirmed the view that "by the laws and usages of nations, conquest is a valid title, while the victor maintains the exclusive possession of the conquered country."[68] This approach is essentially similar to that first suggested by Vattel and Rousseau: as long as one has exclusive possession[69] over a given territory, one is entitled to treat it as one's own, while the sovereignty of the ousted government is "of course, suspended."[70] "[M]ilitary conquest completely displace[s] the sovereignty of the prior possessor."[71]

At the same time, American jurists were influenced by the European literature on international law in general and on the laws of war in particular. Betsy Baker Röben has described in her work[72] a large informal group of liberal American and European international lawyers who corresponded regularly and shared their scholarship.[73] Included in this group were Heffter and Bluntschli, the Europeans, and Halleck and Lieber, the Americans.[74] Heffter's 1844 book had considerable influence in America, which grew even stronger with the publication of the French versions (the first in 1857),[75] and was regarded as one of the two most important authorities on international law for Americans along with Wheaton's 1836 *Elements of International*

68. *Fleming v. Page,* 9 How. 603, 50 U.S. 603, 612, 13 L. Ed. 276 (1850) at 50 U.S 603, 615. On this doctrine, see also William Birkhimer, *Military Government and Martial Law,* 3rd ed. (Kansas City, Mo: F. Hudson, 1914), 54–58.

69. The key test is possession: "while the victor maintains the exclusive possession of the conquered country." *United States v. Rice,* above, note 66, ibid. See also Halleck, *International Law,* 780 (same emphasis).

70. *U.S. v. Rice,* above note 66, ibid.

71. See the decision of the U.S. Court of Appeals in *State of Netherlands v. Federal Reserve Bank,* 201 F2d 455, 461 (2d Cir. N.Y. 1953) (citations omitted): "The nineteenth century American view that military conquest completely displaced the sovereignty of the prior possessor, was substantially modified by the Regulations respecting the Laws and Customs of War on Land, ratified by the United States as an annex to the Fourth Hague Convention of 1907. Since the adoption of these Regulations it is generally agreed that the occupant does not succeed to sovereignty over the occupied territory, but has only limited administrative authority."

72. Betsy Röben, *Johann Caspar Bluntschli, Francis Lieber und das moderne Völkerrecht, 1861–1881* (Baden-Baden: Nomos Verlagsgesellschaft, 2003); Betsy Baker Röben, "The Method behind Bluntschli's 'Modern' International Law," *Journal of the History of International Law* 4 (2002): 249.

73. Röben, *Bluntschli,* at 67–68.

74. Lieber was born in Germany in 1800. He moved to the United States in 1827. See G. Rolin-Jaequemyns, "François Lieber," *Revue de Droit international et de legislation comparée* 4 (1872): 700–705.

75. In the Preface to the 1866 French edition, Heffter noted the success of his earlier versions. The book had been favorably mentioned by American, British, and Russian authors and translated into Greek, Russian, and Polish. It was subsequently translated also into Japanese and Spanish (see Preface of the 8th German edition by Geffken, 1888).

Law.[76] Francis Lieber regarded Heffter as the "acknowledged highest authority on the L. of nations on the continent of Europe,"[77] and the contemporary American writing on international law drew heavily on his book.

Halleck's book on the laws of war[78] turns to both Heffter and the U.S. case-law in the chapters devoted to military occupation. His theory consolidated the two radically different approaches—the British approach and Heffter's—into one, with the outcome a distinction based on the occupant's subjective intention. Once an occupant has successfully secured control over the enemy territory and the ousted government is incapable of regaining that territory through military efforts, the occupant may opt to treat the area as subject to military occupation, during which it "can, at his pleasure, either change the existing laws, or make new ones."[79] However, the occupant can also gain sovereign title over the territory by executing an authoritative and unequivocal sovereign act, such as annexation or incorporation, thereby manifesting its intention to retain the occupied territory as its own.[80]

This distinction had little impact from the perspective of international law, because it still enabled the unilateral acquisition of enemy territory through the use of force. But the distinction was invaluable to upholding the U.S. federal system of government: Occupation in and of itself did not yet render an area subject to U.S. laws or, in particular, the Constitution.[81] Extending U.S. law to these territories could be effected only by an act of Congress, not a presidential act,[82] for the president, acting through his armed forces, had no constitutional authority to do so.[83] This purely domestic distinction was clarified by Chief Justice Taney:

> As regarded all other nations, [the occupied Mexican territory] was a part of the United States, and belonged to them as exclusively as the territory included in our established boundaries. . . . But yet it was not a part of this Union. For every nation which acquires territory by treaty or conquest holds it according to its own institutions and laws. And the relation in which [the

76. Röben, *Bluntschli,* at 69–70.

77. Ibid., 69, n. 411 (citing Lieber's letter from 1863 and other letters). See also Silja Vöneky, "Der Lieber's Code und die Wurzeln des modernen Kriegsvölkerrecht," *Zeitschrift fur Ausländisches öffentliches Recht und Völkerrecht* 62 (2002): 424–60.

78. Halleck, *International Law.*

79. Ibid., 781.

80. Ibid., 811–12.

81. Halleck attributed this to the peculiar nature of the U.S. governmental structure. Ibid., 784.

82. Ibid., 785.

83. Under the U.S. constitutional arrangement, the president, as commander-in-chief, can wage war and therefore conquer territory but cannot "extend the limits, or enlarge the boundaries of the Union." Ibid., 784–85.

occupied territory] stood to the United States while it was occupied by their arms did not depend upon the laws of nations, but upon our own Constitution and acts of Congress.[84]

In other words, under this "somewhat peculiar and anomalous"[85] doctrine, the American occupying army enjoyed the best of all worlds: It was not constrained by international law from acting as it pleased vis-à-vis the enemy government, because its very possession of the occupied territory gave it exclusive title and unfettered discretion. At the same time, it was not constrained by its own domestic law, which did not automatically extend to areas not yet part of the Union.[86] This doctrine suited well the needs of an expanding nation[87] and, consequently, guided American conduct throughout the nineteenth century.[88]

The definition of an occupied area was predicated on actual possession. As a result, an occupant's authority was contingent on its remaining in control of the specific area over which it asserted authority.[89] This distinction explains Chief Justice Marshall's reference in 1828[90] to occupation as distinct from conquest, in a case that raised a question about the status of Florida. In a paragraph that some[91] later inaccurately regarded as anticipating the newly evolving norm of international law, Justice Marshall stated, "The usage of the world is, if a nation be not entirely subdued, to consider the holding of conquered territory as a mere military occupation, until its fate shall be determined at the treaty of peace. If it be ceded by the treaty, the acquisition is confirmed, and the ceded territory becomes a part of the nation to which it is annexed."[92]

This passage made it clear that Marshall did not have in mind a new

84. *Fleming v. Page*. See above, note 68, ibid.

85. Halleck, *International Law*, 784–85.

86. The same rationale applied to the so-called insular cases, where the Supreme Court asserted that the U.S. Constitution does not automatically extend to areas (such as Hawaii, the Philippines, and Puerto Rico) that have come under American control. See, e.g., *DeLima v. Bidwell*, 182 U.S. 1 (1901), *Goetze v. United States*, 182 U.S. 221 (1901).

87. For example, this doctrine was invoked to set up governments in New Mexico and California in 1846 and 1847, respectively. Birkhimer, *Military Government*, at 55–56.

88. *The Netherlands Case*, above note 71 (describing American practice until ratifying the 1907 Hague Regulations). The incorporation of Hawaii in 1898 is a case in point.

89. "The government of the conqueror being *de facto* and not *de jure*, it must always rest upon the fact of *possession*, which is adverse to the former sovereign, and therefore can never be inferred or presumed. . . . Not only must the possession be actually acquired, but it must be *maintained*." Halleck, *International Law*, 780 (emphasis in original).

90. *American Insurance Company v. Canter*, 26 U.S. 511.

91. Von Glahn presented this case as a departure from the British approach. See Gerhard von Glahn, *The Occupation of Enemy Territory* (Minneapolis: University of Minnesota Press, 1957), 7.

92. *American Insurance Company v. Canter*, above note 90, at 542.

concept of occupation when he noted that the U.S. government "possesses the power of acquiring territory, either by conquest or by treaty."[93] It must be concluded that Marshall made the distinction between conquest and "mere" military occupation to explain why it was not necessary to prove in court actual and uninterrupted U.S. possession of Florida: the formal cession of title by Spain was sufficient to grant the U.S. formal title without proof of actual possession.[94]

When Francis Lieber drafted his renowned Lieber Code in 1863,[95] his most immediate concern was the U.S. Civil War, and his reference to occupied territories was necessarily aimed at regulating the Union's occupation of Confederate territories. The instructions set meaningful constraints on occupying armies: they authorized the occupation authorities to make new laws, but only "as far as military necessity requires,"[96] and required the occupant, *inter alia*, "to be strictly guided by the principles of justice, honor, and humanity"[97] and to "acknowledge and protect . . . religion and morality; strictly private property; the persons of the inhabitants, especially those of women: and the sacredness of domestic relations."[98] The Code did not address the question of sovereignty: in this Civil War, it was not at issue.

The Lieber Code opened new horizons for European governments and jurists seeking new modalities for the regulation of the conduct of warfare. What fascinated the Europeans was not the ideas embedded in the Code,

93. Ibid.

94. This was also Halleck's interpretation when he referred, inter alia, to this case while emphasizing that "[d]uring mere military occupation the sovereignty of the conqueror is unstable and incomplete." Halleck, *International Law,* 791.

95. Instructions for the Government of Armies of the United States in the Field (Lieber Code), 24 April 1863.

96. Lieber Code, Art. 3: "Martial Law in a hostile country consists in the suspension, by the occupying military authority, of the criminal and civil law, and of the domestic administration and government in the occupied place or territory, and in the substitution of military rule and force for the same, as well as in the dictation of general laws, as far as military necessity requires this suspension, substitution, or dictation." According to Robert J. Futrell, "Federal Military Government in the South, 1861–1865," *Military Affairs* 15.4 (1951): 190–91, the Lieber Code was interpreted by the Union's various military governments to allow them considerable latitude. The Federal military governors "assumed a broad direction of Southern civil affairs." These governors issued orders to protect public order and public health, regulated, inter alia, the sale of liquor and gambling, organized local militias, introduced new taxes, and, in general, "made themselves masters of the Southern population." The secretary of war of the Confederate states criticized the Code for allowing the military governors unfettered discretion under the concept of "military necessity" (cited in Doris Appel Graber, *The Development of the Law of Belligerent Occupation, 1863–1914* [New York: Columbia University Press, 1949], 17–18).

97. Lieber Code, Art. 4.

98. Ibid., Art. 37. See also Arts. 5, 6, 31, 38.

as these ideas were borrowed from Europe and had been discussed already by Halleck.[99] Rather, what was novel to them was the very system of a code: the possibility of a common text, potentially the basis of a treaty. As a matter of substance, however, the novelty of the Lieber Code should not obscure the fact that, under prevailing American doctrine, occupants could, if they so desired, extend their sovereignty unilaterally based on their ability to control enemy territory.

Before turning attention back to Europe to trace the evolution of the law of occupation there, I will briefly outline the American position in this context up until 1907, when it joined the Second Peace Conference at The Hague. In its relations with its neighbors and enemies, the U.S. government sometimes hid its stance that it had absolute authority over occupied areas. General Taylor's proclamation to the people of Mexico on June 4, 1846, was a distorted paraphrasing of the Rousseau-Portalis doctrine: "[W]e come to overthrow the tyrants who have destroyed your liberties; but we come to make no war upon the people of Mexico, nor upon any form of free government they may choose to select for themselves."[100]

President McKinley's order to the Secretary of War on July 18, 1898, upon the occupation of Santiago de Cuba stated, among other things, "Though the powers of the military occupant are absolute and supreme and immediately operate upon the political condition of the inhabitants, the municipal laws of the conquered territory, . . . are considered as continuing in force, so far as they are compatible with the new order of things, until they are suspended or superseded by the occupying belligerent . . . This enlightened practice is, so far as possible, to be adhered to in the present occasion."[101]

During the International American Conference of 1889–1890, all the participants except for the U.S. supported a text declaring that "the principle of conquest shall never hereafter be recognized as admissible under American public law." The agreed-upon compromise would have provided that the principle of conquest would not be recognized as admissible "during the continuance of the treaty of arbitration," but the treaty never came into effect.[102] The occupations of Hawaii, The Philippines, and Puerto Rico reflected the same unique American view on the unlimited authority of the occupant.[103] The U.S., then, made no contribution to the development of

99. See above, notes 78–82. Bluntschli, Lieber's closest colleague, deemed the Lieber Code "particularly noteworthy because it annunciates the modern rules with clarity and energy." Bluntschli, *Das Beuterecht*, at 66.

100. John Basset Moore, *A Digest of International Law* (Washington: Government Printing Office, 1906), 7:273.

101. Ibid., 262.

102. Ibid., 315–16.

103. See *The Netherlands* decision, above note 71. In 1901, the U.S. Supreme Court

the international doctrine on occupation during the period of its crystallization. When it ratified the Hague Regulations in 1907, the doctrine had already taken shape.

B. Back in Europe: The Franco-Prussian War and Its Aftermath

The occupation of parts of France by the Prussian Army during the 1870–1871 War provided an opportunity for Europe to assess the prospects and limits of the laws of war in general and of the law of belligerent occupation in particular. Edgar Löning indicated that Heffter's distinctions were implemented by the Prussian Army.[104] The Prussian Army divided the area under its control into three governments-general: Alsace, Lorraine, and a third region consisting of the rest of the territories.[105] All three administrations, each of which was headed by a military governor-general and a civil commissioner as an associate, declared that French law would remain in effect as long as the state of war did not require its suspension.[106] Concurrently, however, certain proclamations made by Prussian governor-generals addressing the local populations in their jurisdictions indicated an intention to treat the areas as subject to German sovereignty. Upon assuming his post, the Governor-General of Alsace issued a declaration to the inhabitants of Alsace informing them that the territories under his jurisdiction "are withdrawn, by the very occupation, from [French] imperial sovereignty, and in its stead German authority is established."[107] A declaration to the people of Strasbourg was similarly formulated, proclaiming that the city had been newly reunited ("*de nouveau réunie*") with Germany.[108]

The validity of these declarations and other acts and policies of the Prussian occupation authorities was the subject of much debate among

(in *Dooley v. United States,* 182 U.S. 222 [1901]) reaffirmed Halleck's description of the doctrine, in a case concerning duties imposed on individuals in occupied Puerto Rico in 1898–1900.

104. Löning, *Die Verwaltung,* 13–15.

105. G. Rolin-Jaequemyns, "Chronique du droit international," *Revue de Droit international et de legislation comparée* 2 (1870): 645, at 691. Bordwell mentions a forth district. See Percy Bordwell, *The Law of War between Belligerents* (Chicago: Callaghan, 1908), 98.

106. Rolin-Jaequemyns, "Chronique du droit international." See also Löning, *Die Verwaltung;* Coleman Phillipson, *Alsace-Lorraine, Past, Present and Future* (London: T. F. Unwin, 1918), 155; Graber, *Development of the Law,* 268–70.

107. Declaration of 30 August 1870. "[C]es territories se touvent, par ce fait même, soustraits à la souveraineté imperiale, en lieu et place de laquelle est établie l'autorité des puisances allemandes." Quoted in A. Lorriot, *De la nature de l'occupation de guerre* (Paris: Lavauzelle, 1903): 76–77.

108. Declaration of 8 October 1870, reprinted in Lorriot, *De la nature de l'occupation,* at 42.

jurists. Beyond the partisan views, this debate helped to highlight issues that warranted further refinement. Rolin-Jaequemyns, the Belgian jurist who co-founded the *Institut de droit international* (IDI) and the first professional journal on international legal affairs,[109] examined these issues closely in a series of articles he wrote. He sought not to make judgments but, rather, to extract general principles. Among those principles he suggested was a limitation on the occupant's exploitation of local resources. The occupant, per Rolin-Jaequemyns, was entitled to use only those local resources necessary for maintaining its troops and was prohibited from enrichsing itself from the resources of the occupied territory. It was required to use local resources in moderation proportionate to their availability.[110] This limitation on the occupant's authority meant that it was not entitled to exploit immovable resources and was restricted to enjoying only the fruits of those resources accrued through regular use.[111]

The Franco-Prussian War and the Prussian demand to annex Alsace and Lorraine also brought to the fore the link between the laws of war and the need to ensure regional stability. A right to conquest created incentive to resort to arms, and an internationally accepted constraint on this right could diminish that incentive.[112] Bismarck himself explained his government's demands by invoking security concerns,[113] and German scholars sought general justifications for these claims.[114]Asserting that the right of conquest did not exist, Rolin-Jaequemyns argued that an occupant had no right to demand cession of the territory, but, rather, such a demand must be negotiated and supported by morality and public utility considerations.[115]

The 1870–1871 War prompted Europe-wide efforts to clarify the rules of warfare. Fedor de Martens wrote in 1901[116] that, during the war, both

109. See Koskenniemi, *Gentle Civilizer,* 13–15.

110. G. Rolin-Jaequemyns, "Essai complémentaire sur la guerre franco-allemande dans ses rapports avec le droit international," *Revue de droit international et de legislation comparée* 3 (1871): 335.

111. Ibid., 357.

112. A. de Montluc, "Le droit de conquéte," *Revue de droit international et de legislation comparée* 5 (1873): 581.

113. André Merquiol, *Les occupations etrangères en France au XIXme siècle* (Nice: Imprimerie de "L'Eclaireur de Nice," 1944): 51–53.

114. Phillipson, *Alsace-Lorraine*, at 145–47, cites German writers who, although writing generally about the illegitimacy of conquest, stated that Germany's demand to annex Alsace-Lorraine was not a conquest, but, rather, a "restoration" or a response to earlier French provocations.

115. G. Rolin-Jaequemyns, "Note," *Revue de droit international et de legislation comparée* 5 (1873): 588, 589. Among these considerations, he mentioned the historic and ethnic ties of the population in the ceded territory and evident considerations of security.

116. de Martens, *La paix et la guerre,* 93–98.

sides had accused each other of violations of the laws of war, while public opinion had called for a clarification of these laws before a new war were to occur. This generated private initiatives to study the subject and put forth proposals to governments. Private societies—such as the IDI and International Law Association—formed with this as their founding purpose, while publicists and scholars called for a convening of a conference on the laws of war, eventually initiated by the Russians.[117]

The debates in Brussels and, later, in The Hague over the details of the regime of occupation were intense and complex. As a full discussion is beyond the scope of this essay, I will confine myself to outlining the different stages of the codification of the concept of occupation. The Heffterian concept of occupation was at no time in dispute;[118] the Russian text presented before the 1874 Brussels Conference gave quite clear expression to the concept.[119] Finding the right formula to describe the occupant's authority in the occupied territory proved to be more difficult, however.[120] In this context, we may recall, a gap existed between the more permissive approach advocated by

117. Martens credited himself with the initiative. In January 1873, he published an article in a St. Petersburg journal, in which he stated that a code on military regulations was a prerequisite in an era of general conscription: "Au moment où le service militaire obligatoire est en vue d'être introduit chez nous . . . l'opportunité de fixer par la loi les droits et les devoirs des troupes s'impose impérieusement. Il serait desirable que chaque défenseur de la patrie entrât en campagne, non seulement armé d'aprés toutes les règles de l'art militaire, mais encore pénétré de cet vérité que la guerre n'est pas une lutte physique, qu'aucune prescription de droit et de morale ne contient." This article caught the attention of the emperor and his ministers (de Martens, *La paix et la guerre,* at 102).

118. Jean De Breucker, "La Declaration de Bruxelles de 1874 concernant les lois et coutumes de la Guerre," *Chronique de Politique Étrangère* 27 (1974): 22 (noting that the parties to the Brussels negotiations could not deny the validity of Heffter's distinction between occupation and conquest).

119. Article 1: L'occupation par l'ennemi d'une partie du territoire de l'État en guerre avec lui y suspend, par le fait même, l'authorité du pouvoir legal de ce dernier et y substitute l'authorité du pouvoir militaire de l'État occupant. See *Annuaire de l'institut de droit international* 1 (1877): 277, 278.

120. This distinction between general recognition of the principle and the details implied by the principle for an occupation regime is reflected in the description of the project to assess the Brussels text undertaken by the *Institut de droit international.* See Session de La Haye (1875), *IDI Examen de la Déclaration de Bruxelles de 1874* (Rapporteur: M. Gustave Rolin-Jaequemyns) (rep. in http://www.idi-iil.org/idiF/resolutionsF/1875_haye_02_fr.pdf). The project was to focus on the implications of the fact that occupation is a provisional regime:

"VI. Les dispositions du projet de Déclaration relatives à l'occupation du territoire ennemi sont l'application de ce principe vrai: que le seul fait de l'occupation ne confère aucun droit de souveraineté, mais que la cessation de la résistance locale et la retraite du gouvernement national, d'une part, la présence de l'armée envahissante, de l'autre, créent pour celle-ci et pour le gouvernement qu'elle représente un ensemble de droits et d'obligations essentiellement provisoires. Le projet tend surtout, dans cet ordre d'idées, à tracer les limites de ces

Heffter and the rather restrictive stance taken by Fiore, who insisted on the occupant's obligation to respect the public order of the ousted government.[121] The Russian draft allowed the occupant rather broad powers, whereby it could, "in accordance with the demands of the war and in view of the public interest, maintain the obligatory force of the laws that had been in force in peacetime, modify them, or suspend them entirely."[122]

In contrast, the final text of the Brussels Declaration presented a more restrictive formula: "[The occupant] shall take all the measures in his power to restore and ensure, as far as possible, public order and safety [and] shall maintain the laws which were in force in the country in peacetime, and shall not modify, suspend or replace them *unless necessary*."[123] The basic principles of the Brussels Declaration met with scholarly approval. In 1875, the IDI declared that, although there was room for improvement, the new rules on occupation as suggested by the 1874 Brussels Declaration were essentially more favorable to peaceful citizens and public and private ownership in occupied territories than what had been provided by practice thus far and by the teachings of most scholars.[124] The IDI subsequently adopted the same rules in its Oxford Manual on Land Warfare (1880).[125]

The limits on the occupant's powers were tested when Russia occupied Bulgaria between 1877 to 1878, during the Russo-Turkish War. Russia wasted little time reorganizing the local administrative system, a move that was hardly in line with the occupant's duty to preserve indigenous institutions "unless otherwise necessary." However, de Martens gave several reasons for the legality of these measures. In his view, they in fact were

---

droits, et à déterminer ces obligations, dictées par la nécessité de maintenir l'ordre social et de protéger la sécurité individuelle et la propriété privée, en l'absence momentanée de tout gouvernement régulier."

121. See above, notes 54–60 and accompanying text.

122. "Article 2: L'ennemi qui occupé en territoire peut, selon les exigencies de la guerre et en vue de l'intérêt public, soit maintenir la force obligatoire des lois qui étaient en vigueur en temp de paix, soit les modifier, soit les susprendre entièrement." See *Annuaire de l'institut de droit international* 1 (1877): 277, 278.

123. Project of an International Declaration concerning the Laws and Customs of War. Brussels, 27 August 1874, Articles 2 and 3 (http://www.icrc.org/ihl.nsf/FULL/135?OpenDocument).

124. "VI. Les règles tracées à cet égard sont sans doute susceptibles d'améliorations de détail, mais, dès à présent, elles sont au fond plus favorables aux citoyens paisibles et aux propriétés publiques et privées du pays occupé, que la pratique suivie jusqu'ici et que la doctrine de la plupart des auteurs." *IDI Examen de la Déclaration,* above note 120.

125. Article 44 of the Manual: "Art. 44: The occupant should maintain the laws which were in force in the country in time of peace, and should not modify, suspend, or replace them, unless necessary." *Institut de droit international,* Session d'Oxford (1880); Manuel des lois de la guerre sur terre (Rapporteur: M. Gustave Moynier) (rep. in http://www.idi-iil.org/idiF/resolutionsF/1880_oxf_02_fr.pdf).

necessary because it had been impossible to restore the local regime from which the Bulgarians had suffered for centuries; the Brussels principles had been aimed at benefiting the local populations and, thus, were irrelevant when their application would only harm those populations. Furthermore, de Martens explained, a "transformative policy" is justified when the main purpose of a war was to annex a province or to "change or ameliorate" its administration.[126]

de Martens indicated, however, that these legal questions were given significant consideration, noting the "great number" of articles in the "turcophile European press" that condemned Russia for violating the laws of war.[127] Regardless, the smaller states of Europe were far from pleased with the Brussels formula and were perhaps even alarmed by Russia's interpretation of the rules of occupation. Thus, when the 1899 Hague Peace Conference provided an opportunity for these states to renegotiate the Brussels text, they cleverly turned their weakness into a weapon. During the negotiations, it became clear that two camps of negotiators had formed, the potential occupants and the potential occupied,[128] and that the latter were being asked to legitimate future actions of the former that might prove to be counter to their interests. The concern with legitimation led the Belgian delegate to suggest that most of the issues in dispute be left "floating in the shadows."[129] But de Martens, who chaired the session as the Russian delegate, managed to convince the smaller states to stay in the game, noting that they could benefit from the imposition of clear limitations on the authority of occupants.[130] Convinced, the smaller states succeeded in extracting stricter restrictions on the occupant's power, most notably a formulation that was aimed at further binding occupants to the legal sta-

126. Fedor de Martens, *Traité de droit international,* trans. Alfred Leo (Paris: Marescq, 1877), 3:257: "L'occupation prend un autre aspect quand elle n'a pas un caractère temporaire et qu'elle a lieu en vue d'une annexion, ou si le but même la guerre est de changer ou d'améliorer l'organisation d'une province appurtenant àl'ennemi. Dans ce cas, la puissance, qui procède à une annexion, a tout à fait le droit de transformer complètement les institutions régnantes et l'ordre établi, afin de les mettre en harmonie avec ses interérêts politiques, ou afin de procurer quelque avantage aux habitants." ("The occupation acquires a different aspect when it is not of a temporary nature but instead annexation is envisioned or the aim of the war itself was to change or ameliorate the organization of a province belonging to the enemy. In this case, the power that executes annexation has the right to transform the ruling institutions and establish order, so as to harmonize them with its political interests or to procure some advantage for the inhabitants.") de Martens, *La paix et la guerre,* at 267–96.

127. de Martens, *La paix et la guerre,* at 271.

128. de Lapradelle, "La conference de la paix," *Revue générale de Droit International Public* 6 (1899): 736–38.

129. Session of 6 June 1899, quoted in Lapradelle, "La conference," at 736–37.

130. Ibid., at 738.

tus quo in occupied territories: "[The occupant] shall take all steps in his power to re-establish and insure, as far as possible, public order and [civil life], while respecting, *unless absolutely prevented,* the laws in force in the country.[131] Thus, in the 1899 Hague Regulations, Fiore's notion finally won out.

C. Different Conceptions of Occupation beyond Europe

The rationale for the concept of occupation as the ultimate manifestation of national sovereignty was not applied beyond Europe. In the colonial context, because the colonialists did not recognize the sovereignty of the "uncivilized" nations, the temporary nature of occupation was regarded as simply inapplicable. As discussed above,[132] there was a doctrinal reason for the limited territorial scope of the European concept of occupation. Because the doctrine was meant to safeguard national sovereignty, it could not apply to regions whose sovereignty was not recognized. The prevailing view among the mainly European powers was that sovereignty, as a "gift of civilization,"[133] did not extend beyond the circle of self-defined "civilized," mainly Christian nations. Thus, the term "occupation" of "*terra nullius*" served, at the time, to denote one of the several ways of acquiring sovereignty over the non-Christian world, in addition to discovery, conquest, and cession.[134]

131. Art. 43, Hague Regulations. See above note 1.

132. See above note 24 and accompanying text.

133. Koskenniemi, *Gentle Civilizer,* at 98. On the modes of unilateral acquisition of non-Christian territories, see Korman, *Conquest,* at 42–66.

134. As Chief Justice Marshal observed with respect to the rights asserted by the Europeans concerning the New World (Johnson and Graham's *Lessee v. M'Intosh,* 21 U.S. 543, 572–73 [1823]), "On the discovery of this immense continent, the great nations of Europe were eager to appropriate to themselves so much of it as they could respectively acquire. Its vast extent offered an ample field to the ambition and enterprise of all; and the character and religion of its inhabitants afforded an apology for considering them as a people over whom the superior genius of Europe might claim an ascendancy. The potentates of the old world found no difficulty in convincing themselves that they made ample compensation to the inhabitants of the new, by bestowing on them civilization and Christianity, in exchange for unlimited independence. But, as they were all in pursuit of nearly the same object, it was necessary, in order to avoid conflicting settlements, and consequent war with each other, to establish a principle, which all should acknowledge as the law by which the right of acquisition, which they all asserted, should be regulated as between themselves. This principle was, that discovery gave title to the government by whose subjects, or by whose authority, it was made, against all other European governments, which title might be consummated by possession. The exclusion of all other Europeans, necessarily gave to the nation making the discovery the sole right of acquiring the soil from the natives, and establishing settlements upon it. It was a right with which no Europeans could interfere. It was a right which

III. Conclusion

The story of the evolution of the law of belligerent occupation in the nineteenth century reflects both evolving ideas and changing national interests. These ideas and interests pushed the legal doctrines along several different paths over the years and caused much confusion in the legal literature. Eventually, by the early twentieth century, with the codification of the laws of war in the U.S. and Europe and the consolidation of colonial and American territorial gains, the core meaning of occupation as a temporary and limited regime had gained general acceptance. But this meaning was soon to be challenged. Over the course of the twentieth century, numerous occupants would disregard their obligations, invoke exceptions to the doctrine, or resort to such contemporaneous concepts as national self-determination and human rights law to claim expanded authority. Thus, the doctrine on occupation, just like its mirror-image, the doctrine on sovereignty, continued to be shaped by the ideas of the day and by political realities.

---

all asserted for themselves, and to the assertion of which, by others, all assented. Those relations which were to exist between the discoverer and the natives, were to be regulated by themselves. The rights thus acquired being exclusive, no other power could interpose between them."

[7]

OCCUPATION UNDER THE LAWS OF WAR: I

ELBRIDGE COLBY

It is the fashion to date events in political, economic and social life in their chronological relation to those armed conflicts which have been the turning points and remain, to a man retracing the progress of nations, as conspicuous guide posts of history. Thus we have the phrases *"ante bellum"* and *"post bellum."* But there is a further use of Latin quite appropriate to this analysis, a use more common to the courts of law than either of the two phrases already mentioned that slip so trippingly off the tongues of the generality of mankind. Many a judge and jurist, many an advocate and publicist, has employed in the midst of learned argumentation the words *"flagrante bello"* or else *"nondum cessante bello."* Here in the dead speech of ancient Rome, still occasionally living on the lips of modern men, are appropriate distinctions with regard to the status of territory occupied by troops of a foreign nation.

If the occupation takes place, *ante bellum,* prior to open and acknowledged hostilities, it is deemed "intervention" or else becomes a cause of war and is merged in character and results with purely belligerent activities.[1] In such circumstances it is not occupation at all, neither in popular parlance nor in law.

If the occupation exists after the signing of the treaty of peace, *post bellum,* it exists by virtue of the treaty. Incidents relating to such occupation are to be scrutinized only in the light of the status created by the terms of the treaty of peace. If that treaty provides for the transfer or cession of the occupied territory into the hands of the occupying power, problems as to government and the administration of justice are questions of constitutional law, to be decided as such,[2] for the treaty by ratification and proclamation becomes the supreme law of the land and

---

[1] Although politically the entry of troops into China in 1900 has been deemed intervention, a United States Circuit Court legally reasoned and determined that a state of war existed. *Hamilton* v. *McClaughry* (C. C. Kan. 1905) 136 Fed. 445. Such was undoubtedly the case, for organized hostilities resulted. Vera Cruz in 1914 was similar. See declaration of Mexican Government. This was "an initiation of war". American Year Book (1914) 235. Only the lack of organized hostilities makes the situation in Santo Domingo "intervention" rather than belligerent occupation.

[2] *Cross* v. *Harrison* (U. S. 1853) 16 How. 164; *Leitensdorffer* v. *Webb* (U. S. 1857) 20 How. 176; Sutherland, *Constitutional Power and World Affairs* (1919) 82, 83; *Downes* v. *Bidwell* (1901) 182 U. S. 244, 21 Sup. Ct. 770; *Dorr* v. *United States* (1904) 195 U. S. 138, 24 Sup. Ct. 808; *Balzac* v. *Porto Rico* (1921) 258 U. S. 298, 42 Sup. Ct. 343; *De Lima* v. *Bidwell* (1901) 182 U. S. 1, 21 Sup. Ct. 743; *Dooley* v. *United States* (1901) 182 U. S. 222, 21 Sup. Ct. 762; *Sanchez* v. *United States* (1910) 216 U. S. 167, 30 Sup. Ct. 367.

forms the essential determining part of that constitutional law on which any mooted questions are decided.[3] Whatever is done, is done, not by the laws of war, but by the peace-time authority of the government newly become sovereign in that territory. Even if nothing is done, and war-time conditions are permitted to continue until legislatively changed, the delay is presumed consistent with policy.[4] In the meanwhile military personnel usually continue in control and their acts continue to be valid, even to the establishment of courts of justice.[5]

If the *post bellum* occupation is only temporary, and it is contemplated in the terms of the treaty of peace that it will cease upon the fulfillment of certain conditions,[6] such occupation is "military in name only"[7] and has no reference to the laws of war—only to the contractual relations established by the treaty. It is proper to avoid altogether the term military occupation and to designate such activity simply as a "garrisoning."[8]

The other is the type which is, though governed completely by the laws of war, that occupation of territory which takes place *flagrante bello* or, if an armistice be signed and peace not yet definitely concluded, *nondum cessante bello*. This is what is known as military occupation,[9] sometimes called military government.[10] The most appropriate term for it, however, would seem to be "belligerent occupation"[11] for this phrase implies that conditions of war exist, that the occupa-

[3] *United States* v. *Percheman* (U. S. 1833) 7 Pet. 51; Treaty of Frankfort, Herslet, Vol. iii, No. 446, arts. ii, ix. *Henderson* v. *Poindexter* (U. S. 1827) 12 Wheat. 530, 535.

[4] *Cross* v. *Harrison, supra,* footnote 2; *Santiago* v. *Nogueras* (1908) 214 U. S. 260, 29 Sup. Ct. 608.

[5] *Leitensdorfer* v. *Webb, supra,* footnote 2.

[6] *E.g.,* Allied occupation of France in 1871, under the Treaty of Frankfort, Herselet, Vol. iii, No. 446, arts. vii, viii; Chilean Occupation of Tacna-Arica, Treaty of Ancon (1883) art. iii; 74 British and Foreign Papers, 349; 10 Martens, *Nouveau Recueil Général de Traités* (2nd ser.) 191; Treaty of Paris, Dec. 11, 1898, (1898) 30 Stat. 1754, arts. 1, 16; Haskins and Lord, *Problems of the Peace Conference* (1920) 131, 144; League of Nations, *Official Journal* (1921) pp. 683-686; *Agreement Supplementary to the Treaty.* Sen. Doc. 81, 66th Cong. 1st Sess. 362.

[7] General Leonard Wood, *The Military Government of Cuba* (1903) 21 Ann. of the Amer. Acad. of Pol. Sci. 153.

[8] This is the view of Bray, *Occupation Militaire,* 127, following Fiore, who seems to be alone among writers on the subject in so holding, but it seems sound, nevertheless. For example such is the state of affairs in Haiti today, by virtue of the Treaty of Peace and Amity of 1915, (1915) 39 Stat. 1654, where that status did not even follow a war; and such was the position of the United States troops in Coblenz, who carefully refrained from interference in any local matters that did not affect their own safety, not even in possible revolution. See R. S. Baker, *America and the World Peace,* N. Y. Times, July 23, 1922; Hyde, *International Law* (1922) 791.

[9] *American Ins. Co.* v. *Canter* (U. S. 1828) 1 Pet. 511; and *Sanchez* v. *United States, supra,* footnote 2.

[10] See Birkhimer, *Military Government and Martial Law* (1892) 21.

[11] This is the term suggested by Hyde, *op. cit.,* footnote 8.

tion is founded upon force, that the laws are laws of war. In using this term there is little likelihood of confusing the subject under discussion with treaty rights,[12] with civil affairs administered by army officers in ceded territory,[13] or with martial law.[14]

Such belligerent occupation may exist only in connection with armed conflict where frontiers have been crossed. It usually exists only within the territories of a national enemy.[15] Yet it has been known to exist, in a legal sense, within rebel territory,[16] when an insurrection against the established government had well defined geographical limitations.[17] It has even been known to exist in neutral territory, as during the Russo-Japanese war in China,[18] and during the World War in Luxemburg, China, and Greece.[19] Never could it be said to exist in

---

[12] *Supra*, footnote 4.

[13] *De Lima* v. *Bidwell*, *supra*, footnote 2; *Sanchez* v. *United States*, *supra*, footnote 2, deal with acts by such governments, functioning after the exchange of ratifications, under constitutional law rather than under the laws of war.

[14] In the United States "martial law" appears only in home territory where belligerency does not exist; in England the term is applied to all law administered by the army including that in occupied territory. See the *British Manual of Military Law* (1914) 3, par. 15.

[15] See Birkhimer, *op. cit.*, footnote 10, p. 21, defines it is follows: "Military government is that which is established by a commander over occupied enemy territory."

[16] "When a rebellion becomes organized and attains such proportions as to be able to put a formidable military force in the field, it is usual for the established government to concede to it some belligerent rights." *Williams* v. *Bruffy* (1877) 96 U. S. 176, 186. See also Vattel, *The Law of Nations* (1916) bk. 2, c. 18, § 293; (1869) 9 Ops. Atty. Gen. 140; 1 Moore, *A Digest of International Law*, (1906) 43, 49-51; and *Underhill* v. *Hernandez* (1897) 168 U. S. 250, 18 Sup. Ct. 83.

The contrary opinion was held by British officers operating in the southern states during the American Revolution who continued to ridicule the idea of observing capitulations with citizens, insisting that those who claimed to be members of an independent state were but vanquished traitors who owed their lives to British leniency. 6 Bancroft, *History of the United States* (Cent. ed. 1879) 381-382.

[17] *Tyler* v. *Defrees* (U. S. 1870) 1 Wall. 331, 345; *Dow* v. *Johnson* (1879) 100 U. S. 158, 170; *Miller* v. *United States* (U. S. 1870) 11 Wall. 268, 306-307; *Coleman* v. *Tennessee* (1878) 7 U. S. 509, 516-517. This conception was made more readily possible by the Presidental Proclamation of Aug. 16, 1861, stating which states were "in insurrection." See (1861) 12 Stat. 1262. This proclamation granting the rights of belligerents to the Confederates not only set a magnanimous example to other nations regarding internal rebellions, Alvarez, *Le Droit International Americain* (1910) 71, but was also responsible for the establishment of well-defined laws of war for the United States Army (1863) Gen. O. 100, and for the opportunity granted the Supreme Court of the United States to embody in many subsequent decisions sound legal interpretations concerning the effects of belligerent occupation on the laws of occupied territory. See also 1 Moore, *op. cit.*, footnote 16, pp. 57-58; and with regard to Iquique duriug a Peruvian revolution (1869) 9 Op. Atty. Gen. 140.

[18] See Ariga, *La Guerre Russo-Japonaise* (1908) 429-432.

[19] 2 Garner, *International Law and the World War* (1920) 237, 239, 241 255. It is, however, claimed that the occupation of Salonica in 1915 was initiated with the consent of the Venizclist ministry, which would give a slightly different aspect to the case. Villari, L., *Macedonian Campaign* (1922) 23-25.

allied territory, for in such a case the friendly ally would conduct its own government and the troops would be assisting by invitation and not exercising any belligerent power against the sovereign state or the people in the lands they occupied.

One of the most interesting cases on the law of military forces which has ever been decided in America, laid down the principle that in home territory martial law could not be valid if the courts of the country were open and conducting their affairs.[20] A recent writer has remarked: "The question, in any case, is simply whether the government is powerless."[21] The distinction is rather generally[22] accepted as sound regarding home territory,[23] and sound also with regard to military government set up during belligerent occupation under the laws of war. For before belligerent occupation is entitled to recognition as such, it is necessary "that the authority of the State to which the territory belongs should have ceased there to be exercised."[24] "The government of the conqueror being *de facto* and not *de jure* in character, it must always rest upon the fact of possession which is adverse to the former sovereign.......The criterion......is the driving out of enemy authorities or their submission to the dominant power."[25] It is a matter of fact, not a matter of law. Attempts to say too precisely what are the legal conditions for its existence frequently meet an impasse, as for instance in the Russo-Japanese War, when the local officials had no authority to retire in the face of a force which was not a national enemy, and an army had no belligerent and hostile justification for compelling their departure, since China—though the battle ground of the armies—was still a neutral nation.[26] In the Annex to Hague Convention IV of 1907 the following words are used: "Territory is considered occupied when it is actually placed under the authority of

[20] *Ex parte Milligan* (U. S. 1866) 4 Wall. 2.

[21] See Glenn, *The Army and the Law* (1918) 190.

[22] For a convenient discussion of the increasing acceptance of this doctrine, see Glenn, *op. cit.*, footnote 21, pp. 186-190.

[23] This conception is used as a basis of judgment in *Handlin* v. *Wickliffe* (U. S. 1870) 12 Wall. 173, 175, and phrased thus: "If......the civil Constitution of the State was in full operation, independent of military control, the authority derived from the appointment by the military governor ceased......"

[24] Birkhimer, *op. cit.*, footnote 10, p. 21. See also 2 Oppenheim, *International Law* (1920) §§ 166, 167.

[25] Birkhimer, *op. cit.*, footnote 10, p. 48, citing *Thorington* v. *Smith* (U. S. 1868) 8 Wall. 1 and *Fleming* v. *Page* (U. S. 1850) 9 How. 602. See also Wright, *Enforcement of International Law through Municipal Law* (1916) 208, who says: "The law of military government, therefore, is a matter governed by international law."

[26] Ariga, *op. cit.*, footnote 18, pp. 429-432. A circumstance somewhat similar arose in 1806 when Napoleon occupied Hesse-Cassel to avoid dangers arising from the armed neutrality of the Elector, though at the Peace of Tilsit that territory was treated as if it were conquered instead of merely occupied. 2 Phillimore, *International Law* (3d ed. 1879) 842.

the hostile army."[27] Of course mere raids do not constitute occupation, nor invasions which do not attempt to establish any administration. But the actual size and distribution of the occupying forces are immaterial. The test of occupation is its effectiveness. Prussian occupation of portions of France in 1870-1871 was maintained by the mere ability to assert essential power.[28] The extent of the occupation is likewise determined by the test of effectiveness in permanently eliminating the authority of the original government and continuously maintaining the authority of the occupant. It is not the use of mere "flying colnmns"[29] but the results of their work, by which we must judge. If the damage they do is merely occasional, they are merely raiders and temporary invaders in the districts where they roam, and occupation does not exist.[30] If they take possession of the municipal offices and establish their authority,[31] even if they come and go in the manner of a ranging police force like the state troopers of New Jersey, New York, and Pennsylvania, reinforcing only when necessary the will and acts of their agents, then the outlying districts may be said to be occupied. Such occupation, depending upon fact rather than upon law, has no relation to geographical boundaries of former political units. It exists only by force, and where that force fails it cannot be said to exist.[32] "It is manifest," says Phillimore, "that the conquest......must not be the mere conquest of a capitol but of a country."[33] Whatever proclama-

[27] (1907) 36 Stat. 2227, art. 42.

[28] "One could go for miles within the occupied territory without seeing a single Prussian soldier," Bordwell, *Law of War Between Belligerents* (1908) 92-93; also Hall, *International Law* (8th ed., 1924) 501, footnote 1. It is doubtful, though, if even this extreme, sound position could justify the Isle-Adam incident of September, 1870, where a patrol entered the town and retired, returning the next day to collect arms, was ambushed by some non-villagers, and in retaliation gave the town to pillage "because of the rising against them." Bray, *op. cit.*, footnote 8, pp. 171-172.

[29] Bordwell, *op. cit.*, footnote 28, p. 92. See also Oppenheim, *op. cit.*, footnote 24, p. 501, footnote 1; Jacomet, *Les Lois de la Guerre Continentale* (1913) 69; and 1 Busch, M., *Bismarck* (1898) 476, citing remarks of 1871: "We should from time to time send a flying column wherever they show themselves recalcitrant and shoot, hang and burn."

[30] U. S. Army, *Rules of Land Warfare* (1914) § 288.

[31] 2 Oppenheim, *op. cit.*, footnote 24, §167. Bordwell, *op. cit.*, footnote 28, p. 297.

[32] "An occupation giving the right to the conqueror to exercise governmental authority must be not only invasion, but also possession of the enemy's country ......The military occupation by the United States, during and after the War with Spain, of the Philippine Islands, and the conduct of the military government thereof, did not extend to places which were not in actual possession of the United States until they were reduced to such possession. *MacLeod* v. *United States* (1912) 229 U. S. 416, 33 Sup. Ct. 955.

[33] 3 Phillimore, *op. cit.*, footnote 26, p. 823.

tions may say,[34] and whatever dependence municipal law may place upon them,[35] in international law occupation depends solely upon the fact of possession and rule. Indeed, no proclamation is necessary, though they are usually issued[36] to let the inhabitants know what to expect.[37] A proclamation is, however, useful. It may serve as political propaganda, as did Kearny's and Stockton's in the Mexican War, as did Napoleon's extremely adroit one at Alexandria in 1798.[38] It may give due notice to inhabitants as to the new state of affairs, the extent of the new authority, and their new duties and rights,[39] in order to simplify procedure and eliminate future misunderstandings. A proclamation serves the further useful purpose of standing as evidence of intention to occupy—though not necessarily as proof of occupation—and might reasonably be cited when questions arise as to whether or not

---

[34] An interesting conflict between international law and municipal law is found in *Van Deventer* v. *Hancke* (1903) Transvaal Sup. Ct. 401, where in spite of the fact that the acts in question were undoubtedly those of a *de facto* government and took place prior to British possession though subsequent to the Proclamation of Annexation, the British court was compelled to refrain from questioning the correctness of Crown proclamations and to hold the British occupation effective on a date when it really was not so. The following is a neutral remark on the topic: "Le gouvernement britannique......entendit, avant toute annexion et en vertu de la seule occupation de territoire envahi par ses armées, astreindre tous les habitants au devoir de fidélité envers lui." Despagnet, *La Guerre Sud-Africaine* (1902) 213-214.

[35] There is no real contradiction between the Philippines and the Transvaal cases mentioned in footnotes 32 and 34, above. In the Transvaal case, the proclamation announced an annexation which was later rendered effective, and the original state was completely extinguished and rendered powerless to protest. In the Philippines case, the presidential Executive Order did not speak in terms of geography, as did the Transvaal proclamation, but extended the regulations in question only "upon the occupation and possession of parts aud places...... by the forces of the United States"—thus making actual military accomplishment the standard of judgment, which is indeed a far sounder one than political pronouncements of belligerent iutentions as yet unaccomplished. The difference is a difference in the type of executive declaration, not in the manner of the court decision. Indeed, with a somewhat similar matter, opposing Haitian claims to the island of Navassa, the United States Supreme Court did not hesitate to declare: "Who is the sovereign *de jure* or *de facto* of a territory is not a judicial but a political question, the determiuation of which by the legislative and executive departments of any government conclusively binds the judges as well as all other officers, citizens, and subjects of government." *Jones v. United States* (1890) 137 U. S. 202, 11 Sup. Ct. 80. See a similar decision in a British court in *Mighell* v. *Sultan of Johore* [1894] L. R. 1 Q. B. 149.

[36] *Rules of Land Warfare* (1912) § 292 (18) (19) (20) (22) *Planters' Bk.* v. *Union Bk.* (U. S. 1879) 6 Wall. 483; 1 Smith, *War with Mexico*, 291, 296, 335; *British Manual Military Law* (1914) § 347. 2 Hyde, *op. cit.*, footnote 8, p. 369, footnote 1.

[37] "Issued merely from abundant caution, as a useful warning to those whom it may concern." Holland, *Letters upon War and Neutrality* (3d ed. 1918) 112.

[38] So characterized, and summarized in 8 Cambridge Modern History (1909) 599. Commandant Guitry, *L'Armé de Bonaparte en Egypte*, 87.

[39] *Cf.* discussion of Gen. Pershing's 1918 proclamations and texts, in Smith, H. A., *Military Government* (1920) 88, 99-101. Wellington deemed a proclamation necessary. 115 Hansard, *Parliamentary Debates* (3d ser. 1891) 880 cited in Hall, *International Law* (4th ed.) 489.

the occupation is complete and disputes as to whether or not flying columns function merely as harrassing units or as upholders of scattered administrative elements. In such a proclamation, however, expectation should not outrun accomplishment. Its statements regarding territorial limits of control should be based upon achieved results. It should be a record of events. If it is such, it will be a valuable historical document, not because it announces a policy, not because it advertises the fact of occupation, but chiefly because it will tell of the scope of that occupation already established. It records, but does not create, occupation. The occupation itself extends to the territory where the authority of the hostile army has been established and can be exercised.[40] It exists where it exists because it is a fact, not because it is law;[41] it is founded on military might *flagrante bello* or else *nondum cessante bello;* it is a belligerent act, maintained by belligerent methods and for belligerent purposes.

In its purpose and methods belligerent occupation limits its own life. Founded on force, it may be overthrown by force. If the invasion which made it possible is repulsed after a lapse of time, the occupation necessarily ceases. As a fact it has ceased to exist. It does not cease, though, simply because the armed soldiers who established it pass on to wage their continued campaign against the national armies of the native country.[42] In such cases, to protect their rear, they leave details and administrative agents behind to maintain their authority over the disarmed and powerless inhabitants. Occupation does cease definitely when a military reverse or a strategic withdrawal permits the original officials to return and institute again the functions and processes of their administration. It likewise ceases with the treaty of peace, whatever the fate of the territory. If the occupied lands are returned to the possession of the original owner, the national sovereignty reasserts itself. If the occupied lands are ceded to the occupant, belligerent occupation forthwith ceases simply and obviously because belligerency has come to an end. The same officials may administer the government. They may conform to the same laws. They may be the identical officers of the army who acted in the identical capacity before. But "the government so established....ends with the restoration of peace, and the resumption of the regular municipal government of peace."[43] Though the military commander may still govern, because his own government

[40] Annex to Hague Convention, IV of 1907, art. 42; (1907) 36 Stat. 2277.

[41] Bynkershoek, *Law of War* (1810) 56; "Occupation which is had in war consists more in fact than in Law."

[42] 2 Oppenheim, *op. cit.*, footnote 29, §168.

[43] *Isbell* v. *Farris* (Tenn. 1868) 5 Cold. 426.

so wishes, with an "actual or implied consent",[44] he administers the laws of peace and not of war. His authority is no longer to promote warfare, but to preserve peace.[45] It would be unwise to say, however, that an armistice terminated belligerent occupation.[46] In 1918 indeed it actually created a belligerent occupation of the Rhineland.[47] On one view of this case, the march into Germany of the allied and associated powers might be said to be a contractual act similar to those already mentioned as *post bellum* occupations, but it seems that the warrant for this march was belligerent, because armistices are belligerent acts, and quite different from treaties. Not by armistices, therefore, but by treaties, is belligerent occupation terminated.[48] In fact, the period between the signing of an armistice and the ratification of a treaty of peace, is the only period which can appropriately be described by the terms *nondum cessante bello.* During this period control is purely based on belligerent force; the occupation is a belligerent occupation; the occupation as a belligerent fact ceases and the permanent sovereignty commences at the exchange of the ratifications of the treaty.[49]

"The holding of a conquered territory is regarded as a mere military occupation until its fate shall be determined at the treaty of

---

[44] *Ex parte Milligan, supra,* footnote 20.

[45] Sutherland, *op. cit.,* footnote 2, pp. 81, 82. See citations above, footnotes 1 and 2, notably the analysis of the changing status of Porto Rico as set forth in *De Lima* v. *Bidwell, supra,* footnote 2 and in *Sanchez* v. *United States, supra,* footnote 2.

[46] 2 Oppenheim, *op. cit.,* footnote 29, §231, is quite emphatic in declaring that an armistice, though a temporary cessation of hostilities, is "in no wise to be compared with peace, and ought not to be called temporary peace." He cites, most aptly, the Franco-German armistice of January 28, 1871, the purpose of which was expressly declared to be "the creation of the possibility for the French Government to convoke a Parliamentary Assembly which could determine whether or not the war was to be continued." (§233.)

[47] *Text of Armistice Signed by Germany* (1918) 9 Cur. Hist. Mag. 364. This is to be distinguished from the Treaty occupation. (1919) Sen. Doc. No. 75, 66th Cong. 1st Sess.; 2 Hyde, *op. cit.,* footnote 8, p. 362.

[48] This has been the practice of the United States. It has been announced "that a state of war existed between Spain and the United States, and the Island (of Porto Rico) remained Spanish territory....until April 11, 1899, when ratifications of the treaty of peace were exchanged." *Ex parte Ortiz* (C. C. Minn. 1900) 100 Fed. 955. "The holding of a conquered territory is regarded as mere military occupation until its fate shall be determined at the treaty of peace." *American Ins. Co.* v. *Canter, supra,* footnote 9.

[49] *Armstrong* v. *Bidwell* (C. C. N. Y. 1903) 124 Fed. 690; *De Lima* v. *Bidwell supra,* footnote 2; *Dooley* v. *United States, supra,* footnote 2; *Ponce* v. *Roman Catholic Church* (1908) 210 U. S. 296, 307, 28 Sup. Ct. 737; *Sanchez* v. *United States, supra,* footnote 2; *DePass* v. *Bidwell* (C. C. N. Y. 1903) 124 Fed. 615, 619; *Howell* v. *Bidwell* (C. C. N. Y. 1903) 124 Fed. 688; *Isbell* v. *Farris, supra,* footnote 43; *Ochoa* v. *Hernandez* (1913) 230 U. S. 139, 159, 33 Sup. Ct. 1033. There should, however, be noted the following *contra* cases, though of very old date, where the end of the war was considered to have come at the signing of the peace treaty, not at the ratification thereof. *Bain* v. *The Speedwell* (U. S. 1784) 2 Dall. 40; *The Mentor* (1799) 1 C. Rob. 179.

peace."[50] This is the modern doctrine. There was a time when war was considered a method primarily of acquiring territory instead of fighting for trade privileges and economic rights. What a nation conquered, it held. Sometimes seizures were traded against one another over the diplomatic tables of peace congresses. But usually military conquest meant ownership. Then the entire complexion of the world changed. Small professional armies were replaced by huge national forces. Intricacies of governmental administration, of military supply, and of economic coördination of national resources increased to such an extent that military commanders aimed to seize a capital city and there dictate their terms, rather than merely to occupy and hold the districts which they coveted. As the decades passed, occupation became more and more merely a means of war instead of an end of war. It was in purpose as well as in fact belligerent, an act of war, without necessarily any prospects of permanence.[51] Still, though, the old notion of transferred sovereignty remained, even if only in the sense of temporary sovereignty. There is some question as to whether a treaty clause stipulating cession actually transfers the territory or merely recognizes the fact of cession already accomplished by belligerent occupation. But it seems that, in view of the many precedents of withdrawal from conquered districts, in view of the occasional cession in treaties of lands not involved in hostilities, the safest procedure is to view cession a function of treaties, and belligerent occupation as involving only a temporary

[50] *American Ins. Co.* v. *Canter*, *supra*, footnote 9.

[51] We find such opposite expressions in modern times as these: "To complete the right of property, *the right to the thing*, and *the possession of the thing itself*, should be united. This is the general law of property and applies, I conceive, no less to the right of territory than to other rights." Sir William Scott in *The Fama* (1805) 5 C. Rob. 106, 125. "The acquisition of land by conquest shall not......be recognized under American Public Law." Resolutions at International American Congress, 1889-1890, 1 Moore, *op. cit.*, footnote 16, p. 292; 7 *id.* p. 318. "Conquest does not give title. It merely creates occupation." Bordwell, *op. cit.*, footnote 28, pp. 57-58. "Various and many treaties of peace fortify the sound international doctrine that *conquest* and *occupation* of territory are distinct public acts, both to the state and to the individual." 3 Phillimore, *op. cit.*, footnote 26, p. 785. "Le transfert de la souverainetè en droit, avec toutes les consequences juridiques qu'il entraine, ne se produit que par la cession contractuelle du territoire a la conelusion de la paix, c'est-a-dire par l'annexion proprement dite". Despagnet, *op. cit.*, footnote 34, p. 144. "The courts have held that under the Constitution Congress has no power to declare wars for conquest; hence the United States cannot acquire new territory by conquests." Wright, *op. cit.*, footnote 25, p. 25, citing *Fleming* v. *Page*, *supra*, footnote 25. "By the law of nations, the *occupatio bellica* transfers the sovereign power to the conqueror." Birkhimer, *op. cit.*, footnote 10, p. 28, citing (1857) 8 Ops. Atty. Gen. 365, 369. "The principle that the wishes of a population are to be consulted when the territory which they inhabit is ceded has not been adopted into international law, and cannot be adopted into it until title by conquest has disappeared". Hall, *op. cit.*, footnote 39, p. 49. "......a conquerer prescribes the limits of the right of conquest......" and the terms and conditions of peace. *The Cherokees and their Lands* (1830) 2 Ops. Atty. Gen., 321, 323, citing Marshall in *Johnson* v. *McIntosh* (U. S. 1823) 8 Wheat. 543, 588.

transfer of sovereignty if any at all. Practices may differ slightly on account of varying constitutional restrictions upon the foreign relations powers and the war powers of the agents of different governments which carry on wars, but in the long run we must depend upon international rather than upon municipal law for our conception as to the true world-wide conception of belligerent occupation.[52] Formerly it used to be said that "the intention of the conqueror is not merely to invade one district, but the whole of the hostile empire, and to make his own all the countries belonging to it "[53] Then under the influence of Rousseau and Locke and in view of the practices of the armies of the French Revolution,[54] the strict rule was relaxed and military occupation was looked upon as temporary,[55] as limited to the period of belligerency in its effects. However the old practices persisted in leaving their impress on modern theory. Jurists have compared the administration of occupied territory with the administration of national affairs by revolutionary officials and have said that the conqueror sets up a *de facto* government and that to such a government "obedience in civil and local matters" is "not only a necessity but a duty."[56] "By the conquest and military occupation of Castine," said Mr. Justice Story, speaking of the British control of the Maine town in 1814, "the enemy acquired that firm possession which enabled him to exercise the full rights of sovereignty over that place. The sovereignty of the United States over the territory was, of course, sus-

---

[52] *Rutledge* v. *Fogg, Ex'r* (Tenn. 1866) 3 Cold. 554; Birkhimer, *op. cit.*, footnote 10, p. 28, citing Maine, *International Law* (1888) 179; *30 Hogsheads of Sugar* v. *Boyle* (U. S. 1815) 9 Cranch 191, citing *Fleming* v. *Page, supra,* footnote 25, pp. 615-616 and *Cross* v. *Harrison, supra,* footnote 2, citing 2 Bl. Comm. *107; 4 *id.* pp. 414-415, and Dana's Wheaton, *International Law* (8th ed. 1866) §345, holds that "mere occupation and control" are insufficient and that to it should be added express transfer in capitulations or in treaty or else "a long lapse of time". *Cf.* also Sutherland, *op. cit.*, footnote 2, footnote 80.

[53] Bynkershoek, *op. cit.*, footnote 41, p. 48.

[54] Title VI, Const. of 1791. Anderson, *Constitutions and Documents*, 93. Also French Decree of May 22-27, 1790, art. 4, see 1 Duvergier, *Collection Complète des Lois* (1824) 191. For brief historical survey of change in point of view on this point, see 2 Westlake, *Principles of International Law* (2d ed. 1910) 95, 96.

[55] Heffter, *Le Droit International Publique de L'Europe* (1866) §§132-133. See the very able survey of British cases appearing in the opinion of the court in *The Gerasimo* (1857) 11 Moore P. C. 88. Note also the dictum in *United States* v. *Hayward* (C. C. Mass. 1815) 2 Gall. 485: "A territory conquered by the enemy is not to be considered as incorporated into the dominions of that enemy, without a renunciation in a treaty of peace, or a long and permanent possession." Nashville, Tenn., though occupied by Union troops, was held to be "enemy territory" on account of the Presidential proclamation of Aug. 16, 1861, (1861) 12 Stat. 1262, regarding states in insurrection. *Hamilton* v. *Dillin* (U. S. 1874) 21 Wall. 73.

[56] *Thorington* v. *Smith, supra,* footnote 25. See also 1 Bluntschli, *Le Droit International* (1895) §§ 35, 36a, 42, 64, and Ordonnance of Andjuar, 1823, in 5 Pasquier, *Memoires du Chancelier,* 517.

pended, and the laws of the United States could no longer be rightfully enforced there..... By the surrender the inhabitants passed under a temporary allegiance to the British government."[57] This is one point of view, then, that "sovereignty passes immediately upon effectual occupation of the territory"[58] even though such sovereignty is ouly temporary and the title is only valid "while the victor maintains exclusive possession of the conquered territory."[59] This conception has been maintained by Birkhimer, who declares: "The unlawfulness of trade with the enemy extends not only to every place within his dominions and subject to his government, but also to all places in his possession or military occupation, even though such occupation has not ripened into a conquest or changed the national character of the inhabitants."[60] The United States Supreme Court has adopted this theory, holding, in the case of a ship belonging to and carrying produce from a Danish citizen to Santa Cruz then occupied by Great Britain as an act of war, that "for belligerent and commercial purposes" Santa Cruz was properly to be considered "a part of the domain of the conqueror."[61]

---

[57] *United States* v. *Rice* (U. S. 1819) 4 Wheat. 246. Commenting upon this case, Chief Justice Chase in *Thorington* v. *Smith, supra,* footnote 25, declared: "It is not to be inferred from this that the obligations of the people of Castine as citizens of the United States were abrogated. They were suspended merely by the presence, and only during the presence, of the paramount force". This principle was followed in a naturalization and citizenship case in 1830, arising out of the capture of Charlestown by the British in 1780. *Shanks* v. *Dupont* (U. S. 1830) 3 Pet. 242, 246.

[58] Wright, *op. cit.,* footnote 25, p. 208, who states it as a doctrine, but does not agree with it. In 1814, Moose Island fell to the British and American inhabitants were required to take the oath of allegiance to the crown of Great Britain, and the Islands of Passamaquoddy Bay were taken because it was felt that they belonged to Great Britain by the treaty of 1783. See 4 McMaster, *History of the People of the United States* (1883) 130, 131, 133; Daily American Advertiser, Aug. 1, 1814. Wright, *Control of American Foreign Relations* (1922) 297, further states that a Congressional declaration of war "authorizes the President to both occupy and militarily govern enemy territory, although it does not authorize him to annex it". Ch. de Visscher, *L'Occupation de Guerre* (1918) 34 Law Quart. Rev. 72, likewise holds that military occupation in itself is not a source of sovereignty.

[59] *Fleming* v. *Page, supra,* footnote 25, and *American Ins. Co.* v. *Canter, supra,* footnote 9. An interesting example of this attitude is found in the declaration of the incoming Governor General of Alsace in 1870, though of course this declaration was motivated by the apparent intention of the Germans to regain and retain that province: "Les événements de la guerre ayant amené l'occupation d'une partie du territoire française par les forces allemandes, ces territoires se trouvent par ce fait même soustraits à la souveraineté impériale, et en place de laquelle est établie l'autorité des puissance allemandes". Hall, *op. cit.,* footnote 39, p. 486.

[60] *Op. cit.,* footnote 10, p. 229, citing Halleck, *International Law* (4th ed. 1908) c. 1, §20; Woolsey, *Introduction to Study of International Law* (5th ed. 1885) §124; 1 Kent, *Commentaries* (14th ed. 1896) 68 (c); and *contra, The Hoop* (1799) 1 C. Rob. 196, 209.

[61] *30 Hogsheads of Sugar* v. *Boyle, supra,* footnote 52.

The Judicial Committee of the Privy Council of Great Britain took a contrary stand,[62] in the case of a ship and a cargo belonging to a Moldavian under the Moravian flag captured during the Crimean war while Russia occupied those districts with the express policy of not altering their political status and of not incorporating them into the Russian Empire. "The mere possession of a territory," said the court, "does not of itself necessarily convert the territory so occupied into hostile territory, or its inhabitants into enemies." Yet, for purposes of trading with the enemy acts, and for determination of nationality and jurisdiction, it seems that there must be a change. Modern war is so much an economic affair in its causes and in its conduct. It is so much a popular affair with its conscriptions and selective service. For the period of the war, all occupied territory must be considered as part of the resources of the occupant. He can levy large contributions. He can develop to his own advantage such natural resources as will assist him in prosecuting his campaign with weightier or more numerous pieces of material. When you try to fix "an iron ring" around Germany or any other nation and have to enlarge its diameter and circumference because of certain military successes which the armies of that nation may have had, you must include within your ring all the land in rear of his armies. He will use that territory as if it were his own, working civilians in factories, coal mines, and in productive agricultural lands, repressing non-essential industries there as thoroughly as he represses them in his own hard-pressed districts behind his original frontiers. For all practical purposes, the territory has changed hands. True it is only a temporary transfer, subject to being changed back with the changing fortunes of war, either as an incident to the successful campaigns or as a provision of treaty stipulations. But for the time being it is enemy territory, so far as the ousted nation is concerned.

Belligerent occupation is an incident of war. It is a means of carrying on a war. It is "a legitimate method of warfare."[63] The soldiers say that "the seal of victory is the occupation of territory."[64] It adds to

---

[62] *The Gerasimo, supra,* footnote 55. This matter was summarily decided, almost in an introductory manner, while the greater part of the decision was taken up with the problem as to whether or not the fact of occupation needed to be supplemented by cession or conquest to make the occupied territory a part of the dominions of the occupant. The opinion states: "the proposition...... cannot be maintained......(that it is) sufficient that the territory in question should be occupied by a hostile force, and subjected, during its occupation, to the control of the hostile power, so far as such power may think fit to exercise control."

[63] Wright, *op. cit.,* footnote 58, p. 297.

[64] Major R. Cheneoux-Trench, in Gold Medal Prize Essay for 1922, *Scientific Inventions and Sciences* (1923) 68 Journ. Roy. Unit. Serv. Inst. 199, cited in (1923) Chem. Warfare 2.

the resources of the occupying power in men, money, and provisions; and subtracts from those same resources of the enemy. Its purpose is military.[65] War is the litigation of nations. Questions in dispute are settled by force. Belligerent occupation is a forceful seizure and maintenance of firm possession of enemy property. The orders of military commanders have no further permanent efficacy than such as they draw from the force which makes them possible and upholds them.[66] Army officers are usually in control.[67] Obviously what governs is not law at all, but merely expedient regulations designed to accomplish military ends that are deemed necessary. In some respects the Hague Conventions restrict action, but even they can be avoided on a just plea of military necessity, of reprisals, or of superior orders and national policy. Wellington, in the House of Lords in 1851. called it "neither more nor less than the will of the general who commands the army....no law at all."[68] As far as municipal law is concerned the supreme power is "the arbitrary will of the commander exercised without reference to any principle and subject to no limitation or, as said by Sir Matthew Hale 'something indulged, rather than allowed as law.' The power, whatever it may be called, is one which finds no limitations in the Constitution, or in the general laws of the land. Its arbitrary and absolute character is shown by the ancient maxim by which it is characterized: 'The will of the conqueror is the law of the conquered.' "[69] The United States Supreme Court has stated the situation succinctly:

"The conquering power has a right to displace the pre-existing authority, and to assume, to such extent as it may deem proper, the exercise by itself of all the powers and functions of government. It may appoint all the necessary officers and clothe them with designated powers, larger or smaller, according to its pleasure. It may prescribe

[65] Magoon, *Reports on the Law of Civil Governments in Territory Subject to Military Occupation* (1902) 11, citing *Ex parte Milligan, supra,* footnote 20.

[66] *Varner* v. *Arnold* (1880) 83 N. C. 206, cited by 7 Moore, *op. cit.,* footnote 16, p. 268.

[67] The Japanese once tried to utilize as administrators former consuls, secretaries of foreign affairs, officials from open ports, but found civilians ineffective and inappropriate, possibly because a rule of force is best administered by a man with the prestige and power of military uniform and rank, admittedly because they were unfitted to coöperate with the army in the issuing of orders and the infliction of purely military punishments. The Japanese social, almost caste, distinctions between civil and military personnel were also attributed as reasons for the failure of the experiment. Ariga, *La Guerre Sino-Japanaise* (1896) 178. Disastrous results, though dissimilar, followed the mixing of civilians and soldiers in ruling Belgium in 1793. 7 Cambridge Modern History, 418. A similar experiment was attempted at San Francisco in 1846. *Trenouth* v. *San Francisco* (1879) 100 U. S. 251.

[68] 115 Hansard, *op. cit.,* footnote 39, p. 880.

[69] Sutherland, *op. cit.,* footnote 2, p. 80 concerning General Butler at New Orleans it was decided that "his will was law". *United States* v. *Diekelman* (1875) 92 U. S. 520, 526.

the revenues to be paid, and apply them to its own use or otherwise. It may do anything necessary to strengthen itself and weaken the enemy. There is no limit to the powers that may be exerted in such cases, save those which are found in the laws and usages of war."[70]

The Hague Convention and Annex covering this matter are really very scant in extent, and very superficial in character. In the very preamble of that document it is frankly admitted that "all the circumstances" have not been covered and that "unforeseen cases" will arise.[71] And such things are left in vague and general terms—and therefore meaningless since they can be interpreted in various ways and always in view of that elastic doctrine of military necessity—to "the principles of the law of nations, the usages among civilized peoples, the laws of humanity, and the dictates of the public conscience." Truly as ex-Senator Sutherland has remarked,[72] concerning the maxim about the will of the conqueror being the law of the conquered:

> "The harshness of this ancient rule, in actual practice, has long since passed away. As administered under the usages of modern and civilized nations, military government is tempered by the dictates of fairness and humanity, and kept, as far as possible, within the bounds of necessity; the civil rights of the inhabitants are interfered with as little as possible; and the municipal laws, at the time in force within the occupied territory, are followed and enforced unless they tend to interfere with the prosecution of military operations, or the acomplishment of the objects for which the warfare was inaugurated. Nevertheless, as long as actual warfare continues, the ancient maxim is the yard-stick by which the power is ultimately measured."

There was a time when pillage invariably followed a successful assault.[73] The ravages of the Thirty Years War, including the sack of Magdeburg, were once considered normal acts of war, justified in intent and result as a means of crippling the enemy.[74] There was a time, "when

---

[70] *New Orleans* v. *Steamship Co.* (U. S. 1874) 20 Wall. 387, 394. Cited with approval in *Daniel* v. *Hutcheson* (1893) 86 Tex. 51, 61, 22 S. W. 933; Magoon, *op. cit.*, footnote 65, p. 13.

[71] (1907) 36 Stat. 2277.

[72] Though this dictum was not delivered from the bench of the Supreme Court where he now sits but from a lecture rostrum during the World War, it must nevertheless be taken in a very special sense, for at the time when he was speaking most Americans were engaged in assimilating without deliberation the anti-German propaganda then being spread broadcast by the Committee on Public Information in an attempt to incite the nations for war purposes because of the supposedly awful things the soldiers of the Central Powers, and the High Command itself, had been doing in occupied Belgium. The quotation is from *Constitutional Powers and World Affairs* (1919) 80.

[73] Nys, *Les Origines du Droit International* (1894) 221; 1 Walker, *History of the Law of Nations* (1899) 132.

[74] Hall, *op. cit.*, footnote 39, p. 442, footnote 1.

arms were once taken up, all reverence for divine and human law was thrown away, just as if men were thenceforth authorized to commit all crimes without restraint."[75] But within a century the American government has laid it down that "men who take up arms against one another in public war do not cease on this accout to be moral beings, responsible to one another and to God."[76] And the British government has announced to its men in uniform: "The dictates of religion, morality, civilization, and chivalry ought to be obeyed."[77]

It is clearly within the interests of the occupying government to maintain order and tranquillity in the occupied territory. This is for the general facilitation of such military operations as may still be in progress as well as for general prevention of anarchy and the maintenance of decency and order. Within the territory are soldiers carrying out the wishes of one belligerent, and civilians obligated by nationality to the other belligerent. All of these are subject to the will of the supreme commander of the occupation army. But in different ways and for different purposes.

Law in modern times is primarily territorial in effect. Jurisdiction is in general limited by national frontiers. Yet to this sound theory armed forces form a distinct exception. Military law is non-territorial and is personal in effect.[78] It is applicable to persons subject thereto, wherever they may be, provided only they be officers or soldiers in the army, or civilians connected therewith.[79] In all matters that affect the relations of soldiers with one another, military law governs, and is administered through courts-martial,[80] and this is true whether the army be at home or abroad. "Wherever they are, they remain subject to the articles of war, army regulations, and the general orders of the War Department."[81] Disorders and neglects to the prejudice of good order and

[75] Grotius, *De jure Belli et Pacis* (1625) § 28.

[76] (1863) Gen. O. 199, § 15. Not repeated in (1914) *Rules of Land Warfare* § 12.

[77] *British Manual of Military Law* (1914) c. 14, par. 39.

[78] (1912) Dig. Ops. J. A. G., p. 511, no. VIII B; Wright, *op. cit.*, footnote 25, p. 38.

[79] U. S. Army, *Manual for Courts Martial* (1921) 47; *British Manual of Military Law* (1914) 576.

[80] Excepting only, of course, those instances which come before Courts of Inquiry (M. C. M., 1921, par. 3d, 447-475) which are not now so rare as hitherto, on account of the operation of §246 of the Act of Congress approved June 4th, 1920.

[81] Wright, *op. cit.*, footnote 25, p. 38. The British book, *Manual of Military Law* (1914) c. 1, par. 3, says: "In peace and in war, at home and abroad, at all times and in all places, the conduct of officers and soliders as such is regulated by military law." The Japanese practice is exemplified in the following case; from the instructions of Marshall Oyama to the commander of the Second Army: "Les actes illégaux et coupables commis par un Japonais qui se trouvera sur le territoire occupé, punissibles en vertu du code pénal militaire et du code d'instruction criminelle militaire, seront déférés au conseil de guerre." Ariga, *op. cit.*, footnote 67, p. 188.

military discipline and conduct of a nature to bring discredit upon the military service committed by members of the occupant army are subject to the military jurisdiction of that army, and only to that jurisdiction. This has been maintained with reference to troops in friendly foreign territory,[82] in cases of invasion or intervention where a state of war seems to but does not legally exist,[83] in rebel territory,[84] and—very naturally—in hostile territory.[85] They are "exempt from the civil and criminal jurisdiction" of an enemy's territory.[86] "When our armies marched into the enemy's country," says the Supreme Court, "their officers and soldiers were not subject to its laws."[87]

It is not proper, I believe, to go so far as to say that "criminal jurisdiction over the soldier, when in the enemy's country, is exclusively vested in the court martial."[88] It is true that this was the principle followed by Pershing in Germany and Luxemburg, when he specifically forbade members of the American or allied forces being tried by the military commissions or provost courts, which he had established as an incident to the occupation of the Rhine districts.[89] It is true that at Matamoras in 1846, Taylor hesitated to bring offenders before a military court and shipped them back to the States,[90] and also that at Puebla in 1847 General Worth actually went so far in agreeing that "Mexican law, to be administered by Mexican authorities, should remain in force"

---

[82] *The Exchange* (U. S. 1812) 7 Cranch 116, 139; The *contra* case of *The People* v. *McLeod* (N. Y. 1841) 25 Wend. 483; 26 Wend. 663; 2 Moore, *op. cit.*, footnote 16, pp. 24-25, is not really so, because diplomatic action sustained in this matter the validity of international law as against the municipal law of New York State and Congress made haste to enact legislation, Rev. Stat. §753, U. S. Comp. Stat. (1916) §1281; 2 Moore, *op. cit.*, footnote 16, 30, which would prevent future contraventions of the international rule. Also discussed in *Coleman* v. *Tennessee, supra,* footnote 17.

[83] *Hamilton* v. *McClaughry, supra,* footnote 1.

[84] 24 Ops. Atty. Gen. 570, to the Secretary of War, January 26th, 1903. "The parties to a civil war usually concede to each other belligerent rights". *The Prize Cases* (1862) 67 U. S. 635, 666.

[85] *Coleman* v. *Tennessee, supra,* footnote 17; *Dow* v. *Johnson, supra,* footnote 17, p. 165; (1849) 5 Ops. Atty. Gen. 58; *Mitchell* v. *Clark* (1883) 110 U. S. 633, 648, 4 Sup. Ct. 170; *Freeland* v. *Williams* (1889) 131 U. S. 405, 416, 9 Sup. Ct. 763; also Birkhimer, *op. cit.*, footnote 10, p. 29.

[86] *Cf.* Glenn, *op. cit.*, footnote 21, pp. 90-97. It was so announced in the ordinance of the governor general of Rheims, Nov. 5, 1870, Bray, *op. cit.*, footnote 8, p. 307.

[87] *Dow* v. *Johnson, supra,* footnote 17, p. 165, followed in *Freeland* v. *Williams, supra,* footnote 85, p. 416.

[88] Glenn, *op. cit.*, footnote 21, p. 93.

[89] Smith, *op. cit.*, footnote 39, p. 103, par. 15; Gen. John J. Pershing, *Final Report* (1919) 88.

[90] 2 Smith, *op. cit.*, footnote 36, p. 211. For facts of disorders, see Smith, *American Rule in Mexico* (1918) 22 Amer. Hist. Rev., 287. The text of Scott's memorandum to the Secretary of War on the need of new rules is given in Appendix. Townsend, *Anecdotes of the Civil War,* 279-283.

with regard to soldiers that General Scott had to correct the error.[91] We have contrary precedent established as early as 1862 by General McClellan at Yorktown who ordered that "acts commonly recognized as crimes against society" by "soldiers, officers, or other persons connected with the army" were "punishable by a court or military commission."[92] We find in the Manual of Military Law governing such things in the British Army,[93] that though "officers, men, and followers of the occupying force.... are dealt with by the military law of their army" an "exceptional" kind of court-martial may be devised for the punishment of offenses committed by them against the laws of war. Also, the practice of Pershing to the contrary notwithstanding, the newest edition of the Manual for Courts-Martial in the United States Army gives military commissions express statutory jurisdiction over certain offenses,[94] and they have been permitted to assume jurisdiction in cases of such offenses as forcing a safeguard or intimidation of persons bringing supplies.[95] The Manual quite evidently intends that "offenders against the laws of war, and under martial law, and military government" may be tried by military commissions even if they be part of the army itself, for it distinctly states that in such cases "the General Court Martial has concurrent jurisdiction with military commissions and provost courts."[96] The courts-martial do not, then, have exclusive criminal jurisdiction over the military, at least in law.

Yet, as regards purely military offenses such as are specified in the Articles of War, it would seem best to follow the practice of Pershing. The form and procedure of the courts-martial are more fixed and less liable to error; it has been more clearly and completely settled by statute, executive order, and custom; it has a well recognized[97] and clearly derived jurisdiction.[98] It is intended for the scrutiny and judgment of offenses committed by soldiers against other soldiers and against military laws. It is the more familiar to the personnel who will be proceeding in judgment, as well as to the military persons who appear before

[91] 2 Smith, *op. cit.*, footnote 36, pp. 70-71. "No one connected with the army could be tried by Mexican tribunals." 2 Smith *id.*, p. 230.

[92] *Army of the Potomac*, Gen. O. 2, April 7, 1862, cited in (1861) 9 Rebellion Record, pt. 3, p. 77.

[93] C. 14, par. 365; c. 5, pars. 1, 24, 25.

[94] *Articles of War* (1920) 80, 81 82, cited M. C. M. p. 2.

[95] *Articles of War* (1920) 78, 88.

[96] U. S. Army, *Manual for Courts Martial* (1921) 2.

[97] *Deming* v. *McClaughry* (C. C. A. 8th Cir. 1902) 113 Fed. 639, 650; *aff'd.*, *McClaughry* v. *Deming* (1902) 186 U. S. 49, 63, 22 Sup. Ct. 786; *Grafton* v. *United States* (1907) 206 U. S. 333, 347-348, 27 Sup. Ct. 749; *Dynes* v. *Hoover* (1857) 61 U. S. 65, 81; (1865) 11 Ops. Atty. Gen. 19, 21; *Hamilton* v. *McClaughry*, *supra*, footnote 1.

[98] U. S. Const., Amend. V; Act of Congress approved June 4th, 1920, 41 Stat. 759, U. S. Comp. Stat. (Supp. 1923)§1715a; Presidential Executive Order, December 17, 1920; U. S. Army, *Manual for Courts-Martial* (1921) 26, especially.

the bar. General McClellan, in the instance cited, tried to preserve as much business as possible for courts-martial by prescribing that "no acts already recognizable by courts martial shall be tried by military commissions." And the present American Manual, though stating that "the rule has not always been strictly observed" and instancing the exceptions already mentioned, declares:

> "It has generally been held that military commissions have no jurisdiction of such purely military offenses specified in the Articles of War as those articles expressly make punishable by sentence of courts-martial except where the military commission is given express statutory jurisdiction of the offense; and in repeated instances where military commissions have assumed such jurisdiction, their proceedings have been declared invalid in general orders."[99]

We next approach an anomalous situation in law. Suppose,—and it is scarcely necessary to so suppose, for the thing frequently happens,—there is a matter which concerns soldiers and civilians. One of the parties is a non-resident and subject to the military law of the army, simply because it is non-territorial and personal in effect. The other is subject to the authority of both the quasi-judicial tribunals, established and the army, not on account of any personal relations—for by nationality and preference he is bound elsewhere—but simply because he happens to be within the territories for the time being controlled by that army. For instance, if a street fight occurs between the two with no assignable cause or fault on either side, and the parties are brought up for punishment, the authority and jurisdiction over one is personal and over the other territorial, over the one permanent and over the other temporary, over the one for violation of military law and over the other for violation of the laws of war. The soldier would likely be tried by court-martial for committting acts to the prejudice of good order and military discipline, or of such a nature as to bring discredit upon the military service, under the Ninety-Sixth Article of War, if not specifically for assault with intent to do bodily harm. The civilian would likely be tried by military commission for disorder, breach of the peace, acts against a member of the occupying force,—in fact for generally acting so as to disturb the firm hold of the occupant and to distract his attention from the weightier matters of war. The instance is exaggerated. Yet it shows exactly what would be the situation if these two hypothetical persons committed their offenses independently of one another, in time and

---

[99] U. S. Army, *Manual for Courts Martial* (1921) 3.

place. The army man would be tried by court-martial. The civilian would be brought before a military commission.[100]

Nevertheless, the difference, as far as the civilian inhabitant is concerned is merely a difference in form. Both the courts-martial and the military commissions derive their authority from the commander of the occupying force. Punishment will be inflicted upon the man by a government which has forced itself upon him. The ultimate power of punishment is that created by belligerent occupation. It is of little consequence whether such government be called a military or a civil government; its character is the same, and the source of its authority the same; in either case it is a government imposed by the laws of war, and so far as it concerns the inhabitants of such territory, those laws alone determine the legality or illegality of its acts.[101] That is, when they are not determined by the circumstances of an offense or the necessities of the moment.[102]

ELBRIDGE COLBY

FORT BENNING, GA.

---

[100] According to the U. S. Army, *Manual for Courts Martial* (1921) 2-3, "The General Court Martial has concurrent jurisdiction with military commissions and provost courts to try any offender who by the law of war is subject to trial by military tribunals". Yet the practice of Pershing, already noted, not to try civilians before courts-martial seems sound. It is of course provided that spies shall be tried by court-martial, this specifically in the Articles of War.

[101] 2 Halleck, *op. cit.*, footnote 60, p. 466.

[102] Ariga, *op. cit.*, footnote 67, p. 214.

[8]

OCCUPATION UNDER THE LAWS OF WAR: II

ELBRIDGE COLBY

II

We have already seen that this belligerent occupation, the crossing of a political frontier, the traversing of an imaginary geographical boundary line, has no effect upon the legal status of the soldier. He remains in the same status as before, subject to the same discipline and laws. We have next to consider the actual legal status of the inhabitant of the occupied territory, in his relation to the occupying belligerent.

It is quite apparent that since "by the conquest and occupation of enemy territory, the government previously existing is, *ipso facto*, overthrown,.... from the necessity of the case, in order that anarchy may be prevented, lawlessness restrained, private property protected, and the lives and liberties of the inhabitants safeguarded, the military commander of the successful armies must have power to maintain temporarily such government as the exigencies of the situation may require."[103] Everyone in the territory is subject to his rule, natives,[104] his own nationals,[105] and neutrals.[106] No considerations should prevent his successful maintenance of his position, which was assumed and is to be held for military purposes. The most isolated transgressions against members of the occupying army,[107] as well as disorders and disturbances of the peace caused by combinations of citizens,[108] have been severely dealt with. At Pavia and Verona and Strassburg and in the Peninsula, harsh

---

[103] Sutherland, *op. cit.*, footnote 2, p. 79. It has been said that this results from "The duty to provide for the security of persons and property". *The Grapeshot* (U. S. 1869) 9 Wall. 129, 132.

[104] *Fleming* v. *Page, supra,* footnote 25, p. 615; *United States* v. *Rice, supra,* footnote 57, p. 253; *Thorington* v. *Smith, supra,* footnote 25, p. 10; 1 Bluntschli, *op. cit.*, footnote 56, §§35, 36a, 42, 64.

[105] *The Ouachita Cotton* (U. S. 1867) 6 Wall. 521; *The Sea Lion* (U. S. 1866) 5 Wall. 630, 632; *Coppell* v. *Hall* (U. S. 1868) 7 Wall. 542; *McKee* v. *United States* (U. S. 1868) 8 Wall. 163; *United States* v. *Lane* (1868) 8 Wall. 185.

[106] Proclamation of Kinchou, Nov. 12, 1894; Ariga, *op. cit.*, footnote 67, p. 185. See Instructions to 2nd Army, re Port Arthur, Ariga, *loc. cit.*, p. 188 McClellan at Yorktown included "inhabitants or other persons." *Army of the Potomac,* Gen. O. 2, *op. cit.*, footnote 92. The ordinance of the Governor General of Rheims, Nov. 5, 1870, included everyone who committed *"crimes, délits et contraventions ......contre les puissances alliées, leurs armées, et les personnes de leur suite."* Bray, *op. cit.*, footnote 8, p. 307. In California in 1847 a British subject was convicted and punished for receiving deserters, Thomas, *Military Government* 230; Borchard, *Diplomatic Protection* (1916) 208, 251.

[107] Bordwell, *Law of War* (1908) 94-95, citing 4 Archives Diplomatiques 1163.

[108] 6 Rebellion Records, ser. i, p. 717.

measures have been the rule. In New Mexico and California, the United States was lenient for reasons of policy in view of the intended permanence of the occupation.[109] And of necessity. Indeed the necessity is not so much the general requirement of law and order either. It is military necessity, the necessity of maintaining the "firm occupation." Vattel tells how the Genoese rose and drove the Austrians out of their city.[110] Whatever the theoretical legal status of the inhabitants may be, the fact is that they are controlled by the occupant.

There are some who speak of a "temporary allegiance"[111] and of a choice "between the ousted and the *de facto* government."[112] When Commodore Connor took military possession of Tampico in 1846, he told the inhabitants that he would not interfere with their municipal regulations, their religion, nor their property, but that any breach of good faith on their part would "expose them to serious evils."[113] Thus there has grown up the idea of a quasi-contract. "*Apres que la lutte a cessé, tous ceux qui restent dans le pays, ceux surtout qui y continuent leur commerce, leurs affaires ou leurs travaux, acceptent implicitement pour leurs personnes et leurs biens la protection de l'occupant. En échange de la securité qui leur est garantié, ils sont tenus de respecter l'autorité de fait établie sur le territoire.*" So speaks the French writer, Bray.[114] But more recently the English authority, Oppenheim, has spoken quite distinctly to the opposite effect, saying: "Inhabitants do not owe an atom of allegiance to the occupying power."[115] He further declares that the moral obligation to behave is not founded on any quasi-contract with the occupant, but merely on a mutual duty of fellow citi-

[109] Thomas, *op. cit.,* footnote 106, pp. 113, 160, 193-194.

[110] Bk. iii, c. 15, §228.

[111] Birkhimer, *op. cit.,* footnote 10, p. 37. This is really the doctrine of *United States* v. *Rice, supra,* footnote 57, p. 246.

[112] Birkhimer, *op. cit.,* footnote 10, p. 9.

[113] 1 Smith, *op. cit.,* footnote 36, p. 280, citing Archives U. S. Navy Dept., Captain's letter; House Doc. 1, 30th Cong. 2d Sess., p. 1171, 1173; House Doc. 4, 29th Cong. 2d Sess. p. 381, and New York Evening Post, November 18, 1847. A similar distinction was made by the Prussian King in 1870, Bray, *op. cit.,* footnote 8, p. 76. Gen. Butler's Proclamation of May 1, 1862 in New Orleans was enforced as a quasi-contract against the occupant. *Planters' Bk.* v. *Union Bk., supra,* footnote 36.

[114] *Op. cit.,* footnote 8, p. 170. The stand of Birkhimer, *op. cit.,* footnote 10, p. 37, is similar: "Those who remain quietly in the occupied district, transacting their ordinary business, should receive the care of, and they owe temporary allegiance to the government established over them. Allegiance is a duty owing by citizens to their government, of which, so long as they enjoy its benefits, they cannot divest themselves. It is the obligation they incur for the protection afforded them. It varies with and is measured by the character of that protection......Under military government this allegiance is said to be temporary only. It is not wholly different in kind, but in degree falls far short of that owing by native born or naturalized subjects to their government."

[115] *On War Treason* (1917) 33 Law Quart. Rev. 266, 269-273. This problem will of course not arise when the occupation is of neutral territory. Ariga, *op. cit.,* footnote 67, pp. 429-432.

zens to preserve one another from harm at the hands of their ruler.[116] But it seems useless to determine the theory of this matter definitely. The occupant holding by force will rule by force in everything that concerns himself.[117] There is even an instance of drastic punishment meted out to a whole town because the citizens did not give warning of the approach of raiders who destroyed an important strategic bridge.[118] It makes no difference whether they are brought before courts-martial for their alleged offences, or before military commissions,[119] for both exist simply as agents of the occupant, both are probably composed of army officers of the nations which have invaded their land, and both will reach their findings and sentences in accordance with the same laws, the laws of war. By tradition and training, the inhabitants must be expected to sympathize with the ousted government, particularly in these modern days when nationalism has become so intense and so universal a thing as a result of democratic theory, wide-spread education, and effective war-time propaganda. Their natural and acquired inclinations and tendencies will still remain in their minds and hearts, and will only be prevented from resulting in overt acts by threats of superior force, indeed, by threats of personal force.

The facts in the matter are simply as stated by Birkhimer—who argues for temporary allegiance: "Those who remain under military government are subject to the orders of the conqueror, and are not for the time being subject to the laws of the displaced State or its mandates."[120] "They are under no obligations to recognize the authority

---

[116] See Oppenheim, *Legal Relations Between Occupying Power and Inhabitants* (1917) 33 Law Quart. Rev. 363, citing 1 Guelle, *Precis des Lois de la Guerre sur Terre* (1884) 130, and Fiore, *International Law* (1918) § 1457.

[117] Note the declaration of Bordwell, *op. cit.*, footnote 28, p. 93; "It is entirely proper to require the cooperation of the inhabitants and local authorities in the suppression of acts of lawlessness, even though such acts be committed with patriotic intent." The control of the commander is nowhere made so apparent as in the fact that during the South African War, the British permitted continuing local and newly established courts to apply the Transvaal law, even in matters affecting the army and its interests, which they never would have done unless their control had been complete. Spaight, *War Rights on Land* (1911) 357-358. The Japanese have combined local laws with their own. Ariga, *op. cit.*, footnote 67, p. 213.

[118] Bray, *op. cit.*, footnote 8, pp. 213-214.

[119] "The General Court Martial has concurrent jurisdiction with military commissions and provost courts to try any offender who by the law of war is subject to trial by military tribunal." U. S. Army, *Manual for Courts-Martial* (1921) p. 2, citing Arts. of War 12, 15. Note that during the Mexican war "when Mexicans were placed before an American military commission they were permitted to bring counsel." 2 Smith, *op. cit.*, footnote 36, p. 230. Even Chinese were tried by the Japanese military code for acts against that army. Ariga, *op. cit.*, footnote 67, p. 210.

[120] Birkhimer, *op. cit.*, footnote 10, p. 198. This principle was followed by the United States in 1898. 7 Moore, *op. cit.*, footnote 16, p. 261; (1913) Sen. Doc. 173, 63 Cong. 1st Sess. pp. 473-479. Even the theory of temporary sovereignty is denied by Ch. de Visscher, *op. cit.*, footnote 58.

of a State which can only command their services without the power to protect them if they obey. To do this is but to invite severest measures of repression on the part of the military governmental authorities."[121] Whether or not there is a complete substitution of sovereignty,[122] or a temporary allegiance,[123] the legal government is deprived of the power to exercise publicly its rights of sovereignty.[124] Said Black: "Occupation entitles the enemy to the sovereignty and gives him civil dominion as long as he retains his military possession. The inhabitants who remain and submit, and strangers who go there during the occupation of the enemy, must take the law from him as the ruler *de facto*, and not from the government *de jure* which has been expelled."[125] The inhabitants remain citizens of their original state; but they are like those who live in a foreign land and who, for a time and in certain limits, submit to another power.[126] Of course the submission is by compulsion and not by choice. They retain their allegiance, and can be called to account for variations therefrom after the conclusion of the peace and the re-entry of the original government into the occupied regions. Such variations should not transpire of the free will of the inhabitant, but only when compelled by paramount force. But if, in choosing "between the ousted and the *de facto* governments" they do impair that initial and primary allegiance,[127] if they do more than merely submit to superior and more immediate power, they are guilty of treason and may be punished therefore as soon as the rightful government regains control,[128] even if the transgressor be an alien[129] or an alien

[121] Birkhimer, *op. cit.*, footnote 10, p. 4. See the dictum of the same author cited above in footnote 114 that, "The obligation they incur for the protection afforded them,....varies with and is measured by the character of that protection." (p. 37.)

[122] Alvarez, *op. cit.*, footnote 17, p. 358, discusses and denies this, citing interesting decisions. This was the principle adopted by the Germans in Alsace in 1870. Hall, *op. cit.*, footnote 39, p. 486. And by the Americans in New Mexico in 1846. 1 Smith, *op. cit.*, footnote 36, pp. 291, 296; Thomas, *op. cit.*, footnote 106, pp. 103-104.

[123] *Shanks* v. *Dupont, supra,* footnote 57; *United States* v. *Rice, supra,* footnote 57; *United States* v. *Hayward, supra,* footnote 55; Halleck, *op. cit.*, footnote, c. 32, § 14; Dana's Wheaton, *op. cit.*, footnote 52, p. 436, note 169; 60, Phillimore, *op. cit.*, footnote 26, § 592.

[124] Bray, *op. cit.*, footnote 8, p. 151.

[125] (1909) 9 Ops. Atty. Gen. 140. See also 1 Moore, *op. cit.*, footnote 16, pp. 45-51.

[126] 4 Lueder, *Handbuch des Volkerrechts von Holtzendorff*, 512, § 118.

[127] Birkhimer, *op. cit.*, footnote 10, p. 9.

[128] "When the law of peace is supplanted by the law of war......it does not abandon its claim to continued authority. All paragraphs of the domestic code threatening punishment for treason remain in force". Smith, M., *Militarism and Statecraft* (1918) 176-177. It should also be mentioned in connection with this statement that the book which contains it may have been written by an American during a war in which the national enemy, Germany, was being widely and vigorously flayed, for conduct in the occupied territories of France and Belgium.

[129] *Carlisle* v. *United States* (U. S. 1872) 16 Wall. 147, 155; *Jager* v. *Attorney*

enemy.[130] Bray objects that the Brussels Conference and the Institute of International Law had offered solutions of this difficulty entirely too theoretical to be of value and says the soundest view is to leave the matter in the domain of unwritten law under the sanction of public opinion. He shows that, on account of the usual insufficiency of even the best of maps, the occupant has on the score of military necessity the right even to impress guides. In any event he holds that the use of force or threats will relieve the inhabitants of the offence of treason, quoting Bluntschli's remark that an isolated individual cannot resist an army and ought to give way to threats.[131] It has been well said:

> "Only extreme duress imposed by the invader can protect the inhabitants, in case these render services to the invading army, against subsequent accountability to their own courts in case of a change in the fortunes of war or after the conclusion of peace. Here the one punishment has to overbid the other; the invading army cannot dispense with the services of the inhabitants; it is obliged to demand them at every step. These services have to be secured only through fear of severer and more certain punishment than that threatened by domestic law. In such cases interest and fear must silence patriotism and the sense of right in the hostile population. This is certainly far from moral, but it is a military necessity and the inevitable result of military invasion."[132]

Truly might we repeat, with regard to this matter, the ancient legal maxim: *inter arma silent leges*. Arguments as to the existence or non-existence of a "temporary allegiance" are futile in the face of circumstances. Certainly the allegiance to the rightful government is temporarily suspended when the acts of the invading army so operate, though not permanently as we have seen,[133] and only by means of bayonet and bullet. For the time being it is exclusively the interpretation of military

General of Natal (1907) L. R. App. 326. See the Franco-Prussian controversy over the furnishing of lists of persons of an age suitable for military service. 4 Archives Diplomatiques 201; Bray, *op. cit.*, footnote 8, pp. 93-94.

[130] *Jager* v. *Atty. Gen. of Natal, supra*, footnote 129; and Bray, *op. cit.*, footnote 8, p. 306, citing Art. 77 of the French Penal Code and a decision of the French Court of Cassation, July 16, 1874.

[131] Bray, *op. cit.*, footnote 8, pp. 216-224.

[132] Smith, *op. cit.*, footnote 128, pp. 176-177, citing 13 General Julius von Hartmann, *Militarishe Notwendigkeit und Humanitat in Deutsche Rundschau*, 464.

[133] General Kearny, at Santa Fe, August 22, 1846, declared all inhabitants to be henceforth American citizens and formally absolved them from all allegiance to the Mexican Government, but was obviously exceeding his rights in so doing, as was pointed out even in the United States less tban twelve months later. 1 Smith, *op. cit.*, footnote 36, pp. 296, 516; see Thomas, *op. cit.*, footnote 106, pp. 103-104. He likewise proclaimed a new code of laws partly Mexican and partly new. House Doc. 60, 30th Cong. 1st Sess., reprinted as (1912) Sen. Doc. 896, 62d Cong. 2d Sess. See the remarks of Royce, relative to the laws of Massachusetts, who claimed that Kearny exceeded his orders. 17 Congress. Globe, July 10, 1848, pp. 933-935.

authority which is valid. "There is for Halluin," said the Commandant of the town in 1915, "neither a prefecture nor a French Government. There is only one will, and that is the will of German military authority."[134]

There is still another set of relations to be considered, the relations of inhabitants of the occupied territory with one another. "So far as practicable," declares Birkhimer,[135] "municipal laws of the district occupied and all causes between the inhabitants therein were not interfered with" by the Union armies in 1862. The same procedure was followed in New Orleans.[136] In Memphis, in matters affecting only the inhabitants in their dealings with each other, the local law was enforced "in its criminal and civil branches."[137] Bray says that municipal or provincial laws which concern only private interests are retained,[138] and that even penal laws may properly be enforced as between the inhabitants, because in these the invader has no special interest.[139] As between one another there is fundamentally and legally no change; and this is usually true in fact as well as in law. *"La conquête les fait seulement changer de maître,"* remarked Vattel.[140] "Their relations to each other....remain undisturbed."[141] The occupant is "forbidden as a general rule to vary or suspend laws affecting property and private personal relations, or which regulate the moral order of the community."[142] Even during the German occupations of the World War, concerning which many protests have been made,[143] the Belgian codes remained in force except in-

---

[134] Massart, *Belgians under the German Eagle* (1916) 193.

[135] *Op. cit.,* footnote 10, p. 100.

[136] Birkhimer, *op. cit.,* footnote 10, p. 70, mentioning specifically misdemeanors not interfering with the laws or forces of the United States, crimes of an aggravated nature, disturbances not caused by combinations of citizens, and "civil causes between party and party."

[137] 2 Rebellion Record, *op. cit.,* footnote 92, pt. 3, p. 77; 14 *id.* p. 334; 17 *id.* pt. 2, p. 41; and 9 *id.* p. 20.

[138] *Op. cit.,* footnote 8, p. 304. Also so held by 2 Halleck, *op. cit.,* footnote 60, p. 444; Birkhimer, *op. cit.,* footuote 10, p. 92, and in *American Ins. Co.* v. *Canter, supra,* footnote 9.

[139] Bray, *op. cit.,* footnote 8, p. 298, where he remarks that such euforcements are generally lost sight of and over shadowed by the numerous special and novel proceedings resulting from the new regulations imposed by the occupant.

[140] *Op. cit.,* footnote 16, Bk. 3, c. 12, § 200. Followed by the French in Savoy in 1792, 1 Archives Parlementaires (ser. I) 188, and generally later, *id.,* p. 651 *et seq.,* though with exceptions in Belgium and on the Rhine, Moniteur Universal, Dec. 18, 1892 (No. 353).

[141] *United States* v. *Perchman, supra,* footnote 3, p. 87; *Leitensdorffer* v. *Webb, supra,* footnote 2; Magoon, *op. cit.,* footnote 65, p. 14.

[142] Hall, *op. cit.,* footnote 9, p. 489. Bray says the occupant should maintain existing laws "subject to changes made necessary by the state of war." Bray, *op. cit.,* footnote 8, pp. 269-270. When Taylor accepted the surrender of Matamoras in 1846 he allowed "civil laws to continue." Smith, *op. cit.,* footnote 36, 178.

[143] 2 Stowell and Munroe, *International Cases* (1916) 150-151.

sofar as they were expressly abrogated by German legislation or were obviously inconsistent with the changed political situation.[144]

But the master has been changed, even if only for the time being. It has been held to be his duty, even where it is not to his military advantage, "to provide as far as possible for the security of persons and property and the administration of justice."[145] He exercises all civil as well as military authority.[146] Yet in so doing he may utilize local officials who are familiar with local customs and local laws. The mere fact of military occupation does not abrogate or destroy public offices.[147] Sometimes the constitution or the local law forbids officials serving under public enemies.[148] Sometimes they are ordered to retire before an advancing enemy, or—when the advance is so swift that this is impossible —specifically forbidden to serve.[149] Sometimes they may be specifically directed to remain and authorized to carry on so long as they do not assist the enemy in a military manner,[150] in order to take care of the interests of the inhabitants.[151] Sometimes they may flee, without authority,[152] or remain and refuse to continue in office.[153] Yet, if they do remain he is not compelled to utilize their services.[154] His authority is supreme, and he may expel them or render them impotent if he so desires or if their conduct seems to warrant.[155] So supreme is his authority that only their refusal or flight can prevent his using them in purely local matters if he will find them useful. This is a common practice.[156] It has been employed in New Mexico by Kearny,[157] at Rheims by the

[144] Roxburgh, *International Conventions and Third States* (1917) 12, n. 3.

[145] *The Grapeshot, supra,* footnote 103, p. 129; Bray, *op. cit.,* footnote 8, pp. 269-270; Magoon, *op. cit.,* footnote 65, p. 11 citing *Ex parte Milligan, supra,* footnote 20.

[146] *United States* v. *Rice, supra,* footnote 57.

[147] *Ketchum* v. *Buckley* (1878) 99 U. S. 188; *Sanchez* v. *United States, supra,* footnote 2; Magoon, *op. cit.,* footnote 65, pp. 198-201.

[148] 1 Smith, *op. cit.,* footnote 39, pp. 8, 56 regarding Mexican officials; Bray, *op. cit.,* footnote 8, p. 242, regarding the Versailles officials in 1870.

[149] Austrians ordered from Bohemia in 1866. Bray, *op. cit.,* p. 241; Hall, *op. cit.,* footnote 39, p. 498.

[150] Prussian regulations of 1814. See Bray, *op. cit.,* footnote 8, p. 241. French regulations of 1870. Hall, *op. cit.,* footnote 9, p. 490, n. 2.

[151] Bluntschli, *op. cit.,* footnote 56, § 541, quoted approvingly by Hall, *op. cit.,* footnote 39, p. 498, n. 2.

[152] Ariga, *op. cit.,* footnote 67, p. 195. If the occupation is over neutral territory, they have no right to retire. Ariga, *op. cit.,* footnote 18, pp. 429-432.

[153] Under Stockton in California. Birkhimer, *op. cit.,* footnote 10, p. 67.

[154] Oppenheim, *op. cit.,* footnote 29. § 172.

[155] Except, of course, when it is neutral territory which is occupied. *Cf.* Ariga, *op. cit.,* footnote 18, pp. 429-432. It is charged that Chile created a handmade government favorable to itself in Peru, during the War of the Pacific. Maurtua, *Question of the Pacific* (1901) 127; U. S. Foreigu Affairs (1881) 951-952.

[156] Bray, *op. cit.,* footnote 8, pp. 269-270; Hall, *op. cit.,* footnote 39, p. 495.

[157] 1 Smith, *op. cit.,* footnote 36, p. 271.

Germans in 1870,[158] in California by Stockton,[159] in Memphis, Tennessee, during the Civil War,[160] in Mexico during 1846, 1847, 1848, by the Americans,[161] in Cuba by the United States,[162] and again attempted at the occupation of Vera Cruz in 1914.[163] Elections for the filling of vacant offices have even been held, in California,[164] in Mexico,[165] and in China.[166] Special appointments were made from the civil population at Memphis and New Orleans.[167] In California, an "elected" officer was removed by the will of the commander, which even that officer admitted to be supreme.[168] However, this is all in the discretion of the commander. At times it will happen as at Adrianople in 1912[169] and at Dijon in 1870 that all the public services will continue to function as in the past.[170] At other times it will happen as at Strassburg, Nancy, Versailles, and Rheims in 1870 that the municipalities will in general continue, but employees of other services will refuse to work under the invader who will have to take over such departments as the railway and post office.[171] At other times, it will happen as in Mexico, that all local officials will retire or refuse to function, and the invading government will have to settle pressing disputes under purely local law without expert local advice.[172] Sometimes it will happen that the local civil government, as in Germany in 1918, will remain in full possession of its former power and retain jurisdiction over local matters, subject only to the infrequently exerted

---

[158] Bray, *op. cit.*, footnote 8, p. 307, quoting an ordinance of the Governor General which threw the protection of military jurisdiction around the military either as defendant or complainant, and then remarked: "*Sauf ces cas, il n'y a rien de changé dans la compétence des tribunaux et des officiers judiciaires français qui fonctionneront dans les formes légalement constituées avant la guerre.*"

[159] Birkhimer, *op. cit.*, footnote 10, p. 67.

[160] As indicated in footnote 137.

[161] 2 Smith, *op. cit.*, footnote 36, pp. 229-230; Smith, *op. cit.*, footnote 39, pp. 59, 62; (1855) 7 Ops. Atty. Gen., 365.

[162] Magoon, *op. cit.*, footnote 65, p. 203.

[163] Smith, *op. cit.*, footnote 39, p. 65.

[164] 1 Smith, *op. cit.*, footnote 36, 335; Thomas, *op. cit.*, footnote 106, pp. 232-233.

[165] 2 Smith, *op. cit.*, footnote 36, pp. 229-230.

[166] Ariga, *op. cit.*, footnote 67, pp. 195-196.

[167] New Orleans officials were later judged competent because appointed by the occupant power, *i.e.*, by the President as commander-in-chief, so long as the authority continued sovereign by force of arms, and only so long, even those "elected" under his supervision and authority. *Handlin* v. *Wickliffe*, *supra*, footnote 23; *Pennywit* v. *Eaton* (U. S. 1872) 15 Wall. 382; *United States* v. *Reiter* (Pr. Ct. La. 1865) Fed. Cas. 16,146.

[168] Thomas, *op. cit.*, footnote 106, p. 233.

[169] *Report of The Carnegie Commission on The Balkan Wars* (1914) 177.

[170] Bray, *op. cit.*, footnote 8, p. 165.

[171] Bordwell, *op. cit.*, footnote 28, pp. 98-99; Bray, *op. cit.*, footnote 8, pp. 275-279-280. Municipalities are in a special class. Magoon, *op. cit.*, footnote 65, pp. 387-388. There is the question as to their dual functions as corporations and as political units. Generally they are considered non-national. *Cf. Vilas* v. *City of Manila* (1911) 220 U. S. 345, 31 Sup. Ct. 416.

[172] Smith, *op. cit.*, footnote 39, pp. 71-72.

"advice" of specially detailed "officers in charge of civil affairs."[173] Whichever procedure and method may be employed in fact, the doctrine is definite on the point. "The law of the land will have ceased to possess any proper vigor."[174] Participation in the administration of that law,[175] and what parts of the law are to be administered,[176] are questions for the decision of the military commander. If he be wise he will follow the excellent procedure of Wellington.

> "He declared that he had governed strictly by the laws of the country, and governed with such moderation that political servants who had at first fled, or had been expelled, afterwards consented to act under his direction. The judges sat in the courts of law, conducting their judicial business, and administering the law by his authority."[177]

It is to be noted here that though the law administered is the national law, it is administered by the authority of the commander. An interesting and unusual example of this procedure occurred in Mexico in 1914. The refusal of former Mexican officials to serve in their prior capacities and of other qualified Mexicans to substitute for them, finally led to the legal department of General Funston's army acting as an arbitral court to adjust legal difficulties between natives, adjudicating some new cases "under the letter and spirit of the Mexican law", and even in some instances where cases had been settled by Mexican courts then inactive, searching the records and executing judgments in accordance with the Mexican decisions.[178] And perhaps this incident can be contrasted with the British application of their Indian penal and criminal codes throughout Tanganika Territory.[179]

---

[173] Pershing, *op. cit.*, footnote 89, p. 87.

[174] (1856) 8 Ops. Atty. Gen. 365. Naturally, of course, those political laws with reference to recruitings, assemblages, voting, free speech, treason, search warrants, and regular taxation. Bray, *op. cit.*, footnote 8, pp. 281-298, 306.

[175] While Chile was occupying most of Peru, one of her ministers declared: "We should not call on the Peruvian law courts to administer justice; we should administer justice to ourselves;" and the Chilean commander-in-chief plainly ordered that "no acts of government will be permitted to be done, or exercised by any other functionaries than those established by these headquarters." Maurtua, *op. cit.*, footnote 155, pp. 106, 120. It is to be noted however......in connection with footnote 171 above....that it was also ordered: "The municipal authorities shall subsist and continue to receive municipal taxation for the purpose of providing for the necessities for local service." Maurtua, *op. cit.*, p. 120 in view of the fact that the Lieber Instructions and the Brussels declaration were published to the Chilean army at the beginning of the war. Alvarez, *op. cit.*, footnote 17, p. 110.

[176] Oppenheim, *op. cit.*, footnote 116, p. 365, insists that "he respects them and leave them in force unless absolutely prevented by military necessity."

[177] 115 Hansard, *op. cit.*, footnote 39, p. 880.

[178] Smith, *op. cit.*, footnote 39, p. 71.

[179] *Report on Tanganika Territory*, Brit. Parlia. Paper Command (1921) 1428.

Bordwell holds that courts really act under the sovereignty of the conqueror in all respects.[180] But this principle has been denied. Oppenheim has argued that since it is their own law which they enforce it is to their own government that they are responsible.[181] De Vischer has added that "law is an act of sovereignty and sovereignty has not passed to the chief of the armies since force creates no law."[182] This latter author raises the interesting point that because Belgium had ratified the Hague document of 1907 it was under Belgian laws that such courts did function as remained in existence during the German occupation. The Belgian courts pronounced their judgments in the name of the King of the Belgians.[183] Chinese attempts to use the formula "the Empire of Japan" in their official acts were disclaimed by the Japanese.[184] In 1870, French courts continued to render justice in the name of the Emperor, and only ceased when for political reasons, based on a policy of non-recognition, the German occupant refused to permit them to use the name of the Republic and they were unwilling themselves to act in the name of Napoleon who had not only been captured but deposed.[185] At Dijon, though, they were even permitted to employ the name of the Republic.[186] Such a solution of the difficulty is convenient. The rightful sovereign has been driven out. The occupant has no rightful sovereignty, probably not even a temporary sovereignty. There is convenience in it, particularly because it facilitates easy readjustments after the conclusion of the peace. Such judgments will probably stand upon the regaining of the territory by the original holder, because they have been rendered by his officials, under his law, and in his name.[187] They will probably stand also if the territory is eventually ceded to the occupant, because the treaty by which he acquires the land will terminate the old sovereignty as of the date of the ratification,[188] but more especially be-

[180] Bordwell, *op. cit.*, footnote 28, p. 300. This is contrary to the principles laid down in *Rutledge* v. *Fogg, supra*, footnote 52, and contrary to the idea that the sovereignty is not complete until the treaty, noted above.

[181] Oppenheim, *op. cit.*, footnote 116.

[182] Ch. de Vischer, *op. cit.*, footnote 58.

[183] Oppenheim, *op. cit.*, footnote 116, p. 367.

[184] Ariga, *op. cit.*, footnote 67, p. 174.

[185] Bray, *op. cit.*, footnote 8, pp. 314-317; Bordwell, *op. cit.*, footnote 28, p. 99.

[186] Bray, *op. cit.*, footnote 8, p. 165.

[187] Bray, *op. cit.*, footnote 8, pp. 317-319, 321-323, citing a decision to this effect by the French Court of Cassation. An interesting case somewhat analogous is quoted by 7 Moore, *op. cit.*, footnote 16, p. 269, where a clerk of the court fled behind the retiring lines, and the later tribunals decided that during his absence, with the records no one could administer the duties of the office as his deputy. *Herring* v. *Lee* (1883) 22 W. Va. 661. The First Chamber of the Civil Court in France has held that German occupation suspended certain requirements of French Law. New York Times, May 5, 1923, 3b.

[188] An exception to this practice is found in the protocol signed May 26, 1849, the date of exchange of treaty ratifications, which said: "Those are lawful titles to property of every kind, movable or immovable, existing in the ceded territories, which may have been lawful titles under the Mexican law up to the 13th May, 1846." Ops. Atty. Gen. 321, 325.

cause they were rendered with the approval of his official representatives, even though those officials were military agents and not judicial officers. But more of this survival hereafter.

There is next the question as to the government of the territory, How much further can he go, besides governing his own army, punishing trangressions against his army, and either fostering or permitting the normal courts to act in accordance with the law normal in that territory? In New Orleans the acts of the courts established by the invading and hostile occupant were held valid in all cases, civil, criminal, and military.[189] Civil commissions established at Memphis, Tennessee by General Grant acted on the collection of debts and the enforcement of contracts and had their powers and propriety later recognized even by the Supreme Court of the state against whose authority they were established.[190] Other strange methods have been pursued. "At Tampico, Shields appointed three Mexican alcaldes and also (to act with these in cases between Americans and Mexicans) an American court of three American citizens."[191] At Monterey and at Saltillo, "Worth made an admirable governor, sitting four days to hear complaints, and administering substantial justice without reference to legal technicalities."[192] Of course such acts may be ratified after the fact. For instance, the Acts of Congress approved March 3, 1863, and May 11, 1866, extended protection to all persons for acts done under military direction in the prosecution of the Civil War, and prevented recoveries in actions brought later.[193] Then, after the violent War of the Pacific, the Treaty of Ancon declared: "The contracting parties recognize and accept the validity of all administrative and judicial acts during the occupation of

---

[189] *Dow* v. *Johnson*, *supra*, footnote 17; *The Grapeshot*, *supra*, footnote 83; *Mechanics' Bk.* v. *Union Bk.* (U. S. 1874) 22 Wall. 276; *New Orleans* v. *Steamship Co.*, *supra*, footnote 70, p. 394; *Handlin* v. *Wickliffe*, *supra*, footnote 23; *Pennywit* v. *Eaton*, *supra*, footnote 167.

[190] *Hefferman* v. *Porter* (Tenn. 1869) 6 Cold. 391. Little weight should, in sober reason, be attached to the approval granted by the Supreme Court in *Leitensdorfer* v. *Webb*, *supra*, footnote 2, and *Cross* v. *Harrison*, *supra*, footnote 2, to the immediate validity of the acts of the military governments established in New Mexico, for such governments were exceptionally complete and far too complete in abolishing Mexican sovereignty.....in phrases at least..... in changing Mexican laws, prior to the legal transfer of sovereignty. Our intention to annex and our subsequent annexation made certain appearances other than would have been possible if the territory had not been annexed and the same government continued. It is believed that Birkhimer, *op. cit.*, footnote 10, pp. 67, 95, is somewhat too enthusiastic over the importance of these cases. They are perfectly good municipal law. But for international law, the decision in *Hefferman* v. *Porter* is far more significant. The approval after the war by the re-established court of the occupied country of judgments in civil causes rendered by tribunals appointed and established by the belligerent occupant.

[191] 2 Smith, *op. cit.*, footnote 36, p. 461.

[192] 2 Smith, *op. cit.*, footnote 36, p. 213; Smith, *op. cit.*, footnote 90.

[193] *Beard* v. *Burts* (1877) 95 U. S. 434; (1863) 12 Stat. 756, U. S. Comp. Stat. (1916) § 1013; (1866) 14 Stat. 46, U. S. Comp. Stat. (1916) § 1013.

Peru arising from the martial jurisdiction exercised by the Government of Chile."[194] The treaty with Cuba in 1903 ratified all public acts of officers of the United States during the American occupation.[195] A new state constitution for the State of Tennessee "ratified and affirmed" all officers elected under the "military" rule and the acts of those officers "until their successors shall be elected or appointed."[196] Indeed the ultimate validity of acts of government in occupied territory seems to be as much a political as a legal matter, for so few of the possible acts are covered in the Hague stipulations and these with the possibility of pleading military necessity. A single glance at Articles 228-230 of the latest Treaty of Versailles will make the matter plain. German persons responsible for improper acts were to be punished, originally by the Allies as the treaty says, but later actually by the Supreme Court of Leipzig.[197] Nothing was said about the trial of any officer, agent, or person in the "Allied and Associated" armies. And it is not entirely possible that there were absolutely no violations in those armies. Truly we might well cite with approval the statement of the much-maligned Town Commandant of Halluin: "It is not for us to discuss that, for we are not competent, and we shall never arrive at an understanding on this point. It will be the business of the diplomatists and the representatives of the various States after the war."[198] This is believed to be just as sound in international relations and just as moral as the act of war itself and the establishment of legal status by treaties of peace signed at the point of the sword. It is just as correct an assumption in international law as is the assumption in constitutional law that the abolition of a political office in Porto Rico one or two days prior to a Congressional enactment validating all acts of the military government is therefore valid and correct.[199]

The grim arbitrament of war is an assize of force, and it said:

"The right to administer force against force in actual war depends upon the question whether there is a war or not. If there is war, there is the right to repel force by force, but it is found convenient and decorous from time to time, to authorize what are called 'courts' to administer punishments, and to restrain by acts of repression the violence that is committed in time of war, instead of leaving such punishment

[194] Maurtua, *op. cit.*, footnote 155, pp. 203-207.

[195] (1903) 33 Stat. 2249, cited in *De Camara* v. *Brooke* (1908) 209 U. S. 45, 28 Sup. Ct. 439. See in the connection with this case, Magoon, *op. cit.*, footnote 65, pp. 194-209.

[196] *Isbell* v. *Farris, supra*, footnote 43.

[197] *German War Trials*, Brit. Parlia. Papers Command (1921) 1450; Mullins, *The Leipsic Trials* (1921).

[198] Massart, *op. cit.*, footnote 134, p. 192.

[199] *Sanchez* v. *United States, supra*, footnote 2; The Foraker Act (1900) 31 Stat. 79, U. S. Comp. Stat. (1916) § 3753.

and repression to the casual action of persons acting without sufficient consultation, or without sufficient order or regularity in the procedure in which things alleged to have been done are proved. But no attempt to make these proceedings of so-called 'courts-martial' administering summary justice under the supervision of a military commander, analogous to the regular proceedings of courts of justice is quite illusory. Such acts of justice are justified by necessity, by the fact of actual war; and that they are so justified under the circumstances is a fact that it is no longer necessary to insist upon, because it has been over and over again so decided by courts as to whose authority there can be no doubt."[200]

Indeed, it is true that, "whether established or sanctioned, they are nothing more than agents of and subject to the military power, and even their decisions are subject to military control, whenever the commanding officer thinks proper to interfere."[201] It makes no difference in occupied territory. If the supposed judgments are rendered by courts-martial, the authority behind them is the power of the occupying army; if rendered by "military commissions," by "provost courts", or by "military tribunals", or by so-called "civil commissions" established by the military occupant, the authority behind them is always the power of the occupying army; and even if rendered by the continuing courts of the country, whatever the procedure they use, whatever the law they apply, and whatever the name they cite, the authority which makes them possible, which makes the enforcement of their judgments possible, is still the power of the occupying army.[202]

This power exists for the period of the emergency. It is based upon the fact of occupation and the necessity for a proper conduct of further military operations together with the necessity for some rule in the territory. It is as clearly *de facto* government as was the "military representative of the insurrection" which ruled Alabama and Georgia during the Civil War in the 1860's,[203] where the same laws, constitutions, and officers continued state administrations. The French Court of Cassation declared in 1841 that acts which *"troublent la société et compremettent l'ordre public tombent de plein droit aussitôt que l'occupation cesse; si, d'autre part, ils concurrent au bien être de ce pays, et sont conformés aux intentions du souverain légitime, ils persistent jusqu'à leur abrogation expresse."*[204] And the Supreme Court of Ten-

[200] *Tilonko* v. *Attorney General of Natal* [1907] L. R. App. 93.

[201] *Jecker* v. *Montgomery* (U. S. 1851) 13 How. 498, 515.

[202] Magoon, *op. cit.*, footnote 65, p. 14.

[203] *Thorington* v. *Smith*, *supra*, footnote 25; *United States* v. *Ins. Co.* (U. S. 1874) 22 Wall. 99, 101; *Sprott* v. *United States* (U. S. 1874) 20 Wall. 459, 464.

[204] Cited in Hall, *op. cit.*, footnote 39, p. 489. When the French revolutionary armies held Belgium, the French assembly on Dec. 15, 1792 decreed that "in all territories occupied by French troops the new French revolutionary institu-

nessee soundly remarked, in words which well summarize the entire situation:

"The right of a military occupant to govern implies the right to determine in what manner and through what agency such government is to be conducted. The municipal laws of the place may be left in operation, or suspended, or others enforced. The administration of justice may be left in the hands of the ordinary officers of the law, or these may be suspended and others appointed in their places. Civil rights and civil remedies may be suspended, and military laws and courts, and proceedings substituted for them, or new legal remedies and civil proceedings introduced. The power to create civil courts exists by the laws of war in a place held in firm possession by a belligerent military occupant; and if their judgments and decrees are held to be binding on all parties during the period of such occupation, as the acts of a *de facto* government, no valid ground can be assigned for refusing to them a like effect, when pleaded as *res judicata* before the regular judicial tribunals of the State since the return of peace."[205]

This is normal and reasonable. During the occupation something has to be done. The inhabitants have to live together. They have to live in the same community. They have to feed and clothe, not only themselves as individuals, but—in the present complex conditions of social and economic life—they have to feed and clothe one another. They must raise produce and manufacture garments, take these to market and trade with them in the shops.

"The existence of a state of war does not loosen the bonds of society or do away with civil government, or the regular administration of the laws. Order must be preserved, police regulations maintained, crime prosecuted, property protected, contracts enforced, marriages celebrated, estates settled, and the transfer and descent of property regulated precisely as in time of peace."[206]

When the occupant army permits such things to go on, basing the administration which he has the authority to conduct, supervise, or permit upon prior customs in the occupied land, he so permits them

---

tions should be established." And of later campaigns it has been said: "Greatest fact of all, wherever the French emperor's rule extended, there followed the abolition of feudalism and serfdom, the recognition of equality of all citizens before the law, the principles and precepts of the Code Napoleon." 1 Hayes *Modern Europe* (1919) 543. On January 26, 1793, Dumouriez incorporated the Belgian troops in the French army and "after January 31 the only government in the country was that of the French generals assisted by National Commissioners from Paris, who proceeded to use the army to force the Belgians to vote for incorporation." (1909) 7 Cambridge Modern History 478.

[205] *Hefferman* v. *Porter, supra,* footnote 190, p. 397, "The conqueror exercises, for the time being, the powers of a *de facto* government."

[206] *Horn* v. *Lockhart* (U. S. 1873) 17 Wall. 570, 580.

in the interests of continuity. And so, when he retires, the advantages of continuity of custom would naturally require that whatever reasonable has been done should remain valid under the returning government. For example, when the Southern States which had been under the control of the "military representative of the insurrection" were returned to the Union, all acts which took place therein were recognized in the courts of the United States as valid, even those which had to do with Confederate funds and paper money so long as they were not in intent and purpose for the aid and furtherance of the rebellion.[207] This, on the *de facto* government theory, was sustained with regard to Texas, invaded and ruled by the Confederacy.[208] So powerful is the force of this argument for *de facto* government and continuity, that the Belgian Court of Cassation affirmed on that account acts of the occupant German courts, even though it deemed their meddling with the law of tenancy and contracts for hire to be really beyond their power under the laws of war. However, it should be mentioned that in a very similar case, the French Court of Douai held to the contrary, and solely on the ground that the civil court established by the invaders at Maubeuge had acted beyond what the Hague Conventions permitted.[209]

It is on account of the desirability of such continuity in civic, social, and economic life that Birkhimer has been led to deny the usually admitted doctrine that the establishment of military government is primarily of advantage to the invader, enabling him more easily to protect and administer his own forces and more completely to reach the resources of the country.[210] Birkhimer insists that this "is more in appearance than in reality, arising from the circumstances that the occupying army alone has the power to maintain government of any kind."[211] "Such government," he says, "is of most advantage to the inhabitants

[207] *Thorington* v. *Smith*, *supra*, footnote 25; *Keith* v. *Clark* (1878) 97 U. S. 454. There appears to be but one restriction upon the validity of these courts, that they cannot impair the rights of persons compulsorily absent across the hostile lines, and so out of reach of process and unable to receive notice or appear in defense. *Dean* v. *Nelson* (U. S. 1869) 10 Wall. 158; and French decree of Sept. 9, 1870 cited in Bray, *op. cit.*, footnote 8, p. 304. Also *Dorr* v. *Gibboney's Ex'r'x* (C. C. Va. 1878) 3 Hughes 382; *University* v. *Finch* U. S. 1873) 18 Wall. 106.

[208] *Texas* v. *White* (U. S. 1868) 7 Wall. 700.

[209] 2 Garner, *op. cit.*, footnote 19, p. 38.

[210] 1 Clausewitz, *War* (1911) 33, quoted with disapproval, as one would expect in 1918 in Smith, *op. cit.*, footnote 128, p. 180, represents the military, strategic view of the matter when he says: "Invasion is the occupation of the enemy's territory, not with a view to keeping it, but in order to levy contributions upon it or to devastate it." The U. S. War Department specifically ordered General Scott in Mexico to adopt harsher measures in order to make the civilian population feel the hardships of war and be more ready to make peace." 7 Moore, *op. cit.*, footnote 16, pp. 282-285. This course is approved by Hall, *op. cit.*, footnote 39, p. 443 as "relatively merciful."

[211] Birkhimer, *op. cit.*, footnote 10, p. 21.

of the territory over which it is instituted. Without it they would be left a prey to the uncertain demands of a dominant military, which, without perhaps intending it and through mere want of system, might oppress them; with it, so long as they conform to the will of their new rulers, they generally are left unmolested in ordinary domestic and business regulations, and largely in municipal affairs." It is undoubtedly true that the existence of government—and no government is such unless it is present and able to support its dicta—is of advantage to ordinary citizens; even a government by hostile soldiers is better than no government at all. It is also true that it is of advantage to the ordinary citizens to have affairs of municipalities undisturbed, and their continued existence and functioning recognized.[212] When Verdun capitulated during the Franco-Prussian War, and many other towns and cities likewise, the articles specifically provided that "*toutes les administrations publiques, les tribunaux civils, le notariat, le. commerce, et l'in dustrie fonctionneront librement.*"[213] The city of Manila has been held to have gone through a military conquest, a revolution, and a recapture without changing its identity, impairing its charter, or creating new conditions.[214] This was the common conception of southern municipalities which went through the Civil War.[215] Even state laws and provincial entities have been understood as having a continued existence as a body politic, whatever the changes in superior authority.[216] Even Oppenheim, who has been among the most vigorous of modern international law writers in denying rights to occupants, who insists that the enforced obedience is imposed by martial law only, neither by international law nor by the local municipal law, admits that the occupant has a right of administration over the territory. Even Oppenheim says that "all administrative acts which he carries out in accordance with

---

[212] Napoleon at Alexandria in 1798 appointed a "Divan" of nine sheiks to administer municipal affairs under his control. 7 Cambridge Modern History, 603.

[213] Bray, *op. cit.,* footnote 8, p. 159, citing *Receuil des Actes Relatifs a la Paix avec l'Allemagne,* 287-326.

[214] *Vilas* v. *City of Manila, supra,* footnote 171.

[215] *Broughton* v. *Pensacola* (1876) 93 U. S. 266; *Mount Pleasant* v. *Beckwith* (1879) 100 U. S. 514; *Moblie* v. *Watson* (1886) 116 U. S. 289, 6 Sup. Ct. 398; *Shapleigh* v. *San Angelo* (1897) 167 U. S. 646, 17 Sup. Ct. 957; *O'Connor* v. *City of Memphis* (Tenn. 1881) 6 Lea 730. Even amid the Balkan War, at Adrianople, "the municipality retained its powers" during Bulgar occupation. Carnegie Report, *op. cit.,* footnote 169, pp. 108, 117, 211, 212.

[216] *Keith* v. *Clark, supra,* footnote 207; see also *Cohas* v. *Raison* (1853) 3 Cal. 443; *Hart* v. *Burnett* (1860) 15 Cal. 530; *Townsend* v. *Greely* (U. S. 1866) 5 Wall. 326; *Merryman* v. *Bourne* (U. S. 1869) 9 Wall. 592, 602; *More* v. *Steinbach* (1888) 127 U. S. 70, 8 Sup. Ct. 1067; *Los Angeles Milling Co.* v. *Los Angeles* (1910) 217 U. S. 217, 30 Sup. Ct. 452. I believe that *Cross* v. *Harrison, supra,* footnote 2, and *Leitensdorfer* v. *Webb, supra,* footnote 2, may properly be considered *contra* cases, for these decisions validated acts of new governments in accordance with a new law, on the ground of federal authority, not the authority of the local body politic.

the laws of war and the existing local law must be recognized by the legitimate sovereign after the occupation ceases."[217] This view was sustained with respect to Castine and Cebu.[218] As far as its permanent effects, then, the military government may be of advantage to the inhabitants, yet it seems rather exaggeration to state that it is of "most" advantage to them, as Birkhimer does.

The occupation exists to do the enemy damage in a general way.[219] A military government is erected, as we have already seen, to provide for peace and order in the rear of the armies that are holding the rightful owner from his lands, and also to systematize the development of the resources of the occupied land and their utilization by the occupant nation. The first is a military matter, a matter of police and the suppression of violence. It is likely to apply only to those who commonly transgress the public peace, or to those whose national patriotism is too impassioned and unrestrained for their situation. But the development and use of the territorial resources is a different matter, a matter of political policy and of economic program.

It has long been understood that the conqueror may levy taxes, collect customs dues, and require money contributions in the occupied territory. This may be done in order to meet the expenses of a municipality,[220] of a department or district of the country,[221] and of the army of the occupant himself, and should preferably be done in accordance with the normal agencies of taxation in the territory,[222] where these can be obtained and used.[223] It has been assumed that private property is not subject to confiscation,[224] though Birkhimer declared in 1892 that

---

[217] See Oppenheim, *op. cit.*, footnote 116.

[218] *United States* v. *Rice, supra*, footnote 57; *MacLeod* v. *United States, supra*, footnote 32.

[219] 1 Clausewitz, *op. cit.*, footnote 210, p. 33, quoted in Smith, *op. cit.*, footnote 180. *United States* v. *Rice, supra*, footnote 57; *Fleming* v. *Page, supra*, footnote 25; *MacLeod* v. *United States, supra*, footnote 32; Borchard, *op. cit.*, footnote 106, p. 240.

[220] *Rutledge* v. *Fogg, supra*, footnote 52; Maurtua, *op. cit.*, footnote 155, p. 120; *United States* v. *Rice, supra*, footnote 57.

[221] *Cross* v. *Harrison, supra*, footnote 2; Moore, *op. cit.*, footnote 16, pp. 312-314; Oppenheim, *op. cit.*, footnote 24, §§ 148, 170; Hall, *op. cit.*, footnote 39, p. 496; Birkhimer, *op. cit.*, footnote 10, p. 198.

[222] Art. 48, Annex to Hague Convention IV, *op. cit.*, footnote 40.

[223] Art. 51, Annex to Hague Convention IV; Maurtua, *op. cit.*, footnote 155, p. 106; Hurlbut to Blaine: "The Chilean authorities....are carefully examining all sources of internal revenue." Bordwell, *op. cit.*, footnote 28, p. 313; tells of a similar German procedure in 1870-1871. Similarly Napoleon in Egypt had taxes raised as formerly, but for his benefit. 7 Cambridge Modern History, 603.

[224] *Brown* v. *United States* (U. S. 1814) 8 Cranch 110; *United States* v. *1756 Shares of Capital Stock* (C. C. N. Y. 1865) 5 Blatchf. 231; *United States* v. *Klein* (U. S. 1871) 13 Wall. 128, 137; *Lamar* v. *Browne* (1875) 92 U. S. 187, 194; 7 Moore, *op. cit.*, footnote 16, pp. 288-289; Art. 46, Annex to Hague Convention IV, *op. cit.*, footnote 40; *Military Laws of United States* (1914) 1079.

it is only a constitutional provision of municipal law that so forbids.[225] It was held in *Planter's Bk.* v. *Union Bk.*[226] that it was only the quasi-contract established by the proclamation of the commander that "all rights of property of whatever kind will be held inviolate" which invalidated a seizure of funds on deposit in occupied territory belonging to enemies of the occupant. Yet the modern principles are well established since the Hague Conventions; and the Supreme Court of the United States quite correctly stated the matter, though in fact far in advance of the times:

> "It is the usage of all the civilized nations of the world, when territory is ceded, to stipulate for the property of its inhabitants. An article to secure this object so deservedly held sacred, in view of policy, as well as of justice and humanity, is always required and is never refused."[227]

This, even on a permanent transfer of sovereignty, which an occupation is universally considered not to be. It is however understood that, though private property can be confiscated out of hand only in particular emergencies, it may be "requisitioned",[228] even neutral property.[229] Yet even this does not apply to the injury or destruction in the course of operations, when even the government is not responsible.[230] "The right of a state to impress and take private property for the use of the army in the field, on the actual theatre of military operations, is

---

[225] Birkhimer, *op. cit.*, footnote 10, p. 128, citing *Elphinstone* v. *Bedreechund* (1830) 1 Knapp 316; see also *Army of the Deccan* (1833) 2 Knapp 103, 149-151. Citing *United States* v. *Padelford* (U. S. 1869) 9 Wall. 531, 541, Birkhimer goes on to say that "moveable private property can be conveyed with good title if there has been "actual seizure in obedience to orders of the commanding general". *Op. cit.*, footnote 10, p. 176, providing the conqueror remains, no treaty provision forbids, and the doctrine of *post liminium* is extinguished by complete conquest. A similar idea is contained in the dictum that "rights of property not taken by orders of the conqueror remain undisturbed." *Leitensdorffer* v. *Webb*, *supra*, footnote 2, citing Vattel, *op. cit.*, footnote 16, bk. 3, c. 13, § 200 and *United States* v. *Percheman*, *supra*, footnote 3, pp. 86, 87. Again it was declared referring to the provisions of the treaty of Guadaloupe Hidalgo that the rights of private property, consecrated by the law of nations were merely protected by the treaty. *United States* v. *Moreno* (U. S. 1863) 1 Wall. 400, 404.

[226] *Supra*, footnote 36; *Ochoa* v. *Hernandez*, *supra*, footnote 49.

[227] *Henderson* v. *Poindexter*, *supra*, footnote 3. See also Wambaugh, *Monograph of Plebiscites* (1920) 281 *et seq.*

[228] Art. 52, Annex to Hague Convention IV, *op. cit.*, footnote 40.

[229] Because the status of property depends upon its territorial location. *The Chester* v. *The Experiment* (U. S. 1787) 2 Dall. 41; *United States* v. *Gillies* (C. C. Pa. 1865) 1 Pet. 159; *The Venus* (U. S. 1814) 8 Cranch 253; *The Frances* (U. S. 1814) 8 Cranch. 335, 363; *The Mary and Susan* (U. S. 1816) 1 Wheat. 46; *Rogers* v. *Amado* (D. La. 1847) I Newb. Adm. 400; *The William Bagley* (U. S. 1866) 5 Wall. 377; *Gates* v. *Goodloe* (1879) 10 U. S. 612; *Mrs. Alexander's Cotton* (U. S. 1864) 2 Wall. 404, 419; 7 Moore, *op. cit.*, footnote 16, pp. 424-434, cited in Wright, *op. cit.*, footnote 25, p. 173.

[230] *United States* v. *Pacific R. R.* (1887) 120 U. S. 227, 7 Sup. Ct. 490.

perfect, and without it a nation could not exist." Indeed, the United States Supreme Court even recognized this right in Confederate military commanders.[231] If such seizures are not compensated for in cash, formal receipts are given. Payments are to be made "as soon as possible" but that may mean after the conclusion of the peace; it may mean that all claims against the victor nation may be quashed by an article of the Treaty.

Limitations on what might be requisitioned, and on the taking of property against the will of the owner are stricter now than they have been.[232] The words in the regulations may be approximately the same but their meanings are different. "Military necessity" has a new conception. "The needs of the army" have increased. It used to be that you could declare that only food and transportation material might be taken or money contributions for the same.[233] But a modern army in occupied territory needs more than that. War means more than a rifle and a bullet and a dinner for a professional soldier. It is no longer merely a clash between professional warriors. It is an economic conflict as well, in which the entire nation is engaged. During the American Civil War, even, when the famous Lieber instructions set new precedents as to distinctions between combatants and non-combatants, special attention was paid to purely commercial matters, for—as has been well said—"cotton was the principal support of the rebellion."[234] Imagine the "iron ring" of the Allies starving the population of Germany into submission or revolution while the adjoining occupied lands of Belgium and France live on the plentitude of the fields and the warmth of the coal districts, because forsooth these things are private property and may not be taken except only insofar as they apply to the needs of

---

[231] Birkhimer, *op. cit.*, footnote 10, p. 271, citing *Taylor* v. *Nashville and Chatanooga R. R.* (Tenn. 1869) 6 Cold. 646 and *Ford* v. *Surget* (1878) 97 U. S. 594, 596. Notice also the judgment in *Herrera* v. *United States* (1911) 222 U. S. 558, 569, 32 Sup. Ct. 179, as follows: During the war with Spain "Cuba was enemy's country, and all persons residing there pending the war, whether Spanish subjects or Americans, were to be deemed enemies of the United States, their property enemy's property and subject to seizure, confiscation and destruction."

[232] As late as 1833 attempts were made in England to secure an equitable distribution of booty among personnel of a conquering army. *The Army of the Deccan, supra*, footnote 225, pp. 149-151. In 1894, Hall, *op. cit.*, footnote 39, p. 442, said "So long as it is not too harshly enforced, there is little to object to."

[233] Holland, *The Laws of War on Land* (1908) 55, supported by 2 Hyde, *op. cit.*, footnote 8, p. 370, suggested that certain extensions of the former limited view of the amount and purpose of contributions are "reasonable." 2 Hyde, *op. cit.*, p. 371, footnote 4, reiterates with approval the vigorous strictures of Garner on the "notorious abuse" by Germany of *ante bellum* theories, and the use of "sheer power in contempt of the Hague Regulations."

[234] *Sprott* v. *United States, supra*, footnote 203. For modern opinions of the nature of commerce as a nationalistic force, see Johnson, *Commerce and War* (1914) Amer. Assn. Internat. Concil. Bull. No. 77.

the occupying army. If the mines of Northern France were utilized for the benefit of the Teutons, we can at least point out that the mica deposits of German East Africa[235] were utilized by the British "for national purposes" and can feel fairly certain that iron and coal deposits in the Saar Basin or the Black Forest would have been just as unhesitatingly used if the Allies could have penetrated that far and had felt the need. Imagine again the subjects of the German Emperor giving their government all the copper and brass they could find in cellar or attic, and the occupied Belgian and French territory going unsurveyed for these materials. Yet this very matter of the forced sale and requisitioning of copper and brass, for which payment was made at the time,[236] has been vigorously objected to as against the German policy.

The modern practice,—and expectations had best be based upon practice,—granted practically supreme powers to the occupant. His jurisdiction extends to all persons in the district actually occupied; it is territorial because it is based upon the holding of territory. Every one who lives there is under his control. Because they live there they are presumed to be enemies and subject to his will, administered either according to announced principles and local existing laws, or announced by dogmatic proclamation. No one and nothing escapes. "All property within enemy territory is in law enemy property, just as all persons in the same territory are enemies."[237] In accordance with the principle laid down in 1801 by Lord Stowell, that a belligerent character acquired by residence ceases with the end of the period of residence,[238] a Frenchman who worked as a cook in Mexico was deemed to have an enemy character as far as the United States was concerned so long as he resided in Vera Cruz and to have lost that character as soon as he sailed from the port.[239] Similarly an international tribunal, in relation to his residence in Mexico during the American occupation, declared: "According to the municipal law of England, he may be for some purposes still a British subject, but by the rules of international law, he is a Mexican citizen and not a British subject."[240] Over all persons within the limits of his potent control, the commander is the ruler, and he rules those persons and the land within those limits in every way his

[235] *Report on Tanganyika Territory* (1921) Brit. Parlia. Command Papers, No. 1428, p. 67.

[236] 9 Huberich and Speyer, *German Legislation for the Occupied Territory of Belgium* (1915) 389-394.

[237] *Young* v. *United States* (1873) 97 U. S. 39, 60.

[238] *The Indian Chief* (1801) 3 C. Rob. 12.

[239] *United States* v. *Guillem* (U. S. 1850) 11 How. 46, 60.

[240] *The Messrs. Laurent's Case,* 3 Moore, *International Arbitrations* (1898) 2671-2691; *cf. The Baltica* (1857) 11 Moore P. C. 141, 143; *The William Bagley supra,* footnote 229; 3 Moore, *loc. cit.,* pp. 2691-2695.

advantage requires. He can regulate the coming and going of persons.[241] He can permit foreign consuls to continue to function or stop them altogether.[242] He controls all trade.[243] He can fix prices he will pay for articles purchased for the troops.[244] If he can, as an act in support of the war, prescribe rationing and prices of foodstuffs in his own home country, it is equally reasonable to suppose that he can so prescribe in the adjacent territory which he occupies, for otherwise the captured enemy might be in better circumstances than the loyal patriot at home. So extreme is his power that it even extends to foreign ministers, who may be haled before local tribunals in occupied territory.[245] He can continue laws, alter them, or replace them. He is supreme; and he is supreme for the purpose of enabling him to carry on the war successfully. Thus he may act economically as well as against crimes.

It would seem therefore that the proper method of deciding what may be done depends less upon what the theoretical lawyer may decide purely from precedent, than upon what are the characteristics of modern armies and modern warfare. If the practice and the theory go entirely apart, we shall have other commanders declaring, in future cases: *"Oui cela se met dans les livres, mais voila' tout."*[246] Much depends upon circumstances. Theoretically the commander is supreme. Actually he is limited. In dealing with persons within his own army, he must follow the military law of his own country. If he find any of his own citizens in the occupied territory, he is in a strange position. They cannot be tried by the criminal law of his home country, which is territorial in effect and does not extend where complete sovereignty does not reach.[247] In civil causes involving them and native inhabitants, he

[241] Birkhimer, *op. cit.*, footnote 10, p. 204, citing 1 Bluntschli, *op. cit.*, footnote 56, § 8, and *Fleming* v. *Page, supra*, footnote 25, p. 615. See also *Hanauer* v. *Woodruff* (U. S. 1872) 15 Wall. 439, 447; *Ford* v. *Surget, supra*, footnote 231, p. 617; *United States* v. *Diekelman, supra*, footnote 69, p. 526; *The Venice* (U. S. 1864) 2 Wall. 258, 275.

[242] Hinckley, *American Consular Jurisdiction in the Orient* (1906) 176, 179, 180; citing cases in Algiers, Madagascar, Samoa, and Manchuria; 2 Stowell and Munroe, *op. cit.*, footnote 143, pp. 147-150; 2 Hyde, *op. cit.*, footnote 8, p. 385, on occupied Belgium. 7 Richardson, *Messages* (1917) 238, 277, 390, 403; 8, *id.* 72 Regarding Egypt, 2 Buchan, *History of the Great War* (1921) 378; and Villari, *op. cit.*, footnote 19, p. 31, regarding the Allies' expulsion of German, Austrian, Bulgar, and Turk consuls from Salonica.

[243] *Gates* v. *Goodloe, supra*, footnote 229, p. 616; 2 Smith, *op. cit.*, footnote 36, p. 226; 2 Hyde, *op. cit.*, footnote 8, p. 385; (1859) 9 Ops. Atty. Gen. 140; see also *supra*, footnote 214; Magoon, *op. cit.*, footnote 65, pp. 225-228, 316-338.

[244] Ariga, *op. cit.*, footnote 18, pp. 455-459; 9 Huberich and Speyer, *op. cit.*, footnote 236, pp. 389-394.

[245] Halleck, *op. cit.*, footnote 60, c. 9, §12; (1863) G. O. 100, §5. This was done by the Germans even in the neutral territory of Luxemburg. 2 Garner, *op. cit.*, footnote 19, p. 237.

[246] Bray, *op. cit.*, footnote 8, p. 163.

[247] See the case of the Frenchman accused of murder in occupied Catalonia in 1811 over whom the French Assize Court of the Department of the Pyrennées Orientales was decided not to have jurisdiction. Hall, *op. cit.*, footnote 39, p. 484.

has to decide whether or not the local law shall take its course.[248] And, in America at least, he has to be very careful indeed in his own dealings with them, for the celebrated case of *Mitchell* v. *Harmony*[249] made it plain that he could not seize the private moveable property of a citizen of his own country unless there was urgent necessity therefor and that if he did seize it he would be compelled to come into court when he had returned from the war and prove the specific urgent necessity or pay the damages out of his own pocket. All this on the general principle that civil actions can be brought wherever the goods of the defendant can be attached, providing the court wishes to deal with unfamiliar matters and cares to assume jurisdiction.[250] It is true that in some instances he may find protection from his home government.[251] Later legislation[252] or treaty provision[253] may operate to protect him against civil actions. But, generally he may be held responsible by his own courts in civil causes, and in criminal cases as well, yet under military, not civilian, authority, and that only so long as he remains a member of the army.[254]

In other words he is a military commander, carrying out military purposes. His acts are to be judged by military law,—save in a few

---

[248] Japanese instructions in 1895 said *"d'après les lois et coutumes locales, soit que les deux parties soient chinoises, soit que l'une des deux soit japonaise."* Ariga, *op. cit.*, footnote 67, p. 203. Smith, *op. cit.*, footnote 39, pp. 90-91, 97-98, mentions an instance under General Funston in Mexico where acts "clearly contrary to Mexican law" were permitted and recommends such policy in the future, saying—strangely enough—"there is no question of law involved but simply a question of doing justice to an American citizen."—In Germany in 1918-1919 "the interest of American citizens were referred to the American Embassy." Pershing, *op. cit.*, footnote 89, p. 87.

[249] (C. C. N. Y. 1850) 1 Blatchf. 549 and (U. S. 1851) 13 How. 115. *Case of Messrs. Porter* (1861) 10 Ops. Atty. Gen. 212, for a contrary decision, though not a *contra* case, because "If General Johnston had not been justified....by military necessity, he would have been personally liable."

[250] *Montalet* v. *Murray* (U. S. 1807) 4 Cranch 46; *Watts, Watts, & Co.* v. *Union Austriaca* (1918) 248 U. S. 9, 39 Sup. Ct. 1; *Panama R. R.* v. *Napier Shipping Co.* (1897) 166 U. S. 280, 17 Sup. Ct. 572; *The Belgenland* (1885) 114 U. S. 355, 5 Sup. Ct. 860.

[251] *E. g.*, the decision against the naval officer in *The Charming Betsy* (U .S. 1804) 2 Cranch 64, suggested that he be "indemnified by the state" and this was done by Act of Congress, January 31, 1805 (1805) 6 Stat. 56.

[252] The Foraker Act (1900) 31 Stat. 79, U. S. Comp. Stat. (1916) § 3753 was so applied in *Ochoa* v. *Hernandez, supra*, footnote 49; *Beard* v. *Burts, supra*, footnote 193, decided on the basis of Acts of Congress, March 3, 1863 (12 Stat. 756, U. S. Comp. Stat. (1916) § 1013 and May 11, 1866 14 Stat. 46, U. S. Comp. Stat. (1916) § 1013) which extended protection to all persons for all acts they committed in subordination to the military authorities in conducting the war. *Cf.* also *Planters' Bk.* v. *Union Bk., supra*, footnote 36, where the court also suggested an application to the government.

[253] *De Camara* v. *Brooke, supra*, footnote 195, exonerating a commander in occupied territory by virtue of the Platt Amendment of the Act of March 2, 1901, 31 Stat. 897, c. 803, U. S. Comp. Stat. (1916) § 7679 and the treaty with Cuba of May 22, 1903, 33 Stat. 2249.

[254] See (1903) 24 Ops. Atty. Gen. 570.

rare instances,—that is, judged by the military law of his own country which includes the Hague Conventions ratified by his government and incorporated in the instructions to his army. Questions as to whether or not he can adopt novel financial and commercial restrictions and regulations as an agent of the supreme power of the home government applying war powers as against the legislative power to regulate trade,[255] are really questions of constitutional rather than international law. As far as international law is concerned,

> ". . . . . the conquering power has the right to displace the pre-existing authority, and to assume to such extent as it may deem proper the exercise by itself of all the powers and functions of government. It may appoint all the necessary officers and clothe them with designated powers, larger or smaller, according to its pleasure. It may prescribe the revenues to be paid, and apply them to its own use or otherwise. It may do anything necessary to strengthen itself and weaken the enemy. There is no limit to the powers that may be exerted in such cases, save those that are found in the laws and usages of war. These principles have the sanction of all publicists who have considered the subject."[256]

When we speak of the sanctions of international law, we mean in addition to the few items covered by the Hague Conventions, two things: we mean that these things will be determined around the conference table where diplomats frame and sign the treaty of peace; and we mean that these things will be judged in official propaganda, editorial pronouncements, and popular speech and rumor by "the public opinion of the civilized world." If the acts of the conference delegates settle the matter, it is a political judgment. If "the general public opinion of the civilized world", it is not necessarily legal.[257] Both of

[255] Lawrence's Wheaton, *International Law* (6th ed. 1863) 1014, cited by 7 Moore, *op. cit.*, footnote 16, p. 270. See also Magoon, *op. cit.*, footnote 65, pp. 168-169; President Polk's Message of Feb. 10, 1846, 7 Moore, *loc. cit.*, p. 269; *Cross* v. *Harrison*, *supra*, footnote 2, p. 190; *New Orleans* v. *Steamship Co.*, *supra*, footnote 70, p. 394; *Dooley* v. *United States*, *supra*, footnote 2, p. 230; Magoon, *loc. cit.*, p. 227; and President McKinley's Executive Orders relative to the Philippines, Cuba, and Porto Rico (1903) Sen. Doc. 173, 63d Cong. 1st Sess., pp. 475-476, 470, 480; 2 Hyde, *op. cit.*, footnote 8, pp. 385-386. 2 Garner, *op. cit.*, footnote 19, p. 88, grows quite vapid over the German industrial regulations, labor legislations, food conservation and trade restrictions in Belgium. See also (1915) Documents of the Amer. Assn. Internat. Council regarding the European War, Ser. No. X, covering the Declaration of London, contraband commerce and diplomatic correspondence is relative.

[256] *Dooley* v. *United States*, *supra*, footnote 2, p. 231, citing *New Orleans* v. *Steamship Co.*, *supra*, footnote 70.

[257] No more vicious example of this sort of thing can be found than in the official Reports of Majority and dissenting reports of American and Japanese members of the Commission of Responsibilities, Conference of Paris, published *Violations of the Laws and Customs of War* by the Carnegie Endowment for International Peace (1919) 16-19, notably with reference to this topic.

these methods of determining the rights and wrongs of things done *flagrante bello* are unsound. The only remaining method is to check the acts against the Hague Conventions, and if the Hague Conventions do not forbid, or if the Hague Conventions admit of variations on the score of military necessity, the accused individual, army, or nation must be exonerated. In these days when an intense nationalistic spirit is spread throughout the countries of the world by extensive education, when this spirit is fostered by periodical political speeches and maintained by the democratic ideals or popular participation in governmental functions, when this spirit is so readily aroused through the rapid spreading of doctrines by easy transportation and communication, when this spirit is further intensified by theories like "selective service" and "the whole country at war"......then you have a state of affairs which presumes every enemy alien a hostile alien, every enemy resource fair capture, and every enemy protest "partisan propaganda." Amid such a turmoil of nationalistic, chauvinistic, or jingoistic thought and speech, the military commander can depend upon but one thing: military necessity. If he be an able commander, he will keep his troops in order; he will protect those troops against acts of the occupied population; and he will permit civilians to run their own affairs according to their own law, reserving his own time and energy, as much as he can, for the accomplishment of those belligerent ends which are his sole guide and aim. In war things are necessary or not, purely from military standards; and anything that aids the military is necessary. This is the final rule of belligerent occupation. It is the theory underlying each word of the Hague Conventions concerning occupied territory. It is the theory that motivated the famous general orders of Scott in Mexico. It is the theory by which the commander's work will be judged by his own superiors in the army; and, eventually, when the fumes of bitterness have cleared away, by "the general public opinion of the civilized world." Yet, to be just, that opinion must consider the nature of modern war.

Laws of war must be practical, declared Bray. War today is a tiresome, wearing, exhausting method of attrition. Military decisions seem to be secured in wars on a large scale only when the people as well as the armed force have been weakened in money, morale, and bodily strength. To a state surrounded by enemies, every day feeling more and more the lack of food, every day approaching, nearer and nearer, to the desperate situation of a beleaguered city, every day growing more and more frantic, no man in a sane mind can attribute too much blame if all the funds and resources be appropriated which lie within the lines, which have been conquered by his fighting forces and now become "occupied territory." To object strenuously to such conduct during the war itself is, of course, a valid method of propaganda. But to object to it after the peace in supposedly unimpassioned and scholarly studies, as have Garner and Hyde, is to lose sight of the simple facts which make up the intensive and inclusive nature of modern warfare.

It is not my purpose to plead for unlimited power of occupant forces in all circumstances. But when British Orders in Council, and public pronouncements of allied and associated statesmen, journalists, and propagandists announce the intention to "starve Germany out", there is something that can be said on the German side. When war becomes so largely a matter of financial and economic resources rather than military genius and manpower, we must recognize that fact with regard to the desperate activities of our enemies no less than we recognize it ourselves when "organizing for victory". Such a war is not desired by civilians, by army men, or by anyone who desires to see stability and decency in international relations. Yet, hopes for the future are not the facts of the past, nor even fair means of judging events of the present.

ELBRIDGE COLBY

FORT BENNING, GA.

[9]

WHAT IS A MILITARY OCCUPATION?*

By ADAM ROBERTS[1]

I. INTRODUCTION

ALTHOUGH there is a substantial body of international law which relates to military occupation, the scope of application of this law has been perennially problematical. The foreign military involvements of States, not least in the post-1945 world, have taken place in a bewildering variety of circumstances, and have assumed an equally bewildering variety of forms. Many recent and contemporary cases—in eastern Europe, the Middle East, Namibia, northern Cyprus, the Western Sahara, East Timor, Kampuchea and Afghanistan—raise a difficult question: what exactly is a military occupation? Underlying this question are several others: are certain types of occupation, which differ in some respect from what was envisaged in the 1907 Hague Regulations or the 1949 Geneva Conventions, still subject to the rules laid down in these and other agreements? Who determines whether a particular situation is to be called an occupation? Can the relevant body of law be applicable even in situations where the term 'occupation', with all its emotional overtones, is rejected by one or another party? Is there one law of military occupation, or is there a combination of rules which may vary somewhat depending on the type of occupation?

Michel Veuthey has gone so far as to say that 'the concept of "occupation" is juridically inoperative or disputed in practically all contemporary conflicts, including those involving guerrilla warfare.'[2] These are sobering words, and they raise doubts as to whether there is much merit in trying to define exactly what an occupation is, when one knows that in practice States will often disagree about the application of this label to particular situations. Might it not be more useful, as Veuthey suggests, to think rather in terms of basic humanitarian rules which apply to all situations, irrespective of arid academic distinctions and definitions?

Certainly there is no use worrying excessively about the definition of occupation. The core meaning of the term is obvious enough; but, as usually happens with abstract concepts, its frontiers are less clear. There sometimes is genuine difficulty in determining such questions as when an

[1] MA (Oxon.); Alastair Buchan Reader in International Relations, University of Oxford, and Professorial Fellow of St Antony's College.

[2] Veuthey, *Guérilla et droit humanitaire* (2nd edn., 1983), p. 355.

occupation can be said to have ended; and whether a particular situation—say the role of United States and regional forces in Grenada in late 1983—counts as an occupation.

A basic rule to follow when threading one's way through such questions is not to get into definitional and legalistic quibbling if one can avoid it. This rule is increasingly accepted in matters relating to the scope of application of the humanitarian laws of war, especially so far as the definition of 'war' is concerned. Questions such as what exactly a war is, how it is declared, how many types exist, etc., while interesting from many viewpoints, are not of enormous significance so far as the basic issue of the applicability of this body of law is concerned: it has come to be widely accepted that when there is an actual armed conflict between two or more countries, the humanitarian laws of war are applicable.[3] Similarly with occupations, the fact that these can be hard to define, can sometimes happen without being declared, and can have many different causes, characters and consequences, need not necessarily have an effect on the applicability of the relevant parts of the humanitarian laws of war. One might hazard as a fair rule of thumb that every time the armed forces of a country are in control of foreign territory, and find themselves face to face with the inhabitants, some or all of the provisions of the law on occupations are applicable.

The case for such an approach is especially strong in view of the fact that the law on occupations is not a totally discrete entity, different from all other law and applying solely and exclusively to military occupations. On the contrary: (*a*) many laws of war rules which apply in occupations also explicitly apply in other situations—for example, in combat areas, or in the territory of a party to the conflict;[4] (*b*) the category of 'crimes against humanity' applies even more broadly, and depends neither on distinctions between 'war' and 'peace', nor on distinctions between what a State can do in its territory and what it can do in foreign or occupied lands;[5] and (*c*) international conventions on human rights contain some provisions which are not subject to derogation in time of emergency, and are applicable in time of war and occupation.[6]

[3] Stone, *Legal Controls of International Conflict* (1954), pp. 311–13; Draper, *The Red Cross Conventions* (1958), pp. 10–11; Brownlie, *International Law and the Use of Force by States* (1963), pp. 398–401; Skubiszewski in Sørensen (ed.), *Manual of Public International Law* (1968), pp. 808–11; Partsch in Bernhardt (ed.), *Encyclopaedia of Public International Law*, vol. 3 (1982), pp. 25–8.

[4] Perhaps the clearest example of rules of this kind is Articles 13 to 34 of 1949 Geneva Convention IV.

[5] As far as conventions are concerned, the 1948 United Nations Genocide Convention is the main instrument in this area. Article I confirms that genocide 'whether committed in time of peace or in time of war' is a crime under international law.

[6] Non-derogable provisions include the 1950 European Convention on Human Rights, Articles 2, 3, 4 (1) and 7; and the 1966 International Covenant on Civil and Political Rights, Articles 6, 7, 8 (1) and (2), 11, 15, 16 and 18. On human rights in armed conflicts and occupations see also Draper, 'The Status of Combatants and the Question of Guerrilla Warfare', this *Year Book*, 45 (1971), p. 218; Meron, 'Applicability of Multilateral Conventions to Occupied Territories', *American Journal of International*

Even if States dispute the formal applicability of the law on occupations in a particular situation, or challenge the labelling of a military intervention as 'occupation', they still sometimes decide to apply the provisions of the law on occupations—for example, on a *de facto* or *ex gratia* basis, as the most appropriate available outline of the rights and duties of the respective parties to use in the circumstances. Courts, too, have sometimes been guided by aspects of the laws of war, including the law on occupations, even in cases where the *de jure* applicability of the relevant convention was in doubt. International organizations too have sometimes taken a similar line.[7]

This article does not seek to attach any exaggerated importance to the question of how military occupations are either defined or classified. The application of quite basic practical and humanitarian rules cannot be made to depend on an endless series of definitional wrangles and legal niceties. Rather the aim here is to focus attention on a process whereby the law on occupations has come to be regarded as applicable in a wide variety of situations; and also, at the same time, to get away from the *idée fixe* that all occupations are essentially the same in their character and purpose. Even if the application of a single set of rules to a very wide variety of situations presents some difficulties, it is not necessarily absurd or impossible.

II. Indications in the Conventions

The various international conventions on the laws of war contain at least a framework of ideas as to what an occupation is. The most important indications are those in the Hague Regulations, in the 1949 Geneva Conventions and in the 1977 Geneva Protocol I.

(a) *The 1907 Hague Regulations*

The 1907 Hague Regulations, like those of 1899, appear to be based on an assumption that a military occupation occurs in the context of a war, and consists of direct control of one hostile State's territory by a rival hostile State's armed forces. Some of this is evident from the very title of the part of the Regulations which deals with the question of occupation: 'Military Authority Over the Territory of the Hostile State'. The first article in this part of the Regulations—Article 42—establishes an apparently simple factual basis for determining what an occupation is:

> Territory is considered occupied when it is actually placed under the authority of the hostile army.

Law, 72 (1978), pp. 542–57; and the same author's contributions in *Israel Yearbook on Human Rights*, issues for 1978 and 1979.

[7] Examples of such *de facto* applications of the law on occupations are mentioned below, pp. 268, 281–3 and 302–3.

The occupation extends only to the territory where such authority has been established and can be exercised.[8]

The implicit assumption here, that an occupant exercises authority directly, through its armed forces, rather than indirectly, through local agents, is also evident in Article 43, which begins: 'The authority of the legitimate power having in fact passed into the hands of the occupant. . . .' Direct control by the occupant also seems to be taken for granted in Articles 48, 49, 51–3 and 55. An open and identifiable command structure is thus a central feature of the Hague definition of military occupation.

(b) *The 1949 Geneva Conventions*

After the Second World War, the need was felt for a more adequate definition of the cases to which the laws of war, including the law on occupations, applied. As far as occupations were concerned, there had been many, especially in the period 1938–45, which differed in important respects from the implicit definitions of the Hague Regulations. Czechoslovakia and Denmark were leading examples. These occupations did not begin with war between the parties as envisaged at The Hague. Czechoslovakia had been invaded and occupied without military resistance and before the outbreak of the war, not as a consequence of war; and Denmark, which was invaded and occupied during the war, only put up minimum military resistance to the invasion. The forms of administration also differed from what was envisaged at The Hague. In both countries there were periods when the Germans exercised control partly through indigenous governments. Moreover, in Czechoslovakia there were additional complications, not least its purported abolition as a State in March 1939. A clarification was needed that the laws of war applied to these and other types of occupation.

The main result was the adoption of common Article 2 of the four 1949 Geneva Conventions. This states, in full:

> In addition to the provisions which shall be implemented in peacetime, the present Convention shall apply to all cases of declared war or of any other armed conflict which may arise between two or more of the High Contracting Parties, even if the state of war is not recognized by one of them.
>
> The Convention shall also apply to all cases of partial or total occupation of the territory of a High Contracting Party, even if the said occupation meets with no armed resistance.
>
> Although one of the Powers in conflict may not be a party to the present Convention, the Powers who are parties thereto shall remain bound by it in their

[8] Hague Convention IV Respecting the Laws and Customs of War on Land, signed on 18 October 1907, Annex, Article 42: Scott (ed.), *The Hague Conventions and Declarations of 1899 and 1907* (3rd edn., 1918), p. 100.

mutual relations. They shall furthermore be bound by the Convention in relation to the said Power, if the latter accepts and applies the provisions thereof.[9]

The crucial first two paragraphs of the above article were the subject of surprisingly little discussion at the Diplomatic Conference.[10] This suggests that there was general agreement with their provisions, but it makes commentary difficult. However, two points about the first paragraph of the article should be briefly noted. First, the essential meaning of the paragraph is that declarations of war are of no real significance so far as the application of the laws of war is concerned. Technically speaking, the paragraph might be taken to mean that the Conventions are inapplicable in an armed conflict in which *both* parties denied the existence of a state of war, but any such interpretation of the paragraph is challenged by Pictet.[11] Draper is right to have said that the 1949 Conventions 'have reduced the importance of determining whether a legal state of war exists to vanishing point'.[12] Although the word 'occupation' only occurs in the second paragraph, it has been persuasively argued that the Conventions apply to most occupations by virtue of the first paragraph: only those types of occupation which are not opposed militarily (e.g. Czechoslovakia in 1938–9 and Denmark in 1940) are the subject of the second paragraph.[13]

The broad terms of common Article 2 establish that the 1949 Geneva Conventions apply to a wide range of international armed conflicts and occupations—including occupations in time of so-called peace. But they do not thereby end all possibility of dispute about what military occupation is or to what situations the law on occupations is applicable.

In the 1949 Geneva Convention IV (the Civilians Convention), many other provisions besides Article 2 indicate that occupation is conceived of more broadly than in the Hague Regulations. The most notable such provisions are Article 6, which refers to occupations which continue after the end of military operations; and Article 47, which *inter alia* takes account of two possibilities, the first being an occupation in which the authorities of the occupied territory remain in post, and the second being an attempted annexation by the occupant of the whole or part of the occupied territory.

Since 1949 the various new international conventions with a specific

[9] The four Geneva Conventions on the protection of victims of war, signed at Geneva on 12 August 1949, common Article 2: *United Nations Treaty Series*, vol. 75, pp. 31–417.

[10] For evidence of the paucity of discussion of Article 2, paras. 1 and 2, see *Final Record 1949* (n.d.), vol. IIA, p. 620; and vol. IIB, pp. 9–10, 128, 325.

[11] Pictet, *Commentary on Geneva Convention IV* (1958), p. 21.

[12] Draper, op. cit. above (p. 250 n. 3), at p. 25.

[13] Para. 2 'does not refer to cases in which territory is occupied during hostilities; in such cases the Convention will have been in force since the outbreak of hostilities or since the time war was declared. The paragraph only refers to cases where the occupation has taken place without a declaration of war and without hostilities, and makes provision for the entry into force of the Convention in those particular circumstances': Pictet, op. cit. above (n. 11), at p. 21.

bearing on occupations have all echoed the terms of 1949 common Article 2.[14]

(c) *The 1977 Geneva Protocol I*

The most significant post-1949 development, so far as the scope of application of the law on occupations is concerned, is in the 1977 Geneva Protocol I, Article 1, paragraphs 3 and 4:

> 3. This Protocol, which supplements the Geneva Conventions of 12 August 1949 for the protection of war victims, shall apply in the situations referred to in Article 2 common to those Conventions.
>
> 4. The situations referred to in the preceding paragraph include armed conflicts in which peoples are fighting against colonial domination and alien occupation and against racist regimes in the exercise of their right of self-determination, as enshrined in the Charter of the United Nations and the Declaration on Principles of International Law concerning Friendly Relations and Co-operation among States in accordance with the Charter of the United Nations.[15]

The aim of paragraph 4 as quoted above seems to be to try to establish that certain armed conflicts, which might be viewed by some as essentially internal in character, are really international, and hence fully subject to the better developed legal regime governing international armed conflicts. As far as its specific reference to occupation is concerned, the paragraph does not concern itself directly with the definition or scope of 'alien occupation'; and it adds little to the scope of application as spelt out in the 1949 Geneva Conventions themselves. All it really does is to close a tiny technical loophole in common Article 2 of the 1949 Geneva Conventions, by making a little clearer what was already widely accepted—namely, that the law on occupations is applicable even in situations (like the West Bank and Gaza) where the occupied territory was not universally viewed as having been part of 'the territory of a High Contracting Party'. As Bothe, Partsch and Solf say, it appears that the term 'alien occupation' is 'meant to cover cases in which a High Contracting Party occupies territories of a State which is not a HCP, or territories with a controversial international status, and to establish that the population of such territory is fighting against the occupant in the exercise of their right of self-determination.'[16]

Another provision of the 1977 Geneva Protocol I—namely, Article 4—points in the same direction. It contains the statement: 'Neither the

[14] 1954 Hague Cultural Property Convention, Articles 5 and 18; 1977 Geneva Protocol I, Article 1; 1981 United Nations Convention on Certain Inhumane Weapons, Article 1. Texts in Roberts and Guelff (eds.), *Documents on the Laws of War* (1982), pp. 339, 387, 467.

[15] Protocol I Additional to the Geneva Conventions of 12 August 1949, and Relating to the Protection of Victims of International Armed Conflicts, signed at Geneva on 12 December 1977: Misc. No. 19 (1977) (Cmnd. 6927), p. 23.

[16] Bothe, Partsch and Solf, *New Rules for Victims of Armed Conflicts* (1982), pp. 51–2, support the view that this might mean in practice 'the peoples of southern Africa and Palestine'.

occupation of a territory nor the application of the Conventions and this Protocol shall affect the legal status of the territory in question.' Thus the controversial international status of a territory would not be affected by the application of these accords: there would be no implication that it was 'the territory of a High Contracting Party'.

(d) *Other Conventions, etc.*

Other conventions and declarations, outside the laws of war framework, do not add any further general indications as to what an occupation is. Take, for example, various United Nations agreements. The United Nations Charter itself does not contain the word 'occupation'. The 1970 Declaration on Principles of International Law Concerning Friendly Relations and Co-operation Among States in Accordance with the Charter of the United Nations does refer to occupation of 'the territory of a State' but says little.[17] The same is true of the 1970 Declaration on the Strengthening of International Security[18] and the 1974 Definition of Aggression.[19] However, in an *ad hoc* manner various United Nations resolutions dealing with particular territories (and mentioned later in this article) do provide some additional clues about the factual situations and types of status of territory which the term occupation can cover.

(e) *Occupation Essentially International in Character*

Taking the conventions as a whole, it is evident that the concept of military occupation remains essentially international in character. At the heart of almost all treaty provisions and legal writings about occupations is the image of the armed forces of a State exercising some kind of coercive control or authority over inhabited territory outside the accepted international frontiers of their State. However, the conventions are far from clear that the law applies to all possible situations of this type; moreover, they give rather few hints about its possible relevance in any analogous situations which may arise within a State. It will be necessary to turn to other sources, including State practice and judicial decisions, to illuminate these issues.

III. Beginning and End of Occupation

To the extent that there are clearly established factual criteria for determining when occupations begin and when they end, the question of what an occupation is becomes easier to answer. However, while the conventions as cited above do indicate certain criteria, these do not cover all cases.

[17] Approved on 24 October 1970 in GA Res. 2625 (XXV).
[18] Approved on 16 December 1970 as GA Res. 2734 (XXV).
[19] Approved on 14 December 1974 in GA Res. 3314 (XXIX).

(a) *The Beginning of Occupation*

In the great majority of cases, occupations are preceded by invasions. The rather technical issue of the precise moment when an invasion turns into an occupation is not always easy to determine. Invasion itself—the entry of military forces into country controlled by adversaries—is not occupation; and if it consists of a mere raid, or a simple passage across territory, it may not lead to occupation. Most sources follow the Hague Regulations, Article 42, in stating that occupation may be said to begin when the invader actually exercises authority, thus stressing that it is factual criteria that are important.[20]

Even before an occupation begins, relations between the invaders and the inhabitants are subject to numerous provisions of the laws of war, including many of those set out in the 1899 and 1907 Hague Regulations, and in the 1949 Geneva Convention IV. All that happens when an occupation begins is that in addition to the general provisions of the laws of war, the specific provisions relating to occupied territories (which constitute Section III both in the Hague Regulations and in the 1949 Geneva Convention IV) come fully into effect.

Pictet suggests that the Geneva rules governing occupations also apply in the preceding invasion phase:

> There is no intermediate period between what might be termed the invasion phase and the inauguration of a stable regime of occupation. Even a patrol which penetrates into enemy territory without any intention of staying there must respect the Conventions in its dealings with the civilians it meets. When it withdraws, for example, it cannot take civilians with it, for that would be contrary to Article 49, which prohibits the deportation or forcible transfer of persons from occupied territory . . .[21]

Both the United States and United Kingdom military manuals take a similar view, stating that the rules which apply to occupied territory should also be observed as far as possible in areas through which troops are passing and even on the battlefield.[22] All this is evidence of a more general tendency to think of the laws of war as a set of minimum rules to be observed in the widest possible range of situations, and not to worry excessively about the precise legal definition of military occupation. Further evidence of such an approach is to be found in the 1977 Geneva Protocol I, in which most provisions apply quite generally, and only a few are said to apply specifically to occupied areas.[23]

[20] Oppenheim, *International Law*, vol. 2 (7th edn., 1952), pp. 434–6; US, Department of the Army, *The Law of Land Warfare*, Field Manual No. 27-10 (18 July 1956), pp. 138–9; UK, War Office, *Manual of Military Law*, Part III, *The Law of War on Land* (1958), pp. 141–2.

[21] Pictet, op. cit. above (p. 253 n. 11), at p. 60.

[22] US Manual, op. cit. above (n. 20), at p. 138; UK Manual, op. cit. above (n. 20), at p. 141.

[23] In 1977 Geneva Protocol I, Articles 14, 63 and 69 (dealing respectively with medical units, civil defence, and basic needs) are the main provisions whose application is specifically in occupied areas.

Making a proclamation of occupation, like making a declaration of war, may be considered the proper thing to do, but it is not absolutely essential. There is no formal requirement—in the Hague, Geneva or any other conventions in force—that the occupying forces have to issue a formal proclamation of a state of occupation. However, such proclamations are generally considered to be desirable, and are favoured by international practice.[24]

In some instances there may be occupations which do not begin with invasion. Foreign forces may be stationed in a territory by international agreement (with peacekeeping, defence or other specified functions), and then later go beyond that role. For example, from 1920 onwards South Africa's presence in Namibia was under the terms of an international mandate, terminated by the United Nations in 1966. Thereafter, and especially after the advisory opinion of the International Court of Justice in 1971, it was increasingly viewed as an occupation. This and some other possible examples of occupation beginning otherwise than by outright invasion are considered later in this article.

(b) *The Ending of Occupation*

Most legal writings indicate that an occupation ends when the troops leave. As Oppenheim put it, 'Occupation comes to an end when an occupant withdraws from a territory, or is driven out of it'.[25] In many cases such a statement poses no problems. But the occupant has not necessarily withdrawn at the end of all occupations, especially of the post-surrender type, a category to which, in any case, the application of the law on occupations has in the past often been contested.[26]

1. *Military withdrawal*

One post-war example of an occupation which did end with a complete withdrawal of all the occupying forces (in this case by agreement) is Austria. The occupation by the USSR, USA, UK and France, which lasted for more than ten years, was wound up in accord with the Austrian State Treaty, signed by these four countries on 15 May 1955. Later the same day the Austrian foreign ministry published the text of a resolution on Austria's permanent neutrality to be placed before the national legislature. The last Allied troops left Austria on 24 October 1955, and on 25 October Austria became a completely free and sovereign country.[27]

This date of the formal ending of the occupation is not necessarily the same as the date of re-emergence of the Austrian State. Clute has persuasively argued that 28 June 1946—the date of a new agreement

[24] US Manual, op. cit. above (p. 256 n. 20), at p. 140; UK Manual, op. cit. above (p. 256 n. 20), at p. 142.

[25] Oppenheim, op. cit. above (p. 256 n. 20), at p. 436.

[26] On post-surrender occupations, see below, pp. 267–71.

[27] *Keesing's Contemporary Archives*, pp. 14193–8 and 14561.

concluded by the four occupying powers—can be interpreted as the real date of 'the re-emergence of the Austrian State and a government capable of acting on its behalf . . .'. The 1955 Austrian State Treaty 'merely confirmed the existence of an independent Austrian State and contributed to its stability by creating the conditions for a termination of the occupation, but did not create or re-establish the Austrian State'.[28]

Another example of an occupation ending with a negotiated withdrawal by the occupying forces was the Israeli occupation of Sinai which had begun in 1967, and which was concluded with a phased evacuation between 1979 and 1982 in accord with the terms of the Egypt-Israel Peace Treaty signed in Washington in March 1979.[29]

2. *Continued presence of foreign forces*

However, there are instances where an occupation is declared or widely presumed to have ended, but the occupant's forces remain in the country. This can happen, for example, if a treaty ending an occupation is acompanied by another one permitting the presence of foreign forces. Alternatively it may happen in a less formal way.

In Japan on 28 April 1952 a Peace Treaty ending the United States military occupation of the country took effect, and simultaneously a Security Treaty came into force, providing for a continued United States military presence.[30]

Likewise in West Germany on 5 May 1955 a number of agreements took effect simultaneously, including one which ended the last vestiges of the three-power occupation, one which provided for the continued presence of the same three countries' forces in West Germany, and others which provided for the entry of West Germany into the North Atlantic Treaty Organization and the Western European Union.[31]

As for East Germany, a Soviet Government statement of 25 March 1954 ended the Soviet 'supervision of the activities of the German Democratic Republic', and also specified that the Soviet Union would retain in East Germany its functions connected with guaranteeing security.[32]

The city of Berlin meanwhile remains frozen in the time-warp of the four-power occupation. Although the powers of the Allies are minimal

[28] Clute, *The International Legal Status of Austria 1938–1955* (1962), pp. 34–5, 132.

[29] For details of the evacuation see International Institute for Strategic Studies, *Strategic Survey 1979* (1980), pp. 73–8, and *Strategic Survey 1982–1983* (1983), pp. 69–70.

[30] For texts of these two treaties, both of which had been signed on 8 September 1951, see *United Nations Treaty Series*, vol. 136, pp. 46, 216.

[31] For details of the agreements on West Germany see B. Ruhm von Oppen, *Documents on Germany under Occupation 1945–1954* (1955), pp. 600–48. Most of the occupants' powers of intervention in West German domestic affairs had already been abolished in the Convention on Relations Between the Three Western Powers and the Federal Republic, signed on 26 May 1952. Text in ibid., pp. 616–17.

[32] Ibid., pp. 597–8. In 1955 several further steps were taken, including the opening of diplomatic relations between the USSR and GDR on 20 September. However, West German official publications continued for many years thereafter to refer to East Germany as the 'Soviet Occupation Zone'.

and residual, Berlin is a reminder that occupations can assume some very strange forms, and can last for an astonishingly long time.[33]

In some instances, there may have been no formal statement that an occupation has ended, and no withdrawal of the occupying troops, yet the territory ceases to be viewed as occupied. The situation in Hungary after the Soviet suppression of the 1956 Hungarian uprising affords a possible example. A United Nations General Assembly resolution in November 1956 referred to 'the Soviet army of occupation in Hungary'; and a resolution in 1957 said 'the USSR has violated its obligations under the Geneva Conventions of 1949'.[34] However, as events moved on and Kadar consolidated his leadership, there were no more designations of Hungary as an occupied territory, despite the continued presence of Soviet forces.

The possibility that an occupation might gradually fade away was allowed for in 1949 Geneva Convention IV, Article 6, which specified that in occupied territory the Convention shall cease to apply one year after the general close of military operations, but that 'the Occupying Power shall be bound, for the duration of the occupation, to the extent that such power exercises the functions of government in such territory, by the provisions of the following Articles . . .', which are then enumerated. The current status of this provision is discussed later in this article.[35]

3. *Other types of ending*

An occupation can also end without a departure of troops if there is a legitimate transfer of sovereignty. The treaty transfer of territory from Turkey to Greece after the Balkan Wars of 1912–13 is an example. The Permanent Court of International Justice's award in the *Lighthouses* case in 1934 was based on a distinction between the period when Greece was occupant, and later sovereign, of the Ottoman territories concerned.[36]

There have been instances in which some have ceased to view a territory as occupied, not because the situation has stabilized, but rather because resistance has become so widespread that the invader, although he has not withdrawn, is presumed to have lost capacity to exercise authority. This

[33] The legal status of Berlin is the subject of the four-power agreement of 3 September 1971, but this nowhere mentions the word 'occupation', nor indeed the word 'Berlin'. For one earlier assessment of the legal status of Berlin see the chapter by Bishop in Stanger (ed.), *West Berlin: The Legal Context* (1966).

[34] GA Resolutions 1127 (XI) of 21 November 1956, and 1133 (XI) of 14 September 1957. On 27 May 1957 Hungary and the USSR signed a troop-stationing agreement: see below, p. 288.

[35] On occupations one year after the end of military operations see below, pp. 271–3.

[36] *PCIJ, Series* A/B, vol. 62, pp. 4–29. The territories in question had been transferred from Turkey to Greece under the terms of the unratified Treaty of London of 30 May 1913 (Parry, *The Consolidated Treaty Series*, vol. 218, p. 159); the Treaty of Athens of 14 November 1913 (ibid., vol. 219, p. 21); and the Treaty of Lausanne of 24 July 1923 (*League of Nations Treaty Series*, vol. 28, p. 12). On the eventual settlement of the dispute over the lighthouses see the Permanent Court of Arbitration's decision of 24 July 1956 in the *Lighthouses* arbitration between France and Greece (23 ILR 659–81). Another case relating to Greece's acquisitions of territory in the period of the breakup of the Ottoman Empire, and similarly depending on a distinction between a period of occupation and subsequent transfer of sovereignty, was the *Ottoman Debt* arbitration: see below, p. 266 n. 58.

was a significant issue in a number of trials following the Second World War, affecting as it did the question whether the relevant body of law was that which relates to combat or that which relates to military occupations. Different decisons on the matter were reached in different cases, reflecting at least in part the different factual circumstances and issues involved.[37]

The preceding brief survey of the beginning and ending of occupations has suggested that the question of when an occupation can be said to have begun, or ended, is sometimes easy to answer but is by no means always so. Even when it can be answered with confidence, there may still be many gradations between direct foreign military control on the one hand and complete independence and freedom from foreign military forces on the other.

IV. Different Types of Military Occupation

The genus 'military occupation' can be classified in many different ways, depending on the particular purpose for which the classification is made. The principal concern here being the applicability or otherwise of the law on occupations, the types or categories of occupation which appear on the following table are ones which raise different issues as to the applicability of such provisions as those contained in the 1907 Hague Regulations and the 1949 Geneva Convention IV. The question arises as to whether any of these types of occupation is subject in any way to a different international legal regime.

These types or categories of occupation are not mutually exclusive: a given occupation might well fit into two or more of the categories at the same time, and/or at different times. For example, the Allied occupation of the Rhineland at the end of the First World War was a multilateral occupation; and it could additionally in successive periods be fitted into three other categories (first belligerent, then armistice, then peacetime occupation by consent)—a reminder of the artificiality of these categories.

The list is neither exhaustive nor definitive: authorities are not agreed on the exact terms to be applied, and it represents just one attempt at distillation and improvisation. Each type of occupation listed is discussed separately under the relevant heading below.

[37] See, e.g., two cases before the United States Military Tribunals at Nuremberg. In the *Hostages* case (*USA* v. *Wilhelm List et al.*), United States Military Tribunal V ruled on 19 February 1948 that the German armed forces were able to maintain control of Greece and Yugoslavia until they evacuated them in 1944: *Trials of War Criminals before the Nuernberg Military Tribunals*, vol. 11 (1950), pp. 1243–4. In the *Einsatzgruppen* case (*USA* v. *Otto Ohlendorf et al.*), United States Military Tribunal II ruled on 8–9 April 1948 that in parts of the Soviet Union occupied by Nazi Germany 'the so-called partisans had wrested considerable territory from the German occupant, and . . . military combat of some dimensions was required to reoccupy those areas . . . In reconquering enemy territory which the occupant has lost to the enemy, he is not carrying out a police performance but a regular act of war . . .': ibid., vol. 4 (1950), pp. 492–3. See also the substantial discussion of this issue as it had arisen in the post-war French case of *In re Bauer and Others*: United Nations War Crimes Commission, *Law Reports of Trials of War Criminals* (1947–9), vol. 8, pp. 18–19.

Seventeen Types of Occupations

(a) *Wartime and Post-War*

The following types of occupation occur during or directly after wars. The word 'war' is used in a factual sense here, to refer to significant (and in this case international) armed conflict.

1. *Belligerent occupation*

This is the classic type of military occupation. It is sometimes known as *occupatio bellica*,[38] and is more or less synonymous with another commonly used term, 'occupation of enemy territory'. When the term 'belligerent occupation' is used in its strict sense, its key distinguishing characteristics are that it is (*a*) by a belligerent State, (*b*) of territory of an enemy belligerent State, (*c*) during the course of an armed conflict, and (*d*) before any general armistice agreement is concluded.[39] However, the term

[38] In past centuries, the term *occupatio bellica* sometimes carried a more extreme meaning, even implying full acquisition of sovereignty by the occupant.

[39] The definition is adapted from those offered or implied by Graber, *The Development of the Law of Belligerent Occupation 1863–1914* (1949), p. 5; Feilchenfeld, *The International Economic Law of Belligerent Occupation* (1942), p. 6; von Glahn, *The Occupation of Enemy Territory: A Commentary on the Law and Practice of Belligerent Occupation* (1957), p. 28.

is often used more broadly to cover wartime occupations of neutral territory; occupations following armistice agreements; and even occupations after the end of active hostilities.

Belligerent occupation in the strict sense is the type which is most unambiguously subject to the law on occupations. Although the term itself does not appear in any of the relevant conventions, it was with this type of occupation above all in mind that these conventions were drawn up. And it is also probably the type of military occupation which has occurred most frequently in this century.

So central has belligerent occupation been to the development of the law on occupations that it is often called the 'law of belligerent occupation'; and it is often suggested that belligerent occupation is the only type to which the law on occupations is applicable. Thus Freeman wrote in 1946: 'International law knows only two categories of occupation by a conquering State: belligerent occupation properly so-called and assumption of sovereignty over the conquered areas. There is no in-between status.'[40] Von Glahn has likewise written: 'Conventional international law recognizes only one form of military occupation: belligerent occupation, that is, the occupation of part or all of an enemy's territory in time of war; this is the type of occupation covered by the Hague Regulations and the Fourth Geneva Convention of 1949.'[41]

However, there are some kinds of occupation which are not exactly 'belligerent occupations' as that term is usually understood, and to which, nevertheless, the law on occupations is applicable. Especially since the advent of the 1949 Geneva Conventions, common Article 2, the body of law governing occupations has recognized this fact. Therefore in this study the practice of using 'belligerent occupation' as the legally relevant generic term is not followed. Instead this article adopts the position of those writers who have used 'military occupation' or just 'occupation' as the best generic term.[42]

2. *Occupation of neutral territory*

This is the occupation by a belligerent of all or part of the territory of a State which has been neutral in a particular armed conflict. Usually this is but one form of belligerent occupation, because such States normally cease to be neutral at the moment when they are attacked and resist such attack. As Oppenheim has said:

[40] *American Journal of International Law*, 40 (1946), pp. 796–7.

[41] Von Glahn, op. cit. above (p. 261 n. 39), at p. 27. However, this restrictive view is not evident on p. 20 (where he quotes 1949 Geneva Convention IV, Article 2); p. 273; and p. 281, where the Convention's application to post-surrender occupations is well discussed.

[42] Such writers include Spaight, *War Rights on Land* (1911); Hall, *Treatise on International Law* (8th edn., 1924); Fraenkel, *Military Occupation and the Rule of Law: Occupation Government in the Rhineland, 1918–1923* (1944); US Manual, op. cit. above (p. 256 n. 20); and Greenspan, *The Modern Law of Land Warfare* (1959).

Hostilities against a neutral on the part of either belligerent are acts of war, and not mere violations of neutrality. Thus the German attack on Belgium in 1914, to enable German troops to march through Belgian territory and attack France, created war between Germany and Belgium.[43]

In minor instances—for example, when a neutral State wards off a frontier incursion—such a transformation of neutrality into belligerency cannot in every case be taken for granted.[44]

The Hague Regulations are generally accepted as applying to occupations of neutral territory. As Feilchenfeld said in 1942:

> Section III of the Hague Regulations applies expressly only to territory which belongs to an enemy and has been occupied without the consent of the sovereign. It is, nevertheless, usually held that the rules on belligerent occupation will also apply where a belligerent, in the course of the war, occupies neutral territory, even if the neutral power should have failed to protest against the occupation.[45]

The applicability of the Hague Regulations to the Axis occupations of neutral States in the Second World War was accepted in principle by both prosecution and defence at the International Military Tribunal at Nuremberg, and at other post-war trials where the issue arose.

The 1949 Geneva Conventions, in accord with the broad terms of common Article 2, quite clearly apply to occupations of neutral territory.

3. *Occupation of allied territory*

This can occur in a number of circumstances. Its usual form is the recapture of all or part of the territory of an ally from an enemy who has been a belligerent occupant of the territory in question. Such an occupation may be of short duration, pending the return of the legitimate sovereign or the establishment of an indigenous government and administration. In most cases it is likely to be governed by some prior agreement between the occupying power and the government of the occupied State, thus falling into the category of occupation by consent: any such occupation has a special legal character, not only because of its separate legal basis (the particular agreement), but also because the indigenous authorities may be entrusted with wider powers than in a belligerent occupation.

Is the law on occupations applicable in such cases? There has been little writing about this, partly no doubt because relatively fewer problems are anticipated than in other types of occupation. In the writing that exists, broadly similar views are expressed as to the applicability of the law on

[43] Oppenheim, op. cit. above (p. 256 n. 20), at p. 685.

[44] 'The fact of a neutral Power resisting, even by force, attempts to violate its neutrality can not be regarded as a hostile act': 1907 Hague Convention V on Neutrality in Land War, Article 10.

[45] Feilchenfeld, op. cit. above (p. 261 n. 39), at p. 8. Von Glahn takes a similar view in op. cit. above (p. 261 n. 39), at p. 12. Oppenheim, op. cit. above (p. 256 n. 20), at p. 241, states that in certain circumstances an occupant of neutral territory 'does not possess such a wide range of rights with regard to the occupied country and its inhabitants as he possesses in occupied *enemy* territory'.

occupations. Von Glahn has said: 'Unless regulated in advance by treaty with the government involved, the occupant would appear to be bound by the provisions of the Hague Regulations and subsequent international lawmaking treaties.'[46] He does not specify what the continuing role of the Hague Regulations, etc., might be in the event that there is such an agreement or treaty with the government concerned. The British military manual is sceptical about the applicability of the law on occupations to occupations of allied territory, except in those cases where it is not possible to conclude a 'civil affairs' agreement before liberation of that territory: in such cases the law on occupations ought to apply as a minimum standard.[47] Greenspan takes much the same line.[48]

In practice, most occupations of allied territory have been governed by what have come to be known as civil affairs agreements, and not explicitly by the law on occupations, though the former often reflect the language and concepts of the latter. Towards the end of the Second World War the Allies made agreements for strictly temporary military authority over civil administration in France, Belgium, Luxembourg, the Netherlands, Norway, Denmark, French Indo-China and the Netherlands East Indies.[49] As Donnison has said apropos of these occupations:

> In the case of forces operating in friendly territory the legal position is not so clear. There is a conflict between two principles, the one, the continuance or the revival, if the territory has been recovered from enemy occupation, of the sovereignty of the friendly government concerned, the other, the principle of military necessity under which the military commander is entitled to take any measures necessary to the success of his operations. There is not the same body of international law and usage to regulate such a situation as there is in the case of operations in enemy territory.[50]

Much the same view—that in an occupation of allied territory the Hague Regulations are not applicable—was advanced in several Polish judgments after the Second World War so far as the activities of Soviet forces on Polish territory were concerned.[51]

However, in at least one post-war occupation of what was technically allied territory the laws of war appear to have been viewed as applicable. This was in Java, a part of the Netherlands East Indies occupied by Japan in the Second World War and then liberated by the Allies in September 1945 after Japan's surrender. The situation in Java was complicated by the fact that there was tension between local political forces seeking

[46] Von Glahn, op. cit. above (p. 261 n. 39), at p. 27.

[47] UK Manual, op. cit. above (p. 256 n. 20), at pp. 140–1 n. See also US Manual, op. cit. above (p. 256 n. 20), at p. 139.

[48] Greenspan, op. cit. above (p. 262 n. 42), at pp. 211–12, 235–40.

[49] Donnison, *Civil Affairs and Military Government: Central Organisation and Planning* (1966), pp. 121–3. He points out that in the cases of Denmark, France and French Indo-China, agreements were only concluded after the arrival of the Allied forces.

[50] Id., *Civil Affairs and Military Government: North-West Europe 1944–46* (1961), p. 37.

[51] See esp. *Jakub Ł.* v. *Teofil B.*, a 1946 case about a cow which changed hands, 26 ILR 730.

independence, and the Allied occupants who were working in conjunction with the Netherlands, the (absent) colonial power in the area. In the case of *Public Prosecutor* v. *X.* (*Eastern Java*), a Temporary Court Martial at Surabaya held on 9 January 1948:

> The Commanders of an Allied Military Force occupying a territory which it had reconquered from the common enemy did not derive their powers to issue military Ordinances for such a territory from the ordinary laws in force there, but directly from the generally recognized principles of war according to which those who *de facto* exercise authority in such liberated countries are entitled to issue the necessary military regulations.[52]

There may be a case for saying that 1949 Geneva Convention IV is applicable to occupations of allied territory, as it is to the other situations covered in the broad terms of common Article 2. However, in many cases the Convention's application is likely to be restricted because of the provision in Article 4, paragraph 2, that nationals of a co-belligerent State 'shall not be regarded as protected persons while the State of which they are nationals has normal diplomatic representation in the State in whose hands they are'. Commenting on this, Pictet says: 'It is assumed in this provision that the nationals of co-belligerent states, that is to say, of allies, do not need protection under the Convention.'[53]

A quite different form of occupation of allied territory is that which occurs against the will of the occupied State—for example, when the senior partner in an alliance intervenes to prevent his co-belligerent opting out of a war. Typical cases are the German Army's take-overs in northern Italy following the announcement on 8 September 1943 that the Italian Government had surrendered; and in Hungary in March 1944. It was particularly on account of the case of Italy that Article 4, paragraph 2, of 1949 Geneva Convention IV contained the above-mentioned condition that there should be normal diplomatic representation.[54] Where normal diplomatic relations have been broken off, the inhabitants are to be regarded as protected persons. Thus coercive occupations of the territory of co-belligerents are covered by 1949 Geneva Convention IV.

4. *Armistice occupation*

This is an occupation under the terms of an armistice between belligerents. It is sometimes known as mixed occupation, or *occupatio mixta—bellica pacifica*;[55] and is quite widely viewed as one form of

[52] *Annual Digest*, 15 (1948), Case no. 176, p. 535. On the background, see Donnison, *British Military Administration in the Far East 1943–46* (1956), pp. 422–4. However, a 1945 Belgian case indicated that an allied occupying power operating under the terms of a specific agreement may have very restricted rights: below, p. 305 n. 197.

[53] Pictet, op. cit. above (p. 253 n. 11), at p. 49.

[54] Ibid.

[55] The term used by F. Llewellyn Jones in his paper 'Military Occupation of Alien Territory in Time of Peace', *Transactions of the Grotius Society*, 9 (1924), p. 150.

belligerent occupation.[56] The territory concerned may have been under belligerent occupation in the pre-armistice period, or it may be newly occupied.

An armistice can be defined as an agreement (which may be general or local) between belligerents on the suspension of hostilities. It may be of a temporary nature, like a truce or cease-fire, or it may involve a complete cessation of hostilities. The term is now most often used in the latter sense. An armistice is distinct from (though it may precede) a definite treaty of peace.[57]

At the end of the First World War there were many armistice occupations by forces of the Allied powers. For example, Western Thrace, which had been assigned to Bulgaria in 1913 under the terms of the 1913 Treaty of Bucharest, was occupied by the Allied Powers at the end of 1918 following the Armistice Convention of Prilep of 29 September 1918. Subsequently, in accordance with the Peace Treaty of Neuilly of 27 November 1919 (which entered into force on 9 August 1920), the territory was ceded to the Allied Powers—which meant in effect Greece.[58] Other examples in the same period were the occupation of part of Hungary by Serbian troops from November 1918 to August 1921; and the occupation of the left bank of the Rhine under the terms of the Armistice of 11 November 1918 until a more permanent agreement was concluded on 28 June 1919.[59]

During the two world wars, such armistice agreements as provided for occupations usually contained a clause stipulating that the occupant had all the rights of an occupying power, but they also provided for support and co-operation from the occupied country. As Bothe has indicated, this

[56] Schwarzenberger, 'The Law of Belligerent Occupation: Basic Issues', *Nordisk Tidsskrift for International Ret*, 30 (1960), p. 18.

[57] However, some armistices may put an end to a state of conflict or war. See McNair and Watts, *The Legal Effects of War* (4th edn., 1966), p. 15.

[58] The status of Western Thrace between 1918 and 1920 was one of the matters considered in the *Ottoman Debt* arbitration (1925). The Swiss arbitrator, Professor E. Borel, ruled that these were occupied territories up to 9 August 1920, and that no transfer of sovereignty took place before that date: *Reports of International Arbitral Awards*, vol. 1, pp. 554–6. Similarly in the *Thrace (Validity of Wills)* case (1925), a Greek court viewed Thrace as having been occupied (and hence Bulgarian law as having been still applicable) during the period when it was controlled by inter-allied troops, and in particular in early 1920: *Annual Digest*, 3 (1925–6), Case no. 364, p. 477.

Texts of treaties relating to Western Thrace: the 10 August 1913 Treaty of Bucharest in Parry, *The Consolidated Treaty Series*, vol. 218, p. 322; the 1918 Prilep Armistice Convention, including its four secret articles, in Falls, *Military Operations: Macedonia, from the Spring of 1917 to the End of the War* (HMSO, 1935), pp. 252–3; the 1919 Treaty of Neuilly in *American Journal of International Law*, 14 (1920), Supplement, p. 185; the 10 August 1920 Treaty of Sèvres concerning Thrace, by which the Allies ceded the territory in question to Greece, in *League of Nations Treaty Series*, vol. 28, p. 226. The main events affecting the status of Western Thrace were usefully summarized in the *Lighthouses* arbitration between France and Greece (1956): 23 ILR 659 at pp. 666–9.

[59] On the Serbian occupation of part of Hungary, see the case of *I. Vétek* v. *N. Dürnbacher & Co.* in *Annual Digest*, 4 (1927–8), Case no. 386, p. 566.

On the armistice occupation of the Rhineland see the excellent discussion of legal aspects in Fraenkel, op. cit. above (p. 262 n. 42), at pp. 183–9. Note particularly his disquiet (p. 188) at the German view which down-played the applicability of the law of belligerent occupation. For a text of the 1918 armistice see Parry, *The Consolidated Treaty Series*, vol. 224, p. 286.

may suggest that the rights and duties of an occupying power can be determined by two different sources—the law on occupations, and the terms of the armistice. He expresses some scepticism as to whether the status of foreign forces was in fact different in each of these cases.[60]

Since the Second World War, the various armistice agreements which have been concluded have not specifically provided for occupations of territory, although some (for example, after the 1973 Middle East war) were followed by a continuation of an already existing occupation.[61]

It is widely accepted that the Hague Regulations apply to armistice occupations. Some modifications might be included in the armistice agreement, but the Hague Regulations remain important, at the very least, as a set of minimum standards.[62]

The 1949 Geneva Conventions are clearly applicable to armistice occupations.[63] They set some limits to the modifications which can be contained in any agreement (including an armistice agreement) between the parties.[64] However, if an armistice involved a general close of military operations, and lasted for more than one year, then under Article 6 some provisions of Convention IV could cease to apply.[65]

5. *Post-surrender occupation*

This is defined here as the occupation of a country which after taking part in an armed conflict has surrendered completely, and neither continues to maintain armed forces in the field, nor has any allies fighting to redress the situation.[66] It may have a less precarious and temporary character than belligerent occupation. A number of particular types of occupation can be regarded as variants of post-surrender occupation. They include *occupation subsequent to unconditional surrender*; and *post-debellatio occupation*, which can be said to occur when at the end of a war a country is so completely defeated that it has virtually ceased to exist as a State.[67]

[60] Bothe, 'Occupation after Armistice', *Encyclopaedia of Public International Law*, vol. 4 (1982), p. 63.

[61] Ibid., pp. 63–4.

[62] Spaight, op. cit. above (p. 262 n. 42), at pp. 245–8; Feilchenfeld, op. cit. above (p. 261 n. 39), at pp. 6, 110–14; von Glahn, op. cit. above (p. 261 n. 39), at p. 28; UK Manual, op. cit. above (p. 256 n. 20), at p. 130.

[63] Under the first paragraph of common Article 2 of the 1949 Conventions: Pictet, op. cit. above (p. 253 n. 11), at pp. 20–2, 62, 63, etc.

[64] That special agreements may not undermine the principles of the 1949 Geneva Convention IV is spelt out clearly in Article 7; Article 11, para. 5; and Article 47. For an explanation of Articles 7 and 47, confirming the Convention's relevance to armistice occupations, see ibid., pp. 67 and 274–5. See also Castrén, *The Present Law of War and Neutrality* (1954), p. 214.

[65] Pictet is explicit that Article 6 applies to armistices: op. cit. above (p. 253 n. 11), at p. 63. This article is discussed further below, pp. 271–3.

[66] Von Glahn calls this 'hostile occupation': op. cit. above (p. 261 n. 39), at p. 27.

[67] The term *debellatio*, which is the same as 'subjugation', is not always used quite consistently. Schwarzenberger points to its basic meaning when he suggests that it is the process whereby 'armed conflicts are terminated unilaterally by the destruction of a party to the conflict as an independent and organized entity': *International Law as Applied by International Courts and Tribunals*, vol. 2 (1968),

Where a State's forces surrender, but there are still allies who continue the struggle, there is an ordinary belligerent occupation, not a post-surrender occupation as discussed here.[68] In cases where there is an actual instrument of surrender or of capitulation, the legal framework of a post-surrender occupation is likely to be significantly influenced by its terms.[69]

A country's defeat and collapse does not necessarily lead to occupation; or it may lead to occupation of a rather special kind. At the end of the First World War, events at the time of the collapse of the Austro-Hungarian Empire raised the question of whether, within a disintegrating State, and before the entry into force of the various peace treaties, any new political or military entities which emerged within the former empire could be considered in any sense the occupants of the territory which they held, or could at least be subject to the application by way of analogy of the law on occupations. Some cases arising from these events indicate a tendency to view at least part of section III of the Hague Regulations as applicable to the new authorities exercising power in one part or another of the former empire. See particularly the decision in the *Danube Shipping* arbitration (1921), in which it was held that although the situation in the former territory of the Hapsburg Empire at the end of the First World War was not an occupation in the normal sense, and the letter of the Hague provisions did not apply, Articles 46 and 53 should be examined 'to see if they furnish a useful analogy'. However, in the event, the arbitrator decided that the character of the vessels concerned was such that they did not fall within the scope of these articles of the Hague Regulations.[70]

The Allied occupations of Germany and Japan after the Second World War provide much clearer examples of post-surrender occupations, and also of reluctance to be formally bound by the Hague Regulations. Here, as well as elsewhere, the victors desired to exercise their power freely, and in particular to make drastic political and other changes in the defeated States. The basic character of these occupations raised issues to which relatively little attention had been paid by international lawyers. Previously, it had sometimes been assumed that the normal consequence of a State's surrender was its subjugation or possibly even annexation by the

p. 730. See also pp. 63 and 320. Similarly, Alwyn V. Freeman has called it 'annihilation of the enemy's armed forces together with destruction of its government resulting in disappearance of the enemy state as an international person': *American Journal of International Law*, 40 (1946), p. 796. Pictet suggests that the absence of a treaty is a main characteristic when he defines *debellatio* as 'the end of an armed conflict which results in the occupation of the whole of the enemy's territory and the cessation of all hostilities, without a legal instrument of any kind': op. cit. above (p. 253 n. 11), at p. 62 n. But Baxter clearly states that a *debellatio* can take the form of a peace treaty: 'The Duty of Obedience to the Belligerent Occupant', this *Year Book*, 27 (1950), p. 236.

[68] Stone, op. cit. above (p. 250 n. 3), at p. 696.

[69] See, e.g., the discussion of the effects of surrender as the issue had arisen in the post-war Shanghai case *Trial of Lothar Eisentrager (alias Ludwig Ehrhardt) and Others* (1947): United Nations War Crimes Commission, *Law Reports of Trials of War Criminals*, vol. 14, pp. 18–22. See also ibid., vol. 15, pp. 131–2.

[70] *Reports of International Arbitral Awards*, vol. 1, pp. 105, 108. See also the comparable issues raised in *Kotra and Others* v. *Czechoslovakia* (1934), *Annual Digest*, 7 (1933–4), Case no. 221, p. 509.

victor; but this did not happen in the bulk of German or Japanese territory at the end of the Second World War, nor in a number of other instances at that time of post-surrender occupations. What took place instead, especially in Germany and Japan, were occupations which went beyond the letter of the Hague Regulations, yet fell short of annexation or assumption of sovereignty.

With respect to the occupation of Germany which began in 1944–5, a legal memorandum to the Foreign Office in March 1945 set out the basic problem:

> The truth is that the Allies are dealing with a situation without previous parallel; they are proposing to exercise their authority with respect to Germany in order to expel the Nazi system and its manifestations completely and utterly, and to continue this process indefinitely until it has succeeded. These objects, far ranging as they are, do not necessarily amount to annexation and the positive and complete transfer of sovereignty whether by cession or by conquest. But they do undoubtedly go far beyond the exercise of military occupation as limited by previous international law.[71]

After the Germans accepted unconditional surrender on 7 May 1945, Germany was completely occupied by the Allies. What then was the position so far as the application of the Hague Regulations was concerned?[72] On this point Jennings, in his authoritative 1946 article 'Government in Commission', argued persuasively that the law of belligerent occupation had been designed to serve two purposes: first, to protect the sovereign rights of the legitimate government of the occupied territory, and secondly, to protect the inhabitants of the occupied territory from being exploited for the prosecution of the occupant's war. Neither of these purposes had much bearing on the situation the Allies faced:

> Thus the whole *raison d'être* of the law of belligerent occupation is absent in the circumstances of the Allied occupation of Germany, and to attempt to apply it would be a manifest anachronism.[73]

Friedmann adopted a very similar position:

> Nor could even the widest interpretation of the rules of warfare bring the powers claimed and exercised by the allies in Germany within the scope of belligerent occupation ... Even the most elastic interpretation could not bring the wholesale abolition of laws, the denazification procedure, the arrest of thousands of individuals, the introduction of sweeping social reforms, the expropriation of industries, and above all the sweeping changes in the territorial and constitutional

[71] 'Opinion of the Lord Chancellor and the Law Officers of the Crown', March 1945, Public Record Office FO 371/50759 (U 1949). On the British discussion about the legal status of Germany, see Donnison, *Central Organisation*, op. cit. above (p. 264 n. 49), at pp. 125–36.

[72] The position before 7 May 1945 is widely viewed as one of normal belligerent occupation. However, as some anti-Nazi measures taken early in the belligerent phase show, there was not a completely sharp distinction between the two stages of the occupation of Germany.

[73] This *Year Book*, 23 (1946), pp. 135–6.

structure of Germany within the rights of belligerent occupation. These are symbols of sovereign government, yet it is of the essence of belligerent occupation that it does not claim such powers.

. . .

It is not . . . surprising that International Law—inadequate to cope with many problems of our days—should not be fully equipped to deal with an entirely unprecedented situation.[74]

The majority of court decisions took the line that the Allied occupation of Germany after its surrender was not subject to the Hague Regulations.[75] For example, in *Dalldorf and Others* v. *Director of Public Prosecutions* a Control Commission Court of Appeal in the British Zone of Germany ruled on 31 December 1949 that Section III of the Hague Regulations was not applicable to the Allied occupation of Germany after unconditional surrender.[76]

These views as to the legal status of Germany after surrender were by no means uncontested.[77] Nor did such views mean that there was a complete international legal vacuum. Even the post-surrender phase may be said to have been subject to 'such rules of international law as limit the right of any Government to commit acts which constitute crimes against peace and crimes against humanity'.[78]

The 1949 Geneva Conventions appear to have substantially changed the situation. Under common Article 2 it would seem that they are applicable to post-surrender occupations, at least for as long as a state of war between the parties continues—i.e. until there is a proper treaty of peace.[79] In these occupations, as in others, there are limits to the modifications which can be contained in any agreement between the parties.[80] However, under Article 6, which is discussed further below, the application of 1949 Geneva Convention IV may be modified in occupied territory one year after the general close of military operations.

Writers have increasingly inclined to the view that post-surrender occupations have been brought within the scope of the law on occupations. True, in 1952 Oppenheim's *International Law* still took the view that post-surrender occupations are not subject to the customary and conventional rules relating to occupations.[81] Von Glahn agrees with Oppenheim that the Hague Regulations were not applicable to Germany after 1945, but suggests that in future cases the 1949 Geneva Convention IV would be

[74] Friedmann, *The Allied Military Government of Germany* (1947), pp. 65, 67.

[75] For a brief listing of cases see Greenspan, op. cit. above (p. 262 n. 42), at p. 216 n.

[76] *Annual Digest*, 16 (1949), Case no. 159, p. 435.

[77] See the excellent survey of the various theories as to the legal status of Germany from 1945 by Theodor Schweisfurth, in *Encyclopaedia of Public International Law*, vol. 3 (1982), pp. 196–7.

[78] Ibid.

[79] Pictet, op. cit. above (p. 253 n. 11), at p. 22.

[80] 1949 Geneva Convention IV, Articles 7, 47, etc.

[81] Oppenheim, op. cit. above (p. 256 n. 20), at pp. 216, 552–4, 602–5. In none of these passages is there any mention of the 1949 Geneva Convention IV, although it has a bearing on the matter.

applicable.[82] The United Kingdom military manual, and also Greenspan, take a similar line on the applicability of 1949 Geneva Convention IV.[83] Schwarzenberger suggests that in international customary law the only limitations on a victor's discretion are those imposed by the standard of civilization; but he goes on to suggest that even an instrument of unconditional surrender may not free a party from such multilateral engagements as the 1949 Geneva Convention IV, or even possibly the Hague Regulations.[84]

In summary, there have been two main schools of thought about the application of occupation law to post-surrender occupations. The first is that such occupations are quite different in character from belligerent occupations, particularly because they may involve making fundamental and permanent changes altering the whole character of the defeated State. Hence the law on occupations is seen as largely irrelevant. The second view is to accept that post-surrender occupations are bound to be different from belligerent occupations, but nevertheless to urge the applicability of the law on occupations, which is after all capable of being adjusted to a wide variety of circumstances. The facts that 1949 Geneva Convention IV adopts such an approach; that certain derogations can sometimes be permitted (as in the 'unless absolutely prevented' proviso in Hague Regulations Article 43); and that there is some room for special agreements between the parties, all tend to reinforce the second view.

6. *Occupation one year after military operations*

Some occupations continue for a very long time after the end of the fighting, invasion, etc., with which they began. Lengthy occupations of this kind can give rise to special problems, both practical and legal. Also, certain provisions of occupation law—particularly those based on a presumption of a continuing armed conflict—may lose their relevance.

The 1949 Geneva Convention IV, Article 6, paragraph 3, provided that in occupied territory the Convention shall cease to apply one year after the general close of military operations: after that time, to the extent that the occupying power exercises the functions of government in occupied territory, it is only obliged to observe a list of forty-three articles of the 159-article Convention. However, these forty-three articles do include no less than twenty-three of the thirty-two articles of that part of the Convention—section III—which deals most specifically with occupied territories. The forty-three articles which remain in force are important, covering as they do such matters as the humane treatment of protected persons.

[82] Von Glahn, op. cit. above (p. 261 n. 39), at pp. 281, 283. On p. 27 he says of post-surrender and other types of occupation: 'Unless regulated in advance by treaty with the government involved, the occupant would appear to be bound by the provisions of the Hague Regulations and subsequent international lawmaking treaties.'

[83] UK Manual, op. cit. above (p. 256 n. 20), at p. 140 n.; Greenspan, op. cit. above (p. 262 n. 42), at pp. 216–17, 224–7.

[84] Schwarzenberger, op. cit. above (p. 267 n. 67), at pp. 318–19.

The 'one year after' provision was much debated at the 1949 Diplomatic Conference.[85] Pictet states that in drawing up this provision 'the delegates naturally had in mind the cases of Germany and Japan'.[86] The curtailment of the application of parts of the Convention seems to have derived from a reasonable, though hardly infallible, belief that after the cessation of hostilities a time would come when the full application of the Convention was no longer justified, especially if most of the governmental and administrative duties carried out at one time by the occupying power had been handed over to the authorities of the occupied territory. For example, Pictet defended those provisions of Article 6 on the grounds that

> . . . if the Occupying Power is victorious, the occupation may last more than a year, but as hostilities have ceased, stringent measures against the civilian population will no longer be justified.[87]

The 1977 Geneva Protocol I abrogates the 'one year after' provisions as outlined above. Article 3 simply states that 'the application of the Conventions and of this Protocol shall cease . . . in the case of occupied territories, on the termination of the occupation . . .'. Bothe, Partsch and Solf say of this abrogation:

> Article 6 (3) of the Fourth Convention . . . was a special *ad hoc* provision for certain actual cases, namely the occupation of Germany and Japan after World War II. There is no reason to continue to keep in force such provisions designed for specific historic cases. In 1972 the majority of government experts expressed a wish to abolish these time limits.[88]

The abrogation of the 'one year after' rule may reflect in part the proper desire of the international community to maintain the full applicabilty of the law on occupations to areas occupied by Israel since 1967. However, the idea that the law on occupations—or major parts of it—can remain applicable more or less indefinitely, leaves open some disturbing possibilities. For example, one or another party to a conflict might refuse to negotiate a peace treaty, and at the same time seek to have aspects of the status quo within occupied territory preserved. According to Israeli interpretations, this is what Arab States have sought to do in the Middle East since 1967. In this view, the law on occupations is being invoked as an enduring safety net against the consequences of diplomatic immobilism. On the other hand, Israel may see some advantage in the continuation of the status of occupied territory, because this arrangement provides a legal basis for treating the Arab inhabitants of the territories entirely separately

[85] See, e.g., *Final Record 1949*, vol. IIA, pp. 623–5.

[86] Pictet, op. cit. above (p. 253 n. 11), at p. 62.

[87] Ibid., p. 63. Pictet goes on to suggest that in cases where there has been no military resistance, no state of war and no armed conflict, the Convention would remain fully applicable as long as the occupation lasts. However, it is far from clear (*a*) whether this was the intention of the negotiators; and (*b*) what the logic is in treating such occupations differently.

[88] Bothe, Partsch and Solf, op. cit. above (p. 254 n. 16), at p. 59. See also p. 57.

from the citizens of Israel: such a view suggests that the law on occupations could potentially pave the way for a kind of *apartheid*. Whatever the views on such matters, it remains the case that occupations of exceptional length do expose certain inadequacies in a body of law essentially intended for much briefer and more precarious periods of foreign military control.

(b) *Peacetime*

The dividing line between war and peace has never been easy to identify: armed conflicts have often occurred between States without any formal declaration of war, and military interventions have often occurred without the kind of hostilities we associate with the word 'war'.[89] Since 1945 the dividing line between war and peace may have become less significant than it was before, owing partly to the use of the more widely applicable phrase 'use of force' rather than 'war' in the United Nations Charter and subsequent treaties.

Although the types of occupation discussed below belong mainly to peacetime, it is obvious that they may occur shortly before a war, or in its aftermath; or indeed these (or closely analogous types of occupation) could occur in a particular territory or country at the same time as other States are involved in some wider war or armed conflict. Moreover, some 'peacetime' occupations may be very reasonably viewed as crimes against peace, threats to the peace or acts of war.[90]

Two main types of peacetime occupation can be identified, namely, forcible peacetime occupation and peacetime occupation by consent—i.e. resulting from an agreement between the parties.[91] Sometimes the term pacific occupation (*occupatio pacifica*) is applied to both these types of peacetime occupation,[92] sometimes exclusively to the latter type.[93]

Although peacetime occupations have varied particularly widely, and have arisen from a variety of legal bases, some more or less common features may be identified. Examining various nineteenth- and early twentieth-century peacetime occupations, Jones suggested that they often

[89] For a wealth of supporting evidence see Maurice, *Hostilities Without Declaration of War: An Historical Abstract of the Cases in Which Hostilities Have Occurred Between Civilized Powers Without Declaration of War or Warning* (1883); Grob, *The Relativity of War and Peace: A Study in Law, History, and Politics* (1949).

[90] For an excellent discussion see Brownlie, op. cit. above (p. 250 n. 3), at pp. 84–8, 211–12, 384–400. Note particularly the judgment of 14 April 1949 in *US* v. *Weizsaecker and Others*, also cited below (p. 276 n. 102).

[91] Robin, *Des Occupations militaires en dehors des occupations de guerre* (Paris, 1913), pp. 9–11, 719–20, etc. For the most part this work is more interesting for its wealth of historical material than for its sometimes eccentric legal classifications.

[92] *Occupatio pacifica* seemed to be used in this broad sense by Jones in his 1924 article 'Military Occupation of Alien Territory in Time of Peace', loc. cit. above (p. 265 n. 55), at p. 150, but see his note of caution on p. 161. See also Bothe in *Encyclopaedia of Public International Law*, vol. 4, pp. 67–8.

[93] 'Pacific occupation is based on a special agreement or treaty covering the rights and duties of the occupant': Fraenkel, op. cit. above (p. 262 n. 42), at p. 183.

last for a very long time: they may be provisional but they are not necessarily precarious. He further said:

> In the case of pacific occupation it is clear that the rights of the occupant are very much curtailed as compared with those of a belligerent occupant. In the latter case the occupant is an enemy, and has to protect himself against attack on the part of the forces of the occupied State, and he is justified in adopting measures which would justly be considered unwarranted in the case of pacific occupation . . . Belligerent military occupation is now largely regulated by the provisions of the Hague Convention, 1907, and obviously a pacific military occupant can have no powers more extensive than those laid down in the Articles of this Convention.[94]

Analysing judgments arising from military occupations in peacetime, or during an armed conflict not amounting to a war, McNair and Watts indicate that 'there seems to have been a tendency to act upon a basis broadly analogous to that of a belligerent occupation during a war'.[95] The terms of the 1949 Geneva Conventions, and particularly common Article 2, must reinforce such a tendency. They apply to an occupation arising from an armed conflict not constituting a war, and also to other cases of occupation of a territory of a party, even if the occupation meets with no armed resistance.[96]

7. *Forcible peacetime occupation*

This is the occupation of all or part of the territory of a State without the previous consent of the government, but also without causing the outbreak of an armed conflict with that State. Usually it is because the invader has made an implicit or explicit threat to use force, and military resistance against invasion appears hopeless, that this kind of invasion is militarily unopposed. Such interventions have been quite common in the twentieth century and have occurred in a variety of circumstances.

The Hague Regulations have been widely viewed as applicable to forcible peacetime occupations. Since such occupations are by definition not governed in advance by any specific bilateral agreement between occupant and occupied, there has naturally been a strong tendency to apply to this type of occupation the existing body of international law governing belligerent occupations. As regards the invasion of Bulgaria by the Romanian army in 1913, which was a military operation without

[94] Jones, loc. cit. above (p. 265 n. 55), at pp. 159–60. On the general issue of international rules applicable to peacetime occupations see also Robin, op. cit. above (p. 273 n. 91), at pp. 13–15, 630, 722, 731–2; Feilchenfeld, op. cit. above (p. 261 n. 39), at p. 116; Castrén, op. cit. above (p. 267 n. 64), at p. 214; Debbasch, *L'Occupation militaire: pouvoirs reconnus aux forces armées hors de leur territoire national* (1962), pp. 1, 85–7, etc.

[95] McNair and Watts, op. cit. above (p. 266 n. 57), at p. 423. Many of the judgments which they examined in the preceding pages arose from what are here included under the heading of 'peacetime occupations'.

[96] The 1947 Conference of Government Experts had been even more explicit that the Conventions should be applicable to 'cases of occupation of territories in the absence of any state of war': Pictet, op. cit. above (p. 253 n. 11), at p. 18.

any fighting, Grob (discussing the matter hypothetically) favoured the applicability of the Hague Regulations.[97]

Courts have generally supported such a view of forcible peacetime occupations. Thus in a case during the Franco-Belgian occupation of the Ruhr area of Germany in 1923–5, it seems to have been accepted by both German and French parties that the Hague Regulations were applicable, even if there was some inevitable disagreement about how they should be interpreted.[98]

The *locus classicus* of the applicablity of the Hague Regulations to forcible peacetime occupation is the German occupation of Bohemia and Moravia, which had started in March 1939, six months before the outbreak of the Second World War. The International Military Tribunal at Nuremberg said in its judgment in 1946 that the rules of land warfare (including of course the Hague Regulations) applied to the occupation of Bohemia and Moravia, because 'these territories were never added to the Reich, but a mere protectorate was established over them'.[99]

Although the Nuremberg judgment did thus assert the applicability of the Hague rules in Bohemia and Moravia, it did not solve all problems relating to the status of territories occupied in peacetime. For example, the IMT did not explicitly spell out what the status of Bohemia and Moravia had been between the invasion in March 1939 and the outbreak of war in September, a question which was not essential to the case before it. A reasonable inference is that the Hague rules were applicable from the start of that occupation. Such a view on the status of occupied Czechoslovakia had already been taken in August 1943 by the Supreme Court of Victoria, Australia, in the case of ***Anglo-Czechoslovak and Prague Credit Bank*** v. ***Janssen***, in which the court expressed the view that the same rules applied in a military occupation in time of peace as in a belligerent occupation.[100]

The matter of the legal status of Austria, occupied by Germany on 12 March 1938, is complicated by several facts, including: (*a*) that there was a last-minute telegram of invitation, though only from the Interior Minister, and it hardly disguised the reality that Austria was in the process of yielding to brute force; and (*b*) on 13 March Austria was declared a part of the German Reich. There have been several legal theories about this occupation. Clute has expressed scepticism as to whether post-Anschluss Austria is properly viewed as a case of belligerent occupation, and has said that none of the terms applied to this situation seems adequate.[101] It may

[97] Grob, op. cit. above (p. 273 n. 89), at pp. 280–1.

[98] See the report of the cases of *In re Thyssen and Others* and *In re Krupp and Others*, in *Annual Digest*, 2 (1923–4), Case no. 191, pp. 327–8. A critical journalist's account of these two cases is Gedye, *The Revolver Republic* (1930), pp. 102–3.

[99] *The Trial of German Major War Criminals* (London, 1946–51), vol. 22, p. 467. For a text of Hitler's proclamation of 16 March 1939 on the legal and constitutional status of Bohemia and Moravia, see *Keesing's Contemporary Archives*, p. 3486.

[100] *Annual Digest*, 12 (1943–5), Case no. 11, p. 47.

[101] Clute, op. cit. above (p. 258 n. 28), at p. 21.

be that it should have been categorized as an occupation, but in fact it was not widely so viewed, and to the extent that there was not the sharp conflict of allegiance characteristic of most occupations there would have been little point in such a categorization. Post-war decisions indicate an understandable reluctance to view Austria as having been an occupied country. The question of the applicability of the Hague Regulations was not directly tackled by the International Military Tribunal at Nuremberg, but it did come up in other cases. A post-war United States Military Tribunal ruled that the Hague Regulations were not applicable to Austria 1938–45, but added:

> In so ruling, we do not ignore the force of the argument that property situated in a weak nation which falls a victim to the aggressor because of incapacity to resist should receive a degree of protection equal to that in cases of belligerent occupation when actual warfare has existed.[102]

Whatever uncertainties there may be in relation to some past episodes, the present situation is clearer. In accordance with its common Article 2, second paragraph, 1949 Geneva Convention IV is applicable to forcible peacetime occupations. As Bothe has said, 'the notion of "pacific" coercive occupation as distinguished from belligerent occupation does not have any current practical significance'.[103]

The Soviet-led occupation of Czechoslovakia begining on 20–1 August 1968 was a fairly clear example of forcible peacetime occupation, but the application of the Geneva Conventions was little discussed in that case—no doubt partly because the Czechoslovak governmental and legal system continued to function effectively (albeit under obvious constraints) in the months and years after the invasion.[104]

8. *Peacetime occupation by consent*

The idea of 'peacetime occupation by consent' raises problems: if foreign forces are in a country in peacetime, in accordance with an agreement with its government, there is bound to be a presumption against using such terminology to describe the situation: a troop stationing agreement does not create an occupation.[105] In addition, there are bound to be doubts about the relevance of the law on occupations, essentially a

[102] *US* v. *Krauch and Others*, judgment of 29 July 1948, *Annual Digest*, 15 (1948), Case no. 218, p. 672. However, see also the judgments in *US* v. *Weizsaecker and Others*, in which it was held that the German invasions of Austria and Czechoslovakia 'were tantamount to, and may be treated as, a declaration of war': ibid. 16 (1949), Case no. 118, p. 347; and in *US* v. *Uhl*, in which evidence of United States recognition of the consolidation of Austria with Germany was presented: ibid. 12 (1943–5), Case no. 8, pp. 23–9.

[103] *Encyclopaedia of Public International Law*, vol. 4, p. 68.

[104] For a characterization of the Czechoslovak situation as a 'Soviet-led invasion and occupation', see the statements of United States Representative Herbert Reis in the United Nations Committee on Principles of International Law, published in *Department of State Bulletin*, 14 October 1968, pp. 394–401.

[105] Below, pp. 297–8.

part of the laws of war, to a situation characterized both by the absence of armed conflict and by the positive fact of an agreement between the parties.

However, the idea of peacetime occupation by consent is not entirely devoid of meaning or practical importance. It has long been recognized as a distinct type. Sometimes, as noted above, the term 'pacific occupation' (*occupatio pacifica*) has been applied exclusively to this type. Others have preferred the rather more specific term 'conventional occupation'; or, where it is intended as a means of safeguarding the withdrawal of armed forces from foreign territory following the conclusion of a peace treaty, it may be called an 'evacuation occupation'.[106] Whatever term is used, a key distinguishing feature of such an occupation is that it takes place on the basis of a valid agreement or treaty, not obtained by duress against the negotiators, in which the States provide in advance for the occupation of all or part of the territory of one of them. Such an occupation may sometimes be intended as a guarantee that the State whose territory is occupied will execute the terms of a treaty. It will normally only be considered an occupation to the extent that there is an identifiable foreign military command structure actually exercising authority in the territory.

As with other types of occupation involving an element of consent, the invitation, agreement or treaty which brings such an occupation into being is likely to be an important means of stipulating the terms of that occupation, and is likely to vary greatly according to different circumstances. Some writers have gone so far as to suggest that the agreement in question is the only basis for determining the terms of a peacetime occupation by consent.[107]

Peacetime occupations by consent are now fairly rare. One often-cited example is the occupation of the left bank of the Rhine by the Allied and Associated Powers under the terms of the Versailles Treaty signed on 28 June 1919 and of the separate Rhineland Agreement of the same date. This is hardly a paradigmatic example, as it was the continuation of an already existing armistice occupation. The purpose of continuing this occupation of part of Germany was largely to ensure Germany's fulfilment of the provisions of the Treaty of Versailles. The applicability of the Hague Regulations to this occupation was the subject of different interpretations. There was a tendency to argue as to whether the Rhineland Agreement, or the Hague Convention, was the source of the occupants' authority, with the Germans wanting the occupants to have fewer powers than those laid down in the Hague, and the French wanting as many or more.[108] The

[106] Both these terms are used by Robin, op. cit. above (p. 273 n. 91), at pp. 10, 11, 15; and by von Glahn, op. cit. above (p. 261 n. 39), at p. 27.

[107] Robin comes fairly close to this position: op. cit. above (p. 273 n. 91), at pp. 13, 15, 722, etc. Schwarzenberger argues this line on general grounds, without at this point citing cases or authorities: op. cit. above (p. 267 n. 67), at p. 321.

[108] Fraenkel, op. cit. above (p. 262 n. 42), at pp. 100, 184, 192, 199. The text of the Rhineland Agreement is in an Appendix.

Hague Regulations were still important in a number of specific ways. First, they had assisted in working out the terms of the initial agreement: indeed, Article 6 of the Rhineland Agreement explicitly referred to the 1907 Hague Convention. Thereafter they were useful as a stopgap, in matters where problems arose which were not covered by the initial agreement.[109] Courts took the line that the rules drawn up at The Hague were valid not only in regard to an occupation 'based solely on force and on disregard of treaties', but also, *a fortiori*, in regard to an occupation 'which was carried out in virtue of a treaty . . .'.[110]

A very different type of peacetime occupation by consent derives from the practice of sending troops into a country on the basis of an invitation from a host government, and thereafter taking over important administrative or leadership functions in that country. Although those directly involved are likely to find other terms for the situation, the end result may be so similar to a foreign occupation that it might reasonably be so viewed, and the law on occupations might reasonably be regarded as applicable. Take, for example, a deeply divided and weak country, facing civil war. It has an unpopular government with a clear external ideological orientation, which invites in a sympathetic superpower ally. That ally then largely dominates indigenous political developments, and there are even allegations that it had complicity in the assassination of the embarrassingly unpopular head of the government which had invited it in. It also gets deeply involved in counter-insurgency operations against the regime's opponents. This is a rough approximation of the situation in Afghanistan since the Soviet intervention of December 1979.[111] It also bears some similarities to the situation of South Vietnam at the time of United States involvement between the mid-1950s and 1973. The international element in such conflicts appears to be so marked that the better developed body of international law governing international armed conflicts and occupations may well be viewed as applicable.

A central difficulty of applying the law on occupations to situations of this type is likely to be the argument to the effect that the conflict is basically internal, and that foreign forces, acting by invitation, are supposedly not occupants. So far as 1949 Geneva Convention IV is

[109] See, e.g., Feilchenfeld, op. cit. above (p. 261 n. 39), at pp. 118–19.

[110] Judgment of the Military Court of the Belgian Army of Occupation in the Rhineland in the case of *In re Boulanger*, 19 April 1923. See also the same court's earlier judgment in the case of *Auditeur Militaire* v. *Reinhardt and Others*: 'Legally there can be a military occupation even in cases where there is no war properly so-called; there is nevertheless an *occupatio bellica*': *Annual Digest*, 2 (1923–4), Case no. 239, pp. 441, 442.

[111] The situation in Afghanistan has been criticized in successive United Nations resolutions as one of 'foreign armed intervention', without the actual word 'occupation' being used. See, e.g., GA Resolutions 36/34 of 18 November 1981, and 37/37 of 29 November 1982. However, many governments have referred to this situation as an occupation. For example, on 13 July 1982 the Parliamentary Under-Secretary of State, Foreign and Commonwealth Office, wrote that Britain and China 'have similar views on such international issues as the Soviet occupation of Afghanistan and the Vietnamese occupation of Cambodia': this *Year Book*, 53 (1982), p. 353.

concerned, there are two possible answers to this problem. First, Articles 7 and 47 establish that any special agreements (for example, between the authorities of the occupied territories and the occupying power) may not adversely affect the situation of protected persons. It appears that these articles can refer to agreements concluded before as well as during hostilities;[112] and presumably, therefore, before an occupation also. A second and less legalistic answer might be to assert that the Convention embodies important general rules for the protection of civilians from a foreign military power in whose hands they are, and these rules should be faithfully observed irrespective of whether the situation is designated as an 'occupation' or as something else.

(c) *Other Possible Categories*

The types of occupation discussed below can occur in wartime or in peacetime. In every case the actual historical examples mentioned could also fit into one or more of the eight categories already considered.

9. *Occupation of territory whose status is disputed or uncertain*

Many invasions and occupations take place in territories whose previous status was something less than full and internationally accepted sovereignty. It is sometimes claimed that the law on occupations is not formally applicable to such cases, on the grounds that the Hague and Geneva Conventions talk about the occupation of the territory of a hostile State, or of a high contracting party. What if the status of the territory is more confused, or is the subject of competing claims? Throughout this century territorial disputes have often preceded or accompanied military occupations, as illustrated by the cases mentioned earlier of the Greek occupation of Ottoman territories after 1912–13 and the Allied occupation of Western Thrace in 1918–20. In the contemporary world, four principal forms of occupation-cum-territorial dispute may be noted.

First, it may simply be asserted by a State with irredentist claims that the territory which is the subject of dispute is occupied. For example, Japanese leaders of all political persuasions have for a long time, and especially since the early 1970s, called for the return of some or all of four islands at the southern end of the Kuril chain—namely, the Habomais, Shikotan, Kunashir and Iturup—which were occupied by the Soviet Union between 29 August and 4 September 1945. A 'Northern Territories Day' has been marked in Japan by rallies every year since 1981. Often the islands are referred to in Japanese political statements as occupied. However, since 20 September 1945 the Soviet Union has viewed these islands as an integral part of its territory; these islands are the subject of exceptionally tangled territorial disputes; and no Japanese live there now, because the 17,000 Japanese residents had all fled or been forcibly

[112] Pictet, op. cit. above (p. 253 n. 11), at pp. 67–8, 274–5.

'repatriated' to Japan proper by 1949. Thus, whatever the position was in 1945, the law on occupations—which in any case has little to say which is relevant to the actual current situation on the islands—is bound to be viewed by the USSR as inapplicable today.[113]

Secondly, States sometimes invade territory which they have long claimed, and then find themselves in the position of occupant of what they assert to be their own territory. For example, there had been a long-standing dispute between the United Kingdom and Argentina over title to the Falkland Islands before the Argentine invasion of 2 April 1982 and the consequent Argentine occupation. The Argentine authorities saw their action as a reclaiming of national territory: but there does not appear to have been any claim that the laws of war (including the law on occupations) were not applicable. The facts that the inhabitants were clearly foreign so far as the Argentines were concerned, and that a struggle for the territory was continuing, strengthened the case for viewing this as an occupation.[114]

A third and quite distinct kind of situation can arise in territories where a colonial power has embarked on withdrawal. Sometimes, before a new indigenous authority has been able fully to consolidate its position or get its statehood recognized, the territory has been invaded by a neighbour.

Perhaps the clearest example of this was Indonesia's invasion of East Timor on 7 December 1975. Indonesia appears to have had no previous claim to the territory. However, it expressed alarm at the prospect of a revolutionary government there, and intervened to support a coalition of political parties which favoured integration with Indonesia.[115] The ensuing occupation, marked by numerous acts of brutality, was opposed locally by Fretilin guerrillas;[116] and was repeatedly criticized in United Nations General Assembly resolutions, which continued to assert the population's right to self-determination.[117]

A somewhat similar case, at roughly the same time, was the Moroccan intervention in Western Sahara. With Spain, the colonial power, on the

[113] The best account of the dispute concerning the 'northern territories' claimed by Japan is in Stephan, *The Kuril Islands: Russo-Japanese Frontier in the Pacific* (1974), pp. 151-247. He is critical of Japan's handling of the dispute. Other useful sources include *Keesing's Contemporary Archives*, pp. 7732, 7418, 27599, 28292; Whymant, 'Japan Steps up Fight for Return of Lost Islands', *The Guardian* (London), 8 February 1984.

[114] A useful collection of statements on legal aspects of the 1982 Falklands war is Marston, 'UK Materials on International Law 1982', this *Year Book*, 53 (1982), pp. 350-559 *passim*. United Kingdom designations of the situation on the islands after 2 April 1982 as a 'military occupation' are at pp. 351, 352.

[115] For a fine critical survey see Clark, 'The "Decolonization" of East Timor and the UN Norms on Self-Determination and Aggression', *Yale Journal of World Public Order*, 7 (1980), pp. 2-44.

[116] Amnesty International statement of 2 September 1983 to United Nations Decolonization Committee; and reports in *The Guardian* (London), 25 June and 20 July 1983. 'Fretilin' is short for Frente Revolucionaria de Timor Leste Independente.

[117] GA resolutions on East Timor have included 3485 (XXX) of 12 December 1975; 33/39 of 13 December 1978; 36/50 of 24 November 1981; and 37/30 of 23 November 1982. The word 'occupation' does not appear in these resolutions: only 'military intervention', 'continuing critical situation' and 'the humanitarian situation prevailing in the territory'.

brink of departure, an advisory opinion of the ICJ, delivered on 16 October 1975, said that the population of the area had a right to prior consultation about the future of the territory.[118] Morocco, however, asserted its claim to the territory in early November with the 'Green March', in which some 350,000 unarmed Moroccans entered the area. On 14 November a tripartite agreement was announced in which Spain agreed to hand over control to Morocco and Mauritania. In December 1975 and January 1976 Moroccan troops occupied the main towns, and the last Spanish troops left on 12 January 1976. Since then Morocco has extended its control, including areas first held by Mauritania. It has been opposed locally by the Polisario Front (supported *inter alia* by Algeria and Libya), and its policy has been heavily criticized in regional organizations and in the United Nations. For example, a 1979 General Assembly resolution referred to the 'inalienable right of the people of Western Sahara to self-determination and independence', supported the Polisario Front as 'the representative of the people of Western Sahara', and deplored 'the continuing occupation of Western Sahara by Morocco and the extension of that occupation to the territory recently evacuated by Mauritania'.[119]

Fourthly, a belligerent occupation, arising almost as a by-product of a larger international war, may be of territory whose status is not completely clear. For example, Israel had not before 1967 made any territorial claims to the West Bank and Gaza, but nor had it accepted that these territories were part of Jordan or Egypt. When it found itself in control of these territories, Israel argued that the 1949 Geneva Convention IV was not formally applicable. In support of this argument Israel repeatedly referred to the second paragraph of common Article 2, which says the Convention applies to 'occupation of the territory of a High Contracting Party'. It contended that the previous status of the occupied territory had been less clear than that, but said that it would apply the 'humanitarian provisions' of the Convention on a *de facto* basis, as well as offering to co-operate fully with the International Committee of the Red Cross.[120] The Israeli military courts likewise frequently referred to the second paragraph.[121]

[118] See *Western Sahara* advisory opinion, *ICJ Reports*, 1975, pp. 12–176. On the history of the dispute see Shaw, 'The *Western Sahara* Case', this *Year Book*, 49 (1978), pp. 119–54; Brownlie, *African Boundaries: A Legal and Diplomatic Encyclopaedia* (1979), pp. 149–58.

[119] The quotations are from GA Res. 34/37, adopted on 21 November 1979. A similar resolution, 35/19, was approved on 11 November 1980. 'Polisario' is short for Frente Popular para la Liberacion de Saguia el-Hamra y de Rio de Oro.

[120] For an authoritative Israeli statement putting forward such a viewpoint see the article by the former Military Advocate General (1961–8), then Attorney-General of Israel (1968–75), Meir Shamgar, 'The Observance of International Law in the Administered Territories', *Israel Yearbook on Human Rights*, 1 (1971), pp. 262–77. See also the refined and developed presentation in Shamgar (ed.), *Military Government in the Territories Administered by Israel, 1967–1980: The Legal Aspects*, vol. 1 (1982), pp. 13–59. For an earlier exposition of the legal status of the West Bank see Blum, 'The Missing Reversioner: Reflections on the Status of Judea and Samaria', *Israel Law Review*, 3 (1968), pp. 279–301. Blum was later appointed Israeli Permanent Representative to the United Nations.

[121] For a typical reference by a court to the second paragraph of Article 2 of the 1949 Geneva Convention IV, see the judgment of the Military Court sitting in Bethlehem on 11 August 1968 in the

The Israeli interpretation of the second paragraph of Article 2 of the 1949 Geneva Convention IV seems excessively legalistic and has been almost universally rejected.[122] Sometimes it has been rejected on grounds of general principle.[123] However, most of those who have been critical of Israel in this matter of the applicability of the Civilians Convention have, like the Israeli authorities themselves, argued their case with reference to the second paragraph of Article 2.[124] As a result the whole debate on the matter may have been on the wrong foot from the beginning. As noted above, it is in fact the *first* paragaph which applies in cases of belligerent occupation.[125] However, this does not necessarily change things greatly. Shamgar argues that even if one accepts the thesis that it is the first paragraph that applies, one still cannot disregard the reference in the second paragraph to 'the territory of a High Contracting Party', since there would be no logic in an occupation which does not meet with armed resistance being alone subject to this restrictive definition. He therefore indicates that in strictly formal terms the 1949 Geneva Convention IV is not applicable.[126] The weakness of his argument on this point is that he nowhere mentions the existence of a custom of viewing the laws of war, including the law on occupations, as formally applicable even in cases which differ in some respect from the conditions of application as spelt out in the Hague and Geneva Conventions. As far as the Israeli occupation of the West Bank and Gaza is concerned, the majority of the international community, and of international legal opinion, has not accepted that Geneva Convention IV is not formally applicable just because the previous status of the territories may have been slightly different from what those who negotiated the 1949 Geneva Convention IV may have had in mind. The 1977 Geneva Protocol I further clarifies that the 1949 Geneva Convention is applicable in such territories.[127]

case of *Military Prosecutor* v. *Zuhadi Salah Hassin Zuhad*, 47 ILR 490–1. The judge did, however, state: 'I assume that I must resort to the Convention as if it were applicable.'

[122] Of the very many GA resolutions affirming the applicability of 1949 Geneva Convention IV in the Israeli-occupied territories, one which is limited to that issue, and can thus be presumed to serve as an indication of the position taken by States on the matter, is 35/122A of 11 December 1980. The voting was 141 for, 1 against (Israel) and 1 abstention (Guatemala): *Yearbook of the United Nations*, 34 (1980), p. 430.

[123] The ICRC has taken the view, relevant to the Israeli and also to other cases, that there is an occupation (and hence the Civilians Convention is applicable) whenever during an armed conflict 'territory under the authority of one of the parties passes under the authority of an opposing party': *Israel Yearbook on Human Rights*, 1 (1971), p. 260; and International Committee of the Red Cross, *Annual Report* for 1968, 1973, 1975, 1976, 1977, 1978, etc.

[124] Of the many writings asserting the applicability of the 1949 Geneva Convention IV to the areas occupied by Israel since 1967 on the basis of the second paragraph of Article 2, see particularly one by a legal adviser of the United States State Department specializing in Middle Eastern affairs, Stephen M. Boyd, 'The Applicability of International Law to the Occupied Territories', *Israel Yearbook on Human Rights*, 1 (1971), pp. 258–61. On p. 260 he indicates that he is relying on the second paragraph of Article 2; this is confirmed in the subsequent discussion on pp. 366–7.

[125] See the text of Article 2 and the reference to Pictet's commentary on it, above, pp. 252–3.

[126] Shamgar, op. cit. above (p. 281 n. 120), at p. 40.

[127] See above, pp. 254–5 and 272–3.

A number of Israeli writers have argued that it does not matter whether the 1949 Geneva Convention IV is formally applicable or not, as Israel in any case observes the 'humanitarian provisions' of this Convention.[128] However, formal applicability versus *de facto* application is not always a distinction without a difference. This is for two reasons. First, there has never been a full clarification as to whether 'humanitarian provisions' means all of the provisions, or just those which Israel decides to apply. Secondly, the rejection of formal applicability has been frequently referred to in Israeli court proceedings, and has been one factor occasionally making the courts reluctant to base their decisions directly on 1949 Geneva Convention IV.[129] (Another quite separate consideration influencing Israeli courts has been the argument that the courts are bound by customary international law, in which category they have come to include 1907 Hague Convention IV; but not by conventional international law, in which category they include all, or at least some, of 1949 Geneva Convention IV.)[130]

Another possible case of an occupation of a territory whose status is uncertain (at least in the sense that it has never been a sovereign State) is the South African occupation of Namibia, discussed later in this article.[131]

Even from the few cases cited, it is evident that in the contemporary world the previous status of occupied territory tends to be more muddled and complex than the status which appears to have been envisaged in the provisions of the main conventions. However, this does not necessarily prevent the applicability of the law on occupations.[132] The 1977 Geneva Protocol I, Article 4, further confirms that the law is applicable even in cases where there is doubt about the legal status of the territory in question.

[128] See, e.g., the foreword by Haim H. Cohn to the booklet *The Rule of Law in the Areas Administered by Israel* (Israel National Section of the International Commission of Jurists, Tel Aviv, 1981), pp. vii–viii.

[129] See, e.g., the statement of Judge Landau of the Supreme Court in the *Beth-El* case, judgment given 15 March 1979, reprinted in Shamgar, op. cit. above (p. 281 n. 120), at p. 387.

[130] See, e.g., the articles by Nathan and Hadar in ibid., pp. 125–49 and 172–5. Also the judgments in the *Beth-El* case, ibid., pp. 377–81 and 388–90; and in the *Elon Moreh* case, ibid., pp. 419 and 438. The *Elon Moreh* case, judgment given on 22 October 1979, illustrates the potential significance of relying on the Hague rather than the Geneva rules. On the basis of Article 52 of the Hague Regulations (which deals with requisitions) the Supreme Court declared an Israeli civilian settlement near Nablus in the occupied West Bank to be illegal. It took this line mainly because there was sharply conflicting Israeli official evidence as to whether the settlement was needed for security reasons. It did not base its decision on the at least apparently relevant provision of 1949 Geneva Convention IV, Article 49, sixth paragraph: 'The Occupying Power shall not deport or transfer parts of its own civilian population into the territory it occupies.' Thus the Elon Moreh decision had little bearing on such other Israeli settlements as (*a*) did not involve requisitions, or (*b*) were declared by the Israeli authorities to be needed for security. In fact the settlement of Elon Moreh was built. It stands impressively, not far from its original site, on a hill close to and visible from Nablus.

[131] Below, pp. 291–2.

[132] Bothe in *Encyclopaedia of Public International Law*, vol. 4, pp. 64–5.

10. *Occupation with an indigenous government in post*

Although the prevailing image of military occupation is of direct and overt foreign rule, in practice occupants often work through indigenous political forces and institutions. They may leave in power the already existing government of the occupied territory; or set up a new but still indigenous government; or even assist the creation of a new supposedly sovereign State.

The first approach—permitting the existing government to remain in post and exercise the functions of government—was followed, though very imperfectly, in German-occupied Denmark between April 1940 and August 1943; in the Soviet and British occupation of Iran from 1941 to 1946; and in Czechoslovakia after the Soviet-led invasion of August 1968. Sooner or later in all these cases there were significant changes in the leadership of the State, government or ruling party, but these change were not necessarily in themselves unconstitutional. For example, when Dubcek was removed from the post of First Secretary of the Czechoslovak Communist Party in April 1969, and replaced by Husak, the change was achieved by procedures which had every appearance of formal propriety.

The second approach—encouraging the advent to power of new indigenous governmental authorities—is also quite common. The classic example is the Quisling regime in Norway between 1 February 1942 and the end of the war in 1945: this regime was the instrument of the Germans who had invaded the country in April 1940. A more recent example, in a totally different political context, occurred in Kampuchea after the Vietnamese invasion of December 1978, which promptly replaced the genocidal Pol Pot regime with a more acceptable one.[133] Such authorities established under the wing of an occupying power may be mere 'puppet governments', but they may in some cases enjoy a measure of independence, legitimacy or popular support.

The third approach is the encouragement by the occupant of the creation of new purportedly sovereign States, sometimes called 'puppet States'. Examples include the 'State of Manchukuo', set up by the Japanese in Manchuria in 1932; the 'Slovak State', set up after the Germans occupied the bulk of Czechoslovakia in March 1939;[134] and Croatia, after the German occupation of Yugoslavia in April 1941.[135] But these are extreme cases of new 'States' whose claims to be anything

[133] GA Resolutions 35/6 of 22 October 1980 and 36/5 of 21 October 1981 called the situation in Kampuchea since 1978 one of 'foreign armed intervention'. Resolution 37/6 of 28 October 1982 called it one of 'foreign armed intervention and occupation'.

[134] On Slovakia, George Kennan reported to the State Department on about 1 May 1939: 'In internal matters, it has exactly the same independence as a dog on a leash. As long as the dog trots quietly and cheerfully at his master's side—and in the same direction—he is quite free; if he starts out on any tangents of his own, he feels the pull at once': Kennan, *From Prague After Munich* (1968), p. 135.

[135] Crawford, *The Creation of States in International Law* (1979), pp. 63–4. See also his excellent discussion of the maintenance or emergence of statehood during a foreign military occupation on pp. 59–60, 68–9, 281–2.

more than the agent of the occupant were extremely weak. Other cases of the emergence of new States during foreign military occupations are not so easily dismissed. The two Germanies, already mentioned, have established their credentials as States. In Korea, following thirty-five years of Japanese rule there, United States and Soviet forces occupied the southern and northern parts of the country respectively in 1945. After the failure of various talks aimed at unification, new States were eventually proclaimed in the two halves of Korea in August and September 1948. The United States wound up its military government in the South, and in the North all Soviet forces were withdrawn by the end of the year.[136]

Where there are indigenous authorities in post in any of the several fashions indicated above, does the law on occupations apply? The clearest treaty provision on the matter is 1949 Geneva Convention IV, Article 47, which states that protected persons shall not be deprived of the benefits of the Convention 'by any change introduced, as a result of the occupation of a territory, into the institutions or government of the said territory, nor by any agreement concluded between the authorities of the occupied territories and the Occupying Power'. Pictet comments:

> It will be noted that the same clause applies both to cases where the lawful authorities in the occupied territory have concluded a derogatory agreement with the Occupying Power and to cases where that Power has installed and maintained a government in power.[137]

Where there is both an occupying power and an indigenous government, whose job is it to ensure the implementation of the law on occupations? Common sense suggests that this is a shared responsibility. However, the applicability of the law to occupations where indigenous authorities exercise control can present some special problems. Three are indicated below.

First, there is sometimes a risk that an occupying power will allow, or fail to prevent, the indigenous authorities from acting in a manner contrary to the law on occupations. This risk is particularly great in those cases where an occupant permits local leaders of sectional groups (whether regional, ethnic or sectarian) to exercise power. Yugoslavia under the Axis occupation in the Second World War provides a classic example of the disasters which can ensue: the carve-up of the country, the wielding of power by irresponsible gangs, communal violence and massacres.

Echoes of such problems arose in Lebanon following the June 1982 Israeli invasion of southern Lebanon. In contrast to their practice in areas occupied in the June 1967 war, where they promptly set up systems of military administration, in Lebanon the Israelis acted largely through local paramilitary forces of one kind or another. This policy led straight to

[136] On the occupation of Korea, see esp. Soon Sung Cho, *Korea in World Politics 1940–1950: An Evaluation of American Responsibility* (1967), pp. 61–244.

[137] Pictet, op. cit. above (p. 253 n. 11), at p. 275.

disaster in the shape of the massacres at Sabra and Shatilla camps in Beirut in September 1982. This was not just the result of operating indirectly, through local paramilitary forces (a policy which in itself was particularly questionable in a country as bitterly divided as Lebanon), but also of failing to make clear that all the provisions of the law on occupations were fully applicable to the situation.[138] Subsequently there was still a comparative lack of authoritative and clear guidance from the Israeli Government on the legal situation in the occupied areas. However, the Israeli Supreme Court confirmed in several decisions the view that Israel was the occupying power. As it said in 1983 in the *Ansar Prison* case,

> A military force may invade or enter an area in order to pass through it to its intended goal and it may leave that area without establishing any effective control. But if the military force has taken control of the area in an effective and workable manner, then even though its presence in such area is limited in time or its intention is to set up no more than a temporary military control, the situation thereby created is one to which the rules of warfare dealing with belligerent occupation apply. Furthermore, the application of the third chapter of the Hague Rules or of the parallel instructions in the Fourth [Geneva] Convention are not conditioned upon the establishment of a special organizational framework in the form of a Military Government . . .
>
> Allowing the former government to act does not alter the fact that the military force is maintaining an effective military control in the area, nor does it relieve the occupant from the responsibilities for the consequences of such acts as far as the rules of warfare are concerned.[139]

A second and somewhat different problem of indirect control is that, in some occupations at least, there may be room for doubt as to whether international law should seek to govern a wide range of aspects of the relations between indigenous authorities and their own subjects. Such involvement is likely to be dismissed by the authorities as 'impermissible interference'.

For example, following the Turkish invasion of northern Cyprus in July–August 1974, the situation could properly be viewed as one of military occupation; and it was so viewed by the Government of Cyprus and by the United Nations General Assembly.[140] However, the facts that

[138] The Kahan Report, published in early 1983, the *Final Report of the Commission of Inquiry into the Events at the Refugee Camps in Beirut*, contains an authoritative account of these events. It refers on p. 54 to 'the lack of clarity regarding the status of the State of Israel and its forces in Lebanese territory', but does not try to resolve this issue. The report bases its criticisms of certain Israeli actions mainly on a concept of public morality and on the book of Deuteronomy. Relevant international agreements such as the 1949 Geneva Convention IV are not mentioned, even though many Articles (e.g. 4 and 144) were applicable to the situation in the camps, and urgently needed to be implemented.

[139] Judgment delivered 13 July 1983. Telex transcript, pp. 13, 16.

[140] GA Resolutions 33/15 of 9 November 1978 and 34/30 of 20 November 1979 deplored 'the continued presence of foreign armed forces and foreign military personnel on the territory of the Republic of Cyprus and the fact that part of its territory is still occupied by foreign forces'. Resolution 37/253 of 13 May 1983 deplored 'the fact that part of the territory of the Republic of Cyprus is still occupied by foreign forces' and demanded 'the immediate withdrawal of all occupation forces from the Republic of Cyprus'.

the declared aim of this operation was to protect the Turkish minority living in Cyprus from the Greek majority, and that a new political entity (the Turkish Federated State of Cyprus) was set up in 1975, gave this occupation a special colour. Not surprisingly, the Turkish Cypriot authorities did not appreciate the application of the term 'occupation' to their situation.[141] On 15 November 1983 their elected assembly went so far as to claim the status of a sovereign State by approving a Declaration of Independence and proclaiming the 'Turkish Republic of Northern Cyprus'—a move which did not win the hoped-for international recognition. Irrespective of the validity of this last act, an argument could be made that not all aspects of the law on occupations were designed for a situation such as this; and in particular that the prohibitions of making extensive legal and political changes may sometimes be of limited relevance where the desire both of the occupants and of most of the inhabitants of the area actually occupied is precisely to make certain changes. On the other hand, in the *Cyprus* v. *Turkey* cases before the European Commission of Human Rights, the Government of Cyprus vigorously asserted that violations of human rights by Turkey in the Turkish-occupied areas (including the detention or murder of some 2,000 missing Greek Cypriots and the refusal to allow more than 170,000 Greek Cypriot refugees to return to their homes) were contrary to the European Convention on Human Rights, and were matters of legitimate international concern. The applications of the Government of Cyprus were ruled admissible by the European Commission of Human Rights on 26 May 1975 and 10 July 1978—a significant recognition in principle of the applicability of international human rights law to occupied territories.[142]

Thirdly, where there are indigenous authorities in post, occupants often seek to buttress any claims that the situation is not one of occupation at all by using a particular device—a subsequent treaty with the 'host' government for the stationing of foreign armed forces. This happened in Iran, where, following the Anglo-Soviet military intervention on 25 August 1941, a Treaty of Alliance between the UK, USSR and Iran was signed at Teheran on 29 January 1942. Article 4 said:

> The Allied Powers may maintain in Iranian territory land, sea and air forces in such number as they consider necessary . . . It is understood that the presence of these forces on Iranian terrritory does not constitute a military occupation and will disturb as little as possible the administration and the security forces of Iran, the economic life of the country, the normal movements of the population and the application of Iranian laws and regulations.[143]

[141] Nedjatigil, *The Cyprus Conflict: A Lawyer's View* (1981), p. 75. The author, a senior Turkish Cypriot official, asserts that the situation is not one of occupation, partly it would seem on the grounds that the Turkish invasion was sanctioned under the 1960 Treaty of Guarantee, and partly on the grounds that the Turkish forces 'are present in Cyprus to assist the security forces of the Turkish Federated State of Cyprus'. Such considerations may affect one's view of the occupation, but do not necessarily change the fact of its being an occupation of part of the territory of the Republic of Cyprus.

[142] 62 ILR 5 at pp. 5–10, 82–3.

[143] *United Nations Treaty Series*, vol. 93, p. 279.

Similarly, following the Soviet interventions in Hungary in October and November 1956 and in Czechoslovakia in August 1968, treaties on the temporary stationing of Soviet troops were concluded. Both treaties specified that they did not affect the sovereignty of the host State, and that the forces involved would not interfere in its internal affairs.[144]

In theory, such agreements have no more power than any other agreement to affect the application of the 1949 Geneva Convention IV: the provisions of Articles 7, 8 and 47 seem unambiguous. However, the awkward question may be raised: could an agreement on the stationing of armed forces mean that a given situation could no longer be properly regarded as an occupation at all? Whatever the answer to this question, it may well be the case in particular instances that such agreements limit the role of foreign forces so stringently that many of the potential points of friction between the inhabitants and the occupant, which are addressed in the law on occupations, are unlikely to arise in practice. To the extent that this is so, the situation may bear some resemblance to a more normal basing of foreign forces in peacetime.[145]

In general, there does seem to be a tendency in the contemporary world to operate through indigenous political forces, rather than to impose direct external control. The fact that all the major powers subscribe to anti-colonial ideologies or principles of one kind or another has undoubtedly reinforced this tendency. So far as the applicability of the law on occupations is concerned, this tendency poses problems, but they are not insuperable. Even if in some instances the authorities reject any categorization of the situation as occupation, they may still apply the relevant rules; and the international community may put pressure on them to do so.

11. *Subsequent occupation*[146]

This is an occupation by one belligerent which follows an occupation of the same region by another belligerent. In such a case the Hague Regulations and the Geneva Conventions apply without difficulty, except in regard to the continuation or modification of measures adopted by the earlier belligerent occupant. Article 43 of the Hague Regulations, obliging the occupant to respect 'unless absolutely prevented, the laws in force in the country', may not be so relevant in such circumstances. There is a risk that this Article could be used to maintain in force any and every piece of draconian legislation enacted by previous domestic or foreign rulers. Such a possibility may be indicated by Gaza, where various rules from the

[144] Agreement Concerning the Legal Status of Soviet Forces Temporarily Stationed in the Territory of the Hungarian People's Republic, signed in Budapest 27 May 1957, Article 1 (*United Nations Treaty Series*, vol. 407, p. 170). Treaty Between the Government of the USSR and the Government of the Czechoslovak Socialist Republic on the Conditions of Temporary Sojourn of Soviet Forces on the Territory of the Czechoslovak Socialist Republic, signed in Prague 16 October 1968, Article 2 (*International Legal Materials*, 7 (1968), p. 1334).

[145] Below, pp. 297–8.

[146] The term was first used by Feilchenfeld, op. cit. above (p. 261 n. 39), at p. 7.

period when the territory was occupied by Egypt remain in force (as, incidentally, do some laws from the period of the British mandate), alongside more recent Israeli laws and orders.[147]

12. *Multilateral occupation*

A territory may be jointly occupied by several States which are allied to each other, and are perhaps under a unified command system. There have been many such occupations in this century, because of the tendency of States, for many reasons, to use armed force on a multilateral basis. Where a region is so occupied, 'the regular rules on belligerent occupation will then apply, but the jurisdictional relationships between the allies will have to be determined'.[148] In a few cases such occupations have resulted in (or been a disguised form of) division of a country into separate parts.

13. *Occupation by United Nations or similar forces*

Forces acting under the aegis of the United Nations could conceivably be in occupation of all or part of the territory of a State, either in the course of an enforcement action, or in the course of an armed peacekeeping operation. In addition, other international peacekeeping forces (perhaps on the lines of the multinational force in the Lebanon 1982–4) could theoretically find themselves in the role of occupant if, for example, the government which had invited them in collapsed totally, without any successor, and the force stayed on to maintain order.

The general question of whether the laws of war apply to United Nations forces has been much discussed. The United Nations itself is not a party to any international agreements on the laws of war, and these agreements do not expressly provide for the application of the laws of war by United Nations forces. However, it is widely held that the laws of war remain applicable to such forces. The great majority of writers have taken such a view, although with some differences of emphasis on the issue as to whether United Nations forces are bound by every provision of the laws of war, or mainly by customary rules, or by some distillation or adaptation of rules which is relevant to a United Nations force's special character and

[147] However, Israel has taken the view that the rules of international law do not prohibit the liberalization of punitive measures, and in all the territories occupied in 1967 it quite promptly abolished the mandatory death penalty previously imposed by Egypt, Jordan and Syria for a wide range of offences: Shamgar, op. cit. above (p. 281 n. 120), at pp. 45 and 52.

[148] Feilchenfeld, op. cit. above (p. 261 n. 39), at p. 8. See also Baxter, 'Constitutional Forms and Some Legal Problems of International Military Command', this *Year Book*, 29 (1952), pp. 355–7. An instance of costly failure to work out a satisfactory basis for relations between allies was in the confused occupation of parts of Turkey by various Allied powers following the Armistice of Mudros between Britain and Turkey, signed on 30 October 1918: Busch, *Mudros to Lausanne: Britain's Frontier in West Asia 1918–1923* (1976), pp. 62–97. Text of the Mudros Armistice: Parry, *The Consolidated Treaty Series*, vol. 224, p. 169.

purpose.[149] The United Nations Organization itself has in practice accepted the applicability of the general laws of war to its own forces and to those of its adversaries both in enforcement actions and in peacekeeping operations. In the Korean War, despite some ambiguities, forces under the United Nations claimed no exemption from the laws of war; and the fact that the United Nations force in Korea consisted of national contingents voluntarily contributed to a unified command under the delegated operational responsibility of one member State underlined the point that the application of the laws of war was a responsibility of States as well as of the United Nations Organization itself.[150] In subsequent operations, for example in the Middle East, Congo and Cyprus, the United Nations has instructed forces under its authority to observe 'the principles and spirit of the general international Conventions applicable to the conduct of military personnel'.[151] In these operations, too, States have retained a responsibility for their contingents with reference to matters relating to the application of the laws of war.[152] This tendency to stress the responsibility of States may in part be due to the existence of some practical difficulties in implementation of the laws of war by the United Nations as such. Any rule which presumes, for example, that the State applying it has territory of its own, or which depends on the application of a State's own national standards, would create a difficulty because the United Nations lacks these characteristic features of statehood. In this connection it may be noted that the United Nations has never as such assumed custody of prisoners of war.

The more specific question of whether United Nations forces could be considered occupants has been less extensively discussed. It is uncontentious that in an enforcement action United Nations forces could well find themselves in belligerent occupation of territory, and that most or all of the customary and conventional laws of war would then apply.[153] As for

[149] For example, Taubenfeld, 'International Armed Forces and the Rules of War', *American Journal of International Law*, 45 (1951), pp. 671–9; Baxter, loc. cit. (previous note), pp. 357–9; Lauterpacht, 'The Limits of the Operation of the Laws of War', this *Year Book*, 30 (1953), pp. 242–3; Bowett, *United Nations Forces* (1964), pp. 484–516; Seyersted, *United Nations Forces in the Law of Peace and War* (1966), pp. 178–426; the resolutions on the subject adopted by the Institute of International Law in 1971 and 1975, reprinted in Schindler and Toman, *The Laws of Armed Conflicts* (2nd edn., 1981), pp. 815–20; Sandoz, 'The Application of Humanitarian Law by the Armed Forces of the UNO', *International Review of the Red Cross*, 206 (1978), pp. 274–84.

[150] Stone, op. cit. above (p. 250 n. 3), at p. 316; Brownlie, op. cit. above (p. 250 n. 3), at p. 400; Bowett, op. cit. (previous note), pp. 55, 487; Seyersted, op. cit. (previous note), pp. 182–97; Higgins, *United Nations Peacekeeping 1946–1967*, vol. 2, *Asia* (1970), pp. 188–95.

[151] For texts of United Nations Regulations containing these words, see, e.g., Seyersted, op. cit. above (n. 149), at pp. 190, 442; and Higgins, *United Nations Peacekeeping 1946–1967*, vol. 1, *The Middle East* (1969), pp. 288–92.

[152] Seyersted, op. cit. above (n. 149), at pp. 190–2, 321–7. This responsibility of individual States was explicitly recognized in a 1966 Agreement between the United Nations and Sweden relating to the Swedish Contingent to the United Nations Force in Cyprus. Text ibid., p. 445.

[153] Bowett, op. cit. above (n. 149), at pp. 490–1; Seyersted, op. cit. above (n. 149), at pp. 281–3. Both discuss briefly whether United Nations forces might be in a privileged position *vis-à-vis* certain rules. On the essentially American (as distinct from United Nations) character of military government activities during the Korean War, see Kyre, *Military Occupation and National Security* (1968), pp. 43, 69.

United Nations peacekeeping forces, where these act within one State on the basis of status of forces agreements between the United Nations and the host State (such as the United Nations Emergency Force in Egypt in 1956–67) they would not be in occupation of the territory as the term has been traditionally used in international law.[154] It is just conceivable, however, that in different circumstances a peacekeeping force could find itself organizing some kind of 'occupation by consent'. Moreover, if central authority in the host State were to collapse, a peacekeeping force might find itself extending its authority and taking full charge of such matters as public order and safety.

The situation in the Congo during the United Nations operation 1960–4 affords one example illustrating the possibility of a United Nations peacekeeping force finding itself in a role closely analogous to that of an occupant. At the outset, the United Nations Secretary-General, Dag Hammarskjøld, stated that the force, which was 'under the exclusive command of the United Nations', was 'not under the orders of the Government nor can it . . . be permitted to become a party to any internal conflict . . .'.[155] But Congolese political developments made it unclear for a time who was the constitutional government, and there was United Nations intervention in administrative activities and in internal conflict beyond what had originally been envisaged.[156]

14. *Occupation of territory for which the United Nations is responsible*

The possibility of a State's occupation of territory which is under the legal responsibility of the United Nations is indicated by the South African presence in Namibia. In 1966 South Africa's mandate (dating from 1920) was terminated by the United Nations General Assembly, which reaffirmed that the territory had 'international status' and decided that it came henceforth 'under the direct responsibility of the UN'.[157]

[154] The Summary Study on the experience of UNEF which the Secretary-General prepared in 1958 defined its functions in a manner distinguishing it rather clearly from an occupying power. Para. 15 stated: 'The Force has no rights other than those necessary for the execution of the functions assigned to it by the General Assembly and agreed to by the country or countries concerned. The Force is paramilitary in character and much more than an observer corps, but it is in no sense a military force exercising, through force of arms, even temporary control over the territory in which it is stationed; nor does it have military objectives, or military functions exceeding those necessary to secure peaceful conditions on the assumption that the parties to the conflict will take all the necessary steps for compliance with the recommendations of the General Assembly': Higgins, op. cit. above (p. 290 n. 151), at pp. 485–6.

[155] Quoted in Higgins, *United Nations Peacekeeping 1946–1967*, vol. 3, *Africa* (1980), p. 125. On the applicability of the laws of war to United Nations forces in general, and to those in the Congo in particular, see also Simmonds, *Legal Problems Arising from the United Nations Military Operations in the Congo* (1968), pp. 168–74, 174–96. He does not specifically address the question of whether United Nations forces can be military occupants.

[156] Higgins, op. cit. (previous note), pp. 125–210. The text of the status agreement of 27 November 1961 between the United Nations and the Republic of the Congo is on pp. 199–206. See also *inter alia* Abi-Saab, *The United Nations Operation in the Congo 1960–1964* (1978), esp. pp. 54–123.

[157] GA Res. 2145 (XXI) of 27 October 1966. For a text of the League of Nations Mandate of 17 December 1920 see Bentwich, *The Mandates System* (1930), pp. 185–7.

Despite this resolution, South Africa continued to administer the territory. In 1968 the United Nations General Assembly, in deploring South Africa's refusal to withdraw from the territory, passed the first of many resolutions describing the situation there as one of 'foreign occupation' and 'illegal occupation'.[158] In 1971 the International Court of Justice, in an advisory opinion, stated that 'the continued presence of South Africa in Namibia being illegal, South Africa is under an obligation to withdraw its administration from Namibia immediately and thus put an end to its occupation of the territory'. It also said that some multilateral conventions 'such as those of a humanitarian character' may be viewed as binding so far as Namibia is concerned.[159] Since then, numerous United Nations resolutions have expressed concern at the continued illegal occupation of Namibia by South Africa.[160]

There is much room for disagreement as to the exact status of Namibia and the exact extent of the United Nations' responsibility. Sagay has argued that the United Nations Council for Namibia has the full powers of statehood and is the *de jure* government of the territory.[161] Others have suggested that, in view of the limited nature of the United Nations' personality, the organization cannot assume the role of territorial sovereign, but does have a capacity to administer territory.[162] Differences on such points do not necessarily affect the validity of the view that Namibia is under foreign occupation.[163]

15. *Occupation by a non-State entity*

Sometimes in armed conflicts the forces of an organized body which is not recognized as the government of a sovereign State (it may, for example, be a 'liberation movement') may occupy territory of a neighbouring State—for example, with the aim of securing supply routes, base areas or sanctuary. Without entering at all into specifics, the possibility of such a type of occupation is indicated by the entry of Yugoslav partisans into Trieste in the closing phase of the Second World War; the role of forces of the National Liberation Front of South Vietnam in frontier areas of Cambodia up to 1975; and the activities of forces of the Palestine Liberation Organization in parts of Lebanon in the 1970s and early 1980s.

158 GA Resolutions 2372 (XXII) of 12 June 1968 and 2403 (XXIII) of 16 December 1968.

159 *ICJ Reports*, 1971, advisory opinion of 21 June 1971, pp. 58, 55.

160 See, e.g., Security Council Resolutions 366 of 17 December 1974 and 385 of 30 January 1976; GA Resolutions 2871 (XXVI) of 20 December 1971, 35/227 of 6 March 1981 and 37/233 of 20 December 1982.

161 Sagay, *The Legal Aspects of the Namibian Dispute* (1975), pp. 271-83.

162 Brownlie, *Principles of Public International Law* (3rd edn., 1979), pp. 175-9.

163 British Government statements in 1982 indicated that the United Kingdom views Namibia as 'under unlawful occupation by South Africa', but does not accept that Namibia is a sovereign State, and considers that 'the UN General Assembly acted beyond its competence in setting up the UN Council for Namibia with the powers with which it purported to endow it': Marston, 'UK Materials on International Law 1982', this *Year Book*, 53 (1982), pp. 391-3.

The general applicability of the laws of war to certain liberation movements is clear enough.[164] However, the specific possibility of a liberation movement occupying the territory of another State does not appear to have been discussed either at the 1949 or the 1974–7 diplomatic conferences at Geneva—perhaps because liberation movements are widely viewed as underdogs, not overlords. One may hazard the opinion that the law on occupations ought to be applied fully in the event of an occupation by a non-State entity, but some provisions might be hard to implement in cases where the occupant lacks some of the resources which a State enjoys.

16. *'Illegal occupation'*

Many military occupations have been called, usually by their critics, 'illegal occupations'. This term is almost invariably used to refer to an occupation which is perceived as being the outcome of aggressive and unlawful military expansion, or as being maintained in defiance of authoritative pronouncements by international bodies calling for a withdrawal. South Africa's 'illegal occupation' of Namibia, as it was called in the 1971 advisory opinion of the International Court of Justice, is the clearest contemporary example.[165]

Do the same international legal provisions apply to such an illegal occupation as apply to an occupation which is, say, a by-product of fighting a defensive war? There has long been a minority tendency, especially strong in some countries which suffered frightful losses under German occupation in the Second World War, to deny that an aggressor occupant has any rights under the Hague or any other conventions. A number of Soviet writers have taken such a view.[166] Some post-war judgments in Polish courts inclined in the same direction.[167] A number of publications and statements of the Palestine Liberation Organization have also adopted this approach.[168]

However, the view that the laws of war apply equally to all occupations, even to those created by illegal acts of aggression, is persuasive and

[164] 1949 Geneva Convention III, Article 4A (2); 1977 Geneva Protocol I, Articles 1 (4) and 96; Veuthey, op. cit. above (p. 249 n. 2), *passim*.

[165] Above, pp. 291–2.

[166] See particularly Trainin's 1945 article, of which an English translation appeared in *American Journal of International Law*, 40 (1946), p. 555; Tunkin, *Theory of International Law* (1974), p. 411. However, by no means all Soviet international lawyers have taken this line: see Kulski, 'Some Soviet Comments on International Law', *American Journal of International Law*, 45 (1951), pp. 347–9; Kozhevnikov (ed.), *International Law* (Moscow, 1961), pp. 427–30.

[167] See the judgment of the Supreme National Tribunal of Poland in *In re Greiser* on 7 July 1946: *Annual Digest*, 13 (1946), Case no. 166, p. 388; and also the different decisions of the court of first instance, the District Court and the Supreme Court (the latter on 13 April 1948) in the case of *N.* v. *B.*, which concerned the ownership of a mare which had been confiscated and auctioned by the German occupation authorities: 24 ILR 941–3.

[168] Yahia, *The Palestine Question and International Law* (Palestine Liberation Organization Research Center, Beirut, June 1970), p. 184; also statement of the Permanent Observer Mission of the PLO at UNESCO, dated 10 April 1981 and published in UNESCO document 22 C/18 dated 30 August 1983, Annex IV, p. 28, para. 11.

undoubtedly represents the bulk of legal opinion. The International Military Tribunal at Nuremberg unequivocally affirmed the applicability of the 1907 Hague Convention in occupied territory, and referred explicitly to the occupant's rights to collect taxes and make requisitions in kind.[169] A number of other post-war judgments strongly supported the view that international law makes no distinction between a lawful and an unlawful occupant in dealing with the respective duties of occupant and population in occupied territory.[170] This view has been supported by the great majority of writers.[171] However, some writers do envisage that in certain very restricted spheres (for example, in considering title to property) there may be some room for applying a principle of discrimination against aggressor occupants, at any rate after the cessation of hostilities.[172]

The applicability of humanitarian rules to all occupations, whether 'legal' or 'illegal', is indicated by the wording of common Article 2 of the 1949 Geneva Conventions, referring as it does to 'all cases of partial or total occupation . . .'. Furthermore, the preamble of the 1977 Geneva Protocol I reaffirms 'that the provisions of the Geneva Conventions of 12 August 1949 and of this Protocol must be fully applied in all circumstances to all persons who are protected by those instruments, without any adverse distinction based on the nature or origin of the armed conflict or on the causes espoused by or attributed to the Parties to the conflict . . .'.

17. '*Trustee occupation*'

This questionable term was advanced by Allan Gerson in 1973. He indicated that not all the provisions of the law on occupations need necessarily apply in cases (such as the Jordanian occupation of the West Bank from 1948 to 1967 and the Israeli occupation thereafter) characterized, it would seem, by the following features: (*a*) the previous legal status of the territory was not one of full sovereignty; (*b*) the occupation is allegedly 'lawful' rather than 'unlawful'—i.e. is not the result of a war of aggression; and (*c*) the occupant seeks positively to develop the territory in some way—for example, politically or economically. He suggested:

[169] *The Trial of German Major War Criminals* (London, 1946–51), vol. 22, pp. 457, 467. Although the Soviet member of the IMT, General I. T. Nikitchenko, delivered a long dissenting opinion (pp. 531–47), he did not raise any question about the applicability of the Hague Regulations.

[170] See, e.g., the judgment of US Military Tribunal V in the *Hostages* case (*USA* v. *Wilhelm List et al.*), loc. cit. above (p. 260 n. 37), at p. 1247. On the applicability of the Hague Regulations specifically in German-occupied Poland, see the judgment on 10 March 1948 in the *RuSHA* case (*USA* v. *Ulrich Greifelt et al.*) in ibid., vol. 5, p. 154; and the judgment on 29–30 July 1948 in the *IG Farben* case (*USA* v. *Carl Krauch et al.*) in ibid., vol. 8, p. 1137.

[171] See, e.g., Lauterpacht, 'The Limits of the Operation of the Law of War', this *Year Book*, 30 (1953), p. 220; Stone, op. cit. above (p. 250 n. 3), at p. 695; Brownlie, op. cit. above (p. 250 n. 3), at pp. 406–8; McNair and Watts, op. cit. above (p. 266 n. 57), at pp. 371–2.

[172] Lauterpacht, loc. cit. (previous note), pp. 233–7; Morgenstern, 'The Validity of the Acts of the Belligerent Occupant', this *Year Book*, 29 (1952), p. 321 n.; Schwarzenberger, op. cit. above (p. 267 n. 67), at pp. 105–6; Skubiszewski, loc. cit. above (p. 250 n. 3), at p. 811.

Israel should replace Jordan as trustee-occupant for the indigenous Palestinian Arabs. As such, Israel should be held responsible for fostering the political and economic self-determination of the region, unburdened by the traditional restraints imposed by the law of belligerent occupation against alteration of the *status quo ante.*[173]

The problem to which the concept of 'trustee occupation' is addressed is real enough. There are often occasions when it is unrealistic or undesirable to stick strictly to a policy of preserving the *status quo ante.* Such occasions may indeed arise in many occupations with features quite different from those indicated by Gerson and outlined above.

However, Gerson's advocacy of the term suffers from several defects. He appears to assume that the 1949 Geneva Convention IV applies only to 'belligerent occupation' fairly narrowly defined, even though Article 2 clearly makes the Convention much more broadly applicable. Secondly, he bases his argument on the claim, which is not properly substantiated, that in occupation law there is a significant distinction between 'aggressor-occupants' and 'lawful-occupants'.[174] Thirdly, he appears to neglect the extent to which the idea of 'trusteeship' is implicit in all occupation law anyway. The idea that all occupants are in some vague and general sense trustees is nothing new. Sir Arnold Wilson suggested in 1932 that 'enemy territories in the occupation of the armed forces of another country constitute (in the language of Article 22 of the League of Nations Covenant) a sacred trust, which must be administered as a whole in the interests both of the inhabitants and of the legitimate sovereign or the duly constituted successor in title'.[175] The Hague Regulations and the 1949 Geneva Convention IV can be interpreted as putting the occupant in a quasi-trustee role. Von Glahn refers to occupants as exercising 'a temporary right of administration on a sort of trusteeship basis'.[176] All this diminishes still further any case for regarding 'trustee occupation' as a separate category of occupation.

V. Cases Distinct from Military Occupation

Although military occupations are very varied, they are not endlessly so. Not every advance of armed forces into inhabited territory amounts to an occupation, or brings into play the law on occupations. Two possible areas of exception are: (*a*) occupation of one's own territory; and (*b*) stationing of foreign military forces by agreement. In addition (*c*) some other cases distinct from military occupation are briefly enumerated.

[173] Gerson, 'Trustee Occupant: The Legal Status of Israel's Presence in the West Bank', *Harvard International Law Journal*, 14 (1973), pp. 1–49; and his subsequent book, *Israel, the West Bank and International Law* (1978), esp. pp. 78–82. Note his frank recognition on p. 82 that Israel has not in fact assumed the role of trustee occupant.

[174] Gerson, loc. cit. above (previous note), p. 3.

[175] Sir Arnold Wilson, 'The Laws of War in Occupied Territory', *Transactions of the Grotius Society*, 18 (1933), p. 38.

[176] Von Glahn, *Law Among Nations* (4th edn., 1981), p. 673.

(a) *Occupation of One's Own Territory*

In conflicts of various kinds, both international and internal, governments sometimes exercise direct military control within the accepted international frontiers of their State in a manner similar to that of a military occupant. For example, in the course of an international war a State may liberate part of its own territory (or what it views as such) which was previously occupied by an enemy, and then set up a system of military government there pending the re-establishment of the institutions of civil government: this happened, for example, at the end of the Second World War, when the United States reasserted control briefly in the Philippines, and likewise when the British returned to Malaya.

The applicability of the law on occupations to such situations has been the subject of different opinions. A footnote in the British military manual says that military control in such a situation 'is a matter for the domestic law of the belligerent concerned and is not regulated by international law'.[177] The wording of the various international conventions regarding their scope of application tends to support this view. However, in practice there have been instances in which at least some parts of the law have been viewed as applicable, especially where there was a continuing war, and also (as in some colonial territories) a degree of conflict between the returning forces and the inhabitants.[178] For example, the Philippines Supreme Court ruled on 6 October 1949 in *Tan Tuan* v. *Lucena Food Control Board*, which related to a seizure of black market goods on 14 June 1945:

> This phase of the case is controlled by the laws of war . . .
> The fact that this was not foreign territory did not deprive the United States Army of the status of belligerent occupant. Military government may be established not only in foreign territory occupied or invaded in time of war, but also domestic territory in a state of rebellion or civil war.[179]

In civil wars, too, the law on occupations may sometimes be applied. For example, when armed forces are sent to a particular area of their own State to exercise control, the authorities may implicitly or explicitly observe provisions of the law on occupations, even if they are not formally obliged to do so. The fact that the Lieber Code, which contains many provisions on occupations, was issued to Union forces in the American Civil War is an illustration of the possibilities of applying the laws of war to civil as well as international wars. However, when an 'occupation' is within a single sovereign State, the rules of international law which the parties are formally *obliged* to observe are rather few. They include common Article 3 of the 1949 Geneva Conventions, which relates to 'armed conflicts not of

[177] UK Manual, op. cit. above (p. 256 n. 20), at p. 141 n. One of the two cases cited in this footnote of the manual is *Public Prosecutor* v. *X* (*Eastern Java*). But that case was in fact about occupation of allied territory, and the court asserted the applicability of the laws of war in such circumstances. See above, p. 265.

[178] On the somewhat analogous situation in the Falkland Islands after 2 April 1982 see above, p. 280.

[179] 18 ILR 591. For a similar view see also US Manual, op. cit. above (p. 256 n. 20), at p. 10.

an international character' and establishes short but clear principles relating to persons taking no active part in hostilities, including members of armed forces who have laid down their arms, the sick, the wounded, etc.[180] For those States which are bound by it, the rather minimal terms of the 1977 Geneva Protocol II (on non-international armed conflicts) are also applicable. So too is some human rights law. But the question of the law applicable in such essentially internal conflicts is not pursued here.[181]

In internal conflicts which do not amount to a full-blown civil war it is particularly unlikely that the designation of 'occupation' will be accepted. The United Kingdom's role in Northern Ireland is called an occupation by some of its adversaries, but this is not the view taken of it by the British or Irish Governments, or by other States. However, even in this case the relevance of some standards derived from the laws of war as well as other international legal norms came to be accepted.[182]

In most circumstances, however, governments are not only reluctant to be viewed as maintaining an occupation in their own territory or in that with which they are constitutionally linked, but are also likely to reject the application of the law on occupations. In *United States* v. *Vargas*, before a United States District Court in Puerto Rico in January 1974, sixteen defendants of Puerto Rican origin, who objected to being conscripted, cited 1949 Geneva Convention IV, Article 51, in their defence. The judgment in the case stated that Puerto Rico could not be characterized as an occupied territory, and recalled the reaffirmation of Commonwealth status by plebiscite in 1967. The Convention was therefore viewed as not applicable.[183]

(b) *Stationing of Foreign Military Forces by Agreement*

The stationing of foreign military forces on the territory of a State in accordance with the terms of a prior agreement is in most cases

[180] Article 3 was stated by Mr Plinio Bolla, the Swiss delegate at the 1949 Diplomatic Conference, to cover the cases of civil war, wars of resistance and wars of liberation, but not banditry or riots: *Final Record 1949*, vol. IIB, p. 335. This approach is formalized in 1977 Geneva Protocol II, Article 1 (2). For a study of Article 3 see Elder, 'The Historical Background of Common Article 3 of the Geneva Convention of 1949', *Case Western Reserve Journal of International Law*, 11 (1979), pp. 37–69.

[181] On the applicability of the laws of war in this type of situation see Higgins, 'International Law and Civil Conflict', in Luard (ed.), *The International Regulation of Civil Wars* (1972), pp. 169–86; Taubenfeld, 'The Applicability of the Laws of War in Civil War', in Moore (ed.), *Law and Civil War in the Modern World* (1974), pp. 499–517; Veuthey, 'Some Problems of Humanitarian Law in Noninternational Conflicts and Guerrilla Warfare', in Bassiouni and Nanda, *A Treatise on International Criminal Law* (1973), vol. 1, pp. 422–52.

[182] The United Kingdom has fairly consistently taken the view that the situation in Northern Ireland is essentially internal, and has regarded the principles in common Article 3 of the 1949 Geneva Conventions as applicable: see, e.g., *Report of the Committee of Privy Counsellors Appointed to Consider Authorized Procedures for the Interrogation of Persons Suspected of Terrorism*, Cmnd. 4901 (1972), pp. 1, 14–15, 23. However, Lord Gardiner's minority report, which was accepted by the Government, is an interesting example of asserting the wider relevance of certain international legal standards, including some from the 1949 Geneva Conventions, in an internal conflict: ibid., pp. 17–22. On the relevance of human rights law to Northern Ireland, see the materials from the case of *Ireland* v. *United Kingdom* in *Publications of the European Court of Human Rights*, Series B, vols. 23I–23III (1980–1).

[183] Report in *American Journal of International Law*, 68 (1974), pp. 744–5. On the history and status of Puerto Rico, see Carr, *Puerto Rico: A Colonial Experiment* (1984).

fundamentally different from military occupation. This is especially so where the functions of the foreign military forces are limited to the manning of certain bases, or defence against an external adversary; but even if the functions do (as in some peacekeeping operations) involve an element of exerting authority over society or maintaining public order, they do not *ipso facto* become occupations.

The legal framework within which foreign forces operate in a country is generally outlined in the particular agreement concerned.[184] The law on occupations is seldom relevant. Debbasch has expressed a contrary view. She has said that a military occupation occurs whenever armed forces are outside their own national territory, and that 'military bases constitute today in peacetime a living example of the idea of military occupation'.[185] This stretches the meaning of the term 'military occupation' to breaking-point. Although she recognizes a distinction between belligerent occupation and the maintenance of military bases in peacetime, her suggestion that both these situations are subject to a common international legal regime is not persuasive.

There are circumstances in which the stationing of foreign forces by agreement may bear some resemblance to a military occupation. This may be so in cases where the agreement was achieved through duress against the negotiators of the receiving State; where the agreement was concluded after an invasion and occupation had already begun;[186] or where the foreign forces, whose functions were initially presented as limited, come to exercise much more extensive powers.[187] To the extent that such situations do present the types of practical problems addressed in the law on occupations, then the provisions of this body of law may well be viewed as applicable.

(c) *Other Cases Distinct From Military Occupation*

There are many other cases which, despite some superficial verbal or physical similarities with military occupation, are both in law and in fact entirely distinct. For example, in the context of consideration of title to *terra nullius*, the term 'occupation' has a specific meaning which is nothing to do with the concept of 'military occupation' as addressed in the laws of war conventions.[188]

[184] See Lazareff, *Status of Military Forces Under Current International Law* (1971); Vali, *Servitudes of International Law: A Study of Rights in Foreign Territory* (2nd edn., 1958), pp. 208-52.

[185] Debbasch, op. cit. above (p. 274 n. 94), at pp. 2-3.

[186] On such post-invasion agreements in Iran in 1942, Hungary in 1957 and Czechoslovakia in 1968, see above, pp. 287-8. However, there have been many cases in which occupations ended but troops remained under the terms of an agreement: see above, pp. 258-9.

[187] See the general discussion of peacetime occupation by consent above, pp. 276-9, including the reference to South Vietnam and Afghanistan. Note also the case of Namibia, above, pp. 291-2.

[188] On *terra nullius*, and occupation thereof, see Brownlie, op. cit. above (p. 292 n. 162), at pp. 180-1; von Glahn, op. cit. above (p. 295 n. 176), at pp. 316-18; Starke, *Introduction to International Law* (8th edn., 1977), pp. 185-91. A recent use of the term 'occupation' in this sense as part of a claim of title to territory was in the Foreign and Commonwealth Office pamphlet *The Falkland Islands: The*

Some writers have drawn attention to the possibility of fictitious military occupations, in which an invader declares certain areas to be occupied without in fact taking any steps to exercise control there. Clearly these are not military occupations at all, as the factual test of occupation advanced in Article 42 of the Hague Regulations remains important.[189]

Many territories have a status which is less than total independence and sovereignty, but is distinct from occupation not least because of the nature of the constitutional or international legal framework. Examples might include certain colonial possessions, non-self-governing and trust territories, autonomous regions and so on.

VI. General Issues and Conclusions

(a) *The Rationale for the Concept of 'Military Occupation'*

The evidence from conventions, practice, judgments and writings all points unambiguously to the conclusion that the generic term 'military occupation' (or just 'occupation'), though by no means infinitely elastic, is a very broad one. Has it become so broad that it ceases to be either satisfactory as a factual description or useful as an indication that a particular body of law is applicable?

The breadth of the concept of occupation is indicated not so much by showing how many categories can be incorporated in a single typology, but rather by looking at the historical cases themselves, each one unique in purpose, character and outcome. If the term 'occupation' has come to refer to far more types of situation than the classic belligerent occupation indicated in the Hague Regulations of 1899 and 1907, this is not because of any intellectual fashion or progressive legal development, but rather because of the inescapably complex and varied character of military and political events. Indeed, one can say of military occupation, as Clausewitz said of war, that it is not a totally independent phenomenon, but 'a continuation of political intercourse, with the addition of other means'.[190]

Facts (HMSO, May 1982), pp. 3–4. The question of what body of principles or law should govern relations between the occupiers of *terra nullius* and any indigenous inhabitants was of great importance at the time of European colonial expansion: for a classic exposition see particularly the work of the sixteenth-century Spanish professor of theology, Franciscus de Victoria, esp. his *De Indis*, first published in his *Relectiones Theologicae* (1557). However, this question is of much more restricted significance today because there is virtually no *terra nullius* in the contemporary world. In recent cases of invasions of inhabited territory whose status is unclear (e.g. East Timor and Western Sahara), the international community has tended to view it not as *terra nullius*, but as territory whose sovereignty, although yet to be exercised, is vested in the inhabitants, whose wishes regarding forms of statehood or union should be determined by appropriate internationally agreed procedures.

[189] On 'so-called constructive occupation' and 'so-called fictitious occupation', see Oppenheim, op. cit. above (p. 256 n. 20), at p. 435; von Glahn, op. cit. above (p. 261 n. 39), at p. 28. On the significance of effective control as a test of occupation see also McNair and Watts, op. cit. above (p. 266 n. 57), at pp. 368, 372–80. Fictitious 'occupations' occur rarely if at all. The opposite problem—of an area being occupied in fact, but being said to be not occupied—is much more common.

[190] Von Clausewitz, *On War* (Howard and Paret translation, 1976), Book viii, chapter vi.

Occupations may be distinguished from each other not merely by the criterion of the kinds of legal or other circumstances in which they occur (the main approach adopted in this article), but also by the criterion of motive or purpose. Here too there are extreme variations. Even within one single type of occupation discussed earlier there could be any of several completely different motives, and views about these will strongly colour attitudes to any particular given episode. Occupations may be an almost accidental by-product of hostilities, or they may be the main aim of military operations. They are initiated, or later maintained, for a wide variety of ostensible purposes: to implement territorial claims; to put pressure on an adversary either to perform obligations under an already existing treaty, or else to negotiate a peace treaty; to prevent the use of the occupied territory as a military base, including for guerrilla or other attacks against the occupying State; to punish an unfriendly act, with a view to securing reparation for the act complained of; to prevent political or economic developments which cause concern to the intervening power; to re-establish order and stability in a case where government has collapsed or is in danger of so doing; to protect a given area or section of the population against internal disturbances or against foreign attack; or to enable the occupant himself to establish military bases. Other motives, justifications or excuses for occupations are not hard to find.

Faced with such bewildering varieties of types and motives of occupation, what common elements remain? Does occupation have a chameleon-like character, able to assume many different faces, forms and colours, or does it rather consist of many entirely different species?

Within the diversity there is a rationale for the concept of 'occupation'. There are important common features. At the heart of treaty provisions, court decisions and legal writings about occupations is the image of the armed forces of a State exercising some kind of domination or authority over inhabited territory outside the accepted international frontiers of their State and its dependencies. It is above all to this kind of activity that the modern law on occupations applies. Even in specific cases differing in some respects from the most classic forms of occupation, there are some markers which may help to indicate the existence of an occupation, or may suggest the need for the law on occupations to be applied. These include: (i) there is a military force whose presence in a territory is not sanctioned or regulated by a valid agreement, or whose activities there involve an extensive range of contacts with the host society not adequately covered by the original agreement under which it intervened; (ii) the military force has either displaced the territory's ordinary system of public order and government, replacing it with its own command structure, or else has shown the clear physical ability to displace it; (iii) there is a difference of nationality and interest between the inhabitants on the one hand and the forces intervening and exercising power over them on the other, with the former not owing allegiance to the latter; (iv) within an overall framework of a breach of important parts of the national or international legal order, administration and the life of society have to continue on some legal basis, and there is a practical need for an emergency set of rules to reduce the dangers which can result from clashes between the military force and the inhabitants.

(b) *The Designation of Territory as 'Occupied'*

There are often disagreements about applying a politically and emotionally laden term such as 'occupation' to a particular situation. Parties involved—especially those on the side of the intervening forces—are often and understandably reluctant to use the word 'occupation' at all. This may be because of a fear of having to apply the full range of the law on occupations. However, the nexus of rights and duties described in that law is by no means necessarily disadvantageous to the occupant. There may be a much simpler reason for reluctance to use the word 'occupation': the adverse connotations of the word itself. To many, 'occupation' is almost synonymous with aggression and oppression.

Thus there has been widespread use of terms with a supposedly better ring: protectorate, fraternal aid, rescue mission, technical incursion, peacekeeping operation, military administration, civil administration, liberation and so on. Sometimes these terms are used in addition to the term 'occupation', in order to qualify it, to highlight the special features of a situation, and to clarify the purpose of the military action in question. Sometimes, and perhaps more often, these terms are used in total substitution for 'occupation'. Occasionally there may be some merit in not classifying a situation as an occupation: the maintenance of a fiction that a country retains its independence may act as a lever for gradually reasserting independence as a fact.

The question thus arises: who determines whether a particular situation is designated as an occupation? This answers itself in clear cases (such as some of the Second World War occupations) but not in all. The Hague and Geneva Conventions do not provide for a body to determine the circumstances in which they are applicable. Sometimes there is bound to be an element of genuine uncertainty, or of political predilection, in the designation of the status of territory. Where one or other of the parties involved disputes the term 'occupation', it is still open to other States and bodies to make clear that they consider the territory in question to be occupied, and to judge the occupant by the standard of the law on occupations. United Nations General Assembly and Security Council resolutions have often been a main means of expressing such a view.[191] Regional organizations such as the OAU have also played a role in such

[191] Territories designated by the General Assembly as occupied, and mentioned earlier in this article, have included Hungary (in a resolution in late 1956), the Israeli-occupied territories (consistently since 1967), Namibia (consistently since 1968), northern Cyprus (since 1978), Western Sahara (1979–80) and Kampuchea (1982).

designations. The ICRC has often expressed a clear view that a given territory was occupied, and that the parties were obliged to observe the relevant provisions of 1949 Geneva Convention IV, etc. In the case of Namibia, the ICJ said in 1971 that it viewed the territory as occupied.

(c) *Does the Application of the Law Depend on Such Designation?*

It is clear that there has long been a tendency to regard the law on occupations as applicable (whether on a *de jure* or *de facto* basis) to many situations, even where these differ in some important particulars from the picture of occupation presented in the relevant conventions. The question is, could the law be applied even in situations where the very designation of 'occupation' is rejected or disputed? Can one leap-frog the emotive issue of name-calling, and just get on with observing basic humanitarian rules? The additional fact that there have been some clear cases of occupations (including the post-1945 ones in Germany and Japan) to which the law on occupations was not at the time considered applicable could conceivably be a further reason for separating the issues of what a situation is called on the one hand, and what law is applicable on the other. Another consideration is that sometimes there is *de facto* observance of many provisions without any mention being made at all of the law on occupations. Thus in Czechoslovakia after August 1968, although Soviet spokesmen neither used the term occupation nor made any public reference to the Hague or Geneva Conventions, the Warsaw Pact forces on the whole acted with restraint.[192]

Both the ICRC and the United Nations have on numerous occasions asserted the applicability of international humanitarian law to particular situations, irrespective of the issue as to whether they count as international armed conflicts and/or occupations. For example, in 1968–9 the United Nations General Assembly urged that the 1949 Geneva Conventions III and IV be applied in conflicts in the territories under Portuguese administration;[193] in Southern Rhodesia after its unilateral declaration of independence;[194] and in southern Africa generally.[195] (Conversely, in at least one case mentioned earlier in this article, northern Cyprus, the General Assembly described a territory as occupied, but it did not in so many words call for the implementation of these conventions there.)

The tendency to focus on the substantive issue of observance of the law, rather than on the seemingly more semantic issue of the legal designation of a territory, could possibly be strengthened by seeking international

[192] However, in April 1969 Soviet representatives were reported to have threatened further military action in the cities if Dubček was not dismissed from his post as First Secretary of the Czechoslovak Communist Party. In the first month of the occupation over seventy Czechoslovak citizens had been killed: Windsor and Roberts, *Czechoslovakia 1968* (1969), p. 123 n.

[193] GA Res. 2395 (XXIII) of 29 November 1968.

[194] GA Res. 2508 (XXIV) of 21 November 1969.

[195] GA Res. 2547 (XXIV) of 11 December 1969.

agreement (e.g. through a United Nations resolution) to the effect that the law applies in all cases of military occupation or of any other situation where armed forces move in and exercise domination or authority outside the internationally accepted frontiers of their State and its dependencies. Some such wording could provide a parallel, so far as occupations are concerned, for what common Article 2 of the 1949 Geneva Conventions already does for international armed conflicts. That is to say, it could help ensure the application of the law irrespective of formal declarations and designations—whether of war or of occupation. However, such a formula still leaves the application of rules dependent on the outcome of complex arguments—not least about recognition of frontiers. An escape from this problem would probably require general acceptance of the idea that certain rules apply equally in internal and international conflicts. Evidence that such an idea is gaining ground can be found: but so far as occupations are concerned there are difficulties in accepting that a set of rules designed for administering foreign territories with their own institutions and laws can really be viewed as equally applicable in all internal conflicts.

The idea of applying the law on occupations on a purely *de facto* basis and irrespective of how a territory is designated has some point, but it also poses some problems. One is that the law may be only applied in part. A possible example is the Israeli application of 'the humanitarian provisions' of the 1949 Geneva Convention IV in the West Bank and Gaza. Such an approach can provide a basis for a State to limit the applicability of the Convention in one way or another. There is sometimes merit in asserting clearly that a given territory is subject to the full range of occupation law. A further consideration is that the formal designation of territory as occupied does have substantial practical and legal consequences. For example, the question of responsibility for war crimes often hinges on whether an area is considered to have been occupied. So too do questions relating to the applicability of the existing law of the territory concerned, and to the validity of actions by the ousted sovereign in respect of the occupied territory. For all these reasons, the importance of the designation 'occupation' is not likely to disappear.

(d) *Can a Single Set of Rules be Applied in Different Situations?*

Granted that occupation can assume many different forms, that the concept is fuzzy at the edges, and that the law relating to occupations is sometimes even applied in situations where the label 'occupation' is contentious or rejected, a major question remains. Can a single set of rules really be relevant to a very wide variety of different situations? Is it not a triumph of legal presumptuousness over common sense to assert that the same rules apply to, say, the Nazi occupation of Poland after 1939, the Turkish invasion of Cyprus from 1974 and the Vietnamese role in Kampuchea since 1978?

An intellectually tempting but in the end impractical way of tackling this problem might be to say that the law on occupations should revert to its formal diplomatic origins of 1899 and 1907, and should only be viewed as applicable in belligerent occupations—i.e. those in which one belligerent occupies the territory of another during a war. Many writers have implied, but with greater or lesser emphasis, that the rules apply mainly to belligerent occupation quite strictly defined; and legal writings have focused mainly on this category. As Feilchenfeld said in 1942:

> There are, of course, other kinds of occupation, and even other phases and types of belligerent occupation. However, the central body of international law governing occupation problems did not grow up around them; the special rules applying to them are invariably incomplete and controversial, and depend usually on deductions from and modifications of Section III [of the Hague Regulations]; most of them, it will appear, have not been hitherto studied and properly analyzed.[196]

However, any approach which tends to limit the application of the law simply to cases of belligerent occupation has many disadvantages: (*a*) it goes against a large body of practice and court opinion; (*b*) it would leave many activities of armed forces outside their own country in something of an international legal limbo; and (*c*), in any case, belligerent occupations themselves vary enormously in their character and purpose, so such an approach would not only be artificial and arbitrary, but would also still leave us with the original problem that one body of law is applicable to many very different cases. The idea that there is a standard case should not be readily abandoned, and some contemporary occupations (for example, the West Bank and Gaza) are in some ways very close to it. However, a recognition that there is a standard case is not incompatible with an acceptance that the classical conception of belligerent occupation is too rigid, and does not correspond to real life.

A better approach, it is suggested, is to accept that the law on occupations is formally applicable to, and capable of being applied in, a wide variety of situations. Two considerations particularly point to such a course. First, to a large extent the nexus of rights and duties it describes is a body of minimum rules, which any power should be able to follow at any time. Secondly, within the law on occupations there is some allowance for the application of different combinations of rules in different circumstances. For example, the Hague and Geneva conventions contain many provisions permitting the occupant to take certain measures in connection with military operations, or on account of real security needs: where there is no continuing war, or the security situation is more stable, such measures would not be justified. Many other provisions for adjusting the applicable rules to the particular situation may be noted. Some provisions

[196] Feilchenfeld, op. cit. above (p. 261 n. 39), at p. 6. See also von Glahn, op. cit. above (p. 261 n. 39), at p. 28.

which restrict an occupant's freedom of action quite conspicuously, such as the Hague requirement to respect the existing laws of an occupied country, are subject to reasonable provisos of one kind or another allowing for exceptional circumstances.

The adaptability of the law on occupations is further indicated by the scope which exists for special agreements of various kinds between occupant and occupied. While there is obviously a risk that special agreements may (contrary to 1949 Geneva Convention IV) derogate from the rights of the inhabitants, this is by no means always the case. The legal framework negotiated at The Hague and Geneva is not so perfect that it cannot be improved upon, and it is hardly surprising that in some occupations, especially those of allied territory, there have in fact been significant improvements.[197]

Indeed, while it is certainly based on some clear minimum standards, there is an extent to which it is wrong to conceive of the law on occupations as a single set of rules. True, its basic principles and provisions are set out in concise form in the Hague Regulations and the Geneva Civilians Convention, but to these must be added many other elements, involving State practice, case law and writings, as well as other conventions of a more general character. In addition, the parallel stream of the international law of human rights has not only influenced the recent development of the laws of war in the shape of 1977 Geneva Protocol I, but has also been increasingly recognized as having some applicability to occupations in its own right.[198]

Granted that it is a substantial body of law containing many elements of flexibility, the tendency to regard the law on occupations as applicable only on a *de facto* basis rather than *de jure*, or only partially through some of its provisions rather than as a whole, is bound to be viewed with some scepticism. Even the fact that in special cases some States may feel justified in ignoring or violating some provisions of the law on occupations does not necessarily mean that the law is wrong or useless. In municipal law, and indeed in ethical systems, norms are sometimes violated (occasionally even for good reasons), but they can still be important yardsticks by which the activities of individuals and States may be guided at the time and evaluated later. The condition of international society being what it is, the practical need for a body of law derived largely from the law of war, and providing such a yardstick for the activities of armed forces *vis-à-vis* the inhabitants of foreign territories, is likely to remain.

[197] In the case of *Ministère Public* v. *Saelens* a Belgian Court Martial held on 25 October 1945: 'The military police of an allied occupying power is not competent to resort to domiciliary search for the purpose of investigating and repressing offences subject to Belgian law . . . On the contrary, the Convention concluded on May 16, 1944 in London between the Belgian Government and allied Governments provided that Belgians who have committed crimes or delicts against allied armies shall be summoned before Belgian Courts Martial . . .': *Annual Digest*, 13 (1946), Case no. 36, pp. 85–6.

[198] Above, pp. 250, 287.

[10]

THE LEGAL RELATIONS BETWEEN AN OCCUPYING POWER AND THE INHABITANTS.

Lassa Oppenheim

IN my paper on War Treason published on pp. 266–86 of this volume of the L. Q. R. I discussed and rejected the doctrine which asserts that the inhabitants of militarily occupied country owe a temporary allegiance to the occupant. It is advisable to inquire now into the nature of the relations between an occupying power and the inhabitants. It cannot be said at all that the nature of these relations is everywhere clearly recognized and well defined. The literature on the subject is to a great extent obscure, and the echo of the former rule that the occupant at once becomes the sovereign of the occupied territory resounds more or less distinctly in the writings of many publicists, although it is commonly rejected in the crude expression given to it by Twiss (vol. ii, § 64). When Bluntschli (§ 544) says that, while the dominion (*Staatsgewalt*) of the legitimate government is displaced by the military power of the occupant, the inhabitants must render *staatlichen Gehorsam* to the occupying power; when Despagnet (§ 570) says that the *de facto* substitution of the sovereignty of the occupant for the sovereignty of the legitimate government subjects the inhabitants to certain obligations to the occupying power; and when other authors use similar language, the suspicion is roused that they still labour under a remote influence of the nowadays untenable theory that the occupant is for the time being the sovereign of the occupied territory. Indeed, a number of writers, such as Hall (§§ 154 and 155 of the 4th edition) and Calvo (§ 2166 of the 5th edition), have in every point freed themselves from the influence of the theory of substituted sovereignty, yet they have not sufficiently [1] elucidated the nature of the relations between the occupying power and the inhabitants. On the other hand, there is a general agreement on three points. Firstly, every one agrees that through military occupation the authority over the territory

[1] I must reproach myself in this matter, if there be reproach at all. Although throughout my treatise on international law where I treat of occupation, I, of course, avoid calling the authority of the occupant 'sovereignty'—I always deliberately speak of his 'sway' to which inhabitants owe obedience, and assert that this sway is merely military authority,—I have nowhere pointed out, as I ought to have, that the obedience owed to the occupant is imposed upon the inhabitants by his martial law only, and neither by international nor by their own municipal law.

and the inhabitants only *de facto*, and not by right, and only temporarily, and not permanently, passes into the hands of the occupant. Secondly, everybody admits that, since the occupant is *de facto* in authority, he has a right[1] of administration over the territory, with the consequence that all administrative acts which he carries out in accordance with the laws of war and the existing local law must be recognized by the legitimate government after the occupation ceases. Thirdly, everybody admits that, while the occupation lasts, the inhabitants have to render obedience to the occupying power. But there are two questions which require elucidation, namely, of what *kind* the authority of the occupant is, and what *law* it is according to which inhabitants owe obedience to the occupying power.

As regards the *kind of authority* an occupant possesses, Hall and others correctly describe it as mere military authority. 'Occupation is merely a phase in military operations' which will only last a longer or shorter time unless it turns into subjugation or into rightful possession by cession. There is not an atom of sovereignty in the authority of the occupant, since it is now generally recognized that the sovereignty of the legitimate government, although it cannot be exercised, is in no way diminished by mere military occupation. The mere military character of the authority of the occupant finds its expression in martial law, under which a territory and its inhabitants come *ipso facto* by the occupation. The 'Instructions for the Government of Armies of the United States in the Field' of 1863 are very excellent on this point in laying down the following two rules:

'§ 1. A place, district, or country occupied by an enemy stands, in consequence of the occupation, under the martial law of the invading or occupying army, whether any proclamation declaring martial law, or any public warning to the inhabitants, has been issued or not. Martial law is the immediate and direct effect and consequence of occupation or conquest. The presence of a hostile army proclaims its martial law.'

'§ 4. Martial law is simply military authority exercised in accordance with the laws and usages of war. Military oppression is not martial law; it is the abuse of the power which that law confers. As martial law is executed by military force, it is incumbent upon those who administer it to be strictly guided by the principles of justice, honour, and humanity—virtues adorning a soldier even more than other men, for the very reason that he possesses the power of his arms against the unarmed.'

[1] If the occupant had not the *right* of administration over the territory, the legitimate government would not be in *duty* bound to recognize, after the occupation ceases, such acts of the occupant as he carried out in accordance with the local laws and the laws of war.

It must, however, be emphasized that although martial law is military authority and nothing else, this authority is nowadays considerably restricted. In former times the powers of the occupant over the territory and the inhabitants were much wider than they are at present, especially since the Hague Regulations concerning the laws and customs of war on land have been agreed upon which deal in section 3, articles 42–56, with the military authority over an occupied territory. Accordingly, the occupant must take all steps in his power to re-establish and ensure as far as possible public order and safety. He must not alter the local laws according to discretion: he must respect them and leave them in force unless absolutely prevented by military necessity. He must respect family honour and rights, the lives of individuals, private property, religious convictions, and liberty of worship. If he collects the taxes and the like, he is on the other hand bound to defray the expenses of the administration of the occupied territory on the same scale as that to which the legitimate government was bound. If the occupant, besides the ordinary taxes, levies other money contributions, this can only be done for military necessities or for the requirements of the local administration. And there are other well-known restrictions which I need not enumerate here, as they become clearly apparent from section 3 of the Hague Regulations. However, it is necessary to draw attention to the fact that the Hague Regulations do not intend to provide a complete code. The preamble of the fourth Hague Convention, to which are appended the Hague Regulations, distinctly says:

> 'On the other hand, it could not be intended by the High Contracting Parties that the cases not provided for should, for want of a written provision, be left to the arbitrary judgment of military commanders. Until a more complete code of the laws of war can be issued, the High Contracting Powers think it expedient to declare that in cases not included in the Regulations adopted by them, populations and belligerents remain under the protection and the rule of the principles of the laws of nations, as they result from the usages established between civilized nations, from the laws of humanity, and the requirements of the public conscience.'

It is for this reason that such acts of an occupant as are not distinctly prohibited by the Hague Regulations are not necessarily lawful. Besides the restrictions specifically mentioned in the Hague Regulations, the military power of the occupant is restricted by 'the usages established between civilized nations', by 'the laws of humanity', and by 'the requirements of the public conscience'.

Turning now to the question of what law it is according to which inhabitants owe obedience to the occupying power, it is, in the first instance, quite certain that it is not their own municipal law. Municipal law demands obedience to the legitimate sovereign only; the occupant is by no means, and with regard to no point, the legitimate sovereign, although, after the occupation ceases, the legitimate government must recognize all such administrative acts as he carried out in accordance with the local laws and the laws of war. The occupant is an enemy who enters the territory forcibly, drives out the legitimate government, and puts the territory and its inhabitants under his military authority. Any obedience the occupant may demand from the inhabitants is therefore certainly not demanded from them by their municipal law. Bordwell in his work, The Law of War between Belligerents, Chicago, 1908, p. 300, seems to argue that, in so far as the occupant conducts the administration of the territory according to the existing laws, the inhabitants are by their municipal law compelled to render him obedience. He says:

'In so far as the occupant acts as the territorial authority for the purpose of ensuring order and exacting the laws, and not for his own immediate belligerent rights, it would appear to be incontestable that the inhabitant does owe him obedience. It would be a hard rule placing on him the burden of punishing ordinary crime or of carrying out such measures as those of sanitation, if the inhabitants were not to be under any obligation to assist him in them or to render him the obedience due with regard to such things from every inhabitant to the government under which he lives. . . . So long, then, as the occupant is acting as a territorial authority in carrying out the ordinary purpose of government, and not for his own purpose, inhabitants owe him obedience; but when he goes further and takes measures which are for his own belligerent purposes, it would seem that the inhabitants, far from owing him obedience, may still look upon him as the enemy of the government to which they owe allegiance, and, so far as orders are hostile to that government, may disregard them as far as they can reasonably do so. Where certain acts are in themselves offenses against the laws of war, the inhabitants are bound to abstain from them, but this is not because of obedience due to the occupant but of respect due to the laws of war.'

This argumentation of Bordwell, although at the first glance plausible, is misleading. In so far as the occupant conducts the administration of the country according to the existing laws, the inhabitants do not really render obedience to *him* but to their own laws and to their own government. The fact that, while conducting the administration of the country according to the existing laws, the occupant is, so to say, the *locum tenens* of the legitimate government, does not make the obedience to these laws on the part of the inhabitants appear to be an obedience rendered to the occupant personally. Even the German Government seems to recognize this, as becomes apparent from the fact that the Belgian courts of justice are during the present German occupation permitted to continue to pronounce their judgments in the name of the King of the Belgians!

On the other hand, it is sometimes asserted that the inhabitants owe obedience to the occupant according to international law, because occupation is a legitimate aim of warfare, and a belligerent does, therefore, not act unlawfully by occupying enemy territory: further, because international law recognizes that the authority over the territory has *de facto* passed into the hands of the occupant and that he has thereby acquired a temporary right of administration over the territory and the inhabitants; and, lastly, because section 3 of the Hague Regulations imposes a number of duties upon the occupant in the very interests of the inhabitants. The correlative to right is duty, and the correlative to duty is right. If the occupant by taking possession of the territory has acquired a temporary right of administration over the territory and its inhabitants, the inhabitants must be in duty bound to submit to this administration. If the occupant has duties towards the inhabitants, he must have rights, and one of these rights is the right to demand obedience from the inhabitants.

This contention that the inhabitants owe obedience to the occupant, according to international law, is, however, faulty, because it overlooks the fact that international law is a law between States only and exclusively, in no way a law between States and individuals, and cannot therefore directly impose rights and duties upon individuals. To the temporary right of administration acquired by the occupant corresponds, not the duty of the inhabitants to submit to such administration, but the duty of the legitimate government to recognize, after the occupation has ceased, all the legitimate acts of administration carried out by the occupant. The duty imposed upon the occupant by section 3 of the Hague Regulations is indeed imposed upon him in the interest of the inhabitants, but no international law relations are thereby created between him and the inhabitants. The duty imposed upon him creates international law relations between him and the legitimate government. The correlative to this duty upon him is not a right of his to demand obedience from the inhabitants but a right of the legitimate government to demand from the occupant that he carries out his administration of the territory in accordance with section 3 of the Hague Regulations. The legitimate government can *demand* from the occupant that he complies with the duty concerned because he has actual authority over the territory, and therefore, according to international law, a temporary right of administration over it. He must re-establish and ensure public authority and safety by the authority which he actually possesses, namely, military authority.

Now if it is neither municipal law nor international law according to which inhabitants owe obedience to the occupant, what, then, is the law according to which they do owe obedience to him?

If it is any law at all, it is martial law, the martial law of the occupying power *ipso facto* imposed upon the inhabitants by the military occupation of the territory. They owe obedience to him because he holds them in the hollow of his hand; he will crush them if they are not obedient. They must be obedient because he can enforce obedience. His authority is based, not on any law, but on his force; it rests on his bayonets, and on the good will, if any, of the inhabitants. No other law than the martial law of the occupant is at the background of the obedience which inhabitants owe to the occupant!

If that is the correct view, it is neither municipal nor international law which prohibits inhabitants from rising in arms, from giving information to their own government, and from abstaining from other acts inimical to the occupant.

But are not inhabitants at any rate *morally* bound to render obedience to the authority of the occupant, provided he does not demand anything from them which the law of war prevents him from demanding? It is sometimes asserted that the rising in arms against the occupant, the giving of information to their own government, and other acts inimical to the occupant on the part of the inhabitants, are a breach of trust. It is argued that the occupant treats the civil population of the territory leniently, in especial does not take them into captivity, because he trusts that they will not commit any act inimical to his interests, and that therefore such acts are a breach of trust. Guelle in his Précis des lois de la guerre sur terre, 1884, vol. i, p. 130, speaks of a *quasi-contract* between the occupant and the inhabitants according to which the latter tacitly engage to remain 'neutral' in return for the protection which they receive from the occupant. The Italian Fiore—see his Nouveau droit international public, second edition, French translation by Antoine, vol. iii, 1886, § 1457—asserts that, by the submission of the inhabitants to the occupation, a kind of *moral contract* is tacitly established between them and the occupant which imposes upon the inhabitants the duty to abstain from hostilities and the duty to render obedience to the occupant.

Now I do not deny that there are moral relations between the occupant and the inhabitants; since *de facto* relations have arisen between him and them, these relations, like all other human relations, are not free from moral duties as well as moral rights. Nor do I deny that *individual* inhabitants are morally bound not to resort to hostilities in arms, and the like, while the occupation lasts; but this is not the outcome of a moral duty towards the occupant but towards their fellow-citizens, for he who resorts to such hostilities endangers the safety of the other inhabitants, because he gives the occupant an excuse for resorting to reprisals and all other kinds of oppressive measures. And, lastly, I do not deny that the occupant treats the civil inhabitants differently from the members of the armed forces of the enemy because he *expects* them not to commit hostilities, not to give information to the enemy, and the like, and that he considers such acts as a breach of trust which he, therefore, calls 'war rebellion' or 'war treason', as the case may be, although the conception of war treason does not comprise exclusively acts committed by inhabitants of militarily occupied territory. However, these inhabitants are being trusted without having given their consent to being trusted. From the point of view of those who commit acts of 'war rebellion' or 'war treason' there is, therefore, no moral wrong in them. Moreover, the fact that the occupant considers such acts as a breach of trust does not even in his own eyes make them morally wrong in so far as they are committed against his authority. Guelle's tacit quasi-contract is as much a valueless fiction as Fiore's tacit moral contract between the occupant and the inhabitants. They receive the occupant submissively because they cannot help it. They chafe under his yoke while he keeps them by force under his sway. Their patriotism will never agree to the proposition that they are morally bound not to rise in arms and thereby free the country from his sway, or not to give valuable information to their own government, or not to assist soldiers of their own army to avoid captivity, and the like. If they desist from committing such acts, they do it because they are afraid of the punishment threatened by the occupant. And the occupant knows quite well that the inhabitants chafe under his yoke, that they submit to his sway because they cannot help it, that they would do anything to turn him out if he did not succeed in keeping them down by force. States will never consent to a law-making international treaty proposing a rule by which they would be prevented from asking the inhabitants of such of their territory as may come under enemy occupation to rise in arms and drive the occupant out, or according to which States would be prevented from making use of valuable information given to them by inhabitants of territory under enemy occupation, whether such information was given spontaneously or for the asking.

For this reason, just as neither international law nor their own municipal law prevents inhabitants of occupied territory from rising in arms or from giving information to their own government, and the like, so no moral taint is attached to such acts. Neither the prosecutor nor the members of the court martial which pronounced sentence of death against Nurse Cavell, nor the general in command who confirmed this outrageous sentence, would assert that she had committed a moral wrong. The occupant punishes inimical acts because necessity compels him thereto; if he did not punish them, he could not maintain his sway over the occupied territory and its inhabitants. He is justified in threatening, and eventually carrying out, punishments for the purpose of deterrence, although he is by no means justified in pronouncing and carrying out brutal and inhuman sentences. 'Est modus in rebus, sunt certi denique fines.' Natural justice, humanity, and the public conscience of the world demand that punishments which he threatens, pronounces, and carries out, be in due proportion to the harm to his interests comprised in the criminal acts concerned. There is neither a need nor a right of the occupant to set up a reign of terror and frightfulness. Moreover, such a reign is apt to defeat its own ends because it will sooner or later drive the unfortunate population into desperation so that they rise in arms. It will also call forth the righteous wrath of the neutral world and cause the intervention of neutral Powers. On the other hand, a just and humane, albeit stern and not indulgent, rule is apt to reconcile the population to their inevitable fate and make them submit to it, although they may chafe under its yoke.

L. OPPENHEIM.

P.S. It seems advisable to point out that the subject of this paper is only the abstract question as to the nature of the legal relations between an occupying power and the inhabitants. The discussion of the innumerable violations, on the part of the German forces occupying Belgium and other enemy territories, of the Hague Regulations concerning occupation is outside my present scope.

[11]

THE DUTY OF OBEDIENCE TO THE BELLIGERENT OCCUPANT

By MAJOR RICHARD R. BAXTER, B.A., LL.B.[1]

WHEN enemy territory has been subjected to belligerent occupation, the inhabitants of that area are commonly said to be under a duty not to commit acts which would jeopardize the security of the occupant. Violations of this duty of obedience are often described in terms of 'war treason' and 'war rebellion'. However, there has been no agreement on the questions whether the juridical basis for this obligation is to be sought in international law, in the municipal law of the occupied state, or merely in the superior force of the occupant and whether its violations may accurately be described in terms borrowed from municipal law. The ruthlessness and disregard for international law which have characterized the conduct of belligerent occupations during two world wars have raised these questions in a particularly acute form. Although the Geneva Convention relative to the Protection of Civilian Persons in Time of War of 12 August 1949 profited from experience gained since the adoption of Hague Convention No. IV of 1907, it did not purport to be a complete recodification of the law of belligerent occupation.[2] The fundamental question of the relationship existing between the inhabitant and the occupying Power remains for the most part a problem of the common law of war and is illuminated only fitfully by explicit provisions of the new Geneva Convention.

The protection of the civilian population of occupied areas against oppression by the occupant has consistently been a guiding principle of the law of belligerent occupation. In the changing tides of warfare it is essential that, to the maximum extent compatible with the conduct of hostilities, the civilian non-combatant should be safeguarded in his person, his property, his loyalties, and in the legal order to which he is subject. It is inevitable, however, that the inhabitants of an occupied area will chafe under enemy rule and under the restrictions placed upon them in the interest of the occupant's security and that they will in numerous instances, acting either singly or in concert, commit acts inconsistent with the security of the occupying forces. The occupant must undoubtedly have the means of dealing, and dealing severely, with such acts, whether or not they arise from hostile intent. It must be recognized, on the other hand, that there is a tendency for the occupant to project his anger indiscriminately

[1] Of the Judge Advocate General's Corps, United States Army. The opinions expressed in this article are those of the author and do not necessarily reflect the views of the Secretary of Defense, the Secretary of the Army, or the Judge Advocate General of the Army.

[2] Art. 154. See Gutteridge, 'The Geneva Conventions of 1949', in this *Year Book*, 26 (1949), pp. 318–19.

upon the guilty and innocent alike and to impose excessive penalties on the wrongdoers when he is exposed to conduct prejudicial to his safety. On what juridical basis the legitimate protection of the occupant against hostile or dangerous acts may best be reconciled with the protection of civilians against arbitrary and unwarranted penalties and punishments is the problem to which this article is directed. To this end it will be necessary to consider the nature of the duty which the inhabitant owes to the occupant and the propriety of describing acts of resistance as 'war treason' or as 'war rebellion'.

I. *The inhabitant's duty to the occupant*

As the law of belligerent occupation developed out of the law which was at one time applicable to conquered territory and ultimately attained an independent status, theories of the nature of the duty owed to the occupant by the inhabitants of the area he occupies have undergone a corresponding change.

1. *Allegiance*

Prior to the emergence of a distinct law of belligerent occupation during the second half of the eighteenth century and the early nineteenth century, enemy territory occupied by armed forces immediately became part of the territory of the occupying state.[1] The unqualified allegiance of the inhabitants of the area was, as a matter of course, demanded by the occupant, and their relationship to the occupant was left entirely to municipal law.[2] Thus when Louis XIV took Namur in 1692, the magistrates of the city came to him the next day to render him homage as his loyal subjects.[3] Although there were intimations in the great texts of the seventeenth century that mere belligerent occupation of territory is precarious and that the very uncertainty of the fortunes of war demands restraint in the exercise of belligerent 'rights',[4] it remained for Vattel and for Klüber and Heffter in the nineteenth century to assert that sovereignty over an occupied area does not pass to the occupant while hostilities are still in progress. Until a *debellatio*, normally in the form of a peace treaty, which determines the disposition to be made of the territory, the state whose territory it is is deprived only of the exercise of certain attributes of sovereignty.[5]

[1] Nys, *Le Droit international. Les principes, les théories, les faits*, vol. iii (1912), p. 223.

[2] See, e.g., Wolff, *Jus Gentium Methodo Scientifica Pertractatum* (1764), § 892; Heffter, *Das europäische Völkerrecht der Gegenwart* (1st ed., 1884), § 132.

[3] Van Nispen tot Sevenaer, *L'Occupation allemande pendant la dernière guerre mondiale* (1946), p. 157.

[4] Grotius, *De Jure Belli ac Pacis* (1625), Book iii, Ch. vi, iv. 1; Pufendorf, *De Jure Naturae et Gentium Libri Octo* (1688), Book viii, Ch. vi, § 7.

[5] Vattel, *Le Droit des gens* (1758), Book iii, Ch. xiii; Klüber, *Droit des gens moderne de l'Europe* (1831), § 256; Heffter, op. cit., §§ 131–3.

The theory that an occupied territory immediately becomes part of the occupying state was slow to die. An English court could state in 1814 that: 'No point is more clearly settled in the Courts of Common Law than that a conquered country forms immediately part of the King's dominions.'[1] In 1875 Sir Travers Twiss still maintained that a belligerent nation taking possession of an enemy's territory acquires sovereignty over it.[2] A revision of de Martens' text which was published a decade earlier contains a statement that a state which makes itself master of an enemy province may demand homage from the inhabitants.[3] During the war between the United States and Mexico, General Kearney issued a proclamation absolving all persons residing in the occupied portion of Mexico from their allegiance to that republic and claiming them as citizens of the United States—an act which did not pass without criticism in Congress.[4] However, these are but isolated instances during a period of change. Already, during several wars of the eighteenth century, new theories of belligerent occupation had been given application.[5] A demand by the occupant for unqualified and permanent allegiance gradually ceased to have the sanction of law or of general practice.

2. *Temporary allegiance*

In Anglo-American law, as distinguished from that of the Continent, the relationship of the population of an occupied area to the occupant was, during a large portion of the nineteenth century, described in terms of *temporary* allegiance. This view is particularly apparent in the American jurisprudence of the period. It received its first statement in *United States* v. *Hayward*,[6] in which Mr. Justice Story made his celebrated statement that by the military occupation of Castine, Maine, by British forces, the inhabitants thereof passed under a temporary allegiance to the British Government. Subsequent opinions of the United States Supreme Court adopted this principle,[7] but in 1830 the Court tempered its holding by suggesting that the occupation of James Island and Charleston by the British in 1780,

[1] *The Foltina* (1814), 1 Dods. 450, 451, 165 E.R. 1374, 1375. Cf. *The Gerasimo* (1857), 11 Moo. P.C. 88, 14 E.R. 628, which indicates that, at least with respect to the question of the enemy character of occupied territory, the principle enunciated in *The Foltina* had by 1857 ceased to prevail.

[2] *The Law of Nations Considered as Independent Political Communities. On the Rights and Duties of Nations in Time of War* (2nd ed., 1875), § 64.

[3] *Précis du droit des gens moderne de l'Europe* (2nd ed. by Vergé, 1864), § 280.

[4] *House Executive Document No. 19*, 29th Congress, 2nd Session, pp. 20 ff., cited in Thomas, *A History of Military Government in Newly Acquired Territory of the United States* (1904), p. 104. For a criticism of General Kearney's conduct, see the remarks of Mr. Holmes in *Congressional Globe*, 29th Congress, 2nd Session, p. 18.

[5] Nys, op. cit., vol. iii, p. 223. A number of historical instances are collected at pp. 227–33.

[6] (C.C. Mass. 1815), F. Cas. No. 15,336, 2 Gall. 485.

[7] *United States* v. *Rice* (1819), 4 Wheat. 246; *Fleming et al.* v. *Page* (1850), 9 How. 603; *Thorington* v. *Smith* (1868), 8 Wall. 1.

while causing the inhabitants to owe temporary allegiance to Great Britain, did not 'annihilate their allegiance to the state of South Carolina'.[1] This judicial characterization of the effect of belligerent occupation represented the state of the law during the war with Mexico and formed the basis of political pronouncements of the time.[2]

Repeated judicial affirmations of this principle left little room for dissent upon the part of American international lawyers. The duty of allegiance is, according to Halleck, writing in 1861, reciprocal to the duty of protection which rests on the occupant, but because of the incompleteness and instability of occupation, the allegiance is only a temporary or qualified one.[3] In fact, the civilian inhabitants of a place taken by the enemy who are allowed to lay down their arms and return to their peaceful pursuits are 'virtually in the condition of prisoners of war on parole'.[4] Other authors, in extending this characterization to the inhabitants of occupied areas generally, overlooked the fact that Halleck had been speaking of members of defending armed forces who had surrendered and been allowed to assume peaceful occupations.[5] The American writers often speak of an 'implied covenant' or an 'implied parole' to remain quiescent which is imputed to the inhabitants and forms the basis of their allegiance to the occupant.[6] During the nineteenth century Mr. Justice Story's remarks in *United States* v. *Hayward* were also quoted and approved by a number of British writers on the subject.[7]

The adoption of Article 45 of the Regulations annexed to Convention No. IV of The Hague of 1907, which forbade compelling the population of occupied territory to swear allegiance to the hostile Power, eventually

[1] *Shanks* v. *Dupont* (1830), 3 Pet. 242.

[2] In replying to Congressional inquiries concerning the administration of the occupied portion of Mexico, President Polk, in a message to the House of Representatives on 24 July 1848, stated that the inhabitants of this area owed a temporary allegiance to the United States. He quoted extensively from *United States* v. *Rice* (Richardson, *A Compilation of the Messages and Papers of the Presidents, 1789–1897* (1897), vol. iv, p. 595).

[3] *International Law; or, Rules Regulating the Intercourse of States in Peace and War* (1861), p. 791.

[4] Ibid., p. 793.

[5] See, e.g., Rolin-Jaequemyns, 'Chronique du droit international. Essai complémentaire sur la guerre franco-allemande dans ses rapports avec le droit international', in *Revue de droit international et de législation comparée*, 3 (1871), p. 312.

[6] Field, *Draft Outlines of an International Code* (1872), vol. ii, p. 482; Birkhimer, *Military Government and Martial Law* (1892), pp. 38–41. Dana's notes in his edition of Wheaton state that the occupying forces have 'a right to require of the inhabitants an oath or parole, not inconsistent with their general and ultimate allegiance to their own state' to remain quiet and submit to the occupant's authority (Wheaton, *Elements of International Law* (8th ed. by Dana, 1866), p. 436, note. Although Hannis Taylor believed that temporary or qualified allegiance is owed to the occupant, he adopted the view that there is no legal or moral impediment to insurrection by the inhabitants if they are willing to undergo the perils of such an enterprise (*A Treatise on International Public Law* (1901), pp. 585–92).

[7] Phillimore, *Commentaries upon International Law* (3rd ed., 1885), vol. iii, p. 869; Creasy, *First Platform of International Law* (1876), p. 512; Wheaton, op. cit. (3rd English ed. by Boyd, 1889), p. 469.

made this theory untenable. The question of the exaction of an oath of allegiance had previously attracted relatively little attention. The United States *Instructions for the Government of Armies of the United States in the Field*, which came into use during the Civil War, had stated no more than that an oath of fidelity or temporary allegiance might be administered to civil officers in the occupied territory,[1] but Bluntschli's paraphrase of this provision carried an annotation to the effect that an 'oath of citizenship' could not be demanded in occupied territory until the conclusion of peace.[2] A provision substantially similar to Article 45 had originally been drafted at the Brussels Conference of 1874[3] and was repeated in the Oxford Manual prepared by the Institute of International Law in 1880.[4] With the unequivocal statement of the 1899 Regulations, which was repeated without further discussion in 1907,[5] it was hardly possible to argue that an inhabitant owed any duty of allegiance to the occupant. More recently, the Geneva Civilians Convention of 1949 has called attention to the fact that an individual in occupied territory who has committed an offence against the occupying Power is not to be considered as bound to the occupant by any duty of allegiance.[6]

3. *A duty of obedience created by international law*

A third theory of the duty of the inhabitant to the occupant, which stands in roughly chronological succession to the view just described, is cast in terms of a duty of obedience imposed by the law of nations. Although this view of the relationship of persons involved in belligerent occupation would certainly not create any greater latitude to commit acts hostile to the occupant, the difference in terminology is nevertheless significant. It suggests forcefully that the relationship of the inhabitant to the occupant is quite different in nature from the relationship of a citizen to his own country, and correspondingly that acts inconsistent with the security of the occupant and offences against the integrity of the state must belong to two separate bodies of law. In practical terms, it indicates moreover that the inhabitant may not be called upon to do certain acts, such as performing

[1] Art. 26, General Orders No. 100, War Department, Adjutant General's Office, 24 April 1863.

[2] *Das moderne Völkerrecht der civilisirten Staaten* (1868), § 551.

[3] Art. 37. The provision in the *projet* submitted to the Conference by the Russian Government had been that the occupied population could not be required to submit to a 'serment de sujétion perpetuelle' to the enemy (see Art. 49, *Projet*, in *Actes de la Conférence de Bruxelles* (1874)).

[4] Art. 47, 'Manuel des lois de la guerre', in *Annuaire de l'Institut de droit international*, 5 (1881–2), p. 167. In a penal code of war prepared by de Landa in 1878, the requiring of an oath (of apparently any nature) of the population of occupied territory rendered the occupant guilty of an *abus d'autorité* ('Droit pénal de la guerre. Projet de classification des crimes et délits contre les lois de la guerre', in *Revue de droit international et de législation comparée*, 10 (1878), p. 183).

[5] See *The Proceedings of the Hague Peace Conferences. The Conference of 1899* (ed. by Scott, 1920), pp. 63, 428, 487, 557.

[6] Art. 68. See also Art. 67, which provides in part that 'They [the courts of the occupant] shall take into consideration the fact that the accused is not a national of the Occupying Power.'

military service or forced labour or furnishing information on hostile activities, which might properly be expected of one owing allegiance.

Those who adopt the view that a duty of obedience is created by international law assert that the rationale of this principle lies in the consideration that a duty of obedience and submission is owed in return for the protection the inhabitant receives. A number of continental writers find a jurisprudential basis for this duty in what is variously described by Guelle as *une espèce de quasi-contrat*, by Loening as a *communauté de droit*, and by Fiore and Calvo as *une sorte de contrat moral* between occupant and occupied.[1] If an inhabitant breaches this social contract, which concededly is the creation of necessity and not of choice, he is placed outside the protection of the law and may be treated at discretion, subject to the limitations imposed by morality and natural justice. It is obvious that this legal principle, which makes an 'outlaw' of someone who commits some trifling act of hostility against the occupant, is difficult to reconcile with patriotic sentiment. Calvo is forced to concede that although the inhabitant of the occupied area 'ought' to desist from resistance, the same inhabitant has the 'right' and 'an imperious duty' under his own law to take up arms against the occupant and to seek to recover his freedom.[2] This caveat represents in itself a withdrawal from the extreme position taken by several other international lawyers, who had asserted that continued resistance on the part of persons in occupied territory is not sanctioned by international law, should not be required by the occupied state, and is, in virtually all circumstances, 'immoral'.[3]

Other continental writers who do not speak in terms of a social contract nevertheless believe that a duty of obedience, reciprocal to the occupant's duty of protection and like it created by international law, is owed to the occupant.[4] In some British texts the duty is also recognized as being created by international law, but it often appears under a different name, such as a duty of quiescence, as Spaight puts it.[5] Several military manuals, including the German *Kriegsbrauch im Landkriege*,[6] the British *Manual of*

[1] Guelle, *Précis des lois de la guerre sur terre* (1884), vol. i, p. 130; Loening, 'L'Administration du gouvernement-général de l'Alsace durant la guerre de 1870–1871', in *Revue de droit international et de législation comparée*, 5 (1873), p. 72; Fiore, *Trattato di diritto internazionale pubblico* (2nd ed., 1884), vol. iii, pp. 238–9, 245; Calvo, *Le Droit international théorique et pratique* (5th ed., 1896), vol. iv, pp. 216–18.

[2] Loc. cit.

[3] See, e.g., Loening, op. cit., pp. 76–7, in which the author especially praises the efficacy of collective punishments, and Rolin-Jaequemyns, loc. cit., pp. 319, 325.

[4] Pillet, *Les Lois actuelles de la guerre* (1898), pp. 200–1, 207–9; Rolin, *Le Droit moderne de la guerre* (1920), vol. i, p. 429; Fauchille, *Traité de droit international public* (1921), vol. ii, pp. 210–11; Nys, op. cit., vol. iii, p. 108; Mérignhac, *Traité de droit public international* (1912), vol. iii, p. 416; Von Liszt, *Le Droit international* (tr. by Gidel from 8th German ed. of 1913), pp. 326–7.

[5] Lafiti, *Effects of War on Property* (1909), p. 11; Spaight, *War Rights on Land* (1911), p. 323.

[6] (1902), p. 114.

Military Law,[1] and the United States *Rules of Land Warfare*[2] speak in more general terms of a duty of obedience. While the source of the duty is not made plain by these texts, a proper inference would appear to be that it is regarded as lying in international law. An 'oath of neutrality' was demanded of the inhabitants of occupied areas in South Africa during the Boer War,[3] and this practice has received some sanction in the texts of this country.[4] Whether the previous exaction of an oath from a person who commits a hostile or dangerous act serves any sound purpose other than compounding his offence when he violates his pledged word is highly questionable, and there seems an air of unreality about such devices after the passage of half a century. Professor Hyde is probably the only modern authority who sees any efficacy in this procedure, which he compares with giving a bond to keep the peace, the peace in this case being one imposed by international law and its breach accordingly constituting a violation of that law.[5]

For the most part, no distinction is made by these authorities between a duty to refrain from acts endangering the occupant or intended to interfere with his military operations and the individual's duty to comply with the existing municipal law of the occupied area and the measures adopted by the occupant in pursuance of his obligations under Article 43 of the Hague Regulations.[6] Bordwell is a noteworthy exception. Certain acts, he states, such as attacks on troops and what we now refer to as sabotage, are violations of international law and are punishable as such by the occupant. Obedience is similarly owed to the occupant 'acting as the territorial authority in carrying out the ordinary purposes of government, and not for his own belligerent purposes'. But if he acts in a third capacity, that is, in serving his own military interests alone, no obedience is owed to him.[7] These distinctions appear to be excessively subtle, and the first and third aspects of the occupant's function are virtually indistinguishable. Still, his formulation of the law does serve to indicate a useful distinction between

[1] (1929), Amendments No. 12 (1936), p. 72.

[2] Field Manual 27-10, War Department, 1 October 1940, para. 301, repeating the substance of Art. 26, General Orders No. 100 of 1863.

[3] Holland, *The Laws of War on Land* (1908), p. 53.

[4] Ibid.; Wheaton, op. cit. (5th English ed. by Phillipson, 1916), p. 531.

[5] *International Law. Chiefly as Interpreted and Applied by the United States* (2nd rev. ed., 1945), vol. iii, pp. 1898-9. See Wheaton, op. cit. (5th English ed. by Phillipson, 1916), p. 531, for a criticism of the practical utility of the oath.

[6] To 'take all the measures in his power to restore, and ensure, as far as possible, public order and safety'.

[7] *The Law of War between Belligerents* (1908), pp. 299-302. Professor Oppenheim criticized Bordwell's theory concerning the occupant as 'territorial authority' on the basis that when the occupant acts in this capacity, the obedience of which he incidentally receives the benefit is actually directed to the inhabitants' own laws and to their displaced government ('The Legal Relations between an Occupying Power and the Inhabitants', in *Law Quarterly Review*, 33 (1917), p. 366).

measures taken by the occupant on his own behalf and those directed to the normal government of the occupied area without regard to the military advantage, other than the preservation of order, thereby accruing to him. The second category is outside the scope of this article, but it should be noted that its importance is lessening. To an increasing degree even such measures as rationing and price control in occupied areas are inspired by the military needs of the occupant, and deliberate violation of such legislation may be employed as a weapon of resistance against the occupant.[1]

4. *A duty of obedience imposed by municipal law*

A provision of the Belgian Law of 25 May 1910, which approved Convention No. IV of The Hague of 1907, provided that the Hague Conventions and Declarations were to have 'full and complete effect in Belgium'. The Belgian Court of Cassation found in this Law a basis for concluding that a legislative measure of the German occupation authorities dealing with arbitration in rent controversies, having been promulgated in pursuance of Article 43 of the Hague Regulations, drew its legal effect not from the fact that the occupant held legislative power in Belgium but solely because Belgian law directed that it be observed.[2] The decree referred to appears to be a consequence of the occupant's authority and responsibility to secure order in the occupied area rather than of his ability to prevent conduct dangerous to him. The legal principle enunciated in the opinion might accordingly not prove applicable to acts of resistance by inhabitants.

The Court of Cassation's view of the law has been sympathetically received by several Belgian commentators, but has gained little currency elsewhere.[3] Most national courts would, it is submitted, be hesitant to construe the incorporation of the Hague Regulations into municipal law as constituting advance assent to whatever legislative measures the occupant might impose in conformity with those Regulations. De Visscher justly observes that the sovereign is free to determine the attitude to be taken by the population of the occupied area toward the occupant and that the

[1] It was so used in occupied Czechoslovakia during the Second World War (*Four Fighting Years* ('Published on Behalf of the Czechoslovak Ministry of Foreign Affairs (Department of Information)', 1943), p. 121). As the occupying Power, under Art. 55 of the Geneva Civilians Convention of 1949, has the 'duty of ensuring the food and medical supplies of the population', deliberate attempts to keep such articles from the market may constitute an additional drain on the resources of the occupant and may thus be used as a weapon of resistance.

[2] *Procureur Général Près la Cour d'Appel de Liége* v. *Marteaux, Michaux et Consorts et le Comte de Borchgrave d'Alténa* (1916), *Pasicrisie Belge*, 1915–16, vol. i, p. 375, *Belgique Judiciaire*, 1919, cols. 148 ff. But see *Cambier* v. *Lebrun et al.* (1919), *Annual Digest*, 1919–21, Case No. 325, p. 459, in which it was held that 'The decrees of the occupying Power, whatever they may be, do not emanate from the exercise of national sovereignty. They have not the validity of Belgian laws, but are merely commands of the enemy military authority and are not incorporated in the legislation or the institutions of the country.' The Belgian cases on the legislative function of the occupant are discussed in Van Nispen tot Sevenaer, op. cit., pp. 176–203.

[3] Rolin, op. cit., vol. i, pp. 445–7; de Visscher, 'L'Occupation de guerre', in *Law Quarterly Review*, 34 (1918), pp. 78–79.

sovereign will require its submission to the decrees and proclamations of the occupant only for such time as this conformity appears to be in the national interest.[1]

5. *A duty of obedience based exclusively on the power of the occupant*

While the theory that international law imposes a duty of obedience on the inhabitant has received considerable support, it has by no means gained universal acceptance either in the last century or in this. There is a strong tendency in modern law, and, it is submitted, a correct one, to deny that there is any duty of obedience founded on any legal or moral obligation with which international law concerns itself. The occupying Power's ability to enforce respect for its legitimate interests is not a creation of the law. It springs instead from superior military power and from factual capacity to compel obedience. International law suffers the occupant to legislate, but it will not lend its authority or its assistance to the enforcement of such legislation.

Although the theory that international law creates an obligation of obedience seems to prevail in French law, and in continental law generally, there is, even among the protagonists of this view, a disquieting realization that the 'moral contract' or 'community of law' or 'the reciprocal rights and duties of the inhabitant' are created solely by force.[2] Those who attribute a frankly factual basis to such duty are comparatively few in number—Jacomet, Coll, and Lorriot among the French writers.[3] De Visscher similarly recognizes the *de facto* character of the occupant's authority but suggests that the peaceful conduct of the population permits the proper sovereign to claim protection for his people.[4] It is, however, no longer the proper sovereign alone who may claim this protection, as war crimes trials following the Second World War have made plain,[5] and it is also evident that protection may be claimed for the occupied population, at least in the form of certain judicial safeguards, notwithstanding violent individual and collective resistance.[6] In England there has been a more pronounced tendency to find the source of the inhabitant's obligations in the military power of the occupant. In the modern texts, such as those of Hall, Phillipson, Pitt Cobbett, Keith, McNair, and Oppenheim, the question is

[1] Loc. cit. And see Van Nispen tot Sevenaer, op. cit., pp. 148–9.

[2] See authorities cited on p. 240, n. 1, *supra*.

[3] Jacomet, *Les Lois de la guerre continentale* ('Publié sous la direction de la section historique de l'état-major de l'armée', 1913), p. 69; Coll, *L'Occupation du temps de guerre* (1914), pp. 71–72; Lorriot, *De la nature de l'occupation de guerre* (1903), p. 175.

[4] Op. cit., p. 79.

[5] See in this connexion the Declaration of German Atrocities, 1 November 1943, issued following the Moscow Conference.

[6] See p. 255, n. 6, *infra*. The Geneva Civilians Convention of 1949 lends no sanction to the view that the safeguards it affords are contingent on the peaceful conduct of the population. A number of provisions, notably the prohibition on collective penalties and reprisals contained in Art. 33, indicate the contrary to be true.

generally regarded in this realistic fashion.[1] But the principle that international law operates only on states, which seemed to at least one British publicist to be a sufficient explanation for this attitude,[2] has lost some of its persuasiveness since the First World War.

It is difficult to believe that during the Second World War many of those who suffered under German, Italian, or Japanese occupation could have believed that their obedience to the occupation measures of those countries was demanded by any higher moral order or by international law itself, even when such measures were taken in conformity with law. The abstract question of the source of their duty, however, seldom demanded the attention of tribunals concerned with prosecutions for war crimes and collaboration. The relationship of occupant and occupied was more often approached from the standpoint of the propriety under international law of resistance by inhabitants of occupied countries. As this matter lends itself to consideration in connexion with the academic doctrine of war rebellion, comment thereon must be deferred until account has been taken of the historical development of the kindred principles of war treason and war rebellion. It may be observed that these terms are customarily regarded as being descriptive not only of violations of a duty of obedience imposed by international law but also, and more surprisingly, as being the titles ascribed by international law to certain breaches of a duty of obedience attributed exclusively to the military power of the occupant.

II. *War treason*

'War treason' has been variously described, but the majority of definitions agree that it involves the commission of hostile acts, except armed resistance and possibly espionage, by persons other than members of the armed forces properly identified as such. The concept is not peculiar to the law of belligerent occupation, for war treason, it is said, may be committed anywhere within the lines of a belligerent.[3] The term 'war treason' in the sense in which it is now understood in international law was first used in General Orders No. 100, *Instructions for the Government of Armies of the United States in the Field*, which was ostensibly prepared by a board of

[1] Hall, *A Treatise on International Law* (4th ed., 1895), p. 498; Wheaton, op. cit. (5th English ed. by Phillipson, 1916), p. 520; Pitt Cobbett, *Cases on International Law* (5th ed. by Walker, 1937) vol. ii, p. 169; Wheaton, op. cit. (7th English ed. by Keith, 1944), vol. ii, p. 234; McNair, *Legal Effects of War* (3rd ed., 1948), p. 332, n. 2; Oppenheim, *International Law* (6th ed. by Lauterpacht, 1944), vol. ii, p. 343.

[2] See Oppenheim's use of this rationale in 'The Legal Relations between an Occupying Power and the Inhabitants' in *Law Quarterly Review*, 33 (1917), p. 367. Van Nispen tot Sevenaer takes a like view (op. cit., p. 204).

[3] See, e.g., the definitions in Oppenheim, *International Law* (6th ed. by Lauterpacht, 1944), vol. ii, p. 457; British *Manual of Military Law* (1929), Amendments No. 12 (1936), p. 37; United States *Rules of Land Warfare*, para. 205.

army officers in 1862 and 1863 but was actually the work of Dr. Francis Lieber, Professor of History and Political Science at Columbia College in New York. Article 90 of the *Instructions* provided:

> 'A traitor under the law of war, or a war-traitor, is a person in a place or district under martial law who, unauthorized by the military commander, gives information of any kind to the enemy, or holds intercourse with him.'

Successive articles dealt in detail with the offences constituting war treason, including the giving of information to the inhabitant's proper government, service as a guide to the enemy in a 'hostile and invaded district', the misleading of the enemy by guides, and all 'unauthorized or secret communication with the enemy'.[1] The offence could equally be committed by a civilian or by an enemy soldier in disguise who entered the occupied area,[2] but apparently could take place only in occupied or invaded territory.[3] If a successful war traitor returned to his own army and was subsequently taken prisoner, like a spy he could not be punished for his previous offence.[4] Although Lieber claimed that he had been the first to use the term 'war traitor',[5] there were precedents for the concept in the military law of at least three nations, with all of which Lieber may well have been familiar.

The history of *Kriegsverrat*, or war treason, may be traced back to medieval Germanic law, in which it constituted a violation of duties of fidelity toward the lord.[6] Professor Oppenheim suggested[7] that Dr. Lieber, who had seen service in the Prussian army several decades earlier, may have been familiar with the provisions relating to *Kriegsverrat* in the Prussian Military Penal Code of 1845, which contained a stipulation subjecting to extraordinary military jurisdiction '. . . all subjects of the Prussian state or aliens who have, in the theatre of war, caused any danger or prejudice to the Prussian troops, by acts of treason'.[8] Although it is by no means clear from the face of this provision that it applied to occupied areas as well as to territory normally subject to Prussian law, both the previous

[1] Arts. 92, 95, and 98. Art. 97, dealing with guides who mislead, does not specifically mention war treason, but the context of the article suggests that Lieber intended so to characterize such conduct.

[2] See Art. 99, regarding the soldier, not in uniform, who is captured while carrying messages in occupied territory, and Art. 104, which refers to the war traitor who has 'safely returned to his own army'.

[3] Lieber speaks of 'a place or district under martial law' (Art. 90), 'a country or place invaded or conquered' (Art. 92), an 'invaded or occupied territory' (Art. 98), and 'a hostile and invaded district' (Art. 95).

[4] Art. 104. This limitation appears only in the Code and was not adopted in subsequent texts and manuals (see *Rules of Land Warfare*, para. 213).

[5] MS. Notebook by Lieber, Office of the Judge Advocate General of the Army, Washington, D.C., U.S.A.

[6] Pella, 'La Répression des crimes contre la personnalité de l'état', in *Recueil des cours de l'Académie de droit international*, 33 (1930), pp. 690–1.

[7] 'On War Treason', in *Law Quarterly Review*, 33 (1917), p. 281.

[8] *Militärgesetz-Codex für das Preussische Heer*, 3 April 1845, Part 2, Title 1, § 18 (4).

history and subsequent revisions of the Military Penal Code indicate that this was intended. A similar provision in Sections 67, 69, and 70 of the Prussian Penal Code of 1851 made all aliens guilty of an act of treason against the Prussian state or Prussian soldiers amenable to the law of war.[1] The French Code of Military Justice for the Army of 1857, which was an improbable source of inspiration to the ardently francophobe Lieber, contained a like stipulation, subjecting persons within enemy territory to court martial jurisdiction for the commission of certain offences, among which were espionage and treason.[2]

A third possible source of the concept of war treason in Lieber's Code was American practice itself. Reference has previously been made to General Kearney's purported absolution of the inhabitants of occupied New Mexico from their allegiance to the Republic.[3] At that time, treatment as traitors was promised to those found in arms against the United States. When, in 1847, the leader of an uprising in New Mexico was sentenced to death for 'treason against the United States', the Secretary of War advised the local military commander that the offender could not be said to be guilty of that offence, as he owed the United States no allegiance.[4] In March 1863, during the period when General Orders No. 100 was being prepared, General Halleck wrote a letter to the Union commanding officer in Tennessee in which he used the expression 'military treason' as applicable to persons who took up arms against the occupying army or the authority established by it or who furnished information to the enemy without proper authority.[5] He specifically distinguished this species of treason from the normal domestic variety.

Several circumstances indicate that it was the American practice, and more particularly the views of General Halleck, which proved a decisive influence in Lieber's adoption of the term 'war treason'. Lieber had dealt with the law of war in his *Political Ethics*, in a series of lectures he had given at Columbia College in 1861 and 1862, and in a pamphlet on guerrillas which he had prepared at the instigation of Halleck in 1862, but none of these writings adverts to war treason.[6] Indeed, in the last of these, he had

[1] See Loening, op. cit., p. 79.

[2] Loening, op. cit., p. 78. See Dalloz, *Jurisprudence générale*, 1865, Part 1, p. 500; ibid., 1866, Part 1, p. 45, in connexion with the sanctioning of this practice by the French Court of Cassation.

[3] See p. 237, *supra*.

[4] Richardson, op. cit., vol. iv, p. 598.

[5] Quoted in Halleck, op. cit. (3rd English ed. by Baker, 1893), vol. ii, pp. 55–57. General Halleck had also written to the commanding general of the Confederate forces stating that, although the United States did not extort oaths of allegiance, it did reserve the right to punish persons within its lines who were suspected of giving aid and information to its enemies or performing any other 'treasonable act' (quoted in Wheaton, op. cit. (2nd ed. by Lawrence, 1863), p. 625, n. 190).

[6] *Political Ethics* (1838–9), pp. 629–68, 'Lectures on the Laws and Usages of War delivered at the Law School of Columbia College, 1861–62', MS., Johns Hopkins University Library, Baltimore, Md., U.S.A.; *Guerrilla Parties Considered with Reference to the Laws and Usages of War* (1862).

described as espionage acts which he was later to place in the category of war treason.[1] An early draft of General Orders No. 100 refers to treasonable acts committed by inhabitants of occupied territories without the use of the qualifying 'war'.[2] As this draft was submitted to Halleck for his comments, one may surmise that it was he who suggested a more cautious approach to the matter of hostile acts in occupied areas. The expression 'war treason' had the further advantage of being grammatically and logically symmetrical with the term 'war rebel', which Lieber had previously originated. Whatever may have been the influences working on Lieber, he was certainly aware that he was dealing with a species of treason cognizable by international rather than by municipal law. Although General Orders No. 100 was prepared in time of civil war and must undoubtedly have been coloured to a certain extent by the military situation then prevailing, Lieber intended that General Orders No. 100 should constitute a code of the international law of war, and he was assiduous to distinguish those principles applicable only in civil wars from those to be observed in wars between states.[3]

The Supreme Court of the United States had several decades previously committed the jurisprudence of that country to the view that the inhabitant of an occupied area temporarily owes allegiance to the occupant. It was not unnatural therefore that the same obligations that rested on residents of the United States should be imposed on an individual who owed allegiance to the United States by reason of occupation, albeit the allegiance was only temporary, and that violations of the fidelity to which each was bound should be generally described in terms of treason. At the same time, the very characterization of war treason as something apart from treason under municipal law represented in itself a significant departure from what might be considered the logical consequences of the rule of temporary allegiance.[4] This deviation from the archaic rule then accepted by the courts should not, however, blind us to the real importance of the appearance of this new doctrine. For 'war treason' represented a fresh borrowing from domestic law at the very time that the law applicable to occupied areas was becoming a subject for international rather than municipal regulation and had successfully thrown off most of the shackles of the past.

[1] Op. cit., p. 12.

[2] *A Code for the Government of Armies in the Field as Authorized by the Laws and Usages of War on Land*, 'Printed as manuscript for the Board appointed by the Secretary of War "To Propose Amendments or Changes in the Rules and Articles of War, and a Code of Regulations for the Government of Armies in the Field, as authorized by the Laws and Usages of War" ' (February 1863), Art. 54.

[3] Lieber later wrote: 'While writing down this code I felt the high responsibility weighing on me and the gravity as well as the nobleness of this task; I was conscious of doing a piece of work for mankind of historic effect and permanency' (MS. Notebook, *supra*). Sec. X of the Code comprises nine articles applicable to insurrection, civil war, and rebellion. These articles specify the extent to which the Code is applicable under such conditions.

[4] Lieber, in Art. 26, had said no more than that the inhabitant owes a duty of obedience.

Kriegsverrat reappeared in Germany, transformed from a concept of municipal law to one of international law, in Bluntschli's *Das moderne Kriegsrecht der civilisirten Staaten.*[1] Despite this entry of war treason into German law under a new guise, it is probable that the provisions of the German Military Penal Code of 1872 applicable to *Kriegsverrat* were the outgrowth of earlier legislation, rather than of any development in international law. The Code stipulated that war treason was punishable by forced labour 'for at least ten years or in perpetuity' and itemized some twelve offences to be considered as war treason. These included espionage, communication with the enemy, betrayal of fortresses, troops, supplies, and secrets to the enemy, and refusal to obey an order.[2] A modified version of Section 161 of the 1872 Military Penal Code, which was in effect during the Second World War, made acts by the inhabitants of occupied countries against the Reich punishable in the same manner as if they had been committed in Germany. Although this provision of law was invoked by the defence in the *Justice Trial*, the Tribunal, while condemning the indiscriminate characterization of wrongs against the occupying Power as 'high treason', did not find it necessary to determine whether Section 161 was in conformity with international law.[3]

For the international conference on the laws of war which was held in Brussels in 1874, the Russian Government had prepared a draft convention. The *projet* did not refer to war traitors, but communication of information to the enemy by inhabitants of occupied territory was treated under the general heading 'Of Spies'.[4] The draft article was, however, suppressed in conformity with the unanimous opinion of the committee which considered it,[5] and the resulting code contained no reference to war treason or to the duty of the inhabitant to the occupant, the latter being merely enjoined not to require an oath of allegiance.[6] When the Institute of International Law prepared a similar manual at its Oxford meeting in 1880, it contented itself with stating that 'individuals who commit acts of hostility against the occupying authority are punishable' and that if inhabitants do not submit to the orders of the occupying authority, they may be compelled to do so.[7] The proceedings of the Hague Conferences of 1899 and 1907 are devoid of any reference to war treason under that name, and there are only isolated references to the commission of hostile acts by the inhabitants of occupied territory.[8]

[1] (1866), §§ 122, 127. See also *Das moderne Völkerrecht der civilisirten Staaten* (1868), §§ 631–9.

[2] *Militärstrafgesetzbuch*, 20 June 1872, §§ 57 and 58.

[3] *In re Altstötter et al.* (1947), *Law Reports of Trials of War Criminals* (hereinafter referred to as '*War Crimes Reports*'), vol. vi, pp. 53, 61.

[4] *Projet*, Art. 20.

[5] *Actes de la Conférence de Bruxelles (1874)*, p. 44.

[6] See p. 239, n. 3, *supra*.

[7] Arts. 47 and 48, 'Manuel des lois de la guerre', in *Annuaire de l'Institut de droit international*, 5 (1881–2), p. 167.

[8] See the statement of Colonel Gross von Schwarzoff concerning Arts. 44 through 47 of the

If war treason was received with indifference by those actively concerned in the codification of the law of war, it met a lively and far from uniform reception in text-books and monographs. Those who regard it as a useful and accurate category of international law do not greatly exceed those who do not, and it is difficult to segregate proponents and opponents on national lines. Both before and after the First World War, it was, for example, described as an accepted doctrine of international law by a number of continental international lawyers, who believed it to be applicable only to communication with the enemy.[1] On the other hand, it meets with little sympathy at the hands of Pillet and Jacomet, who feared that it was responsible for excessive individual and collective punishments and that it failed to take into account the duty of fidelity which the citizen still owes to his state.[2]

In the British view of international law, war treason embraces a wider range of offences than it does in continental law and includes most of the acts in occupied territory which give aid and comfort to the enemy, with the exception of rebellion and espionage.[3] Professor Oppenheim, more than any other individual, has been responsible for the respectability which war treason has attained in English law.[4] He included a discussion of the 'war crime' of war treason in the first edition of his text in 1906,[5] and the list of offences which he regarded as constituting war treason has, with the deletion of certain psychological warfare activities in occupied territory, remained unchanged to this day.[6] A rationale for the principle is seldom encountered, but Spaight suggests that treason no longer means infidelity to a personal sovereign and is now a proper description of any conspiracy against the established authority in a state. If the occupant becomes 'war ruler' of the occupied area, to conspire against him is as much treason as it is to conspire against the ruler in the accepted sense, since both constitute

Hague Regulations that '. . . these limitations could not be deemed to check the liberty of action of belligerents in certain extreme circumstances which may be likened to a kind of legitimate defense' (Report to the Conference from the Second Commission on the Laws and Customs of War on Land (1899), in *Reports to the Hague Conferences of 1899 and 1907* (ed. by Scott, 1917), p. 149).

[1] Guelle, op. cit., vol. i, pp. 129–30; Mérignhac, op. cit., vol. iii, p. 290; Despagnet, *Cours de droit international public* (4th ed. by Boeck, 1910), p. 855; Fauchille, op. cit., vol. ii, p. 211; Calvo, op. cit., vol. iv, pp. 181–2. Rolin expresses only qualified approval and deplores the invoking of war treason as the basis for indiscriminate application of the death penalty (op. cit., vol. i, pp. 372–5).

[2] Pillet, op. cit., pp. 207–9; Jacomet, op. cit., p. 67. Some of the disquiet which the concept aroused may probably be attributed to anxiety about the use to which it was put by the German armed forces.

[3] See, e.g., Oppenheim, *International Law* (6th ed. by Lauterpacht, 1944), vol. ii, p. 457.

[4] See his *apologia* for war treason in 'On War Treason', in *Law Quarterly Review*, 33 (1917), pp. 266 ff., the writing of which was prompted by Professor Morgan's article, 'War Treason', in *Transactions of the Grotius Society*, 2 (1916), pp. 161 ff.

[5] *International Law* (1906), vol. ii, pp. 162, 268.

[6] Ibid. (6th ed. by Lauterpacht, 1944), vol. ii, p. 457.

the 'established authority' in the state.[1] But such eminent authorities as Holland and Westlake have been unable to reconcile the offence of war treason with the natural impulses of patriotism and the continuing bond of the citizen with his own state and his own government.[2]

War treason has been treated in military manuals since the *Instructions* promulgated by the United States in 1863, and some of Lieber's language is preserved in the current *Rules of Land Warfare* employed by the United States Army.[3] References to the subject are also to be found in the British *Manual of Military Law*[4] and the German *Kriegsbrauch im Landkriege*, published in 1902.[5] The British and American manuals, and Anglo-American law generally, regard war treason as an offence which may be committed not only in occupied territory but also within invaded areas and anywhere within the lines of a belligerent.

In the actual practice of states, however, resort to war treason as a juridical basis for the punishment of hostile acts has been comparatively rare. Persons who withheld arms from the German occupying forces during the Franco-Prussian War were held to be guilty of treason,[6] and in the Russo-Japanese War the Japanese characterized certain acts hostile to them, including espionage and the furnishing of information to the enemy, as 'treasonable'.[7] The peculiar nature of the occupation of the Philippine Islands by the United States following the war with Spain in 1898 occasioned some doubt whether native insurgents could be punished for treason. The matter was not resolved until November 1901, when the Philippine Commission passed an act defining and providing for the punishment of treason.[8] Persons in the Orange Free State who had signed a declaration of neutrality but had subsequently held communication with or aided the enemy were in 1900 considered to be guilty of 'treachery'.[9]

The classic case of war treason, which occurred during the First World War, is the trial of Nurse Edith Cavell for assisting in the escape of British and French soldiers and Belgians of military age from areas occupied by the German army. She was charged with violation of Section 58 of the Ger-

[1] *War Rights on Land* (1911), pp. 333–5.

[2] Holland, op. cit., p. 49; Westlake, *International Law*, Part ii (2nd ed., 1913), p. 100. See also Wheaton, op. cit. (5th English ed. by Phillipson, 1916), p. 528; Morgan, loc. cit.

[3] Paras. 207, 208, and 210 of Field Manual 27–10, 1 October 1940, incorporate the language of Arts. 92, 95, and 91 of General Orders No. 100. These and other paragraphs of the *Rules of Land Warfare* dealing with war treason form the basis of references to this subject in Hyde, op. cit., vol. iii, pp. 1865–6, and Hackworth, *Digest of International Law*, vol. vi (1943), pp. 308–9.

[4] (1929), Amendments No. 12 (1936), p. 37.

[5] Pp. 50–51. See Morgan, *The German War Book* (1915), pp. 121–2.

[6] Bordwell, op. cit., p. 303, citing Bray, *De l'occupation militaire en temps de guerre* (1894), pp. 184–8.

[7] Ariga, *La Guerre russo-japonaise au point de vue continental et le droit international* (1908), pp. 397–401.

[8] Thomas, op. cit., pp. 301–2.

[9] Spaight, op. cit., p. 335.

man Military Penal Code, which defined the offence of 'guiding soldiers to the enemy' as military treason, punishable by death.[1] In spite of the popular excitement which the case aroused at the time, it is difficult to see how the German military forces could have been expected to take anything but the serious view of her acts which their dangerous character demanded. It is reported that the term 'war treason' was, like 'espionage' and 'franc-tireur', given a liberal interpretation by the German army during the First World War, and that it frequently served as an excuse for unwarrantedly severe individual and collective punishment of acts hostile to the German forces.[2]

In the Second World War, occupation practices often so far exceeded the bounds of legally permissible conduct that it is difficult, if not impossible, to subject them to legal analysis. When legal principles were invoked by members of the Axis, their application was part of a concerted scheme of oppression, and the law itself was prostituted to the purposes of the occupation forces. The premature annexation of certain areas by the German Reich would thus become the occasion for the extension of all or a portion of the German Criminal Code to the area so incorporated. Among these provisions would, of course, be Sections 80 to 93*a*, which dealt with treason and like offences, such as damage to weapons and inducement to desertion.[3] An official Polish publication states that a number of individuals in the incorporated portion of Poland were sentenced by German Special Tribunals for *Kriegsverrat*, which it defined as 'a term which means all actions detrimental to the Army of Occupation'.[4] The United States Military Tribunal at Nuremberg recognized in its judgment in the *Justice Trial* the impropriety of applying the German municipal law of treason to offences, however slight, which had been committed by Polish nationals in aid of that portion of Poland illegally incorporated in the German Reich.[5] On the whole, however, even the German authorities appear to have made little use of the concept of war treason.[6]

References to war treason in proclamations and decrees relating to the conduct of the populace in occupied areas are nevertheless the exception, and the rare exception, rather than the rule. Not only in the two World Wars of this century but in all the major conflicts which have taken place since the first codification of the law of war, occupants have set forth in plain and unambiguous language those acts which they consider to be dangerous to them and deserving of punishment.[7] It is obviously in the

[1] For a description of the case see Garner, *International Law and the World War* (1920), vol. ii, pp. 97–105.

[2] Ibid., p. 96.

[3] Lemkin, *Axis Rule in Occupied Europe* (1944), pp. 136, 347.

[4] Polish Ministry of Information, *The New German Order in Poland* (1942), p. 41.

[5] *In re Altstötter et al.* (1947), *War Crimes Reports*, vol. vi, p. 53.

[6] Paoli, 'Contribution à l'étude des crimes de guerre et des crimes contre l'humanité en droit pénal international', in *Revue générale de droit international public*, 49 (1941–5), p. 151.

[7] See, e.g., Proclamation of Viceroy Alexeieff, 3 February 1904 (*Foreign Relations of the United

interest of both the occupant and the occupied that language as straightforward as possible should define their relationship. Prohibition of the commission of war treason would be incomprehensible to the average layman. Even the occupation of Germany after the assumption of supreme authority in that country by the signatories to the Berlin Declaration has not served as a basis for the creation of a category of acts 'treasonable' to the occupants. On the contrary, United States Ordinance No. 1 of Military Government for Germany[1] lists specifically some forty acts which will be punished because of the danger they present to the occupant, but war treason is not among these. Some of the offences might be considered to come within the conventional description of war treason; others are certainly not included.

War crimes trials following the Second World War have added almost nothing of substance to the jurisprudence of war treason. The subject was mentioned in several proceedings in which the accused were charged with failure to afford proper judicial safeguards to persons who had committed sabotage or who had attacked Axis soldiers. In the prosecution of several Japanese on this score, the judge advocates informed the court that inhabitants could legally be punished with death for the commission of war crimes, among which was included war treason.[2] In the *Trial of Wilhelm List and others* for reprisal killings, the United States Military Tribunal at Nuremberg mentioned that hostages might be shot upon the recurrence of certain acts of war treason, notice of which had been given to the civilian population.[3] In the modern case law relating to belligerent occupation, the concept has fallen into disuse.

The activities of British secret agents who were sent into occupied France to assist the resistance movement would appear to fall within that definition of war treason which embraces the hostile activities in occupied territory of military personnel disguised as civilians. However, in the *Natzweiler Trial*,[4] in which several Germans were tried for the summary execution of four British women who had been sent into France as secret

States, 1904, p. 127); German proclamation of 5 September 1914 in Belgium (Huberich and Nicol-Speyer, *German Legislation for the Occupied Territories of Belgium* (1915), p. 1); Japanese proclamations of 25 December 1941 and 10 March 1942 in Hong Kong (described in Ward, *Asia for the Asiatics? The Techniques of Japanese Occupation* (1945), pp. 47, 77); German proclamation to the occupied territory in Belgium, 10 May 1940 (Lemkin, op. cit., pp. 317–18); Proclamation No. 1, Allied Military Government of Occupied Territory [Italy], 25 April 1944.

[1] *Military Government Gazette, Germany, United States Zone*, Issue A, 1 June 1946, p. 57.

[2] *In re Ohashi et al.* (1946), *War Crimes Reports*, vol. vi, p. 27; *In re Kato* (1946), ibid., vol. v, p. 37, both of which cite Oppenheim, the British *Manual of Military Law*, and the corresponding Australian manual. See also *In re Sandrock et al.* (1945), ibid., vol. i, p. 43, in which the defence that a Dutch civilian killed without trial had been guilty of war treason was regarded as irrelevant by the judge advocate, who alluded to the necessity of a trial in any case.

[3] *In re List et al.* (*The Hostages Trial*) (1947–8), *War Crimes Reports*, vol. viii, p. 62.

[4] *In re Rohde et al.* (1946), *War Crimes Reports*, vol. v, p. 54; see also *The Natzweiler Trial* (ed. by Webb, 1949), p. 202.

agents, the judge advocate left open the question whether the agents should be considered as spies or not, since it was clear in any case that they should have been afforded a trial. It does not appear that war treason was mentioned either in this proceeding or in the prosecution of *Schonfeld and others* for the summary execution of several baled-out airmen who were taken in civilian clothes while under the protection of the Dutch resistance movement.[1] The contention of counsel for Von Falkenhorst[2] that commando operations constituted sabotage and 'war treason', justifying denial of quarter to the troops involved, was without basis in law and apparently carried no weight with the court.[3]

III. *War rebellion*

The history of 'war rebellion' has roughly paralleled that of war treason, but the concept itself has proved to be considerably less controversial. The writings of Francis Lieber similarly constitute a point of departure for the development of this doctrine. The draftsman of General Orders No. 100 claimed,[4] and his statement appears to be an accurate one, that he originated the term in his pamphlet on guerrilla parties.[5] He defined the war rebel as a 'renewer of war within an occupied territory', and it is in this sense that the term continues to be understood. It presumably refers to uprisings in arms by groups of persons as distinguished from individual acts of hostility and from such conduct as sabotage committed either by individuals or groups. The latter two categories would probably be referred to as war treason, although the reason for the distinction is obscure.

From Lieber's pamphlet, the concept of war rebellion found its way into his *Instructions*[6] and the writings of Bluntschli[7] and so into European

[1] *In re Schonfeld et al.* (1946), *War Crimes Reports*, vol. xi, p. 64.

[2] *In re Von Falkenhorst* (1946), ibid., p. 27.

[3] Two further cases, one in the First World War and the other in the Second, touch on the subject of war treason, but neither took place in occupied territory. The first of these concerned a German agent, Lody, who was tried and convicted by a British court martial on a charge of having committed war treason in Great Britain. It has been stated that he was so charged because espionage was not at the time a capital offence (Phillipson, *International Law and the Great War* (1915), pp. 213–17; Morgan, 'War Treason', in *Transactions of the Grotius Society*, 2 (1916), p. 169). One of the charges against the German saboteurs, whose case was reviewed by the United States Supreme Court in *Ex parte Quirin* (1942), 317 U.S. 1, was violation of the 81st Article of War, which defines the offence of relieving or attempting to relieve, or corresponding with or giving intelligence to, the enemy. Paras. 205 and 206 of the *Rules of Land Warfare* express the belief that this article of war defines the offence of 'war treason'. Whether the military commission which tried Quirin and his fellow agents considered the charge in this light and whether the accused were found guilty thereof cannot be stated at the present date, as the proceedings of the military commission are not to be released until the World War of 1939–45 is officially declared terminated (*New York Times* newspaper, 9 August 1942, p. 1, col. 4).

[4] MS. Notebook, *supra*.

[5] *Guerrilla Parties Considered with Reference to the Laws and Usages of War* (1862), p. 13.

[6] Art. 85 provided that 'War-rebels are persons within an occupied territory who rise in arms against the occupying or conquering army, or against the authorities established by the same.'

[7] *Das moderne Völkerrecht der civilisirten Staaten* (1868), § 643.

jurisprudence. The necessity of taking harsh measures against armed resistance in occupied areas has seldom been questioned, and the principal source of controversy has been, as was noted in connexion with the general duty owed to the occupant, whether there is any *right* to rebel and whether war rebellion constitutes a violation of any moral or legal obligation. The question arose at the Brussels Conference of 1874 and proved to be insoluble. The preliminary draft which had been drawn up by Russia contained an article providing that individuals in an area where the power of the enemy was already established who rose in arms against him might be referred to justice and would not be considered as prisoners of war.[1] The proposed article was subjected to criticism by the delegates of several of the smaller countries represented at the Conference, notably the Netherlands, Belgium, and Switzerland, who contended that it would be improper to require a state, the territory of which might thereafter be occupied, to concede to the enemy in advance jurisdiction over citizens who were responding to the highest sentiments of patriotism and to a positive duty to defend their country.[2] They conceded that the occupant might be forced to take severe measures against those opposing his authority, but were unwilling to make a *levée en masse* in occupied territory the subject of a blanket prohibition in positive international law. Agreement between the major Powers and these small states having proved impossible, it was decided to omit the draft article[3] and to leave the matter to existing international law, which was at the time itself uncertain.[4] Opposition from several large states defeated a renewed attempt at the Hague Conference of 1899 to reach a modicum of agreement through an ambiguous statement that nothing in the convention was to be construed as precluding 'the population of an invaded country' from fulfilling its 'duty of offering by all lawful means the most energetic patriotic resistance to the invader.'[5]

In the writings of the publicists, varying effects are attributed to revolution by occupied populations. To many it is a violation of international law, which is variously said to produce as its sanction the removal of the occupant's protection, the termination of the protection of the law of war, the offender's prosecution as a 'war criminal' for 'illegitimate hostilities in arms', or his punishment at the unfettered discretion of the occupant.[6] In

[1] *Projet*, Art. 46.

[2] *Actes de la Conférence de Bruxelles* (1874), pp. 158–65.

[3] *Actes*, p. 165.

[4] Graber, *The Development of the Law of Belligerent Occupation 1863–1914* (1949), p. 85.

[5] The provision was proposed by the British technical delegate and was withdrawn in the face of strenuous objection from Russia and Germany (*The Proceedings of the Hague Peace Conferences. The Conference of 1899* (ed. by Scott, 1920), pp. 550–5).

[6] Halleck suggests that the right of an occupied population to revolt rests on the same principle as the right of revolution against any government (op. cit., pp. 792–5). See also Bordwell, op. cit., p. 302; Nys, op. cit., vol. iii, p. 108; Fauchille, op. cit., vol. ii, pp. 210–11; Rolin-Jaequemyns, op. cit., pp. 667–8; *Kriegsbrauch im Landkriege* (1902), p. 50.

the opposing camp are to be found authorities such as de Visscher, Calvo, Hannis Taylor, and Hall, who state that there is a 'right' to revolt and perhaps even a duty, of which international law must take account, imposed by the continuing allegiance of the citizen to his own state.[1] The conflicting views which are taken are, for the most part, the logical concomitants of the diverse theories which have been adopted concerning the general relationship of the occupied population to the occupant. The doctrine of war rebellion appears, however, to have gained a fairly firm footing in Anglo-American law, for it is referred to in the standard texts of both Great Britain and the United States[2] and is described in the military manuals of both countries.[3] It should be noted, however, that whereas war rebellion is recognized as a 'war crime' by Oppenheim, his treatise denies that the inhabitant owes any duty of obedience to the occupant under international law.[4]

In modern warfare, the *levée en masse*, or a general uprising of the populace, has been supplanted by the more subtle tactics of the resistance movement and the underground, which, while generally enlisting the sympathies of a large proportion of the population, are actively conducted by a minority of that group. The occupant is less likely to be faced by open rebellion than he is by guerilla warfare, sabotage, individual armed attacks, and other more refined acts of defiance. Having lost its utility, the conventional concept of war rebellion has, like war treason, passed into desuetude both in the practice of belligerents and in the substantive law applied by war crimes tribunals.[5]

Axis occupation practices exhibited such a callous contempt for the limitations imposed by international law on the conduct of the belligerent occupant that during the last five years courts have been called upon in relatively few instances to consider the conformity of resistance activities with the law of nations. More often cases dealing with the punishment of acts hostile to the occupant were decided on the issue whether the occupation authorities ought to have afforded, and did afford, a fair trial to the accused before his execution.[6] It was sufficient in several other instances to

[1] De Visscher, loc. cit., pp. 76–77; Calvo, op. cit., vol. iv, p. 218; Taylor, op. cit., p. 592; Hall, op. cit., p. 498.

[2] Oppenheim, *International Law* (6th ed. by Lauterpacht, 1944), vol. ii, p. 456; Hyde, op. cit., vol. iii, p. 1794 (citing Lieber but not employing the term 'war rebellion').

[3] *Manual of Military Law* (*1929*), Amendments No. 12 (1936), p. 83, which characterizes war rebellion as 'illegitimate hostilities in arms'; United States *Rules of Land Warfare*, para. 349.

[4] Op. cit. (6th ed. by Lauterpacht, 1944), vol. ii, p. 343.

[5] For an isolated example of the use of the term see *In re Ohashi et al.* (1946), *War Crimes Reports*, vol. v, p. 25.

[6] *In re Von Leeb et al.* (*High Command Trial*) (1948), *War Crimes Reports*, vol. xii, p. 1; *In re Buck et al.* (1946), ibid., vol. v, p. 39; *In re Kato* (1946), ibid., vol. v, p. 37; *In re Yamashita* (1945–6), ibid., vol. iv, p. 1; and *In re Wagner et al.* (1946), ibid., vol. iii, p. 23, are typical examples.

decide that reprisals against resistance activities were excessive or had been taken prematurely.[1] As the result of the prohibition of reprisals and collective punishments and the detailed provisions concerning judicial proceedings in the courts of the occupant which have been incorporated in the recent Geneva Civilians Convention,[2] the pronouncements of war crimes tribunals on these matters have become of diminished practical importance. Nevertheless, those cases in which the propriety of resistance activities has been considered have almost universally reached the conclusion that such acts are not in violation of international law. In the *Trial of Hans Albin Rauter*, who had been a German police official in the Netherlands, the Dutch Special Court of Cassation went so far as to state that resistance is a 'permissible weapon' to use against the occupant.[3] A Norwegian court of appeals rejected the defence raised by German police officials for their conduct in Norway that the activities of the underground movement were acts of illegitimate warfare and therefore might be made the subject of reprisals, which in this case took the form of torture. In the opinion of the Court the underground movement did not constitute a violation of international law, although the activities of members of the movement were presumably violations of a body of local law enforced by the German authorities.[4] This issue was not discussed by the Supreme Court in affirming the decision of the court of first instance, but in the *Trial of Flesch* on similar charges, the Supreme Court affirmed the holding of the court of appeals that underground activities, even in the form of guerilla warfare, were not, in the circumstances, in violation of international law.[5] The military tribunal which tried Wilhelm List did not specifically discuss whether resistance is lawful under international law.[6] It did, however, state that persons guilty of acts of resistance to the occupation forces become 'war criminals *in the eyes of the enemy*'[7] and 'must accept the increased risks involved in this mode of fighting' because it is only in this fashion that the occupant may protect himself against what the Court called 'the gadfly tactics of armed resistance'. The Tribunal concluded that 'We think the rule is established that a civilian who aids, abets or participates in the fighting is liable to punishment as a war criminal under the laws of war.'[8] The language is more suggestive on the whole of a punishment *permitted* by international law than it is of a punishment *imposed* by international law.

The larger question of the obligation of inhabitants to obey the measures

[1] *In re Von Mackensen and Maelzer* (1945), *War Crimes Reports*, vol. viii, p. 1; *In re Flesch* (1946–8), ibid., vol. vi, p. 111.

[2] Arts. 33, 64–78.

[3] *In re Rauter* (1948), *War Crimes Reports*, vol. xiv, pp. 127–9.

[4] *In re Bruns et al.* (1946), *War Crimes Reports*, vol. iii, p. 17.

[5] *In re Flesch* (1946–8), *War Crimes Reports*, vol. vi, pp. 115, 119.

[6] *In re List et al.* (*Hostages Trial*) (1948), *War Crimes Reports*, vol. viii, p. 34.

[7] Emphasis supplied.

[8] *War Crimes Reports*, vol. viii, p. 58.

taken by the occupant for his security was considered by Dutch courts in connexion with the prosecution of collaborationists. Several contractors and police officials raised the defence that they had been legally obligated to obey what they contended to be the lawful commands of the German occupation authorities. The Dutch criminal courts and the Special Court of Cassation held, on the contrary, that the only effective defence to a charge of collaboration was one of *force majeure* and that the mere fact that the Hague Regulations sanctioned the requisitioning of services and the enactment of legislation designed to assure order and protect the occupant created no compulsion for individuals to render services in conformity therewith. The Hague Regulations were not intended to create rights against the population of an occupied territory; they merely limit the *de facto* authority of the occupant. Accordingly, they do not create legal obligations in conscience binding upon the inhabitants.[1]

The Geneva Convention relative to the Treatment of Prisoners of War of 12 August 1949 has removed any lingering doubts about the status of certain organized resistance forces by providing that members of 'volunteer corps', including 'organized resistance movements' operating even in occupied territory, are entitled to be treated as prisoners of war upon capture, if they are commanded by a responsible person, have a fixed distinctive sign, carry arms openly, and conduct their operations in conformity with the laws of war.[2] This provision has been rendered necessary by war-time difficulties in securing recognition as prisoners of war for partisans who had conducted their activities in conformity with international law.[3] Underground movements carrying on clandestine activities and persons who individually make armed attacks on occupying military forces are presumably left to the common law of war, subject to the protection afforded by the Geneva Civilians Convention. For the activities of such persons, the appellation of 'war rebellion' hardly seems appropriate.

IV. *The validity of the traditional concepts*

The presence in international law of a theory which envisages a duty of obedience imposed by that law and characterizes certain acts hostile to the occupant as war treason or as war rebellion can only be explained in terms

[1] *In re Contractor Worp* (1946), *Na-oorlogse Rechtspraak, Tribunalen in Nederland,* 2nd Year, 1946, No. 519; *In re Van Huis* (1946), ibid., 2nd Year, 1946, No. 605; *In re Heinemann* (1946), ibid., 3rd Year, 1947, No. 763. In *In re Van Huis,* the Special Criminal Court of The Hague, in a distinction reminiscent of Bordwell, conceded that measures designed exclusively for the benefit of the occupied country might create legal obligations for individuals.

[2] Art. 4 A (2). This principle had already been anticipated in previous writings, which had specified that members of a *levée en masse* in occupied territory who were taken prisoner by the enemy were not thereby deprived of all legal protection (Westlake, op. cit., Part ii, p. 100; Grob, *The Relativity of War and Peace* (1949), p. 268).

[3] *Report on the Work of the Conference of Government Experts for the Study of the Conventions for the Protection of War Victims,* International Committee of the Red Cross (1947), pp. 107–10.

of history. It is particularly significant that these kindred concepts date from a period which was still one of transition from the rigorous law of conquest to the modern and more enlightened view of belligerent occupation. That they have persisted is the consequence of inertia in the law, which has failed to take account of later developments in warfare and in the law of occupation itself. One need only point out as illustrative of the antiquated state of the law the fact that certain paragraphs about war treason in the United States *Rules of Land Warfare* have remained unchanged over a period of nearly ninety years.[1] It must be observed, moreover, that these concepts have never during their history met wholehearted acceptance as positive international law; their present position is more than precarious.

The essential issue which must be faced in a re-examination of this area of the law is whether a duty of obedience is imposed by international law or is merely a consequence of the armed might of the occupant, who alone creates the duty. There is no doubt that theories of allegiance and temporary allegiance are no longer tenable and belong to the past. As for a duty of obedience imposed by municipal law, it would appear that it lies within the competence of a state to impose such a duty if it believes this course to be desirable. Although it may be determined as a matter of policy that non-resistance or outright collaboration will best serve the national interests of the occupied state, it is improbable that such considerations will carry much persuasion.

In modern war resistance to the occupant is virtually inevitable if hostilities are still in progress. The civilian has not only been drawn into the maelstrom of war; he has voluntarily interjected himself into it. It seems to be a natural phenomenon in modern political societies that the citizen should feel a greater measure of responsibility for the support of his country and its political institutions than was true in an age when wars were fought by professional armies in the interests of absolute monarchs. We must also recognize that in the eyes of a citizen's fellows and in those of the world—indeed, probably in those of the enemy as well—there is no moral taint attached to an act of resistance by a civilian patriot.[2] If international law is to have a moral content, it is difficult to see how an ethical basis can be found for the principle that international law intervenes to quell acts of resistance which, in the moral sense of the world, are regarded as heroic rather than criminal.

The aggressor of today appears to have an initial advantage over defend-

[1] See p. 250, n. 3, *supra*.

[2] Although Oppenheim asserts that the inhabitant's duty of obedience is grounded in the martial law of the occupant rather than in international law, he indicates that making use of treason and espionage, while not illegal, is 'detestable and immoral' ('On War Treason', in *Law Quarterly Review*, 33 (1917), p. 268). This attitude does not appear to be in conformity with modern views of morality in warfare.

ing forces, and an immediate, extensive occupation by the state first to move will in all probability befall the invaded country until defending military forces can be mobilized to drive out the enemy. At the same time that the occupant must continue to have the means of penalizing acts hostile to him or dangerous to his security, the emphasis of modern international law must nevertheless be on the protection of *all* the inhabitants of occupied territory, including those whose conduct is prejudicial to the occupant, against unwarranted severity in the occupant's rule. Yet the theory that international law imposes a duty of obedience serves the interests of the occupant, rather than those of the inhabitant, and may either inflame his passions or offer a rationalization for excessively harsh treatment of those under his protection. The emotional overtones of a belief that some higher legal order forbids and penalizes acts of resistance must inevitably lead to unmerited rigorousness in dealing with such conduct. Although collective punishments and reprisals and the taking and killing of hostages have been forbidden by the new Geneva Civilians Convention and certain maximum limitations have been placed on punishments,[1] there is still room for making penalties more onerous than they should be.

The contract theory which is often adduced as the reason for invoking international law in the suppression of acts of resistance is at best a fiction designed to explain away an unpalatable situation. It is unacceptable on three grounds. It is highly improbable, in the first place, that states or their individual citizens would ever concede that they enter into contractual relationships with the occupant by force of law. Secondly, the 'moral contract' lacks a moral foundation, for not only have the inhabitant and his government never consented to it but the populace has not been benefited by the substitution of the occupant's uncertain protection for that of its own government. Thirdly, it is difficult to depict as quasi-contractual a relationship in which the amelioration of the occupant's rule is not brought about by the peaceful conduct of the occupied population but is the subject of a positive prescription of international law. If acts of resistance were to dissolve the moral contract, which appears to be the logical outcome of this theory, the perpetrators of the hostile acts, and indeed the whole community, would appear to be placed outside the law and subject to whatever punishments the enemy might choose to impose. This conclusion is inconsistent with the view, judicially affirmed, that the protection of international law continues even though hostile acts may be committed against the occupant[2] and with the reaffirmation of this principle in the Geneva Civilians Convention of 1949.[3]

[1] Arts. 33 and 68.

[2] *In re Rauter* (1948), *War Crimes Reports*, vol. xiv, p. 129, concerning which see p. 256, *supra*.

[3] See particularly Art. 33.

The argument that if international law imposes duties on the occupant, it must likewise confer rights on him and create duties for the inhabitants has a certain superficial attractiveness because it suggests symmetry and order in the law. However, such reciprocity of duty is demanded neither by logic nor by law. The position of aliens after reception affords a familiar instance in which the special protection granted by international law does not create in *international* law a corresponding duty upon the part of aliens to respect the laws of the state whose hospitality they enjoy. There is also a peculiar inconsistency between the fact of international law defining the relationship of the individual to the authority placed over him by force of arms and the role assigned to municipal law of defining the inhabitant's obligations to the state of which he is a citizen. The reciprocity principle is, moreover, unsatisfactory from a practical point of view because it disregards the function of the international law of war—the amelioration of the conditions of warfare to the maximum extent compatible with the conduct of hostilities, rather than the provision of a set of rules more appropriate to a parlour game than to the lessening of human suffering.[1] Experience has shown that the attempt to place the source of the duty in the law of nations has probably done more to prejudice the cause of occupied peoples than it has to mitigate the severities of war for the non-combatant. Indeed, if a duty of obedience is imposed by the law of nations, it leads to the inference that the latter lends its active support to the conduct of hostilities and that it is itself a weapon of war in so far as it supplies a means of keeping occupied populations in subjection. There is thus room for the view that international law can only be debased by placing obligations on individuals in this area of the law.

If a person committing acts of resistance is guilty of a violation of international law, it seems strange that the individual's own government may inspire or demand such acts without being subjected to similar penalties. Yet it has never been suggested that a state is guilty of an international delinquency if it calls for acts of resistance or avails itself of the fruit of the forbidden tree.[2] Nor has it been suggested by those who allege that international law creates obligations for persons in occupied territory that the state whose citizens these are has a duty to suppress the patriotic sentiments of those of its people who are under alien military control or to punish its citizens who resist the occupying forces. The resulting proposition that

[1] Such expressions as 'the rules of warfare' and 'the laws and customs of war' have not contributed to efforts to enhance the respect in which the international law of war is held.

[2] Oppenheim, 'On War Treason', in *Law Quarterly Review*, 33 (1917), pp. 268 ff. Art. 24 of the Hague Regulations, which provides that 'the employment of measures necessary for obtaining information about the enemy and the country are considered permissible', indicates that a belligerent may avail himself of the services of the inhabitants of occupied areas for intelligence purposes.

international law imposes the duty of obedience only when an individual is being tried by the occupant for some hostile act is obviously untenable.

The Geneva Civilians Convention affords no basis for the assertion that international law constrains the inhabitant to obedience. Both Articles 27 and 64, which authorize the occupying Power to take 'such measures of control and security . . . as may be necessary' and to subject the population to 'provisions . . . essential . . . to the security of the Occupying Power', are cast in permissive terms. These articles and the requirement of Article 65 that offences punishable under the martial law of the occupant must be announced before individuals may be punished for their commission, indicate in strong terms that, subject to the limitations of the Convention, international law permits the occupant to define the incidents of the inhabitant's duty of obedience and submission.

From whatever perspective the inhabitant's duty to refrain from acts inconsistent with the security of the occupant is examined, the argument that such duty is grounded in international law proves unacceptable. It is not in conformity with the practice of states, it creates difficulties of a practical nature, it is inconsistent with morality and with the fundamental principles of the law of war, and it cannot be reconciled with the most recent expression of the desire of the world to better the lot of the civilian in wartime. The source of the inhabitant's duty of obedience can only be the power of the occupant to demand it. The law must take as its starting-point the fact of military supremacy and then set forth to place limits of reasonableness on the occupant's factual capacity to control those who live within the area he holds.

Notwithstanding Oppenheim's ability to reconcile war treason and war rebellion with his denial that there is any duty of obedience created by the law of nations, the three concepts normally march together. To the extent that these 'crimes' are regarded as violations of such a duty, they are open to the objections to that theory which have just been enumerated. They are unsatisfactory, moreover, on the further grounds that they tend to mislead and corrupt practice and that they today serve no useful purpose in systematizing and clarifying the law.

The very terms 'war treason' and 'war rebellion' carry over from municipal law certain connotations which have no rightful place in the law of nations. The most obvious of these is the normal revulsion occasioned by the conduct of the individual who betrays or takes up arms against the community which gives him its protection. The adoption of these concepts into international law has consequently meant that many hostile acts and acts inconsistent with the security of the occupant have been treated with a cruelty and harshness which they little deserved. If it be asserted that this objection goes only to certain popular misunderstandings of these terms in their application to the law of war, it may properly be replied that a legal concept which in fact serves no practical purpose and has that capacity to mislead which history has made plain, should have no place in the law. In a period in which 'war crimes' have acquired a heinous connotation of their own, it is particularly unfortunate that war treason and war rebellion should form one category with war crimes in their popular sense. Although it is generally recognized that war crimes in the form of acts of resistance are fundamentally different from those offences which have recently attracted public attention,[1] some states will probably be only too willing to characterize any acts committed against them as criminal in an international sense.

The meanings of the two terms are themselves obscure. Continental writers state, for example, that war treason applies only to communication with an inhabitant's own government, while the Anglo-American view seems to be that it applies to a wide range of acts hostile to the occupant, but not necessarily to all such acts. When war treason does consist in the communication of information to the inhabitant's own government, it is often quite difficult to distinguish it from espionage.[2] To suggest that espionage applies only to the communication of information acquired by illicit means does not resolve the difficulty, because it is frequently impossible and legally pointless to determine how the guilty information was acquired. It seems paradoxical as well to afford immunity to the spy who has gathered his information and then returned to his own army but to deny that immunity to him who obtains his information innocently and is subsequently able to return to his own military forces. The fact that espionage is regarded, almost without exception, as not being prohibited by international law,[3] makes it the more peculiar that such a close relation as war treason should ever have been regarded as falling under that law's positive prohibition.

The doctrine of war rebellion raises kindred problems of definition. Is it war treason if three civilians, members of an underground movement, dynamite an enemy barracks and kill soldiers sleeping there, and war rebellion only if the same three were to fire upon enemy soldiers? How many people does it take to make armed resistance war rebellion rather than war treason or some other nameless offence? Whatever the answers to

[1] It was stated by the Tribunal in *Re List et al.* (1948), *War Crimes Reports*, vol. viii, at p. 54, that 'Some war crimes, such as spying, are not common law crimes at all; they being pure war crimes punishable as such during the war and, in this particular case, only if the offender is captured before he rejoins his army.'

[2] See Cohen, 'Espionage and Immunity—Some Recent Problems and Developments', in this *Year Book*, 25 (1948), p. 404.

[3] Oppenheim, *International Law* (6th ed. by Lauterpacht, 1944), vol. ii, p. 329; British *Manual of Military Law* (1929), Amendments No. 12 (1936), p. 36; United States *Rules of Land Warfare*, para. 203. But see Hyde, op. cit., vol. iii, p. 1865, and 'Aspects of the Saboteur Cases', *in American Journal of International Law*, 37 (1943), p. 88.

these questions may be, war rebellion, which evokes images of a mass uprising of the peasants, is an inexact and misleading name for guerrilla warfare, the underground movement, the Fifth Column, the Resistance, and the Maquis. At the time of the promulgation of Lieber's Code nearly a century ago, the means whereby inhabitants could resist the enemy and favour their own government were necessarily limited, and war treason, war rebellion, and espionage may well have exhausted the list of ways in which a civilian living under military rule could aid his own government. In the intervening years, war has assumed a complexity that Lieber could not have envisaged, and as the weapons of warfare have been improved, so also have the weapons of resistance. A great variety of methods of doing injury to the occupant have been added to war treason, war rebellion, and espionage, conceived even in their most inclusive sense.[1] The occupant must have the means not only of penalizing acts which do him actual harm but also of punishing conduct that is potentially dangerous or offers conditions under which harm might be done.[2] He must have the means of dealing with such acts whether they are intended to injure him or are done without that *animus*. A violation of black-out regulations or restrictions on entering prohibited areas or failure to observe curfew have potentialities of interfering with the security of the occupant, and it should hardly be necessary that he have the burden either of proving that they were committed with the intention of harming him or that actual harm was caused him, except in so far as these determinations are made necessary by the restrictions on punishments embodied in Article 68 of the Geneva Civilians Convention.[3] The intent of the actor and the effect on the occupant may be significant, but they should not place artificial restrictions on the exercise of military jurisdiction.[4] A determination whether a given act is war

[1] De Watteville, 'The Military Administration of Occupied Territory in Time of War', in *Transactions of the Grotius Society*, 7 (1921), pp. 135, 138.

[2] See Campbell, 'Some Legal Problems arising out of the Establishment of the Allied Military Courts in Italy', in *International Law Quarterly*, 1 (1947), pp. 192 ff., for an account of the situation faced in territory subject to military occupation.

[3] Which makes intent and effect significant for the purpose of determining the maximum punishments which may be imposed.

[4] Both a literal reading of Art. 68 of the Geneva Civilians Convention and the history of its drafting lead to the inference that offences not 'solely intended to harm the Occupying Power' but nevertheless inconsistent with the occupant's security (e.g., stealing from military stores, counterfeiting of occupation currency, violation of curfew, attempted departure from occupied territory) are not punishable by imprisonment. Although the draft of this article, which was prepared at Stockholm, was liberalized by the addition of imprisonment to internment as the penalty for certain acts, the Report of Committee III to the Plenary Assembly at Geneva states specifically that the category of offences concerned has been restricted to 'those intended *solely* to harm the Occupying Power' (CDG/PLEN 71 Civ, 27 July 1949, p. 47; see also Art. 59, Working Document, Draft Convention for the Protection of Civilian Persons in Time of War (Doc. No. 4)). If restrictions of this nature are placed about the imposition of imprisonment as punishment, it may be anticipated that difficulties of a practical nature may be encountered in the preservation of the occupant's security, unless fines and other penalties not referred to prove adequate deterrents.

treason or merely a violation of the ordinances of the occupant is thus absolutely useless, because the occupant has the means and the authority to punish it under either guise.

Leaving to the occupant the function of defining acts inconsistent with his security ultimately redounds both to his advantage and to that of the civilian inhabitant. The occupying Power must, on the one hand, be accorded wide legislative power to specify such acts without being fettered with the outmoded and academic concepts of war treason and war rebellion. The inhabitant, for his part, should welcome a precise definition of those acts from which he is expected to refrain. It should hardly be necessary to add that the ordinances of the occupant must not exceed the bounds of reasonableness in providing for his security and that measures intended to intimidate and oppress occupied populations without regard to the actual military requirements of the occupant are *ultra vires* and may subject their authors to criminal penalties under the international law of war. It is of particular significance that the concepts of war treason and war rebellion are not to be found in the new Geneva Civilians Convention of 1949. The acts of inhabitants which imperil the security of the occupant are described as 'espionage' or 'sabotage' or 'activity hostile to the security of the Occupying Power', but never by the old names.[1] In refusing to use the language of the text-books, the Geneva Conference appears to have adhered to the actual practice of states.

In the case of collective resistance, guerilla warfare, or sabotage, it may become necessary, of course, for the occupant to use a reasonable amount of force in repelling or subduing the attackers or in preventing their escape. By analogy with municipal law, the occupying forces should be legally privileged to wound or kill those individuals who resist arrest. But if the wrongdoers are once taken prisoner, it would appear that the trial and judicial process recognized by the common law of war and by the new Geneva Convention must be accorded them.

If war treason is not regarded as a proper concept of modern international law concerning occupied areas, there remains the problem of acts of this nature committed within or behind the lines of a belligerent but not in occupied territory. If such acts are committed on the territory of a belligerent, they obviously may be dealt with under the municipal law of the state against whom the hostile acts are taken. In areas subject to military jurisdiction, including the combat zone itself, civilians who abuse their immunity by assisting in battle and military secret agents in disguise may, as circumstances dictate, be characterized as spies or placed in the residual

[1] Arts. 5 and 68. The limitations on capital punishment which Art. 68 imposes appear to pay excessive deference to the civilian engaged in hostile conduct (see Gutteridge, 'The Geneva Conventions of 1949', in this *Year Book*, 26 (1949), p. 324, n. 1).

category of 'unlawful belligerents'.[1] Sabotage and demolition, communications, psychological warfare and intelligence activities, and even certain types of assistance in the form of voluntary labour for the enemy, have as much a military character as actual fighting, whether they are done by civilian volunteers or by disguised members of the enemy army, and are subject to like penalties. It would appear that acts of this nature committed in invaded areas or in the battle zone are not themselves prohibited by international law but merely preclude persons from claiming the immunity afforded by military status and conformity with the law of war.

The status of the enemy secret agent, military or civilian, who is sent into the occupied area appears to have been modified to some degree by the new Conventions. Under the customary law of war, it would appear that he had a right to a prompt trial before a prompt execution.[2] By assuming disguise he forfeited his entitlement to be treated as a prisoner of war and voluntarily threw in his lot with civilians who similarly lacked the immunity conferred by passivity or by membership in the armed forces. Article 5 of the Geneva Civilians Convention, the second paragraph of which refers to the activities of spies, saboteurs, and like persons in occupied areas, was inserted in the draft convention presented to the Geneva Conference in response to the fears of many delegations that the Convention might afford undue protection to secret agents.[3] The relevant portion of the article provides that spies, saboteurs, and persons who are detained under definite suspicion of activity hostile to the security of the occupant lose the right of communication if military security so requires.[4] In the words of the committee which considered the article, such persons are placed in 'solitary confinement'. If the cited provision of the Convention is intended to apply to secret agents who pass through the lines of a belligerent into the territory he occupies, it would appear to indicate that all such persons are now, except in so far as they are deprived of the right of communication, assimilated to the inhabitants of occupied territories. If this is true, then presumably spies benefit from the provision that the death penalty may not be imposed on inhabitants in areas where that penalty was not in force when the occupation began.[5] The spy and the secret agent may, in short, have attained a protected status under inter-

[1] *Ex parte Quirin et al.* (1942), 317 U.S. 1. [2] See p. 252, n. 4, *supra*.

[3] Report of Committee III to the Plenary Assembly (CDG/PLEN. 71 Civ, 27 July 1949), pp. 6–7.

[4] 'Where in occupied territory an individual protected person is detained as a spy or saboteur, or as a person under definite suspicion of activity hostile to the security of the Occupying Power, such person shall, in those cases where absolute military security so requires, be regarded as having forfeited rights of communication under the present Convention.' Persons protected by the Civilians Convention are defined in Art. 4 as being all persons in the hands of a party to the conflict or an occupying power of which they are not nationals with the exception of those persons who are entitled to claim the protection of the other Geneva Conventions of 1949.

[5] Art. 68.

national law. However, the question of the status of such individuals under the new Conventions presents major problems which fall outside the confines of the present article.

V. *Conclusions*

The adoption of the new Geneva Conventions and the general revision of text-books and military manuals which this change in the law has made necessary constitute a suitable occasion for an abandonment of the principles of a duty of obedience imposed by international law, of war treason, and of war rebellion. The practice of states, recent judicial decisions, and the provisions of the new Geneva Conventions provide evidence that these concepts serve neither the interests of occupying Powers nor of occupied populations. In the light of that evidence, the following would appear to be a desirable formulation of the law:

1. Subject to the general limitation of reasonableness and the specific limitations imposed by the Hague Regulations and the Geneva Convention relative to the Protection of Civilian Persons in Time of War, international law permits a belligerent occupant to prohibit and punish, but does not itself prohibit, conduct by the inhabitants of occupied areas which is hostile to him or which is inconsistent with the security of his forces or administration.

2. In conformity with the Geneva Civilians Convention, the occupant must announce in advance those acts which he will penalize. The occupying Power must be recognized to have a wide range of legislative competence to forbid acts which may reasonably be considered to imperil his safety.

3. Like the spy, the individual who commits hostile acts or acts inconsistent with the security of the occupant may not be penalized for such acts after he has joined or rejoined the armed forces of his own state.

Admittedly, the civilian non-combatant is increasingly exposed to the economic and social burdens of war.[1] It is true also that the distinction between combatant and non-combatant grows more difficult to draw as new weapons of mass destruction are developed.[2] The practical difficulties with which the law of war is faced in these areas make it the more imperative that his lot under belligerent occupation, which is particularly appropriate to legal regulation, be made the subject of a body of law which takes account of the present-day needs of the civilian population without doing violence to the legitimate requirements of the occupant. It is in such measures as this that convincing proof may be given that the international law of war has continuing utility and validity.

[1] Gutteridge, op. cit., p. 319.

[2] See Nurick, 'The Distinction between Combatant and Noncombatant in the Law of War', in *American Journal of International Law*, 39 (1945), p. 680.

[12]

Legislation and Maintenance of Public Order and Civil Life by Occupying Powers

Marco Sassòli*

Abstract

Article 43 of the 1907 Hague Regulations is a key provision of the law of belligerent occupation. This essay examines how it has been understood by states and scholars, how it was developed by the Fourth Geneva Convention of 1949 and whether and how it was respected by the US and the UK during their recent occupation of Iraq. Under Article 43, an occupying power must restore and maintain public order and civil life, including public welfare, in an occupied territory. Local legislation and institutions based upon such legislation must be respected by an occupying power and by any local authorities acting under the global control of the occupying power. This general prohibition to change the local legislation also applies to post-conflict reconstruction efforts, including constitutional reforms, and changes of economic and social policies. The author examines the exceptions to the prohibition and assesses whether the widespread legislative activities by the occupying powers in Iraq fall under these exceptions. He then analyses the question of whether the law of military occupation ceased to apply in Iraq on 30 June 2004. It is also suggested that Article 43 applies to some peace operations and provides a useful framework even for those peace operations to which it does not formally apply.

1 Some Legal Questions Raised by Recent Events in Iraq

The US-led military occupation of Iraq which started in 2003 has raised renewed interest in the law of military occupation, a branch of international humanitarian law (IHL) that applies, as part of the *jus in bello*, independently of whether under *jus ad*

* Marco Sassòli is Professor of International Law at the University of Geneva, Switzerland. Email: marco.sassoli@droit.unige.ch. This article is based upon and develops a report submitted by the author to the *Second Informal High-Level Expert Meeting on Current Challenges to International Humanitarian Law*, convened in Cambridge, Massachusetts, on 25–27 June 2004 by the Harvard Program on Humanitarian Policy and Conflict Research and by the Government of Switzerland. The author would like to thank his research assistants, Mr. Danio Campanelli and Ms. Lindsey Cameron, for their invaluable research in preparing this article and for revising the text. Events occurring after 1 Oct. 2004 could not be taken into account in this article.

bellum the war against Iraq was justified under UN Security Council resolutions or a new understanding of self-defence. Of particular relevance were the questions of the extent of the obligation of an occupying power to restore and maintain public order and civil life in an occupied territory and the extent to which an occupying power may change local legislation and institutions in a post-conflict reconstruction effort. Both questions are governed by the nearly 100-year-old Article 43 of the Regulations annexed to the 1907 Hague Convention No. IV Respecting the Laws and Customs of War on Land (hereinafter Hague Regulations).[1] The present contribution aims at understanding the meaning of that article in its contemporary context. It will show whether the claim that existing IHL of military occupation, and in particular Article 43, is 'ill suited' to situations of 'transformational occupation' such as Iraq, is correct.[2] Today, the UN Security Council[3] and the US-led coalition consider that the occupation ended on 30 June 2004, although coalition forces remain in Iraq. In terms of IHL of military occupation, this raises the question of when that law ceases to apply in the event of a handover of the functions of government to a new national government instituted by the (former) occupying powers.

Since 1 July 2004, at the latest, coalition forces may consider their military presence in Iraq to be a sort of peace operation. Beyond the case of Iraq, other occupying powers willing to withdraw as soon as a stable government is established may also be tempted to consider their presence on a territory resulting from an armed conflict as a kind of peace operation. Every occupying power is confronted, when restoring and maintaining public order, with problems more typical of peacekeeping operations than of traditional inter-state warfare. Conversely, the question also arises of whether and when traditional peace operations are subject to Article 43 of the Hague Regulations. This question will therefore be equally considered in this article.

2 Article 43 of the Hague Regulations

Article 43 of the Hague Regulations of 1907 reads in the most widely adopted English translation[4] of the original authentic French[5] text:

> The authority of the legitimate power having in fact passed into the hands of the occupant, the latter shall take all the measures in his power to restore and ensure, as far as possible, public order and safety, while respecting, unless absolutely prevented, the laws in force in the country.

The International Military Tribunal at Nuremberg and the International Court of Justice have recognized that this provision corresponds to customary international

1 Hague Convention (IV) Respecting the Laws and Customs of War on Land and Annex, 18 Oct. 1907, 1 Bevans 631–653 [Hague Regulations].

2 See forcefully Scheffer, 'Beyond Occupation Law', 97 *AJIL* (2003) 842, at 847–853.

3 SC Res. 1546 (2004), para. 2.

4 J. B. Scott (ed.), *The Hague Peace Conventions and Declarations of 1899 and 1907* (3rd edn, 1918).

5 Indeed, only the French text is authentic: D. Schindler and J. Toman, *The Laws of Armed Conflict* (4th edn, 2004), at 56.

law.[6] However, its precise meaning is unclear. In practice, occupying powers have sometimes invoked its vagueness to justify broad legislative powers, and, at other times, have relied on the obligation to respect local laws 'unless absolutely prevented' in order to ignore their responsibility to ensure the welfare and normal life of the local population.[7]

The text of Article 43 seems to deal with the respect of local legislation by the occupying power only when the latter restores or ensures public order and civil life, but legislative history and current practice show that the article constitutes a general rule about the legislative powers of an occupying power.[8]

The two issues – maintenance of public order and safety, and legislative action by an occupying power – are closely interrelated. Human rights and the rule of law (indispensable elements in any peace-building effort) demand that the maintenance of public order be based on law. Both an occupying power and an international civil administration restoring and maintaining public order face the question of what legal basis they may rely on to arrest, detain and punish persons threatening or breaching public order and to what extent they may change local legislation for that purpose. Similarly, concern for civil life and welfare is not only an important aspect of both peace-building and the maintenance of public order, but perforce involves legislative action.

3 Legal Aspects of the Obligation to Restore and Ensure Public Order and Civil Life

A *Field of Application: Not Only Security, But Also Welfare*

Article 43 as quoted above refers to 'public order and safety'. This translation of the authentic French words '*l'ordre et la vie publics*' has been criticized. The meaning of '*la vie publique*' is indeed much broader. The legislative history provides good reasons to consider that it encompasses '*des fonctions sociales, des transactions ordinaires, qui constituent la vie de tous les jours*' ('social functions, ordinary transactions which constitute

6 *Trial of the Major War Criminals*, International Military Tribunal in Nuremberg, published in 41 *AJIL* (1947) 172, in particular at 248–249; *Legal Consequences of the Construction of a Wall in the Occupied Palestinian Territory*, Advisory Opinion, 9 July 2004, International Court of Justice, available at http://www.icj-cij.org/icjwww/idocket/imwp/imwpframe.htm, at paras. 89 and 124. See E. Benvenisti, *The International Law of Occupation* (1993), at 8. Art. 43 reaffirms rules already contained in the 1874 Brussels Declaration (*cf. infra* notes 8 and 9). See also G. Von Glahn, *The Occupation of Enemy Territory – A Commentary on the Law and Practice of Belligerent Occupation* (1957), at 95; D. Kretzmer, *The Occupation of Justice – The Supreme Court of Israel and the Occupied Territories* (2002), at 57.

7 Benvenisti, *supra* note 6, at 11.

8 Schwenk, 'Legislative Power of the Military Occupant Under Article 43, Hague Regulations', 54 *Yale LJ* (1944–1945) 397. In the Brussels Declaration (see *infra* note 9) the obligation to restore and ensure public order and civil life and the obligation to respect local laws, unless in case of necessity, were contained in two distinct Articles (Arts. 2 and 3), which became a single Article in the Hague Regulations. This means that the obligation to respect local laws (and its exception) must be seen as a general principle.

664 EJIL 16 (2005), 661–694

daily life').[9] Many scholars and the Israeli Supreme Court have endorsed this critique. They suggest translating '*la vie publique*' as 'civil life'.[10] This would be in line with the basic premise of IHL, confirmed in the introductory sentence of Article 43, that, if necessary, all functions of government must be provisionally assumed by the occupying power in order to guarantee normal life for the civilian population.

B *An Obligation of Means and Not of Result*

Many aspects of what constitutes 'civil life' and the measures an occupying power must, may or may not take to restore or maintain it are governed in detail by specific provisions of the Hague Regulations themselves,[11] of the Fourth Geneva Convention of 1949 (hereinafter Convention IV)[12] or of the 1977 Protocol Additional I to the Geneva Conventions (hereinafter Protocol I).[13] These provisions are *lex specialis* with respect to the general rule of Article 43 of the Hague Regulations. Under the general rule, as its qualifications 'all measures in his power' and 'as far as possible' confirm, public order and civil life are not results that must be guaranteed by an occupying power, but only aims it must pursue with all available, lawful and proportionate means. One may argue that the required standard of action is below that with which human rights instruments expect states to comply in fulfilling human rights, in particular social, economic and cultural rights,[14] since, as discussed below, the occupying power is not sovereign and its legislative powers are limited. In addition, the means an occupying power may use are limited by the numerous prohibitions laid down in Convention IV (e.g. of collective punishments, house demolitions, deportations, coercion, torture, taking of hostages[15]). The most traditional way of restoring public order is criminal prosecution of those who breach it, but such prosecutions

9 This explanation has been proposed by Baron Lambermont, the Belgian representative at the negotiations for the Brussels Convention of 1874, which never entered into force, but is known as the 'Brussels Declaration', considered to codify many old rules of IHL. Art. 43 of the Hague Regulations combines Arts. 2 and 3 of the Brussels Declaration. See Ministère des Affaires Etrangères de Belgique, *Actes de la Conférence de Bruxelles de 1874*, at 23, reproduced in Schwenk, *supra* note 8, at 393.

10 *Cf. ibid.*, at 393, note 1; Benvenisti, *supra* note 6, at 9; M. S. McDougal and F. P. Feliciano, *Law and Minimum World Public Order* (1961), at 746; K. A. Berriedale, *Wheaton's Elements of International Law* (6th edn, 1929), at 783. Kretzmer, *supra* note 6, at 58. Supreme Court of Israel, *Christian Society for Holy Places v Minister of Defence* (1971), summarized at [1972] *Israel YB Hum Rights* 354.

11 See, e.g., Hague Regulations, *supra* note 1, Art. 46 on family rights, property and religious practice, Arts. 48–52 on taxation, contributions and requisitions, and Arts. 53, 55, and 56 on public property.

12 Thus the Geneva Convention relative to the Protection of Civilian Persons in Time of War, 12 Aug. 1949, 75 UNTS 287 (hereinafter Convention IV), Art. 56 deals with hygiene and public health, Art. 55 with medical and food supplies, Arts. 59–62 with relief, Art. 57 with hospitals, Art. 58 with spiritual assistance, Arts. 51 and 52 with labour, working conditions, and labour market measures and Art. 50(3) with some aspects of education.

13 See also Protocol (No. I) Additional to the Geneva Conventions of 12 Aug. 1949 relating to the Protection of Victims of International Armed Conflicts, 8 June 1977, 1125 UNTS 3 (hereinafter Protocol I), Art. 69 on relief and Arts. 63 and 64(3) on civil defence.

14 The distinction between an obligation to respect, to protect, and to fulfil Human Rights was first suggested by A. Eide, *Right to Adequate Food as a Human Right* (Studies Series No. 1) (1989), at paras. 66–71.

15 Prohibited by Arts. 33, 53, 49, 31, 32, and 34, respectively, of Convention IV, *supra* note 12.

have to comply with the judicial guarantees set out in Convention IV.[16] The latter offers an occupying power the additional option of subjecting persons, under various procedural safeguards, to assigned residence or internment 'for imperative reasons of security'.[17] In my view, this security is not only that of the occupying forces, but, due to the obligation to restore and maintain public order, also that of the inhabitants of the territory. From materials available today it seems that the occupying powers in Iraq created only belatedly a legal basis for administrative detention according to Convention IV, although they had recourse to widespread detention of civilians without trial from the start of the occupation.[18] This would have been a clear violation of IHL, as the latter requires an individual decision 'according to a regular procedure *to be prescribed* by the Occupying Power'.[19]

C *An Obligation Subject to the Limitations Set by Human Rights Law for Any State Action*

Public order is restored through police operations, which are governed by domestic law and international human rights law, and not through military operations governed by IHL on the conduct of hostilities. Police operations are not directed at combatants (or civilians directly participating in hostilities) but against civilians (suspected of crimes or threatening public order). While military operations are aimed at weakening the military potential of the enemy, police operations aim to enforce the law and maintain public order. Police operations are subject to many more restrictions than hostilities. To mention but one example, force may be used against civilians only as a last resort after non-violent means have proved unsuccessful in maintaining law and order. As for the use of firearms,[2] it is an extreme measure in police operations[20] while it is normal against combatants in hostilities.

When lawful or unlawful[21] organized armed resistance continues in an occupied territory, as was the case in Iraq, the distinction between the conduct of hostilities against those directly participating in such resistance on the one hand, and police operations destined to maintain law and order and directed at civilians involved in criminal activity on the other, is more difficult to establish. The response by US forces

[16] See Arts. 66–74 of *ibid*.

[17] Art. 78 of *ibid*.

[18] See Coalition Provisional Authority, Memorandum No. 3 (Revised): Criminal Procedures, 27 June 2004, CPA/MEM/27 June 2004/03, which 'implements' CPA Order No. 7: Penal Code, 9 June 2003, CPA/ORD/9 June 2003/07. This and all the Coalition Provisional Authority documents referred to below are available at http://www.cpa-iraq.org until 30 June 2005.

[19] Art. 78 of Convention IV, *supra* note 12 (emphasis added).

[20] See the Basic Principles on the Use of Force and Firearms by Law Enforcement Officials, adopted by the 9th UN Congress on the Prevention of Crime and Treatment of Offenders, Havana, 27 Aug.–7 Sept. 1990, UN Doc. A/CONF.144/28/Rev.1 at 112 (1990) (Basic Principles).

[21] In Iraq, resistance groups certainly did not comply with the requirements that Art. 4(A)(2) of Convention III relative to the Treatment of Prisoners of War, 12 Aug. 1949, 75 UNTS 135, sets up for members of organized armed resistance groups to benefit from combatant status (in particular the conditions of having a fixed distinctive sign recognizable at a distance, of carrying arms openly, and of complying with the laws and customs of war).

666 EJIL 16 (2005), 661–694

to an RPG attack upon one of their convoys in the midst of Baghdad may, for instance, be considered to be covered by the law on the conduct of hostilities, while their firing upon a car failing to stop at a checkpoint is covered by human rights law applicable to police operations.[22] In the first instance, the deliberate killing of an attacker was lawful and the death of innocent bystanders could be lawful, if such civilian losses were not excessive and all feasible precautionary measures had been taken to avoid or minimize them.[23] In the second instance, international human rights law prescribes that the law enforcement officials must try to arrest the offenders without using firearms, and minimize damage and injury, and respect and preserve human life not only (as *mutatis mutandis* in the conduct of hostilities) of bystanders but also concerning the person to be arrested.[24]

However, the application of international human rights law to police operations in occupied territories raises the question whether that branch applies at all to occupied territories. International human rights law also applies in armed conflicts,[25] but since armed conflicts are situations threatening the life of the nation, most of its guarantees may be suspended under certain conditions.[26] Although both the US and Israel deny it,[27] UN practice and judicial decisions clearly indicate that international human rights law binds an occupying power with respect to the population of an occupied territory.[28]

Human rights law on the conduct of police operations, in particular on the use of firearms, may not be suspended even in a situation threatening the life of the nation,

[22] See for such incidents, e.g., Human Rights Watch, *Hearts and Minds: Post-war Civilian Deaths in Baghdad Caused by US Forces* (2003), available at http://www.hrw.org/reports/2003/iraq1003/iraq1003.pdf, at 38–39 (for the RPG attack) and 34–38 (for the killing of persons at a checkpoint).

[23] See Arts. 51(5)(b) and 57 of Protocol I, *supra* note 13, and the largely corresponding customary law. (See for the latter M. Sassòli, *Bedeutung einer Kodifikation für das allgemeine Völkerrecht, mit besonderer Betrachtung der Regeln zum Schutz der Zivilbevölkerung vor den Auswirkungen von Feindseligkeiten* (1990), at 412–419 and 453–489).

[24] See Basic Principles, *supra* note 20, Arts. 4 and 5.

[25] See the UN Human Rights Committee's General Comments No. 29 (CCPR/C/21/Rev.1/Add.11, of 31 Aug. 2001), at para. 3, and No. 31 (CCPR/C/74/CRP.4/Rev.6, of 21 Apr. 2004), at para. 11; *Legal Consequences of the Construction of a Wall, supra* note 6, at paras. 102–106; *The Legality of the Threat or Use of Nuclear Weapons*, Advisory Opinion [1996] ICJ Rep 226, at para. 25.

[26] See *infra* note 30 and accompanying text.

[27] See for Israel *Legal Consequences of the Construction of a Wall, supra* note 6, at paras. 102 and 110; Roberts, 'Prolonged Military Occupations: the Israeli-Occupied Territories since 1967', 84 *AJIL* (1990) 44, at 71–72 (hereinafter 'Prolonged Military Occupations'). The Coalition Provisional Authority's Administrator in Iraq, Ambassador Paul Bremer, is reported to have stated in a letter to Amnesty International that 'the only relevant standard applicable to the Coalition's detention practices is the Fourth Geneva Convention of 1949': see Amnesty International, *Iraq: Memorandum on Concerns Related to Legislation Introduced by the Coalition Provisional Authority*, 4 Dec. 2003, (MDE 14/176/2003), available at http://web.amnesty.org/library/Index/ENGMDE141762003?open&of=ENG-IRQ.

[28] *Legal Consequences of the Construction of a Wall, supra* note 6, at paras. 107–112; See also references in W. Kälin, *Report on the Situation of Human Rights in Kuwait under Iraqi Occupation*, UN Doc. E/CN.4/1992/26, 16 Jan. 1992, at paras 50–59; *Concluding Observations of the Human Rights Committee: Israel. 18/08/98*, UN Doc. CCPR/C/79/Add.93, at para. 10; *Loizidou v Turkey*, and *Cyprus v Turkey, infra* note 131; General Comment No. 31 of the UN Human Rights Committee (see *supra* note 25), at para. 10; UK, Ministry of Defence, *The Manual of the Law of Armed Conflict* (2004), at para. 11.19 (hereinafter UK Manual).

as far as it protects the right to life, a non-derogable right.[29] Other human rights that do not belong to 'the hard core' may be derogated from in times of emergency, to the extent required by the exigencies of the situation and as long as this derogation is consistent with other international obligations.[30] In my view, under the aforementioned conditions, an occupying power may derogate from certain human rights obligations if necessary to restore and maintain public order in an occupied territory. Even a serious disruption of civil life in an occupied territory could sometimes be considered as 'threatening the life of the [occupied] nation'. While an occupying power may thus derogate from certain provisions of international human rights law, it has no obligation to do so.

D *Evaluation of Coalition Practice in Iraq*

In the early days of the occupation, looting, and not an insurgency, represented the greatest threat to public order and the welfare of the local population. Universities, hospitals and government buildings were dismantled piece by piece and carried off. Water and electricity facilities were looted and personal property was stolen. At the time there were even reports that museums were emptied, which fortunately later proved to be exaggerated. Reports indicate that the Coalition had insufficient forces to provide constant security for all possible targets of looting.[31] In addition, some may have taken the attitude that looting should be permitted as 'a venting of anti-Saddam anger'.[32] In some instances, Coalition forces reportedly refused to assist when, for example, ambulances were stolen, replying that 'they had no orders to intervene'.[33] In my view, allowing a population to vent its anger following a conflict tends to cause more long-term problems of reconciliation and reconstruction than it resolves through catharsis. If indeed it was an intentional practice, it violated Article 43 of the Hague Regulations. However, reports also note that Coalition forces in some areas made considerable efforts to re-establish police stations, courts and prison and detention facilities within a short period of time.[34] Documents from the Coalition Provisional Authority highlight the accomplishments of the occupier in assisting 'the Iraqi government in constructing the means to assume responsibility for internal and

[29] See Basic Principles, *supra* note 20, Art. 8.

[30] *Cf.* Art. 4(1) of the 1966 International Covenant on Civil and Political Rights, 16 Dec. 1966, 999 UNTS 171, Art. 15(1) of the European Convention on Human Rights and Fundamental Freedoms, 4 Nov. 1950, 213 UNTS 221, and Art. 27(1) of the American Convention on Human Rights, 22 Nov. 1969, 1144 UNTS 143, and *Legal Consequences of the Construction of a Wall*, *supra* note 6, at para. 127.

[31] Amnesty International, *Iraq: The Need for Security* (2003) (MDE 14/143/2003), available at http://web.amnesty.org/library/Index/ENGMDE141432003?open&of=ENG-IRQ; BBC News, 12 Apr. 2002, British 'breaching Geneva Convention', available at http://news.bbc.co.uk/go/pr/fr/-/2/hi/uk_news/2940739.stm.

[32] Amnesty International, *Iraq: Looting, Lawlessness and Humanitarian Consequences* (2003) (MDE 14/083/2003), available at http://web.amnesty.org/library/Index/ENGMDE140852003?open&of=ENG-IRQ (quoting an unidentified UK military official).

[33] *Ibid.*, quoting Agence France Presse.

[34] See Amnesty International, *Iraq: The Need for Security*, *supra* note 31. These were open and operational by mid-June 2003 in Basra, for example.

668 EJIL 16 (2005), 661–694

external security'.[35] Taking into account that the obligation to preserve civil life and public welfare is one of means and not of result, the efforts made by the Coalition to create secure conditions once the occupation was established should not be discounted. It would seem, however, that such means and effort were lacking at the outset, although the problem was foreseeable.[36]

The obligation to distinguish between military and police operations and use appropriate force was addressed above. Yet reports of civilian deaths and the use of excessive force against civilians in Iraq abound, including prior to the widespread insurgency.[37] It is not difficult to understand that a soldier, aware that much of the population is armed, may react in ill-considered haste when confronted by an unstable environment. Nonetheless, IHL demands disciplined and professional responses to hard situations. To switch from combat to law enforcement mode,[38] the occupying powers should have deployed other troops more familiar with law enforcement. Such troops are, however, rare in Anglo-Saxon countries where the military and police are traditionally separated, while Latin countries such as France, Italy and Spain have them more readily available with their *gendarmerie*, *carabinieri* and *guardia civil*. The other possibility would have been to train combat troops already in peacetime to switch into the law enforcement mode. It must be hoped that the US and the UK learn those lessons from their experience at the beginning of the occupation.

4 The Principle Concerning Legislation: Occupying Powers Must Leave Local Legislation in Force

Article 43 bars an occupying power from extending its own legislation over the occupied territory or from acting as a sovereign legislator. It must, as a matter of principle, respect the laws in force in the occupied territory at the beginning of the occupation. This is one aspect of the conservative approach of IHL towards belligerent occupation, criticized by some for its rigidity.[39] We shall see, however, that it allows a considerable amount of flexibility.

A *The Meaning of the Term 'Legislation'*

The expression 'laws in force in the country' in Article 43 refers not only to laws in the strict sense of the word, but also to the constitution,[40] decrees, ordinances,[41] court precedents (especially in territories of common law tradition),[42] as well as administrative

[35] Coalition Provisional Authority, *An Historical Review of CPA Accomplishments* (2004), available at http://www.cpa-iraq.org.

[36] Roberts, 'The End of Occupation in Iraq (2004)', International Humanitarian Law Research Initiative, Monitoring IHL in Iraq, available at http://www.ihlresearch.org/iraq/feature.php?a = 51, at 1–2; Scheffer, *supra* note 2, at 853–855.

[37] See, e.g., Human Rights Watch, *supra* note 22; Amnesty International, *supra* note 32.

[38] 'From warrior to police': Human Rights Watch, *supra* note 22, at 4 and 5.

[39] R. Kolb, *Ius in bello, Le droit international humanitaire des conflits armés* (2002), at 186–187.

[40] UK Manual, *supra* note 28, at para 11.11.

[41] Schwenk, *supra* note 8, at 397.

[42] Benvenisti, *supra* note 6, at 16.

regulations and executive orders,[43] provided that the 'norms' in question are general and abstract. While the rule refers to the entire legal system, exceptions apply only to the individual provisions covered by the exceptions that allow an occupying power to legislate, as discussed below.

B *The Relationship between Article 43 and Article 64 of Convention IV*

Article 64 of Convention IV states:

> The penal laws of the occupied territory shall remain in force, with the exception that they may be repealed or suspended by the Occupying Power in cases where they constitute a threat to its security or an obstacle to the application of the present Convention...
> The Occupying Power may, however, subject the population of the occupied territory to provisions which are essential to enable the Occupying Power to fulfil its obligations under the present Convention, to maintain the orderly government of the territory and to ensure the security of the Occupying Power, of the members and property of the occupying forces or administration, and likewise of the establishments and lines of communication used by them.

This provision belongs to the section of the Convention devoted to penal legislation.[44] While the first paragraph explicitly refers to 'penal laws', the 'provisions' referred to in the second paragraph are not so qualified. Many nevertheless apply the second paragraph exclusively to penal legislation.[45] Apart from the context of the section, they may rely on the fact that Article 66 refers to 'penal provisions promulgated... by virtue of the second paragraph of Article 64', which seems to underline that these 'provisions' are 'penal'. However, this reasoning is not compelling. The second paragraph could also have a broader sense and allow an occupying power to subject the local population to any (penal, civil, administrative, etc.) laws essential for the purposes it exhaustively enumerates.[46] For the ICRC *Commentary*, the second paragraph expresses 'in a more precise and detailed form' the terms 'unless absolutely prevented' of Article 43.[47] The preparatory work of Article 64 shows that 'it is not a mere coincidence that the adjective "penal" is missing in the second paragraph'.[48]

[43] Von Glahn, *supra* note 6, at 97 and 99; E. H. Feilchenfeld, *The International Economic Law of Belligerent Occupation* (2000) (reprint of the original 1942 edition), at 89.

[44] According to the ICRC Commentary, the drafters of Convention IV were so concerned about penal laws because Art. 43 was not sufficiently observed in past conflicts on this particular issue. See J. Pictet, *The Geneva Conventions of 12 August 1949: Commentary IV Geneva Convention relative to the Protection of Civilians in Time of War* (1958), at 335.

[45] See for instance Dinstein, 'The International Law of Belligerent Occupation and Human Rights' [1978] *Israel Yb Hum Rights* 114; Kretzmer, *supra* note 6, at 125 and 151; G. Schwarzenberger, *International Law as Applied by International Courts and Tribunals, vol. II – The Law of Armed Conflict* (1968), at 194–195.

[46] Benvenisti, *supra* note 5, at 101.

[47] Pictet, *supra* note 44, at 335. Schwarzenberger, *supra* note 45, at 193.

[48] Benvenisti, *supra* note 6, at 101–103. Drafting Committee No. 2 of Committee III (in charge of the draft convention on the protection of civilian persons in time of war) at the 1949 Diplomatic Conference had a long debate about the future Art. 64 and in particular precisely about whether the adjective 'penal' should be added to the term 'provisions' in the second para. *(cf. Final Record of the Diplomatic Conference of*

The text of the second paragraph of Article 64 seems to permit the introduction of new legislation for a purpose – namely, 'to maintain the orderly government of the territory' – for which the first paragraph does not permit the repeal or suspension of existing penal legislation. However, according to the maxim *lex posterior derogat legi anteriori* any new legislation repeals previous contradictory legislation. The admissibility of penal legislation for the purpose of maintaining orderly government would therefore depend on whether, by chance, any legislation existed on the very same point prior to the occupation.[49] This absurd result can be avoided if we consider that legislation permissible under the second paragraph may necessarily derogate from previous legislation. Also, legislation contrary to the needs of orderly government may be considered an obstacle to the application of the Convention (one of the justifications for derogations under the first paragraph), given that Article 154 also refers to Article 43 of the Hague Regulations, which, of course, obliges an occupying power to maintain such orderly government.

Article 64(2) therefore permits, in the cases it specifies, changes to all existing local laws. It appears to impose fewer restrictions on legislative powers than the negative formulation of Article 43 of the Hague Regulations ('unless absolutely prevented'). The ICRC *Commentary* even qualifies the legislative powers of an occupying power as 'very extensive and complex'.[50] Nevertheless, as only those changes that are 'essential'[51] for the admissible purposes are permitted, Article 64 may be seen as interpreting the expression 'unless absolutely prevented' contained in the Hague Regulations. Compared with the latter, the newest element in Article 64 is the recognition of the power of the occupant to modify the existing laws in order to 'fulfil its obligations under the… Convention'. This may be seen as a simple confirmation of *lex specialis derogat legi generali*. However, it implies that the term 'unless absolutely prevented' refers not only to cases of material but also of legal necessity.

In conclusion, Article 64 certainly provides a *lex specialis* regarding the situations in which an occupying power is absolutely prevented from respecting penal law. In addition, there are good reasons to consider it a more precise, albeit less restrictive,

Geneva of 1949 (1950), iii, at 139). The draft submitted by the ICRC stated: '[t]he *penal* laws of the Occupied Power shall remain in force . . .': *ibid.*, i, at 122 (emphasis added). The UK, whose suggested amendment was closest to the finally adopted text, formulated it without specific reference to *penal* laws: *ibid.*, iii, at 139). The USSR wanted to limit the provision to penal norms: *ibid.*, iia, at 670). The Netherlands, a state having been subjected to occupation, insisted, by way of compromise, on the insertion of an Article clarifying the complementary character of the Hague Regulations and the Geneva Conventions: *ibid.*, iia, at 672). The Drafting Committee finally let Committee III choose between two versions, one referring to 'penal provisions', another one more generally to 'provisions'. The latter was adopted by 20 votes to 8: *ibid.*, iii, at 139). In addition, Art. 154 stating that the Convention was 'supplementary' to the Hague Regulations was added as part and parcel of the compromise reached about Art. 64.

49 Thus, an occupying power could introduce criminal liability of public officials in an occupied territory for unlawful official acts if no such legislation existed, but not if the previous legislation specifically excluded such liability.

50 Pictet, *supra* note 44, at 337.

51 The French term '*indispensable*' is even more restrictive and closer to the Hague Regulations.

formulation of when an occupying power is 'absolutely prevented' from applying existing local legislation.

C *Change of Legislation and Changes to Institutions*

Most writers deal with possible changes to the institutions of the occupied country separately, as if they were regulated by a specific norm. It is submitted that 'the occupant's competence to establish and operate processes of governmental administration in the territory occupied does not extend to the reconstruction of the fundamental institutions of the occupied area'.[52] In my opinion, except for the *lex specialis* on changes affecting courts, judges and public officials,[53] the legal parameter is always Article 43 because local institutions of the occupied country are established by and operate under the law. Institutions and the constitutional order are only one aspect of 'the laws in force in the country'. The exception 'unless absolutely prevented' applies here too. The 'active transformation and remodelling of the power and other value processes of the occupied country'[54] admittedly goes much further than simple legislation. An occupying power will only very exceptionally be 'absolutely prevented' from *not* undertaking it. It may not, for example, transform 'a democratic republic into an absolute monarchy', or 'change the regional or racial organizations of an occupied country', or even transform a liberal into a communist economy.[55]

An exception to this so-called Fauchille doctrine, prohibiting changes to the institutions of the occupied territory,[56] is recognized 'where a political system constitutes a permanent threat to the maintenance and safety of the military forces of the occupant so that there is "absolute necessity" to abolish it' (which is clearly a mere application of the general exception 'unless absolutely prevented').[57] This would distinguish the denazification carried out by the American Military Government at the end of the Second World War[58] from the German attempts to change the regional organization of Belgium during the First World War,[59] which were unanimously considered to be illegal.[60] In my view, the cases of post-World War II Germany and Japan should in any case not be seen as precedents for admissible changes in institutions. First, although every country may normally choose its political, economic and social system[61] and the right to self-determination of peoples bars an occupying power from

52 McDougal and Feliciano, *supra* note 10, at 767.

53 See Arts. 64, 66, and 54, respectively, of Convention IV, *supra* note 12.

54 McDougal and Feliciano, *supra* note 10, at 768.

55 Feilchenfeld, *supra* note 43, at 89–90.

56 P. Fauchille, *Traité de droit international public* (1921), at 228 ('*Comme la situation est éminemment provisoire, il ne doit pas bouleverser les* institutions *du pays*').

57 Schwenk, *supra* note 8, at 403.

58 *Ibid.*, at 407 and McDougal and Feliciano, *supra* note 10, at 770.

59 Germany adopted a series of legislative measures with a view to separating the French-speaking and the Dutch-speaking populations of Belgium (*cf.* von Glahn, *supra* note 6, at 97).

60 Feilchenfeld, *supra* note 43, at 89.

61 *Military and Paramilitary Activities in and against Nicaragua (Nicaragua v United States of America)*, *Merits* [1986] ICJ Rep 14, at para. 258.

672 EJIL 16 (2005), 661–694

making such choices, those two countries had particularly odious regimes that had committed the most serious violations of international law. Second, after World War II, *debellatio* or unconditional surrender were still considered to end the applicability of the law of belligerent occupation,[62] which is clearly no longer the case today because Article 6(3) and (4) of Convention IV extends the applicability of that convention beyond the general close of military operations.[63] Third, Article 47 of Convention IV was only adopted in 1949.

Article 47 refers to institutional changes introduced by an occupying power. It states that protected persons 'shall not be deprived, in any case or in any manner whatsoever, of the benefits of the present Convention by any change introduced, as the result of the occupation of a territory, into the institutions or government of the... territory, nor by any agreement concluded between the authorities of the occupied territories and the Occupying Power, nor by any annexation by the latter of the whole or part of the occupied territory'. This provision is sometimes misunderstood as prohibiting such changes as, for instance, annexations. Such prohibition is, however, an issue of *jus ad bellum*. *Jus in bello* simply continues to apply despite such changes and such changes do not justify violations of its provisions – including those on the admissibility of legislative changes. The ICRC *Commentary* stresses that '[c]ertain changes might conceivably be necessary and even an improvement.... [T]he text in question is of an essentially humanitarian character; its object is to safeguard human beings and not to protect the political institutions and government machinery of the State as such.'[64] That the Coalition established an Interim Governing Council in Iraq,[65] laid ground for a federalist constitutional system,[66] abolished the Ba'ath Party and its system of government[67] and tried to introduce a free-market economy,[68] was

62 Roberts, 'What is Military Occupation?', 55 *BYIL* (1984) 249, at 268–269; O. Debbasch, *L'occupation militaire – Pouvoirs reconnus aux forces armés hors de leur territoire national* (1962), at 250; Gerson, 'War, Conquered Territory, and Military Occupation in the Contemporary International Legal System', 18 *Harv Int'l LJ* (1977) 525, at 530–532; Jennings, 'Government in Commission', 23 *BYIL* (1946) 112; the US Military Tribunal at Nuremberg confirmed in *Altstötter and others (Justice Trial)*, 6 War Crimes Reports (1948) 1 that the law of military occupation did not apply to the Allied military presence in Germany.

63 Art. 3(b) of Protocol I, *supra* note 13, goes even further.

64 Pictet, *supra* note 44, at 274.

65 Coalition Provisional Authority, Regulation No. 6: Governing Council of Iraq, 13 July 2003 CPA/REG/13 July 2003/06.

66 Coalition Provisional Authority, Law of Administration for the State of Iraq for the Transitional Period, 8 Mar. 2004, Art. 4 (Transitional Administration Law).

67 Coalition Provisional Authority, Order No. 1: De-Ba'athification of Iraqi Society, 16 May 2003 CPA/ORD/16 May 2003/01; Coalition Provisional Authority, Memorandum No. 1: Implementation of De-Ba'athification Order No. 1, 3 June 2003 CPA/MEM/3 June 2003/01; Coalition Provisional Authority, Order No. 2: Dissolution of Entities (And Annex), 23 May 2003 CPA/ORD/23 May 2003/02.

68 See especially, Coalition Provisional Authority, Order No. 54: Trade Liberalization Policy 2004 with Annex A, 24 Feb. 2004 CPA/ORD/24 February 2004/54; Coalition Provisional Authority, Order No. 56: Central Bank Law and Annex A, 6 Mar. 2004 CPA/ORD/6 Mar. 2004/56; Coalition Provisional Authority, Order No. 87: Public Contracts, 14 May 2004 CPA/ORD/14 May 2004/87; Coalition Provisional Authority, Order No.39: Foreign Investment (Amended by Order No. 46), 20 Dec. 2003, CPA/ORD/20 Dec. 2003/39; Coalition Provisional Authority, Order No. 64: Amendment to the Company Law No. 21 of 1997, 29 Feb. 2004, CPA/ORD/29 Feb. 2004/64.

therefore not as such a violation of IHL, but every individual measure must be checked hereafter against the exceptions admissible under IHL to the prohibition for occupying powers to change local legislation.

5 Exceptions to the Prohibition to Legislate

The words 'restore and ensure... public order and civil life' in Article 43 could be understood as implying that the occupying power is allowed to take only legislative measures for that purpose, i.e. concerning the 'common interest or the interest of the population'.[69] However, as confirmed by Article 64 of Convention IV and the drafting history of the Hague Regulations and prior international instruments on the same topic, an occupying power may also legislate to promote its own military interests.[70] When Article 64 refers to the security of the occupant's forces, it does no more than confirm, though in more permissive terms, what was already admissible under Article 43.[71]

A *The Occupying Power May Only Legislate for the Time of the Occupation*

The task of restoring or ensuring public order and civil life is limited *ratione temporis* to the period of occupation.[72] In accordance with the aim of Article 43 to maintain the existing legislation as far as possible and to limit changes by an occupying power, and because the occupation does not transfer any title of sovereignty, every legislative change made by the occupying power should be commensurate with the transitional and temporary nature of the occupation.

B *The Occupying Power May Legislate for Reasons Other than Military Necessity*

The meaning of the exception 'unless absolutely prevented' ('*sauf empêchement absolu*') is controversial. Some suggest that it refers to 'military necessity'.[73] The words 'unless absolutely prevented' were, however, a mere reformulation of the term 'necessity' contained in Article 3 of the Brussels Declaration, which, according to its preparatory works, was not meant as a synonym for 'military necessity'.[74] At the other extreme, some authors simply require sufficient justification to deviate from local legislation.[75] Others consider that 'absolute prevention means necessity' and

69 Schwenk, *supra* note 8, at 395, citing Meurer, *Die Volkerrechtliche Stellung der vom Feind besetzten Gebiete* (1915), at 23.
70 See Schwenk, *supra* note 8, at 395–397.
71 Benvenisti, *supra* note 6, at 104. See also Schwarzenberger, *supra* note 45, at 194.
72 Oppenheim, *International Law – A Treatise* (7th edn. by H. Lauterpacht, 1952), ii, *Disputes, War and Neutrality*, at 436 and 437.
73 Schwenk, *supra* note 8, at 393; M. Greenspan, *The Modern Law of Land Warfare* (1959), at 224; Bothe, 'Occupation, Belligerent', in R. Bernhardt (ed.), *Encyclopedia of Public International Law* (1997), iii, at 765.
74 Schwenk, *supra* note 8, at 401.
75 Feilchenfeld, *supra* note 43, at 89.

674 *EJIL* 16 (2005), 661–694

that the adverb 'absolutely' is therefore of small consequence.[76] More generally, it is regretted that Article 43 does not offer a fixed criterion to determine which changes are lawful.[77] After the two world wars, courts have indeed accepted a great variety of legislation by occupying powers (including by those that were finally vanquished) as valid.[78] The practice of Israeli courts concerning legislation in the Israeli occupied territories is also very permissive.[79] Most authors have an intermediate position and mention that, as confirmed by Article 64 of Convention IV, not only the interests of the army of occupation, but also those of the local civilian population may prevent an occupying power from applying local legislation.[80] This broader interpretation also corresponds to the practice of allied occupying powers *during* World War II. Nonetheless, the risk of abuse of a broader interpretation should not be neglected, as it is the occupying power that decides whether a legislative act is necessary, and its interpretation is not subject to revision during the occupation.[81]

C *The Occupying Power May Legislate to Ensure Its Security*

Under both Article 43 of the Hague Regulations and Article 64(2) of Convention IV, the most uncontroversial case of legislation an occupying power may introduce is that which is *essential*[82] to ensure its security. Such legislation may not, however, prescribe any measure specifically prohibited by IHL (such as collective punishment, house demolitions or deportations).[83] Traditional examples of laws that may be suspended are those concerning conscription, rights of public assembly, and bearing arms.[84] In Iraq, the occupying powers introduced, for example, a prohibition on the bearing of arms during assemblies permitted by the Coalition Provisional Authority.[85]

76 Dinstein, *supra* note 45, at 112, citing Schwarzenberger, *supra* note 44, at 193. Dinstein adds that '[t]he necessity ... may be derived either from the legitimate interests of the occupant or from concern for the civilian population'.

77 Vité, 'L'applicabilité du droit international de l'occupation militaire aux activités des organisations internationales', 853 *Int'l Rev Red Cross* (2004) 17. This article is based upon a larger study by R. Kolb, G. Porretto, and S. Vité, *L'Articulation des règles de droit international humanitaire et de droits de l'homme applicables aux forces internationales et aux administrations civiles internationales transitoires* (2003) (mimeotyped version, to be translated and published in English).

78 For examples see reference to various court cases in E. David, *Principes de droit des conflits armés* (3rd edn., 2002), at 511.

79 For the practice of the Israeli Supreme Court see Kretzmer, *supra* note 6, at 61–72.

80 Schwenk, *supra* note 8, at 400; Pictet, quoted *supra* note 64; Debbasch, *supra* note 62, at 172; Von Glahn, *supra* note 6, at 97. A. D. McNair and A. D. Watts, *The Legal Effects of War* (1966), at 369 mention three grounds for being 'absolutely prevented' from respecting local laws, namely the maintenance of order, the safety of the occupier, and the realization of the legitimate purpose of the occupation.

81 Von Glahn, *supra* note 6, at 100. Exceptionally, the ICJ was able in *Legal Consequences of the Construction of a Wall*, *supra* note 6, at para. 137, to give an opinion on whether certain measures taken by an occupying power were necessary.

82 While it is not sufficient that legislation *furthers* its security, an occupying power has broad discretion in deciding what is *essential* to its security.

83 *Cf.* Arts. 33(1), 49(1), and 53 of Convention IV, *supra* note 12.

84 UK Manual, *supra* note 28, at para. 11.25.

85 Coalition Provisional Authority, Order No. 19: Freedom of Assembly, 9 July 2003 CPA/ORD/9 July 2003/19, ss. 2 and 6.

D *The Occupying Power May Adopt Legislation Essential for the Implementation of IHL*

The reference in Article 64 to legislation essential for (or an obstacle to) the respect of 'Convention [IV]' must be extended to all applicable IHL, since IHL cannot possibly require specific conduct from an occupying power and also prohibit it to legislate for that purpose. To fulfil its various duties under IHL in a non-arbitrary way compatible with the principles of the rule of law, and to respect the principle *nullum crimen sine lege* in the field of penal law, an occupying power must legislate, including by abrogating provisions of the local legislation contrary to IHL. Examples given in the preparatory works for the necessity to legislate are provisions in the fields of child welfare, labour, food, hygiene and public health.[86] The ICRC *Commentary* mentions 'provisions which adversely affect racial or religious minorities' as examples of laws which may be abrogated. Examples of such changes in Iraq were Orders ensuring fundamental standards for persons detained.[87]

Like any state party to Convention IV, an occupying power must also legislate to try persons having committed grave breaches, if such legislation does not yet exist in the occupied territory.[88] The Coalition Provisional authority in Iraq, however, went one step further. It not only adopted (through the Governing Council for which it is responsible under Article 47 of Convention IV) legislation criminalizing international crimes committed by the former regime.[89] This was certainly lawful. It could then have brought such crimes either before its own (military) courts,[90] or before existing Iraqi courts, which it must 'let continue to function'.[91] It chose neither of those two options, but preferred to create a new Iraqi court for that purpose,[92] an option which is not offered by Convention IV and is certainly not necessary in order to respect IHL, as the other two kinds of tribunals could have done the job. Therefore, in my view, the Iraqi Special Tribunal established on 10 December 2003 by the Interim Governing Council under an explicit delegation of authority by the occupying powers,[93] violated IHL and, as it was not lawfully constituted, it could not today try Iraqis accused of international crimes unless the new Interim Government of Iraq were to establish it again. The conduct of the Council could in any case be attributed to the occupying powers even without the delegation of authority.[94]

86 See *Final Record*, *supra* note 48, iia, at 672 and 833.

87 See Coalitional Provisional Authority, Order No. 10: Management of Detention and Prison Facilities, 5 June 2003 CPA/ORD/5 June 2003/10 and Coalition Provisional Authority, Memorandum No. 2: Management of Detention and Prison Facilities, 8 June 2003 CPA/MEM/8 June 2003/02.

88 UK Manual, *supra* note 28, at para. 11.26, note 54.

89 See Governing Council, The Statute of the Iraqi Special Tribunal, 10 Dec. 2003, 'Annex' to CPA Order No. 48, *infra* note 92. See especially Section Three: Jurisdiction and Crimes.

90 See Art. 66 of Convention IV, *supra* note 12.

91 See *ibid.*, Art. 64(1)

92 See Coalition Provisional Authority, Order No. 48: Delegation of Authority Regarding an Iraqi Special Tribunal, 10 Dec. 2003 CPA/ORD/9 Dec. 2003/48.

93 See *supra* notes 89 and 92.

94 See *infra*, section 6.A.

676 EJIL 16 (2005), 661–694

E *May the Occupying Power Legislate to Implement International Human Rights Law?*

It was explained above that international human rights law also binds occupying powers in respect of the treatment of the local population.[95] The specific provisions of IHL provide for a *lex specialis* on the issues they regulate.[96] However, many issues such as freedom of the press, freedom of opinion, the right to form trade unions or the right to social security are not dealt with by IHL.[97] On other issues, such as the moment from which an accused must have access to defence counsel, human rights as interpreted by treaty and UN Charter-based mechanisms are more specific. In both cases, human rights standards therefore apply, but in the former case they may be subject to derogations.

The occupying power therefore has an obligation to abolish legislation and institutions which contravene international human rights standards. While it may derogate from certain provisions due to a situation of emergency, it is certainly not obliged to do so and may therefore change any legislation contrary to the full guarantees of international human rights law.

That IHL does not mention this additional exception to the continuing applicability of local legislation can be easily explained by the fact that when the Hague Regulations were adopted in 1907, international human rights law did not yet exist, and in 1949, when Convention IV was drafted, it had just come into being.[98] Today, an occupying power has a strong argument that it is 'absolutely prevented' from applying local legislation contrary to international law.

Human rights, e.g. the right to a fair trial, women's rights, and in particular social and economic rights often require the state to take positive (including legislative) action. Thus, one may even go so far as to allow the occupying power to adopt new, additional laws that are genuinely necessary to protect international human rights law. In Iraq, the Coalition prohibited, for example, child labour.[99] The property reconciliation and claims institutions it established may also come under this category.[100]

[95] See *supra* notes 25–28.

[96] See *Legal Consequences of the Construction of a Wall*, *supra* note 6, at para. 106.

[97] Roberts, *supra* note 27, at 73, also mentions that 'discrimination in employment, discrimination in education and the import of educational materials . . . are addressed in considerable detail in certain human rights agreements, and are not so addressed in the law on occupations. In respect of such issues, the application of international human rights standards is highly desirable.'

[98] In 1949, a proposal by the Mexican Delegation to the effect that local legislation could be modified by the occupier only if it violated the 'Universal Declaration of the Rights of Man' was rejected (see *Final Record*, *supra* note 48, iia, at 671).

[99] See Coalition Provisional Authority, Order No. 89: Amendments to the Labor Code – Law No. 71 of 1987, 5 May 2004, CPA/ORD/05 May 2004/89.

[100] See, e.g., Coalition Provisional Authority, Regulation No. 4: Establishment of the Iraqi Property Reconciliation Facility, 14 Jan. 2004 CPA/REG/14 Jan. 2004/04, Regulation No. 8: Delegation of Authority Regarding Establishment of a Property Claims Commission (Amended by Reg. 12), 14 Jan. 2004, CPA/REG/14 Jan. 2004/08, and Regulation No. 12: Establishment of the Iraq Property Claims Commission (As Amended and Restated) with Annex A, 24 June 2004, CPA/REG/24 June 2004/12, which recognizes 'that large numbers of people from different ethnic and religious backgrounds in Iraq have been uprooted and forced to move from their properties . . . ' and attempts to set up a mechanism to resolve property disputes primarily related to the Kurdistan Regional Government area.

However, international human rights law often provides only a framework and leaves the state great latitude on how to implement it. As long as local legislation falls within this latitude, an occupying power may certainly not replace it. As the ICRC *Commentary* emphasizes, occupying authorities may not change local legislation 'merely to make it accord with their own legal conceptions',[101] including where those conceptions are also perfectly compatible with international human rights standards.

A difficult question arises when local legislation is clearly contrary to (or insufficient under) human rights standards. May an occupying power then exercise (provisionally) the latitude granted to states on how they implement international human rights law? In my view, while such exercise of discretion is contrary to the right to self-determination and to the principle that legislation must be based upon the will of the people,[102] it is inherent in the situation of occupation and must therefore be accepted until the local people can exercise their right to self-determination. An occupying power must, however, take into account, while exercising such discretion, that it is not the sovereign – it may introduce only as many changes as is absolutely necessary under its human rights obligations and must stay as close as possible to similar local standards and the local cultural, legal and economic traditions. Consequently, in my view, the proper test cannot be whether a similar law exists in the occupier's own country.[103] If, for instance, an Anglo-Saxon power occupies a country of Roman-German penal law tradition, the legislation of which would not offer the necessary guarantees of a fair trial, the former could not introduce an adversarial criminal procedure, but only those changes which make an inquisitorial trial compatible with the right to a fair trial. Similarly, an occupying power with a free labour market could not change the local labour legislation to allow free hiring and firing in order to implement the right to work.

A special problem arises in relation to the right to self-determination of peoples. First, while this is a human right, it applies only to peoples. Not every population of an occupied territory is a people. If part of an existing country is occupied where a part of a people lives, it would clearly be incompatible with international law for an occupying power to encourage the 'self-determination' of the population of that territory. May an occupying power, however, take legislative action to further the exercise of the right to self-determination of a genuine people living in an occupied territory? In my view, this right cannot be implemented by an occupying power. It is too closely linked to the wishes of the people and the ways in which this right can be satisfied are too manifold. Some would add that the very fact of occupation is incompatible with the right to self-determination. The best way to respect it for an occupying power is not to legislate, but to withdraw. This is, however, an issue of *jus ad bellum* and this argument cannot be used to deny an occupying power the right to legislate under *jus in bello*. An occupying power confronted with a people in an occupied territory may

[101] Pictet, *supra* note 44, at 336.

[102] *Cf.* Art. 21(3) of the Universal Declaration of Human Rights, GA Res. 217(III), UN GAOR, 3d Sess. Supp. No. 13, UN Doc. A/810 (1948), 71.

[103] As suggested by Dinstein, *supra* note 45, at 113.

therefore be considered to be allowed to legislate in order to create conditions necessary to the exercise by that people of its right to self-determination and to abrogate legislation making such an exercise impossible.

F *The Occupying Power May Legislate Where Necessary to Maintain Public Order*

Beyond the protection of its own security, under the explicit wording of Article 43, the protection of the security of the local population is a legitimate aim for legislation by an occupying power. As it must restore and maintain public order, it may also legislate where absolutely necessary for that purpose. In Iraq, it might be that the imposition of longer prison sentences for acts of looting or sabotage of infrastructure was justified under this exception.[104] The simultaneous denial of pre-trial bail in such cases[105] was, however, probably not compatible with human rights standards, which do not include the seriousness of the suspected crime amongst the valid reasons for denial of bail.[106]

G *May the Occupying Power Legislate to Maintain Civil Life in an Occupied Territory?*

The most important contribution of an occupying power to civil life in an occupied territory is to maintain the orderly government of the territory. Article 64(2) of Convention IV explicitly allows it to legislate for that purpose. Beyond that, it must also ensure civil life among the inhabitants of the territory and may legislate for that purpose if the existing legislation or its absence absolutely prevents it from accomplishing that aim. This includes regulations fixing prices or securing the equitable distribution of food and other commodities, calling up, if necessary, the inhabitants for police duty to assist the regular police in the maintenance of public order, for help with fire fighting or to perform other duties that may be required of citizens for the public good.[107] In practice, aside from the case of legislation contrary to human rights standards already mentioned, legislative action by the occupying power to ensure civil life will mainly be necessary where a failed state is occupied. Here again it must stay as close as possible to similar local standards and the local cultural, legal and economic traditions.

104 See Coalition Provisional Authority, Order No. 31: Modifications of Penal Code and Criminal Proceedings Law, 10 Sept. 2003, CPA/ORD/10 September 2003/31.

105 See *ibid.*, s. 6.

106 According to Art. 9(3) of the International Covenant on Civil and Political Rights, 'it shall not be the general rule that persons awaiting trial shall be detained in custody, but release may be subject to guarantees to appear for trial, at any other stage of the judicial proceedings, and, should occasion arise, for execution of the judgement'. In its *General Comment No. 08: Right to liberty and security of persons (Art. 9) 30/06/82*, the Human Rights Committee stated that 'pre-trial detention should be an exception and as short as possible'. In *Communication No 526/1993: Spain. 23/06/97*, it emphasized that 'bail should be granted, except in situations where the likelihood exists that the accused would abscond or destroy evidence, influence witnesses or flee from the jurisdiction of the State party'. In my view, denial of pre-trial bail because of the seriousness of the suspected crime violates the right to be presumed innocent.

107 UK Manual, *supra* note 28, at paras. 11.16 and 11.25.1. For other examples see reference to various court cases in David, *supra* note 78, at 507.

In Iraq, the occupying powers addressed, for example, the problem of a number of different series of Iraqi Dinar notes circulating in order to help stabilize the economy and to instil public confidence.[108] They also adopted changes to the traffic code.[109] The first change could have been considered necessary to maintain economic life. Other measures went clearly beyond what is necessary for that purpose and therefore in my view violated IHL. The occupying powers simplified, for example, the procedure of concluding public contracts and liberalized trade and foreign investment.[110] On the latter, they allowed foreign investors to completely own Iraqi companies with no requirements for reinvesting profits back into the country – something that had previously been restricted by the Iraqi Constitution to the citizens of Arab countries.[111] Neither human rights nor economic life made such a change, affecting the right of the Iraqi people to freely dispose of its wealth and resources, necessary.[112]

H *May an Occupying Power Legislate to Enhance Civil Life in an Occupied Territory?*

Sooner or later, a prolonged military occupation faces the need to adopt legislative measures in order to let the occupied country evolve.[113] As the legislative function is a continuous, necessary function of every state on which the evolution of civil life depends, a legislative vacuum created by the disruption of the legitimate sovereign must at a certain point in time be filled by the occupying power.[114] It has been suggested that the exception of Article 43 must be interpreted more extensively the longer an occupation lasts.[115] This is particularly evident for the rules on taxation. Article 48 of the Hague Regulations does not seem to exclude tax increases, especially if

> such changes . . . have been made desirable . . . . in the case of an extended occupation, [through] general changes in economic conditions. . . . If the occupation lasts through several years the lawful sovereign would, in the normal course of events, have found it necessary to modify tax legislation. A complete disregard of these realities may well interfere with the welfare of the country and ultimately with 'public order and safety' as understood in article 43.[116]

[108] Coalition Provisional Authority, Order No. 43: New Iraqi Dinar Banknotes, 14 Oct. 2003, CPA/ORD/14 October 2003/43.

[109] Coalition Provisional Authority, Order No. 86: Traffic Code with Annex A, 20 May 2004, CPA/ORD/20 May 2004/86.

[110] See *supra* note 68.

[111] See Order 39, *supra* note 68, ss. 7(2)(d), 11.

[112] Equally critical are Roberts, *supra* note 36, at 7, and Catán, 'Iraq Business Deals May be Invalid, Law Experts Warn', *Financial Times*, 2 Nov. 2003; Eviatar, 'Free-Market Iraq? Not So Fast', *NY Times*, 10 Jan. 2004, B9.

[113] Lerquin, 'The German Occupation in Belgium and Article 43 of The Hague Convention of the 18th October 1907', 1 *International Law Notes* (1916) 55.

[114] L. von Kohler, *The Administration of the Occupied Territories, Vol. I – Belgium* (1942), at 6, cited in McDougal and Feliciano, *supra* note 10, at 746, writes that 'the life of the occupied country is not to cease or stand still, but is to find continued fulfilment even under the changed conditions resulting from occupation'.

[115] Kolb, *supra* note 39, at 186.

[116] Feilchenfeld, *supra* note 43, at 49. See also Roberts, *supra* note 27, at 44.

In Iraq, although the occupation did not last for a very long period, the occupying powers legislated to introduce 'an efficient and modern income tax system'.[117]

Here too the risk of abuse exists. Article 43 was originally adopted under the influence of weaker countries that were more susceptible to occupation and thus wished to oblige likely occupants to take care of the civilian population. However, the tendency of the 20th-century state to become more active in regulating economic and social relations and the practice of occupants during the two World Wars have led to the concern that occupying powers invoke their obligation to restore civil life to justify a broad use of legislative powers, thus reversing the original aim of this norm.[118]

I *The Occupying Power May Legislate Where Explicitly Authorized to do so by a UN Security Council Resolution*

Even apart from the case of a peace operation dealt with below, the UN Security Council may mandate or authorize an occupying power to take certain steps to create conditions in which the population of the occupied territory can freely determine its future life under the rule of law and enjoy the respect of human rights. It may consider that this necessitates the establishment of new local and national institutions and legal, judicial and economic reform. According to the principles of the rule of law – which are essential to any peace-building effort – all this implies the need to adopt legislation which may go further than what can be justified under the exceptions to the principle of Article 43 discussed up to this point.[119] Only Security Council resolutions can justify such fundamental changes and the devolution of wide legislative powers to local authorities remaining under the global control of the (former) occupying power. Some authors go even one step further and claim that the Security Council may end the occupation altogether, not by changing the facts on the ground, but by requalifying a belligerent occupation as an international transitional administration.[120]

Assuming that the International Court of Justice was correct when it held that Article 103 of the UN Charter makes not only the UN Charter but also binding UN Security Council resolutions prevail over any other international obligation,[121] such

[117] Preamble to Coalition Provisional Authority, Order No. 49: Tax Strategy of 2004 with Explanatory Note and Annex, 20 Feb. 2004, CPA/ORD/20 Feb. 2004/49. See also Coalition Provisional Authority, Order No.37: Tax Strategy for 2003, 19 Sept. 2003, CPA/ORD/19 Sept. 2003/37.

[118] Benvenisti, *supra* note 6, at 9–11. See also McDougal and Feliciano, *supra* note 10, at 747, Debbasch, *supra* note 62, at 172, and Schwarzenberger, *supra* note 45, at 200–201.

[119] First, the very constitution of new local authorities necessitates changes which go beyond the simple implementation of political rights under international human rights law. Secondly, as long as the occupation lasts, local authorities, even if freely elected (see *infra* note 131) are subject to the same restraints under IHL as the occupying power (see *infra*, at 6. A.). Newly established national authorities will, however, never comply with the limitations of legislative powers discussed hitherto.

[120] Vité, *supra* note 77, at 28. See also Ottolenghi, 'The Stars and Stripes in Al-Fardos Square: The Implications for the International Law of Belligerent Occupation', 77 *Fordham L Rev* (2004) 2177.

[121] Order of 14 April 1992 in *Questions of Interpretation and Application of the 1971 Montreal Convention arising from the Aerial Incident at Lockerbie (Libyan Arab Jamahiriya v US)* [1992] ICJ Rep 126.

resolutions authorizing legislative changes in an occupied territory prevail over the restrictions of Articles 43 of the Hague Regulations and 64 of Convention IV. IHL obligations, however, fall under *jus cogens*.[122] Many consider that even Security Council resolutions may not derogate from *jus cogens*.[123] The International Court of Justice has, on the contrary, called upon the Security Council to take action to bring violations of IHL to an end.[124] However, the question of whom could determine that a given Security Council resolution violates *jus cogens* is unclear.

In my view, any derogation from IHL by the UN Security Council must be explicit. Its resolutions must be interpreted whenever possible in a manner compatible with IHL. First, as mentioned, even the Security Council must comply with *jus cogens*. Second, the mandate of the Security Council to maintain international peace and security consists of enforcing *jus ad bellum*. Just as a state implementing *jus ad bellum* by using force in self-defence or under UN Security Council authorization has to comply with IHL, it follows that any measure authorized by the Council must be implemented in a manner that respects IHL.[125] A simple encouragement of international efforts to promote legal and judicial reform by an occupying power is certainly too vague to justify an occupying power to legislate beyond what IHL permits. I would therefore reject the claim of the new UK Military Manual that UN Security Council Resolution 1483 (2003) justifies US and UK legislation in this field when it simply 'requests the Secretary-General to appoint a Special Representative... whose independent responsibilities shall involve..., in coordination with the [occupying powers], assisting the people of Iraq through:... encouraging international efforts to promote legal and judicial reform'.[126] Such involvement may only have been justified under the exception for legislation necessary under international human rights law. I would similarly reject the claim by the UK Secretary of State for Foreign and Commonwealth Affairs that 'Security Council Resolution 1483 provides a sound legal basis for the policy goals of the CPA Foreign Investment Order' discussed above.[127] Here too, the resolution

122 Draft Articles on Responsibility of States for internationally wrongful acts, United Nations, International Law Commission, *Report on the work of its fifty-third session* (23 April–1 June and 2 July–10 August 2001), UN GAOR, 55th Sess., Supp. No. 10, UN Doc. A/56/10, available at http://www.un.org/law/ilc/reports/2001/2001report.htm, at 29–365, para. 5 to Art. 40, referring to Nuclear Weapons, *supra* note 25, at para. 79. See also *Report of the International Law Commission on the work of its thirty-second session* in *Yearbook of the International Law Commission* (1980), ii, Part Two, at 46, para. 28, and *Prosecutor v Kupreskic*, Case No. IT-95-16-T, Judgment, para 520 (ICTY Trial Chamber 14 Jan. 2000). Scheffer, *supra* note 2, at 852, considers that '[g]iven the widely varying circumstances that may trigger and even justify military occupation, it would be a mistake to regard many of the codified provisions of occupation law as peremptory norms of international law'. The ICJ disagrees, because it applied rules on state responsibility for serious breaches of peremptory norms of international law to violations of IHL of military occupation (see *Legal Consequences of the Construction of a Wall*, *supra* note 6, at para. 159).

123 See Separate Opinion of Judge Lauterpacht in the *Case concerning Application of the Convention on the Prevention and Punishment of the Crime of Genocide (Bosnia and Herzegovina v. Yugoslavia), Provisional Measures, Order of 13 September 1993* [1993] ICJ Rep 325, at 440–441, paras. 100–102.

124 *Legal Consequences of the Construction of a Wall*, *supra* note 6, at para. 160

125 See Meron, 'Prisoners of War, Civilians and Diplomats in the Gulf Crisis', 85 *AJIL* (1991) 104, at 106.

126 See UK Manual, *supra* note 28, at para. 11.11, n. 15, and SC Res. 1483 (2003), para. 8(i).

127 See HC Debs., 20 Nov. 2003, vol. 413, col. 1304W and *supra* notes 110–112.

682 EJIL 16 (2005), 661–694

simply mentions among the responsibilities of the Special Representative the promotion, in coordination with the occupying powers, of 'economic reconstruction and the conditions for sustainable development'.[128] The mentioned Order therefore violated international law.

6 When does International Humanitarian Law of Military Occupation Cease to Apply, particularly in Iraq?

A *IHL of Belligerent Occupation Applies to Local Authorities Acting under the Global Control of an Occupying Power*

As mentioned above, Article 47 of Convention IV states that protected persons 'shall not be deprived' of the benefits of IHL 'by any change introduced, as the result of the occupation of a territory, into the institutions or government of the . . . territory, nor by any agreement concluded between the authorities of the occupied territories and the Occupying Power'. Understood in conformity with the general rules on state responsibility for conduct directed or controlled by a state,[129] this means that a government instituted by the occupying power, such as the Interim Governing Council in Iraq before 30 June 2004, may not subject the local population to changes going beyond those which could be introduced by the occupying power itself. This raises the question of when the devolution of governmental authority to a national government is effective enough to end the applicability of IHL on belligerent occupation altogether. Article 6(3) of Convention IV prescribes that the Convention ceases to apply '[i]n the case of occupied territory . . . one year after the general close of military operations; however, the Occupying Power shall be bound, for the duration of the occupation, to the extent that such Power exercises the functions of government in such territory, by the provisions [of the most important articles for our discussion, such as Articles 47 and 64].' The decisive factor is, therefore, who effectively exercises governmental authority. Article 3(b) of Protocol I goes further in prescribing that IHL applies until the termination of the occupation, but such termination must also depend upon who exercises effectively governmental authority.

[128] SC Res. 1483 (2003), para. 8(e).

[129] See Art. 8 of the Draft Articles, *supra* note 122. The ICRC Commentary to Art. 29 of Convention IV considers that when a violation has been committed by local authorities, 'what is important is to know where the decision leading to the unlawful act was made, where the intention was formed and the order given' (Pictet, *supra* note 44, at 212.). In the *Tadic* case, the International Criminal Tribunal for the Former Yugoslavia held, however, that overall control is the appropriate standard, and not effective control over the conduct to be attributed to a given state (*Prosecutor v Tadic*, Case No. IT-94–1, Judgment, paras. 116–144 (ICTY, Appeals Chamber 15 July 1999)).

B *The End of Occupation through Devolution of Governmental Authority to New National Authorities: The Case of Iraq*

Many would make that end depend on the (democratic) legitimacy of a new national government,[130] given that, taking into account the right of the local people to self-determination, a democratic election cannot be considered as a change 'introduced' by the occupying power, even if it was held under the latter's initiative and supervision. That democratically elected government could then end the occupation, even though troops of the former occupying power remain present on the territory of the state, by freely agreeing to their presence.[131] The main problem with this line of argument is that the legitimacy of the new government is often controversial (as is the question of whether the new government's consent to the continued presence of foreign troops is freely given). International human rights law provides only insufficient indications of such legitimacy, through the right to self-determination, political rights and the rights of minorities.[132] International recognition of such legitimacy, in particular by the UN Security Council, may offer a clearer indication.

In the case of Iraq, Security Council Resolution 1546 (2004), '[l] *looking forward* to the end of the occupation and the assumption of full responsibility and authority by a fully sovereign and independent Interim Government of Iraq by 30 June 2004', explicitly welcomes that 'by 30 June 2004, the occupation will end'.[133] In my view, this cannot be seen as an application of the rules of IHL on the end of application of the law of military occupation to the facts on the ground. Under IHL, the law of military occupation would have continued to apply. The resolution was adopted when the US-led coalition itself admitted that it was still exercising effective control over Iraq and its wording does not make this determination dependent upon an effective change on the ground. As for the facts, more than 100,000 Coalition troops remain in Iraq, they are involved in daily fighting, they are not put under the direction of the Iraqi provisional government and the latter may not even ask them directly for their withdrawal from Iraq. All Resolution 1546 foresees is that the 'mandate for the multinational force shall be reviewed at the request of the Government of Iraq'.[134] When evaluating whether the Interim Government was, in terms of Article 47 of Convention IV, a change introduced by the occupying power, one has to admit that it was not directly chosen by the occupying powers, but under the supervision of a UN representative. On the other hand, the US had an important word to say on its

[130] This appears to be the ICRC position, which requalified the conflict in Afghanistan into a non-international armed conflict once the Karzai government was elected by the Loya Jirga (see Roberts, 'The Laws of War in the War on Terror', 32 *Israel Yearbook of Human Rights* (2002) 193).

[131] See, however, the precedent of Northern Cyprus. The European Court of Human Rights considers it to be occupied by Turkey and attributes the conduct of local authorities, though freely elected, to Turkey in *Loizidou v Turkey, Merits*, ECHR (1996), Series VI, 2216 at 2235–2236, para. 56, and *Cyprus v Turkey*, 10 May 2001, at paras. 69–77, available at http://hudoc.echr.coe.int.

[132] See Arts. 1, 25, and 27 of the International Covenant on Civil and Political Rights, 19 Dec. 1966, 999 UNTS 171 (entered into force 23 Mar. 1976).

[133] SC Res. 1546, *supra* note 3, at para. 2.

[134] *Ibid.*, at para. 12.

684 EJIL 16 (2005), 661–694

composition, the new Prime Minister has a long record of US connections,[135] before the elections held in January 2005 the Government could not yet possibly be considered as democratically legitimated, and, finally, it is very doubtful whether it has greater control over the reality in Iraq than the US and its coalition partners have.

Resolution 1546 must rather be seen as a decision overriding the rules of IHL on the subject. As seen above, such a decision is valid under Article 103 of the UN Charter. It is nevertheless regrettable and a dangerous precedent to make thus the (end of) the application of IHL dependent on criteria which are at best related to the desired legitimacy of the new government and at worst to the needs of a US administration in an election year, as both considerations blur the fundamental separation between *jus ad bellum* (the rules on the legitimacy of the use of force) and *jus in bello* (the rules on how force may be used, which comprise IHL).[136]

C *IHL Rules Applicable after the Official End of Occupation in Iraq*

One could object to the aforementioned line of argument that in an Annex to Resolution 1546, US Secretary of State Colin Powell promises in writing that coalition forces 'are and will remain committed at all times to act[ing] consistently with their obligations under the law of armed conflict, including the Geneva Conventions'.[137] This astonishing promise is difficult to interpret.

First it could mean that while the occupation ends from the point of view of *jus ad bellum* (and for the consumption of the US and Iraqi public opinion), the *jus in bello* of military occupation continues to apply, as the applicability of the *jus in bello* depends on the factual situation.[138] Those espousing this interpretation stress that the occupying powers otherwise would have had to release or transfer to the Iraqi authorities all civilian prisoners on 30 June 2004, which they did not do, and would lack a legal basis for administratively detaining persons newly arrested.[139] The second possible

135 Roberts, *supra* note 36, at 8.

136 See Protocol I, *supra* note 13, at preambular para. 5; the US Military Tribunal at Nuremberg in the case of *Wilhelm List et al.*, 8 July 1947–19 Feb. 1948, Law Reports of Trials of War Criminals, viii (The United Nations War Crimes Commission), at 34–76 (see for this and other references M. Sassòli and A. Bouvier, *How Does Law Protect in War?* (1999), at 83–87, 665, 681, 682); Greenwood, 'The Relationship Between *jus ad bellum* and *jus in bello*', 9 *Review of Int'l Studies* (1983) 221; Bugnion, 'Guerre juste, guerre d'agression et droit international humanitaire', 847 *Int'l Review of the Red Cross* (2002) 523; H. Meyrowitz, *Le principe de l'égalité des belligérants devant le droit de la guerre* (1970).

137 Letter of 5 June 2004 by Secretary of State Colin Powell to the President of the Security Council, annexed to SC Res. 1546 (2004).

138 This position is forcefully supported by Roberts, *supra* note 36, at 14–16. Amnesty International, 'Iraq, Human Rights Protection and Promotion Vital in the Transitional Period', (2004) (MDE 14/030/2004), available at http://web.amnesty.org/library/Index/ENGMDE140302004?open&of=ENG-IRQ, at 2, writes that IHL of military occupation continues to apply if the multinational forces continue to exercise effective control over Iraq.

139 Amnesty, *supra* note 138. Art. 77 of Convention IV reads: '[p]rotected persons who have been accused of offences or convicted by the courts in occupied territory, shall be handed over at the close of occupation, with the relevant records, to the authorities of the liberated territory'. In his letter (*cf. supra* note 137), Secretary of State Powell announces that the multinational forces will have recourse to 'internment where this is necessary for imperative reasons of security'. As occupying powers, they would have a legal basis for such internment in Art. 78 of Convention IV, *supra* note 12.

interpretation is that while the situation in Iraq is no longer governed overall by IHL of military occupation (and in particular the interplay of Article 47 of Convention IV and Article 43 of the Hague Regulations as discussed in this section no longer applies to conduct of the Iraqi Interim Government), the Coalition forces themselves will apply it to their conduct. This would be in line with the ICRC Commentary[140] and an ICTY decision[141] arguing that the concept of occupation under Convention IV is broader than the same concept as defined in Article 42 of the Hague Regulations, which reads: 'Territory is considered occupied when it is actually placed under the authority of the hostile army. The occupation applies only to the territory where such authority is established, and in a position to assert itself.' Convention IV would apply as soon as individuals fall into the hands of the occupying power. Such a theory, however, begs the crucial question when the state into whose power those individuals fall may be classified as the 'occupying power.'[142] Furthermore, the dividing line between the broader and the narrower concept cannot in my view correspond to the distinction between the Hague Regulations and Convention IV. Some of the provisions of the latter too, such as Article 50 on education and Article 64 on criminal legislation presuppose actual control.

The third possible meaning of the promise made by the Secretary of State is that it constitutes a reminder of Article 6(4) of Convention IV, which states, after enumerating in paragraphs 1–3 when the Convention ceases to apply, that 'Protected persons whose release, repatriation or re-establishment may take place after such dates shall meanwhile continue to benefit by the present Convention'. The many persons the US-led coalition continues to hold after 1 July 2004 remain protected by IHL of belligerent occupation. Reportedly, some Coalition officials argue that those detainees were constructively released, although they are still held by Coalition forces, because the latter detain them now under the authority of the Iraqi Government. In my opinion, this is an absurd claim, because IHL applies according to the facts and protection needs and not according to brilliant legal constructions.[143]

Even correctly interpreted, Article 6(4) of Convention IV does not cover persons arrested by Coalition forces after 1 July 2004.[144] Such persons would only be covered by Article 3 common to the Geneva Conventions. More generally, the US and UK forces would become simple allies of the Iraqi Interim Government in a non-international

[140] Pictet, *supra* note 44, at 60.

[141] *Prosecutor v Naletilić and Martinović*, Case No. IT-98–34-T, Judgment, paras. 218ff (ICTY Trial Chamber, 31 Mar. 2003).

[142] *Ibid.*, at para. 221.

[143] See US Military Tribunal at Nuremberg, *US v Alfried Krupp*, The United Nations War Crimes Commission, Law Reports of Trials of War Criminals, x, 1949, 130, partly reproduced in Sassòli and Bouvier, *supra* note 136, at 668, and *Prosecutor v. Tadic*, *supra* note 129, at para. 166.

[144] Interestingly enough, IHL of international armed conflicts contains no provision similar to Art. 2(2) of Protocol [No. II] Additional to the Geneva Conventions of 12 Aug. 1949, and relating to the Protection of Victims of Non-International Armed Conflicts, 8 June 1977, 1125 UNTS 609, which applies to non-international armed conflicts, and reads: 'those deprived of their liberty ... after the conflict for the same reasons [i.e. reasons related to the conflict] shall enjoy the protection [of the provisions relating to persons whose liberty has been restricted and penal prosecutions] until the end of such deprivation ... of liberty'.

686 EJIL 16 (2005), 661–694

armed conflict, bound by Article 3 common to the Conventions.[145] The fourth possibility is therefore that Secretary Powell is simply referring to that common article.

The fifth and final possibility, which would address the concern just mentioned, is that the Coalition forces will no longer apply IHL of military occupation, but other rules of IHL on the conduct of hostilities and detention as soon as they are involved in combat, arrests or detention. The problem with this suggestion is that Convention IV contains no section on arrest and detention other than provisions applicable on a party's own territory[146] and provisions applicable in occupied territory.[147] If Iraq is not an occupied territory, under the mere wording of Convention IV, there are no rules of IHL of international armed conflicts on how US forces have to treat persons in their power, as the US will certainly not consider that it acts on its own territory and because the rules on the treatment of protected persons on a party's own territory are in any case completely inadequate for the situation in Iraq.

This may be one of the few fields in which Convention IV needs an update: the protection of civilians who are in the power of a belligerent, but are neither on a territory occupied by that belligerent nor on that belligerent's own territory. The reality elsewhere, e.g. in Afghanistan and in peace operations, contradicts the assumption of Convention IV that every civilian affected by an international armed conflict is perforce either on the territory of the belligerent in whose power he or she is or on an occupied territory. This assumption could only be maintained by adopting and pushing further, for the purposes of Convention IV, the functional and flexible concept of occupation mentioned above in connection with the second possible meaning of the letter by the Secretary of State.[148] Everyone who is in the hands of a belligerent that acts in an international armed conflict outside its own national territory could be considered to be perforce on a piece of earth 'occupied' by that belligerent. Such a concept would, however, probably be opposed by states not wishing to be labelled as occupying powers where they have no effective overall control of a territory.

7 Application of Article 43 to Peace Operations

The concept of 'peace operations' increasingly covers operations with peace enforcement elements.[149] It is used for both UN-run and UN-authorized operations.[150]

[145] This is envisaged by Amnesty, *supra* note 138, at 2, if the occupation has in fact ended.

[146] See Sections II, I, and IV of Part II of Convention IV, *supra* note 12.

[147] See *ibid.*, Sections III, I, and IV.

[148] See *supra* notes 140–142.

[149] T. Findlay, *The Use of Force in UN Peace Operations* (2002), at 375, indicates that there is a growing consensus that some type of peace enforcement in UN peace operations is possible and desirable. This concept remains controversial, however. While not dealing explicitly with the term 'peace enforcement', the *Report of the Panel on United Nations Peace Operations* supports a robust mandate. See *Brahimi Report*, 21 Aug., 2000 (A/55/305, S/2000/809), at para. 49.

[150] A. Roberts and R. Guelff (eds.), *Documents on the Laws of War* (3rd ed., 2002), at 26, indicate that the term applies to UN run and UN authorized peace operations. It refers to 'peacekeeping operations, whether conducted under UN *or other* auspices . . . ' (emphasis added). The *Brahimi Report* considers the 'NATO-led operations' in Kosovo which facilitate the functioning of UNMIK in the context of peace operations (*supra* note 149, at para. 104).

Indeed, no clear-cut definition of 'peace operations' exists. As the term is not only used for UN-run operations, i.e. not only those established by the UN and placed under its command and control, one might fear that its use depends more on the (claim of) legitimacy and international support for the operation, than on objective criteria.

A *Controversies whether IHL Applies to UN-run Operations*

Traditionally, peace operations are run by international organizations. The latter, and in particular the United Nations, are not party to the treaties which set out IHL. As for customary IHL, the denial by the UN that it is *de jure* subject to IHL raises some doubts as to whether the IHL rules that are customary between states are also customary in armed conflicts involving international organizations. The UN has repeatedly recognized that it is bound by the 'principles and spirit' of IHL. This ostensibly vague commitment does not necessarily imply a lack of will to respect IHL, but may be due to the fact that some provisions of IHL cannot be applied to the UN since it lacks, for instance, a territory, a penal system, or a population.[151] Certainly, in practice, all peace operations are carried out by national contingents that are bound by IHL by virtue of the engagement of their sending states. Is that sufficient to make IHL applicable, even if the organization has command and control? Sending states have at least the general international law obligation not to contribute, through their contingents, to violations of IHL and in particular the obligation 'to ensure respect for' IHL under Article 1 common to the Geneva Conventions.[152]

As for the applicability of IHL of military occupation to peace forces, some object to the very possibility that at least UN peace forces could be subject to the obligations of an occupying power. It is significant in this respect that the 'UN Secretary-General's Bulletin on Observance by United Nations Forces of IHL', which refers to many rules of IHL to be respected by UN forces when engaged as combatants in armed conflicts, does not mention one single rule of IHL of belligerent occupation.[153] Opponents to the applicability of IHL argue that the rights and obligations accruing to occupying powers under IHL flow from the conflict inherent in the relationship between traditional occupying powers and occupied territories and are therefore not relevant to the altruistic nature of a peace operation which is deployed in conformity with the general interest.[154] They argue, as a protective force, peacekeepers are accepted – if not

[151] David, *supra* note 78, at 203–204.

[152] See on the whole debate whether IHL applies to UN operations Greenwood, 'International Humanitarian Law and United Nations Military Operations', 1 *Yb Int'l Humanitarian L* (1998) 3; C. Emanuelli, *Les actions militaires de l'ONU et le droit international humanitaire* (1995); C. Emanuelli (ed.), *Les casques bleus: policiers ou combattants?* (1997); D. Shraga, 'The United Nations as an Actor Bound by International Humanitarian Law', in L. Condorelli, A.-M. La Rosa, and S. Scherrer (eds.), *Les Nations Unies et le droit international humanitaire, Actes du Colloque international à l'occasion du cinquantième anniversaire des Nations Unies, Genève, 19, 20 et 21 octobre 1995* (1996), at 317.

[153] UN Doc. ST/SGB/1999/13 of 6 Aug. 1999, also reproduced in Sassòli and Bouvier, *supra* note 136, at 460.

[154] Shraga, *supra* note 152, at 328; Vité, *supra* note 77, at 19.

688 EJIL 16 (2005), 661–694

welcomed – by the local population, and thus do not require the strictures of IHL. This rather rosy view of relationships between peacekeepers and local populations is not always borne out by experience. Moreover, if the local population accepts the peacekeepers, this will only facilitate compliance with the obligations of IHL. The level of altruism or good intentions may be difficult to measure and will change according to one's perspective; thus, altruism is not a sound basis for determining whether IHL applies to a given conflict. If we adopt it, why should operations carried out by individual states or regional organizations claiming that their motives are purely altruistic be subject to IHL? In my view, to oppose the applicability of IHL of military occupation to UN peace operations based on the alleged nature of the operation disregards reality and introduces a *jus ad bellum* argument into the discussion of whether *jus in bello* applies.[155] Another line of argument simply holds that IHL of belligerent occupation cannot apply to transitional international civil administrations because such administrations proceed, under their Security Council mandate and subsequent practice, to make changes in local legislation and institutions which would not be admissible under IHL of military occupation.[156] This argument, however, begs the question.

In my view, when the UN or a regional organization enjoys 'the effective control of power . . . over a territory . . ., *without the volition of the sovereign of that territory*,' it is an occupying force.[157]

What is even more doubtful is whether the law of military occupation applies to UN-run peace(keeping) forces, meeting no armed resistance, if the latter or a UN civil administration effectively run the territory. Common Article 2(2) of the Geneva Conventions, which provides that those Conventions 'shall also apply to all cases of partial or total occupation of the territory of a High Contracting Party, even if the said occupation meets with no armed resistance', suggests an affirmative answer. Australia considered that IHL of military occupation applied *de jure* to its UN operation in Somalia, which did not meet armed resistance by the territorial sovereign.[158] Most would, however, object that Article 2(2) is an exception clause applying IHL beyond armed conflicts, which must be limited to situations where the foreign military presence is that of another state and not that of the international community organized through the UN. In any case, IHL of military occupation would only apply if the international territorial administration is run or *de facto* controlled by military forces.

155 *Ibid.*, at 27, replies that the Security Council does not derogate from IHL but creates a situation to which IHL on its own terms does not apply.

156 *Ibid.*, at 24.

157 See Benvenisti, *supra* note 6, at 3 (emphasis added); Hoffman, 'Peace-enforcement Actions and Humanitarian Law: Emerging Rules for "Interventional Armed Conflict" ', 837 *Int'l Rev Red Cross* (2000) 193, at 203 and 204; Levrat, 'Le droit international humanitaire au Timor oriental: entre théorie et pratique', 841 *Int'l Rev Red Cross* (2001) 77, at 95–96; Cerone, 'Minding the Gap: Outlining KFOR Accountability in Post-Conflict Kosovo', 12 *EJIL* (2001) 469, at 483–485. Roberts, *supra* note 62, at 291 (citing D. Bowett, *United Nations Forces: a Legal Study of United Nations Practice* (1964)) writes that most or all customary or conventional laws of war would apply.

158 M. J. Kelly, *Restoring and Maintaining Order in Complex Peace Operations* (1999), at 178.

Article 2(2) of Convention IV extending the applicability of IHL of military occupation to cases meeting no armed resistance does not cover every international *de facto* presence not meeting the consent of the sovereign, but only belligerent, i.e. military presences not meeting armed resistance, the difference being that a military occupier could have overcome armed resistance if it had existed, while a civilian presence could not have done so.

B *Applicability of IHL to UN-authorized Operations*

Beyond the aforementioned controversy whether IHL (including its rules on belligerent occupation) applies to UN-run operations, the fundamental separation between *jus ad bellum* and *jus in bello*[159] entails that IHL, including Article 43, certainly applies to any other case of belligerent occupation, whether the occupying power acts upon UN authorization, in self-defence, or in violation of *jus ad bellum*. The distinction between *jus ad bellum* and *jus in bello* dictates that the fact that the UN Security Council authorized military intervention has no impact on the applicability of IHL, as part of *jus in bello*, to the resulting occupation. In my view this must necessarily also be the case if an international administration results from a UN authorized peace-enforcement operation.[160] The same must *a fortiori* be true if the conflict itself was not authorized, but the resulting occupation is explicitly authorized by the UN Security Council or if the latter does so implicitly by mandating the occupying power with certain peace-building tasks (as was arguably the case in Iraq).[161]

In my view, the question turns – as for the qualification of any other foreign military presence – on the issue of whether the sovereign of the territory on which peace operations (whether civil or military) are deployed consents to that deployment or not. It is widely accepted that IHL does not apply to peacekeeping forces if and for as long as the sovereign/host government has consented to the deployment of troops on its territory.[162] Consent excludes the possibility of the occupation being described as 'belligerent'. If the consent vanishes, according to some authors, IHL could subsequently become applicable.[163] I have some doubts, however, whether the simple disappearance of the legal basis for a foreign military presence makes the law of armed conflicts applicable.

According to this view, IHL is not applicable to the international territorial administrations in place in Kosovo and East Timor for the simple reason that the states concerned consented to the presence of foreign troops and administrators on the relevant territories.[164] Conversely, an international administration put in place without the

[159] See *supra* note 136.

[160] Apparently *contra* are Kolb *et al.*, *supra* note 77, at 112.

[161] Vité, *supra* note 77, at 20–21, considers that IHL does not apply if an occupation has been authorized by the Security Council as part of a peace operation.

[162] Roberts, *supra* note 62, at 291.

[163] *Ibid.*; Vité, *supra* note 77, at 21.

[164] Kelly, McCormack, Muggleton and Oswald, 'Legal Aspects of Australia's Involvement in the International Force for East Timor', 841 *Int'l Rev Red Cross* (2001) 101, at 115; Sassòli, 'Droit international pénal et droit pénal interne: le cas des territoires se trouvant sous administration internationale', in M. Henzelin and R. Roth, *Le Droit Pénal à l'épreuve de l'internationalisation* (2002), at 144.

690 *EJIL* 16 (2005), 661–694

consent of the sovereign or host government would trigger the application of IHL to that administration. Some protest that sovereigns of some territories occupied by UN forces in a peace operation may not consent to the operation (whereas others would), which means that we would treat differently situations which demand on their facts to be treated identically, notably from the point of view of protection of civilians.[165] However, in the Westphalian system, the consent of a state is a factor which carries significant legal consequences.

For the occupation of Iraq, Security Council Resolution 1483 (2003) acknowledged the status of the Coalition as occupiers and reminded them of their obligations under IHL. Some considered that this same resolution authorized the occupation of Iraq by the Coalition forces.[166] Indeed, it transferred some peace-building tasks, such as the creation of conditions 'in which the Iraqi people can freely determine their own political future' to the occupying powers, or at least accepted that the occupying powers perform such tasks. Even if this authorized the US-led Coalition (called 'Authority') to exercise the functions of government of Iraq, this would not have made IHL of military occupation inapplicable. The US and the UK indeed never so claimed.

C *Particularities in Applying Article 43 to Peace Operations Subject to IHL*

Several issues arise as to the application of IHL when the UN is involved in a peace operation to which IHL applies. Particularly, as alluded to in the discussion on exceptions to the prohibition to legislate, the Security Council mandate may entail significant derogations from the general principle that local legislation should be left in force, if it considers changes going beyond those permitted by Article 43 indispensable for peace-building purposes. Such authorization must, however, be explicit in the Security Council resolution. A peace operation occupier should interpret the mandate in a manner compatible with IHL whenever possible.[167] Some authors consider that IHL only applies 'unless and until the Security Council use[s] its Chapter VII powers to impose a different regime'.[168] They can base their argument upon Article 103 of the UN Charter.[169] Formally, one could not object to a Security Council resolution even ending an occupation altogether, not by changing the facts on the ground, but by requalifying a belligerent occupation as international transitional administration[170] and deciding that IHL does not apply to that administration. A conclusion such as this, which is contrary to the very core idea that the applicability of IHL depends on the facts and not on legal qualifications, should only be drawn if such intent is made very explicit by the Security Council.

165 Vité, *supra* note 77, at 23.

166 See, for e.g., Stahn, 'Enforcement of the Collective Will After Iraq', 97 *AJIL* (2003) 804, at 822. See also Grant, 'The Security Council and Iraq: An Incremental Practice', 97 *AJIL* (2003) 823, at 825. For a contrary view, see Falk, 'What Future for the UN Charter System of War Intervention?', 97 *AJIL* (2003) 590, at 596.

167 See *supra*, at 5. I.

168 Greenwood, *supra* note 152, at 28.

169 See *supra* note 121, and accompanying text.

170 Vité, *supra* note 77, at 27.

D *Utility of Applying IHL by Analogy to an International Territorial Administration in Peace Operations even if IHL is not Applicable*

Even if IHL is not formally applicable to international civil administrations by virtue of the consent by the sovereign or host government concerned to the mission or for other reasons outlined above, IHL of military occupation provides practical solutions to many problems confronted by a civil or military administration.[171] It offers a normative framework adequate for the maintenance of civil life and public order which has, first, the advantage of being accepted by all states independently of the legitimacy of the international presence on a territory. Second, that framework is pre-existing, which facilitates its immediate application when an international administration starts and avoids '*à la carte*' solutions adopted by the international presence, which are arbitrary (because they are not ruled by a normative framework) or at least perceived as arbitrary. Third, that framework also applies independently of the legitimacy of the presence of the former sovereign and of the feelings of the local population.[172] Fourth, all armed forces and their military lawyers are familiar with the framework since they must comply with it in case of armed conflict. Accordingly, some authors would prefer that the Security Council explicitly determine, when setting up an international civil administration, that IHL of belligerent occupation applies subsidiarily as long as new legislation is not adopted by the administration.[173]

Many principles of IHL of belligerent occupation, such as the right of the local population to continue life as normally as possible[174] and the right for the international presence to protect their security, seem appropriate, as does the obligation to restore and maintain public order and civil life in the territory. As seen above, IHL offers answers to some of the main legal questions for administrators of territory under civil transitional administration who have the responsibility of restoring public order and civil life: On what legal basis may they arrest, detain and punish persons threatening public order? When may they change local legislation? IHL grants to the occupying power the right to have recourse to administrative detention.

IHL also provides a helpful separation with respect to penal law between fields covered by new legislation and applied by a new (at least provisionally international) justice system and those which are governed by local legislation enforced by the local justice system. Under IHL, foreign personnel apply the legislation they create and do not interfere with the handling of individual cases by the local justice system. In a

[171] Sassòli, *supra* note 164, at 141–149; Vité, *supra* note 77, at 29–33; Kelly *et al.*, *supra* note 164, at 115; David, *supra* note 78, at 501; UN Department of Peace-Keeping Operations, Lessons-Learned Unit, *Comprehensive Report on Lessons-Learned from the United Nations Operation in Somalia*, Apr. 1992–Mar. 1995 (Sweden, 1995), at para 57, available at http://www.un.org/Depts/dpko/lessons/UNOSOM.pdf.

[172] Sassòli, *supra* note 164, at 145. Kelly, *supra* note 158, at 311, and Vité, *supra* note 77, at 29–30, support this line of argument.

[173] Vité, *supra* note 77, at 30. In my view this is not very realistic and as far as Art. 43 of the Hague Regulations is concerned it means that the latter would not apply, as it precisely restricts a foreign administration from legislating.

[174] This is what J. Pictet, *The Principles of International Humanitarian Law* (1967), at 50, calls the principle of normality.

territory under international administration, we can distinguish between criminal cases which go to the heart of the objectives of the international presence and those which relate to local law. The first could be decided by the international administration's own tribunals, which would apply the law and procedure that have been established by the administration. All other affairs would be left to the competence of local justice institutions, even if personnel must first be trained.

While awaiting the development of competent local institutions, persons suspected of serious crimes against local law could be held under administrative detention. This would be justified by imperative reasons of security, because security would be threatened by a failure to respond to such acts as well as the acts of vengeance which flow from that failure. From a humanitarian perspective, provisional administrative detention is sometimes preferable to condemnation or acquittal by a biased tribunal in an irregular procedure.[175] This solution would also avoid situations like in Kosovo where foreign judges study, interpret and apply law that they do not know, and where international administrators modify laws for simple reasons of convenience.[176] Given the ideals of judicial independence and the rule of law which must be transmitted to the local population, it is preferable that there be a separation between the areas of competence of the international administration and those of the local administration-in-training. Through the administration period, more and more areas can be successively given back to the local justice system.[177]

There are some limits to the analogy, however. With respect to international civil administrations, derogations from the principle that local legislation may not be altered may be explicitly mandated by the Security Council, and/or more easily be assumed to be implicit in the Security Council mandate. Indeed, where IHL applies *de jure*, the argument was that the Security Council could not easily be considered to want to deviate from the applicable legal regime. Here, the latter is not applicable, but simply provides solutions for problems not governed by any applicable pre-existing legal regime. In addition, there may be a significant difference between situations for which IHL relating to military occupation was created and territories under international administration. In the first situation, protection of the local population consists in particular of a guarantee of the greatest possible continuity from the situation prior to occupation. An international civil administration, on the other hand, is often instituted to change the prior situation. This distinction does not seem to be taken into account in the rules of IHL. However, the population of a territory placed under administration no longer needs to be protected from the previous competent authorities, but against the new authorities. Independence, autonomy, or the introduction of social, legal or economic changes cannot be achieved during the transitional period. During this period, it would not be shocking to apply, as a matter of principle and subject to the many exceptions mentioned above, prior laws not incompatible with the objectives of the transitional administration.

[175] Sassòli, *supra* note 164, at 146.
[176] *Ibid.*, at 128, 146–147.
[177] *Ibid.*, at 147.

Some authors suggest that only the humanitarian rules of IHL apply to international civil administrations, not those fixing the attributes of the occupying power.[178] In my view, protection of war victims and rights of the occupying power are two sides of the same coin. All rules of IHL are humanitarian. Israel has tried to argue that the same distinction exists between humanitarian and other rules of IHL with which it has to comply in the Occupied Palestinian Territories.[179] This distinction was not accepted by other states and has resulted in abuses.

The main disadvantages of the application of IHL by analogy as suggested here are that it depends on the good will of the international administration and that different contingents may have a divergent practice in this respect.[180] In the absence of such analogy, however, the practice will by definition be even less coherent and predictable.

Finally, UN soft law human rights standards,[181] such as the Code of Conduct for Law Enforcement Officials[182] and the Basic Principles on the Use of Force and Firearms by Law Enforcement Officials[183] may also be given greater scope in the context of an international civil administration. While soft law as such is not binding upon states, a UN-run operation, whether *de jure* subject to Article 43 or not, may be considered to be legally bound since that soft law has been adopted by the UN General Assembly, the supreme organ of the UN.[184]

8 Conclusion

Practice, including in Iraq, has shown that occupying powers and international civil administrations, which do not comply with the regime outlined in this article and are either less active in restoring and maintaining public order and civil life or go further in terms of legislation, encounter serious problems among the population concerned or the international community. Our analysis proves that in this field as in others the existing rules of IHL are flexible enough to provide realistic solutions to problems appearing in contemporary conflicts. Such flexibility, unfortunately, stems in part from the possibility that the UN Security Council has to derogate in a given case from the normally applicable rules of IHL, a possibility which is not satisfactory from a humanitarian point of view and which also raises concerns from the point of view of the rule of international law because of the selective and short-term political

[178] Vité, *supra* note 77, at 27–28 and 32.

[179] See on this distinction made by Israel concerning the territories it occupies, Roberts, *supra* note 27, at 62; *Legal Consequences of the Construction of a Wall*, *supra* note 6, at para. 93, and references in Sassòli and Bouvier, *supra* note 136, at 802–872.

[180] Vité, *supra* note 77, at 32.

[181] For an overview of the UN standards as applicable to the maintenance of law and order by UN peace operations see United Nations Crime Prevention and Criminal Justice Branch, *UN Criminal Justice Standards for Peace-Keeping Police (The Blue Book)* (Vienna: Office of Crime Control and Drug Prevention, 1994), available at http://www.uncjin.org/Documents/BlueBook/BlueBook/index.html.

[182] G.A. Res. 34/169, annex, 34 UN GAOR Supp. No. 46 at 186, UN Doc. A/34/46.

[183] *Supra* note 20.

[184] *Cf.* Kolb *et al.*, *supra* note 77, at 166; Art. 10 of the UN Charter.

approach of the Council. These concerns are obviously even more acute when the Council is dominated, as is the case concerning Iraq, by the actual occupying powers.

In any case, as it is not the sovereign and in order to respect the right to self-determination of peoples, an occupying power may, while exercising the discretion that human rights instruments (or the Security Council mandate) leave to states setting up (their) institutions and economic and social policies, introduce only as many changes as absolutely necessary under human rights obligations (or the Security Council mandate) and must stay as close as possible to similar local standards and the local cultural, legal and economic traditions. To paraphrase the ICRC Commentary, occupying authorities may not change local legislation 'merely to make it accord with their own [constitutional, economic or social] conceptions'.[185] If Cuba occupied Switzerland it may not introduce a communist economy, and if Switzerland occupied France it may not introduce federalism, although both countries are certainly convinced that their system is best for the maintenance of civil life. In this respect, the economic changes made by the US and the UK in Iraq certainly went beyond a sustainable interpretation of IHL liable to be applied in other cases to other occupying powers. Furthermore, it is my view that even a UN administration should not introduce such fundamental changes, but at the outmost suggest them to the population of the territory it administers as a solution to their problems.

[185] Pictet, *supra* note 44, at 336.

[13]

GOVERNMENT IN COMMISSION

By R. Y. JENNINGS

Fellow of Jesus College, Cambridge

THIS article is an attempt to assess the juridical basis of the occupation and government of Germany by the four Allied Powers—the United Kingdom, the United States, the Union of Socialist Soviet Republics, and France—and to consider the effects of that occupation on the status of Germany in international law. While the régime established by the occupation is in its nature provisional and liable to continual changes, it has nevertheless given rise to problems which are of general interest for international law and which merit examination. However, before turning to the law it will be convenient briefly to describe the facts of the occupation and to examine the provisions of the main documents involved.

I. *The establishment of the machinery of occupation and control*

By the beginning of May 1945 it was apparent that the German forces were incapable of offering further resistance to the Allied offensive. On Monday, 7 May, an unconditional surrender of the German armed forces was signed at Rheims by General Jodl, and on the following day von Krosigk, the Foreign Minister of Admiral Dönitz's government, broadcast the news of the surrender to the German people. On 9 May a document similar to the one signed by General Jodl was signed at Berlin by Field-Marshal Keitel, Admiral Flensburg, and Air Colonel General Stumpf, in the presence of Air Chief Marshal Tedder, General Spaatz, Marshal Zhukov, and General de Lattre de Tassigny. This document, called the Final Act of Unconditional Surrender, states *inter alia* that the signatories are 'acting by authority of the German High Command' and that 'this act of military surrender is without prejudice to, and will be superseded by, any general instrument of surrender imposed by or on behalf of the United Nations and applicable to Germany and the German armed forces as a whole'.[1] It contains no reference to Admiral Dönitz's government. This

[1] See *The Times* newspaper, 11 May 1945. The full text of the *Final Act of Unconditional Surrender* is as follows:

'1. We the undersigned, acting by authority of the German High Command, hereby surrender unconditionally to the Supreme Commander, Allied Expeditionary Force, and simultaneously to the Supreme High Command of the Red Army, all forces on land, at sea, and in the air who are at this date under German control.

'2. The German High Command will at once issue orders to all German military, naval, and air authorities and to all forces under German control to cease active operations at 23.01 hours, Central European Time, on May 8, 1945, to remain in the positions occupied at that time and to disarm completely, handing over their weapons and equipment to the local allied commanders or officers designated by representatives of the Allied Supreme Commands. No ship, vessel, or aircraft is to be scuttled, or any damage done to their hulls, machinery, or equipment, nor to

government was never recognized in any way by the Allies; indeed, on 24 May it was announced from the Headquarters of 21st Army Group that all the members of this self-styled acting government, as well as members of the German High Command, had been taken into custody as prisoners of war.[1]

Already in February 1945, at the Crimea Conference, Mr. Winston Churchill, President Roosevelt, and Marshal Stalin had agreed on 'common policies and plans for enforcing the unconditional surrender terms which we shall impose together on Nazi Germany after German armed resistance has been finally crushed'.[2] The unconditional surrender of Germany now having been accomplished, the agreed plans were put into operation by the Berlin Declaration of 5 June, and three Statements of the same date dealing respectively with the zones of occupation in Germany, the control machinery in Germany, and consultation with governments of other United Nations.[3]

The Berlin Declaration, signed by Field-Marshal Montgomery, General Eisenhower, Marshal Zhukov, and General de Lattre de Tassigny, consists of a statement of the principles governing the Allied assumption of authority in Germany, followed by fifteen Articles setting forth the immediate requirements with which Germany is to comply. The statement of principles must be cited in full:

DECLARATION REGARDING THE DEFEAT OF GERMANY AND THE ASSUMPTION OF SUPREME AUTHORITY WITH RESPECT TO GERMANY BY THE GOVERNMENTS OF THE UNITED KINGDOM, THE UNITED STATES OF AMERICA AND THE UNION OF SOVIET SOCIALIST REPUBLICS, AND THE PROVISIONAL GOVERNMENT OF THE FRENCH REPUBLIC

The German armed forces on land, at sea and in the air have been completely defeated and have surrendered unconditionally and Germany, which bears responsibility for the war, is no longer capable of resisting the will of the victorious Powers.

machines of all kinds, armament, apparatus, and all the technical means of prosecution of war in general.

'3. The German High Command will at once issue to the appropriate commanders, and ensure the carrying out of, any further orders issued by the Supreme Commander, Allied Expeditionary Force, and by the Supreme Commander of the Red Army.

'4. This act of military surrender is without prejudice to, and will be superseded by, any general instrument of surrender imposed by or on behalf of the United Nations and applicable to Germany and the German armed forces as a whole.

'5. In the event of the German High Command or any of the forces under their control failing to act in accordance with this act of surrender, the Supreme Commander, Allied Expeditionary Force, and the Supreme High Command of the Red Army, will take such punitive or other action as they deem appropriate.

'6. This act is drawn up in the English, Russian, and German languages. The English and Russian are the only authentic texts.'

[1] *The Times* newspaper, 24 May 1945.

[2] *The Times* newspaper, 13 February 1945.

[3] The Declaration and the three Statements are published by H.M. Stationery Office as Cmd. 6648.

The unconditional surrender of Germany has thereby been effected, and Germany has become subject to such requirements as may now or hereafter be imposed upon her.

There is no central Government or authority in Germany capable of accepting responsibility for the maintenance of order, the administration of the country and compliance with the requirements of the victorious Powers.

It is in these circumstances necessary, without prejudice to any subsequent decisions that may be taken respecting Germany, to make provision for the cessation of any further hostilities on the part of the German armed forces, for the maintenance of order in Germany and for the administration of the country, and to announce the immediate requirements with which Germany must comply.

The Representatives of the Supreme Commands of the United Kingdom, the United States of America, the Union of Soviet Socialist Republics and the French Republic, hereinafter called the 'Allied Representatives', acting by authority of their respective Governments and in the interests of the United Nations, accordingly make the following Declaration:

> The Governments of the United Kingdom, the United States of America and the Union of Soviet Socialist Republics, and the Provisional Government of the French Republic, hereby assume supreme authority with respect to Germany, including all the powers possessed by the German Government, the High Command and any state, municipal, or local government or authority. The assumption, for the purposes stated above, of the said authority and powers does not effect the annexation of Germany.
>
> The Governments of the United Kingdom, the United States of America and the Union of Soviet Socialist Republics, and the Provisional Government of the French Republic, will hereafter determine the boundaries of Germany or any part thereof and the status of Germany or of any area at present being part of German territory.

The actual machinery of government by which the supreme authority assumed in the Declaration is exercised is outlined in the three Statements. The decision to divide Germany into occupation zones had already been made known in the official announcement made after the Crimea Conference.[1] This decision is carried into effect in the first of the three Statements, by which Germany within her frontiers as they were on 31 December 1937 is 'for the purposes of occupation' divided into four zones: an eastern zone to the Union of Socialist Soviet Republics; a north-western zone to the United Kingdom; a south-western zone to the United States; and a western zone to France. The occupying forces in each zone are placed under a Commander-in-Chief designated by the responsible Power. The area of Greater Berlin, however, constitutes a special area occupied by forces

[1] See *The Times* newspaper, 13 February 1945. The official announcement states *inter alia*: 'Under the agreed plans the forces of the three Powers will each occupy a separate zone of Germany. Coordinated administration and control have been provided for under the plan through a Central Control Commission consisting of the Supreme Commanders of the three Powers with headquarters in Berlin.

'It has been agreed that France should be invited by the three Powers, if she should so desire, to take a zone of occupation, and to participate as fourth member of the Control Commission. The limits of the French zone will be agreed by the four Governments concerned through their representatives on the European Advisory Commission.'

of each of the four Powers and governed by an Inter-Allied Governing Authority (known also by its Russian name of *Kommandatura*) consisting of four Commandants appointed by their respective Commanders-in-Chief who are to 'direct jointly its administration' and who serve in rotation as Chief Commandant.

That the zones are fundamental to the whole Allied government and administration is shown by the Statement on Control Machinery in Germany, which establishes a Control Council for the government of Germany as a whole and formulates its relationship to the government of the zones in the following terms:

> 'In the period when Germany is carrying out the basic requirements of unconditional surrender, supreme authority in Germany will be exercised, on instructions from their Governments, by the British, United States, Soviet and French Commanders-in-Chief, each in his own zone of occupation, and also jointly in matters affecting Germany as a whole. The four Commanders-in-Chief will together constitute the Control Council. Each Commander-in-Chief will be assisted by a Political Adviser.[1]
>
> '2. The Control Council, whose decisions shall be unanimous, will ensure appropriate uniformity of action by the Commanders-in-Chief in their respective zones of occupation and will reach agreed decisions on the chief questions affecting Germany as a whole.'

Under the Control Council is a hierarchy of committees and departments which together provide a machinery of central government known collectively as the Control Authority. Immediately subordinate to the Control Council there is a permanent Co-ordinating Committee composed of the Deputies of the Commanders-in-Chief. Its function is to advise the Control Council and to administer the carrying out of the Control Council's decisions. In practice the Co-ordinating Committee tends to be the more important body, for it is here that the main work of hammering out a common policy takes place. Both the Control Council and the Co-ordinating Committee are served by an Allied Secretariat (A.S.E.C.). Subordinate to the Co-ordinating Committee are the Directorates, which correspond to the usual departments of a central government.[2] The outstanding feature of the whole organization of the Control Authority is the provision at all stages for the equal representation of the four Allied Powers and the requirement at all stages that decisions shall be unanimous. The require-

[1] This formula is repeated in slightly different language in the Potsdam Declaration of 2 August 1945: '1. In accordance with the agreement on control machinery in Germany, supreme authority in Germany is exercised, on instructions from their respective Governments, by the commanders-in-chief of the armed forces of the United States of America, the United Kingdom, the Union of Socialist Soviet Republics, and the French Republic, each in his own zone of occupation, and also jointly, in matters affecting Germany as a whole, in their capacity as members of the Control Council.'

[2] The Allied Statement on *Control Machinery in Germany* (Cmd. 6648) lays down the following divisions 'subject to adjustment in the light of experience': Military; Naval; Air; Transport; Political; Economic; Finance; Reparation; Deliveries and Restitution; Internal Affairs and Communications; Legal; Prisoners of War and Displaced Persons; Man-power.

ment of unanimity is not confined to the Control Council but operates at all levels of the Control Authority. Thus, before a draft measure can be adopted it must secure unanimous approval in Sub committee, Directorate, Co-ordinating Committee, and in the Control Council itself.

The relationship between the Allied Governments, the Control Council, and the Zone Commanders is not free from difficulty. It is nowhere precisely defined in the instruments; nevertheless, there are certain necessary implications which give some indication of the true position. By the Berlin Declaration, supreme authority over the whole of Germany is assumed by the four Allied Governments. This can only mean that the supreme authority over the whole of Germany was thereby vested in the four Governments jointly. There could be no question of each of those Governments having an original authority in its own zone, for the zones themselves were only subsequently established by an exercise of that joint authority. By the Allied Statement on *Control Machinery in Germany*, the *exercise* of this supreme authority was, as we have seen, devolved through two channels: first, the Zone Commanders, acting on instructions from their Governments, are to exercise supreme authority each in his own zone; secondly, the Control Council, by agreed decisions, is to exercise supreme authority in the chief questions affecting Germany as a whole. This machinery, it will be noticed, does not create a simple hierarchy of authority, with the Zone Commands subordinated to the Control Council and the Control Council in turn subordinated to the Allied Governments. It creates two distinct areas of authority: first, the authority exercised by each Zone Commander in his own zone, and secondly, an overriding authority in the Control Council in matters, affecting Germany as a whole, on which the Control Council is able to reach an agreed decision. But whether exercising authority in their own zones, or through the Control Council for Germany as a whole, the Commanders-in-Chief are the instrumentalities not of their own Governments, but of the four Allied Governments jointly. The undivided supreme authority continues to reside in the four Governments jointly, as provided in the Berlin Declaration; it is merely the *exercise* of that authority that is devolved on a zonal basis by the Statement on Control Machinery. Thus, the jurisdiction of the Control Council in Germany as a whole, is not produced by a coalescence of four separate authorities but is delegated to it directly by the four Governments acting together. However, the strictly consensual basis of the Control Council's procedure tends to make it in practice little more than a machinery for the auto-limitation of the Zone Commanders' authority; for the unanimity rule, coupled with the fact that the Control Council is composed of the Zone Commanders themselves, means in effect that the Control Council is powerless to legislate when the Commander-in-Chief of any particular zone refuses to agree. The Commanders-in-Chief, whether acting as Zone Commanders or as members of the Control Council, act on instructions from their respective Governments. Consequently, the extent to which the Control Council is able to provide an effective central organ of government for Germany as a whole depends directly on the extent to which the four Allied Governments can agree among themselves on a common policy to be followed in the exercise of the supreme authority which they have jointly assumed. An attempt to formulate the broad lines of such a common policy was made in the Potsdam Declaration of 2 August 1945.[1] The interpretation of parts of this Declaration has notoriously been a matter of acute controversy. Nevertheless, it does provide the essential basis for the successful working of the control machinery. The Control Council legislation already promulgated shows that substantial co-operation has been found possible in practice, and uniform legislation has been achieved on a number of important topics.[2]

The first formal meeting of the Control Council was held under the chairmanship of General Eisenhower on 30 July 1945. At the conclusion of this meeting an official communiqué was issued stating that future sessions of the Council would be held regularly on the 10th, 20th, and 30th of each month, and at any other time at the request of any member of the Council. After its fourth meeting on 30 August a Proclamation was issued and broadcast to the German people; it announced that in virtue of the supreme authority and powers assumed by the four Allied Governments in their Declaration of 5 June, the Control Council had now been established and that supreme authority in matters affecting Germany as a whole had been conferred upon the Control Council, but all military laws, orders, and decrees issued by the Commanders-in-Chief for the adminstration of their respective zones would continue in force in those zones.[3] This Proclamation of course in no way altered the law or machinery of government; it is

[1] See *The Times* newspaper, 3 August 1945.

[2] Control Council legislation is published in the *Official Gazette of the Control Council for Germany* (hereafter called *Official Gazette*) published by the Allied Secretariat in Berlin. It may also be consulted in the *Military Government Gazette, Germany, British Zone of Control*, published by H.M. Stationery Office.

By Control Council Directive no. 10, dated 22 September 1945, it was decided that all legislative action by the Control Council should be in one of the following forms:

'(*a*) *Proclamations*: to be issued to announce matters or acts of especial importance to the occupying powers or to the German people, or to both.

'(*b*) *Laws*: to be enacted on matters of general application, unless they expressly provide otherwise.

'(*c*) *Orders*: to be issued in other cases when the Control Council has requirements to impose on Germany and when laws are not used.

'(*d*) *Directives*: to be issued to communicate policy or administrative decisions of the Control Council.

'(*e*) *Instructions*: to be issued in cases when the Control Council wishes to impose requirements direct upon a particular authority.'

[3] See *Official Gazette*, p. 4.

simply a formal publication of the existing state of affairs to the German people.

The picture of the machinery of central government would be incomplete without mention of two provisions which will be of considerable importance in attempting to assess the juridical nature of the Allied régime. The first is the formal statement that these arrangements for the government of Germany are purely temporary, being intended to 'operate during the period of occupation following the German surrender, when Germany is carrying out the basic requirements of unconditional surrender', and that 'arrangements for the subsequent period will be the subject of a separate agreement'.[1] The second is the announcement of the Allied Governments that in the exercise of the supreme authority assumed in the Berlin Declaration it is their intention to consult with the Governments of other United Nations.[2]

Such in outline is the Allied machinery for the government of the occupation zones and of Germany as a whole. It will be remembered, however, that the supreme authority assumed in the Berlin Declaration includes not only the powers of central government but also all powers of local government. The inter-Allied arrangements do not provide any uniform method for the exercise of local governmental powers;[3] no doubt there would necessarily be much improvisation in the early stages of the occupation, and there would probably be considerable divergence between local governmental machinery in the different zones. The general policy has been, as far as possible, to reconstitute the general pattern of local government as it existed in the Weimar Republic. This policy was carried out in the British zone either by the deployment of detachments of Military Government, or by personnel of the Control Commission. The weakness of this system of military or Control Commission administration at all levels was of course that it failed to provide for the re-education of the German people in democratic responsibility and to lay the necessary foundations for the gradual return to some form of self-government. The second stage therefore in the development of local government has been to encourage Germans with sound political records to take part in it. Little could be done in this direction until Nazi sympathizers had been identified; but once this process was under way, Germans who were known to have been loyal

[1] See para. 8 of the Statement on *Control Machinery in Germany*, Cmd. 6648.

[2] See Statement of the Allied Governments on *Consultation with Governments of other United Nations*, Cmd. 6648.

[3] However, the general policy to be followed is laid down in the Potsdam Declaration of 2 August 1945: '9. The administration of affairs in Germany should be directed towards the decentralization of the political structure and the development of local responsibility. To this end (i) local self-government shall be restored throughout Germany on democratic principles, and in particular through elective councils, as rapidly as is consistent with military security and the purposes of military occupation. . . .'

supporters of the former Republic began to be appointed, even to important administrative posts. In pursuance of the same policy, some of the more important towns were given consultative committees to serve as links between the administration and the people. There is no doubt, of course, that the early revival of some of the more important German administrative units was dictated by the necessities of the situation as much as the result of a conscious policy of re-education. Thus, in the British zone, the urgent task of repairing damaged highways and bridges had to be met by reopening the Frankfurt office of the Reichsautoamt; similarly for railways, the Reichsbahndirektionen of Essen and Münster were early functioning under Allied supervision. Thus the outlines of the machinery of local government are tolerably clear: it is a system of indirect government carried on through local institutions modelled in the main on those of the Weimar Republic,[1] in which Germans with sound political records play increasingly important roles. Of course, all these local institutions, whether staffed by Military Government or by Germans, are in every way completely under the authority of the Zone Commanders-in-Chief and the Control Commission; there has never been any question of a division of ultimate responsibility.

II. *The meaning and effect of the assumption of supreme authority*

We must now consider the nature and extent of the rights which the Allied Powers have assumed over Germany and the consequent modification of the status of Germany in international law. The effect of the Allied Declaration of 5 June 1945 has been considered by the English courts in the case of *Rex* v. *Bottrill, ex parte Kuechenmeister.*[2] Kuechenmeister, a German national, had permanently resided in the United Kingdom since 1931, during which year he had married an Englishwoman. During the war he was interned as an enemy alien and it was now proposed to deport him. He applied to the court for a writ of habeas corpus. Counsel for the applicant accepted the proposition that the court will not issue habeas corpus on the application of an enemy alien;[3] but he argued that Kuechenmeister was no longer an enemy alien because the effect of the Allied Declaration of 5 June was to destroy the existence of Germany as a sovereign state, from which conclusion it also followed that there could no longer be a state of war between Great Britain and Germany, and, further, that there was no longer a status of German nationality in international law. In answer to this argument the Attorney-General, opposing

[1] A few of the institutions established by the Nazi Government were preserved, e.g. the Landwirtschaftsämter and the Landesbauernschaften.

[2] Proceedings in the King's Bench are reported in All E.R., [1946] i. 635; for the decision of the Court of Appeal see L.R. [1947] K.B. 41.

[3] *R.* v. *Vine Street Police Station Superintendent, ex parte Liebmann,* [1916] 1 K.B. 268.

the application, put before the court a certificate signed by Mr. Ernest Bevin, Secretary of State for Foreign Affairs, in the following terms:

'(1) That under paragraph 5 of the Preamble to the Declaration dated June 5, 1945, of the unconditional surrender of Germany, the Governments of the United Kingdom, the United States of America, the Union of Soviet Socialist Republics, and France assumed supreme authority with respect to Germany, including all the powers possessed by the German Government, the High Command, and any State, municipal, or local government or authority. The assumption for the purposes stated above does not effect the annexation of Germany.

'(2) That in consequence of this declaration, Germany still exists as a State and German nationality as a nationality, but that the Allied Control Commission are the agency through which the Government of Germany is carried on.

'(3) No treaty of peace or declaration by the Allied Powers having been made terminating the state of war with Germany, His Majesty is still in a state of war with Germany, although, as provided in the declaration of surrender, all active hostilities have ceased.'[1]

The Court of Appeal upheld a decision of the Divisional Court refusing the application. It was held that the certificate of the Secretary of State was conclusive on the Court for the facts alleged in it, and in any case the action of the Executive taken in the interests of the safety of the state must be above challenge by habeas corpus. 'In our municipal law,' said Lord Justice Scott in the Court of Appeal, 'whether or not it differed in that respect from international law, a state of war could continue with a State in spite of the fact that that State no longer had any independent central government.'[2] The actual decision of the Court rests, of course, on doctrines of English constitutional law; for the international lawyer the interest of the case lies in the propositions enunciated in the certificate of the Secretary of State. Although the certificate is conclusive of such matters in English law, it is not of itself conclusive in international law, and it will be convenient to consider the several propositions *seriatim*, together with certain other aspects of the operation of the Berlin Declaration not touched on in this case.

The continued existence of the German state

The Berlin Declaration states that the Allies have assumed 'supreme authority' over Germany, but that this does not effect the annexation of Germany. It has been argued that this is an assumption of sovereignty over Germany and that consequently Germany, lacking the prerequisite of an independent government, can no longer be said to exist as a state in the

[1] See *The Times* newspaper, 4 April 1946.

[2] In *Netz* v. *Ede*, [1946] Ch. 224, it was likewise argued for the plaintiff that, Germany being 'merely a certain geographical area governed by the Allied Control Commission', the United Kingdom was no longer at war with Germany. Wynn-Parry J. did not find it necessary to decide this question as he held himself bound by the Statement of Claim, which did not plead that the plaintiff had ceased to be an alien enemy.

sense of international law.[1] On the other hand, it is evident from *Rex* v. *Bottrill* that the British Government, at any rate, relies on the continued existence of Germany as a state. Which of these two contradictory views of the effect of the Berlin Declaration is correct?

The view that the German state has ceased to exist rests very largely on the—it is submitted mistaken—assumption that the Allies have in fact vested themselves with full sovereignty over Germany in the ordinary sense of that term. The Berlin Declaration is obviously a carefully drafted document and it is significant that, far from declaring that the occupying Powers have assumed the sovereignty over Germany, it studiously avoids any reference to sovereignty. It speaks only of an assumption of 'supreme authority' (*l'autorité suprême: oberste Regierungsgewalt*), which is not necessarily the same thing. For the 'supreme authority' assumed by the occupying Powers is not without qualification: it is assumed for certain stated purposes;[2] it is 'without prejudice to any subsequent decisions that may be taken respecting Germany'; it is a provisional régime to provide for 'the period when Germany is carrying out the basic requirements of unconditional surrender';[3] furthermore, it is specifically stated that 'the assumption, for the purposes stated above, of the said authority and powers does not effect the annexation of Germany'. Admittedly, sovereignty is not a term with a very precise legal connotation; nevertheless, it is quite clear that the powers assumed by the Allies fall something short of what is generally understood by sovereignty, and the content and legal effect of those powers must be established by an analysis of the Berlin Declaration, and not by an analysis of the general concept of sovereignty.[4]

[1] See Professor Kelsen's lucid article in *American Journal of International Law*, 39 (1945), p. 518; also the argument of learned counsel for the applicant in *Rex* v. *Bottrill, ex parte Kuechenmeister*, loc. cit.

[2] See paragraphs 2 and 3 of the preamble to the Berlin Declaration, *supra*, p. 114.

[3] See the Statement by the four Allied Governments on *Control Machinery in Germany*, Cmd. 6648.

[4] An instructive analogy is provided by the machinery employed at the end of the First World War for the transference of certain former German territories to the Mandatory Powers. By Article 119 of the Treaty of Versailles, Germany renounced in favour of the Principal Allied and Associated Powers all rights and titles over her overseas possessions. Construing this clause in *Rex* v. *Jacobus Christian, S.A.L.R.*, [1924] App. Div. 101, the Supreme Court of South Africa said: 'The expression "renounce in favour of" is sometimes used in the Treaty as equivalent to "cede to".... Not so with the overseas possessions; or at any rate such of them as fall within the operation of Article 22. They were not by Article 119 ceded to all or any of the Principal Powers, any more than the City of Danzig was ceded to them under Article 110. The animus essential to a legal cession was not present on either side. For the signatories must have intended that such possessions should be dealt with as provided in part 1 of the Treaty; they were placed at the disposal of the Principal Powers merely that the latter might take all necessary steps for their administration on a mandatory basis. The intention of the signatories seems to have been to place certain overseas possessions relinquished by Germany upon a basis new to international law, and regulated primarily by Article 22 of the Treaty.'

Similarly, in Germany, the Allies have assumed supreme authority in order to impose upon Germany a special and temporary régime, also new to international law, and without prejudice to the ultimate disposal of German territory and German government.

If, indeed, the correct view is that the German state has ceased to exist, it would seem to follow that there has been a state succession, and that certain of the rights and duties of the former German state have passed by succession to the Allied states; for example, it would then be arguable that parts of the German debts are now chargeable on the public funds of the Allied states. It cannot be supposed that such a result was within the intention of the Allied Powers in making the Berlin Declaration. On the contrary, the expressed intention is that the assumption of supreme authority over Germany is not to effect the annexation of Germany, and this qualification of the rights assumed is an essential part of the instrument which must, if possible, be interpreted in such a way as to give undoubted effect to the qualification. If the qualification that Germany is not annexed is to be given any substantial content it can only be interpreted to mean that the Allied régime stops short of creating any sort of identity between the German state and the Allied states. In so far as there is any succession, it must be a succession of governments and not of states; or to put it another way, it means that in so far as the Control Authority is acting as 'the agency through which the Government of Germany is carried on', its acts are in law attributable not to the Allied states but to the state of Germany, which is accordingly deliberately maintained in being as a legal person.

Thus to draw a distinction between government and state and to assume plenary powers of government unaccompanied by annexation of the state is admittedly unprecedented, and the question remains how far such a result is possible in law. There is, indeed, nothing novel in the idea that the persons who control one legal entity may also control a distinct legal entity. If the controlling shareholders of company X are also the controlling shareholders of company Y, the common lawyer finds no difficulty in still regarding company X and company Y as distinct legal persons; and there is no logical difficulty in applying the same reasoning to the artificial legal persons we call states. However, this does not dispose of the substantial objection that a state must nevertheless have an *independent* government if it is to qualify as a state in the sense of international as opposed to municipal law. It may very well be that Germany still exists as a legal person properly called a state but that, having no independent government, that legal personality is reduced to the sphere of constitutional law and has no validity in international law; just as Virginia is unquestionably a legal entity properly called a state in American constitutional law but, nevertheless, has no separate legal personality in international law. The criterion of statehood in international law must be the enjoyment of a sufficient degree of independent government, and the rule is fundamental to the international system: a state obviously could not be permitted to multiply itself by the creation of subsidiary states on the analogy of the subsidiary companies of company law and to claim for those subsidiary states legal personality in international law, including for example the right of separate representation on international assemblies. But in considering the relevance of this rule to the present status of Germany, the decisive factor is the purely temporary nature of the régime set up in the Berlin Declaration. For this is a question not of the emergence of a new state but of the continued existence of an old state with a long history of independence. The presumption is therefore of her continued existence as a state,[1] and a merely provisional arrangement for carrying on her government through an agency set up by the four occupying Powers does not upset that presumption. It is of course true that the Allies have not yet finally committed themselves on the future of Germany, but their present intention is clearly that after a period of control and re-education in democratic responsibilities, Germany may be granted a new government which it is hoped will prove itself fitted eventually to resume the powers of the government of the German state.[2]

Continuance of the state of war

The certificate of the British Secretary of State declares that, no treaty of peace or declaration of peace terminating the state of war with Germany having been made, His Majesty is still in a state of war with Germany. Presumably this is also the attitude of the other occupying Powers. The technical possibility of the continuance of the state of war clearly depends upon the continued existence of the German state, for there could be no relationship of war with a state which no longer exists: that indeed is why the books usually cite subjugation as a mode of terminating the state of war, for they assume that subjugation includes annexation and in so far as annexation terminates the existence of the annexed state it must also terminate any relationship of war with that state. If, however, we are correct in saying that Germany not having been annexed the state of Germany continues to exist, it follows that a state of war between the occupying Powers and Germany remains technically possible. The fact that the Allies

[1] See Baty, *The Canons of International Law* (1930), p. 7. See also Halleck, *International Law* (Sir Sherston Baker's ed., 1878), vol. ii, p. 470, where, discussing the nature of conquest, he says: 'The title of the original owner prior to the conquest is, by the very nature of the case, admitted to be valid. His rights are, therefore, suspended by force alone. If that force be overcome, and the original owner resumes his possession, his rights revive, and are deemed to have been uninterrupted.' If the original owner resumes at the will of the conqueror it is an *a fortiori* case.

[2] See Potsdam Declaration, reported in *The Times* newspaper, 3 August 1945: 'It is not the intention of the allies to destroy or enslave the German people. It is the intention of the allies that the German people be given the opportunity to prepare for the eventual reconstruction of their life on a democratic and peaceful basis. If their own efforts are steadily directed towards this end it will be possible for them in due course to take their place among the free and peaceful peoples of the world.'

have taken over the government of Germany does not alter this position, for war is a relationship between states, not between governments. The absence of any treaty of peace or declaration of peace is not in itself conclusive that the state of war persists, for it is well known that belligerents may drift into a state of peace on the simple cessation of hostilities.[1] The mere cessation of hostilities, however, does not of itself end war; there must also be a cessation of the *animus belligerandi*, and where, as in the case before us, a belligerent state issues a categorical assertion that the relationship of war persists between it and another state and acts on that assumption,[2] there does not seem to be any real room for doubt that there is a continuing state of war in the technical sense.

The continuance of the state of war with occupied Germany is admittedly a new departure in international law. In these peculiar circumstances the state of war has become so refined and technical as practically to alter the character of the concept; for it is no longer a part of the machinery for the conduct of hostilities but has become part of the machinery of control of an already conquered enemy. It is a two-edged weapon of control, for not only does it mean that Germany can herself be treated as an enemy state, but also that her foreign relations can be conducted in accordance with the Allies' own state of belligerency. Thus, for example, in providing for the representation of third states in Germany, the occupying Powers have drawn up a sharp distinction between members of the United Nations, neutral states, and states at war with any of the occupying Powers.[3] The prolongation of the state of war after the assumption of supreme authority over the whole territory of the enemy is indeed to claim the best of both worlds; the conqueror enjoys the rights conferred by his conquest yet stops short of permitting his conquest to resolve the state of war.

German nationality

Given the continued existence of the German state it follows that German nationality also continues to exist. This point need not be laboured. As Germany has not been annexed, the inhabitants do not acquire any other nationality, and to hold that they are all now stateless would be repugnant to both law and common sense. However, the position of German nationality law under the occupation régime does merit consideration. In accordance with the accepted doctrine of international law, the investitive

[1] See Oppenheim, *International Law* (6th ed. by Lauterpacht 1940), vol. ii, pp. 465 ff. See also McNair, *Legal Effects of War* (2nd ed. 1944), p. 6.

[2] As for example in the continued application of the British Trading with the Enemy legislation to Germany.

[3] The Statement on *Control Machinery in Germany* (Cmd. 6648) provides for liaison between the Control Council and 'other United Nations Governments chiefly interested' by means of military missions. For the position of representatives of countries at war with any of the four Powers and of neutral countries, see p. 126 note 2.

and divestitive facts of German nationality are governed not by international law but by German municipal law. The ruthless denationalization policy followed by the Nazi Government is notorious; and it was primarily the rule of international law that nationality is a matter governed exclusively by municipal law that made it peculiarly difficult to make an effective attack on the denationalization policy on legal grounds. In Germany to-day the gulf between international and municipal law has been bridged. The supreme authority assumed by the occupying Powers obviously includes competence to modify the German nationality laws by Control Council legislation, and the Control Council has not been slow to change those laws so as to bring them into conformity with the requirements of natural justice. Control Council Law No. 1 of 20 September 1945[1] repeals some twenty-seven 'laws of a political or discriminatory nature upon which the Nazi régime rested', including the Reich Citizenship Law (Reichsbürgergesetz) of 15 September 1935.[2] The effect of the repealed Nazi legislation and of the Decrees made under it was to provide for the denationalization of German citizens in two cases. Firstly it provided a discretionary power to denationalize Germans who, without the permission of the German Government, had accepted service with a foreign government, and who disobeyed an order of the German Government to return to Germany.[3] The second case was not discretionary but automatic: by Section 1 of the 11th Decree in connexion with Reich citizenship of 25 November 1941[4] all Jews living abroad at the time of the coming into force of the said Decree were thereby automatically deprived of their German nationality. The effect of Control Council Law No. 1 is to abolish these two categories of denationalization, but the abrogation has no retrospective effect, so that persons who had already been deprived of their German nationality in pursuance of the Nazi legislation do not now regain it.[5]

The foreign relations of Germany

Given the premiss that the German state still exists, it follows that Germany remains a subject of international law capable of relations with third

[1] See *Official Gazette*, p. 6. [2] *R.G.Bl.I.* 1146.

[3] Action under this first category has caused great hardship, for many persons so liable to denationalization do not know whether they were in fact deprived of their nationality or not. The Office of the High Commissioner for Refugees has accordingly provided a service for searching the Reichsanzeiger to enable these unhappy people to discover whether or not they are still German nationals. [4] *R.G.Bl.I.* 722.

[5] Persons who were thus deprived of their German nationality while resident in the United Kingdom have found themselves in an anomalous position owing to the decisions of the English courts (see *The King* v. *Home Secretary*, [1945] 1 K.B. 7) that the German Decree of 1941 was a war measure of the German Government and therefore its effect could not be recognized by the English courts, and that no government could in time of war validly denationalize its subjects resident in enemy territory. Thus these unfortunate persons are still regarded as German nationals by English law but are stateless according to German municipal law even as modified by the Control Council.

states, and continuing to bear rights and duties *vis-à-vis* third states; but as long as the Allies exercise supreme authority in Germany it also follows that the foreign relations of Germany are conducted on behalf of the German state by the Allied Representatives. These principles are set forth in Control Council Proclamation No. 2 of 20 September 1945, addressed to the German people and containing 'certain additional requirements arising from the complete defeat and unconditional surrender of Germany with which Germany must comply'.[1]

'The Allied Representatives will regulate all matters affecting Germany's relations with other countries. No foreign obligations, undertakings or commitments of any kind will be assumed or entered into by or on behalf of German authorities or nationals without the sanction of the Allied Representatives.'

Furthermore the Proclamation makes it clear that the foreign relations of Germany will be conducted by means of machinery provided by the Allied Government of Germany, that the machinery of the former German Government is to be liquidated and that the Allied Government of Germany assumes complete control over the diplomatic, consular, and commercial representatives of third states in Germany.[2] At the time of writing (October 1946), no diplomatic, consular, or commercial machinery of representation has yet been provided by the Allies to fill the gap created by the abolition of the machinery of the former German Government, but it is understood that the provision of some such machinery is under active consideration by the Allied Control Authority. In the meantime it would seem that German foreign relations must be regarded as being provisionally in a state of suspense.[3]

Had Germany been annexed by the Allies the position would of course have been simpler: the foreign relations of Germany would have become in law and in fact the foreign relations of the annexing Powers. There would

[1] *Official Gazette*, pp. 8–19.

[2] Section III, s. 7 of Proclamation No. 2 provides:

'7. (*a*) In virtue of the unconditional surrender of Germany, and as of the date of such surrender, the diplomatic, consular, commercial and other relations of the German State with other States have ceased to exist.

'(*b*) Diplomatic, consular, commercial and other officials and members of service missions in Germany of countries at war with any of the four Powers will be dealt with as the Allied Representatives may prescribe. The Allied Representatives may require the withdrawal from Germany of neutral diplomatic, consular, commercial and other officials and members of neutral service missions.

'(*c*) All German diplomatic, consular, commercial and other officials and members of German service missions abroad are hereby recalled. The control and disposal of the buildings, property and archives of all German diplomatic and other agencies abroad will be prescribed by the Allied Representatives.'

[3] As already mentioned, provision is made for the representation of certain of the United Nations in the Joint Statement on *Control Machinery in Germany*, section 5 of which provides that: 'Liaison with the other United Nations Governments chiefly interested will be established through the appointment by such Governments of military missions (which may include civilian members) to the Control Council. These missions will have access through the appropriate channels to the organs of control.'

have been a succession of states. But as Germany is not annexed and as the German state continues to exist there can be no question of a state succession. Liabilities incurred and rights acquired by the Allied Government of Germany as against third states will inhere in the German state and not in the Allied states; although of course the position is somewhat complicated by the fact that the Allied states necessarily also bear a measure of international responsibility for their conduct of the government of Germany, so that it may often be a nice question whether a third state's right of redress lies against the state of Germany or against one or all of the Allied states.

With regard to already existing treaty rights and obligations the Proclamation provides:

> '6. The Allied Representatives will give directions concerning the abrogation, bringing into force, revival or application of any treaty, convention or other international agreements, or any part or provision thereof, to which Germany is or has been a party.'

This, on the face of it, does no more than announce that the Allied Representatives are henceforward responsible for the conduct of Germany's treaty relations. It remains, however, to consider how far the Allied Representatives are bound to observe the existing treaty obligations of Germany towards third states; or, to put the same question another way, how far there is a succession of obligations as well as of rights from the former German Government to the Allied Government of Germany. If the occupation were one of the normal varieties of military occupation there would be no succession, for the legitimate government would itself remain liable, even though the possibility of fulfilling those obligations might temporarily be in suspense. Where, however, as in the present case, the former government is entirely replaced by the Allied Representatives, the position is different. According to the ordinary principles of governmental succession and the continuity of states it would seem that the Allied Government in Germany inherits the treaty relations of the former German Government intact, including both rights and obligations; except of course political treaties and the like which, being personal to the Nazi Government, have obviously been rendered obsolete by the changed circumstances, and also treaties which are abrogated or suspended by Germany's belligerency. It is apparent, however, that there is a certain reluctance to admit that the Control Authority is in the full sense of the word the Government of Germany for international purposes. It is referred to merely as the agency through which the government of Germany is for the time being carried on.[1] It may be that in thus defining the Control Authority as a provisional

[1] The following answers were given to questions in the House of Commons on 20 March 1946 (Hansard, *Parliamentary Debates*, vol. 420, p. 1856):

'*Mr. John Foster* asked the Secretary of State for Foreign Affairs whether the Allied Control Council is for international purposes the recognized Government of Germany.

'*Mr. Bevin*: The Allied Control Council is the agency through which the government of

device for the interim administration of the country and the carrying into effect of certain specific policies, the Allies seek to avoid responsibility for treaty commitments of the former German Government, and this interpretation of the position would explain the very consensual language of paragraph 6 of the Proclamation quoted above, which seems to assume that the Allied Representatives have a discretion to determine which of the treaties entered into by the former German Government shall once more be put into operation. Nevertheless, as regards third states, there would seem to be no valid reason why the occupying Powers should assume all the rights of government without incurring the corresponding liabilities. In any case, there should be no room for doubt that treaties which secure rights of third states against German property or territory will be binding on the Allied Representatives on the ordinary principles of *res transit cum suo onere.*

The control and disposal of property

The Allied Control Council has assumed extensive powers of disposal over property, mainly as a necessary preliminary step in implementing the policy of the Potsdam Declaration of breaking the concentration of German economic power in cartels and other monopolistic concerns and the removal as reparations of productive power surplus to the requirements of a peaceful economy. The details of the Control Council's property legislation are not relevant to this paper, but it will be necessary to refer briefly to some of the main provisions in so far as they raise questions of general principle.

Control Council Proclamation No. 2[1] places an embargo on the unauthorized disposal of certain kinds of property subject to the jurisdiction of the Control Council. It forbids the disposal in any way whatever without the sanction of the Allied Representatives of three kinds of property: (i) German public property whether situated inside or outside Germany; (ii) property situated outside German territory of any person resident or carrying on business in Germany; (iii) the property, whether situated inside or outside Germany, of such companies, associations, and concerns as may be designated by the Allied Representatives.[2] These provisions are not, how-

Germany is carried on, but its position and that of Germany itself are without precedent. The foreign relations of Germany as a State are in abeyance, and the status and functions of the Control Council for international purposes must, therefore, develop according to circumstances.

'*Mr. Foster*: Which is the recognized Government of Germany?

'*Mr. Bevin*: The Allied Control Council is absolutely responsible, but there are many other things such as pre-war debts and obligations, which have not yet been definitely transferred.'

[1] See *Official Gazette*, pp. 8–19.

[2] Proclamation No. 2 of 20 September 1945, Section V: '14. (*a*) The property, assets, rights, titles and interests (whether situated inside or outside Germany) of the German State, its political subdivisions, the German Central Bank, State or semi-State, provincial, municipal or local authorities or Nazi organizations, and those situated outside Germany of any person resident or carrying on business in Germany, will not be disposed of in any way whatever without the sanction of the Allied Representatives. The property, assets, rights, titles and interests (whether situated inside

ever, to be deemed to prevent sales or transfers to persons resident in Germany for the purpose of maintaining or carrying on the day-to-day national life, economy, and administration.[1] The German authorities are also to furnish the Allied Representatives with full information concerning property, assets, and the titles thereto, including information concerning and documents of title to German property and assets situated in the territories of any of the United Nations.[2] Property, assets, rights, titles, and interests situated inside Germany may not be removed outside Germany or transferred to any person resident or carrying on business outside Germany without the sanction of the Allied Representatives.[3] All gold and silver in coin or bullion situated in Germany, all foreign currency held by Germans, and all money tokens issued or prepared for issue by Germany in the territories formerly occupied by her or elsewhere are to be handed over in full to the Allied Representatives.[4]

For the administration of the vesting and marshalling of German external assets, Control Council Law No. 5 establishes a *German External Property Commission*, composed of representatives of the four occupying Powers and constituted as 'an inter-governmental agency of the Control Council vested with all necessary powers and authority'.[5] The preamble states that the reason for the establishment of the Commission is the determination of the Control Council 'to assume control of all German assets abroad and to divest the said assets of their German ownership with the intention thereby of promoting international peace and collective security by the elimination of German war potentials'.[6] By Articles II and III certain kinds of property are automatically vested in the Commission.

> 'All rights, titles and interests in respect of any property outside Germany which is owned or controlled by any person of German nationality inside Germany are hereby vested in the Commission.'
>
> 'All rights, titles and interests in respect of any property outside Germany which is owned or controlled by any person of German nationality outside Germany or by any branch of any business or corporation or other legal entity organised under the laws of Germany or having its principal place of business in Germany are hereby vested in the Commission.'[7]

or outside Germany), of such private companies, corporations, trusts, cartels, firms, partnerships and associations as may be designated by the Allied Representatives will not be disposed of in any way whatever without the sanction of the Allied Representatives.'

[1] Proclamation No. 2, Section V, sub-section 14 (*d*).

[2] Proclamation No. 2, Section V, sub-section 14 (*b*).

[3] Proclamation No. 2, Section V, sub-section 14 (*c*).

[4] Proclamation No. 2, Section V, sub-section 15.

[5] Control Council Law No. 5 of 30 October 1945 is published in the *Official Gazette*, pp. 27–31.

[6] See also the Potsdam Declaration: '18. Appropriate steps shall be taken by the Control Council to exercise control and the power of disposition over German-owned external assets not already under the control of the United Nations which have taken part in the war against Germany.'

[7] Article III defines 'any person of German nationality outside Germany' as applying 'only

The question of compensation to the original owners of titles thereby vested in the Commission is left to be 'decided at such time and in such manner as the Control Council may in the future determine'.[1] The Commission is to dispose of the property or the proceeds of its realization 'pursuant to such further directives as the Control Council may issue from time to time'.[2] Article IX contains the proviso that Articles II and III 'shall not apply to assets subject to the jurisdiction of the United Kingdom, British Dominions, India, Colonies and Possessions, the Union of Soviet Socialist Republics, the United States, France and any other United Nations determined by the Control Council'.

Law No. 9 of 30 November 1945[3] is more radical, in providing for the actual seizure of property owned by the I.G. Farbenindustrie, 'in order to ensure that Germany will never again threaten her neighbours or the peace of the world, and taking into consideration that I.G. Farbenindustrie knowingly and prominently engaged in building up and maintaining the German war potential'. Accordingly it is provided that all properties and assets of any nature which were, on or after 8 May 1945, owned or controlled by I.G. Farbenindustrie A.G., are seized by and the legal title therefor vested in the Control Council, and the seized plants and properties are to be controlled by a Committee consisting of four Control Officers appointed by the respective Zone Commanders. The ultimate disposal of the plant and properties is to be made in accordance with a programme of destruction, dispersal, and making available for reparation.[4]

For the legal basis of the Control Council's competence thus to dispose of German property it is not necessary to go beyond the supreme authority wielded by the Council in the government of Germany which obviously must include power of disposal over all German property and assets, both public and private, and whether situated within German territory or not. The familiar distinction between public and private property drawn by the laws of war finds no place here, for the power involved is not a belligerent right but a right of government. Moreover, by virtue of the supreme authority the power of disposal includes the competence to pass a good title.

Complications are introduced, however, when the subject-matter is not

to a person who has enjoyed full rights of German citizenship under Reich Law at any time since 1 September 1939 and who has at any time since 1 September 1939 been within any territory then under the control of the Reich Government but shall not apply to any country annexed or claimed to have been annexed by Germany since 31 December 1937'.

[1] Article V. [2] Article VI.

[3] See *Official Gazette*, pp. 34–5.

[4] A four-power Agreement on the destruction of German war and industrial potential is reported in *The Times* newspaper, 3 October 1946. The ownership of certain basic German industries situated in the British zone is being vested in the Commander-in-Chief with a view to their eventual nationalization. See the speech of Mr. Bevin, British Foreign Secretary, in the House of Commons on 22 October 1946 (reported in *The Times* newspaper, 23 October 1946) where he says, 'the exact form of this public ownership and control is now being worked out'.

German but foreign property. There is no difficulty indeed where the rights annexed are existing German rights over foreign property, as, for example, in the seizure of charter-party rights over foreign shipping:[1] for this is no more than a compulsory assignment of contractual rights and is not inconsistent with the foreign ownership of the property. Different considerations apply if rights of disposal are claimed inconsistent with foreign ownership in property. Proclamation No. 2 of the Control Council provides that all property in Germany belonging to or held for countries, or nationals of countries, or persons resident in or carrying on business in countries, 'against which any of the United Nations is carrying on hostilities', is to be 'taken under control and will be preserved pending further instructions'. Further, that all property in Germany held for or belonging to private individuals, private enterprises, and companies of countries (other than the above countries and Germany) which have at any time since 1 September 1939 been at war with any of the United Nations will likewise be 'taken under control and will be preserved pending further instructions'.[2] These requirements do not, of course, amount to an assertion of title or power of disposal of such property by the occupying Powers; they merely provide for the safe custody of such property without prejudice to its ultimate disposal, and at the time of writing the policy of the occupying Powers in regard to such property has not yet become apparent. Nevertheless, an important question of principle is raised. The right to deal with such property other than in accordance with the rights of the owners might be asserted by the occupying Powers either as a war right or as a consequence of the conquest of the country involved, and it is important to note that in exercising such a right the Control Council must be regarded as the agent of the Allied Powers themselves and not of the German state; in short, that their action would be attributable in law to the Allied states and not to the German state. For in their capacity as the government of the German state the occupying Powers could not assert rights based on the existence of a state of war, or on the consequences of successfully waged war, between themselves and another country which country has never been in a state of war with Germany. The states which bear the rights exercised must also bear the corresponding responsibilities. Thus, the

[1] Control Council Proclamation No. 2, Section VII, provides *inter alia:*

'23. (*c*) Foreign merchant shipping in German service or under German control will likewise be made available to the Allied Representatives for such use and on such terms as they may prescribe. In the case of such foreign merchant vessels which are of neutral registration, the German authorities will take all such steps as may be required by the Allied Representatives to transfer or cause to be transferred to the Allied Representatives all rights relative thereto.

'24. Any existing options to repurchase or reacquire or to resume control of vessels sold or otherwise transferred or chartered by Germany during the war will be exercised as directed by the Allied Representatives. Such vessels will be made available for use by the Allied Representatives in the same manner as the vessels covered by sub-paragraphs 23 (*b*) and (*c*) above.'

[2] Proclamation No. 2 of 20 September 1945, Section V, sub-section 16.

German state cannot be held responsible for any claims arising out of the exercise of such rights by the Allied Government of Germany. In considering questions of responsibility towards third states it will constantly be important to bear in mind this duality of function of the Allied Representatives in Germany and to ask whether any particular act of government called in question is attributable to the German state or to one or all of the Allied states.

Judicial reform

It will be evident from the nature of the Allied occupation that the law in force in Germany remains the German municipal law, although of course the Control Council, being the Government of Germany, is fully competent to change or modify this law in any way. This situation would require no further comment were it not for the fact that so much of the German municipal law under the Nazis was a denial of the most elementary principles of natural law and justice, with the consequence that the Control Council is not merely competent to modify those laws but is under a plain duty to do so.[1] The abrogation of the Nazi denationalization laws has already been noticed,[2] and this is not the place to enter upon a detailed examination of the many reforms of the private law that have already been accomplished. Mention must be made, however, of the reform of the judicial system. The abolition of the Nazi system of justice and the re-establishing of the rule of law was urgently necessary not only on grounds of general principle but also as part of the programme of destroying the totalitarian state; for the substantial reason behind the introduction of the Führer-Prinzip and such-like notions into the legal system was still further to enhance the power of the executive and to free it from checks by the judiciary. Control Council's Proclamation No. 3[3] lays down the fundamental principles of a 'new democratic judicial system based on the achievements of democracy, civilization and justice'. The first need was clearly to abolish discriminatory practices based on racial theories: the first article of the Proclamation therefore provides,

> 'All persons are equal before the law. No person, whatever his race, nationality or religion, shall be deprived of his legal rights.'

Next the Proclamation guarantees certain fundamental rights to accused persons. No person is to be deprived of life, liberty, or property without due process of law. Crime is limited to offences defined by the law, and conviction by 'analogy' and so-called 'sound popular instinct' (*gesundes*

[1] Indeed it could hardly be argued that even a mere belligerent occupant is required by Article 43 of The Hague Regulations to respect the laws in force in the country to the extent of respecting laws which are contrary to natural justice.

[2] See above at p. 125.

[3] See *Official Gazette*, p. 22.

Volksempfinden) is prohibited. In any criminal prosecution the accused is to have 'the rights recognized by democratic law', viz. speedy and public trial, the right to be informed of the nature and cause of the accusation, the right to be confronted with witnesses against him, process for obtaining witnesses in his favour, and the right to assistance by counsel. All sentences on persons convicted under the Hitler régime on political, racial, or religious grounds are quashed. Finally, after abolishing the extraordinary Hitler courts, the Proclamation lays down the fundamental principles of judicial independence from the executive, and opens judicial office to 'all who accept democratic principles without account of their race, social origin or religion', their promotion to be based solely on merit and legal qualifications.

The machinery of the new justice is constituted by the Control Council's Law No. 4 of 30 October 1945.[1] It is a reversion to the structure of courts of the Weimar Republic, re-establishing the threefold system of Amtsgerichte, Landsgerichte, and Oberlandsgerichte. Their jurisdiction is to be as laid down by the law in force on 30 January 1933, with a few minor changes, except that certain offences affecting Allied forces or subjects are reserved to the Allied military courts.

III. *The Allied occupation and international law*

There remains the question, What is the legal basis and justification of the rights assumed by the occupying Powers? The importance of the question is obvious, and it must be answered by the application of general principles of international law. It will be appreciated at once that the Berlin Declaration of 5 June creates a situation that does not fit easily, if it fits at all, into orthodox legal categories. Nevertheless, it is not sufficient merely to describe the Allied occupation as *sui generis*, for to do so is to beg the question of the basis and limits of its legality. It must be assumed that behind the orthodox categories of situations there are general principles of law applicable to new situations.

The main principles of the law governing military occupations of territory are well established. A clear distinction is drawn between mere belligerent occupation and other forms of occupation, the reason being that belligerent occupation is regarded as a purely provisional status in which the occupant's rights are limited by the laws of war, particularly as they are defined in Articles 42 to 56 of The Hague Regulations, by which the belligerent occupant's rights are in general limited to those necessary either for the prosecution of the war or for the day-to-day administration of the territory. He does not in any sense enjoy sovereignty, for until the con-

[1] *Official Gazette*, pp. 26–7.

quest is completed the sovereignty is still vested in the legitimate government of the territory. The position is put very clearly by Halleck, who writes with great authority on these matters:

> 'The term *conquest*, as it is ordinarily used, is applicable to conquered territory the moment it is taken from the enemy; but, in its more limited and technical meaning, it includes only the real property to which the conqueror has acquired a *complete title*. Until the ownership of such property so taken is confirmed or made complete, it is held by the right of *military occupation* (*occupatio bellica*), which, by the usage of nations and the laws of war, differs from, and falls far short of, the right of *complete conquest* (*debellatio, ultima victoria*).'[1]

The practical basis of this doctrine is that although the acquisition of title to territory by force of arms is a concession to the rule of might that must be allowed by a comparatively undeveloped system of law, the law is nevertheless strong enough to insist that in order to confer title the conquest shall in fact be complete; it is not complete so long as the final issue of the conflict remains in any doubt, and as long as the final issue of the arbitrament of force is in doubt an occupation of enemy territory is at most a belligerent occupation and cannot legitimately be enlarged. In Hall's phrase, the occupier is a mere belligerent occupier so long as 'the intention or proved ability to appropriate his enemy's territory is still wanting'.[2]

However, when considering the implications of the classic statements of the law it must be borne in mind that the writers are naturally assuming as a fact that a war will follow the ordinary sequence of events followed by all the wars with which they were familiar; namely, that the final victory of one side (*ultima victoria*) results, if not in treaty arrangements, then in the annexation of the defeated state and the consequent ending of the state of war,[3] so that *ultima victoria* and *debellatio* are always thought of as being, if not the same thing, at any rate necessarily coincidental. We must be careful not to mistake these assumptions of fact for assumptions of law, for this has led to the canvassing of two heresies: (i) that belligerent occupation and annexation constitute a sort of legal dichotomy so that anything short of complete annexation must be at most belligerent occupation; and (ii) that there cannot be more than belligerent occupation so long as a state of technical war continues to exist,[4] even though hostilities have ceased in the complete defeat of one of the belligerents.

The fallacy of this too literal interpretation of the older formulations of

[1] *International Law* (Sir Sherston Baker's ed. 1878), vol. ii, p. 444. Halleck here uses the term 'military occupation' as equivalent to what we have called 'belligerent occupation'.

[2] *International Law* (8th ed. 1924), p. 553.

[3] For by annexation the annexed state ceases to exist and there can be no war with a state which no longer exists.

[4] See, e.g., a learned comment in this *Year Book*, 19 (1938), p. 237, on *Bank of Ethiopia* v. *National Bank of Egypt*, [1937] 1 Ch. 513, by an anonymous contributor who says, *inter alia*: 'The test [of belligerent occupation] is whether the war is over or not, and for the court whether the government have recognized that it is over.'

the law becomes apparent when we consider the present position of the occupying Powers in Germany, for here the events have not at all followed the normal sequence assumed by the commentators. The Allies have enjoyed a final victory as decisive as any in the history of warfare: not only is the whole of German territory under Allied occupation, not only have her fighting services surrendered unconditionally, but her former legitimate government has been completely destroyed. But this supreme example of what Halleck calls *ultima victoria* has resulted, as we have seen, neither in the annexation of the defeated state nor in the termination of the technical state of war. Far from the *ultima victoria* and *debellatio* being coincidental, the Allied régime which we have to consider is a régime interposed between *ultima victoria* and *debellatio*. Into which category then does this novel régime fall? Is the crucial test the *ultima victoria* or the *debellatio*? It is submitted first that the Allied occupation is certainly not a belligerent occupation, and secondly that on the contrary the Allies enjoy a good title to supreme authority, by subjugation.

A brief consideration of the position in Germany to-day will suffice to demonstrate that a final victory which results in the destruction of the government of the occupied territory and the cessation of all hostilities is of itself sufficient to end the status of belligerent occupation whether or not it be accompanied by the ending of a purely technical state of war.[1] The law of belligerent occupation is designed to serve two purposes. First, it is intended to protect the sovereign rights of the legitimate government of the occupied territory, and the denial of sovereignty to the occupant is therefore accompanied by the corollary that the sovereignty still resides in the legitimate government. In Germany there is no longer in existence any German government in which the sovereignty could be said to reside. In these circumstances it must be not only lawful for the occupant to assume powers over and above those necessary for the day-to-day administration of the territory: it is his duty to do so, because being in sole control of the territory he must assume responsibility for carrying on all aspects of government. To insist that the Allied occupation should conform to the limits of The Hague Regulations would be to insist on the maintenance of a governmental vacuum; it is inconceivable that that is the law. Secondly, the law of belligerent occupation is designed to protect the inhabitants of the occupied territory from being exploited for the prosecution of the occupant's war in ways which are forbidden by the ordinary rules of war. Clearly this principle again can have no application in a war which is a

[1] This is not to say, of course, that *ultima victoria* is invariably the proper criterion of belligerent occupation, for there may be *debellatio* without *ultima victoria* as when indecisive fighting is brought to an end by a treaty between the belligerents; such a treaty of peace would end all possibility of belligerent occupancy as plainly as *ultima victoria* unaccompanied by *debellatio* does in the case before us.

purely technical status in which all possibility of active hostilities has ceased. Thus the whole *raison d'être* of the law of belligerent occupation is absent in the circumstances of the Allied occupation of Germany, and to attempt to apply it would be a manifest anachronism.

However, the legal basis of the Berlin Declaration of 5 June cannot be established merely by demonstrating the inapplicability of The Hague Regulations to the case. The assumption of supreme authority must be supported by a demonstration of positive title, and this brings us to our second submission that the Allies enjoy a good title by subjugation. A successful belligerent may acquire title to his enemy's *imperium* either by treaty of cession or by subjugation. The former German Government having ceased to exist, there can be no question of a transfer of title by treaty, so the question resolves itself into whether or not the occupying Powers can claim title to supreme authority as a result of subjugation.

Among the writers there is general agreement on the essentials of subjugation or conquest.[1] Bouvier defines conquest as 'the acquisition of the sovereignty of a country by force of arms, exercised by an independent power which reduces the vanquished to the submission of its empire'.[2] 'There is subjugation', says Rivier, 'when a war is terminated by the complete defeat of one of the belligerents, so that all his territory is taken, the authority of his government suppressed, and he ceases in consequence to exist as a State.'[3] In an illuminating discussion of the law Halleck says, 'By the term *conquest* we understand the *forcible* acquisition of territory admitted to belong to the enemy. It expresses not a *right*, but a *fact* from which rights are derived. Until the fact of conquest occurs there can be no rights of conquest.'[4] Oppenheim defines subjugation as 'extermination in war of one belligerent by another through annexation of the former's territory after conquest, the enemy forces having been annihilated'.[5] It will be seen that all these definitions have this in common: they all expressly or impliedly postulate the extinction of the vanquished state by annexation to the conquering state as an essential ingredient of subjugation.[6] Now it is, of course, true that the mere fact of final victory over the enemy is not of itself sufficient to confer any sort of title on the victor, for this in itself does not produce legal results; there must also be an assumption and exercise

[1] The terms 'subjugation' and what some of the older writers call 'conquest in its technical sense' are, of course, synonymous.

[2] *Law Dictionary* (1856), see under 'conquest'.

[3] *Droit des Gens* (1896), vol. ii, p. 436.

[4] Op. cit., p. 470.

[5] *International Law* (6th ed. by Lauterpacht, 1940), vol. ii, p. 467.

[6] See also Westlake, *International Law* (1910), pt. i, p. 64: 'The extinction of a State by conquest will take place when the conquering power has declared its will to annex it, and has established its authority throughout the territory, any opposition still made being on the scale of brigandage rather than of war, and no corner remains in which the ordinary functions of government are carried on in the name of the old State.'

of the rights to which title is claimed by virtue of the conquest.[1] But must the rights assumed amount to complete annexation of the state in order to confer a good title? The writers speak only of annexation because they assume that a victor who does not reinstate the legitimate government and make a treaty with it will always annex. The Berlin Declaration shows that there is a third possible course which had not occurred to the writers; that is, to draw a distinction between the government and the state, and to assume all the powers of the former while stopping short of annexing and therefore extinguishing the latter. If, after the German surrender, the Allies had indeed annexed the German state there could have been no doubt about the nature of their right in law to do so; the circumstances would have fitted neatly and unquestionably into the familiar category of subjugation. But if as a result of the Allied victory and the German unconditional surrender Germany was so completely at the disposal of the Allies as to justify them in law in annexing the German state, it would seem to follow that they are by the same token entitled to assume the rights of supreme authority unaccompanied by annexation; for the rights assumed by the Allies are coextensive with the rights comprised in annexation, the difference being only in the mode, purpose, and duration of their exercise, the declared purpose of the occupying Powers being to govern the territory not as an integral part of their own territories but in the name of a continuing German state. It is not suggested, of course, that an assumption of anything less than supreme authority could be justified in law by subjugation; if the Allies had chosen only to assume rights over Germany which left even the German Government in existence there could have been no question of title by subjugation because such rights would in law remain vested in the legitimate government unless and until they were ceded by treaty. Where, however, the former government is completely extinguished, the whole of its authority being assumed by the conqueror, there must be a good title to those rights by virtue of subjugation. The fact that the conqueror chooses to exercise those rights as the government of the still existing though conquered state—in short, to take its government into commission—cannot vitiate his entitlement to those rights, any more than a finder in English law would forfeit his legal title to the thing he finds by immediately declaring a trust of it.

It remains to consider the Final Act of Unconditional Surrender.[2] This

[1] For, as Oppenheim points out, 'a belligerent, although he has annihilated the forces and conquered the whole of the territory of his adversary, and thereby brought the armed contention to an end, may nevertheless not choose to exterminate the enemy State by annexing the conquered territory, but may conclude a treaty of peace with the expelled or imprisoned head of the defeated State, re-establish its Government, and hand back to it the whole or part of the conquered territory. Subjugation takes place when a belligerent, after having annihilated the forces and conquered the territory of his adversary, destroys his existence by annexing the conquered territory' (op. cit., vol. ii, p. 467).

[2] See above at p. 112, note 1.

document was executed by representatives of the German High Command. It is generally accepted law that an instrument of surrender executed by military authorities is a purely military instrument and cannot do more than regulate the surrender of the military forces, unless, indeed, it be afterwards ratified by the political authorities.[1] It may be said that when the representatives of the German High Command executed this instrument there were no longer any German political or other authorities, and that, the High Command being the only German organization capable of exercising any authority in respect of Germany, the High Command must therefore be regarded as having been competent to act not only on behalf of the armed forces but also for Germany as a whole. It is not necessary to decide this question, for the Final Act of Unconditional Surrender does not purport to do more than to effect the surrender of the armed forces. It does, however, state that it is without prejudice to, and will be superseded by, any general instrument of surrender imposed by, or on behalf of, the United Nations and applicable to Germany and the German armed forces as a whole.[2] This imposed general instrument of surrender is the Berlin Declaration of 5 June 1945 which begins by reciting the fact of the 'unconditional surrender of Germany'.[3] This Declaration is not executed by any of the former German authorities, political or otherwise; it is executed by the occupying Powers by virtue of an authority over Germany which they already possess, and the mere fact of its unilateral imposition is evidence of the accomplished fact of the unconditional surrender of Germany as a whole. What is the relevance of this fact of unconditional surrender to the title of the occupying Powers to supreme authority in Germany? International law knows no title by surrender; where there is a surrender by the political authorities of a state the title is either conferred by cession or is acquired by subjugation. The Final Act of Unconditional Surrender of Germany is not a treaty executed by the former Government of Germany whereby that Government has abdicated its authority to the Allies; if it were, it would have conferred a title derived from the authority of that former Government. On the contrary, the former German Government had already ceased to exist; Admiral Dönitz's self-styled government was never recognized, was not in fact capable of exercising authority, was of doubtful legitimacy even in German municipal law, and in any case never executed the instrument of surrender. Obviously, therefore, the title of the occupying Powers is an original title by subjugation, and the juridical significance of the instrument of unconditional surrender is that it provides the best possible evidence of the complete conquest which is an essential ingredient of title by subjugation.[4]

[1] See Oppenheim, op. cit., p. 430. [2] Para. 4. [3] See above at p. 113.

[4] On the *original* nature of title by subjugation see Halleck, op. cit., at p. 470, where he dis-

Thus far we have considered the Allied occupation of Germany only in relation to what may be called the ordinary law of nations, and that relation is of obvious importance. Nevertheless, it would be a grave error to permit the consideration of the ordinary rules governing military occupations to obscure the fact that in the Allied occupation of Germany there are involved higher and much more important principles of international law and government. The rules of the ordinary law, formulated in the late nineteenth and early twentieth centuries, before the Covenant of the League of Nations, the Briand–Kellogg Pact, and the Charter of the United Nations, belong to a stage of international law which took aggressive war for granted and had temporarily abandoned the attempt to distinguish between just and unjust wars. This is not to say that these rules are obsolete; but it is certain that they are of themselves totally inadequate to meet contemporary needs. To hold that when a state wages aggressive total war contrary to its most solemn covenants, its occupation and control thereafter by members of the United Nations is in the last resort to be judged and limited by the ordinary laws of military occupation, would be to admit an anachronism of the most damaging kind.[1] Municipal law does not deal with a criminal by applying the individualistic concepts of the law of property.

It is not suggested, of course, that there are already formulated and accepted rules of this higher law; the most that can be claimed is that the situation in Germany provides an occasion appropriate for the development of a new legal technique and that this aspect of the situation should be recognized when considering the legality of the occupation and of the acts of the occupying Powers. It is possible, however, to lay down certain general principles by which the occupation ought to be judged and to which it ought to conform. First, if the occupying Powers are to claim rights under an international constitutional law, those rights must be exercised for constitutional purposes; that is to say, not for the individual benefit or aggrandizement of the occupying Powers (apart from the enforcement of just reparation) but in the interest and for the benefit of the

cusses the nature of 'conquest', using the term in the sense of completed conquest or subjugation: 'The rights of conquest are derived from *force* alone. They begin with possession, and end with the loss of possession. The possession is acquired by force, either from its actual exercise, or from the intimidation which it produces. There can be no antecedent claim or title, from which any *right* of possession is derived: for if so, it would not be a *conquest*. The assertion and enforcement of a *right* to possess a particular territory do not constitute a *conquest* of that territory.'

[1] See the Judgment of the International Military Tribunal at Nuremberg, *The Times* newspaper, 1 October 1946: 'In the opinion of the Tribunal the solemn renunciation of war as an instrument of national policy necessarily involves the proposition that such a war is illegal in international law; and that those who plan and wage such a war, with its inevitable and terrible consequences, are committing a crime in so doing. War for the solution of international controversies undertaken as an instrument of national policy certainly includes a war of aggression, and such a war is therefore outlawed by the pact.'

community of nations at large. Such a programme, indeed, the main item of which must be the effective control and re-education of a recalcitrant member of that community, the occupying Powers have laid down for themselves in the Potsdam Declaration of 2 August 1945.[1] Secondly, the occupation can no longer be considered the concern only of the occupying Powers themselves, but becomes the common concern of all the United Nations. If the government of Germany is to be carried on in the name of the United Nations, the ultimate responsibility of the occupying Powers must also inhere in the United Nations, who must, moreover, be allowed more than a nominal part in the determination of the policy to be followed. This principle again has been clearly recognized by the occupying Powers in their own declaration and Statements.[2]

IV. *Summary of conclusions*

The main propositions submitted in this article may be summarized as follows:

1. Supreme authority in Germany has been assumed by, and is vested in, the four Allied Governments jointly.

2. The exercise of that authority has been devolved upon the Commanders-in-Chief, each in his own zone, and jointly in the chief matters affecting Germany as a whole, thus providing a machinery through which the government of Germany can be carried on pending a final settlement. In exercising that authority, the Commanders-in-Chief are the agents of the four Allied Governments jointly, from whom their authority is derived.

3. Meanwhile, the German state still exists, having been deliberately kept in being by the Berlin Declaration of 5 June 1945.

4. A state of technical war continues to exist between the United Kingdom and the state of Germany.

5. The Allied occupation is not a belligerent occupation within the meaning of Articles 42–56 of The Hague Regulations.

6. The title of the Allied Governments to the rights they have assumed is founded in a form of completed conquest or subjugation; for although subjugation in its ordinary meaning is a conquest coupled with annexation of the enemy state, the same legal principles apply to a conquest coupled

[1] See *The Times* newspaper, 3 August 1945.

[2] See, for example, the Statement of the four occupying Governments of 5 June 1945: 'By the Declaration regarding the defeat of Germany issued at Berlin on the 5th June, 1945, the Governments of the United Kingdom, the United States of America and the Union of Soviet Socialist Republics, and the Provisional Government of the French Republic have assumed supreme authority with respect to Germany. The Governments of the four Powers hereby announce that it is their intention to consult with the Governments of other United Nations in connection with the exercise of this authority.'

See also the Berlin Declaration (p. 113 above) stated to be made by the Allied Representatives 'acting by authority of their respective Governments and in the interests of the United Nations'. Also para. 4 of the Final Act of Unconditional Surrender, quoted above in note 1, pp. 112–13.

with an assumption of the enemy's governmental powers, always provided the former enemy Government has ceased to exist. This new departure, which uses conquest to provide a machinery of international control instead of a machinery of aggrandizement, is a sublimation of the old law of conquest which may prove to be an important advance in international law.

7. The foreign relations of the German state are generally in a state of suspense, but the Allied Representatives may act on behalf of the German state in that regard and, in so far as they do so, the rights acquired and the obligations incurred will attach to the German state.

8. How far the Allied Representatives are bound to bring into renewed operation still-existing German treaties with third states entered into by the former German Government is a matter of some doubt. Those treaties clearly still bind the German state, but their operation might be regarded as being suspended pending the formation of a new German Government. There can be no doubt, however, that in so far as the Allied Representatives exercise rights under these treaties, or acquire control of German property to which they attach, the Allied Representatives are bound by the corresponding obligations. It must be noted, however, that such obligations would attach to the Allied Representatives, not to the Allied states; there is no succession of states, the question being only how far there is a succession of governments.

It is scarcely necessary to add that conclusions drawn little more than twelve months after the inception of the experiment in Germany are necessarily tentative. It would be foolish at this stage[1] to attempt any final assessment. The success or failure of the experiment is a matter which still lies in the future. Events are moving rapidly and there may be radical changes both in the structure and in the policy of the occupation. This much may be said, however: if properly used, this novel machinery of taking the government of a state into commission may add a powerful new instrument of control to the vocabulary of international law.

[1] October 1946.

[14]

PROLONGED MILITARY OCCUPATION: THE ISRAELI-OCCUPIED TERRITORIES SINCE 1967

*By Adam Roberts**

To what extent are international legal rules formally applicable, and practically relevant, to a prolonged military occupation? The question has assumed prominence because of the exceptional duration of the occupation by Israel of various territories that came under its control in the war of June 5–10, 1967. The situation there has had two classic features of a military occupation: first, a formal system of external control by a force whose presence is not sanctioned by international agreement; and second, a conflict of nationality and interest between the inhabitants, on the one hand, and those exercising power over them, on the other. In highlighting these features, the Palestinian uprising, or *intifada,* which began in Gaza and the West Bank in December 1987, has added urgency to the question of the law applicable to prolonged occupations.

There is a simple answer, and a perfectly serious one, to the central question addressed here. Israel has given express commitments over the years to implement the terms of a large number of treaties, and is also, like all states, bound by international customary law. These are solemn obligations. There is no need to engage in the laborious business of seeking to prove that any or every commitment passes an artificial test of "applicability" in a given situation. Rather, the burden of proof lies on an obligated state to show, if it can, that in the actual situation a given commitment does not apply. Hence, it can be asserted, simply but also persuasively, that the Israeli occupation of various territories has been, and continues to be, covered by a wide range of agreements, with which Israel must conform.

This simple answer, though important as a starting point, is not the last word on the subject because of two main considerations, which form the raison d'être of this article. First, in a number of statements Israeli spokesmen and courts have suggested that certain international rules were never formally applicable to the occupied territories, or else that their application may be qualified in some ways owing to special circumstances, one being the long duration of the occupation. The validity of these Israeli statements needs to be examined. Second, even if it is accepted that the rules governing occupations should be applied (whether out of formal legal obligation or as a matter of policy), the question remains whether these rules are relevant to the practical problems that arise in a prolonged occupation—and, indeed,

* Montague Burton Professor of International Relations, Oxford University; and Fellow of Balliol College.

This is an extensively revised version of a paper presented at a conference on the administration of occupied territories, Jerusalem, Jan. 22–25, 1988, organized by al-Haq, Ramallah. A book of papers from the conference, edited by Emma Playfair, will appear in due course.

whether implementation of the rules is likely to serve their underlying purposes. In particular, are the rules a straitjacket that inhibits political, legislative and economic change?

Although the present writer is a specialist in international relations rather than international law, the focus here is on legal issues. There are good reasons for this so far as the Israeli-occupied territories are concerned. First, the very concept of occupation, with its implicit assertion that external military control is temporary, is a triumph of legal thinking. Second, the appeal to general norms and standards has had great practical significance as regards the Israeli occupation: much of the international comment on it, especially within the framework of the United Nations, has emanated from legal as well as other considerations, or at least has been expressed in legal language.

Nevertheless, there are some hazards in discussing burning political issues in legal terms. Other methodologies—those of history and political science, even strategy and arms control—are necessary complements to law, and may be just as likely to assist understanding and to promote solutions. Moreover, while most international lawyers are, quite properly, cautious in their application of rules and principles to particular cases, sometimes law may get misused. The language of law can easily become a language of right and wrong, of moralistic reproach, of the clothing of interest in the garments of rectitude, of the concealment of factual changes with legal fictions, of refined scholasticism in the face of urgent practical problems, and of the facile application of general rules without a deep understanding of situations that are unique. Such approaches are hardly the highest expressions of law; nor are they necessarily the best way of addressing complex and multilayered international problems such as those encountered in the occupied territories.

Addressing as it does the single question of the rules applicable in a prolonged occupation, this article makes no attempt to assess the conduct of the Israeli occupation overall, or to cover the huge range of legal and practical issues to which it has given rise. For example, nothing is said here on such important and frequently raised matters as ill-treatment of detainees, since the basic pertinent rules are clear and are not affected by the duration of the occupation.

The article is divided into nine parts. The first three, which examine the law on occupations, are the most general; the rest deal centrally with the Israeli-occupied territories.

I. Purposes of the Law on Occupations

There is no single authoritative exegesis of the various purposes served by that part of the laws of war relating to military occupations—what is called here the "law on occupations." However, those purposes can be inferred from the principal conventions, from the events that gave rise to them, from their negotiating history, from military manuals, from court judgments and from writings.

The law on occupations is both permissive (accepting that an occupant exercises certain powers) and prohibitory (putting limits on the actions of various parties, including occupying powers). Briefly summarized, it can have the following purposes:

- Ensuring that those who are in the hands of an adversary are treated with humanity. (In this respect the rules on occupations serve a similar purpose to those on prisoners of war and internees.)

- Harmonizing these humanitarian interests with the military needs of the occupant.

- Preventing the imposition of disruptive changes in the occupied territory, and preserving the rights of the sovereign there. (Where the eventual disposition of territories awaits the outcome of peace negotiations, or the hold of the occupant might be reversed by the fortunes of war, there is a need for rules to inhibit any unilateral, drastic and permanent changes in the political, economic, social and legal orders.)

- Preserving military discipline among the occupying forces. (Occupations typically present problems—such as uncontrolled exercise of power, numerous points of friction between occupants and inhabitants—that can easily lead to looting, general disorder and a breakdown of military discipline. A modicum of rules is one safeguard against these dangers.)

- Reducing the risk that relations between occupant and occupied will get out of hand and lead to renewed conflict.

- Improving the chances that, if an occupant finds part of its own territory occupied, its population will in turn be treated with due regard to international norms. (Sometimes military occupations in war are concurrent, with each side holding some of the other's territory; or they may be consecutive, with a country that had been an occupant having part of its territory occupied. Either circumstance can give an additional incentive for observing rules.)

- Helping to maintain friendly relations between the occupying power and foreign states—whether allies, adversaries or neutrals.

- Facilitating the prospects for an eventual peace agreement.[1] (The prohibition of annexation of occupied territory, and the rules against transfers of populations into and from occupied territories, partly reflect this purpose.)

Whether the law has always succeeded in serving these purposes may be debated. Moreover, in any given situation determining the particular policies that will best reflect these purposes may well be a matter of delicate political judgment. However, the purposes themselves are enduring. They are not purely and simply humanitarian, but also practical—arising as they do from the interests and experiences of states over a long period.

As far as prolonged occupations are concerned, some or all of these purposes may remain important. Yet some may come to be seen as of less

[1] This can be inferred from, e.g., D. A. GRABER, THE DEVELOPMENT OF THE LAW OF BELLIGERENT OCCUPATION 1863–1914: A HISTORICAL SURVEY 37–40 (1949).

importance: to the extent that this is so, the detailed rules intended to reflect these purposes may be called into question.

II. Prolonged Occupations as a Distinct Category

An important, but implicit, assumption of much of the law on occupations is that military occupation is a provisional state of affairs, which may end as the fortunes of war change, or else will be transformed into some other status through negotiations conducted at or soon after the end of the war. However, many episodes during this century have called into question the assumption that occupations are of short duration. As Doris Appel Graber already noted in 1949:

> Considering the complexity of modern occupations, such as those during World War I and II in which large areas were occupied for long periods of time, raising a multitude of legal questions about the rights and duties of occupants in particular situations and the legal effects of the occupant's actions after the war, the rules laid down in the landmark codes of the 1863–1914 period and expounded in the literature and in military manuals seem fragmentary indeed and inadequate to guide occupation policies. But . . . they were developed in a relatively peaceful period in which no major wars occurred and in which belligerent occupations were generally of short duration so that occupants were not forced to assume the full governmental burdens which had rested on the displaced sovereign. Consequently, while general principles were evolved, few specific rules developed because of a lack of factual situations requiring application of specific rules often enough to permit their growth into law.[2]

In the period since the Second World War, there has been no shortage of cases of prolonged occupation, many of which have raised complex questions about the applicability and utility of international rules—rules that have of course developed significantly since Graber wrote. These occupations seem yet another proof of the paradox "Rien ne dure comme le provisoire."

The precise definition of "prolonged occupation" is likely to be a pointless quest. For the purpose of this article, it is taken to be an occupation that lasts more than 5 years and extends into a period when hostilities are sharply reduced—i.e., a period at least approximating peacetime.

A few examples from the post-1945 period are mentioned below. While by no means the only cases that might be viewed as prolonged occupations, they are sufficient to indicate how varied in character and purpose such occupations can be. Many of them have raised difficult questions: what body of international law applies in circumstances where the entire purpose of an occupation is (or ought to be) to bring about political change, rather than simply to preserve the status quo? And what rules apply when an occupation takes place (or continues) in peacetime?

[2] *Id.* at 290–91.

The Allied Occupations of Germany and Japan

The Allied occupations of Germany and Japan after the Second World War lasted for 10 and 6 years, respectively.[3] They defied the neat legal categories on which the law on occupations often seems to be based. These were not cases of subjugation and annexation; hence, they were military occupations of a kind. However, the victors wished to exercise their powers freely, and to make drastic political changes. They were not willing to be formally bound by the Hague Regulations.[4] One of the most cogent presentations of the argument for the Allied position suggested that the law of belligerent occupation had been designed to serve two purposes: (1) to protect the sovereign rights of the legitimate government of the occupied territory, and (2) to protect the inhabitants from being exploited for the prosecution of the occupant's war. Since neither of these purposes had much bearing on the situation the Allies faced, to have applied the law would have been "a manifest anachronism."[5] While this view of the applicability of the Hague Regulations was by no means uncontested, it did largely prevail. For those who found the Hague Regulations inapplicable, what rules of international law did apply to the Allied occupation of Germany after its unconditional surrender? Theodor Schweisfurth has said convincingly that this phase was subject to "such rules of international law as limit the right of any Government to commit acts which constitute crimes against peace and crimes against humanity."[6] Clearly, in these exceptional cases of prolonged occupation, any rules that could be interpreted as limiting the Allies' right to bring about significant political changes in the former Axis countries were deemed to be irrelevant.

Current and future military occupations, even postsurrender ones, cannot be governed by so few formal international rules as were these post-1945 cases. This is due to two legal developments. First, the fourth Geneva Convention would appear to be applicable to a future postsurrender occupation by virtue of its common Article 2.[7] Second, the development of

[3] The U.S. military occupation of Japan ended on Apr. 28, 1952, with the entry into force of the Peace Treaty between the two countries. The occupation by the three Western powers of West Germany ended on May 5, 1955. The Soviet occupation of East Germany can be said to have formally ended with the opening of diplomatic relations between the two countries on Sept. 20, 1955, following a Soviet government statement of Mar. 25, 1954. The city of Berlin remains in some technical sense occupied, and hence qualifies as a case of prolonged occupation, but the powers of the Allies are minimal.

[4] Convention respecting the Laws and Customs of War on Land, with annexed Regulations, Oct. 18, 1907, 36 Stat. 2277, TS No. 539, 205 Parry's TS 277.

On the UK discussion about the legal status of defeated Germany, see especially F. S. V. DONNISON, CIVIL AFFAIRS AND MILITARY GOVERNMENT: CENTRAL ORGANIZATION AND PLANNING 125–36 (1966).

[5] Jennings, *Government in Commission*, 23 BRIT. Y.B. INT'L L. 112, 135–36 (1946).

[6] *Germany, Occupation After World War II*, [Instalment] 3 ENCYCLOPEDIA OF PUBLIC INTERNATIONAL LAW 191, 196–97 (R. Bernhardt ed. 1982).

[7] Convention relative to the Protection of Civilian Persons in Time of War, Aug. 12, 1949, 6 UST 3516, TIAS No. 3365, 75 UNTS 287. *See* COMMENTARY ON THE GENEVA CONVENTIONS OF 12 AUGUST 1949: GENEVA CONVENTION RELATIVE TO THE PROTECTION OF CIVILIAN PERSONS IN TIME OF WAR 22 (J. Pictet ed. 1958) [hereinafter Pictet]; G. VON GLAHN,

international human rights law since 1945 has greatly enlarged the scope of rules of international law that place limits on the right of any government to commit whatever actions it pleases against those under its control. (This point will be discussed in part VI below.)

The U.S. occupation of the Ryukyu Islands, including Okinawa, lasted for 27 years, ending on May 14, 1972, in accord with the terms of the U.S.-Japanese Okinawa treaty of June 17, 1971.[8]

South Africa's Occupation of Namibia

The presence of South Africa in Namibia after its international mandate there was terminated by the United Nations in 1966 was increasingly viewed as an occupation—especially after the advisory opinion of the International Court of Justice in 1971.[9] In this case, as in that of the Israeli-occupied territories, the international community made clear that it would like to see certain positive changes introduced, leading to the emergence of a new sovereign state. Agreements signed in New York on December 22, 1988, specified that the South African presence in Namibia would come to an end after elections in November 1989.[10]

THE OCCUPATION OF ENEMY TERRITORY: A COMMENTARY ON THE LAW AND PRACTICE OF BELLIGERENT OCCUPATION 281, 283 (1957); UK WAR OFFICE, THE LAW OF WAR ON LAND: BEING PART III OF THE MANUAL OF MILITARY LAW 140 (1958); and M. GREENSPAN, THE MODERN LAW OF LAND WARFARE 216–17, 224–27 (1959).

There might thus seem to be at least a theoretical possibility that a future postsurrender occupation would be subject to the Geneva Convention but not to the Hague Regulations, inasmuch as the latter stress mainly the preservation of the status quo against the background of war, while the former puts somewhat more emphasis on the protection of the individual inhabitants. (Israeli courts have to some extent reversed this formula, having relied more on the Hague than the Geneva rules.) However, most, if not all, future postsurrender occupations would be brought within the ambit of the Hague Regulations because of several factors, including (1) they are customary in character; and (2) in relations between powers bound by the 1899 or 1907 Hague Conventions, the fourth Geneva Convention (Art. 154) states that it is "supplementary" to the Hague Regulations.

[8] Agreement concerning the Ryukyu Islands and the Daito Islands with related arrangements, June 17, 1971, United States-Japan, 23 UST 446, TIAS No. 7314. *See also* KEESING'S CONTEMPORARY ARCHIVES 24,715 (1971).

[9] Legal Consequences for States of the Continued Presence of South Africa in Namibia (South West Africa) notwithstanding Security Council Resolution 276 (1970), 1971 ICJ REP. 16 (Advisory Opinion of June 21).

Key UN resolutions on Namibia include the following. Before 1971: GA Res. 2145 (XXI) (Oct. 27, 1966) (terminating South Africa's mandate); GA Res. 2372 (XXII) (June 12, 1968) (referring several times to South Africa's "occupation" of South West Africa and proclaiming that it "shall henceforth be known as Namibia"); and SC Res. 284 (July 29, 1970). After the Court's advisory opinion, a consistent stream of UN resolutions referred specifically to South Africa's "illegal occupation" of Namibia. *See, e.g.*, SC Res. 301 (Oct. 20, 1971); SC Res. 366 (Dec. 17, 1974); SC Res. 385 (Jan. 30, 1976); GA Res. 2871 (XXVI) (Dec. 20, 1971); GA Res. 41/39 (Nov. 20, 1986); SC Res. 601 (Oct. 30, 1987); and GA Res. 43/26 (Nov. 17, 1988).

[10] *See* Agreement among the People's Republic of Angola, the Republic of Cuba, and the Republic of South Africa, Dec. 22, 1988, UN Doc. S/20346 (1988), *reprinted in* 28 ILM 957 (1989) (providing for implementation of SC Res. 435 (Sept. 29, 1978) on steps to establish

This occupation raised the question of what bodies of international law should be applied. In its 1971 advisory opinion, the International Court of Justice said that some multilateral conventions "such as those of a humanitarian character" may be viewed as binding as regards the occupation of Namibia.[11] For the purposes of the question it was addressing, it was not essential for the Court to specify which humanitarian conventions it had in mind: the important point is the endorsement of the applicability of international rules even though this occupation was seen as being marked by several exceptional features. In 1971 the UN General Assembly specifically urged South Africa to comply with the third and fourth 1949 Geneva Conventions in Namibia.[12]

The occupation of Namibia also raised the question of the legitimacy of resistance movements. This old and difficult question in the laws of war received in this case a simple answer. The General Assembly consistently supported the legitimacy of the armed struggle of the South West Africa People's Organization.[13] So, notably, did Vice-President Ammoun in his separate opinion to the 1971 ICJ judgment on Namibia.[14]

Some Other Recent Cases of Prolonged Occupation

The presence of Turkish forces in northern Cyprus since the invasion of July 20, 1974, has been viewed in some resolutions of the UN General Assembly as an occupation.[15]

The presence of Moroccan forces in Western Sahara since they intervened in December 1975 and January 1976 has similarly been viewed in some resolutions of the General Assembly as an occupation.[16]

The presence of Vietnamese forces in Kampuchea following the invasion of December 27, 1978, was also seen in some General Assembly resolutions as an occupation.[17] On April 5, 1989, the Governments of the three countries of Indochina (Vietnam, Laos and Kampuchea) announced that all Vietnamese "volunteer troops" would be withdrawn from Kampuchea by

Namibian independence); Agreement between the Government of the Republic of Cuba and the Government of the People's Republic of Angola for the Conclusions of the Internationalist Mission of the Cuban Military Contingent, Dec. 22, 1988, UN Doc. S/20345 (1988), *reprinted in* 28 ILM 959 (1989) (providing for staged withdrawal of Cuban troops from Angola). Elections to a constituent assembly were held in Namibia on Nov. 7–11, 1989. The last South African troops stationed in Namibia withdrew to their own country on Nov. 23–24, 1989.

[11] 1971 ICJ REP. at 55.

[12] *See, e.g.,* GA Res. 2871, *supra* note 9.

[13] *See, e.g., id.;* GA Res. 2403 (XXIII) (Dec. 16, 1968); and GA Res. S-14/1 (Sept. 20, 1986).

[14] 1971 ICJ REP. at 70.

[15] *See* GA Res. 33/15 (Nov. 9, 1978); GA Res. 34/30 (Nov. 20, 1979); and GA Res. 37/253 (May 13, 1983). In subsequent years, the question of Cyprus has been deferred by the General Assembly.

[16] GA Res. 34/37 (Nov. 21, 1979); and GA Res. 35/19 (Nov. 11, 1980). Subsequent resolutions do not use the term "occupation" but do reaffirm the need for self-determination. *See, e.g.,* GA Res. 43/33 (Nov. 22, 1988).

[17] GA Res. 37/6 (Oct. 28, 1982); GA Res. 40/7 (Nov. 5, 1985); and GA Res. 43/19 (Nov. 3, 1988).

September 30, 1989, regardless of whether or not a political solution to the Kampuchean conflict had been found.[18]

Many other situations quite widely viewed as occupations could be cited. For example, the intervention of Soviet forces in Afghanistan between December 1979 and the conclusion of their phased departure on February 15, 1989, was called an occupation by many governments.[19]

* * * *

The idea that "prolonged occupation" is a special category of occupation should be set in the proper context, namely, that there are many different types of occupation: the present writer has tentatively suggested seventeen types—a listing that is far from exhaustive. Neither the law as laid down in international conventions nor state practice justifies the restrictive approach of viewing the law on occupations as applying only to the classic case of belligerent occupation, in which one belligerent occupies the territory of another belligerent during an armed conflict. The law on occupations has in fact been applied to a wider range of cases than this: it is properly viewed as being formally applicable to, and capable of being applied in, many types of occupation—and, indeed, many situations to which the opprobrious term "occupation" is not actually attached. It contains some notable elements of flexibility.[20]

While the frequent occurrence of long occupations is beyond dispute, there are some grounds for doubt about the value of regarding them as constituting a special category. The danger in making such a suggestion is that it may seem to imply the further suggestion that those parts of the laws of war that deal with military occupations may not be fully applicable, and that departures from the law may be permissible. These conclusions would pose problems, especially if the applicability of major conventions were put in doubt, if the criteria for permitting departures from the law were vague and subjective, or if it were unclear what bodies have authority to suggest or make departures. However, it may be that departing from occupation law is not the only legal issue to be faced. There may also be some scope for variations *within* the framework established by existing international law. The laws of war treaties that govern occupations contain some scope for variations.

[18] KEESING'S RECORD OF WORLD EVENTS 36,588 (1989). Vietnam was subsequently reported to have completed this withdrawal in the week ending Sept. 30, 1989, but without supervision by international observer forces.

[19] *See, e.g.*, British statement of July 13, 1982, *quoted in* 53 BRIT. Y.B. INT'L L. 352 (1982).

[20] Occupations that have differed in some respects from the classic case of a belligerent occupation include that of the Rhineland after 1918, the Franco-Belgian occupation of the Ruhr in 1923–1925, the German occupation of Bohemia and Moravia from March 1939, and Namibia since 1971. In these cases, certain courts and tribunals have accepted the use of the term "occupation" and the applicability of international rules, including, e.g., the Hague Regulations. Roberts, *What Is a Military Occupation?*, 55 BRIT. Y.B. INT'L L. 249, 275, 278, 291–92 (1984).

Further, in a prolonged occupation the applicability of other bodies of law—including the international law of human rights—assumes special importance.

While there may be some dangers in regarding "prolonged occupation" as a special category, there are also very good reasons for doing so. At present, there is a distinct risk that the law on occupations, if not adapted to special problems arising in a prolonged occupation, could be used or abused in such a way as to contribute to leaving a society politically and economically undeveloped. During a long occupation, many practical problems may arise that do not admit of mere temporary solutions based on the idea of preserving the status quo ante: decisions may have to be taken about such matters as road construction, higher education, water use, electricity generation and integration into changing international markets. Such decisions, although they involve radical and lasting change, cannot be postponed indefinitely. Nor can the setting up of political institutions be postponed indefinitely without creating the theoretical possibility (and in the West Bank and Gaza it is more than theoretical) that the law on occupations could be so used as to have the effect of leaving a whole population in legal and political limbo: neither entitled to citizenship of the occupying state, nor able to exercise any other political rights except of the most rudimentary character. If there is any risk at all that the law on occupations might provide, paradoxically, the basis for a kind of discrimination that might bear comparison with apartheid, the causes of that risk need to be identified, and possible solutions explored.

The category of prolonged occupation overlaps in certain respects with another category—peacetime occupation. Some writers have taken the view that in peacetime occupations the rights accruing to an occupant may be more limited than in the classic case of belligerent occupation. Thus, F. Llewellyn Jones wrote in 1924:

> In the case of pacific occupation it is clear that the rights of the occupant are very much curtailed as compared with those of a belligerent occupant. In the latter case the occupant is an enemy, and has to protect himself against attack on the part of the forces of the occupied State, and he is justified in adopting measures which would justly be considered unwarranted in the case of pacific occupation. . . . Belligerent military occupation is now largely regulated by the provisions of the Hague Convention, 1907, and obviously a pacific military occupant can have no powers more extensive than those laid down in the Articles of this Convention.[21]

Following this general approach, it could be argued that in a prolonged occupation, as in a pacific one, the rights of the occupants are vastly curtailed. This conclusion is very persuasive; and it conforms with the approach adopted in the fourth Geneva Convention, discussed in the next part. However, this conclusion can hardly follow automatically in all cases, or on all issues. For example, if there is extensive and violent opposition to the occu-

[21] Jones, *Military Occupation of Alien Territory in Time of Peace*, 9 GROTIUS SOC'Y, TRANSACTIONS 149, 159–60 (1924). *See also* Roberts, *supra* note 20, at 273–79.

pation, or a general terrorist threat to the nationals of the occupying power, there may be a situation somewhat akin to war, in which the prolongation of certain emergency measures can be justified.

In a prolonged occupation there may be strong reasons for recognizing the powers of an occupant in certain specific respects—for example, because there is a need to make drastic and permanent changes in the economy or the system of government. At the same time, there may be strong reasons for limiting the occupant's powers in other respects. An examination of past occupations suggests that any variations in the rules may have a more complex and multifaceted character than simply the curtailment of the rights of one party or another.

III. Prolonged Occupations in the Principal Conventions

The following are the main conventions that set out rules relating to the conduct of military occupations. All of them entered into force within 1–3 years of the date of signature.

The fourth 1907 Hague Convention has 37 states parties.[22] Whether or not a state is a party to this Convention is of limited significance, because the annexed Hague Regulations have since at least 1946 been widely and authoritatively viewed as embodying customary international law.[23]

The fourth 1949 Geneva Convention (like the other three 1949 Geneva Conventions) has 166 states parties.[24] This remarkably high number is one of several factors that have strengthened arguments that the Conventions are, in whole or in substantial part, declaratory of customary international law.[25]

[22] Also, 18 out of the 48 states parties formally bound by the very similar terms of the second 1899 Hague Convention did not become parties to the 1907 agreement. Convention with respect to the Laws and Customs of War on Land, July 29, 1899, 32 Stat. 1803, TS No. 403. Most of the provisions of the regulations annexed to these two Conventions are identical.

Information about states parties to the second 1899 Convention and the fourth 1907 Convention supplied by the depositary (the Netherlands Ministry of Foreign Affairs), and valid as of July 1, 1988. *See* DOCUMENTS ON THE LAWS OF WAR 44 and 58–59 (A. Roberts & R. Guelff 2d ed. 1989) [hereinafter Roberts & Guelff].

In addition, some states became bound by these two Hague Conventions through general declarations of succession to treaties (e.g., at the time of independence), even if they have not so notified the depositary. This explains why some sources give higher figures for states parties. According to the U.S. Department of State, the number of parties to the second 1899 Convention and the fourth 1907 Convention are 56 and 43, respectively. DEPARTMENT OF STATE, TREATIES IN FORCE: A LIST OF TREATIES AND OTHER INTERNATIONAL AGREEMENTS OF THE UNITED STATES IN FORCE ON JANUARY 1, 1989, at 363 and 363–64.

[23] For the leading judgment to this effect, see 22 TRIAL OF THE MAJOR WAR CRIMINALS BEFORE THE INTERNATIONAL MILITARY TRIBUNAL, NUREMBERG 497 (1948). Note also Meron's statement that "the customary law status of the Regulations annexed to the Convention is universally recognized." T. MERON, HUMAN RIGHTS AND HUMANITARIAN NORMS AS CUSTOMARY LAW 226 (1989).

[24] International Committee of the Red Cross [ICRC], List of Signatures, Ratifications, etc. (Jan. 31, 1989); and Addendum (Feb. 7, 1989).

[25] For an excellent discussion, see Meron, *The Geneva Conventions as Customary Law*, 81 AJIL 348 (1987). *See also* T. MERON, *supra* note 23, at 41–62.

The 1954 Hague Cultural Property Convention has 75 states parties; 63 of these are also bound by the 1954 Hague Protocol.[26] Various important powers—including China, Japan, the United Kingdom and the United States—are not yet formally bound by this Convention.

The 1977 Geneva Protocol I has 92 states parties.[27] Several important powers—including France, India, Indonesia, Japan, the United Kingdom and the United States—are not formally bound by this Protocol. However, some of its provisions are viewed as embodying customary law; and other provisions may be viewed, even by nonparties, as meriting inclusion in the rules governing their military operations.[28]

In none of the above agreements is any formal limit set on the duration of an occupation. Inasmuch as the subject of duration is addressed at all, it is more in writings and judgments than in conventions.[29] Meir Shamgar is correct in saying:

> According to International Law the exercise of the right of military administration over the territory and its inhabitants had no time-limit, because it reflected a factual situation and pending an alternative political or military solution this system of government could, from the legal point of view, continue indefinitely. Military government does not derogate from the potential rights of either party but represents a minimum standard imposed by the Law of Nations and is co-extensive in time and space to the effective rule of the military.[30]

This is certainly a good starting point for considering the whole question of prolonged occupation. The proposition that the basic rules codified in the law on occupations must continue to be observed for as long as the occupation lasts is a useful compass bearing to guide one through this difficult subject.

[26] Convention and Protocol for the Protection of Cultural Property in the Event of Armed Conflict, May 14, 1954, 249 UNTS 240. Information about states parties supplied by the depositary (UNESCO), and valid as of July 1, 1988. *See* Roberts & Guelff, *supra* note 22, at 367–70.

[27] Protocol Additional to the Geneva Conventions of 12 August 1949, and Relating to the Protection of Victims of International Armed Conflicts (Protocol I), *opened for signature* Dec. 12, 1977, 1125 UNTS 3. For information about states parties, see ICRC, List of Signatures, Ratifications, etc. (Nov. 3, 1989). The figure 92 includes the USSR, which ratified this Protocol (and Protocol II, on noninternational armed conflicts) on Sept. 29, 1989.

[28] *See, e.g.,* President Reagan's Letter of Transmittal of Protocol II to the U.S. Senate, S. TREATY DOC. NO. 2, 100th Cong., 1st Sess., at III (1987); and T. MERON, *supra* note 23, at 62–70.

[29] Although a great deal of published writing has some bearing on the subject, very few papers or articles have been specifically devoted to prolonged occupation either in general or in the Arab-Israeli context. There have not been any such articles in some of the journals where they might have been expected, e.g., the *Israel Yearbook on Human Rights*, the *Revue Egyptienne de Droit International* and the *Palestine Yearbook of International Law*. Falk, *Some Legal Reflections on Prolonged Israeli Occupation of Gaza and the West Bank*, 2 J. REFUGEE STUD. 40 (1989), is very much the exception.

[30] Shamgar, *Legal Concepts and Problems of the Israeli Military Government—the Initial Stage*, in 1 MILITARY GOVERNMENT IN THE TERRITORIES ADMINISTERED BY ISRAEL: THE LEGAL ASPECTS 13, 43 (M. Shamgar ed. 1982) [hereinafter MILITARY GOVERNMENT]. For statements on the same issue in Supreme Court judgments, see *infra* text at notes 177 and 178.

The "One Year After" Provision of 1949

While the condition of military occupation (or, more euphemistically, "military administration") may continue indefinitely, there is, or used to be, one formal provision for variation of the rules on the grounds of duration. This was Article 6, paragraph 3 of the fourth 1949 Geneva Convention:

> In the case of occupied territory, the application of the present Convention shall cease one year after the general close of military operations; however, the Occupying Power shall be bound, for the duration of the occupation, to the extent that such Power exercises the functions of government in such territory, by the provisions of the following Articles of the present Convention: 1 to 12, 27, 29 to 34, 47, 49, 51, 52, 53, 59, 61 to 77, 143.[31]

These provisions represent one attempt to address the issue of prolonged occupation. However, they are of little importance, for four main reasons.

First, Article 6, paragraph 3 has featured very little in legal analyses of prolonged occupations in the past 40 years; and the Israeli authorities have never invoked it as a means of reducing their obligations.[32]

Second, in particular cases, including the Israeli-occupied territories, there might be scope for debate about whether, or when, there was, in the words of Article 6, a "general close of military operations."[33] The renewed outbreak of international war in 1973 has been only one of several events that might have given rise to the argument that, even if military operations had earlier been viewed as closed, they had now reopened and, in consequence, the fourth 1949 Geneva Convention was again applicable *in toto.*

Third, even if Article 6, paragraph 3 were invoked, many important provisions of the Convention would remain in force. The burden of the article is that from 1 year after the general close of military operations an occupying power is only obliged to observe 43 of the 159 articles of the Convention. However, these 43 do include no less than 23 of the 32 articles of that part of the Convention—section III—which deals most specifically with occupied territories. The 43 articles are important, covering as they do such matters as the humane treatment of protected persons.

In section III (Articles 47–78), the nine articles by which the occupying power would cease to be bound in a long occupation are 48 (dealing with

[31] Fourth Geneva Convention, *supra* note 7, Art. 6, para. 3.

[32] E. Cohen, Human Rights in the Israeli-Occupied Territories 1967–1982, at 51 (1985). Cohen also reports the opinion of Shabtai Rosenne, a legal adviser to the Israeli foreign ministry, given in a 1977 interview, that

> the period of one year after the general cessation of hostilities set by the framers of Article 6 was arbitrary. While not admitting to the applicability of the Convention to the Israeli occupied territories, he felt that all the humanitarian provisions of the Convention, and not just those provided in Article 6, should be applied *de facto* . . ..

Id. at 62 n.103.

[33] For an analysis written in 1969 or 1970 claiming that there had been no "general close of military operations" and that the Geneva Convention therefore remained fully applicable, see Hammad, *The Culprit, the Targets and the Victims,* in 2 The Arab-Israeli Conflict 366 (J. N. Moore ed. 1974).

foreign nationals in occupied territory), 50 (care and education of children), 54 (status of public officials and judges), 55 (food and medical supplies of the population), 56 (medical and hospital services), 57 (requisitioning of civilian hospitals), 58 (ministers of religion and articles for religious needs), 60 (relief consignments) and 78 (assigned residence and internment). The contents of these articles suggest that the framers of the 1949 Geneva Conventions may have optimistically assumed that, in the course of time, the rigors of occupation would gradually ease, and more and more responsibilities would be handed over to the institutions of the occupied territory.

The records of the 1949 Diplomatic Conference confirm this assumption. They show that the "one year after" provision in Article 6 was the subject of much debate.[34] In his *Commentary*, Jean Pictet states that in drawing up this provision, "the delegates naturally had in mind the cases of Germany and Japan." He goes on to defend the provision on the grounds that "if the Occupying Power is victorious, the occupation may last more than a year, but as hostilities have ceased, stringent measures against the civilian population will no longer be justified."[35]

The final reason for doubting the importance of the provisions of Article 6, paragraph 3 of the fourth Geneva Convention is that Article 3(b) of Additional Protocol I effectively abrogates the "one year after" provision —at least so far as the parties to the Protocol are concerned. It states that "the application of the Conventions and of this Protocol shall cease, . . . in the case of occupied territories, on the termination of the occupation." Bothe, Partsch and Solf say of this abrogation:

> Article 6(3) of the Fourth Convention . . . was a special *ad hoc* provision for certain actual cases, namely the occupation of Germany and Japan after World War II. There is no reason to continue to keep in force such provisions designed for specific historic cases. In 1972 the majority of government experts expressed a wish to abolish these time limits.[36]

The abrogation of the "one year after" rule may reflect in part the proper desire of the international community to maintain the applicability of the law to occupations in general, and to areas occupied by Israel since 1967 in particular. However, the abandonment of Article 6, paragraph 3 has had little practical relevance to the Israeli-occupied territories. This was more because of the factor already mentioned (these provisions of Article 6 were

[34] *See, e.g.*, 2A FINAL RECORD OF THE DIPLOMATIC CONFERENCE OF GENEVA OF 1949, at 623–25.

[35] Pictet, *supra* note 7, at 62–63. In addition, Pictet suggests that where there has been no military resistance, no state of war and no armed conflict, the Convention will remain fully applicable as long as the occupation lasts. However, it is far from clear (1) whether this was the intention of the negotiators; and (2) what the logic is in treating such occupations differently.

[36] M. BOTHE, K. PARTSCH & W. SOLF, NEW RULES FOR VICTIMS OF ARMED CONFLICTS 59, also 57 (1982). *See also* COMMENTARY ON THE ADDITIONAL PROTOCOLS OF 8 JUNE 1977 TO THE GENEVA CONVENTIONS OF 12 AUGUST 1949, at 68 (Y. Sandoz, C. Swinarski & B. Zimmermann eds. 1987).

not invoked by Israel anyway) than because of the more legalistic point that Israel has neither signed nor ratified Protocol I.

In general, the "one year after" provision of 1949 must be viewed as a legal oddity. It may have correctly identified a problem—that the rules designed for belligerent occupation during a war may require some modification in a prolonged occupation—but the solution it proposed was not equally appropriate to all occupations, and it has not commended itself greatly to military administrators, inhabitants of occupied territories or international lawyers.

Other Possibilities of Variations

The main conventions relating to military occupations do not provide for any other variation in the rules specifically because of the length of an occupation. This omission does not mean that the conventions are inflexible or cumbersome on this matter. Rather, they contain a modest number of rules, intended primarily to prevent repetition of the worst excesses of previous occupation regimes. They do not govern all aspects of life, and their provisions leave substantial room for different policies, practices and administrative systems. There are in fact many general possibilities for variations, and these could be germane in a prolonged occupation, as well as in other cases.

The scope for variation within the existing conventions is illustrated by the matter of the occupant's structure of authority, which can assume many different forms. The 1907 Hague Regulations refer variously to "the hostile army," "the occupant," "a commander-in-chief," "the commander in the locality occupied," "an army of occupation" and "the occupying State" as the bodies or individuals that exercise authority in occupied territory.[37] The fourth Geneva Convention, which refers throughout to the "Occupying Power" as the body with authority in occupied territory, says nothing about the precise administrative form of the occupation regime. Protocol I is identical in this regard. There is widespread agreement that the occupying power has substantial discretion as to whether it operates through a military or a civil administration, and whether through an imposed administrative system or indigenous authorities.[38]

[37] 1907 Hague Regulations, *supra* note 4, Arts. 42, 43, 48, 49, 51, 52, 53 and 55.

[38] In K.N.A.C. v. State of the Netherlands, 16 Ann. Dig. 468 (Dist. Ct. The Hague 1949), the court said:

> Though the régime envisaged by the Hague Regulations for occupied territory comprised a military administration with civil departments subordinate to it, the setting up by the Occupant of a separate civil administration to control the existing civil administration left functioning, was not forbidden and must, on the contrary, be held to be a permissible complement of the maintenance of the latter administration in office.

Id.

In the Ansar Prison case (No. H.C. 593/82) (July 13, 1983), telex transcript 13, the Israeli Supreme Court said, apropos of Israel's occupation of parts of Lebanon: "the application of the third chapter of the Hague Rules or of the parallel instructions in the Fourth [Geneva] Convention are not conditioned upon the establishment of a special organizational framework in the

Some possibilities of variations are also evident in the rules on taxation. The Hague Regulations state in Article 48:

> If, in the territory occupied, the occupant collects the taxes, dues, and tolls imposed for the benefit of the State, he shall do so, as far as is possible, in accordance with the rules of assessment and incidence in force, and shall in consequence be bound to defray the expenses of the administration of the occupied territory to the same extent as the legitimate Government was so bound.[39]

Commenting on this article, Ernst Feilchenfeld says:

> The provision would not seem to exclude, as has been asserted, taxation increases, particularly such changes as have been made desirable through war conditions or, in the case of an extended occupation, general changes in economic conditions.
>
> . . . [I]f the occupation lasts through several years the lawful sovereign would, in the normal course of events, have found it necessary to modify tax legislation. A complete disregard of these realities may well interfere with the welfare of the country and ultimately with "public order and safety" as understood in Article 43.[40]

Special agreements between the high contracting parties are allowed for in the fourth Geneva Convention. Such agreements can be about practically any matter, as long as the principle spelled out in Article 7, paragraph 1 is observed: "No special agreement shall adversely affect the situation of protected persons, as defined by the present Convention, nor restrict the rights which it confers upon them." In section III (on occupied territories), Article 47 further specifies that protected persons shall not be deprived of the benefits of the Convention "by any agreement concluded between the authorities of the occupied territories and the Occupying Power."[41]

IV. The Israeli-Occupied Territories

In the wake of the June 1967 war, Israel was in control of the following territories.

The West Bank. This is the area, previously under Jordanian rule, that lies between the River Jordan and Israel proper (i.e., Israel in its pre-1967 borders). On December 17, 1967, the Israeli military government issued an order stating that "the term 'the Judea and Samaria Region' shall be identi-

---

form of a Military Government . . .." For extracts and a short summary of this leading judgment, see 13 Isr. Y.B. Hum. Rts. 360 (1983).

On various possible forms of administrative structure under occupation, see U.S. Dep't of the Army, The Law of Land Warfare 10, 139 and 141 (Field Manual No. 27-10, 1956); and UK War Office, *supra* note 7, at 145. For an indication that there are limits to the constitutional changes an occupying power may bring about, see Pictet, *supra* note 7, at 273.

[39] 1907 Hague Regulations, *supra* note 4, Art. 48.

[40] E. Feilchenfeld, The International Economic Law of Belligerent Occupation 49 (1942).

[41] Fourth Geneva Convention, *supra* note 7, Arts. 7(1) and 47.

cal in meaning for all purposes . . . to the term 'the West Bank Region'." This change in terminology, which has been followed in Israeli official statements since that time, reflected a historic attachment to these areas and rejection of a name that was seen as implying Jordanian sovereignty over them.[42] The 1978 Camp David accords, signed by Egypt and Israel, contained extensive provisions for a "self-governing authority" in the West Bank and Gaza; these provisions—heavily criticized by Arab governments, by the leadership of the Palestine Liberation Organization (PLO) and by the residents of the territories—were never implemented.[43]

The Gaza Strip. This area was administered from 1948 to 1967 by Egypt, which did not claim sovereignty over it. Israeli official statements generally refer to it as "the Gaza Region." Gaza was mentioned both in the 1978 Camp David accords and in the 1979 Israel-Egypt Treaty of Peace (see below).

East Jerusalem. This area, previously part of the West Bank, came under Israeli law, with extended boundaries, on June 28, 1967, and was formally annexed on July 30, 1980.[44]

The Golan Heights. This area, part of Syria, has been under Israeli control since 1967. In the 1973 Middle East war, Israel gained additional Syrian territory in the area. Following the 1974 Israeli-Syrian disengagement agreement, Israel withdrew from all this additional territory, and also from some areas occupied in the 1967 war, including the devastated town of Quneitra.[45] Israeli law was extended to the Golan Heights on December 14, 1981.[46]

The Sinai Peninsula. This area, part of Egypt, came under Israeli control in 1967. For administrative purposes, the Israeli authorities divided it into two military government units: Northern Sinai (which was comparatively more inhabited), and Central and Southern Sinai (containing only a sparse Bedouin population). Israel withdrew progressively from Sinai—initially under two partial disengagement agreements, concluded in 1974 and 1975;[47] and

[42] Rubinstein, *The Changing Status of the "Territories" (West Bank and Gaza): From Escrow to Legal Mongrel*, 8 TEL AVIV U. STUD. IN L. 61 (1988). On Jordan's 1988 disengagement from the West Bank, see *infra* text at note 120.

[43] Camp David Agreements, Sept. 17, 1978, Egypt–Israel–United States, 17 ILM 1466 (1978).

[44] The enabling legislation for the extension of Israeli law and of municipal boundaries was the Municipalities Ordinance (Amendment No. 6) Law, June 27, 1967, 21 LAWS OF THE STATE OF ISRAEL 75 (1967). The act of annexation was the Basic Law: Jerusalem, Capital of Israel, July 30, 1980, 34 *id.* at 209 (1980). For a succinct Israeli exposition, see Y. BLUM, THE JURIDICAL STATUS OF JERUSALEM (Jerusalem Papers on Peace Problems No. 2, Hebrew University, 1974).

[45] Agreement on Disengagement between Israeli and Syrian Forces, May 31 and June 5, 1974, 13 ILM 880 (1974). The Israeli military withdrawal to the new lines was completed by June 26, 1974.

[46] Golan Heights Law, Dec. 14, 1981, 36 LAWS OF THE STATE OF ISRAEL 7 (1982).

[47] Agreement on Disengagement of Forces in Pursuance of the Geneva Peace Conference, Jan. 18, 1974, Egypt-Israel, 13 ILM 23 (1974), which provided for the withdrawal of all Israeli forces from the areas they had held west of the Suez Canal since the cease-fire at the end of the

then under the 1979 Peace Treaty, which laid down a timetable for phased total Israeli withdrawal, completed on April 25, 1982.[48] In 1989 Israel withdrew, additionally, from a small remaining disputed area at Taba.[49]

Although East Jerusalem and the Golan Heights have been brought directly under Israeli law, by acts that amount to annexation, both of these areas continue to be viewed by the international community as occupied, and their status as regards the applicability of international rules is in most respects identical to that of the West Bank and Gaza.[50]

In addition to the above territories, Israel briefly occupied parts of southern Lebanon during the Litani operation of March–June 1978. It occupied larger areas of Lebanon following the invasion of June 1982, and has maintained a security zone in the south since its withdrawal from the rest of the country in 1985. Although Israel did not establish a formal military-administrative system in Lebanon along the same lines as in other areas, its position was properly viewed as that of an occupant.[51]

For the most part, the Israeli occupation of territories since 1967 does belie the assumption that occupation is temporary. However, this brief listing shows that prolonged occupation does not necessarily mean permanent control: at least some areas, Sinai and part of the Golan, were returned (to Egypt and Syria, respectively) after long spells under Israeli control.

A full political analysis of the reasons for the exceptional length of this occupation is beyond the scope of this article. The problems of ethnicity and nationhood in the Middle East, which are thrown into such sharp relief in

---

1973 war, and for an Israeli pullback east of the canal to the area covered by the Mitla and Giddi Passes; and Agreement on the Sinai and Suez Canal, Egypt-Israel, Sept. 4, 1975, and various associated agreements, 14 ILM 1450 (1975), which provided for an Israeli withdrawal from a further 2,500 square miles of occupied Egyptian territory in Sinai, including the oil fields at Ras Sudar and Abu Rudeis, in return for certain Egyptian political undertakings, and on the basis of major pledges and commitments by the United States. Full implementation of the latter agreement was completed on Feb. 22, 1976.

On the background, content and implementation of these agreements, and the role of the United States and United Nations, see KEESING'S CONTEMPORARY ARCHIVES 26,317, 27,429 and 28,381 (1974, 1975 and 1977).

[48] Treaty of Peace, Mar. 26, 1979, Egypt-Israel, 18 ILM 362 (1979). Article II stated: "The permanent boundary between Egypt and Israel is the recognized international boundary between Egypt and the former mandated territory of Palestine. . . . without prejudice to the issue of the status of the Gaza Strip."

[49] Agreement Regarding the Permanent Boundary Between Egypt and Israel, Feb. 26, 1989, 28 ILM 611 (1989). This Agreement followed the Egypt-Israel arbitral tribunal award of Sept. 29, 1988, 27 ILM 1421 (1988). The disputed area at Taba was returned to Egypt on Mar. 15, 1989.

[50] *See, e.g.,* UN General Assembly and Security Council resolutions, *infra* notes 79, 86–88 and 153. The Israeli laws on the status of East Jerusalem and the Golan Heights do not use the word "annexation" and do not extend Israeli citizenship to the local population.

[51] It was so viewed by the Israeli Supreme Court in the Ansar Prison case, *supra* note 38, 13 ISR. Y.B. HUM. RTS. at 362–63. A question in the Knesset on Mar. 23, 1983, yielded the answer that the provisions of the fourth Geneva Convention were applied in Lebanon "on humanitarian grounds," implying that the Convention was not viewed as formally applicable. Rubinstein, *supra* note 42, at 63.

the occupied territories, have deep historical roots. The outside powers involved in the area in the past, including Britain, did not resolve these problems and may have made them worse. Throughout this century, most attempts to achieve a negotiated settlement of Jewish-Arab tensions in the Middle East have failed. Since 1967, Israel has maintained its occupation for a mixture of reasons that have included understandable security concerns, religious-fundamentalist expansionism and inertia. The situation was made more difficult to the extent (which is a matter of debate) that the PLO, Arab states and/or Israel failed to come forward with credible proposals for the future of the occupied territories. Such proposals necessarily involve grasping many extremely painful nettles: acceptance of the existence of Israel; the creation of a Palestinian state that might be radical, or unstable, or both; and possible conflict within Arab states, or between them, if the Palestinian cause or the PLO leadership is alleged to have been "betrayed" in a diplomatic compromise. Numerous other real or presumed obstacles to political settlement could be cited: various aspects of PLO, and Israeli, activities and pronouncements; and Israel's refusal to engage in direct talks with the PLO. At the superpower level, there has been a long history of disagreement between the United States and the USSR on the nature of the Middle East conflict and possible means of its amelioration. In this, as in some other cases of prolonged occupation, there can be no assumption that apportionment of blame for the length of the occupation will be a productive exercise, or will yield simple answers.

The Israeli occupation since 1967 has contained many special features quite apart from its unusual duration. These features, which inevitably inform the discussion in this article, include (1) the undecided previous legal status of the West Bank and Gaza; (2) the dispute over whether the Palestinians constitute an appropriate unit of self-determination; (3) the persistence of a threat to Israel itself, and of various types of violent incidents, all of which have tended to erode neat distinctions between "war" and "peace"; and (4) the existence among Israelis of expansionist and annexationist ideas of various kinds, which call into doubt the very idea of Israel as having only a provisional role in the occupied territories.

V. Applicability of the Law on Occupations to the Israeli Occupation

To consider how the law may be interpreted or varied to take account of the prolonged character of a particular occupation, it is first necessary to survey, at least briefly, some of the main viewpoints on what laws of war rules have been viewed as applicable to that occupation anyway.

The facts about states parties to treaties are straightforward: the states most directly involved (Israel, Egypt, Jordan and Syria) are formally bound by the principal international agreements governing occupations as follows:[52]

[52] See *supra* notes 22–27 for the sources of depositary information about the states parties to these agreements, their customary law status, and details of declarations, reservations, etc.

The fourth 1907 Hague Convention. None of the states involved has ever been a formal party. However, in view of the customary law status of the Regulations annexed to the Convention, all are bound.

The four 1949 Geneva Conventions. Israel and Jordan ratified these agreements in 1951, Egypt in 1952, and Syria in 1953.

The 1954 Hague Cultural Property Convention, and Protocol. Egypt ratified both in 1955, Jordan both in 1957, and Syria both in 1958; Israel ratified the Convention in 1957, and registered its accession to the Protocol in 1958.

The 1977 Geneva Protocol I. Israel has not made any indication of adherence; Egypt has signed but not ratified; Jordan ratified in 1979; and Syria acceded in 1983.[53]

The Official Israeli View

Israeli positions on the applicability of international legal norms in the occupied territories are complex and occasionally misunderstood. There have been some variations over time, and in different forums. They have to be seen against the background of changing political views about the significance or otherwise of the "green line" separating Israel proper from the land held since 1967; and official use of such terms as "administered territories," rather than the blunter "occupied territories." The seminal legal statement remains that by Shamgar in 1971, which first advanced the argument that the terms of an agreement whose *de jure* applicability might be in doubt could nevertheless be applied on a *de facto* basis.[54]

This principle applies particularly to the fourth 1949 Geneva Convention. Since the end of the June 1967 war, Israel has never stated that the Convention is formally applicable in the occupied territories on a *de jure* basis. However, it has indicated, along the lines advanced by Shamgar in 1971, that it is willing to observe the "humanitarian provisions" of this Convention.[55] For some years, Israel's voting on UN General Assembly

[53] Syria, at accession in November 1983, made a declaration that its accession to Protocol I in no way amounts to recognition of Israel or the establishment of any relations with it regarding the application of the Protocol.

In a note to the depositary, Israel objected to this declaration: "the Geneva Conventions and the Protocols are not the proper place for making such hostile political pronouncements, which are, moreover, in flagrant contradiction to the principles, objects and purposes of the Conventions and the Protocols." The Syrian declaration "cannot in any way affect whatever obligations are binding . . . under general international law or under particular conventions." As for the substance of the matter, Israel would adopt towards Syria "an attitude of complete reciprocity." Roberts & Guelff, *supra* note 22, at 466–67.

[54] Shamgar, *The Observance of International Law in the Administered Territories*, 1 ISR. Y.B. HUM. RTS. 262–77 (1971). This very influential article was first presented at a symposium at Tel Aviv University in 1971, when the author was Attorney General.

[55] *Id.* at 266; and Rubinstein, *supra* note 42, at 63. The latter refers to Order No. 3 as evidence that immediately after the 1967 war it seemed clear that the Convention would apply to the territories. However, that proclamation was in fact issued during the war; and, as he notes, the section mentioning the Convention was repealed soon after the war.

resolutions reflected the view that the applicability of the Convention was an open question; but since 1977, it has voted against *de jure* applicability.[56]

As to the 1907 Hague Regulations, whose provisions are briefer and more general, the present position is simpler. Their applicability, whether on a *de facto* or a *de jure* basis, is widely accepted.[57] Esther Cohen has gone so far as to say that "no problem arises in regard to the Hague Regulations. . . .. The official Israeli position is that these Regulations are applicable to the Israeli-occupied territories . . .." She has indicated that the only real question about the applicability of the Regulations concerns areas (East Jerusalem and the Golan Heights) that Israel has in effect sought to annex.[58] However, in the late 1970s, some authoritative statements cast doubt on the formal applicability of the Hague Regulations.[59] Some Supreme Court judgments before 1979 avoided expressing a view on whether the Hague Convention applied to the administered areas.[60] Since the 1979 decision of the Supreme Court in the *Beth-El* case, a more positive view about the applicability and justiciability of the Hague Regulations has prevailed, based largely on acceptance that they are part of customary law.[61]

Israel deserves credit for acknowledging openly, albeit inadequately, the relevance of international legal standards. Its position contrasts with those of the many occupying powers in the past 40 years that have avoided expressing any view on the applicability of international legal agreements: such powers have included the Soviet Union in Hungary (1956), Czechoslovakia (1968) and Afghanistan (1979); and South Africa in Namibia. Israel also deserves credit for cooperating with the International Committee of the Red Cross, which has played an important role in the occupied territories by performing a wide range of tasks, including, in particular, monitoring conditions of detention.[62]

Nevertheless, Israel's position regarding the fourth Geneva Convention is unsatisfactory in several respects, and merits closer scrutiny. The scope of

[56] Resolutions on the applicability of the fourth Geneva Convention on which Israel abstained: GA Res. 3092A (XXVIII) (Dec. 7, 1973); GA Res. 3240B (XXIX) (Nov. 29, 1974); and GA Res. 31/106B (Dec. 16, 1976). Since 1977, Israel has always voted against the applicability of the Convention: *see infra* note 87.

[57] *See* Shamgar, *supra* note 54; *see also* Shamgar, *supra* note 30, at 48; Nathan, *The Power of Supervision of the High Court of Justice over Military Government*, in MILITARY GOVERNMENT, *supra* note 30, at 109, 129, 131–32 and 163–66. Nathan says re the Preamble to the Hague Convention: "This language would appear to express the intention of the parties . . . that insofar as the Regulations embody norms of international law, these are binding as minimum standards of international law, even in situations not directly covered by the Regulations." *Id.* at 132.

[58] E. COHEN, *supra* note 32, at 43, 51 and 58 nn.49, 50.

[59] For elements of such doubt about the fourth Hague Convention, see the Israeli Ministry of Foreign Affairs, Memorandum of Law (Aug. 1, 1977), 17 ILM 432, 432–33 and 442 (1978) (on offshore oil exploration in the Gulf of Suez). *See also infra* note 162 and accompanying text.

[60] *See infra* note 175 and accompanying text.

[61] *See infra* text at notes 166–79.

[62] See the ICRC statement on the 20th anniversary of the occupation, ICRC BULL., No. 137, June 1987, at 1, noting that the ICRC has had free access to all the occupied territories, but listing a number of "persistent violations" of the fourth Geneva Convention.

application of the Convention is stated in common Article 2, whose first two paragraphs read as follows:

> In addition to the provisions which shall be implemented in peacetime, the present Convention shall apply to all cases of declared war or of any other armed conflict which may arise between two or more of the High Contracting Parties, even if the state of war is not recognized by one of them.
>
> The Convention shall also apply to all cases of partial or total occupation of the territory of a High Contracting Party, even if the said occupation meets with no armed resistance.[63]

The publicly stated grounds for Israel's skepticism about the applicability of the Convention relate to the pre-1967 status of the West Bank and Gaza. Before 1967, Israel did not accept that these territories were part of Jordan and Egypt, respectively. The territories therefore could not be viewed as "the territory of a High Contracting Party" within the meaning of the second paragraph of common Article 2; rather, they had been under Jordanian and Egyptian occupation. Israel expressed concern that by accepting the automatic application of the Convention, it might appear to accord Jordan and Egypt the status of an ousted sovereign with reversionary rights.[64]

This Israeli interpretation is open to several serious objections. Four principal ones are: (1) It has sometimes been based on what appears to be a technical error. To refer to the terms of the *second* paragraph of common Article 2 is of limited relevance, because it is in fact the *first* paragraph that applies when a belligerent occupation begins during a war. As shown above, this paragraph says nothing about "the territory of a High Contracting Party," referring simply to "all cases of declared war or of any other armed conflict" arising between two or more of the high contracting parties.[65] (2) The Israeli interpretation was never relevant to those occupied territories (Sinai and the Golan) whose pre-1967 status was not disputed by Israel,

[63] Fourth Geneva Convention, *supra* note 7, Art. 2, paras. 1–2.

[64] The clearest expositions of this Israeli view are in Blum, *The Missing Reversioner: Reflections on the Status of Judea and Samaria*, 3 ISR. L. REV. 279 (1968); Shamgar, *supra* note 30, at 13–60; and Farhi, *On the Legal Status of the Gaza Strip*, in MILITARY GOVERNMENT, *supra* note 30, at 61–83.

Crown Prince Hassan Bin Tallal of Jordan has denied that Jordan's position in the West Bank up to 1967 was that of occupant. He does not specify the precise status Jordan did have there. He argues that even if Jordan was a belligerent occupant up to 1967, it would not follow that Israel was free of legal limitations after 1967—especially in light of the provisions of the Geneva Convention. H. BIN TALLAL, PALESTINIAN SELF-DETERMINATION: A STUDY OF THE WEST BANK AND GAZA STRIP 67–68 (1981).

[65] For an authoritative Israeli statement relying on the second paragraph of common Article 2, see Shamgar, *supra* note 54, at 262–77. See also his revised presentation (responding to the argument that the relevant paragraph is the first, not the second) in Shamgar, *supra* note 30, at 37–40.

For a commentary on Article 2, see Pictet, *supra* note 7, at 21, which leaves little room for doubt that it is the first paragraph that is relevant to the territories occupied by Israel in the 1967 war.

which were therefore clearly "the territory of a High Contracting Party." (3) It has not been advanced consistently: similar objections could be, but seldom have been, made about the applicability of the Hague Regulations, which contain a similar assumption; namely, that occupied territory is "territory of the hostile state." (4) The Israeli position ignores or understates the precedents for viewing the laws of war, including the law on occupations, as being formally applicable even in cases that differ in some respect from the conditions of application spelled out in the Hague Regulations and the Geneva Conventions.[66]

In fact, Israel has got into a little-noted logical muddle on the applicability of the Hague and Geneva Conventions. Distinguished Israeli lawyers have asserted that the status of belligerent occupation is dependent on the continued existence of a state of war between two countries. As Yoram Dinstein put it in 1978: "Belligerent occupation continues as long as the occupant remains in the area and war goes on. That is to say, it is terminated if the occupant withdraws from the area or the war comes to a close (either with the occupant's victory or his defeat)."[67] Likewise, the Supreme Court indicated in a judgment on March 15, 1979, that the application of the law was linked to a state of belligerency.[68] However, since the Israeli-Egyptian Peace Treaty of March 26, 1979, there has been no state of belligerency between Israel and Egypt. Thus, the Gaza Strip has even more certainly than before not been "territory of the hostile state." Yet Israel has continued to justify its powers and actions there with reference to the law of belligerent occupation, including the Hague Regulations.[69] This is reasonable; but it shows that Israel itself, when it chooses, is prepared to depart from its own strict legal logic about the circumstances in which the relevant rules and conventions are applicable.

Several Israeli writers have argued that whether the fourth Geneva Convention is formally applicable or not is academic because of Israel's stated willingness to observe the "humanitarian provisions."[70] However, formal applicability versus *de facto* application is not always a distinction without a

[66] *See supra* note 20.

[67] Dinstein, *The International Law of Belligerent Occupation and Human Rights*, 8 ISR. Y.B. HUM. RTS. 105 (1978).

[68] Justice Witkon, judgment in the Beth-El case (H.C. 606/78 and 610/78), *translated in* MILITARY GOVERNMENT, *supra* note 30, at 371, 374:

> Each of us obviously knows of recent political developments that have occurred in our region, of the peace negotiations . . . . We deal with the rights of the parties according to the existing situation prevailing between Israel and the Arab countries. This situation is one of belligerency, and the status of the respondents in respect of the occupied territory is that of an occupying power.

On the *Beth-El* case, see also *infra* text at notes 166–71.

[69] *See* Dinstein, *The Israel Supreme Court and the Law of Belligerent Occupation: Reunification of Families*, 18 ISR. Y.B. HUM. RTS. 173, 173–74 (1988).

[70] *See, e.g.*, Haim H. Cohn, *Foreword* to THE RULE OF LAW IN THE AREAS ADMINISTERED BY ISRAEL, at vii–viii (Israel National Section of the International Commission of Jurists, 1981); M. BENVENISTI, THE WEST BANK DATA PROJECT: A SURVEY OF ISRAEL'S POLICIES 37 (American Enterprise Institute, 1984); and Shamgar, *supra* note 30, at 32–33 and 42–43.

difference, for three main reasons. First, although the term "humanitarian provisions" is often interpreted to mean all of the provisions, Israel has never definitively clarified this point by specifying which provisions it regards as humanitarian. Second, the rejection of formal applicability has frequently been referred to in Israeli court proceedings, and has in the past been one of several factors making the courts reluctant to base their decisions fairly and squarely on the fourth Geneva Convention.[71] Third, the hint of *ex gratia* about Israel's application of the Convention could be construed as carrying an implication that it might unilaterally interpret, or eventually abrogate, its terms.

Israel's refusal to accept the full *de jure* applicability of the fourth Geneva Convention has not proved persuasive. It has been criticized by many legal writers, including some in Israel itself;[72] and, as mentioned below, it has been decisively rejected by virtually all the members of the international community—at least if their votes in the United Nations are a guide.[73]

PLO Views

There has never been a full and authoritative exposition of PLO views on the international legal status of the territories occupied by Israel since 1967. The PLO has been in something of a quandary, principally because of the organization's commitment in the 1968 Palestinian National Covenant: "Palestine, with the boundaries it had during the British mandate, is an indivisible territorial unit."[74] Consequently, for a long time the PLO was reluctant to draw clear legal distinctions between the lands controlled by Israel before and after June 1967. The fact that until 1984 the PLO had no specialized agencies concerned with legal aspects of the Palestine question contributed to the confusion.[75]

The PLO has sometimes advanced the view that Israel is an aggressor or illegal occupant, and as such has no rights over the inhabitants under international law. The concept of "illegal occupation," and the related proposition that an illegal occupant has no rights, have precedents, not least in the writings of some Soviet and Polish lawyers about the Nazi occupations in the Second World War.[76] In 1970 a PLO Research Center Publication took this

[71] On the Supreme Court's position in this regard, see *infra* text at notes 165–73.

[72] For a reasoned account and criticism by a leading Israeli international lawyer, see Dinstein, *supra* note 67, especially at 106–08. *See also* E. COHEN, *supra* note 32, at 51–56; and Rubinstein, *supra* note 42, at 63–67. For a critical view by a British academic, see J. R. GAINSBOROUGH, THE ARAB-ISRAELI CONFLICT: A POLITICO-LEGAL ANALYSIS 159 (1986).

[73] *See infra* notes 86–88 and accompanying text.

[74] Art. 2, Palestinian National Covenant, adopted by the PLO at its National Congress in Cairo in July 1968. The boundaries of Palestine during the British Mandate (which ended in 1947) encompassed all of the territory of Israel in its 1949–1967 frontiers, plus the Gaza Strip and the West Bank; they had also encompassed Jordan until 1922. For the text and exposition of Article 2, including discussion of whether it involves a claim to Jordan, see Y. HARKABI, THE PALESTINIAN COVENANT AND ITS MEANING 33–39 and 113 (1979).

[75] 2 PALESTINE Y.B. INT'L L. 191 (1985).

[76] *See especially* Trainin, *Questions of Guerrilla Warfare in the Law of War, trans. from Russian and reprinted in* 40 AJIL 534, 535 (1946).

line.[77] Likewise, in 1981 a PLO document submitted to UNESCO about Military Order 854 of July 6, 1980 (which sought to bring higher education in the occupied territories under Israeli control), challenged the right of the Israeli authorities to justify it "on the basis of statements 'under international law' made by foreign authors in completely different contexts . . . because the existing occupation . . . has been illegalized by the Community of Nations which unanimously requested putting an end to it on various occasions and in many resolutions."[78]

What these Palestinian writers appear to be suggesting is not that the law on occupations is not applicable at all, but rather that Israel cannot claim any rights under that law. This argument is questionable on several grounds. First, it is debatable whether Israel was an "aggressor" in 1967, or acted out of a basically defensive intent. There is also reason to doubt whether the occupation itself (as distinct from some of the actions by the occupying power) has been definitively considered illegal by the international community.[79] But these points pale into insignificance beside the cardinal principle that the laws of war, including the law on occupations, are widely viewed as applying equally to all states, whether aggressors or victims of aggression. Moreover, it seems strange to insist that Israel or any other country could be expected to carry out all its obligations under the conventions, without at the same time having certain rights, or at least being "suffered" by international law to take certain actions.

This Palestinian view has not commanded any significant international support, and by no means all Palestinian writers on these matters have

[77] F. YAHIA, THE PALESTINE QUESTION AND INTERNATIONAL LAW 184 (PLO Research Center, Beirut, 1970).

[78] UNESCO Doc. 22 C/18 (Aug. 30, 1983).

[79] The term "illegal occupation" has been used sparingly in UN resolutions. As regards the Israeli-occupied territories, GA Res. 32/20 (Nov. 25, 1977) expressed concern "that the Arab territories occupied since 1967 have continued, for more than ten years, to be under illegal Israeli occupation." The term was also used in GA Res. 33/29 (Dec. 7, 1978). These resolutions were the exception rather than the rule. The voting figures for each resolution, showing countries for and against and abstentions (102-4-29 and 100-4-33, respectively), contain substantially fewer votes in favor than most General Assembly resolutions criticizing the Israeli occupation attracted in those years.

Some resolutions have implied the illegality of the occupation per se, without actually using the term "illegal occupation." For example, GA Res. 43/54A (Dec. 6, 1988) "[*c*]*ondemns* Israel's continued occupation of the Palestinian territory occupied since 1967, including Jerusalem, and the other occupied Arab territories, in violation of the Charter of the United Nations, the principles of international law and the relevant resolutions of the United Nations." Voting was 103-18-30.

The great majority of the numerous resolutions of the UN General Assembly and the Security Council on the Israeli occupation have not stated that it is illegal per se. They have deplored Israel's conduct of the occupation, have condemned as illegal the purported annexation of parts of the occupied territories (including Jerusalem), and have called upon Israel to put an end to its occupation of Arab territories—but have not stated that the fact of the occupation is in itself illegal. *See, e.g.*, GA Res. 41/63 (Dec. 3, 1986) and GA Res. 43/58A–G (Dec. 6, 1988). The omission of the term "illegal occupation" from most UN resolutions on the Arab-Israeli conflict is in sharp contrast to its repeated use in those on Namibia. *See supra* note 9.

subscribed to it.[80] In statements in the last few years, the PLO has not reiterated the view, and indeed may have retreated from it in changing its policy in the direction of gradual acceptance of the existence of Israel.[81] However, there does not appear to have been a clear PLO statement formally renouncing this view.

The Idea of "Trustee Occupation"

International laws and institutions, including the United Nations, have long recognized the reality that certain territories and peoples are not self-governing, and that outside powers can exercise certain trustee-like functions in such territories.[82] Could Israel's occupation be viewed as at least an analogous case?

The idea that Israel's occupation of the West Bank might be of a special kind termed "trustee occupation" was advanced by Allan Gerson in 1973 and 1978.[83] His reasoning in support of this proposition was, briefly, as follows: Since Israel's rights to sovereignty over the West Bank are not superior to those of either Jordan or the indigenous population, Israel's status is that of occupant, not lawful sovereign. Yet the law of belligerent occupation imposes heavy constraints on the alteration of the political status quo ante—constraints that may be contrary to the interests of the inhabitants of the West Bank, as any momentum towards self-determination may be stifled. This reasoning reflects real concerns and points to a central problem in applying the law on occupations in these territories.

Nevertheless, there is doubt about the extent to which "trustee occupation" can usefully be viewed as a distinct legal category. Gerson himself leaves some doubt about what body of law would apply in such a case. In fact, as noted above, under its common Article 2, the fourth Geneva Convention is applicable to a wide range of occupations and not just to "belligerent occupation" narrowly defined. Moreover, some idea of "trusteeship" is implicit in all occupation law anyway. Finally, the central question, which has become even more difficult since Gerson wrote, is whether Israel could be viewed, either by Palestinians or by the international community, as an appropriate trustee for Palestinian interests. However, he does frankly accept that Israel has not in fact assumed the role of "trustee occupant."[84]

[80] Palestinian works that appear to accept that the occupied territories are subject to the normal rules relating to occupations include R. SHEHADEH, OCCUPIER'S LAW: ISRAEL AND THE WEST BANK (Institute for Palestine Studies, Washington, D.C., 1985); and Kassim, *Legal Systems and Developments in Palestine,* 1 PALESTINE Y.B. INT'L L. 19, 29–32 (1984). However, neither of these studies contains a sustained and concentrated discussion of what parts of international law are applicable in the occupied territories.

[81] *See infra* text at note 121.

[82] See, e.g., the provisions regarding non-self-governing territories, and also regarding the trusteeship system, in UN CHARTER Arts. 73–85.

[83] Gerson, *Trustee Occupant: The Legal Status of Israel's Presence in the West Bank,* 14 HARV. INT'L L.J. 1 (1973); A. GERSON, ISRAEL, THE WEST BANK AND INTERNATIONAL LAW 78–82 (1978).

[84] A. GERSON, *supra* note 83, at 82.

The View of the International Community

The view that the fourth Geneva Convention is applicable, and should be applied, in all the territories occupied by Israel since 1967 has been very widely held internationally. Indeed, a remarkable degree of unanimity prevails on this matter. Countless international organizations, both intergovernmental and nongovernmental, have taken this view.[85] Within the UN General Assembly, it has been upheld from the beginning of the occupation.[86] Since 1973, Israel has completely lacked positive support in the voting on General Assembly resolutions on this specific issue.[87] Since the beginning of the occupation, the Security Council has also consistently urged the applicability of the Convention.[88]

* * * *

[85] The ICRC has done so consistently. See ICRC, *Annual Reports* for 1968 and subsequent years; and its statement, *supra* note 62.

[86] The first such resolution, urging in general terms respect for the principles contained in the third and fourth 1949 Geneva Conventions, was GA Res. 2252 (ES-V) (July 4, 1967) (116-0-2) (the figures in parentheses are votes for, votes against and abstentions).

In 1968 came the first of a stream of resolutions making specific comments about the occupied territories, and calling on Israel to comply with the fourth Geneva Convention, as well as with various other agreements, including the 1948 Universal Declaration of Human Rights. *See* GA Res. 2443 (XXIII) (Dec. 19, 1968) (60-22-37). Similar resolutions in the first 5 years of the occupation included GA Res. 2727 (XXV) (Dec. 15, 1970) (52-20-43); and GA Res. 3005 (XXVII) (Dec. 15, 1972) (63-10-49). The resolutions in this period attracted less support than the 1967 resolution cited above, and less than those from 1973 onwards mentioned in note 87. There are many possible reasons for this: one that should not be overlooked is that in these years the resolutions tended to combine statements about what law was applicable with other, more contentious statements.

[87] See, e.g., the following resolutions (in all cases of a negative vote, i.e., from 1977 onwards, it is Israel's):

GA Res. 3092A (XXVIII)	(Dec. 7, 1973)	(120-0-5)
GA Res. 3240B (XXIX)	(Nov. 29, 1974)	(121-0-7)
GA Res. 32/5	(Oct. 28, 1977)	(131-1-7)
GA Res. 35/122A	(Dec. 11, 1980)	(141-1-1)
GA Res. 38/79B	(Dec. 15, 1983)	(146-1-1)
GA Res. 41/63B	(Dec. 3, 1986)	(145-1-6)
GA Res. 43/58B	(Dec. 6, 1988)	(148-1-4)

The United States voted for these resolutions in some years (1973, 1974 and 1980), and abstained in the others. However, the United States continued to state that it viewed the Convention as applicable. "The United States recognizes Israel as an occupying power in all of these territories and therefore considers Israeli administration to be subject to the Hague Regulations of 1907 and the 1949 Fourth Geneva Convention concerning the protection of civilian populations under military occupation." U.S. DEPARTMENT OF STATE, COUNTRY REPORTS ON HUMAN RIGHTS PRACTICES FOR 1987, 100th Cong., 2d Sess. 1189 (1988).

[88] For example, SC Res. 237 (June 14, 1967), adopted unanimously (4 days after the cease-fire came into effect), recommended to the governments concerned "the scrupulous respect of the humanitarian principles governing the treatment of prisoners of war and the protection of civilian persons in time of war contained in the Geneva Conventions of 12 August 1949."

SC Res. 446 (Mar. 22, 1979), adopted by 12 votes to none, with 3 abstentions (Norway, the United Kingdom and the United States), reaffirmed the applicability of the fourth Geneva Convention, as well as opposing the establishment of Israeli settlements in the occupied territories.

None of the various attempts to argue that Israel's occupation of foreign territory is such a special case that some of the normal provisions of the law on occupations do not apply to it has proved persuasive: indeed, all these attempts have been based, in varying degrees, on dubious interpretations of the body of conventional and customary law relating to occupations. The better view is that both the fourth 1949 Geneva Convention and the 1907 Hague Regulations are applicable. However, serious problems remain: not only of getting their applicability accepted, and seeing that their basic provisions are applied, but also of relating the law to particular problems of prolonged occupation.

VI. Applicability of Human Rights Law

This is not the place to examine all the arguments concerning the applicability of the international law of human rights to military occupations generally.[89] Suffice it to say that (1) this question is but a part of the larger one of the applicability of multilateral conventions in occupied territories;[90] (2) the main impetus for UN action after 1945 to develop human rights law was the near-universal reaction against Nazi oppression in Germany and in German-occupied territories in the Second World War;[91] (3) the scope-of-application provisions of human rights accords do not exclude their applicability in principle, even if they do, as noted below, permit certain derogations in time of emergency; (4) the idea of "respect for human rights in armed conflicts" has been stressed in numerous UN and other resolutions since at least the late 1960s;[92] and (5) in some decisions, international courts and tribunals have affirmed the applicability of human rights law in occupied territories either implicitly (Namibia[93]) or explicitly (northern Cyprus[94]).

SC Res. 605 (Dec. 22, 1987) was strongly critical of Israeli conduct and reaffirmed that the Convention "is applicable to the Palestinian and other Arab territories occupied by Israel since 1967, including Jerusalem." This resolution was adopted by 14 votes to none, with one abstention (the United States). Two weeks later, SC Res. 607 (Jan. 5, 1988), adopted unanimously, reaffirmed the applicability of the Convention.

[89] *See* Roberts, *The Applicability of Human Rights Law During Military Occupations*, 13 REV. INT'L STUD. 39 (1987).

[90] *See* Meron, *Applicability of Multilateral Conventions to Occupied Territories*, 72 AJIL 542 (1978), *reprinted* (with slight alterations) *in* MILITARY GOVERNMENT, *supra* note 30, at 217.

[91] W. BISHOP, JR., INTERNATIONAL LAW: CASES AND MATERIALS 470 (3d ed. 1971).

[92] See, e.g., GA Res. 2444 (XXIII) (Dec. 19, 1968) (adopted unanimously), which is on respect for human rights in armed conflicts generally; and the numerous General Assembly resolutions urging respect for human rights in specific armed conflicts and occupations, including those on the Israeli-occupied territories cited in note 99 *infra*.

[93] In its advisory opinion on Namibia, the International Court of Justice may have had human rights law in mind (as well as the laws of war, often called international humanitarian law) when it pointed to the applicability of "certain general conventions such as those of a humanitarian character." 1971 ICJ REP. at 46, 55 and 57.

[94] The European Commission of Human Rights ruled applications by the Government of Cyprus in respect of the Turkish occupation admissible in *Cyprus v. Turkey*. *See* 1975 Y.B. EUR. CONV. ON HUM. RTS. 82 (Nos. 6780/74 and 6950/75, Decision of May 26, 1975); and 1978 *id.* at 100 (No. 8007/77, Decision of July 10, 1978). The European Convention for the

The more specific question of the applicability of human rights law in the Israeli-occupied territories has been extensively discussed.[95] Cohen has suggested that in a prolonged occupation certain human rights accords may provide a useful guide for an occupying power, and should therefore be followed as a matter of policy:

> [T]he concept of human rights was taken into account in drafting the Geneva Conventions, including the Fourth Geneva Convention.
>
> Nevertheless, the Fourth Convention was designed to protect the civilian population under an essentially temporary occupation. While the Convention remains applicable to a large extent during the prolonged belligerent occupation phase, it is insufficient to ensure adequate protection for the needs of the civilian population during that phase. Further protection is called for. It is submitted that the Universal Declaration and the International Covenants on Human Rights may be used to guide the belligerent occupant in the administration of the territory occupied, just as civilian governments may be guided by these laws in the administration of their own territories.
>
> Thus, in certain areas not covered by the Convention, such as economic rights, which involve a certain dynamism and initiative in order to avoid the stagnation which would result in their violation, the concept of human rights can serve to breathe new life into an otherwise stalemated situation.[96]

The Israeli Government has frequently indicated a skeptical attitude towards the applicability of human rights instruments. One official publication has implied that human rights are totally dependent on the existence of peace; it has cited Article 4 of the 1966 International Covenant on Civil and Political Rights selectively, conveniently omitting all reference to those clauses of the article which spell out that certain general obligations, and certain specific provisions of the Covenant, continue to apply even in time of public emergency.[97]

Protection of Human Rights and Fundamental Freedoms, Nov. 4, 1950, 213 UNTS 221, Art. 1, states that the high contracting parties shall secure certain rights and freedoms to everyone "within their jurisdiction." The Commission found:

> [T]his term is not equivalent to or limited to "within the national territory" of the High Contracting Party concerned. . . . [T]he High Contracting Parties are bound to secure the said rights and freedoms to all persons under their actual authority and responsibility, not only when that authority is exercised within their own territory but also when it is exercised abroad.

1978 Y.B. EUR. CONV. ON HUM. RTS. at 230.

[95] *See particularly* Meron, *The International Convention on the Elimination of All Forms of Racial Discrimination and the Golan Heights*, 8 ISR. Y.B. HUM. RTS. 222 (1978); and Meron, *West Bank and Gaza: Human Rights and Humanitarian Law in the Period of Transition*, 9 *id.* at 106 (1979); *see also* Meron, *supra* note 90.

[96] E. COHEN, *supra* note 32, at 29.

[97] MINISTRY OF DEFENCE, CO-ORDINATOR OF GOVERNMENT OPERATIONS IN JUDEA-SAMARIA AND THE GAZA DISTRICT, JUDEA-SAMARIA AND THE GAZA DISTRICT: A SIXTEEN-YEAR SURVEY (1967–1983) 60 (1983). For the International Covenant on Civil and Political Rights, Dec. 16, 1966, see 999 UNTS 171.

A particularly clear exposition of the Israeli view on the applicability of human rights accords is contained in a memorandum prepared by the Office of the Legal Adviser in the Israeli Foreign Ministry in 1984. Written in response to an inquiry about the applicability of seven human rights accords, the memorandum asserts that Israeli policy in the West Bank and Gaza was in accord with the provisions of the 1950 Agreement on the Importation of Educational, Scientific and Cultural Materials; the 1960 Convention against Discrimination in Education; and the 1966 International Convention on the Elimination of All Forms of Racial Discrimination. However, in respect of some other agreements (the 1948 Universal Declaration of Human Rights and the two 1966 International Covenants), the memorandum says:

> The unique political circumstances, as well as the emotional realities present in the areas concerned, which came under Israeli administration during the armed conflict in 1967, render the situation *sui generis*, and as such, clearly not a classical situation in which the normal components of "human rights law" may be applied, as are applied in any standard, democratic system in the relationship between the "citizen" and his government. Hence the criteria applied in the areas administered by Israel, in view of the *sui generis* situation, are those of "humanitarian law", which balances the needs of humanity with the requirements of international law to administer the area whilst maintaining public order, safety and security.[98]

This passage contains a serious argument, namely, that much human rights law is about the relations between the citizen and his own government and is therefore not necessarily appropriate to the rather different circumstance of occupation. Nevertheless, it is doubtful whether human rights law only applies in "a classical situation," and the memorandum itself does not view all human rights law in this rather limited way. Its insistence that the relevant criteria are those of "humanitarian law" (i.e., the Hague Regulations and the Geneva Conventions) seems evasive in view of the elements of ambiguity in Israel's attitude towards the applicability of the fourth Geneva Convention.

A very strong case can be made for asserting the general applicability of human rights standards to military occupations, but this does not solve many problems. The relevance of the international law of human rights to the prolonged Israeli occupation needs to be assessed in individual cases, taking the following points into account.

1. There are different views on the exact legal status of some international agreements relating to human rights, including the 1948 Universal Declaration, whose applicability in the occupied areas has been urged in numerous UN General Assembly resolutions.[99]

[98] Office of the Legal Adviser, memorandum (Sept. 12, 1984), *written for, and contained in*, A. ROBERTS, B. JOERGENSEN & F. NEWMAN, ACADEMIC FREEDOM UNDER ISRAELI MILITARY OCCUPATION 80, 81 (World University Service, London/International Commission of Jurists, Geneva, 1984).

[99] *See, e.g.*, GA Res. 2443 (XXIII) (Dec. 19, 1968); GA Res. 2546 (XXIV) (Dec. 11, 1969); GA Res. 2727 (Dec. 15, 1970); and the subsequent annual resolutions entitled "Report of the

2. Fewer states are parties to the international conventions on human rights than to the Geneva Conventions. For example, on December 31, 1988, the four Geneva Conventions had 165 states parties, including all the states in the area; whereas the two International Human Rights Covenants had 92 and 87 parties, respectively. Egypt, Jordan and Syria are parties to both Covenants. Israel has signed both but has not ratified them.[100]

3. Many human rights conventions permit derogations from some of their provisions, for example, in time of public emergency. Israel is obviously inclined to view its military occupation, especially in the context of continuing armed conflict or internal revolt, as constituting such an emergency.

4. Over a wide range of issues, the laws of war rules regarding military occupations, as laid down in the Hague Regulations and the Geneva Conventions, may offer more extensive, detailed and relevant guidance than can the general human rights conventions;[101] and their supervisory machinery may be more appropriate to the circumstances.

5. On a few specific issues, there may be an element of conflict between the law on occupations and human rights law. For example, Article 13(1) of the Universal Declaration says: "Everyone has the right to freedom of movement and residence within the borders of each state." Article 78, paragraph 1 of the fourth Geneva Convention says: "If the Occupying Power considers it necessary, for imperative reasons of security, to take safety measures concerning protected persons, it may, at the most, subject them to assigned residence or to internment."[102]

6. There are some issues (such as discrimination in employment, discrimination in education and the import of educational materials) that are addressed in considerable detail in certain human rights agreements, and are not so addressed in the law on occupations. In respect of such issues, the application of international human rights standards is highly desirable.

Special Committee to Investigate Israeli Practices Affecting the Human Rights of the Population in the Occupied Territories." For the Universal Declaration of Human Rights, see GA Res. 217A (III), UN Doc. A/810, at 71 (1948).

[100] *See* note 24 *supra* and accompanying text. For the Covenant on Civil and Political Rights, *supra* note 97, and the Covenant on Economic, Social and Cultural Rights, GA Res. 2200 (Dec. 16, 1966), see MULTILATERAL TREATIES DEPOSITED WITH THE SECRETARY-GENERAL: STATUS AS AT 31 DECEMBER 1988, at 120, 130, UN Doc. ST/LEG/SER.E/7 (1989).

Syria, at accession to the Covenants in April 1969, made a declaration to the same effect as that of its declaration on Protocol I, *supra* note 53. In a note to the depositary in July 1969, Israel objected to this declaration.

[101] Possible overlap between human rights law and the laws of armed conflict was raised in *Cyprus v. Turkey* where, because of the applicability of the third Geneva Convention on prisoners of war, the European Commission of Human Rights did not find "it necessary to examine the question of a breach of Article 5 of the European Convention on Human Rights with regard to persons accorded the status of prisoners of war." *See* T. MERON, HUMAN RIGHTS LAW-MAKING IN THE UNITED NATIONS 212 n.229 (1986) (quoting Eur. Comm'n of Hum. Rts., Report on Applications Nos. 6780/74 and 6950/75 (Cyprus v. Turk.) 109 (1976, declassified in 1979)). *See also supra* note 94.

[102] Fourth Geneva Convention, *supra* note 7, Art. 78, para. 1.

7. Some human rights accords contain procedures for dealing with an issue, for example, enabling individuals to raise a matter directly with some outside institution, of a kind lacking in laws of war rules.

8. In the event that there is a significant change in status of the territories, with Israel and other states viewing the occupation phase as ending, the role of the law on occupations would probably be attenuated, and human rights law might be the principal body of international law to remain applicable.

VII. Views of the International Community

The Israeli occupation since 1967 has attracted a vast amount of international attention: from writers, including many in Israel and the occupied territories;[103] from nongovernmental organizations, especially those concerned with law and human rights; and from governments. Governmental interest has been evident at several levels: neighboring states, inter-Arab organizations, the nonaligned movement, the members of the European Communities, the two superpowers and the United Nations system.

This high degree of international interest has many causes. Politically, the occupation has been an appropriate target for the prevailing values and rhetoric of anticolonialism. The importance of the Middle East in power politics, and the key role of its oil resources, especially after 1973, has meant that the occupation could not be ignored. In any case, it is proper that there should be international concern about the effects of a prolonged occupation, particularly where there is a plain conflict of interest between occupier and occupied. Further, in common Article 1 of the four 1949 Geneva Conventions the states parties "undertake to respect and to ensure respect for the present Convention in all circumstances." An additional basis for international interest in the territories is the large number of refugees there who are entitled to, and do, receive international assistance.

The preoccupation of the United Nations with the occupied territories has been especially noteworthy, and controversial. Many aspects of UN involvement have attracted considerable, and often justified, critical comment—especially the work of the Special Committee to Investigate Israeli Practices.[104] Dinstein has written that "Israel is averse to proposals that the

[103] Critical work in English from the occupied territories includes many publications of the Palestinian affiliate of the International Commission of Jurists, al-Haq/Law in the Service of Man, Ramallah; and R. SHEHADEH, *supra* note 80, which summarizes a range of complaints against Israeli practices.

[104] The work of the Special Committee to Investigate Israeli Practices Affecting the Human Rights of the Population in the Occupied Territories has illustrated the political hazards that can attend efforts to evaluate Israeli actions by reference to international legal standards. Since it was set up in 1968, the committee has submitted annual reports, published by the United Nations. *See, e.g.*, its 15th report, UN Doc. A/38/13 (1983). In the eyes of many Israelis, the committee was biased from the beginning and its reports one-sided. For a critical Israeli review, see Shefi, *The Reports of the UN Special Committees on Israeli Practices in the Territories*, in MILITARY GOVERNMENT, *supra* note 30, at 285. The committee's work may have reinforced two already existing tendencies in Israel: distrust of international organizations and reliance on unilateral, rather than multilateral, approaches.

legality of the measures taken by its military government in the occupied territories will be subjected to scrutiny by international organizations (especially the United Nations, which it regards as totally dominated by hostile countries)."[105] Persistent attempts in the 1980s to deprive Israel of the right to participate in various UN bodies, although unsuccessful, have not enhanced Israeli respect for the Organization.[106] The General Assembly's attitude to Israel has often been strident and denunciatory—most notably in the 1975 resolution equating Zionism with "racism and racial discrimination."[107] Phraseology in some General Assembly resolutions suggests that in occupations, as in war, the laws of war can easily get used for political propaganda. Such resolutions have probably had little effect other than to strengthen Israel's sense of isolation and defiance of international opinion. However, many UN resolutions have spelled out important positions on fundamental legal questions. These include the resolutions, already noted, on the applicability of international law to this occupation[108] and other resolutions, mentioned below, on additional key aspects of the legal framework of a prolonged occupation.

The Status of Territory and Self-Determination

When a prolonged occupation occurs because of ancient rivalries and deep-seated territorial-cum-political disputes, there well may not be a status quo ante to which states can easily revert as part of a diplomatic settlement. Moreover, during a prolonged occupation the aspirations of the inhabitants, and of the international community, may change. Thus, questions are raised about the extent to which the ousted sovereign, who had control before the occupation, continues to have rights with respect to the territory; and whether the inhabitants of the occupied territory have a right of self-deter-

---

For another critical view of the committee's work, see Alderson, Curtis, Sutcliffe & Travers, *Protection of Human Rights in Israeli-Occupied Territories,* 15 HARV. INT'L L.J. 470 (1974). They suggest that the General Assembly, through the committee and through its resolutions concerning rights in the occupied territories, has had little discernible effect other than to antagonize Israel and add another element of contention to the disputes between Israel and its neighbors. *Id.* at 481. They conclude that parties to the fourth Geneva Convention need to

> perfect and reaffirm the enforcement procedures prescribed in that agreement. They cannot rely exclusively upon United Nations action to ensure conformity with its provisions. A consistent theme in United Nations pronouncements on the enforcement of the Convention has been that it is only the parties themselves which are, in the last analysis, in a position to implement the procedures and exert the pressures which will make the Convention work.

Id. at 482.

[105] Dinstein, *supra* note 69, at 174. Note also Schachter's observation, in *Self-Defense and the Rule of Law,* 83 AJIL 259, 263 (1989): "That states generally do not welcome international scrutiny of their defensive measures is hardly surprising. This attitude is especially marked when armed force is actually used, even though seen by the user as legitimate self-defense." The same attitude characterizes military occupants.

[106] *See* Tabory, *Universality at the UN: The Attempt to Reject Israel's Credentials,* 18 ISR. Y.B. HUM. RTS. 189 (1988).

[107] GA Res. 3379 (XXX) (Nov. 10, 1975).

[108] *See supra* notes 86–88 and accompanying text.

mination and, if so, how any such right may be recognized and exercised. While there cannot be absolute answers to these questions, the case of the West Bank and Gaza suggests some partial answers and points to the emergence of procedures for addressing them.

The international community has favored self-determination in respect of several recent and contemporary occupations—for example, in Kampuchea, Namibia and Western Sahara.[109] However, the case for self-determination has not been pressed where the occupied territory is widely accepted as being part of an existing state, from which it has been forcefully separated and to which it may be expected eventually to revert. A case in point is northern Cyprus: any act of self-determination there might well be seen as a threat to the sovereignty and territorial integrity of Cyprus, and as a victory for the Turkish invasion and occupation.

The idea of Palestinian self-determination, which has been extensively advanced since 1967, is not new. There are strong grounds for doubt whether the West Bank and Gaza were, before 1967, simply integral parts of Jordan and Egypt, respectively.[110] There was also, even before 1967, some evidence of a tendency to view the inhabitants of Palestine as a people, and as candidates for self-determination—despite uncertainty and disagreement as to the geographical area in which it was to be exercised.[111]

In the period since June 1967, Palestinian nationalism has grown within the occupied territories.[112] Moreover, in many different ways the international community has come to accept the propositions that there is a Palestinian people; that it has a right of self-determination; and that this right is to be exercised in the West Bank and Gaza, rather than in the whole of former mandatory Palestine. None of these propositions is self-evident, and in the nature of things their acceptance by the international community has been slow and uneven; for example, Palestinian self-determination was not mentioned in UN Security Council Resolutions 242 and 338.[113] Significant

[109] *See, e.g.*, GA Res. 36/5 (Oct. 21, 1981); and GA Res. 43/19 (Nov. 3, 1988) (both on Kampuchea); GA Res. 2403 (XXIII) (Dec. 16, 1968); and GA Res. 43/26 (Nov. 17, 1988) (both on Namibia); and GA Res. 38/40 (Dec. 7, 1983); and GA Res. 43/33 (Nov. 22, 1988) (both on Western Sahara).

[110] *See supra* text at note 64.

[111] On the evolution within the international community of the idea of Palestinian self-determination, see especially S. & T. Mallison, *The Juridical Bases for Palestinian Self-Determination*, 1 PALESTINE Y.B. INT'L L. 36 (1984). On the emergence of nationalism among the Palestinian Arabs, see the important study by an Israeli scholar, Y. PORATH, THE EMERGENCE OF THE PALESTINIAN-ARAB NATIONAL MOVEMENT 1918–1929 (1974).

[112] On political developments in the West Bank, see particularly two fine studies by an Israeli and a Palestinian academic, respectively: M. MA'OZ, PALESTINIAN LEADERSHIP ON THE WEST BANK: THE CHANGING ROLE OF THE MAYORS UNDER JORDAN AND ISRAEL (1984); and E. SAHLIYEH, IN SEARCH OF LEADERSHIP: WEST BANK POLITICS SINCE 1967 (1988). In 1979–1980 Ma'oz was an adviser on Arab affairs to the Israeli Defense Minister, and to the Coordinator for Activities in the Territories.

[113] SC Res. 242 (Nov. 22, 1967) provided for Israeli withdrawal from territories occupied in the 1967 war, coupled with a termination of all claims or states of belligerency. SC Res. 338 (Oct. 22, 1973) reaffirmed Res. 242 and called for negotiations "aimed at establishing a just and durable peace in the Middle East." These resolutions, accepting as they did Israel's right to

landmarks in the international acceptance of Palestinian aspirations have included General Assembly resolutions from 1969 onwards reaffirming "the inalienable rights of the people of Palestine";[114] the September 1978 Camp David Agreements between President Sadat, Prime Minister Begin and President Carter, with their proposals for a self-governing authority for the West Bank and Gaza for a transitional period of 5 years;[115] the June 1980 Venice declaration of the heads of government of the nine member states of the European Communities, calling for recognition of two principles—the right to existence of all the states in the region and the legitimate rights of the Palestinian people;[116] the peace plan, adopted by the Arab summit at Fez in September 1982 and accepted by the PLO, calling for a settlement based on Israeli withdrawal from the territories occupied in 1967;[117] the September 1983 Geneva declaration on Palestine;[118] and the short-lived Jordan-PLO accord of February 1985.[119]

In 1988 and 1989, many important diplomatic developments took place. King Hussein of Jordan changed the framework of discussion significantly on July 31, 1988, by accepting "the wish of the PLO, the sole legitimate representative of the Palestinian people, to secede from us in an independent Palestinian state," and indicating that he would dismantle "the legal and administrative links" between Jordan and the West Bank.[120] On November 15, the Palestine National Council, in making a declaration of independence, proposed an international conference on the Middle East on the basis of Security Council Resolutions 242 (1967) and 338 (1973), and thus implic-

---

exist, and making no specific mention of Palestinian self-determination, were for many years viewed with deep suspicion by the PLO.

[114] The first such resolution was GA Res. 2535B (XXIV) (Dec. 10, 1969). Another key resolution was GA Res. 2672C (XXV) (Dec. 8, 1970), which recognized that "the people of Palestine are entitled to equal rights and self-determination, in accordance with the Charter of the United Nations." These early resolutions attracted only modest support: votes for and against and abstentions were, respectively, 48-22-47, and 47-22-50.

[115] Camp David Agreements, *supra* note 43. For a succinct account of the negotiation of these accords, referring to memoirs of participants, see S. SOFER, BEGIN: AN ANATOMY OF LEADERSHIP 189–200 (1988). According to Sofer, as late as March 1978, "Sadat was inclined to agree that a Palestinian state should not be established." *Id.* at 187.

[116] KEESING'S CONTEMPORARY ARCHIVES 30,635 (1980).

[117] The Arab Peace Plan, adopted by the Twelfth Arab Summit Conference, held at Fez, Sept. 6–9, 1982, went some way towards accepting the existence of Israel. For details, including extracts from the Fez summit declaration, see KEESING'S CONTEMPORARY ARCHIVES 32,037 (1983). It was subsequently supported in numerous General Assembly resolutions, e.g., GA Res. 43/54A (Dec. 6, 1988), and at the extraordinary summit meeting of the Arab League at Algiers on June 7–9, 1988.

[118] This declaration was issued at the conclusion of the UN International Conference on the Question of Palestine, held at Geneva, Aug. 29–Sept. 7, 1983, *reprinted in* 1 PALESTINE Y.B. INT'L L. 66 (1984).

[119] The text of the Jordanian-Palestinian Accord, Feb. 11, 1985, together with indications of the PLO Executive Committee's desired alternative wording, is *reprinted in* 2 PALESTINE Y.B. INT'L L. 224 (1985). On the demise of the accord, see Roberts, *Decline of Illusions: The Status of the Israeli-occupied Territories over 21 Years,* 64 INT'L AFF. 345, 353–54 (1988).

[120] N.Y. Times, Aug. 1, 1988, at A1, col. 6.

itly accepted the existence of Israel and a two-state solution to the problem of Palestine.[121] The proclamation of the State of Palestine was widely, though not of course universally, acknowledged in the international community.[122] Subsequent clarifications by PLO Chairman Yasir Arafat in Geneva on December 13 and 14, including reiterations in a new form of earlier statements renouncing terrorism, led to the first official direct talks between U.S. and PLO officials, which began in Tunis on December 16.[123]

All these developments were followed by a period of continued infiltration and incidents on the ground, and diplomatic stalemate. On May 14, 1989, the Israeli cabinet approved Prime Minister Shamir's plan for elections among Palestinians in the occupied territories, leading to a strictly limited autonomy. The PLO rejected it, while indicating that certain elements could be incorporated into a framework for an overall settlement. Shamir remained hostile to any Palestinian state, telling the Knesset on May 17 that he ruled out trading land for peace. The Egyptian Government announced a ten-point plan aimed at overcoming these differences in September 1989, following extensive consultations with key parties: it contained detailed proposals for internationally supervised elections in the West Bank (including East Jerusalem) and Gaza, and envisaged negotiations on a final settlement in 3 to 5 years' time.[124]

These diplomatic moves came on top of some other demographic and political developments that have weakened, if not undermined, extreme positions on both sides: by the late 1980s, neither the complete abolition of Israel nor complete Israeli settlement and domination of the occupied territories could be presented with the same conviction as in earlier periods.[125]

The effect of all these developments should not be exaggerated. They could not in themselves dissolve the encrusted bitterness of a long-standing and violent dispute, they could not alleviate deep fears on both sides about security and they could not prevent the growth of religious fundamentalism among Arabs and Israelis. They have had, at best, a limited effect in persuading Israelis and Palestinians to work towards pragmatic compromise. The Israeli Government remains obdurate; while on the Palestinian side, the belief that self-determination is an internationally recognized right still

[121] For a succinct summary of the 19th session of the PNC, held in Algiers, Nov. 12–15, 1988, see KEESING'S RECORD OF WORLD EVENTS 36,438 (1989). On the evolution of Palestinian thinking that led to the events at the end of 1988, see Sayigh, *Struggle Within, Struggle Without: The Transformation of PLO Politics since 1982*, 65 INT'L AFF. 247 (1989).

[122] Evidence of a degree of international acceptance of the PLO's move was GA Res. 43/177 (Dec. 15, 1988), which acknowledged the proclamation of the State of Palestine by the Palestine National Council and decided that the designation "Palestine" should be used in place of "Palestine Liberation Organization" in the UN system, without prejudice to the observer status and function of the PLO within the system. The vote was 104-2-36, the two votes against being those of Israel and the United States. UN Press Release GA/7814, at 112 (Jan. 16, 1989).

[123] Int'l Herald Trib. (Paris), Dec. 17–18, 1988, at 1.

[124] KEESING'S RECORD OF WORLD EVENTS 36,599 and 36,670 (1989); and report from Cairo, The Times (London), Sept. 13, 1989, at 12, col. 7.

[125] *See, e.g.*, Y. HARKABI, ISRAEL'S FATEFUL DECISIONS (1988); and Roberts, *supra* note 119.

sometimes involves a corollary reluctance to think in terms of a transitional period before full independence, or to accept that there might be any obligation on Palestinians to demonstrate (to Arab states as much as to Israel) that a future Palestinian state would be a stable and responsible member of international society, accepting frontiers, regimes and rules of coexistence.

Despite the many problems associated with them, the diplomatic and political moves since the occupation began together have reinforced the view of the West Bank and Gaza as territories that jointly are a candidate for self-determination, and have weakened alternative views. The idea that either of these territories might revert eventually to the state that previously controlled it is effectively dead. Thus, the acts of the international community indicate that the implicit assumption of the law on occupations—that occupied territory is "territory of a High Contracting Party"—need not be a straitjacket when it comes to consideration of the future status of a land and its people.

Professor Richard Falk, in proposing a formal international convention on prolonged occupation, has suggested that if an occupation is not terminated after, say, 10 years, some political procedure needs to be established whereby the inhabitants can secure and exercise a right of self-determination.[126] Although the Falk proposal would accord with the expressed views of the international community on the West Bank and Gaza, it may be doubted whether an international convention would actually add clarity or force to what is already a strong demand. Moreover, it is not self-evident that in all cases of occupations, a formal requirement for some mechanism of self-determination after a specified period would be superior to the normal processes of bargaining for a political settlement. In some cases, the international community is unlikely to favor self-determination by the people in the territory deemed to be occupied, e.g., northern Cyprus.

The emphasis placed by the international community on Palestinian self-determination has not meant a complete abandonment of Jordanian and Egyptian responsibility for the West Bank and Gaza, respectively. With Israeli consent, the ousted administering powers have maintained a modest degree of involvement in various spheres, including some educational matters. Until the Palestinians actually exercise self-determination, and decide on the form of a future Palestinian entity, the Governments of Jordan and Egypt are likely to continue to have an important role in the territories—or at least in negotiations on their future.

The Legitimacy and Treatment of Resistance

In most cases of prolonged occupation, resistance emerges in some form, whether violent or nonviolent. However, the main international conven-

[126] Prof. Falk's article, *supra* note 29, was originally a paper presented on July 8, 1988, at an international symposium at Oxford. In this paper he also suggested that the proposed convention should specify that international human rights law, as well as the law of war, applies in a prolonged occupation.

tions on occupations say little about its legitimacy or otherwise, and only slightly more about the treatment of those involved in it. The most detailed rules governing the treatment of resisters are in Articles 5, 49 and 68 of the fourth Geneva Convention. There is also a much larger, but widely dispersed, body of case law, especially from the time of the Second World War.

The legitimacy of resistance in occupied areas, and of support from abroad for such resistance, has always been a difficult question for diplomatic conferences, courts, writers on the laws of war and governments. It has been raised in sharp form by events in the 1980s in Afghanistan, Nicaragua, Namibia and elsewhere. What is the status of combatants other than the members of the regular armed forces of a country? Is popular resistance (whether violent or nonviolent) a breach of a notional contract between occupier and occupied?[127] Is active outside support of resistance in occupied areas justified? Is the recovery of lost territories, including those under prolonged occupation, a justification for war?[128] These questions, which are by no means new, do not admit of absolute answers: it is placing too heavy a burden on international law to expect answers from it, but it can offer some criteria and guidelines.

In the post-1945 period, following Allied support for resistance in Axis-occupied countries, and the ending of the European colonial empires, the international community has tended not only to support self-determination in principle, but also—and increasingly—to view resistance against outside domination as justifiable. The 1974 UN Definition of Aggression contained the statement:

> Nothing in this Definition . . . could in any way prejudice the right to self-determination, freedom and independence, as derived from the Charter, of peoples forcibly deprived of that right . . ., particularly peoples under colonial and racist régimes or other forms of alien domination; nor the right of these peoples to struggle to that end and to seek and receive support, in accordance with the principles of the Charter . . . .[129]

As a corollary of this approach, a degree of recognition has been granted to certain liberation movements. Thus, on November 13, 1974, PLO Chairman Arafat addressed the UN General Assembly. On November 22 of that year, the Palestine Liberation Organization was one of several national liberation movements accorded observer status in the General Assembly and UN-sponsored conferences.[130]

[127] A famous exploration of resistance is Baxter, *The Duty of Obedience to the Belligerent Occupant*, 27 BRIT. Y.B. INT'L L. 235 (1950).

[128] For a brief, skeptical discussion of this issue in relation to the 1973 war, which Egypt and Syria justified partly as a war for the recovery of territory under prolonged Israeli occupation, see W. O'BRIEN, THE CONDUCT OF JUST AND LIMITED WAR 286 (1981).

[129] Definition of Aggression, Art. 7, Annex to GA Res. 3314 (XXIX) (Dec. 14, 1974). See also the similar formula in the Declaration on Principles of International Law concerning Friendly Relations and Co-operation among States in accordance with the Charter of the United Nations, Annex to GA Res. 2625 (XXV) (Oct. 24, 1970).

[130] GA Res. 3237 (XXIX) (Nov. 22, 1974). On recognition, see also *supra* note 122.

In countless statements, UN bodies have criticized the actions taken by Israel in response to resistance of one kind or another. For example, a telegram dispatched by the UN Commission on Human Rights on March 8, 1968, called on Israel "to desist forthwith from acts of destroying homes of the Arab civilian population in areas occupied by Israel."[131] Eighteen years later, in 1986, a General Assembly resolution called on Israel "to release all Arabs arbitrarily detained or imprisoned as a result of their struggle for self-determination and for the liberation of their territories."[132] In 1988, almost a year after the outbreak of the *intifada,* a General Assembly resolution stated that it

> [*c*]*ondemns* Israel's persistent policies and practices violating the human rights of the Palestinian people in the occupied Palestinian territories, including Jerusalem, and, in particular, such acts as the opening of fire by the Israeli army and settlers that result in the killing and wounding of defenceless Palestinian civilians, the beating and breaking of bones, the deportation of Palestinian civilians.[133]

Much Israeli policy and practice in dealing with resistance has deserved criticism. The above-quoted resolution was properly critical of the policy of "force, power and beatings" enunciated by Minister of Defense Rabin on January 20, 1988. This approach—though subsequently clarified by the Attorney General in a ruling that beatings could only be administered to subdue rioters while resisting arrest—led to the issuing of certain orders that were criticized by an Israeli military court in 1989 as "manifestly illegal."[134]

Yet the General Assembly's tendency to criticize almost all Israeli actions against resistance has resulted in failure to take note of those that have recognized legal standards in the treatment of resisters; and an equal failure

[131] Mentioned in GA Res. 2443 (XXIII) (Dec. 19, 1968). House demolitions have been widely criticized as an extrajudicial measure of collective punishment.

[132] GA Res. 41/63A (Dec. 3, 1986). In logic, one could question the claim that the Arabs have been detained "arbitrarily," when the reason for their detention occupies the rest of the same sentence in the resolution. In reality, however, it does appear that many cases of detention and imprisonment have been arbitrary.

[133] GA Res. 43/21 (Nov. 3, 1988). In April 1989, the ICRC stated

> that it had been extremely concerned for some time by the increasingly frequent use of firearms against civilians in the occupied territories, and by acts of physical violence against defenceless people. Over the past 16 months, more than 400 Palestinians and around 17 Israelis have been killed, while thousands of people have been injured. In addition, the institution stated that the evacuation of the wounded, the work of medical staff and the smooth running of hospitals in the occupied territories were hampered by Israeli forces.

ICRC BULL., No. 160, May 1989, at 1.

[134] Judgment of an Israeli military court, May 25, 1989, hearing the case of four soldiers accused of manslaughter of a Palestinian beaten to death after trying to protect his son from arrest. The four were convicted on the lesser charge of brutality. The court said that, under Israeli law, obeying orders is no defense if, as in this case, they were manifestly illegal. Charles Richards, reporting from Jerusalem, concluded: "Prosecutions and disciplinary actions have been rare; the army protects its own. . . . Since the Uprising began in December 1987, two soldiers have been convicted of manslaughter. Nearly 500 Palestinians have been shot dead or beaten to death in this period." The Independent (London), May 26, 1989, at 12, col. 1.

to note that the dilemmas Israel faces are difficult and its rights under the law on occupations real. Consequently, General Assembly resolutions bearing on the treatment of Palestinian resistance have had diminished impact, having been easy for Israelis to dismiss.

In general, United Nations involvement in the subject of resistance has been highly controversial, and has contributed to criticism of the Organization. It has sought simultaneously to maintain the Charter prohibitions on the use of force and to offer an "innovatory adumbration of the principles of the Just War."[135] UN support for struggles of national liberation has often been expressed rhetorically, without addressing important issues. One finds little awareness of the Burkean distinction between the possible existence of a right (e.g., of resistance, or of recovery of territory through war) and the wisdom of actually exercising that right in a given situation. Further, one finds little serious discussion of choice of means of pursuing a given right; for example, UN resolutions have given no clue as to whether liberation struggles ought to be fought within limits derived from, or akin to, the laws of war. This omission has been especially serious since terrorist attacks against wholly innocent civilian targets were already alarmingly widespread in the early 1970s. The record of the United Nations in this respect has not been wholly negative: it has, of course, been involved in drawing up conventions and resolutions dealing with various aspects of terrorism, and it has been increasingly critical of this phenomenon.[136] The real criticism is that UN resolutions have lacked intellectual coherence, and (for a time at least) they lost sight of laws of war principles as a possible restraint not just on occupying powers, but also on liberation movements.

The issue of making legal restraints clearly applicable to liberation struggles is addressed in Geneva Protocol I, which includes within its scope of application "armed conflicts in which peoples are fighting against colonial domination and alien occupation and against racist régimes in the exercise of their right of self-determination."[137] This formula, which is echoed in countless UN documents, clearly includes the peoples of southern Africa and Palestine.[138] If implemented, Protocol I would require any liberation movement to observe extensive restrictions as regards methods of operation, weaponry and targets. The provisions in respect of such movements, and, indeed, whether the Protocol encompasses such movements at all, have inspired considerable debate, especially in the United States.[139] Nevertheless, the Protocol does establish that there are rules that would apply to

[135] Howard, *The UN and International Security*, in UNITED NATIONS, DIVIDED WORLD 31, 37 (A. Roberts & B. Kingsbury eds. 1988).

[136] For results of the UN consideration of terrorism, including the texts of conventions on the subject, see especially GA Res. 3166 (XXVIII) (Dec. 14, 1973); GA Res. 34/146 (Dec. 17, 1979); and GA Res. 40/61 (Dec. 9, 1985).

[137] Protocol I, *supra* note 27, Art. 1(4).

[138] M. BOTHE, K. PARTSCH & W. SOLF, *supra* note 36, at 51–52. Since neither South Africa nor Israel has become party to the Protocol, its formal applicability to these territories is of course doubtful.

[139] The main positions are outlined in *Agora: The U.S. Decision Not to Ratify Protocol I to the Geneva Conventions on the Protection of War Victims*, 81 AJIL 910 (1987); and its continuation, 82 AJIL 784 (1988); *see also* Gasser's further letter, 83 AJIL 345 (1989).

participants in liberation struggles as well as to other types of combatant—which is more than can be said of some UN resolutions.

Palestinian Deportations, Israeli Settlements

Over 20 years, no aspect of life can remain static. The changes in the demography of the occupied territories have been particularly significant. In September 1967, the Palestinian population of the West Bank and Gaza was just under one million. By the end of 1987, it reached an estimated 1,424,100 (860,000 in the West Bank and 564,100 in the Gaza Strip).[140] This growth is remarkable, considering that it has taken place against a background of substantial labor emigration, especially in the oil boom of the 1970s. Among Israelis, these figures have caused much concern because they suggest that within decades there might be an Arab majority in the overall area comprising Israel and the occupied territories.[141] For Palestinians, too, there are major causes of concern on demographic matters: deportations of Palestinians and Israeli settlements.

In accord with the view that occupation is a provisional state of affairs, the imposition of demographic changes within occupied territory has long been seen as undesirable. The fourth Geneva Convention appears to be precise on the question, stating as it does in the first and sixth paragraphs of Article 49:

> Individual or mass forcible transfers, as well as deportations of protected persons from occupied territory to the territory of the Occupying Power or to that of any other country, occupied or not, are prohibited, regardless of their motive.
>
> . . . .
>
> The Occupying Power shall not deport or transfer parts of its own civilian population into the territory it occupies.[142]

The individuals deported from the occupied territories fall into two broad categories: political leaders and those alleged to be involved directly in hostile activities. The deportations began in 1967 in the first months of the occupation, have particularly affected the leadership and have involved well over a thousand persons.[143] Some of the deportations have been de-

[140] CENTRAL BUREAU OF STATISTICS, STATISTICAL ABSTRACT OF ISRAEL 1988, at 705.

[141] Unofficial Israeli projections for mandatory Palestine as a whole (i.e., Israel, the West Bank and Gaza) suggest that by the year 2010 there will be parity between the Jewish and Arab populations. *See* M. BENVENISTI, THE WEST BANK DATA BASE PROJECT 1987 REPORT 5 (1987). An accelerated influx of Soviet Jews in the 1990s could upset these forecasts.

[142] Fourth Geneva Convention, *supra* note 7, Art. 49, paras. 1 and 6.

[143] E. COHEN, *supra* note 32, at 106–07, reports figures indicating that over 1,100 people were deported from the West Bank and Gaza between 1967 and 1977. She quotes a senior military official as saying that only 68 of these were genuine deportations—i.e., cases in which the individuals concerned were (1) recognized officially to be residents of the occupied territories, and (2) not transferred as part of an exchange with an Arab state. The deportations aroused opposition both internally and internationally; in 1980 they were discontinued, recommencing following a cabinet decision of Aug. 4, 1985.

A figure of 2,000 deportations for the whole period 1967–1986, apparently from the West Bank alone, is given in M. BENVENISTI, THE WEST BANK HANDBOOK: A POLITICAL LEXICON 87 (1986).

fended, e.g., in Supreme Court decisions, on a variety of grounds, such as that these deportations were quite different in character and intent from those which took place in the Second World War; that the individuals concerned were not "protected persons"; and/or that they were being deported, not to "any other country," but to a country (e.g., Jordan) whose nationals they were.[144] Such arguments could not allay the deep fears among the Palestinian population that the deportations actually carried out by Israel were the thin end of the wedge, to be followed by larger expulsions. One disturbing aspect of the Israeli swing to the right as a result of the Palestinian uprising has been an apparent increase in the numbers of Israelis favoring deportations. According to a survey conducted for Tel Aviv University, four Israelis in every ten support the idea of "transferring" the Arab populations out of the West Bank and the Gaza Strip.[145]

The growth of Israeli settlements in the occupied territories, which has been most marked since 1977, has similarly fueled fears of mass expulsions. At the end of 1976, after almost a decade of occupation, there were an estimated 3,176 Jewish settlers in the West Bank. By April 1987, there were approximately 65,000 Jews living in the West Bank, and 2,700 in the Gaza Strip.[146] As with deportations, so with settlements: there have been some claims that Israeli practices are compatible with international norms, including those of the fourth Geneva Convention. A distinction has been drawn between the transfer of people—which is forbidden under Article 49—and the voluntary settlement of nationals on an individual basis; and it has been asserted that there is nothing wrong with settlements in the sense of army bases where soldiers are engaged in agriculture for part of the time.[147] Civilian settlements have also been called necessary for the occupying power's security, and therefore essential if the occupying power is to preserve public order and safety.[148]

[144] For discussions of the legality of the deportations, see Dinstein, *Refugees and the Law of Armed Conflict*, 12 ISR. Y.B. HUM. RTS. 94 (1982); Shefi, *supra* note 104, at 304–06; E. COHEN, *supra* note 32, at 104–11. For a well-argued critique of the legality of deportations (mainly those of 1985–1986), see J. HILTERMANN, ISRAEL'S DEPORTATION POLICY IN THE OCCUPIED WEST BANK AND GAZA (Al-Haq/Law in the Service of Man, 1986). For a 1988 Supreme Court case involving deportations, see *infra* text at note 181. For a recent affirmation of the illegality of deportations, under both the Geneva Convention and customary law, see T. MERON, *supra* note 23, at 48 n.131.

[145] OBSERVER (London), June 12, 1988, at 22, col. 5. In the November 1988 election, one party, Moledet, ran on this issue; it secured under 2% of the total vote and won only two seats in the Knesset.

[146] M. BENVENISTI, *supra* note 141, at 51–55; and M. BENVENISTI, *supra* note 143, at 66. The figures for settlers in the West Bank do not include the large number (80,000 in 1985, and still growing) in the extended municipal boundaries of Jerusalem.

[147] For an analysis suggesting that some Israeli settlements are compatible with the fourth Geneva Convention, see Dinstein, *supra* note 67, at 124. See also text at notes 169, 173 and 174 *infra*, for statements in the Supreme Court on the status and meaning of Article 49, paragraph 6.

[148] See, e.g., the material on various Supreme Court cases involving settlements in MILITARY GOVERNMENT, *supra* note 30, at 152–53, 158, 313–19, 371–97, 404–41. *See also infra* text at notes 166–74 (referring to the *Beth-El* and *Elon Moreh* cases).

Such arguments are far from convincing. In particular, even if voluntary settlement of nationals on an individual basis were permissible under Article 49, the ambitious settlements program of the 1980s, which was planned, encouraged and financed at the governmental level, does not meet that description.[149] Moreover, it is doubtful whether the settlements program was primarily intended to contribute to the occupying power's security and whether, in the event, it has contributed to that end; by causing friction with the Palestinian inhabitants of the territories, the program may even have added to the work of the Israel Defense Forces (IDF).[150] The settlements program is quite simply contrary to international law. However, it is now so far advanced, and so plainly in violation of the Geneva Convention, that it actually creates a powerful reason for Israel's continuing refusal to accept that the Convention is applicable in the occupied territories on a *de jure* basis.

The international community has taken a critical view of both deportations and settlements as being contrary to international law. General Assembly resolutions have condemned the deportations since 1969, and have done so by overwhelming majorities in recent years.[151] Likewise, they have consistently deplored the establishment of settlements, and have done so by overwhelming majorities throughout the period (since the end of 1976) of the rapid expansion in their numbers.[152] The Security Council has also been

[149] *See, e.g.*, M. BENVENISTI, *supra* note 141, at 51–65.

[150] On unauthorized violence by settlers, see the Ministry of Justice report J. KARP ET AL., REPORT OF THE INQUIRY TEAM *RE* INVESTIGATION OF SUSPICIONS AGAINST ISRAELIS IN JUDEA AND SAMARIA (1984).

[151] The first was GA Res. 2546 (XXIV) (Dec. 11, 1969). The following resolutions condemning deportations received overwhelming majorities: GA Res. 41/63E (Dec. 3, 1986) (131-1-21); and GA Res. 43/58E (Dec. 6, 1988) (152-1-1). The United States abstained on these resolutions. However, the "United States has stated that deportation is inconsistent with the Fourth Geneva Convention." DEPARTMENT OF STATE, *supra* note 87, at 1193.

[152] See, e.g., the following examples, at 4-year intervals:

GA Res. 31/106A	(Dec. 16, 1976)	(129-3-4)
GA Res. 35/122B	(Dec. 11, 1980)	(140-1-3)
GA Res. 39/95C	(Dec. 14, 1984)	(143-1-1)
GA Res. 43/58C	(Dec. 6, 1988)	(149-1-2)

The United States voted against the 1976 resolution above, and abstained on the others. When it abstained on GA Res. 32/5 (Oct. 28, 1977) (131-1-7), the U.S. representative said that the United States opposed the Israeli settlements, but that it had accepted a special responsibility as cochairman of the Geneva Peace Conference on the Middle East, requiring it to remain impartial when the complex issues to be considered there were involved. 1977 UN Y.B. 317–18.

For a clear statement of the U.S. view that Israel's establishment of civilian settlements in the occupied territories is inconsistent with international law, see the letter of Herbert J. Hansell, Legal Adviser, Department of State, to House Comm. on International Relations (Apr. 21, 1978), 17 ILM 777 (1978). On U.S. policy towards settlements in 1989, see text at note 184 *infra*.

The General Assembly has shown some consistency in criticizing other cases of demographic changes imposed by foreign occupation forces. See, e.g., its expressions of concern "about reported demographic changes being imposed in Kampuchea by foreign occupation forces" in GA Res. 40/7 (Nov. 5, 1985), and GA Res. 43/19 (Nov. 3, 1988).

critical of deportations and settlements;[153] and other bodies have viewed them as an obstacle to peace, and illegal under international law.[154]

Long-Term Economic Change

The idea that occupation is temporary, and that an occupying power has a role in some respects akin to that of a trustee, finds reflection in a number of rules on economic matters, particularly the 1907 Hague Regulations (Articles 48–56). Some of the foundations of the Hague rules now seem dated, especially the insistence (objectionable to Communist countries) that private property merits a higher degree of protection than state property. However, few in number and antique as they are, these rules do establish some important principles, such as on taxation.[155]

In the West Bank and Gaza since 1967, extensive economic changes have been brought about in such key areas as agriculture, land ownership, use of water resources, the road system, building construction and taxation. Labor has become more mobile: large numbers work daily in Israel, and many have left on a longer-term basis to work abroad.[156] Not all these changes have been for the worse. For example, living standards rose, at least up to the mid-1970s. Nevertheless, some actual and planned economic measures have caused concern, on several grounds: discrimination against Palestinian economic activity, creation of an economy dependent on that of Israel and use of certain resources in the territories for the benefit of Israelis rather than Palestinians.

The international community has made many pronouncements on economic aspects of the Israeli occupation. The numerous references in the annual reports of the UN Special Committee on Israeli Practices have been reflected in the annual General Assembly resolutions on the reports.[157]

[153] *See, e.g.*, SC Res. 469 (May 20, 1980) (on deportations; quoting the fourth Geneva Convention, Art. 49, and calling on Israel to rescind the expulsion of the mayors of Hebron and Halhoul, and the Sharia Judge of Hebron); and SC Res. 465 (Mar. 1, 1980) (calling settlements a "flagrant violation of the Geneva Convention"). The latter resolution, which also criticized Israel's purported annexation of Jerusalem, was adopted unanimously, but the U.S. Government subsequently stated that it was retracting its vote. For an account of "the highly publicized snafu" over this vote, see Z. BRZEZINSKI, POWER AND PRINCIPLE: MEMOIRS OF THE NATIONAL SECURITY ADVISER, 1977–1981, at 441 (rev. ed. 1985). Brzezinski presents much interesting material on the Carter administration's thinking on the settlements; *see, e.g.*, *id.* at 110, 258, 263 and 440–42. See also SC Res. 607 (Jan. 5, 1988), adopted unanimously, calling on Israel to refrain from deporting any Palestinian civilians from occupied territory.

[154] See, e.g., the June 1980 Venice declaration of the nine EEC countries, *supra* note 116 and accompanying text, which was blunt on the settlements issue.

[155] *See, e.g.*, text at note 177 *infra*.

[156] On economic developments in the West Bank and Gaza, see Graham-Brown, *The Economic Consequences of the Occupation*, in OCCUPATION: ISRAEL OVER PALESTINE 167 (N. Aruri ed. 1984); and M. BENVENISTI, publications cited in notes 70, 141 and 143 *supra*.

[157] See, e.g., GA Res. 41/63D (Dec. 3, 1986), which includes in its litany of complaints of Israeli policies and practices the following economic items:

> (c) Illegal imposition and levy of heavy and disproportionate taxes and dues;
>
> . . .

Other General Assembly resolutions have also addressed the legality of certain Israeli economic activities and plans. From 1973 to 1983, a series of resolutions on "Permanent Sovereignty over National Resources in the Occupied Arab Territories" asserted that Israel, as an occupying power, has very limited economic rights, and condemned Israel for alleged exploitation of resources.[158] Resolutions in the period 1981–1984 demanded "that Israel cease forthwith the implementation of its project of a canal linking the Mediterranean Sea to the Dead Sea."[159] All these resolutions reflect the underlying principle that an occupying power, even in a prolonged occupation, has particularly to avoid making drastic changes in the economy of the occupied territory—especially those which are of an exploitative character, or which would result in binding the occupied territory permanently to the occupying power. However, the international community has not been inflexible in its interpretation of this principle.[160]

Oil was a subject of some contention in Israel's relations with Egypt, and with the United States. The oil fields in the Sinai Peninsula, which were operated during the Israeli occupation and returned to Egypt in November 1975, were not the main problem. Difficulties principally arose over prospecting for additional oil in Sinai and the Gulf of Suez, raising questions about an occupant's right to make so significant a change in the economy of

(f) Confiscation and expropriation of private and public Arab property in the occupied territories and all other transactions for the acquisition of land involving the Israeli authorities, institutions or nationals on the one hand and the inhabitants or institutions of the occupied territories on the other;

. . .

(m) Interference with the system of education and with the social and economic and health development of the population in the Palestinian and other occupied Arab territories;

. . .

(o) Illegal exploitation of the natural wealth, resources and population of the occupied territories.

158 The first was GA Res. 3175 (XXVIII) (Dec. 17, 1973). It referred to the fourth Geneva Convention. It was not until the fifth resolution on this subject, GA Res. 32/161 (Dec. 19, 1977), that specific reference was made to the Hague Convention, which is more germane to the exploitation of natural resources. These resolutions received substantial, but not overwhelming, support. The voting on the last in this series, GA Res. 38/144 (Dec. 19, 1983), was fairly typical: 120 for, 2 against and 18 abstentions.

159 If constructed, part of the canal would allegedly have gone through the Gaza Strip. The first General Assembly resolution criticizing it was GA Res. 36/150 (Dec. 16, 1981). The 1984 version, GA Res. 39/101 (Dec. 14, 1984), stated that the canal, "if constructed, is a violation of the rules and principles of international law, especially those relating to the fundamental rights and duties of States and to belligerent occupation of land." This received 143 votes for, 2 against and 1 abstention.

160 One piece of evidence of discrimination by the international community is that there has been little, if any, international comment or censure regarding one apparent infringement by Israel of the law on occupations—the building of the main road from Jerusalem to Tel Aviv on a natural line that passes through what before 1967 was a demilitarized zone between the West Bank and Israel. Although this road in effect annexes a small portion of territory, Jordan and other states acquiesced in it.

an area, and about its position regarding maritime matters. A Memorandum of Law by the U.S. Department of State of October 1, 1976, concluded firmly: "International law does not support the assertion of a right in the occupant to grant an oil development concession."[161] An Israeli response dated August 1, 1977, included this statement bearing on prolonged occupation: "if over a long period, such as in the case of the present occupation of Sinai, oil exploitation had been prevented, the development of the territory would have been delayed by that number of years."[162] Although in the eyes of the international community there was considerable doubt about the legitimacy of Israel's oil exploitation policy, it does not appear in the end to have been an obstacle to peace with Egypt.[163]

VIII. Israeli Supreme Court Judgments on Prolonged Occupation

In a large number of cases, especially before the Supreme Court of Israel, questions of an inherently long-term character, or involving specific consideration of the prolonged nature of the occupation, have arisen. What follows is not in any sense a comprehensive survey of these cases, or even an account of the main issues raised in them, but rather a distillation intended to convey some of the main lines of the Supreme Court's thinking on a few such questions.

An innovation was made in the territories occupied by Israel after the June 1967 war, namely, the establishment of a right to petition the Israeli Supreme Court against arbitrary or illegal acts by the occupant. The Court asserted its competence to review the legislation and acts of the military commander and other authorities in the West Bank and Gaza. The effectiveness of the Court in bringing rules of law, including those of international law, to bear on Israeli occupation policy has been much discussed.[164]

[161] U.S. Dep't of State, Memorandum of Law (Oct. 1, 1976), 16 ILM 733, 752 (1977). This memo stated that concessions granted to Amoco by Egypt were valid, "whether granted prior to or post June 1967." *Id.*

[162] Memorandum of Law, *supra* note 59, 17 ILM at 434 (submitted to the U.S. Department of State on Oct. 27, 1977). On Mar. 26, 1978, two wells in the Alma field in the Gulf of Suez began operation under a concession granted by Israel to the Neptune Oil Co. *Id.* at 432. All Sinai was returned to Egypt by Apr. 25, 1982.

[163] *See further* Gerson, *Off-Shore Oil Exploration by a Belligerent Occupant: The Gulf of Suez Dispute,* 71 AJIL 725 (1977); and Claggett & Johnson, *May Israel as a Belligerent Occupant Lawfully Exploit Previously Unexploited Oil Resources of the Gulf of Suez?,* 72 AJIL 558 (1978).

[164] Nathan, *The Power of Supervision of the High Court of Justice over Military Government,* in MILITARY GOVERNMENT, *supra* note 30, at 109, 133. For other Israeli assessments, see Domb, *Judgments of the Supreme Court of Israel Relating to the Administered Territories,* 11 ISR. Y.B. HUM. RTS. 344 (1981); Negbi, *The Israeli Supreme Court and the Occupied Territories,* JERUSALEM Q., No. 27, Spring 1983, at 33; and E. COHEN, *supra* note 32, at 80–92.

Many inhabitants of the occupied territories with whom I discussed the matter in November–December 1983 and January 1988, welcomed this right of petition, and noted that it had fostered a few out-of-court settlements of certain issues, but argued that, overall, very few practical results had been achieved. These sources were critical of the tendency of the Court (1) to accept "security" as a justification for the acts of the occupant, and (2) to accept certain limits on the formal applicability or justiciability of the fourth Geneva Convention. For a critical Palestinian view, see R. SHEHADEH, *supra* note 80, at 95–100.

In reviewing acts by the occupant, the Supreme Court has had regard, inter alia, to the relevant rules of international law. However, it was not self-evident which rules of international law were to be applied by the Court or exactly how it was to apply them. The Court has had to take into account not only the Israeli Government's position on the *de jure* applicability of the 1907 Hague and 1949 Geneva Conventions, but also complex questions of justiciability: do these agreements impose obligations and create rights directly enforceable under Israeli municipal law before an Israeli court? In addressing this issue, the Court has suggested that customary international law, including the Hague Convention, is justiciable; whereas conventional international law (in which category it has tended to include the Geneva Convention) is more problematical in this regard.[165]

Cases about Israeli Settlements

The matter of Israeli settlements, so central to any consideration of the long-term impact of the occupation, highlights the significance of relying more on the Hague Convention than on the Geneva Convention.

In the *Beth-El* case, the Court reached its key decision on settlements. The petitioners were inhabitants of the West Bank who owned land there that was being requisitioned by the Israeli authorities for Jewish settlement. In his judgment, given on March 15, 1979, Justice Witkon addressed the question

> whether the petitioners as protected persons may themselves claim their rights under these Conventions in a municipal court of the occupying power or whether only states, parties to the Conventions, are competent to claim the rights of the protected persons, and this clearly on the international level alone. The answer to this question depends [on] whether a provision of an international convention which it is desired to enforce has become part of the municipal law of the state whose court is asked to deal with the issue or whether that provision remains the term of an agreement merely between states and has not been incorporated into municipal law. In the first case, we speak of customary international law, recognized by the municipal court so long as the term is not in conflict with some provision of the municipal law itself, and in the second case we speak of conventional international law, binding . . . only on states *inter se.*[166]

Justice Witkon then referred to certain judgments of the Supreme Court indicating that "both Conventions are in the nature of conventional international law and were therefore not to be invoked in an Israeli municipal court." However, he went on to state that he had changed his mind following publication of an article by Dinstein: "I am now persuaded that the Hague Convention is accepted as customary law under which actions may be

[165] *See, e.g.*, Nathan, *supra* note 164, at 125–49; and Hadar, *The Military Courts,* in MILITARY GOVERNMENT, *supra* note 30, at 171, 172–75. Also the judgments in the *Beth-El* and *Elon Moreh* cases, *infra* text at notes 166–74. For a critique of the view that the fourth Geneva Convention does not embody customary law, see T. MERON, *supra* note 23, at 45–50.

[166] Beth-El case, *supra* note 68, at 378. For a short report of this case, see 9 ISR. Y.B. HUM. RTS. 337 (1979).

brought in a municipal court . . .. It is otherwise with the Geneva Convention."[167]

On settlements, Justice Witkon said that "as regards the pure security aspect, it cannot be doubted that the presence in occupied territory of settlements—even 'civilian' settlements—of citizens of the occupying power contributes appreciably to security in that territory and makes it easier for the army to carry out its task."[168]

In the same case, Justice Landau, concurring, raised some specific objections to the idea that Article 49, paragraph 6 of the fourth Geneva Convention had become customary law.[169] He also supported the Israeli settlements against the obvious objection that there was an inconsistency between the temporary character of an occupation and the construction of permanent settlements. Referring to the advocates for the petitioners and the respondents, he said:

> Mr. Khoury asks how a permanent settlement can be established on land requisitioned only for temporary use. This is a good question. But Mr. Bach's answer, that the civilian settlement can only exist in that place as long as the IDF occupy the area by virtue of the Requisition Order, commends itself to me. This occupation can itself come to an end some day as a result of international negotiations . . ..[170]

All the opinions in the *Beth-El* case emphasized Israel's unique security problems as a basis for justifying the settlements.[171] The petition objecting to the requisition of land was dismissed.

It was on the basis of Article 52 of the Hague Regulations (which deals with requisitions) that the Supreme Court, in its famous judgment of October 22, 1979, in the *Elon Moreh* case, declared an Israeli civilian settlement near Nablus in the West Bank to be illegal.[172] Because the decision was based on this provision, it had little bearing on settlements that did not involve requisitions or were officially declared essential to Israeli security. In his judgment, Justice Landau said that he "excluded Article 49(6) of the Geneva Convention altogether from consideration because it belongs to conventional international law which does not legally bind an Israeli court."[173] In concurring, Justice Witkon said: "The question whether voluntary settlement falls under the prohibition of 'transferring sections of the

[167] Beth-El case, *supra* note 68, at 379. The article in question was Dinstein, *The Judgment in the Rafiah Approach Case,* 3 TEL AVIV U.L. REV. 934 (Hebrew 1974).

For critiques of the Supreme Court's view that the fourth Geneva Convention does not have the status of customary law, see T. MERON, *supra* note 23, at 5–6 n.5, and 48 n.131; and Rubinstein, *supra* note 42, at 65–67.

[168] Beth-El case, *supra* note 68, at 377.

[169] *Id.* at 387–90. See also Justice Witkon's statement that "the provisions of the Geneva Convention regarding the transfer of population from or to occupied territory do not come under already existing law. They are intended to enlarge, and not merely clarify or elaborate the duties of the occupying power." *Id.* at 380.

[170] *Id.* at 392.

[171] *Id.* at 374–77, 392–93, 395–97.

[172] Elon Moreh case, No. H.C. 390/79, *reprinted in* MILITARY GOVERNMENT, *supra* note 30, at 404, 419–26 and 437–38. For a short report, see 9 ISR. Y.B. HUM. RTS. 345 (1979).

[173] Elon Moreh case, *supra* note 172, at 419.

population' within the meaning of Article 49(6) of the Geneva Convention is not an easy one and, as far as we know, no answer has yet been found in international jurisprudence."[174] The only practical effect of the decision in this case was that Elon Moreh was built a short distance away from its original site.

Cases about Other Matters

Numerous other Supreme Court judgments have tackled issues, including economic ones, directly related to the prolonged character of the occupation.

In *Christian Society for the Holy Places v. Minister of Defence,* the Court considered whether an order by the Regional Commander of Judea and Samaria was *ultra vires* Article 43 of the Hague Regulations, which requires the occupant to respect, "unless absolutely prevented, the laws in force in the country." The case arose from an employment dispute, and the order in question was an amendment of a Jordanian law so as to make it possible to appoint members of an arbitration council. The petitioner's position was dismissed by a majority decision. Justice Sussman, in upholding the legality of the order, observed that the occupant has a duty in respect of the population's welfare:

> A prolonged military occupation brings in its wake social, economic and commercial changes which oblige him to adapt the law to the changing needs of the population. The words "absolutely prevented" in Article 43 should, therefore, be interpreted with reference to the duty imposed upon him *vis-à-vis* the civilian population, including the duty to regulate economic and social affairs. In this context, it is of special importance whether the motive for the change was the furtherance of the occupant's interests or concern for the welfare of the civilian population. In Sussman's opinion, the appointment of persons to the arbitration council was done for the purpose of enabling an institution established by the Jordanian Law to function. The Order only completed the machinery set up under Jordanian Law, which would not otherwise have been able to operate. Therefore the Order did not constitute an excess of jurisdiction.[175]

[174] *Id.* at 438.

[175] Christian Soc'y for the Holy Places v. Minister of Defense, No. H.C. 337/71, 26(1) Piskei Din 574 (1972), *as summarized in* 2 Isr. Y.B. Hum. Rts. 354, 355 (1972). Justice Cohn's dissenting opinion is at p. 355. On the application of particular treaties, the summary states that the Court

> refrained from considering two issues: first, whether the Hague Convention applied to the administered areas, and second, whether the two aforementioned Conventions [i.e., the fourth Hague Convention and the fourth Geneva Convention] constitute law which could be invoked in an "internal" dispute between a State and its citizens. The Court explained that it avoided these questions because Counsel for the State chose not to raise them, as he based the defense of the respondents on the argument that they observed the Conventions properly.

Id at 356. See also the interesting discussion of this case, and the implications of prolonged occupation, in Dinstein, *supra* note 67, at 112–14.

In *Jerusalem Electricity Co. Ltd. v. Minister of Energy*, the legality of the occupant's purchase of the undertaking that supplied electricity to the West Bank was considered. The Supreme Court declared that the notice on the purchase of the petitioner's undertaking was null and void. Justice Cahan said:

> [G]enerally, in the absence of special circumstances, the Commander of the region should not introduce in an occupied area modifications which, even if they do not alter the existing law, would have a far-reaching and prolonged impact on it, far beyond the period when the military administration will be terminated one way or another, save for actions undertaken for the benefit of the inhabitants of the area.[176]

The *Abu Aita* case centered on whether the imposition of a new tax (value added tax) was contrary to Articles 48 and 49 of the Hague Regulations. In his carefully argued judgment of over a hundred pages, given on April 5, 1983, Justice Shamgar referred to the significance, so far as a prolonged belligerent occupation is concerned, of the above-mentioned judgment in *Christian Society for the Holy Places.* He stated that international law prescribes no limits to the duration of a belligerent occupation. He went on to endorse the criterion, advanced by Dinstein, that in most instances legislative steps taken by the occupant should be regarded as legitimate if the occupant takes equal legislative steps towards its own population; but he noted that this criterion is not exhaustive, and that situations may occur in an occupied territory that demand legislative steps not required in the home country. He also accepted that the new tax was genuinely necessary.[177]

In *Cooperative Society v. Commander of the IDF Forces in the Judea and Samaria Region*, the Court considered the occupant's authority to construct new roads in the region and to expropriate private lands for the purpose. The petitioners' application was dismissed. A central issue was whether the occupant had authority to initiate "a civil project of long-range permanent implications lasting beyond the duration of the belligerent occupation." Justice Barak said that, in defining the scope of the authority of a military administration, one must bear in mind the distinction between one of short duration and one that is prolonged. He cited Dinstein in noting that "the needs of the civilian population become more valid and tangible when the

[176] Jerusalem Elec. Co. v. Minister of Energy, No. H.C. 351/80, 35(2) Piskei Din 673 (1981), *summarized in* 11 ISR. Y.B. HUM. RTS. 354, 357 (1981).

[177] Abu Aita case, Nos. H.C. 69/81 and 493/81, 37(2) Piskei Din 197 (1983), *translated in* 7 SELECTED JUDGMENTS OF THE SUPREME COURT OF ISRAEL 6, 98–99 (1988). For a summary, see 13 ISR. Y.B. HUM. RTS. 348 (1983). The article by Dinstein to which Shamgar referred was *The Legislative Power in Occupied Territories*, 2 TEL AVIV U.L. REV. 505 (1972 Hebrew). *See also* Dinstein, *supra* note 67, at 112–13; and his analysis of this case, Dinstein, *Taxation under Belligerent Occupation*, in DES MENSCHEN RECHT ZWISCHEN FREIHEIT UND VERANTWORTUNG 115 (J. Jekewitz et al. eds. 1989).

In a subsequent case, 'Atiah v. IDF Commander in Gaza Strip, No. H.C. 118/84, 38(3) Piskei Din 107 (1984), *summarized in* 15 ISR. Y.B. HUM. RTS. 276 (1985), which concerned the treatment of mentally ill accused persons, the Supreme Court ruled that there was no obligation to make legislation in the occupied territories conform to Israeli legislation on similar matters; discretion for such conformity was vested in the commander of the region.

occupation is drawn out." Therefore, though the Hague Regulations had been codified against the background of a short occupation, "nothing prevents the development—within their framework—of rules defining the scope of a military government's authority in cases of prolonged occupation."[178] Barak concluded:

> The authority of a military administration applies to taking all measures necessary to ensure growth, change and development. Consequently, a military administration is entitled to develop industry, commerce, agriculture, education, health, welfare, and like matters which usually concern a regular government, and which are required to ensure the changing needs of a population in a territory under belligerent occupation.[179]

In *Mustafa Yusef v. Manager of the Judea and Samaria Central Prison,* the six petitioners, convicted of homicide by a court in Israel and sentenced to long prison terms, objected to their transfer from a prison in Israel to the newly opened Judea and Samaria Central Prison. Their petition was not successful. Justice Barak said in his judgment:

> The right to a "civilized human life in prison" is granted to every "criminal" or "security" prisoner, both in Israel and in the Region. It is the duty of a military administration—in particular one of prolonged duration—to be concerned with the welfare of the inhabitants of the occupied territory, and this concern includes maintaining a minimal standard of prison conditions.[180]

The legality of deportations has been examined in several Supreme Court decisions. In the *Afu* case, the Court asserted by a majority decision on April 10, 1988, that Article 49 of the fourth Geneva Convention prohibits "only such, especially collective, deportations as are carried out for purposes similar to those underlying the deportations by the Nazi authorities during the Second World War."[181] Individual, security-motivated deportations are not prohibited. This holding is hard to reconcile with the clear language of Article 49, paragraph 1, and has been criticized.[182]

Supreme Court Judgments: Some General Considerations

The judgments of the Israeli Supreme Court in cases arising from the occupation have been numerous, lengthy, erudite and carefully argued. Many have reflected key aspects of international law, and have related them to the multitude of problems thrown up in this prolonged occupation. Even

[178] Cooperative Soc'y v. Commander of IDF Forces in Judea and Samaria Region, No. H.C. 393/82, 37(4) Piskei Din 785 (1983), *summarized in* 14 ISR. Y.B. HUM. RTS. 301, 307–08 (1984) (referring to Y. DINSTEIN, THE LAWS OF WAR 216 (1983 Hebrew)).

[179] 14 ISR. Y.B. HUM. RTS. at 309.

[180] Mustafa Yusef v. Manager of the Judea and Samaria Central Prison, No. H.C. 540-6/84, 40(1) Piskei Din 567 (1986), *summarized in* 17 ISR. Y.B. HUM. RTS. 309, 312 (1987).

[181] T. MERON, *supra* note 23, at 48 n.131 (referring to Afu case, Nos. H.C. 785/87, 845/87 and 27/88 (1988)).

[182] *Id.* (referring also to Dinstein, *Deportation from Administered Territories,* 13 TEL AVIV U.L. REV. 403 (1988)). For the text of Article 49, paragraph 1, see *supra* text at note 142.

though the *de jure* applicability and justiciability of the fourth Geneva Convention have been questioned, the Court has increasingly taken for granted the *de facto* applicability of its provisions. Nevertheless, problems remain.

1. Applicability *de jure* of the fourth Geneva Convention to the occupied territories. Has the Court accepted too easily, without full scrutiny of all relevant issues, the position of the Israeli Government?

2. Justiciability of the fourth Geneva Convention. The Court has relied heavily on the assumption that the incorporation of provisions of international conventions into municipal law is a principal form of evidence that such provisions have the status of customary international law. Has it placed excessive reliance on this one form of evidence of customary law?

3. Interpretation of the fourth Geneva Convention. The Court has often interpreted the Convention's provisions in a relative way that is not easily squared with their language or with the interpretations placed on them by other states.

4. Views of governments and international organizations. The Court's judgments contain very little reference to the opinions of governments and the resolutions of international organizations (e.g., the United Nations, UNESCO, the ICRC) on matters relating to the occupation. There is an argument for taking some account of such statements—at least in cases where they reveal a high degree of agreement among states or address issues on which there is a need to interpret existing legal provisions, for example, in the light of new circumstances.

5. Israeli settlements. The Court has sometimes appeared not just reluctantly to accept, but positively to espouse, the debatable argument that settlements contribute to Israel's security. Further, its view that their apparently permanent character is not inconsistent with the provisional character of the occupation, though justified by the example of the now-abandoned settlements in Sinai, invites skepticism.

6. The principle of equal legislative treatment. The judgment in the *Abu Aita* case relied on an interesting, but potentially problematical, criterion for judging new legislation: whether the occupying power takes equal legislative steps towards its own population. As the judgment itself implied, legislation that is suitable for one society (with its own laws and customs, ethnic and religious composition, and state of development) may not be at all suitable for another, very different society. Such an approach could also have the effect of integrating the occupied territory into that of the occupant, and separating it from other states with which the inhabitants may want association.

7. The changing needs of the population. The argument made in several judgments—that in a prolonged occupation, new (and sometimes long-term) measures have to be taken in response to new problems—is powerful. However, it raises the question of exactly what individual or institution is able to assess and respond to the changing needs of the population, and by what means those needs or wishes should be determined.

Overall, the question arises whether the approach adopted by the Supreme Court—on the applicability, justiciability and interpretation of international conventions—has not had the effect of reducing the Court's possibilities of intervention. Is there an extent to which the Court has served as a buffer to soften the apparent conflict between international legal provisions, on the one hand, and Israeli policy and practices, on the other?

IX. Issues and Conclusions

Prolonged Occupations Generally

1. Prolonged occupations, lasting more than 5 years, have not been uncommon in the post-1945 world. Although attaching the opprobrious label "occupation" to a given situation is always controversial, many situations have been so identified by the international community, and some have not ended quickly. Condemnation of occupations, especially prolonged ones, is natural; but there is a need also to understand why they occur, and how the interests of the occupants and the inhabitants can be balanced.

2. Some or all of the underlying purposes of the law on occupations remain relevant in prolonged occupations. However, there may sometimes be tension among the various purposes; and difficult matters of political judgment are often involved in determining what particular policies flow from them.

3. The one diplomatic attempt to establish which rules apply to an occupation on the basis of its duration—namely, Article 6, paragraph 3 of the fourth 1949 Geneva Convention—indicated that fewer rules would apply in a prolonged occupation. It was based on the assumption, confounded in the Israeli-occupied territories, that as time went by indigenous institutions would take over more and more responsibilities. The provision has never been formally implemented, was in effect rescinded by Protocol I and must be regarded as a failure.

4. Any effort to get formal international agreement on a body of rules to apply specifically to all prolonged occupations is likely to fail, partly because prolonged occupations differ in their character and purpose, as recent and contemporary cases (including Kampuchea, Namibia and northern Cyprus) demonstrate. Further, it has been hard enough to get states to agree on the existing rules on occupations; to try to revise these rules, subdivide them or create special permutations of them would create acrimony and invite legalistic chaos. If prolonged occupations deserve a special body of rules, then why not occupations in which the indigenous government remains in post? Or occupations of territory whose status is in dispute? The most that could reasonably be expected is some broad guidelines as to the principles that might inform any departure from or addition to the existing law—but even that would be difficult.

5. If a formal international agreement on the problems raised by prolonged occupations is unlikely, it may be more profitable to consider other means by which such problems might be tackled—especially the emergence of procedures, both national and international, for interpreting and implementing law in the light of changing conditions.

6. In an occupation, including a prolonged one, international organizations can have a number of important roles. They can remind all concerned of their obligations under international law; indicate which policies, or international legal provisions, remain not merely applicable but in urgent need of being applied; interpret legal provisions in the light of new circumstances; suggest appropriate action where there is a conflict between legal principles or provisions; engage in fact-finding or arbitration in respect of particular issues; and provide peacekeeping or observer forces to facilitate total or partial withdrawals by the occupant.

Whatever view is taken about the quantity, the quality and the precise status in international law of the many UN resolutions on particular occupations (those relating to Israel are considered further below), their existence does suggest that the international community already has machinery for addressing certain questions that arise in such cases. Granted the reluctance of sovereign states to accept international scrutiny of how they use their armed force, this machinery will always need to be used with care.

7. Specific causes for concern about the relevance of the existing law on occupations to prolonged occupations include, but are not limited to:

(a) The law on occupations, especially as interpreted in some writings and military manuals, seems to allow, or suffer, the occupant to have a very large measure of authority, especially regarding the occupant's own security, the maintenance of public order, the keeping in force of already existing public order legislation, control of the media and prohibitions on political activity. This degree of authority may be acceptable in a war, but can it be acceptable indefinitely? Statements by international bodies suggest that there is a widely held view that in a prolonged occupation, especially if it extends into something approximating peacetime, an occupant cannot exercise the draconian powers that may be permissible in a shorter occupation; the interests and wishes of the inhabitants must be accorded greater weight.

(b) The conventions sometimes seem to be based on assumptions about a territory—that its previous status as part of a sovereign state was clear, and its previous legal and political order was satisfactory—that are open to question in many recent and contemporary prolonged occupations.

(c) The conventions governing military occupations say little about certain issues that inevitably crop up in a prolonged occupation, including the safeguarding and promotion of the economic life of occupied territories.

(d) The conventions say little about the treatment of those involved in resistance activities of whatever kind (whether violent or nonviolent), apart from a few key references in the fourth Geneva Convention (Articles 5, 49 and 68).

8. Causes for concern such as those listed above may be perfectly genuine, but they do not suggest that the relevant international agreements (especially the Hague Regulations and the fourth Geneva Convention) should cease to be viewed as formally applicable. These agreements are not

a rigid straitjacket, but a flexible framework. They leave room for special agreements between the parties if they are willing to conclude them; for interpretation by policy makers in accord with their basic purposes and principles; for elucidation by various bodies; and for supplementation from other sources: from case law, writings and other international agreements.

9. There are grounds for viewing international human rights law as applicable to occupations, including prolonged ones. Certain provisions of this body of law—for example, prohibitions of discrimination in education and of racial discrimination generally—usefully supplement the Hague and Geneva rules on occupations. In addition, some human rights conventions offer procedures of a kind lacking in laws of war conventions. However, the application of some provisions is not free from difficulties, especially in time of armed conflict or internal uprising.

10. The questions whether there is a right of resistance in territories under occupation (especially when prolonged), whether foreign states are justified in assisting such resistance, and whether states are justified in going to war to recover occupied territories have cropped up in many recent conflicts. It is doubtful whether general answers in international law can be particularly helpful when the circumstances of each case, including the purpose and character of the occupation, vary so greatly. Some statements on these matters made in UN General Assembly resolutions have been vulnerable to other criticisms as well. They have drawn attention neither to the key importance of the choice of means involved in pursuing any such rights, nor to the related issue of the application of laws of war limitations to the armed actions of liberation movements.

Israeli-Occupied Territories

11. Israel deserves credit for accepting the relevance in these territories of international legal norms, including those outlined in the fourth Geneva Convention. However, its position that the latter is not necessarily applicable on a *de jure* basis is unconvincing.

12. During the long occupation, a continuous and, in the 1980s, increasingly strong litany of complaints has emerged about numerous aspects of Israel's rule: the annexation of East Jerusalem and the Golan Heights, the establishment of Israeli settlements, deportations of inhabitants, the treatment of institutions of higher education, the acquisition of land, the conduct of the judicial system, conditions of detention, and so on. Such complaints have often been expressed in legal form, as violations of particular international legal provisions or, indeed, of fundamental principles of humanitarian law. They are thus testimony to the continued salience, if not always to the efficacy, of international law in a prolonged occupation.

13. Both Israelis and Palestinians can point to ways that, in their view, the whole framework of the law on occupations has in some sense been abused by the adversary in this prolonged occupation:

(a) Israelis could argue that the law on occupations has provided a safety net, enabling the Palestinians to escape the consequences of their leaders' folly, or that of some Arab governments, in not negotiating seriously about the future of the territories—a safety net that it is not necessarily reasonable to maintain indefinitely. A related Israeli argument has been that the law is being used in a one-sided way if Palestinians claim legal rights at the same time as their leaders support "terrorism" (itself a violation of the laws of war) or deny Israel's right to exist—a violation of even more fundamental norms.

(b) A concern widely shared by Palestinians is that the law on occupations has afforded Israel a cloak of legitimacy: while apparently respecting international law, Israel has actually interpreted it to suit its purposes. The Israelis are seen as claiming all the rights of belligerent occupants but shirking some of their legal obligations, and as introducing a system of permanent control under the legal cover that it is temporary. A further concern is that the law on occupations provides a basis for putting the inhabitants in a separate legal category and denying them normal political activity, keeping them in effect permanently under Israeli control, but as second-class citizens or worse. From this perspective, the longer the occupation lasts, the more akin to colonialism it seems.

Both these positions are serious. They point to the hazards of using the law on occupations selectively: the Palestinian tendency to take little account of the corrosive effects of terrorism is one example; so is the Israeli tendency to see in the law on occupations a justification for preventing or strictly controlling political activity indefinitely.

14. Consideration of the practical relevance of the two main instruments on occupations (the Hague Regulations and the fourth Geneva Convention) to the situation in the territories is likely to yield the conclusions that both are of key importance in the various fields they address; that neither has lost its relevance because of passage of time; and that the Convention is germane to a wider range of currently critical problems, including treatment of detainees and the legality of deportations and settlements. The Convention has also been cited far more frequently in resolutions of international bodies.

15. The question whether, and if so to what extent, the fourth Geneva Convention embodies customary law has become important in respect of the Israeli occupation and needs to be further considered. Some relevant facts to be taken into account include the large number of states parties, the time that has elapsed since 1949, resolutions of international bodies, incorporation into domestic legislation, state practice and the opinions of writers. To the extent that its provisions are accepted as embodying customary law, the terms of the Convention might be taken into greater account by at least some Israeli decision makers and courts.

16. Any consideration of how to get the law on occupations properly implemented has to start with the fact that the Government of Israel has responsibility for these territories. (Indeed, there has always been some doubt whether other states would rush to pick up that responsibility if given the chance.) Israel does have a certain discretion in interpreting and applying the law on occupations—especially as that law, like much law, involves

balancing different considerations. In these circumstances, criticisms of Israeli policy that are seen as ill-considered, intemperate or unfair are obviously not likely to be heeded. Israel will pursue policies based on its view of its own interests, and up to a point it is right that it should do so. International law and the national interest of states—even occupying powers—should not be seen as necessarily incompatible.

17. Some Israeli legal practices in this occupation have been notably innovative. One example is the abolition of capital punishment for murder, which shows that the duty in Article 43 of the Hague Regulations to respect, "unless absolutely prevented, the laws in force in the country" need not be a bar to progressive legislation.

18. Another significant innovation is the right to petition the Israeli Supreme Court in respect of arbitrary or illegal acts by the occupant. Whatever the arguments about the effectiveness of this right in practice, and about the actual decisions reached by the Court, this innovation has potential as one additional means of bringing international law and occupation policy into some kind of relation with each other. (The other such means to have emerged in this occupation has been the United Nations, especially the General Assembly, discussed below. A difficulty is that the Supreme Court and the General Assembly have reached different conclusions on key matters and have largely ignored each other's positions.)

International Interest in the Israeli Occupation

19. The interest of the outside world in events in the Israeli-occupied territories is legitimate not only because an interest in human rights anywhere is legitimate, but also because the territories and those inhabitants who are refugees have a special status. There is no reason for this interest to decline, or to be viewed as less legitimate, on account of the great length of the occupation; rather the reverse.

20. The interest of the outside world has been manifested through mechanisms somewhat different from the formal system enunciated in the fourth Geneva Convention. Some of the bodies that have exerted significant influence in the occupied territories are indeed mentioned in the Convention: the International Committee of the Red Cross, as well as individual governments, which have a responsibility under Article 1 to "ensure respect for the Convention in all circumstances." On the other hand, the formal system of protecting powers, mentioned extensively in the Convention, has not operated. Numerous UN bodies, not mentioned in the Convention, have had an important role.

21. The outside power with the greatest capacity to influence Israel on adhering to the law on occupations is the United States. Indeed, the United States played a central role in negotiations leading to Israeli withdrawals from Sinai and part of the Golan Heights. It may have been partly because of positions adopted by the United States that Israel has not annexed the West Bank and Gaza: against the objections of so important an ally, Israel could not throw the restraints of international law out the window, even if it

wished to do so.[183] In the past, the United States has sometimes been diffident about restraining extreme Israeli policies, such as the extension of Israeli law to the Golan Heights in 1981, the invasion of Lebanon in 1982, and the building of settlements in the Golan Heights, the West Bank and Gaza. The reasons for past U.S. diffidence have included not just the much-vaunted Jewish lobby, but also a legitimate opposition to terrorism and to some of the PLO's aims; a genuine commitment to Israel's survival; a concern that extreme pressure could be counterproductive; a stated desire to maintain a degree of independence so as to sustain credibility in pursuit of a negotiated settlement; and perhaps a lack of confidence in the Government's own judgment (especially in view of Vietnam), combined with exaggerated respect for Israeli judgment. Further, in the early Reagan years, which were so fateful in the Middle East, the U.S. administration went through a phase of, at best, lukewarm support for multilateral legal agreements and procedures. In 1988 and 1989, U.S. policy on a range of issues connected with the occupation began to change, as indicated by Secretary of State James Baker's statement on May 23, 1989, that Israel should "forswear annexation" of the West Bank and Gaza Strip, and "stop settlement activity there. For Israel now is the time to lay aside once and for all the unrealistic vision of a greater Israel."[184]

22. The United Nations, and in particular the General Assembly, is sometimes seen as having done little but pass resolutions indiscriminately condemnatory of all aspects of Israeli policy. Although this is more a criticism of the member states than of the Organization as such, the United Nations is vulnerable to the charge of rebuking Israel endlessly, while maintaining a diplomatic silence in respect of certain brutalities committed by other governments, including some Arab governments. The Special Committee to Investigate Israeli Practices has been widely criticized. The potential of UN resolutions has been undermined by political partiality and intellectual inconsistency. The General Assembly's espousal in 1975 of the resolution equating Zionism with racism was the most spectacular, but not the only, example of a denunciatory and self-defeating approach. Too often, UN member states have seemed content to cast votes on the subject and leave it at that; painstaking fact-finding, authoritative argument and diplomatic dialogue have sometimes been lacking. All this has conveyed the unfortunate impression that the law on occupations is a stick with which to beat occupants and a mechanism of political warfare, rather than a serious means of seeking to reconcile the conflicting interests of the parties. Elements in the approaches taken at the United Nations have made careful and sober consideration of some issues more difficult and may have reduced the Organization's chances of exercising a useful role in mediation or negotiation. For the future, there is a case for reconsideration of the UN mechanisms both for the investigation of facts concerning prolonged occupations and for the articulation of opinion about them.

[183] A point argued impressively by Arthur Hertzberg, *Israel and the West Bank: The Implications of Permanent Control*, 61 FOREIGN AFF. 1064, 1072–75 (1983).

[184] The Independent (London), May 24, 1989, at 11, col. 1.

23. UN resolutions, though open to criticism, have had some consistency and utility. They have criticized other occupying powers and not just Israel. Many General Assembly and Security Council resolutions on the Israeli-occupied territories have usefully reaffirmed the value of key legal provisions and related these to changing factual situations. On basic matters, such as whether the West Bank and Gaza should eventually revert to the states that formerly controlled them or form a new state based on self-determination for the inhabitants, UN resolutions have been the principal means of expressing the changing views of the international community. On some issues, the United Nations has shown discrimination in its response to developments in the occupied territories: many extreme and one-sided resolutions have attracted fewer votes than more dispassionate ones.

24. During the Israeli occupation, international organizations not only have passed resolutions but have assumed other important roles. They have acted in mediatory, humanitarian and peacekeeping capacities. From the beginning, the International Committee of the Red Cross has engaged in a wide range of activities, including observing prison conditions, arranging prisoner transfers, making private representations to the Israeli Government and issuing public statements about the international legal provisions applicable in the territories. The UN Relief and Works Agency for Palestine Refugees in the Near East (UNRWA) has continuously assisted those inhabitants of the West Bank and Gaza classified as refugees, and it has served as an important point of contact between the territories and the UN system. In schools in the occupied territories, the extremely sensitive problem of eliminating objectionable material in textbooks from Jordan and Egypt was eventually resolved through the good offices of UNESCO.[185] The United Nations has provided peacekeeping and observer forces in Sinai and the Golan Heights to facilitate Israeli withdrawals from occupied territory. As to the future, there have been several suggestions that UN peacekeeping or observer forces could have a role in monitoring elections in the West Bank and Gaza.

25. The International Court of Justice has not been asked to consider issues arising from the Israeli-occupied territories. Its important advisory opinion on Namibia of 1971 stands as a reminder that it can play a role in clarifying certain legal questions in a prolonged occupation. It has sometimes been suggested that the General Assembly or the Security Council might refer certain legal matters to the Court, in accord with Article 96 of the UN Charter and Article 65 of the ICJ Statute. Theoretically, many questions might be put to the Court: for example, whether the fourth Geneva Convention is applicable in the occupied territories on a *de jure* basis and in its entirety; whether the Convention embodies customary law, and if so to what extent; whether, in a prolonged occupation, there might in principle be some room for variations within, or even departures from, the law on occupations, and if so on what grounds; whether international

[185] *See* A. GERSON, *supra* note 83, at 181–83; and the 1983 Report of the Commissioner General of UNRWA, 38 UN GAOR Supp. (No. 13) at 12, UN Doc. A/38/13 (1983).

human rights instruments are applicable in occupied territories; and whether settlements by nationals of the occupying power, or deportations of inhabitants, or major plans for new roads tying the territories to Israel proper accord with international law. Not all such questions are necessarily amenable to resolution by a legal body of this kind; and any such resolution would not of itself necessarily change political and military realities. The principal ground for considering the proposal at all is that, more than two decades after this occupation began, there is still basic disagreement about what parts of international law are formally applicable to the situation in the territories.

The Ending of Prolonged Occupations

26. Consideration of prolonged occupations, against the background of more than 20 years of Israeli occupation, should encourage some reflection about how occupations end. One idea, widely accepted by lawyers and politicians, is of international negotiation leading to a formal treaty that terminates the occupation at a single point in time. However, the end of many occupations (and also colonial regimes) has included the gradual emergence (or re-emergence) of autonomous political institutions within the territory, which assume increasing responsibilities culminating in sovereignty and independence. Past events there suggest that such a process would not be easy to initiate today in the West Bank and Gaza. However, some such process is envisaged in several current diplomatic proposals and should not be ruled out entirely on the all-too-familiar grounds of "all or nothing." Such a process could be especially important in view of the continuing need for Palestinians to show the rest of the world (including their Arab neighbors as well as Israel) that they can conduct their affairs in a responsible and effective way. Since many occupations have only ended when the occupying power has made its own decision, in its own interest, that the time for termination has come, the value of steps that might provide a basis for an occupant to reach that decision is clear. The PLO still has a long way to go to get over encrusted suspicions, and to demonstrate clearly its acceptance of Israel, its opposition to terrorism and its commitment to democracy.

27. Prolonged occupation may be a feature of the contemporary world, but it does not necessarily mean permanent occupation. Some long-standing and contentious cases of foreign military involvements—the Soviet Union in Afghanistan, Vietnam in Kampuchea, and South Africa in Namibia—have been drawing to a close. As for the Middle East, the Soviet Union now looks more willing to treat Israel in a less ideological manner than hitherto, and to assist more constructively in diplomatic negotiations. However, the problem of the Israeli occupation remains outstandingly difficult to resolve: Israel has greater grounds than some other recent occupying powers to be concerned about threats to its security; the presence of settlers in the occupied territories makes withdrawal more difficult; the political strength in

Israel of territorial claims is considerable; and drawing the borders of any future Palestinian state raises tangled problems, especially regarding Jerusalem.

28. The Israeli occupation, unlike some others, is therefore likely to be yet further prolonged. In these circumstances, the law on occupations cannot conceivably eliminate the fundamental conflict between the Israeli occupants and the Palestinian inhabitants. At most, it can mitigate some of the worst effects of that conflict. In particular, it can remind all concerned of the provisional status of the occupation and deter further drastic steps that would militate against an eventual settlement. If such modest functions are not to be wasted, the parties involved will need, not just to use law, but to demonstrate statesmanship.

[15]

TRANSFORMATIVE MILITARY OCCUPATION: APPLYING THE LAWS OF WAR AND HUMAN RIGHTS

*By Adam Roberts**

Within the existing framework of international law, is it legitimate for an occupying power, in the name of creating the conditions for a more democratic and peaceful state, to introduce fundamental changes in the constitutional, social, economic, and legal order within an occupied territory? This is the central question addressed here. To put it in other ways, is the body of treaty-based international law relating to occupations, some of which is more than a century old, appropriate to conditions sometimes faced today? Is it still relevant to cases of transformative occupation—i.e., those whose stated purpose (whether or not actually achieved) is to change states that have failed, or have been under tyrannical rule? Is the newer body of human rights law applicable to occupations, and can it provide a basis for transformative acts by the occupant? Can the United Nations Security Council modify the application of the law in particular cases? Finally, has the body of treaty-based law been modified by custom?

These questions have arisen in various conflicts and occupations since 1945—including the tragic situation in Iraq since the United States–led invasion of March–April 2003. They have arisen because of the cautious, even restrictive assumption in the laws of war (also called international humanitarian law or, traditionally, *jus in bello*) that occupying powers should respect the existing laws and economic arrangements within the occupied territory, and should therefore, by implication, make as few changes as possible. This conservationist principle in the laws of war stands in potential conflict with the transformative goals of certain occupations.

This survey suggests that the law on occupations remains both viable and useful, and has proved reasonably flexible in practice. The article explores two particular ways that potential conflicts between the conservationist principle on the one hand, and transformative goals on the other, may be mitigated. One is the application of international human rights law, which offers principles and procedures that can help to define the means and ends of an occupation. Another is the involvement of international organizations, especially the United Nations, that can assist in setting or legitimizing certain transformative policies during an occupation.

The existence of a possible legal justification for pursuing transformative projects in military occupations might be thought to have two consequences, but neither of them follows automatically from it. First, it is no basis for general optimism about transformative occupations. Law may allow for certain possible courses of action, but that does not mean that transformative goals are always desirable or attainable. Only in exceptional circumstances are occupations likely to bring about a successful democratic transition in a society. There is ample ground for skepticism about the propositions that democracy can be spread by the sword, and that the

* Montague Burton Professor of International Relations, Oxford University; Fellow, Balliol College. This article is a product of research conducted under the auspices of the Oxford Leverhulme Programme on the Changing Character of War. A version will appear in due course in INTERNATIONAL LAW AND ARMED CONFLICT: EXPLORING THE FAULTLINES (Michael N. Schmitt & Jelena Pejic eds., 2006) (essays in honor of Yoram Dinstein).

holding of multiparty elections in itself constitutes evidence that a society is moving beyond authoritarianism.[1]

Second, a legal framework for a transformative project under the *jus in bello* does not mean that, under the *jus ad bellum*, states can be said to be vested with anything approaching a general right to invade other sovereign states with the stated purpose of reforming their political systems in a democratic direction. Since at least the time of the French Revolution of 1789, there have been many visions and projects of democratic transformative conquest. In contemporary international law a transformative political purpose does not on its own justify intervention.

The question of whether intervention on transformative grounds can be justified overlaps with the longstanding and contentious question of "humanitarian intervention." A strong tradition of skepticism has developed among international lawyers about whether, in the absence of specific UN Security Council authorization, any "right of humanitarian intervention" obtains.[2] However, there is scope for a nuanced view that allows for some possibility of humanitarian intervention even without specific Security Council authorization. In such a view, it is neither logical nor helpful to frame the consideration of interventions in humanitarian crises in terms of a general "right" of humanitarian intervention. Rather, humanitarian intervention should be seen as an occasional necessity, requiring that the legal issues on both sides be finely balanced, and that the states taking military action accept a degree of legal risk. If it were accepted along these lines that on rare occasions intervention on humanitarian grounds might be justifiable, even without explicit Security Council authorization, each individual case of intervention would need to be based on meticulous consideration of the factual situation and legal issues involved.[3]

The question of whether an occupant is entitled to transformative goals is in principle distinct from the question of the original reason for the intervention. The distinction is especially important because, at least in some cases, an occupation may be initiated primarily as a response to the international conduct of the target state—such as offensive military operations or violations of its international commitments on any of a wide range of matters. In such cases the transformative purpose of an occupation may at best be a secondary reason for invading, or may emerge as a goal only after the armed conflict and/or the resulting occupation has commenced. Yet an element of artificiality marks the proposition that transformative goals may be acceptable, but only as a byproduct of military action, not as its real justification.

Several episodes, including events in the defeated Axis countries after 1945 and Iraq since 2003, indicate that a transformative political purpose can often arise in occupations, and also in some other situations resembling occupations in certain respects (such as UN administrations of postconflict territories). In the cases where occupation law is applicable, the lawfulness, or lack of it, of such a purpose has to be assessed partly as a question relating to the lawful powers of occupants.

This survey, which focuses mainly on the *jus in bello* question of the limits of the powers of an occupant, is divided into four main parts. The first part looks at certain underlying rules of the laws of war that set a framework of minimal alteration of the existing order in the occupied

[1] On the distinction between the external trappings of democracy and political systems in which freedom is deeply entrenched, see especially FAREED ZAKARIA, THE FUTURE OF FREEDOM: ILLIBERAL DEMOCRACY AT HOME AND ABROAD (2003).

[2] Yoram Dinstein has been characteristically consistent, clear, and unequivocal in denying the existence of such a right. YORAM DINSTEIN, WAR, AGGRESSION AND SELF-DEFENCE 70–73, 90–91, 315 (4th ed. 2005).

[3] For elaboration of such a view, see Adam Roberts, *The So-Called "Right" of Humanitarian Intervention*, 2000 Y.B. INT'L HUMANITARIAN L. 3.

territory, and considers certain challenges to them. The second part discusses the applicability of the international law of human rights to military occupations. Because this is a relatively new and controversial issue, this part includes not only a general discussion, but also brief reference to certain occupations and analogous situations in which this question has arisen. The third part examines post-1945 foreign military presences with a fundamentally transformative purpose, and considers, inter alia, the implications of such a purpose for the law governing occupations. This part focuses on the role of international organizations (especially the United Nations), and on Iraq since 2003. The fourth part suggests some general conclusions about transformative military presences, with an eye mainly to the challenges to, and continuing relevance of, the laws of war and also human rights law.

I. THE LAWS OF WAR

The assumption that, the occupant's role being temporary, any alteration of the existing order in occupied territory should be minimal lies at the heart of the provisions on military occupation in the laws of war. Three aspects of the law relating to occupied territories exemplify this requirement: the prohibition of annexation, the rules regarding the occupant's structure of authority, and the rules regarding the maintenance of existing legislation in occupied territory. The first, the prohibition on annexation, has survived, battered but unbowed. The second and third are under much greater pressure. Each is considered in turn.

All three of these rules are related to the understanding of occupation as a concomitant of war and a temporary state of affairs pending a peace agreement. In this sense these rules fit well within the mainstream of the *jus in bello*. However, occupation has long been accepted as not always a mere temporary phase during a war. For example, there is a tradition of thought about *post-debellatio* occupation, which occurs when a country is so completely defeated at the end of a war that it has virtually ceased to exist as a state.[4] Modern transformative occupations can be distinguished from *post-debellatio* occupation, but they do bear certain similarities to it. In the period since 1945, several occupations have endured long after the hostilities that caused them: the Israeli-occupied territories, northern Cyprus, and Iraq are cases in point. This phenomenon has given rise to thoughtful consideration by some writers as to whether occupation law faces a crisis of relevance. At the most general level, it has been asked whether occupation law should be viewed as coming under a new umbrella labeled *jus post bellum*, but this suggestion has been tempered by awareness of the importance of effective implementation of the present body of occupation law, which is seen as remaining relevant to many problems raised in modern occupations.[5]

Prohibition of Annexation

The rule of international customary law that prohibits unilateral annexation of territory, at least while a conflict is still continuing, is a necessary foundation for the whole idea that occupation is subject to a distinct regulatory framework. The rule serves as a reminder of the limits imposed on an occupying power—limits that might also have implications for "transformative" occupations. Although annexation and transformation are conceptually and legally very

[4] Adam Roberts, *What Is a Military Occupation?* 1984 BRIT. Y.B. INT'L L. 249, 267.

[5] Daniel Thürer & Malcolm MacLaren, *"Ius post bellum" in Iraq: A Challenge to the Applicability and Relevance of International Humanitarian Law? in* WELTINNENRECHT: LIBER AMICORUM JOST DELBRÜCK 753 (Klaus Dicke et al. eds., 2005).

different, they do have one thing in common—they tend to involve extending to the occupied territory the type of political system adhered to by the occupying power.

Many acts of annexation have been defended by the rhetoric of transformation. Thus, when in September 1911, Italy presented an ultimatum to the Ottoman government, it complained that Tripoli and Cyrenaica had been left in a "state of disorder and neglect," insisting that "these regions should be allowed to enjoy the same progress as that attained by other parts of Northern Africa. This transformation, which is required by the general exigencies of civilization, constitutes, so far as Italy is concerned, a vital interest. . . ."[6] In November 1911, Italy decreed the subjection of Tripolitania and Cyrenaica to complete Italian sovereignty. Many saw this annexation as illegal. As Sir Thomas Barclay wrote, shortly after:

> If annexation could be decreed by an invader without the consent of the invaded Power the whole population of the annexed territory might at once be made to pass under the allegiance of the invading sovereign, its legitimate acts of defence be made rebellious and punishable as such and the troops opposed to the invader be made to forfeit their right to be treated as belligerent. This is a *reductio ad absurdum* of any such proposition.[7]

Modern practice, which finds expression in several international agreements, denies the right in most circumstances to annex occupied territory unilaterally—i.e., to change its legal status to that of a component part of the occupant's sovereign state. Even if the whole country is occupied, and the legitimate government goes into exile and does not participate actively in military operations, the occupant does not have any right of annexation.[8]

If the occupying power does (illegally) annex the whole or part of the occupied territory, the population must not by that act be deprived of the benefits of the Fourth Geneva Convention of 1949.[9] An example of the international community's observation of this principle in response to an attempted annexation occurred on August 2, 1990, when Iraq occupied Kuwait. On the same day the UN Security Council demanded that Iraq "withdraw immediately and unconditionally," and on August 6, declaring itself "[d]etermined to bring the invasion and occupation of Kuwait by Iraq to an end," the Council imposed economic sanctions on Iraq.[10] On August 8, Saddam Hussein announced the merger of Kuwait with Iraq—i.e., annexation. On the following day, the Security Council decided "that annexation of Kuwait by Iraq under any form and whatever pretext has no legal validity, and is considered null and void."[11] The Council subsequently stated explicitly that "the Fourth Geneva Convention applies to

[6] Ultimatum from Italy to Turkey Regarding Tripoli (Sept. 26, 1911), 6 AJIL Supp. 11, 11 (1912).

[7] THOMAS BARCLAY, THE TURCO-ITALIAN WAR AND ITS PROBLEMS 45 (1912). On the strong international Muslim feeling about this conquest, see the additional chapter by the Rt. Hon. Ameer Ali at 101–08. See *id.* at 109 for the text of Italy's ultimatum of September 26, 1911 (also *supra* note 6), and *id.* at 113 for its Decree of Annexation of November 1911.

[8] The prohibition on annexations is part of customary law and finds expression in Article 2(4) of the UN Charter and in the Declaration on Principles of International Law Concerning Friendly Relations and Co-operation Among States in Accordance with the Charter of the United Nations, GA Res. 2625 (XXV), annex (Oct. 24, 1970). *See also* Georg Schwarzenberger, *The Law of Belligerent Occupation: Basic Issues*, 30 NORDISK TIDSSKRIFT FOR INT'L RET 10, 12–18 (1960).

[9] Convention Relative to the Protection of Civilian Persons in Time of War, Aug. 12, 1949, Art. 47, 6 UST 3516, 75 UNTS 287 [hereinafter Geneva Convention IV].

[10] SC Res. 660 (Aug. 2, 1990), 29 ILM 1325 (1990); SC Res. 661, pmbl. (Aug. 6, 1990), 29 ILM 1325 (emphasis omitted). The texts of these and all other Security Council and General Assembly resolutions and certain other UN documents mentioned in this survey are available at <http://www.un.org/documents>.

[11] SC Res. 662, para. 1 (Aug. 9, 1990), 29 ILM 1327 (1990).

Kuwait."[12] Thus, in this case at least, the most drastic form of transformation of a territory and its political order—namely, incorporation into another state—was viewed as clearly contrary to international law; and the rules governing occupations remained a valid benchmark by which the actions of the occupant were to be judged.

Other cases of annexation or quasi annexation demonstrate that the prohibition of annexations, while crystal clear in theory, is by no means as straightforward in practice. A principal problem is that many cases of annexation or attempted annexation have taken place in circumstances where the original status of the annexed territory was itself less than one of full sovereignty. The Chinese invasion of Tibet (1950), the Indian invasion of Goa (1962), and the Indonesian invasion of East Timor (1975) are all cases in point. Only the last of these three actions was eventually reversed, in 1999–2002.

Annexation has often been seen, quite naturally, as linked to aggression. Many international lawyers have propounded the principle that unilateral acts inconsistent with fundamental rules of international law should be viewed as null and void, and no prescriptive rights should accrue in favor of the aggressor. Thus, annexation resulting from aggression should not be recognized. Yoram Dinstein raises the interesting question of the long-term effectiveness of the legal principle of nonrecognition. "If the *de facto* control of the territory annexed by the aggressor continues uninterrupted for generations, the non-prescription rule may have to give way in the end. International law must not be divorced from reality."[13]

What if an occupation arises, not from an act of aggression, but following a defensive war in which a state defending its territory occupies neighboring lands? This is one factually well-grounded view of the position of Israel regarding the territories occupied since 1967. In certain parts of these territories (the Golan Heights, and East Jerusalem with extended boundaries) subsequent acts of annexation or quasi annexation have been taken, mainly in the form of applying Israeli law to them. The overwhelming tendency of states and international bodies has been not to recognize these purported annexations but, rather, to view the law on occupations as remaining applicable to the situation. The general prohibition on annexation, in other words, continues to be seen as a key principle, even though it is under pressure.

Despite its undeniable importance, annexation is by no means the only way that fundamental and lasting change may be brought about in a territory. One of the common ways for occupying forces to change the political order in occupied territory is by attempting, not an act of annexation, but changes, for example, in the composition of the government, and in the constitutional or legal system. These changes may be aimed at achieving what is in effect the opposite of annexation: the full resumption of sovereignty by the territory concerned. There is nothing new about such practices. As Sharon Korman has written in *The Right of Conquest*, the post-1789 French revolutionaries believed that they had replaced the old-fashioned right of conquest with a new principle—the right of peoples to determine their political affiliations freely:

> Thus, in accordance with the principle of "no conquests" which it had proclaimed in 1790, revolutionary France declined to invoke the right of conquest in the countries to which its arms were supposedly bringing liberty. But if it no longer substituted its own sovereignty *directly* in the occupied territories, it did so in an *indirect* manner. Judging that the people were the sole sovereign, it overthrew the ancient sovereignty of "usurper" kings, only to

[12] SC Res. 670, para. 13 (Sept. 25, 1990), 29 ILM 1334 (1990); SC Res. 674, pmbl. (Oct. 29, 1990), 29 ILM 1561.

[13] DINSTEIN, *supra* note 2, at 171.

establish in their place popular authorities which it placed under the "revolutionary guidance" of France.[14]

This episode serves as a useful reminder that transformative occupations have a long history. They arguably grew out of the disapproval of annexations but are not their opposites in all respects. Indeed, in many cases, from the French Revolution to twentieth-century Germany and Japan, and twenty-first-century Iraq, transformative occupation may be considered to have emerged as a more honorable, but still deeply controversial, successor to the discredited notion of annexation.

The Occupant's Structure of Authority

The occupant, including such occupying forces or officers as are mentioned in the conventions, usually exercises authority by virtue of its effective factual control rather than any legal entitlement. That factual power is accorded a degree of recognition in the conventions, which reflect the assumption that the occupant maintains a structure of authority and extensive responsibilities in the occupied territory. Transformation, which necessarily involves handing over power to authorities that come from within the territory, threatens this assumption.

What is an occupation administration supposed to look like? The 1907 Hague Regulations refer variously to "the hostile army," "the occupant," "a commander-in-chief," "the commander in the locality occupied," "an army of occupation," and "the occupying state" as the entities exercising authority in occupied territory.[15] The Regulations clearly imply that a well-ordered chain of military command and legal responsibility emanates from the government of the occupying state: and, indeed, most occupation administrations have had such a character.

The Fourth Geneva Convention refers throughout to the "Occupying Power" as the body with authority in occupied territory.[16] This term applies essentially to the central government of the state whose forces have carried out the invasion and occupation. Nothing is said in this Convention about the precise administrative form of the occupation regime. Additional Protocol I of 1977 also uses the term "Occupying Power" without defining it or suggesting the administrative forms it might assume.[17] Thus, the Geneva stream of law establishes that the government of the occupying state bears responsibility for actions taken in occupied territory, but it does not elaborate on the brief references in the Hague Regulations as to who exerts this authority on the spot.

Many writers, properly stressing the idea of temporary trusteeship, which is found at the core of much occupation law, have indicated that the constitutional changes an occupying power

[14] SHARON KORMAN, THE RIGHT OF CONQUEST: THE ACQUISITION OF TERRITORY BY FORCE IN INTERNATIONAL LAW AND PRACTICE 122 (1996). For a historical perspective on transformative occupations, see also Nehal Bhuta, *The Antinomies of Transformative Occupation*, 16 EUR. J. INT'L L. 721 (2005).

[15] Regulations Respecting the Laws and Customs of War on Land, Arts. 42, 43, 48, 49, 51, 52, 53, 55, annexed to Convention Respecting the Laws and Customs of War on Land, Oct. 18, 1907, 36 Stat. 2277, 1 Bevans 631 [hereinafter Hague Regulations].

[16] In Geneva Convention IV, *supra* note 9, the term "Occupying Power" appears in Articles 4–6, 30, 47–61, 63–68, 70–75, 78, and 143. A continuing role for the authorities of the occupied territories is implicitly envisaged in Articles 6 and 47.

[17] Protocol Additional to the Geneva Conventions of 12 August 1949, and Relating to the Protection of Victims of International Armed Conflicts, *opened for signature* Dec. 12, 1977, Arts. 14, 15, 63, 64, 69, 85, 1125 UNTS 3 [hereinafter Protocol I]. The same term is used in the UNESCO Convention for the Protection of Cultural Property in the Event of Armed Conflict, May 14, 1954, Art. 5, 249 UNTS 240.

may bring about are limited. Jean Pictet, commenting on Article 47 of the Fourth Geneva Convention, has expressed this view:

> During the Second World War Occupying Powers intervened in the occupied countries on numerous occasions and in a great variety of ways, depending on the political aim pursued; examples are changes in constitutional forms or in the form of government, the establishment of new military or political organizations, the dissolution of the State, or the formation of new political entities.
>
> International law prohibits such actions, which are based solely on the military strength of the Occupying Power and not on a sovereign decision by the occupied State. Of course the Occupying Power usually tried to give some colour of legality and independence to the new organizations, which were formed in the majority of cases with the co-operation of certain elements among the population of the occupied country, but it was obvious that they were in fact always subservient to the will of the Occupying Power. Such practices were incompatible with the traditional concept of occupation (as defined in Article 43 of the Hague Regulations of 1907) according to which the occupying authority was to be considered as merely being a *de facto* administrator.[18]

Pictet's underlying idea, that the occupying power normally has the role of de facto administrator, is indeed justified. However, in the sweeping form in which he presents it, his condemnation of political interventions by occupying powers is open to challenge. Occupants often attempt to disguise or limit their own role by operating indirectly: by setting up some kind of quasi-independent puppet regime; by operating through the existing system of government, which remains in post within occupied territory; by establishing an international administration of the territory; or by introducing a new constitutional system. Sometimes they may seek to justify such actions as steps toward creating a new democratic system of government in the occupied territory. Particularly strong reasons can argue for doing so if a war is concluded without any prospect that the territory will simply revert to its former rulers.[19]

Although many of the wide variety of governmental arrangements imposed by occupying powers undoubtedly differ from what is envisaged in the Hague Regulations and the Fourth Geneva Convention, states have been reluctant to conclude that in every case such practices are unlawful. Specifically, they hesitate to condemn in principle the introduction of constitutional democracy in the occupied territory. However, the emergence of a legitimate government inevitably modifies the responsibilities and structure of authority of the occupant.

Existing Legislation of the Occupied Territory

What are the rules under occupation law that govern the nature and extent of changes that can be introduced within occupied territory? On the face of it, they are straightforward. Their basics are enshrined in the much-quoted words of the 1907 Hague Regulations, which provide in Article 43:

[18] INTERNATIONAL COMMITTEE OF THE RED CROSS [ICRC], COMMENTARY ON THE GENEVA CONVENTION (IV) RELATIVE TO THE PROTECTION OF CIVILIAN PERSONS IN TIME OF WAR 273 (Jean Pictet gen. ed., 1958), *available at* <http://www.icrc.org/ihl>.

[19] In regard to Israel's role in the West Bank, the term "trustee occupation" was proposed by Allan Gerson in 1973. He suggested that since this occupation had certain special features, not all the provisions of the law on occupations need necessarily apply. He himself conceded that Israel had not in the end assumed the role of "trustee occupant." ALLAN GERSON, ISRAEL, THE WEST BANK AND INTERNATIONAL LAW 76–82 (1978).

> The authority of the legitimate power having in fact passed into the hands of the occupant, the latter shall take all the measures in his power to restore, and ensure, as far as possible, public order and safety, while respecting, unless absolutely prevented, the laws in force in the country.[20]

This article presents some problems. The assumption that the previous ruler of a territory was a "legitimate power" is not easy to square with U.S. or indeed many other views of Adolf Hitler and Saddam Hussein. The article's implication that the "laws in force in the country" were basically satisfactory has often been called into question by events. The escape clause, "unless absolutely prevented," has provided a basis for introducing certain changes to the laws of occupied territories.

The basic requirement to respect the existing legal framework of a territory has long been under pressure, for a variety of reasons. This apparently straightforward rule needs interpretation in light of the particular facts of a situation, and the particular nature of certain laws. In practice, certain types of law (e.g., laws relating to military conscription and to national elections) are often suspended during occupations.[21] Moreover, in occupations of countries that had previously been under dictatorial or extremist rule, numerous other laws may be suspended. In the occupation of parts of Italy and Germany toward the end of World War II, the Allies abolished fascist laws. They did so right from the start, during the belligerent occupation phase before the Italian armistice and the German surrender. This measure might appear to have transgressed the letter of Article 43. However, many writers indicated that the nature of the Axis regimes and their laws was such as to "absolutely prevent" the Allies from accepting their continuation.[22]

Against this background, in the negotiations leading to the 1949 Geneva Civilians Convention, the extent to which an occupying power can legitimately alter the laws in force in occupied territory was naturally discussed. The states concerned eventually agreed on a modest modification of Article 43 of the Hague Regulations, allowing a little more scope for changes in the existing local laws. This is Article 64 of the Civilians Convention:

> The penal laws of the occupied territory shall remain in force, with the exception that they may be repealed or suspended by the Occupying Power in cases where they constitute a threat to its security or an obstacle to the application of the present Convention. Subject to the latter consideration and to the necessity for ensuring the effective administration of justice, the tribunals of the occupied territory shall continue to function in respect of all offences covered by the said laws.
>
> The Occupying Power may, however, subject the population of the occupied territory to provisions which are essential to enable the Occupying Power to fulfil its obligations under the present Convention, to maintain the orderly government of the territory, and

[20] Hague Regulations, *supra* note 15, Art. 43; *see also id.*, Art. 23(h). For a useful discussion of Article 43 and its flexibility in practice, see Marco Sassòli, *Legislation and Maintenance of Public Order and Civil Life by Occupiers*, 16 EUR. J. INT'L L. 661 (2005).

[21] U.S. DEP'T OF ARMY, LAW OF LAND WARFARE 143 (Field Manual No. 27–10, 1956); UNITED KINGDOM [UK] WAR OFFICE, THE LAW OF WAR ON LAND, BEING PART III OF THE MANUAL OF MILITARY LAW 145 (1958) [hereinafter 1958 UK MANUAL]. Its successor, the 2004 triservice manual, states that the occupant may suspend or amend existing laws of the occupied territory in certain defined circumstances. UK MINISTRY OF DEFENCE, THE MANUAL OF THE LAW OF ARMED CONFLICT 278–79, 284 (2004) [hereinafter 2004 UK MANUAL].

[22] F. S. V. DONNISON, CIVIL AFFAIRS AND MILITARY GOVERNMENT: NORTH-WEST EUROPE 1944–46, at 381–82, 477–78 (1961); C. R. S. HARRIS, ALLIED MILITARY ADMINISTRATION OF ITALY 1943–1945, at 14 (1957); 2 L. OPPENHEIM, INTERNATIONAL LAW: A TREATISE 446–47 (Hersch Lauterpacht ed., 7th ed. 1952); *see also* 2004 UK MANUAL, *supra* note 21, at 143.

> to ensure the security of the Occupying Power, of the members and property of the occupying forces or administration, and likewise of the establishments and lines of communication used by them.[23]

The negotiation in 1949 that preceded this text included proposals that would have more explicitly acknowledged the right of the occupying power to change the laws. The U.S. delegate, Robert W. Ginnane, proposed replacing draft Article 55, which became the above-quoted Article 64, with a much shorter, simpler, and (for the occupying power) more permissive text: "Until changed by the Occupying Power the penal laws of the occupied territory shall remain in force and the tribunals thereof shall continue to function in respect of all offences covered by the said laws."[24]

The Soviet delegate, Platon Dmitrievitch Morosov, spotted the obvious problem with this proposal, "that it gave the Occupying Power an absolute right to modify the penal legislation of the occupied territory. Such a right greatly exceeded the limited right laid down in the Hague Regulations . . . ."[25] Less powerful but no less perceptive, the distinguished French international lawyer Paul de Geouffre de la Pradelle, representing Monaco, suggested that, in the case of occupied Germany after World War II, U.S. modification of the laws of the country was acceptable, but that this modification did not provide a basis for a general rule:

> What would be the position in the opposite case, that of an invader other than a democratic Power, who exercised that right? Under the United States amendment the invader could change the penal legislation of the occupied territory. The Committee should think very carefully before amending the wording of the Convention in the way suggested.[26]

In the discussion that followed, Mexico suggested "the adoption of a wording to the effect that the Occupying Power could only modify the legislation of an occupied territory if the legislation in question violated the principles of the 'Universal Declaration of the Rights of Man'."[27] This solitary reference to a human rights benchmark was not followed up at the conference.[28] Yet in the long run, the issue of human rights was to have a profound effect on the rules governing occupations. It was to supply one basis for altering the laws of the occupied territory.

Overall, the rule that the laws in force in the country should be respected continues to provide an important benchmark for occupants. In many cases, however, occupants, for a wide variety of reasons, have changed laws in the occupied territory without incurring international criticism. Transformative occupations increase the pressure for changing those laws. As a result, if Article 64 of the Fourth Geneva Convention were rewritten today, pressure would be

[23] Geneva Convention IV, *supra* note 9, Art. 64. In the 1958 UK Manual it was implied that an occupant may also repeal or suspend laws if in the occupied territory there is no "adequate legal system in conformity with generally recognised principles of law." 1958 UK MANUAL, *supra* note 21, at 145. In similar spirit, its 2004 successor states: "The occupying power should make no more changes to the law than are absolutely necessary, particularly where the occupied territory already has an adequate legal system." 2004 UK MANUAL, *supra* note 21, at 284.

[24] 3 FINAL RECORD OF THE DIPLOMATIC CONFERENCE OF GENEVA OF 1949, at 139, amend. 294; *see* 2A *id.* at 670. The draft text of Article 55 that the United States sought to replace is in *id.* at 858. A useful report on Article 55 appears in *id.* at 833. These negotiations on the text of the Civilians Convention were conducted in the conference's Committee III.

[25] 2A *id.* at 670.

[26] *Id.* at 671.

[27] *Id.*

[28] See the further discussion in *id.* at 672, and the report back by the Drafting Committee, *id.* at 771. In the index of contents of the four volumes of the *Final Record*, there is no entry for "human rights" or "Universal Declaration."

applied to provide for laws of the occupied territory to be repealed or suspended in two additional types of circumstance—where they hamper the exercise by the inhabitants of fundamental human rights and the implementation of transformative purposes approved by the UN Security Council.

In the Civilians Convention, one other provision might at first sight seem relevant to transformative occupations but actually illustrates failure to come to grips with them. In Article 6, which addresses occupations that continue for more than a year after the end of a war and envisages the progressive handing over of the functions of government by the occupant, it is stated:

> In the case of occupied territory, the application of the present Convention shall cease one year after the general close of military operations; however, the Occupying Power shall be bound, for the duration of the occupation, to the extent that such Power exercises the functions of government in such territory, by the provisions of the following Articles of the present Convention: 1 to 12, 27, 29 to 34, 47, 49, 51, 52, 53, 59, 61 to 77, 143.[29]

Thus, if the occupant is still in charge one year after the war, Article 64 with its moderate conservationist thrust is among the many that would still apply. However, Article 6 provides no other guidance on the extent to which an occupant pursuing long-term transformative goals may make changes in existing legislation. In any case, the "one year after" rule is widely seen as bearing little or no relevance to actual occupations, and it was effectively rescinded by a provision of Additional Protocol I, as between states parties to the latter.[30] Despite its limitations, Article 6 is a reminder of the old and important fact that not all occupations can be subject to exactly the same rules.

II. The International Law of Human Rights

Traditionally, the laws of war have been seen as the main—even the only—branch of international law applicable to occupations. However, there is no a priori reason why multilateral conventions on other matters should not be applicable to occupied territories. Increasing evidence indicates that one other body of law may be especially relevant: human rights law. Setting out as it does to spell out certain fundamental human rights, human rights law is not specifically tailored to the situation considered here—military occupation. Like the law on crimes against humanity, it has a wider scope of application than the laws of war: it applies in peacetime, and it applies within states, affecting, for example, the relations between governments and their own subjects.

Human rights law developed from custom over a long period. A key document in its codification was the 1948 Universal Declaration of Human Rights.[31] Adopted by the UN General Assembly, the Declaration did not take the form of a legally binding instrument, and it does not contain the normal machinery whereby states can become parties to it. Rather, it commands the status of an authoritative guide to the relevant parts of the UN Charter. It was followed by the conclusion of a large number of human rights treaties, four leading examples of which are the 1950 European Convention for the Protection of Human Rights and Fundamental Freedoms (ECHR),[32] the 1966 International Covenant on Civil and Political

[29] Geneva Convention IV, *supra* note 9, Art. 6(3).

[30] Protocol I, *supra* note 17, Art. 3(b).

[31] Universal Declaration of Human Rights, GA Res. 217A (III), UN Doc. A/810, at 71 (1948).

[32] European Convention for the Protection of Human Rights and Fundamental Freedoms, Nov. 4, 1950, 213 UNTS 221 [hereinafter ECHR].

Rights,[33] the 1966 International Covenant on Economic, Social and Cultural Rights,[34] and the 1984 UN Convention Against Torture.[35]

Some have viewed such instruments as the 1948 Universal Declaration and the two 1966 Covenants as together constituting an "International Bill of Human Rights," an authoritative interpretation of the UN Charter's human rights clauses that hence is binding on all states, establishing a human rights standard of universal applicability.[36] This view, as indicated below, is contested.

The application of international human rights law to several occupations has been urged since the mid-1960s. However, experience has shown that the application of international human rights law in this way can give rise to considerable problems. Before certain grounds for caution are addressed, the overall relationship between this branch of law and the laws of war needs to be examined.

Relationship Between Human Rights Law and the Laws of War

International human rights law is in some respects a new body of law that has been evolving quite rapidly since the end of World War II. It is therefore not surprising that the relationship of human rights law to armed conflict in general, or to occupations in particular, should still be in need of exploration.[37]

That human rights law and the problem of war and military occupation are indeed connected is indicated by the origins of the modern movement for human rights law. It can be said to have begun with the international concern about the disregard for human rights shown in many occupied countries, as well as in the territory of Germany itself and that of its allies, during World War II. As William Bishop wrote: "The greatest impetus for United Nations action for international protection of human rights grew out of the almost universal reaction against the German Nazi oppressions of persons in Germany and in the territories occupied by Germany during World War II."[38]

This concern not only contributed to the development of the body of human rights law, but also had its effect on international agreements on the laws of war. This influence is evident in the terms of the four 1949 Geneva Conventions. As Dietrich Schindler has written, with that tinge of optimism that occasionally marks his commentary on the Conventions: "[A] tendency may be detected in the *Geneva Conventions of 1949* for their provisions to be considered not only as obligations to be discharged by the High Contracting Parties but as individual rights of the protected persons."[39]

[33] International Covenant on Civil and Political Rights, Dec. 16, 1966, 999 UNTS 171 [hereinafter ICCPR].

[34] International Covenant on Economic, Social and Cultural Rights, Dec. 16, 1966, 993 UNTS 3 [hereinafter ICESCR].

[35] Convention Against Torture and Other Cruel, Inhuman or Degrading Treatment or Punishment, *opened for signature* Dec. 10, 1984, 1465 UNTS 85 [hereinafter Convention Against Torture].

[36] Frank C. Newman, *The International Bill of Human Rights: Does it Exist? in* CURRENT PROBLEMS OF INTERNATIONAL LAW: ESSAYS ON UN LAW AND ON THE LAW OF ARMED CONFLICT 107 (Antonio Cassese ed., 1975).

[37] Many works on human rights law make little or no reference to the problems of armed conflict and military occupation. *See, e.g.*, PAUL SIEGHART, THE LAWFUL RIGHTS OF MANKIND: AN INTRODUCTION TO THE INTERNATIONAL LEGAL CODE OF HUMAN RIGHTS (1985).

[38] WILLIAM W. BISHOP JR., INTERNATIONAL LAW: CASES AND MATERIALS 470 (3d ed. 1971).

[39] Dietrich Schindler, *The International Committee of the Red Cross and Human Rights,* INT'L REV. RED CROSS, No. 208, Jan.–Feb. 1979, at 3, 7.

Additional Protocol I on international armed conflict overlaps with human rights law much more directly than the 1949 Conventions, which it supplements. Article 72 specifies that the provisions outlined in that section of the Protocol are additional not only to the rules in the Fourth Geneva Convention, but also "to other applicable rules of international law relating to the protection of fundamental human rights during international armed conflict." Moreover, Article 75 (on fundamental guarantees) is directly derived from the 1966 International Covenant on Civil and Political Rights. In the 1977 Additional Protocol II on noninternational armed conflict, Article 6 (on penal prosecutions) is similarly derived from the same 1966 Covenant.[40] True, the various instruments of human rights law are not mentioned by name in Geneva Protocols I and II, but their presence is there nonetheless.

Further evidence of a connection between human rights law and the laws of war is the fact that it was a UN conference on human rights (held in 1968 in Tehran) that marked the first occasion when the United Nations showed real interest in the further development of the laws of war. This concern contributed to the diplomatic process that led, inter alia, to the conclusion of Protocols I and II.[41] UN committees and conferences have often discussed laws of war issues under the heading "respect for human rights in armed conflicts."[42]

Writers on the law of armed conflict were not all equally alert to the possible significance of human rights law in occupied territories. To be sure, in 1944 Ernst Fraenkel, in *Military Occupation and the Rule of Law*, did urge that an "international bill of rights" should apply to an occupation regime "at least after the purely military phase of the occupation has ended."[43] However, in works published in the 1950s the question received only modest attention. No specific reference to human rights law appeared in Gerhard von Glahn's *The Occupation of Enemy Territory*, published in 1957.[44] The British *Manual of Military Law*, published in 1958, referred to human rights only in general terms.[45]

Gradually, a change set in as writers came to recognize the potential applicability of human rights in occupied territories. Morris Greenspan, in his major work *The Modern Law of Land Warfare*, published in 1959, briefly adverted to human rights accords—notably, the 1948 Universal Declaration and the 1950 European Convention—and evidently accepted their applicability.[46] Martin and Joan Kyre, in a study of U.S. policy on military occupations published in 1968, noted the significance of the Universal Declaration of Human Rights for military

[40] Protocol Additional to the Geneva Conventions of 12 August 1949, and Relating to the Protection of Victims of Non-international Armed Conflicts, *opened for signature* Dec. 12, 1977, Art. 6, 1125 UNTS 609.

[41] On the various factors leading to the negotiations, which were ultimately to result in the 1977 Geneva Protocols I and II, see particularly Frits Kalshoven, *Reaffirmation and Development of International Humanitarian Law Applicable in Armed Conflicts: The Conference of Government Experts, 24 May–12 June 1971*, 1971 NETH. Y.B. INT'L L. 68.

[42] See, for example, the two-volume survey prepared by the UN Secretariat, Respect for Human Rights in Armed Conflicts: Existing Rules of International Law Concerning the Prohibition or Restriction of Use of Specific Weapons, UN Doc. A/9215 (1973).

[43] ERNST FRAENKEL, MILITARY OCCUPATION AND THE RULE OF LAW 205 (1944).

[44] However, see Gerhard von Glahn, *The Protection of Human Rights in Time of Armed Conflicts*, 1971 ISR. Y.B. HUM. RTS. 208, 213–14, where he accepts the applicability, in time of armed conflicts, of fundamental human rights.

[45] 1958 UK MANUAL, *supra* note 21, at 143. Its 2004 successor includes reference to the applicability of human rights law. 2004 UK MANUAL, *supra* note 21, at 282.

[46] MORRIS GREENSPAN, THE MODERN LAW OF LAND WARFARE 161 n.34; 247 n.123; 250 n.133; 504 n.393 (1959); *see also* Morris Greenspan, *The Protection of Human Rights in Time of Warfare*, 1971 ISR. Y.B. HUM. RTS. 228, 229 (stating that human rights instruments "apply in war as well as in peace").

occupations, but regretted "a shift in mood within the United States away from internationalism" that had restricted the U.S. role in helping to develop the international law of human rights.[47]

The relation between human rights law and the laws of war began to attract international attention in the late 1960s and early 1970s. This notice was due in part to the adoption of the two International Human Rights Covenants in 1966; international concern over various wars of the period, including in Vietnam; and the Israeli occupation of certain Arab territories in the 1967 war. Many writers recognized a relationship between the two bodies of law, even if it was not a simple one. G. I. A. D. Draper wrote in 1971:

> Human Rights do not dissolve in time of war or public emergency affecting the life of the nation, but are subject to a controlled and limited derogation from specific Human Rights to be justified by the extent of that emergency.
>
> . . . The precise relation between the law of war and the regimes of Human Rights has not yet been elaborated.[48]

Professor Draper also said, in an article published in 1971 in the *Israel Yearbook on Human Rights*: "The essential nexus between the law of war and the regime of human rights has been made in theory, viz., that the former is an essential part of the latter. The law of war is a derogation from the normal regime of human rights . . . ."[49]

The idea that the law of war could be seen, in large measure, as one important body of rules and principles for safeguarding human rights in situations of armed conflict and occupation was supported by many other writers. Dinstein, in an article in 1978, also in the *Israel Yearbook*, entitled *The International Law of Belligerent Occupation and Human Rights*, actually wrote almost entirely about the rules laid down in the laws of war. This approach followed quite naturally from the fact that he was preoccupied with the problem of belligerent occupation, especially that of the Israeli-occupied territories, and not with transformative occupation, as the following passage indicates:

> The government of an occupied territory by the occupant is not the same as a State's ordinary government of its own territory: a military occupation is not tantamount to a democratic regime and its objective is not the welfare of the local population. Most peacetime human rights are suspended in time of belligerent occupation.[50]

In a work published in 1980 exploring the relation of human rights law to the laws of war, Aristidis Calogeropoulos-Stratis stressed the applicability in time of armed conflict of certain human rights instruments.[51] In a 1993 study specifically devoted to military occupations, Eyal Benvenisti reached a more nuanced conclusion, which is especially relevant to cases of transformative occupations:

[47] MARTIN & JOAN KYRE, MILITARY OCCUPATION AND NATIONAL SECURITY 97 (1968).

[48] G. I. A. D. Draper, *The Status of Combatants and the Question of Guerilla [sic] Warfare*, 1971 BRIT. Y.B. INT'L L. 173, 218.

[49] G. I. A. D. Draper, *The Relationship Between the Human Rights Regime and the Law of Armed Conflicts*, 1971 ISR. Y.B. HUM. RTS. 191, 206.

[50] Yoram Dinstein, *The International Law of Belligerent Occupation and Human Rights*, 1978 ISR. Y.B. HUM. RTS. 104, 116; *see also* Yoram Dinstein, *Human Rights in Armed Conflict: International Humanitarian Law, in* HUMAN RIGHTS AND INTERNATIONAL LAW: LEGAL AND POLICY ISSUES 345 (Theodor Meron ed., 1984).

[51] ARISTIDIS S. CALOGEROPOULOS-STRATIS, DROIT HUMANITAIRE ET DROITS DE L'HOMME: LA PROTECTION DE LA PERSONNE EN PÉRIODE DE CONFLIT ARMÉ (1980).

> In the interplay between the conflicting interests, the law of occupation concedes that certain civil and political rights will from time to time be subjected to other concerns. Ultimately, as in other cases, the occupant is required to balance its interests against those of the occupied community. Thus, as hostilities subside, and security interests can permit, the occupant could be expected to restore civil and political rights. Under such circumstances, the human rights documents may well serve as guidance for reestablishing civil and political rights in the occupied territory.[52]

In 2004 Kenneth Watkin suggested that, in general, the use of force in armed conflict is increasingly assessed through human rights law as well as international humanitarian law. In briefly considering the specific case of military occupation, he indicated that both normative regimes may come into play, but that the use of force within occupied territory (for example, against an insurgency) is not always amenable to a human rights framework.[53]

On specific issues, especially those relating to individual liberty and political freedoms, there is an element of tension between human rights law and the law on occupations. For example, Article 9 of the International Covenant on Civil and Political Rights prohibits arbitrary detention and requires that "[a]nyone who is arrested shall be . . . promptly informed of any charges against him."[54] By contrast, the first paragraph of Article 78 of the Fourth Geneva Convention states: "If the Occupying Power considers it necessary, for imperative reasons of security, to take safety measures concerning protected persons, it may, at the most, subject them to assigned residence or to internment."[55] Even though the second paragraph adds that such measures must be made "according to a regular procedure," this provision is more draconian than those of the Covenant. The tension between these two approaches is mitigated by the fact that, in time of public emergency threatening the life of the nation, states may derogate from certain obligations under the Covenant, whereas the Convention has to be considered the *lex specialis* for occupations.

In many occupations one basis for asserting the applicability of human rights law may be its near-universal character, as a body of law subscribed to equally by the occupying state and by the occupied state. However, in some occupations the question has arisen as to whether certain specific obligations under human rights law of the occupying power extend to territories that it occupies. An example is the application of the European Convention on Human Rights (which offers not merely a statement of principles, but also an unusually strong legal procedure for obtaining redress) in territories outside those of states parties to the Convention.

The overall question of whether human rights treaties apply extraterritorially is still contested. Michael Dennis of the U.S. Department of State, in a general survey of the subject, goes so far as to conclude:

> The obligations assumed by states under the main international human rights instruments were never intended to apply extraterritorially during periods of armed conflict. Nor were they intended to replace the *lex specialis* of international humanitarian law. Extending the protections provided under international human rights instruments to

[52] EYAL BENVENISTI, THE INTERNATIONAL LAW OF OCCUPATION 189 (1993).

[53] Kenneth Watkin (deputy judge advocate general/operations, Canadian Forces), *Controlling the Use of Force: A Role for Human Rights Norms in Contemporary Armed Conflict*, 98 AJIL 1, 1–2, 26–28 (2004).

[54] ICCPR, *supra* note 33, Art. 9(2).

[55] Geneva Convention IV, *supra* note 9, Art. 78(1).

situations of international armed conflict and military occupation offers a dubious route toward increased state compliance with international norms.[56]

This conclusion is based on serious considerations, including a strict interpretation of Article 2, paragraph 1 of the International Covenant on Civil and Political Rights, under which a state is obliged to ensure the Covenant's rights "to all individuals within its territory and subject to its jurisdiction."[57] The core of Dennis's argument is that both these conditions must be met. Yet it remains unconvincing to argue that human rights law cannot apply at all to situations that arise in a military occupation. A clearer distinction than Dennis offers needs to be drawn between armed conflict (where the application of human rights law is more problematic) and occupation; and also a further distinction between occupation in general and the holding of certain specific persons by outside forces. In the latter situation the application of human rights law may be particularly appropriate. Such distinctions have not always been clearly drawn in addressing the extraterritorial application of human rights norms. For a territory that is indeed occupied—i.e., under the control of the occupying power—a stronger prima facie case that human rights law should apply can be made than for situations of armed conflict. Where prisoners or internees are held under the direct control of the occupant, the case may be stronger still. To the extent that an occupying power exercises control, which it certainly should do in its own prisons, it has the kind of administrative apparatus necessary to make human rights protection effective.[58]

The implementation of human rights law may be advocated as a matter of legal obligation, or as a matter of choice irrespective of whether, as a matter of law, the occupant is required to implement it. Such advocacy of implementation may come from interested parties from two different perspectives: (1) the inhabitants, or outside bodies claiming to act on their behalf, may invoke human rights standards so as to bring pressure to bear on the occupant—e.g., to ensure the human rights of inhabitants, internees, and others; and (2) an occupant with a transformative project may view human rights norms as constituting part of the beneficent political order being introduced into the territory, which has been the U.S. position in the UN Security Council from 2003 onward as far as Iraq has been concerned, but it is not clear how far it has percolated through the U.S. government.

The relation between human rights law and the laws of war is not just a simple confrontation between the *lex generalis* of human rights and the *lex specialis* of the laws of war. In occupations some practical issues can arise (such as discrimination in employment, discrimination in education, and the importation of educational materials) that are addressed in considerable detail in certain human rights agreements but are not so addressed in the law on occupations. Or human rights law may offer procedures for individual complaint and redress that are unknown to the laws of war. As regards such issues, international human rights standards may not merely fill in gaps in the laws of war, but also provide procedures for assisting in the implementation of key provisions of those laws.

In short, the relation between the laws of war and human rights law under conditions of occupation is extraordinarily complex. More than any writings or theories, events would be the

[56] Michael J. Dennis, *Application of Human Rights Treaties Extraterritorially in Times of Armed Conflict and Military Occupation*, 99 AJIL 119, 141 (2005). This article is part of *Agora: ICJ Advisory Opinion on Construction of a Wall in the Occupied Palestinian Territory, id.* at 1 [hereinafter *Agora*].

[57] ICCPR, *supra* note 33, Art. 2(1).

[58] See also the further discussion of Dennis's article as it relates to the Israeli-occupied territories and Iraq, in text at notes 74 and 76 *infra*.

engine to reveal the complexity of the interrelations, the different perspectives on them, and their importance in transformative occupations.

Application of Human Rights Law to Particular Occupations

The general principle that human rights law can apply to military occupations is now widely, but by no means universally, accepted. Evidence for this proposition can be found in statements since the mid-1960s by international, and in some cases national, bodies of various types.

The United Nations role. The United Nations has played a major part in urging the application of human rights rules to occupations. Of the various UN organs, the General Assembly has played the most prominent (and often contentious) role in this regard. Starting in 1968, it has urged the observance of human rights law in armed conflicts and military occupations generally.[59] It has also done so, not always with perfect evenhandedness, with respect to particular occupations. The occupation that has received the most attention from the General Assembly, both in general and as regards the application of human rights, is that by Israel of the territories taken over in 1967: the application of human rights law to these territories has been urged in numerous UN resolutions.[60]

Although the Security Council has frequently urged respect for human rights in armed conflict generally, for a long time it did not address the more specific issue of human rights in occupations to the same extent as the General Assembly. This posture has begun to change. Where UN bodies established by the Security Council have had a major role in administering post-conflict territories, as in Kosovo and East Timor (situations in some ways comparable to occupations), these bodies have placed emphasis on human rights law, while keeping silent about the application of the laws of war.[61] Following the commencement of the U.S.-led occupation of Iraq in 2003, the Security Council emphasized the importance of human rights law as well as the laws of war.[62]

Namibia: The 1971 ICJ advisory opinion. Several occupied territories have been viewed by international tribunals as subject to human rights law. With respect to Namibia, it may have been partly with human rights law in mind (as well as the humanitarian laws of war) that the International Court of Justice, in its 1971 advisory opinion, pointed to the applicability of "certain general conventions such as those of a humanitarian character."[63]

Czechoslovakia after 1968: Charter 77. The range of circumstances in which human rights law may be relevant is extremely wide, but the classic situation to which such law applies is in the relations between the government of a state and its own citizens. This situation can arise in some occupations when an indigenous government has been left in post or a new one has been put in place. In such instances, which might be viewed by some as occupations, but where

[59] *See, e.g.*, Respect for Human Rights in Armed Conflicts, GA Res. 2444 (XXIII) (Dec. 19, 1968) (adopted unanimously).

[60] UN General Assembly resolutions specifically urging the application of human rights in the Israeli-occupied territories include GA Res. 2443 (XXIII) (Dec. 19, 1968); GA Res. 2546 (XXIV) (Dec. 11, 1969); GA Res. 2727 (Dec. 15, 1970); and the subsequent annual resolutions entitled "Report of the Special Committee to Investigate Israeli Practices Affecting the Human Rights of the Population of the Occupied Territories."

[61] On the foundational regulations of the Kosovo and East Timor administrations, see *infra* notes 130 and 131.

[62] *See* text at notes 75, 136, 152 *infra*.

[63] Legal Consequences for States of the Continued Presence of South Africa in Namibia (South West Africa) Notwithstanding Security Council Resolution 276 (1970), Advisory Opinion, 1971 ICJ REP. 16, para. 122 (June 21). Note also the references to human rights law in *id.*, paras. 92, 131.

that status is strongly contested by some or all of the parties concerned, human rights law may take on special importance. For example, the indigenous government may reject the pejorative label of occupation, but it may accept the application of human rights standards. One such case was Czechoslovakia following the formal entry into force in 1976 of that country's ratification of the two 1966 UN Human Rights Covenants. Both the Communist government (grudgingly) and its critics accepted in principle that international human rights instruments were applicable. The idea of the "Charter 77" movement was conceived on the day—November 11, 1976—when an official ordinance was published in Prague relating to Czechoslovakia's accession to these two conventions. Vladimir Kusin records a conversation in a Czech home on that day:

> We stood in the kitchen door and she said "Something ought to be done about it" and made three more steps and turned on the tap to make water run over our voices.... The day was Thursday, 11 November 1976, when they began selling *Collection of Laws* No. 23 which contained among other things the Foreign Minister's ordinance of 10 May 1976, numbered 120 and bearing a title full of hope: International Covenant on Civil and Political Rights and International Covenant on Economic, Social and Cultural Rights.[64]

In the late 1970s and 1980s, human rights law provided one framework for dialogue both within Eastern European states and between them and the West. The 1975 Helsinki Final Act of the Conference on Security and Co-operation in Europe[65] (not a legally binding document as such) and the diplomatic procedures established under it played a part in this process. Those involved in resisting the occupation of Czechoslovakia and its consequences were left with no doubt about the significance of human rights principles.

Northern Cyprus since 1974: role of the European Convention. Both the European Commission of Human Rights and the European Court of Human Rights have confirmed the general principle of the applicability of human rights law to the areas of northern Cyprus occupied by the armed forces of Turkey in 1974. In three decisions in 1975, 1978, and 1996 in cases brought by Cyprus against Turkey, the Commission ruled that applications by the government of Cyprus regarding the Turkish occupation were admissible.[66] The cases concerned the application of the European Convention on Human Rights, Article 1 of which states that the high contracting parties shall secure certain rights and freedoms to everyone "within their jurisdiction."[67] The Commission found (in the words of its decision in the second case):

> [T]his term is not equivalent to or limited to "within the national territory" of the High Contracting Party concerned.... [T]he High Contracting Parties are bound to secure the said rights and freedoms to all persons under their actual authority and responsibility, not only when that authority is exercised within their own territory but also when it is exercised abroad.[68]

[64] VLADIMIR V. KUSIN, FROM DUBČEK TO CHARTER 77: A STUDY OF 'NORMALISATION' IN CZECHOSLOVAKIA 1968–1978, at 304 (1978). On the role of human rights accords in the Charter 77 movement, see also VÁCLAV HAVEL ET AL., THE POWER OF THE POWERLESS 69–78 (1985). The text of the original Charter 77 declaration, published at the beginning of January 1977 and referring extensively to international human rights agreements, is reprinted in *id.* at 217.

[65] Conference on Security and Co-operation in Europe: Final Act, Aug. 1, 1975, 73 DEP'T ST. BULL. 323 (1975), *reprinted in* 14 ILM 1292 (1975).

[66] Cyprus v. Turkey, App. Nos. 6780/74, 6950/75, 2 Eur. Comm'n H.R. Dec. & Rep. 125 (1975); Cyprus v. Turkey, App. No. 8007/77, 13 Eur. Comm'n H.R. Dec. & Rep. 85 (1978) [hereinafter Cyprus v. Turkey II]; Cyprus v. Turkey, App. No. 25781/94, 86–A Eur. Comm'n H.R. Dec. & Rep. 104 (1996).

[67] ECHR, *supra* note 32, Art. 1.

[68] Cyprus v. Turkey II, *supra* note 66, at 149.

In the third of these cases on northern Cyprus, and the first of them to be referred to the European Court of Human Rights, the Court reaffirmed earlier decisions of the Commission, and indicated that Turkey had extensive responsibilities under the European Convention on Human Rights. This also confirmed the Court's earlier decisions in the *Loizidou* case.[69]

These conclusions did not mean that the law of armed conflict was supplanted by human rights law. On the contrary, when in the first case the detention of Greek military personnel in Turkey was raised, the Commission ruled that the law relating to prisoners of war, the Third Geneva Convention of 1949, was applicable, and that the Commission therefore did not need to "examine the question of a breach of Article 5 of the European Convention on Human Rights with regard to persons accorded the status of prisoners of war."[70]

Israeli-occupied territories: 2004 ICJ advisory opinion in the "Wall" *case*. The application of human rights norms to the Israeli-occupied territories is a much-contested matter. In many statements the Israeli authorities have denied that human rights law is formally applicable to the territories occupied since 1967. The question has been explored in depth in numerous writings, and in decisions of the Supreme Court of Israel.[71] This extensive body of experience of problems relating to the application of human rights norms in occupied territories is beyond the scope of this article.

However, the advisory opinion of the International Court of Justice in the *Wall* case in 2004 merits attention here because it is so definite, so wide-ranging in its scope, and so controversial. The ICJ concluded "that the International Covenant on Civil and Political Rights is applicable in respect of acts done by a State in the exercise of its jurisdiction outside its own territory."[72] In the occupied territories, therefore, Israel was deemed to be bound by its terms. This forthright conclusion, like other parts of this advisory opinion, appears to be weakened by some shaky legal reasoning.[73] Dennis has criticized this part of the opinion on the grounds that the Court (1) placed a questionable interpretation on the preparatory work for the International Covenant on Civil and Political Rights; (2) paid remarkably little attention to the role of the Palestinian Authority as a body that may have responsibilities for implementing human rights law in the areas under its control; and (3) assumed too easily that the law of armed conflict had only limited applicability to the situation on account of the (highly contestable) argument that, under the rule in Article 6 of the 1949 Geneva Civilians Convention that becomes effective "one year after the general close of military operations,"certain provisions of the Convention no longer applied to the territories occupied in 1967.[74] These and other specific criticisms of the ICJ advisory opinion are serious, and suggest that the Court has done less than it may have thought to advance the view that human rights law does apply in at least some circumstances in occupied territories.

[69] Cyprus v. Turkey, 2001–IV Eur. Ct. H.R. at 22–26. On *Loizidou v. Turkey*, see 310 Eur. Ct. H.R. (ser. A) at 23 (1995) (Preliminary Objections); 1996–VI Eur. Ct. H.R. 2216, 2234–35 (Merits).

[70] Cyprus v. Turkey, App. Nos. 6780/74, 6950/75, 4 Eur. H.R. Rep. 482, 533 (1982) (Commission report).

[71] *See* ISR. Y.B. HUM. RTS. (almost all issues); ESTHER COHEN, HUMAN RIGHTS IN THE ISRAELI-OCCUPIED TERRITORIES 1967–1982 (1985); Adam Roberts, *Prolonged Military Occupation: The Israeli-Occupied Territories Since 1967*, 84 AJIL 44, 70–74 (1990).

[72] Legal Consequences of the Construction of a Wall in the Occupied Palestinian Territory, Advisory Opinion, 2004 ICJ REP. 136, para. 111 (July 9). The Court focused particularly on the ICCPR, *supra* note 33, Art. 12, guaranteeing freedom of movement.

[73] For a range of views on the ICJ advisory opinion on the security barrier, see the nine contributions in *Agora*, *supra* note 56.

[74] Dennis, *supra* note 56, at 122–37.

Iraq: UK Court of Appeal in 2005. The promotion of human rights was proclaimed as one purpose of the occupation of Iraq in two UN Security Council resolutions passed in May 2003 and June 2004 with the support of the United States and the United Kingdom.[75] Curiously, in some American discussion of the application of human rights law to the U.S.-led coalition's occupation of Iraq, including the article by Dennis cited above, this fact has been ignored.[76] Yet important questions have been raised about whether the actions of U.S.-led coalition forces could be governed by human rights law as well as by the laws of war.

The fact that a situation, or an individual, is within the control and authority of an outside power was a key consideration in a UK Court of Appeal decision in December 2005 involving the coalition forces in Iraq from 2003 onward. The *Al-Skeini* case was brought on behalf of Iraqi families who claimed that six deceased relatives had been mistreated and killed by British troops in southern Iraq, and that such acts were violations of the European Convention on Human Rights and the national legislation based on that Convention, the UK Human Rights Act, 1998. Five of the relatives had died as a result of incidents resulting from the activities of British Army patrols. The sixth, Baha Mousa, died after having been taken into the custody of British forces. These incidents all happened between August and November 2003. The key issue in the case was the extent of applicability of British and European human rights norms. As Lord Justice Brooke stated in his leading judgment, the case

> is about acts done by the soldiers of an army which, with others, has overthrown the government of a sovereign state and is temporarily in occupation of the territory of that state pending the establishment of a new national government. This is why it is being contended that the United Kingdom was obliged to secure to the citizens of that part of Iraq which its forces occupied the rights and freedoms defined in the ECHR because, it is said, those citizens were temporarily within this country's jurisdiction.[77]

He drew a distinction between the applicability of laws of war and human rights rules to the overall situation in southern Iraq, stating that "[i]n my judgment it is quite impossible to hold that the UK, although an occupying power for the purposes of the Hague Regulations and Geneva IV, was in effective control of Basrah City for the purposes of ECHR jurisprudence at the material time."[78] He continued:

> It would indeed have been contrary to the Coalition's policy to maintain a much more substantial military force in Basrah City when its over-arching policy was to encourage the Iraqis to govern themselves. To build up an alternative power base capable of delivering all the rights and performing all the obligations required of a contracting state under the ECHR at the very time when the [Governing Council of Iraq] had been formed, with [the Coalition Provisional Authority's] encouragement, as a step towards the formation by the people of Iraq of an internationally recognized representative Government, would have run right against the grain of the Coalition's policies.[79]

The conclusion of the case was as follows: "[T]he UK did not possess Article 1 jurisdiction in relation to those killed in the first five incidents with which we are concerned, and that the

[75] SC Res. 1483 (May 22, 2003), 42 ILM 1016 (2003); SC Res.1546 (June 8, 2004), 43 ILM 1459 (2004); *see* text at notes 136, 152, respectively.

[76] Dennis, *supra* note 56, at 120 & n.13.

[77] Regina, *ex parte* Al-Skeini v. Sec'y of State for Def., [2005] EWCA Civ 1609, para. 5, *available at* <http://www.bailii.org>.

[78] *Id.*, para. 124.

[79] *Id.*, para. 125 (citation omitted).

appeals of the first five claimants must be dismissed."[80] The case of Mr. Mousa, however, was different. The UK government, after initially taking the opposite view, had conceded that in his case it was exercising extraterritorial jurisdiction for purposes of the European Convention on Human Rights. Accordingly, the Court had only to consider whether the UK Human Rights Act applied to this case. It did so decide, and therefore concluded that the case on behalf of Mr. Mousa is justiciable in UK courts.[81] The judgments in this case, including the separate opinions of Lord Justices Sedley and Richards, recognized that the issues were complex and would need further consideration by the House of Lords.[82] As far as the application of human rights law is concerned, the Court of Appeal has drawn a vital distinction between situations where an individual is plainly under the control of UK forces (e.g., because of being in custody) and those where, even in times of occupation, individuals are not under such control.

Human Rights Law: Criteria for Assessment

A range of experience in the years since 1945 leads to the conclusion that human rights law is widely, but not yet universally, seen as applicable in occupied territories; and that in many cases the responsibility for applying the law lies with the occupant. However, the precise relevance of human rights law in times of foreign military occupation needs to be carefully examined in any particular instance. What follows is a first attempt at enunciating criteria for assessing the relevance and applicability of human rights law in circumstances of occupation.

Before considering criteria that might point to the relevance of human rights law, certain grounds for caution, five of them in particular, should be plainly laid out.

First, commentators have expressed different views on whether the scope of application of human rights agreements—especially the 1966 International Covenants—encompasses occupied territories.[83]

Second, many human rights conventions permit parties to derogate from some of their provisions, for example, in times of public emergency threatening the life of the nation. Some military occupations occur in circumstances (which may well include a continuing armed conflict) that could be viewed by at least one party as constituting such an emergency.

Third, more states are parties to the four 1949 Geneva Conventions (and with fewer declarations and reservations) than to the conventions on human rights. No fewer than 193—virtually all—states are parties to the four 1949 Geneva Conventions, and 165 to their 1977 Additional Protocol I.[84] By contrast, the two 1966 International Covenants on Civil and Political Rights, and on Economic, Social and Cultural Rights have 156 and 153 parties, respectively; and the 1984 Convention Against Torture has 141.[85] Thus, there is further scope for debate as to whether a particular human rights convention is applicable in the event that either the occupying power is not a party to the convention, or the power that previously held the territory

[80] *Id.*, para. 142.

[81] *Id.*, paras. 142, 143, 147.

[82] *Id.*, paras. 147 (Brooke), 206 (Sedley), 210 (Richards).

[83] These differences of view, which are not new, resurfaced over post-2003 Iraq. The strongest critique of the proposition that human rights law is applicable in times of occupation is that by Dennis, *supra* note 56, at 119–41.

[84] Figures of states parties to the Geneva Conventions and Additional Protocols from the ICRC as of July 21, 2006, are available at its Web site, <http://www.icrc.org>.

[85] These figures are current as of June 30, 2006. Figures of states parties to the ICCPR, *supra* note 33, the ICESCR, *supra* note 34, the Convention Against Torture, *supra* note 35, and other human rights treaties are available from the United Nations at <http://www.ohchr.org/english/>.

is not—or at any rate was not when the occupation began. Debate on this issue is not likely to be entirely eliminated by claims that human rights law is binding on all states.

Fourth, human rights agreements were not drawn up with the circumstances of armed conflict and occupation primarily in mind. The Universal Declaration of Human Rights does not specifically refer in any of its provisions to human rights in armed conflict.[86] Indeed, some human rights agreements—for example, the 1966 Covenant on Economic, Social and Cultural Rights—have the character more of a program than of a binding set of detailed rules. No human rights agreement draws distinctions between different categories of individuals in the way that the laws of war do.

The final ground for caution in assessing the applicability of human rights law to occupations is that over a wide range of issues, the laws of war rules regarding military occupations, as laid down in the Hague Regulations and the Geneva Conventions, may offer more extensive, detailed, and relevant guidance than the general human rights conventions; and their supervisory machinery, although allowing less room for legal redress than some human rights treaties, may be more appropriate to the circumstances.

Despite these considerations, human rights conventions can play an important role in some situations that either constitute occupations, or closely resemble occupations in certain key respects. They may impose formal obligations on parties; be instrumental in political debate, as a basis for assessing the actions of external powers and local actors; provide legal procedures for taking action; or serve as one basis for pursuing transformative goals. These conventions can be particularly relevant in the following instances:

— If it is claimed—for example, on the basis of a status-of-forces agreement, a purported mandate to act as liberator, and the existence of an indigenous government—that there is no occupation at all. This could well be the case with some "transformative" projects in the wake of military interventions. Whether or not such a denial of occupation is legally defensible in the circumstances, it may suggest that human rights law is the most useful set of standards to which to appeal.

— If an occupation is deemed to continue in some form, an indigenous government is in post, and problems revolve around the relations between individual citizens and their own government. In such a case, many issues concerning the relations between inhabitants and their own governmental authorities could properly be considered as human rights matters.

— If the provisions of a human rights instrument have been incorporated into the domestic law of the occupied territory and/or the occupying power.

— If some individuals or groups of people in occupied territory (e.g., certain terrorist suspects) are considered by the detaining power not to fall within the various broad categories of protected persons as laid down in, say, the four 1949 Geneva Conventions and the 1977 Protocols. There may be human rights protections that relate to their situation.

— If applicable human rights instruments in the circumstances concerned deal with subject matter that fills gaps in the law of war on occupations—e.g., importing of educational materials. Partly because of the broad subject matter coverage, they may be cited particularly often in occupations that continue for a long time, even into something approximating peacetime, and that present problems different from those addressed by the laws of war.

[86] Schindler, *supra* note 39, at 7.

— If a human rights agreement contains procedures for dealing with an issue of concern, for example, enabling individuals to raise a matter directly with some outside institution. The role of the European Court of Human Rights in situations involving the use of force is evidence of possibilities in this regard.

— If a specific issue arising in an occupation involves violations of those parts of human rights law that are not derogable in times of crisis;[87] or, alternatively, if the power against which a claim is made has not made a derogation in respect of the occupation.[88]

— If the occupant and/or international bodies properly refer to human rights law as providing a legal basis for changing certain laws of the occupied territory, or even as setting goals for a transformative occupation. For example, Article 1 of the 1966 International Human Rights Covenants contains implications for political arrangements under occupations: "All peoples have the right of self-determination. By virtue of that right they freely determine their political status . . . ."[89]

In such instances human rights conventions can reinforce the idea that there are some important basic rules to be applied, and principles to shape the conduct of the states and individuals involved. Each of the eight instances listed above could take place in a transformative occupation.

III. Post-1945 Occupations with a Transformative Purpose

Many interventions and occupations since 1945 have been more than mere byproducts of war: they have often been designed to affect the political order in the territory concerned. Cases during the Cold War years include, for example, Czechoslovakia after 1968, northern Cyprus after 1974, Cambodia after 1978, and Grenada in 1983.

This part looks selectively at foreign military presences aimed at a fundamental democratic transformation, and considers their possible implications for the law on occupations. Put crudely, the traditional assumption of the laws of war is that bad (or potentially bad) occupants are occupying a good country (or at least one with a reasonable legal system that operates for the benefit of the inhabitants). In recent years, especially in some Western democratic states, various schools of thought have been based on the opposite idea, crudely summarized as good occupants occupying a bad country (or at least one with a bad system of government and laws).

Both of these crude views of occupations are questionable. The second view—of the occupant as the bringer of progress—can lead to a dangerous mix of crusading, self-righteousness, and self-delusion. Yet this view is the product of serious considerations based on actual events, including the post–World War II occupations, the interventions since the end of the Cold War, and the case of Iraq. Each will be considered in turn.

Postsurrender Occupations at the End of World War II

The Allied occupations of Germany and Japan after World War II typify postsurrender occupations, and also reluctance to be formally bound by the Hague Regulations. Here, as well

[87] Nonderogable provisions include the ECHR, *supra* note 32, Arts. 2, 3, 4(1), 7; and the ICCPR, *supra* note 33, Arts. 6, 7, 8(1) & (2), 11, 15, 16, 18.

[88] For example, the United Kingdom did not make a derogation in respect of the European Convention on Human Rights in connection with the occupation of Iraq from 2003 onward. In general, it might be hard to argue that there was a "threat to the life of the nation" arising from the occupation of a distant country.

[89] ICCPR, *supra* note 33, Art. 1; ICESCR, *supra* note 34, Art. 1.

as elsewhere, the victors desired to exercise their power freely, and in particular to make drastic political and other changes in the defeated states. The basic character of these occupations raised issues to which relatively little attention had been paid by international lawyers. Previously, it had sometimes been assumed that the normal consequence of surrender by a state was its subjugation, or possibly even annexation, by the victor; but this fate did not befall the bulk of German or Japanese territory at the end of the war, or some other occupied territories at that time. What took place instead, especially in Germany and Japan, were occupations that went beyond the letter of the Hague Regulations, yet fell short of annexation or assumption of sovereignty.

With respect to the occupation of Germany, which began in 1944–1945, a legal memorandum to the UK Foreign Office in March 1945 set out the basic problem:

> The truth is that the Allies are dealing with a situation without previous parallel; they are proposing to exercise their authority with respect to Germany in order to expel the Nazi system and its manifestations completely and utterly, and to continue this process indefinitely until it has succeeded. These objects, far ranging as they are, do not necessarily amount to annexation and to the positive and complete transfer of sovereignty whether by cession or by conquest. But they do undoubtedly go far beyond the exercise of military occupation as limited by previous international law. . . . Looking, therefore, at the matter broadly, we cannot regard the international law which will apply to the case now in prospect as limiting the right of the Allies to those attaching to a mere military occupation unless there is a positive assumption of sovereignty as a whole.[90]

After the Germans accepted unconditional surrender on May 7, 1945, Germany was completely occupied by the Allies. What, then, was the position so far as the application of the Hague Regulations was concerned?[91] On this point Robert Jennings, in an authoritative article in 1946, argued persuasively that the law of belligerent occupation had been designed to serve two purposes: first, to protect the sovereign rights of the legitimate government of the occupied territory, and second, to protect the inhabitants of the occupied territory from being exploited for the prosecution of the occupant's war. Neither of these purposes had much bearing on the situation the Allies faced: "Thus the whole *raison d'être* of the law of belligerent occupation is absent in the circumstances of the Allied occupation of Germany, and to attempt to apply it would be a manifest anachronism."[92]

Wolfgang Friedmann adopted a very similar position:

> [E]ven the widest interpretation of the rules of warfare [could not] bring the powers claimed and exercised by the allies in Germany within the scope of belligerent occupation. . . . [E]ven the most elastic interpretation could not bring the wholesale abolition of laws, the denazification procedure, the arrest of thousands of individuals, the introduction of sweeping social reforms, the expropriation of industries, and above all the sweeping

[90] Opinion of the Lord Chancellor and the Law Officers of the Crown (Mar. 1945), typescript copy of FO 371/50759 (U 1949), Public Record Office (now National Archives). On the British discussion about the legal status of Germany, see F. S. V. DONNISON, CIVIL AFFAIRS AND MILITARY GOVERNMENT: CENTRAL ORGANIZATION AND PLANNING 125–36 (1966).

[91] The position before May 7, 1945, is widely viewed as one of normal belligerent occupation. However, as some anti-Nazi measures taken early in the belligerent phase show, there was not a completely sharp distinction between the two stages of the occupation of Germany.

[92] R. Y. Jennings, *Government in Commission*, 1946 BRIT. Y.B. INT'L L. 112, 136.

> changes in the territorial and constitutional structure of Germany within the rights of belligerent occupation. These are symbols of sovereign government, yet it is of the essence of belligerent occupation that it does not claim such powers.
>
> . . . .
>
> . . . It is not . . . surprising that International Law—inadequate to cope with many problems of our days—should not be fully equipped to deal with an entirely unprecedented situation.[93]

A curious aspect of the legal arrangements for the post–World War II occupations was Article 107 of the UN Charter. It states, in full: "Nothing in the present Charter shall invalidate or preclude action, in relation to any state which during the Second World War has been an enemy of any signatory to the present Charter, taken or authorized as a result of that war by the Governments having responsibility for such action."

Article 107 can be seen as a way of keeping the Allied occupations of Germany and Japan outside the control of the UN Security Council. It is also a spiritual precursor of an approach that has sometimes surfaced in the thinking of the U.S. government, which views certain governments (and particularly that of the United States) as entitled to take action internationally with only a restricted role for the UN Security Council. Following the 2005 UN World Summit, Article 107 may be in process of being consigned to legal oblivion, but its unilateralist spirit is not entirely dead.[94]

After the entry into force of the 1949 Geneva Conventions, it became doubtful whether a claim could ever again be made that an occupation fell outside the framework of the laws of war, or would not be subject to certain conservationist provisions. The scope of application of the Conventions, as outlined in common Article 2, was "to all cases of partial or total occupation of the territory of a High Contracting Party." Although Article 6 of the 1949 Civilians Convention did allow for the cessation of certain rules one year after the general close of military operations, the occupant (if still exercising governmental functions) would have remained bound by many conservationist rules.[95]

International Military Actions Since the End of the Cold War

Since the end of the Cold War, international circumstances have created strong pressures, and also opportunities, for military action to help bring about change in certain states. The international problems that have led to this tendency have included:

- — internal repression within states, in many cases leading to large numbers of internally displaced persons and refugees;
- — civil wars within states (which may cause concern on humanitarian grounds because of their capacity to spread, and also because of their tendency to cause refugee flows); and
- — toleration by certain states of terrorist activities aimed at targets abroad.

[93] W. FRIEDMANN, THE ALLIED MILITARY GOVERNMENT OF GERMANY 65, 67 (1947).

[94] In the UN World Summit Outcome document of September 16, 2005, the United Nations member states declared that "we resolve to delete references to 'enemy States' in Articles 53, 77 and 107 of the Charter." GA Res. 60/1, para. 177, at 38 (Oct. 24, 2005).

[95] Geneva Convention IV, *supra* note 9, Arts. 2, 6. On the meaning and status of Article 6, see *supra* text at notes 29–30.

These problems are serious, and a complete refusal by the international community to tackle them is not an option. Of the many effects of international interventions since 1989, one of the most striking is the tendency for refugees to return in large numbers. Another is the attempt to bring about political change in the territory concerned—not always with success.

Many post–Cold War military actions have been characterized by a tendency to avoid being seen as occupations, or even being thought of as amenable to the application of occupation law. A possible rationale for this approach is that in most cases involving a foreign military presence with a transformative purpose and some participation in governmental functions, this presence has been accorded a degree of formal consent by the government of the country concerned. Examples of a foreign military presence with consent include (1) Haiti (1994–2000 and from 2004 onward); (2) Bosnia and Herzegovina (from December 1995 onward); (3) Albania (March–June 1997); (4) Kosovo (from June 1999 onward); (5) East Timor (October 1999–May 2002); and (6) Afghanistan (from December 2001 onward). Further factors in all these cases are that the UN Security Council formally authorized (although not always from the start) the foreign military presence in the territory concerned; that the foreign presence had a multinational character; that the intervention was preceded by Council expressions of concern over the humanitarian situation in the territory; and that human rights were emphasized as one key concern of the intervening forces.

Neither the fact of formal consent of the government of the country nor formal UN authorization makes it impossible for the law on occupations to be considered applicable to these cases. When troops from abroad interact with the population of another country, there must always be a strong case for viewing the law on occupations as a necessary safety net. However, the law on occupations is not the only lens through which one can examine this wide range of interventionist activity.[96]

Of these six cases, the one most similar to post-2003 Iraq is the U.S.-led external involvement in Afghanistan. In Afghanistan the United States had a clear transformative purpose; there, as in Iraq, the major U.S.-led military action was aimed explicitly at deposing the ruling regime; and the deposition did not end all armed opposition. The two situations differed mainly in that the establishment of a foreign military occupation regime was not necessary in Afghanistan. After the fall of the Taliban and the accession to power of the Afghan Interim Authority on December 22, 2001, the coalition's role was essentially to aid the government.

Iraq Since 2003

There was a precedent, of sorts, in Iraq: the "safe haven" established in northern Iraq in 1991. The U.S.-led military intervention that began on April 17, 1991, resulting in the establishment of the zone, enjoyed neither the specific authorization of the UN Security Council, nor, initially, the consent of the Iraqi government, whose forces had only a few months before been repulsed from Kuwait. After the initial phase, northern Iraq was protected from Iraqi government incursions almost entirely through the establishment of a U.S.-initiated air exclusion zone. The history of this protected zone illustrates certain transformative possibilities of foreign military involvement. However, the zone never assumed the character of anything approaching a full occupation regime. Initiated to enable large numbers of refugees from the region to return home, it resulted in the application of enough coalition military pressure to keep Hussein's

[96] A useful study of cases of international administration since 1995 is RICHARD CAPLAN, INTERNATIONAL GOVERNANCE OF WAR-TORN TERRITORIES: RULE AND RECONSTRUCTION (2005).

forces out of northern Iraq, enabling the Iraqi Kurds to develop their own administrative structures in the region. Here, indeed, was a transformation facilitated by a foreign military role: but that role took the form of a short-term military presence on the ground, followed by a more remote one in the air that could not be viewed as an occupation.

Transformation as one basis of the decision to use force in Iraq. The military operations launched in Iraq on March 19–20, 2003, raised numerous issues relating to the *jus ad bellum.* These are not reviewed here, partly because of the familiar principle that the laws of war apply irrespective of the legality or otherwise of the original resort to force. However, one question must be briefly addressed: is transformation a legitimate reason for resorting to force? This question is distinct from whether transformation is a legitimate goal once force has (for whatever reason) been used.

The case of Iraq confirms that a complex mixture of political motives may underlie intervention, and a no less complicated mixture of legal and other justifications. The U.S.-led invasion followed a prolonged and confused legal-cum-political debate, in which the stated purposes of intervention varied not just over time, but also within and between different U.S. agencies and participating states.

On March 20, 2003, the United States made a statement to the United Nations seeking to justify the military operations that had just commenced. The purpose of the action was specified very precisely: "These operations are necessary in view of Iraq's continued material breaches of its disarmament obligations under relevant Security Council resolutions, including resolution 1441 (2002). The operations are substantial and will secure compliance with those obligations."[97] As to the basis of authority to use force, the statement made a claim of continuing or revived authority on the basis of earlier resolutions: "The actions being taken are authorized under existing Council resolutions, including its resolutions 678 (1990) and 687 (1991)."[98] No mention at all was made of a politically transformative purpose or the prevention of terrorism.

In reality, the idea of political transformation had long been one significant element in U.S. debates about Iraq. As early as 1998, the joint houses of Congress, in passing the Iraq Liberation Act, had called for the United States "to support efforts to remove the regime headed by Saddam Hussein from power in Iraq and to promote the emergence of a democratic government to replace that regime."[99] However, this clarion call for transformation did not exist in a vacuum, since it was based on complaints about Iraq's conduct, including violations of international rules. The Act cited Iraq's conduct in the war against Iran of 1980–1988, its invasion and occupation of Kuwait in 1990–1991, its orchestration of a failed plot to assassinate President George H. W. Bush in 1993, its repression of the Kurds, its violation of the disarmament conditions of the 1991 cease-fire, and its denial of democracy.[100] In subsequent U.S. debates and decision making, regime change featured not simply as a likely consequence of intervention, but a principal purpose of it. It was claimed that enforced regime change would lead to substantial beneficial consequences both within Iraq and in the region generally.

[97] Letter Dated 20 March 2003 from the Permanent Representative of the United States of America to the United Nations Addressed to the President of the Security Council, UN Doc. S/2003/351.

[98] *Id.*

[99] H.R. 4655, §3, 105th Cong. (1998), passed by the House of Representatives on October 5, 1998, 144 CONG. REC. H9483 (daily ed. Oct. 5, 1998), and the Senate on October 7, 1998, *id.* at S11,811 (Oct. 7, 1998), as Pub. L. No. 105-338.

[100] H.R. 4655, *supra* note 99, §2.

In Britain no significant body of opinion supported the idea that transformation— however desirable in principle it might be—was in itself a justification for going to war in Iraq. In April 2002, when he met with President George W. Bush in Crawford, Texas, Prime Minister Tony Blair

> said that the UK would support military action to bring about regime change, provided that certain conditions were met: efforts had been made to construct a coalition/shape public opinion, the Israel-Palestine Crisis was quiescent, and the options for action to eliminate Iraq's [weapons of mass destruction] through the UN weapons inspectors had been exhausted.[101]

The memorandum of July 21, 2002, which recorded this position, also stated: "US views of international law vary from that of the UK and the international community. Regime change per se is not a proper basis for military action under international law. But regime change could result from action that is otherwise lawful."[102] Blair subsequently stated that regime change and weapons of mass destruction (WMD) "were linked in the sense that it was the regime that was producing the WMD."[103] In the House of Commons debate just before the war, he stated:

> I have never put the justification for action as regime change. We have to act within the terms set out in resolution 1441—that is our legal base. But it is the reason why I say frankly that if we do act, we should do so with a clear conscience and a strong heart.[104]

The thrust of public presentations of government policy involved alleged Iraqi noncompliance with disarmament obligations. In a secret memorandum to the prime minister on the legality of military action against Iraq, dated March 7, 2003, the attorney general, Lord Goldsmith, developed the argument that "a violation of Iraq's obligations under resolution 687 which is sufficiently serious to undermine the basis of the cease-fire can revive the authorisation to use force in resolution 678."[105] The final paragraph of the memorandum expressed nervousness about political transformation as a rationale for the use of force. It did so in the context of a discussion of proportionality—which, famously, is a matter that constitutes a link between the *jus ad bellum* and the *jus in bello*. The paragraph reads:

> 36. Finally, I must stress that the lawfulness of military action depends not only on the existence of a legal basis, but also on the question of proportionality. Any force used pursuant to the authorisation in resolution 678 (whether or not there is a second resolution):
>
> — must have as its objective the enforcement [of] the terms of the cease-fire contained in resolution 687 (1990) and subsequent relevant resolutions;
>
> — be limited to what is necessary to achieve that objective; and

[101] Conditions for Military Action, Secret Cabinet Office paper, para. 2 (July 22, 2002), partially leaked in SUNDAY TIMES (London), May 1, 2005, and published in full in SUNDAY TIMES (London), June 12, 2005, at 10, *available at* <http://www.downingstreetmemo.com/cabinetofficetext.html>, *and* <http://www.informationclearinghouse.info/article9112.htm>.

[102] *Id.*, para. 11.

[103] Secret Downing Street memo of the Prime Minister's meeting, Ref. S 195/02 (July 23, 2002), published in SUNDAY TIMES (London), May 1, 2005, at 7, *available at* <http://www.downingstreetmemo.com/timelinehome.html>, *and* <http://www.informationclearinghouse.info/article8709.htm>.

[104] Tony Blair, statement opening the debate on Iraq, HANSARD, House of Commons, pt. 365, col. 772, Mar. 18, 2003, *available at* <http://www.parliament.uk/hansard/hansard.cfm>.

[105] Lord Goldsmith, attorney general, Iraq: Resolution 1441, para. 7 (Mar. 7, 2003) (secret memo to prime minister, released on April 28, 2005), *at* <http://www.number-10.gov.uk/files/pdf/Iraq%20Resolution%201441.pdf>.

— must be a proportionate response to that objective, ie securing compliance with Iraq's disarmament obligations.

That is not to say that action may not be taken to remove Saddam Hussein from power if it can be demonstrated that such action is a necessary and proportionate measure to secure the disarmament of Iraq. But regime change cannot be the objective of military action. This should be borne in mind in considering the list of military targets and in making public statements about any campaign.[106]

Dinstein developed a justification for the use of force against Iraq that was similar to that of Lord Goldsmith, but with certain differences. Deploring the confusion in rationales for the Iraq action, and noting that the political considerations that had resulted in intervention were broader than the legal ones, Dinstein sought to reduce the chaos of arguments about the legal basis of the 2003 action to some kind of order. He argued that the original 1991 coalition's use of force over Kuwait had been lawful not only because it had been authorized by Security Council Resolution 678 of November 29, 1990, but also because it was a lawful exercise of collective self-defense following the attack on Kuwait. He went on to suggest that "the legal basis of the 2003 hostilities was a revival of the Coalition's right to use force against Iraq consequent upon the Iraqi material breach of the cease-fire" that had been concluded between Iraq and the coalition in 1991.[107] He did not devote attention to the U.S. emphasis on regime change as a reason for the use of force, but was critical of U.S. notions of preventive self-defense. Compared with Goldsmith's argument, this analysis was less dependent on Security Council resolutions, and put more emphasis on a continuing right of self-defense as a basis for responding to violations of the terms of the 1991 cease-fire.

The legal justifications of the 2003 Iraq intervention advanced by Goldsmith and Dinstein are stronger than most. However, like all views of the Iraq intervention, they are by no means free of problems. Both of these justifications relied heavily on the propositions that Iraq had engaged in major violations of the cease-fire deal, that these had become very serious by 2003, and that the crisis was so severe as to justify the fateful step of invasion and regime change, as distinct from continuing and adapting the policy of containment.

There were, and are, many grounds for reservations over the coalition governments' assessments in 2002–2003 of evidence of Iraqi breaches of the terms of the cease-fire. True, these assessments were largely shared by other governments and their intelligence services. Yet it was not, and is not, obvious that a crisis had developed over Iraqi weapons in March 2003 of such gravity as to justify withdrawing the inspectors and resorting to full-scale invasion. Hans Blix, charged with conducting UN inspections in Iraq, had doubted the accuracy of the assessments made about Iraq in Washington and London in March 2003.[108]

The debate about Iraq in the years before the outbreak of war in March 2003 revealed a difference of view between the United Kingdom and the United States over whether the political transformation of Iraq, or of the region more broadly, could serve as a reason for intervention. The United Kingdom felt more strongly that, on its own, regime change was an insufficient reason in international law. The project of political transformation of Iraq, and of the Arab world more generally, was particularly strong in the United States for years before 2003, to the point where it constituted a significant part of the rationale for intervention—and was perhaps

[106] *Id.*, para. 36.

[107] Yoram Dinstein, *The Gulf War, 1990–2004 (and Still Counting)*, 2005 ISR. Y.B. HUM. RTS. 1, 5.

[108] HANS BLIX, DISARMING IRAQ: THE SEARCH FOR WEAPONS OF MASS DESTRUCTION (2004).

more important in the minds of some policymakers than disarmament. Many advocates of transformative intervention saw something artificial in a situation where the law is such that a real reason for intervention—turning a dictatorship into a democracy—could play at best a minimal part in the debate about the legal justification of military action.

Transformative occupation of Iraq from April 2003. Since the initial U.S.-led invasion and subsequent military presence obviously occurred without the agreement of the government of Hussein, and involved direct responsibility for running the country, the resulting situation was much closer to a military occupation than in most cases of foreign military presence after the Cold War. Naturally, a wide range of laws of war issues arose, in light of which the policies of the coalition authorities were extensively justified and critically scrutinized.[109]

The occupation of Iraq was not well planned. As early as July 2002, a UK government memorandum had noted: "There was little discussion in Washington of the aftermath after military action."[110] Some senior officers in the Pentagon with legal expertise were told not to bother themselves with plans for the occupation, and a State Department study preparatory to the occupation was ignored. The undertaking was also marked by conceptual confusion, especially in the United States. In the public debate on the matter in Washington, D.C., in the first few months of 2003, some policymakers made the basic error of asserting that, because the action amounted to a liberation of Iraq, it was not an occupation at all. A typical comment was that by Paul Wolfowitz, U.S. deputy secretary of defense and a leading advocate of the intervention. In February 2003, shortly before the military action, he said: "[W]e're not talking about the occupation of Iraq. We're talking about the liberation of Iraq. . . . Therefore, when that regime is removed we will find [the Iraqi population] . . . . basically welcoming us as liberators."[111] U.S. officials made countless similar statements.

This view was accompanied by a U.S. tendency—not confined to the government—to ignore or downplay certain laws of war rules,[112] which led to some corrective statements by international lawyers. Dinstein wrote:

> The Coalition was very eager to present its forces in Iraq as an army of liberation. But notwithstanding the fact that the overthrow of the Saddam Hussein regime brought liberation to the Iraqi people, it must be appreciated that—pursuant to international law—the legal status of the Coalition forces in Iraq is not that of liberators but that of belligerent occupants.[113]

[109] Two assessments of the Iraq occupation in relation to the laws of war that address many issues not tackled here are Michael N. Schmitt & Charles H. B. Garraway, *Occupation Policy in Iraq and International Law, in* 9 INTERNATIONAL PEACEKEEPING: THE YEARBOOK OF INTERNATIONAL PEACE OPERATIONS, 2004, at 27 (2005); Thürer & MacLaren, *supra* note 5.

[110] Secret Downing Street memo of the Prime Minister's meeting, *supra* note 103.

[111] Paul Wolfowitz, Interview with Melissa Block (National Public Radio, Feb. 19, 2003), *available at* <http://www.defenselink.mil/transcripts/2003/t02202003_t0219npr.html>. Sixteen months later, this interview was cited critically by Senator Hillary Rodham Clinton when Wolfowitz gave testimony to the U.S. Senate Committee on Armed Services on the transition in Iraq (June 25, 2004), *available at* <http://www.defenselink.mil/speeches/2004/sp20040625-depsecdef0541.html>.

[112] There was no reference at all to the laws of war rules on occupations in an otherwise thoughtful study of Iraq by two U.S. nongovernmental institutions in which international lawyers were strongly represented. *See* PUBLIC INTERNATIONAL LAW & POLICY GROUP, & CENTURY FOUNDATION, ESTABLISHING A STABLE DEMOCRATIC CONSTITUTIONAL STRUCTURE IN IRAQ: SOME BASIC CONSIDERATIONS (May 2003), *available at* <http://www.pilpg.org>.

[113] Yoram Dinstein, Jus in Bello *Issues Arising in the Hostilities in Iraq in 2003*, 2004 ISR. Y.B. HUM. RTS. 1, 12.

In the Middle East, where concern about the Israeli-occupied territories is widespread, the United States would understandably wish to avoid the odium accompanying the term "occupation." However, it was a legal and political mistake to counterpose "liberation" and "occupation" as opposites, hence to imply that the law governing occupations was scarcely relevant. A legally sounder approach, one that would have elicited less political scorn, would have stated from the start that the United States, while its intention was to liberate Iraq, accepted that one main body of international rules that should govern the conduct of its forces was the law of occupation. Eventually, after the main combat phase in Iraq, the United States and its coalition partners did adopt this position. Security Council Resolution 1483 of May 22, 2003, mentioned further below, marked their acceptance that occupation law applied to their presence in Iraq, and at the same time reflected their intention to achieve a fundamental transformation of the constitution and laws of the country.

While the intervention was still in its major combat operations phase, concerns surfaced in some parts of the coalition governments that the transformative project for Iraq might violate the legal norms governing occupations. On March 26, 2003, in a detailed memorandum spelling out his advice to the British Cabinet on the same day, Attorney General Goldsmith stated:

> In short, my view is that a further Security Council resolution is needed to authorise imposing reform and restructuring of Iraq and its Government. In the absence of a further resolution, the UK (and US) would be bound by the provisions of international law governing belligerent occupation, notably the Fourth Geneva Convention and the 1907 Hague Regulations.[114]

The attorney general went on to note in particular that "the imposition of major structural economic reforms would not be authorised by international law."[115] On a separate point, he stated that

> a further complicating factor for the United Kingdom is the extent to which the ECHR [European Convention on Human Rights] and other international human rights instruments are likely to apply to any territory of which the UK is the Occupying Power. I am advising the Ministry of Defence separately on the extent of our ECHR obligations in Iraq.[116]

Following this memorandum, the UK government did publicly emphasize the framework of Hague and Geneva law. In a statement in the House of Commons on April 14, 2003, outlining plans for Iraq's reconstruction, Prime Minister Blair said: "In the first phase, the coalition and the Office of Reconstruction and Humanitarian Assistance will have responsibility under the Geneva and Hague conventions for ensuring that Iraq's immediate security and humanitarian needs are met."[117] He also stressed that the United Nations would have a "vital role." He did not use the term "occupation"; instead, he said, optimistically: "Iraq is a nation with a creative people, potentially wealthy, with a dynamic and prosperous future ahead of it. They do not need to be run from the outside by the US, the UK or the UN, and they will not be."[118]

The occupation had already begun during the course of the fighting, when progressively more areas of Iraq came under coalition control. Although in particular places and phases determining exactly when occupation began could be difficult, there was apparently no dispute in

[114] Lord Goldsmith, Iraq: Authorisation for an Interim Administration (Mar. 26, 2003), *in* John Kampfner, *Blair Was Told It Would Be Illegal to Occupy Iraq*, NEW STATESMAN (London), May 26, 2003.

[115] *Id.*

[116] *Id.*

[117] Tony Blair, Statement on Iraq, HANSARD, House of Commons, pt. 384, col. 616 (Apr. 14, 2003).

[118] *Id.*, cols. 616–17.

principle about the status of these areas as "occupied territory," as was confirmed by the use of this term in a Security Council resolution of March 28.[119]

The countrywide occupation administration is described in some official documents as having begun on April 16, 2003, one day after a meeting of various Iraqi factions, held at a makeshift U.S. air base near Ur, agreed on a thirteen-point plan (including as point 10 the dissolution of the Ba'ath Party) for steering Iraq to a democratic future.[120] This plan was seen by the United States and its coalition partners as providing some kind of mandate for embarking on drastic change. The next day General Tommy Franks, commander of the coalition forces, issued a "Freedom Message to the Iraqi People." While not using the word "occupation," he announced: "I am creating the Coalition Provisional Authority [CPA] to exercise powers of government temporarily. . . ."[121] In this message he also announced a range of transformative policy measures, including the disestablishment of the Ba'ath Party. Oddly, this manifesto for the transformation of an entire country—a document later briefly claimed by the CPA to be foundational in character—was little noted at the time and has been hard to locate subsequently.[122] The same day, April 16, was also the date on a message issued by General Franks, "Instructions to the Citizens of Iraq," containing down-to-earth advice aimed at ensuring the safety of the population and the coalition forces, which was also little noted.[123]

There was some early confusion about which person, and indeed organization, was in charge. The occupation was initially perceived as being under General Jay Garner, director of the Office of Reconstruction and Humanitarian Assistance (ORHA), which had been set up within the Department of Defense in January to meet the challenges of reconstructing Iraq. He had been present at the meeting near Ur on April 15, and arrived in Baghdad on April 20. Within less than three weeks he was sidelined. On May 6, in a statement that made no reference to the Coalition Provisional Authority, President Bush appointed Ambassador L. Paul Bremer as U.S. presidential envoy to Iraq, stating that, as "the senior Coalition official in Iraq," he would be responsible for overseeing reconstruction and institution-building efforts, while

[119] SC Res. 1472 (Mar. 28, 2003), 42 ILM 767 (2003). The preamble stated:

> *Noting* that under the provisions of Article 55 of the Fourth Geneva Convention . . . , to the fullest extent of the means available to it, the Occupying Power has the duty of ensuring the food and medical supplies of the population; it should, in particular, bring in the necessary foodstuffs, medical stores and other articles if the resources of the occupied territory are inadequate.

The word "humanitarian" features fourteen times in this resolution.

[120] 13-Point Statement on a Democratic Iraq (Apr. 15, 2003), GUARDIAN UNLIMITED, Apr. 16, 2003, *at* <http://www.guardian.co.uk/Iraq/Story/0,2763,937856,00.html>.

[121] General Tommy R. Franks, Freedom Message to the Iraqi People (Apr. 16, 2003). There is a question regarding its status. It was referred to as an important foundational document in certain later statements, including CPA Order No. 2 of May 23, 2003, *see* text at note 144 *infra*. An Arabic text of the "Freedom Message" was probably delivered by air over Iraq. However, the message does not appear to have been mentioned in the main daily press conferences given by the U.S. military at that time, or in the English-language international press. Its text is hard to locate on the Internet: it was not on the CPA, Pentagon, State Department or related Web sites when searched in March–May 2006. It was not noted at all in a study of the basic CPA framework, L. ELAINE HALCHIN, THE COALITION PROVISIONAL AUTHORITY (CPA): ORIGIN, CHARACTERISTICS, AND INSTITUTIONAL AUTHORITIES (Congressional Research Service, updated June 6, 2005), *available at* <http://www.fas.org/man/crs/RL32370.pdf>. Nor is its existence noted in many later books about the 2003 Iraq war. However, it can be found (in English), Ref. IZ C148, on the Aerial Propaganda Leaflet Database of the Web site of the PsyWar Society, at <http://www.psywar.org/apdsearchform.php>.

[122] *See supra* note 121.

[123] Tommy R. Franks, Instructions to the Citizens of Iraq: Coalition Provisional Authority Directive (Apr. 16, 2003). For an English-language text, see Ref. IZ C149, at PsyWar Society Web site, *supra* note 121.

General Franks would retain command of coalition military personnel in the area.[124] On May 9, President Bush gave Bremer the formal letter of appointment as presidential envoy "with full authority over all U.S. government personnel, activities and funds there." Shortly thereafter, Secretary of Defense Donald H. Rumsfeld designated him as administrator of the CPA.[125] On May 12, Bremer arrived in Baghdad, and for the following thirteen months he was effectively in charge but under an arrangement that divided power between the administrator and CPA on the one hand, and the military chain of command on the other, both reporting to the secretary of defense.[126]

The term "Coalition Provisional Authority" came into prominence only from May 8 onward. On that day, without mentioning the word "occupation," the United States and the United Kingdom informed the president of the UN Security Council that "[t]he States participating in the Coalition will strictly abide by their obligations under international law, including those relating to the essential humanitarian needs of the people of Iraq."[127] They had created the "Coalition Provisional Authority, which includes the Office of Reconstruction and Humanitarian Assistance, to exercise powers of government temporarily, and, as necessary, especially to provide security, to allow the delivery of humanitarian aid, and to eliminate weapons of mass destruction."[128]

In the first regulation of the CPA, which he signed on May 16, 2003, Bremer outlined its basis of authority and goals in the opening words:

> *Pursuant* to my authority as Administrator of the Coalition Provisional Authority (CPA), relevant U.N. Security Council resolutions, including Resolution 1483 (2003), and the laws and usages of war,
>
> I hereby promulgate the following:
>
> *Section 1*
> *The Coalition Provisional Authority*
>
> (1) The CPA shall exercise powers of government temporarily in order to provide for the effective administration of Iraq during the period of transitional administration, to restore conditions of security and stability, to create conditions in which the Iraqi people can freely determine their own political future, including by advancing efforts to restore and establish national and local institutions for representative governance and facilitating economic recovery and sustainable reconstruction and development.
>
> (2) The CPA is vested with all executive, legislative and judicial authority necessary to achieve its objectives, to be exercised under relevant U.N. Security Council resolutions, including Resolution 1483 (2003), and the laws and usages of war. This authority shall be exercised by the CPA Administrator.[129]

[124] Statement by the White House Press Secretary (May 6, 2003), *available at* <http://www.whitehouse.gov/news/releases/2003/05/20030506-5.html>.

[125] L. PAUL BREMER (with Malcolm McConnell), MY YEAR IN IRAQ: THE STRUGGLE TO BUILD A FUTURE OF HOPE 12–13 (2006).

[126] For an intelligent and historically informed account of the structure and role of the CPA by one of its constitutional advisers, see NOAH FELDMAN, WHAT WE OWE IRAQ: WAR AND THE ETHICS OF NATION-BUILDING (2004).

[127] Letter Dated 8 May 2003 from the Permanent Representatives of the United States of America and the United Kingdom of Great Britain and Northern Ireland to the President of the Security Council, UN Doc. S/2003/538.

[128] *Id.*

[129] CPA Regulation No. 1, §1, ¶1 (May 16, 2003), *available at* <http://www.iraqcoalition.org/regulations/index.html#Regulations> [hereinafter CPA Regulations & Orders]. CPA regulations, orders, and other materials

In its reference to a key UN Security Council resolution, and in encompassing executive, legislative, and judicial authority, this passage is virtually identical to the equivalent part of Regulation No. 1 in two cases of international administration that were not considered to be occupations: the UN Administration in Kosovo in 1999,[130] and the Transitional Administration in East Timor in the same year.[131] A notable difference is that, whereas the regulations for Kosovo and East Timor had referred to "internationally recognized human rights standards," the CPA regulation refers to "the laws and usages of war." This reflects the view that, of the three cases, only Iraq was an occupation.

The process by which the CPA emerged was more obscure than in these two earlier cases: it has given rise to three basic questions.

First, when was the CPA established? The simple answer would be April 16, 2003, the date of General Franks's "Freedom Message" and his CPA directive. However, one finds little evidence that the CPA existed as an actual administrative body in April. As noted, the letter of May 8 refers to it as already existing. It appears to have gradually come into existence, and to have assumed a form distinct from the military chain of command in Iraq, in the first half of May.

Second, what was the CPA's status in U.S. law? While it had close connections with the Department of Defense, it may not have been a federal agency.[132] It was mainly, but not exclusively, an American entity, constituting the administrative arm of a U.S.-led multinational coalition, but its exact status in U.S. law remains unclear.

Third, did the UN Security Council supply a legal framework for the CPA's work? The CPA's first regulation, issued on May 16, twice referred to the Council's Resolution 1483 as providing a guiding framework, even perhaps a degree of legal authorization. However, Resolution 1483 was actually passed by the Security Council only on May 22—six days after the regulation that invoked its name. This is odd. Nevertheless, the principal terms of Resolution 1483 had been on the table two weeks in advance, when the United Kingdom and Spain submitted a draft text.[133]

As eventually passed on May 22, Resolution 1483 noted the letter of May 8 from the United States and the United Kingdom, and then used the term "occupying powers" when it referred to the "specific authorities, responsibilities, and obligations under applicable international law of these states as occupying powers under unified command ('The Authority')." Immediately thereafter, it indicated that "other States that are not occupying powers are working now or in the future may work under the Authority":[134] this statement raised the interesting possibility that, in an occupation with transformative purposes, some countries involved may collaborate with the occupying powers without themselves being so labeled. Such status, however, does not imply a complete escape from the law on occupations. The resolution went on to state that the Council "*[c]alls*

are also available on the CPA Web site at <http://www.cpa-iraq.org/#>. After the CPA's role ended on June 28, 2004, it was originally indicated that the Web site would remain open for historical purposes only until June 30, 2006, but it in fact remained open after that date.

[130] On the Authority of the Interim Administration in Kosovo, UNMIK/Reg/1999/1, §1, ¶1 (July 25, 1999), *available at* <http://www.unmikonline.org/regulations/index.htm>.

[131] On the Authority of the Transitional Administration in East Timor, UNTAET/Reg/1999/1, §1 (Nov. 27, 1999), *available at* <http://www.un.org/peace/etimor/untaetR/r-1999.htm>.

[132] HALCHIN, *supra* note 121, at 8–42 *passim*.

[133] By the morning of May 9, 2003, the BBC and news agencies already had a draft text of what was to become, thirteen days later and after further amendment, Security Council Resolution 1483 (full draft text on file with author).

[134] SC Res. 1483, *supra* note 75, pmbl. The resolution passed by a vote of 14-0. Syria was absent from the meeting.

upon all concerned to comply fully with their obligations under international law including in particular the Geneva Conventions of 1949 and the Hague Regulations of 1907."[135]

Resolution 1483 also proclaimed certain objectives for the occupation. Apart from some broad indications in the preamble, these objectives are mainly to be found in paragraph 8, which deals with the role of the UN special representative for Iraq. The special representative was mandated, in coordination with the CPA, to assist the people of Iraq through

> (c) working intensively with the Authority, the people of Iraq, and others concerned to advance efforts to restore and establish national and local institutions for representative governance, including by working together to facilitate a process leading to an internationally recognized, representative government of Iraq;
>
> . . .
>
> (g) promoting the protection of human rights;
>
> . . .
>
> (i) encouraging international efforts to promote legal and judicial reform.[136]

Taken as a whole, the purposes of the occupation as outlined in Resolution 1483 went beyond the confines of the Hague Regulations and the Fourth Geneva Convention. Yet the resolution did not explain the relation between the transformative purposes of this occupation and the more conservative purposes of the existing body of law on occupations. These two things were set out separately. Subsequent resolutions, reaffirming the transformative purposes of the occupation, did not address this disjunction between occupation law and transformative purpose.[137]

In late 2003, David Scheffer, noting the significance of Resolution 1483, observed that it "rested uncomfortably within occupation law" and that the latter "was never designed for such transforming exercises."[138] Concerned about the emerging confusion in Iraq, he suggested: "The legal environment in Iraq would be better rationalized with a fresh UN mandate setting forth the responsibilities and mission objectives of the military powers operating in Iraq and by establishing UN civilian administrative functions that would assume powers held by the Authority under Resolution 1483."[139]

Some have argued that, from the start of the occupation of Iraq, the United States should have sought an even more central role for the United Nations. Gregory Fox, who is skeptical about the transformative project, and shows respect for the conservationist principle, suggests that a stronger and clearer Security Council mandate would have been needed to buttress the drastic series of reforms attempted in Iraq. Such a mandate "would have superseded the conservationist principle by invoking a superior international obligation and could have provided an opportunity to make clear that a consensus within the United Nations supported reform in Iraq."[140]

Unfortunately, arguments for a more central UN Security Council role in the transformation of Iraq are not persuasive. After the Council divided so bitterly on the use of force in the

[135] *Id.*, para. 5.

[136] *Id.*, para. 8.

[137] *See, e.g.*, SC Res. 1511 (Oct. 16, 2003), 43 ILM 254 (2004).

[138] David J. Scheffer, *Beyond Occupation Law*, 97 AJIL 842, 845, 849 (2003). His excellent discussion of the relation between transformative and conservationist objectives in Iraq is part of the continuation of *Agora: Future Implications of the Iraq Conflict*, 97 AJIL 803.

[139] Scheffer, *supra* note 138, at 859.

[140] Gregory H. Fox, *The Occupation of Iraq*, 36 GEO. J. INT'L L. 195, 296 (2005).

months leading up to the war, that it could have given more extensive support for the reform effort in Iraq than it actually did is hardly imaginable; and the extent of that mandate, as indicated above, was impressive. In no previous case had the Council been so closely involved in setting the framework for an occupation at all—let alone by explicitly backing some of the occupant's transformative projects.

The actual conduct of the occupation was seriously flawed from the start.[141] It had begun badly in April with the conspicuous failure to carry out a basic duty of occupying forces: the prevention of looting. Since some fighting was still going on, prevention of looting may not have been the top priority of the coalition forces, but the episode was an early indication of a lack of preparedness. It demonstrated that, whereas it had proved possible to do "invasion-lite" in Iraq, "occupation-lite" was not an option. Troops were needed on the ground for public order and guard duties, and they were not available. Astonishingly, even nuclear facilities were left unprotected.[142]

Subsequently, cases involving a pattern of maltreatment of prisoners in coalition hands came to light—a problem that led to numerous reports and several trials. In addition, the understandable U.S. emphasis on force protection inevitably brought about the occasional taking of lives of Iraqi citizens if there was even a possibility that they, or their locations, posed a threat to the occupation forces. As a result of these factors, what was intended as a liberation looked very different to many Iraqis.

In the occupation of Iraq, the inevitable legal interplay between the contending imperatives of conservation and reform played out mainly in favor of drastic change. Some change was necessary and effective, such as the introduction of a new currency. However, some policies of the CPA caused considerable controversy. Three much-criticized CPA orders illustrate the point. All could be seen as in tension with the conservationist assumptions of the law of the Hague Regulations and the Fourth Geneva Convention. They also raised a question about the prudence of the ambitious transformative policy of the CPA, and in particular about the wisdom of a decision-making procedure that (paradoxically for a body supposedly imposing liberal values) allowed little room for serious internal discussion or consultation with allies.

The first such example is CPA Order No. 1, De-Ba'athification of Iraqi Society, which was issued on May 16, 2003. Implementing the announcement in the "Freedom Message" of April 16 that had "disestablished the Ba'ath Party of Iraq," it went on to specify that four categories of senior party members were banned from future employment in the public sector.[143] This major decision was not the product of consultations, and took no account of the more subtle approach to Ba'ath Party members that had been taken in the years since 1991 in the Kurdish-run areas of northern Iraq.

The second such example is CPA Order No. 2, Dissolution of Entities, issued on May 23, 2003. Reconfirming the "Freedom Message" of April 16, it announced the abolition, as of April 16, of the Ministry of Defense; the Ministry of Information; the Ministry of State for Military Affairs; the Iraqi Intelligence Service; the National Security Bureau; the Directorate of National Security; the Special Security Organization; Saddam Hussein's bodyguards; the

[141] For useful accounts of the Iraq events, drawing attention to the limitations of the plans and activities of ORHA and CPA, see especially ANTHONY H. CORDESMAN, THE IRAQ WAR: STRATEGY, TACTICS, AND MILITARY LESSONS 493–516 (2003); MICHAEL GORDON & BERNARD TRAINOR, COBRA II: THE INSIDE STORY OF THE INVASION AND OCCUPATION OF IRAQ 152–63 (2006); DAVID L. PHILLIPS, LOSING IRAQ: INSIDE THE POST-WAR RECONSTRUCTION FIASCO 121–68 (2005).

[142] Ian Traynor, *Nuclear Looting Alarms UN Watchdog*, GUARDIAN, May 14, 2003, at 16.

[143] CPA Order No. 1 (May 16, 2003), *available at* CPA Regulations & Orders, *supra* note 129.

army, air force, and navy; the Air Defense Force; and twelve other regular military, paramilitary, and other organizations.[144] Administrator Bremer has sought to justify the abolition of the army on the grounds that many units had disbanded in the wake of the invasion anyway, and to have recalled them would have been to end up with a largely Sunni force.[145] Yet this was a drastic step, leaving a vast cadre of unemployed and embittered military personnel.

The third such example is CPA Order No. 39, Foreign Investment, issued on September 19, 2003, with (in theory) immediate effect. The order allowed foreign investors to own Iraqi companies fully without being required to reinvest profits into the country, a privilege that had previously been restricted by the Iraqi Constitution to citizens of Arab countries.[146] In the following months, this measure did not have the intended effect of opening Iraq up to foreign investment, mainly because the insurgency, which the order can have done nothing to check, made outsiders cautious. The order's sweeping terms raised concerns—within the CPA, and inside and outside Iraq—that the transformation being imposed was more extensive than the law permitted and the situation warranted. This dramatic act of economic transformation, unlike the political changes, lacked a convincing mandate either in human rights law or in Security Council resolutions.

Within three months of the end of major combat operations, announced by President Bush on the USS *Abraham Lincoln* on May 1, 2003, a major insurgency developed. Some evidence suggests that the insurgency was preplanned by the Iraqi authorities, well before the U.S.-led invasion of March 2003—as Bremer has asserted.[147] The presence of a foreign military force in a region with long memories of colonialism, war, and foreign occupation was always likely to cause tension. The emergence of resistance illustrates a potential hazard, and vulnerability, of transformative occupations. Any attempt at a major restructuring of society was likely to provoke opposition, especially when a large segment of that society—in this case the Sunni Muslim population—saw reforms as threatening a long-established pattern of political and economic dominance. The speedy dismissal of huge numbers of officials and the wholesale disbanding of the Iraqi army added to the risks. The insurgency was mainly centered in three of Iraq's eighteen provinces but had effects throughout the country. Using tactics that were a nightmare inversion of the notions of combat enshrined in the laws of war, the insurgency made the achievement of transformation very much more difficult. By attacking a wide range of outsiders—soldiers, UN officials, International Committee of the Red Cross personnel, civilians, and aid workers—the insurgents discouraged the outside world from sending troops or other personnel to Iraq. The UN special representative for Iraq, Sergio Vieira de Mello, was assassinated in an attack in Baghdad on August 19, 2003, which destroyed much of the UN headquarters there.[148] This was a clear sign that the insurgents were aiming at vulnerable targets, and sought to stop international assistance for the transformation project. By using suicide bombers who were indistinguishable in appearance from civilians, the insurgents increased the

[144] CPA Order No. 2 (May 23, 2003), *available at id.*

[145] BREMER, *supra* note 125, at 54–59.

[146] CPA Order No. 39 (Sept. 19, 2003), *available at* CPA Regulations & Orders, *supra* note 129.

[147] BREMER, *supra* note 125, at 126–27.

[148] The attack on the UN headquarters in Baghdad occurred five days after the passage of Security Council Resolution 1500 of August 14, 2003, establishing the UN Assistance Mission for Iraq. (The vote was 14 in favor, with Syria abstaining.) After the bombing, UNAMI was unable to function as planned in Iraq. Security Council Resolution 1546 of June 8, 2004, *supra* note 75, para. 7, cautiously provided for the resumption of its activities "as circumstances permit."

tension between coalition personnel and ordinary Iraqis, any of whom might pose a hidden threat.

The U.S. administration, with its self-generated illusions about liberation and transformation, had not anticipated such a sustained insurgency. President Bush, when asked in December 2005 whether he now acknowledged that the mission had not gone as originally planned, and in particular that the U.S. forces had not been welcomed as liberators, gave this characteristic reply, which merits inclusion in a lexicon of Bushisms: "I think we are welcomed, but it was not a peaceful welcome."[149] U.S. public support for the intervention in Iraq declined sharply between March 2003 and the summer of 2005 for two reasons: first, the change of objective from restraining Iraq's weapons capability to participation in an internal political struggle; and second, the high human cost and halting progress of the occupation.[150]

Considering the circumstances of insurgency, a remarkable degree of political transformation was achieved in Iraq. The movement toward Iraqi self-rule, though facing difficult problems and subject to constant criticism, was brisk. The Governing Council of Iraq, established under the wing of the CPA, held its first meeting on July 13, 2003. A notably high number of voters turned out in the elections for the Transitional National Assembly in January 2005, the referendum on the new Constitution in October 2005, and the elections for the National Assembly in December 2005. This participation was evidence that the transformative project, flawed as it may have been, struck a chord with Iraqis. Finally, on May 21, 2006, after many delays, the National Assembly approved a new national unity government. Meanwhile, the huge refugee flows out of Iraq (mainly to Syria and Jordan) confirmed the limits of what had been achieved.

The process by which the Iraqi occupation had formally ended on June 28, 2004, illustrates a problem of transformative occupations.[151] While all such occupations aim at establishing a political order based on the principle of self-government, determining at what point one can say that the transformation has been achieved, and the government of the occupied territory is in a position to exercise the powers of sovereignty, is genuinely difficult. This question is much easier to answer when a more conventional occupation ends in a more traditional way, either as a result of reconquest of the territory by its original ruler, or as part of the terms of a peace agreement. Where what is involved is a gradual transfer of powers to the indigenous authorities as their capacity to govern is built up, there is bound to be an arbitrary element in fixing on a single date as the symbolic ending of the occupation. Political controversy figured in this case as well, since critics viewed the formal ending as concealing continued U.S. dominance of a puppet government.

At the United Nations, the ending of the occupation, within a framework laid down by the U.S. government, was provided for in Security Council Resolution 1546 of June 8, 2004. It began by "*[w]elcoming* the beginning of a new phase in Iraq's transition to a democratically elected government, and *looking forward* to the end of the occupation and the assumption of full responsibility and authority by a fully sovereign and independent Interim Government of

[149] President George W. Bush, Interview with Brian Williams (NBC television news, Dec. 12, 2005), *available in* LEXIS, News Library, Transcripts File.

[150] This is the conclusion of the most thorough assessment of the subject, Richard C. Eichenberg, *Victory Has Many Friends: U.S. Public Opinion and the Use of Military Force, 1981–2005*, 30 INT'L SECURITY 140, 176 (2005).

[151] For a fuller exposition, completed at the time of the transfer of authority in June 2004, see Adam Roberts, *The End of Occupation: Iraq 2004*, 54 INT'L & COMP. L.Q. 27 (2005).

Iraq by 30 June 2004."[152] The resolution reaffirmed "the right of the Iraqi people freely to determine their own political future and control their own natural resources."[153] It laid down a detailed road map for Iraq's future political development, including the holding, before January 31, 2005, at the latest, of democratic elections to the Transitional National Assembly. (These were in fact held on January 30, 2005.) The resolution welcomed the fact that Iraqi security forces were "responsible to appropriate Iraqi ministers," and that there was to be a "full partnership between Iraqi security forces and the multinational force."[154] It contained extensive provisions on the roles of the multinational force and the Iraqi government, both of which were envisaged as taking a wide range of security measures. It referred three times to the promotion of human rights in Iraq as a key goal.

The new situation after June 28, 2004, was not just an occupation by another name. There were real differences, including the fact that the Interim Government had an explicitly recognized right to demand the withdrawal of the U.S.-led forces in Iraq. As the Security Council put it in the same resolution: "the mandate for the multinational force shall be reviewed at the request of the Government of Iraq or twelve months from the date of this resolution, . . . and [the Council] *declares* that it will terminate this mandate earlier if requested by the Government of Iraq."[155]

Yet the prospect that there would be continuing significant similarities with an occupation found reflection in certain provisions of the resolution about the application of international rules. A preambular clause inserted fairly late in the long negotiations over the text recognized the continued application of international humanitarian law: "*Noting* the commitment of all forces promoting the maintenance of security and stability in Iraq to act in accordance with international law, including obligations under international humanitarian law, and to cooperate with relevant international organizations."[156] The inclusion of this clause can be interpreted as one way of conceding that, even if the occupation was theoretically over, the likelihood remained that uses of force, perhaps even exercises of administrative authority, that closely resembled a situation of occupation would occur. This scenario, of course, has been played out repeatedly in the two years since the occupation notionally ended. Indeed, many continued to use the term "occupation" with respect to Iraq and will no doubt do so as long as coalition forces are present and exercise significant influence in the management of the country.

In addition, the first operative paragraph of Resolution 1546 confirmed the incomplete nature of the transfer of sovereignty for which the resolution provided. It stated that the Security Council

[152] SC Res. 1546, *supra* note 75, pmbl. This resolution, which passed unanimously, was a substantially revised version of earlier drafts; the first had been presented at the United Nations on May 24, 2004. See also the detailed listing of the broad range of tasks of the multinational force (including even internment), and the assurance about the continued fulfillment of obligations under the law of armed conflict, contained in the letter of June 5, 2004, from the U.S. secretary of state to the president of the Security Council, annexed to the resolution.

[153] *Id.*, pmbl.

[154] *Id.*, para. 11.

[155] *Id.*, paras. 9, 12. See also the text of letters (both dated June 5, 2004) from the prime minister of the Interim Government of Iraq and the U.S. secretary of state to the president of the Security Council, annexed to the resolution.

[156] *Id.*, pmbl. There had been no equivalent clause in the draft of Resolution 1546 presented at the United Nations by the United States and the United Kingdom on May 24, 2004. The revised draft presented on June 1 had included the clause in a shorter version than the final one. Only the final text, which was first circulated on June 7, contained the phrase "including obligations under international humanitarian law."

> *Endorses* the formation of a sovereign Interim Government of Iraq, as presented on 1 June 2004, which will assume full responsibility and authority by 30 June 2004 for governing Iraq while refraining from taking any actions affecting Iraq's destiny beyond the limited interim period until an elected Transitional Government of Iraq assumes office as envisaged in paragraph four below.[157]

This important limitation on "taking any actions affecting Iraq's destiny beyond the limited interim period" reportedly resulted from pressure by various Iraqi groups fearful that the position of Kurds, Shiites, or others might be undermined irrevocably by actions taken by the "sovereign" Interim Government. This constraint placed the Interim Government, paradoxically, in a position analogous to that of an occupying power. The CPA interpreted the provision as limiting the Interim Government's power to conclude treaties. The constraint bears obvious similarities to the obligations on occupying powers to refrain from making fundamental changes in the legal system of the occupied territory, and to behave generally in a trusteelike manner. The fact that the term "caretaker government" was often used with reference to the Interim Government confirmed this interpretation. Thus, ironically, a transformative occupation challenging the very foundations of the law of the Hague Regulations and the Fourth Geneva Convention had the effect of leading to a reassertion of the conservative principles that underlie occupation law—even at the moment when the occupation was deemed to be at an end.

IV. CONCLUSION: THE RELEVANCE OF THE LAWS OF WAR AND HUMAN RIGHTS

The idea of achieving the transformation of a society through a military intervention is far from new. It was a key element in much European colonialism and in France's wars after the Revolution of 1789. The United States, with its long-held vision of itself as reformer of a corrupt international system, has been particularly attracted by the idea, but has devoted surprisingly little attention either to the checkered history of transformative interventions or to the prescriptive question of how they should be conducted.[158]

The need for foreign military presences with transformative political purposes is not going to disappear. The U.S. government belatedly recognized this circumstance (and implicitly recognized that mistakes had been made in Iraq) in 2004–2005, when it established the Office of the Coordinator for Reconstruction and Stabilization. Based in the State Department, the office was charged with leading U.S. government civilian capacity "to prevent or prepare for post-conflict situations, and to help stabilize and reconstruct societies in transition from conflict or civil strife, so they can reach a sustainable path toward peace, democracy and a market economy."[159] Similarly, in December 2005, the United Nations established a Peacebuilding Commission, an advisory body to assist in postconflict peacebuilding and recovery.[160]

Transformative military presences may be attempted by states, coalitions, and international bodies, including the United Nations. While the management of such projects largely consists in the prudent and informed conduct of policy, the laws of war and human rights continue to

[157] *Id.*, para. 1.

[158] One post-2003 U.S. attempt to look at the matter, which it does from a policy rather than a legal perspective, is David M. Edelstein, *Occupational Hazards: Why Military Occupations Succeed or Fail*, 29 INT'L SECURITY 49 (2004).

[159] U.S. Dep't of State, Office of the Coordinator for Reconstruction and Stabilization (established by presidential directive Dec. 7, 2005), *at* <http://www.state.gov/s/crs/>.

[160] The establishment of the Peacebuilding Commission was recommended in the September 2005 World Summit Outcome document, *supra* note 94, paras. 97–105, and implemented on December 20, 2005, in concurrent Resolutions 60/180 of the General Assembly, and 1645 and 1646 of the Security Council.

regulate the conduct of those engaged in them. In the light of the experiences of transformative military presences, the following conclusions can be offered about the law relating to these enterprises.

Jus Post Bellum

Underlying all consideration of transformative occupation is the fact that it is not a temporary wartime occupation, liable to be ended by the fortunes of war or a peace agreement. Rather, it typically arises *after* a war—whether civil or international—and/or after a foreign military intervention; and it is likely to end in a different way, as stable government emerges in the territory itself. In such circumstances, the *jus in bello* is unlikely to be a perfect fit. It might even be tempting to invoke an emerging or future *jus post bellum* as a better basis for handling these situations.

The idea of military intervention with a transformative purpose stands in tension with the existing system of international law as it applies to states. Under the *jus ad bellum*, a transformative goal is not a valid basis for resorting to force. As for the *jus in bello*, at least some aspects of the laws of war as they address occupations conflict with the transformative intentions of outside powers. Sobering evidence of this conflict is that two of the most successful transformative occupations of the twentieth century—those of Germany and Japan from 1945 onward—were explicitly conducted outside the framework of the law of the Hague Regulations, with their assumption that the occupant has a largely conservationist role.

"Occupation" Not a Completely Distinct Category

In the post–Cold War international system, democratic transformation has been a declared goal of many foreign military and administrative presences of theoretically distinct types. These include some (such as those in Kosovo and East Timor in 1999) that have not been considered to be occupations—partly, it appears, because there was a degree of consent from the state concerned and/or from the population of the area where the troops and administrations were deployed; and perhaps also because the administrations were UN-led rather than U.S.-led. While the foreign military presence in Iraq from May 2003 onward resembled some of these other cases in its powers and declared purposes, it was explicitly viewed as an occupation for the good reason that it plainly lacked the consent of the government of the state concerned. Yet even after the resumption of Iraqi sovereignty on June 28, 2004, the situation continued to exhibit certain features comparable to those of an occupation. In general, the similarity of different situations—some viewed as occupations, some not—raises a question about the extent to which military occupation is a distinct category, and points to the conclusion that the law governing occupations may have some application to certain situations not specifically called occupations. In addition, human rights law can apply to occupations, as well as to a range of comparable situations.

These conclusions suggest that in all military interventions, however labeled, a case can be made for developing a common legal approach involving a proper balance between the laws of war and human rights law. Steven Ratner has argued that the case for achieving such a balance is particularly strong in transformative occupations.[161]

[161] Steven R. Ratner, *Foreign Occupation and International Territorial Administration: The Challenges of Convergence*, 16 EUR. J. INT'L L. 695 (2005).

Human Rights Law

Human rights norms are increasingly recognized as applicable in military occupations, and also in situations that resemble military occupations in various ways yet are distinct from the classic case of occupation. Their application, by no means free of difficulty, offers some important opportunities—especially where the inhabitants find themselves within the power of the outside forces. These opportunities include (1) individuals can press cases in certain regional courts (specifically, the European Court of Human Rights and the Inter-American Court of Human Rights) in ways that the laws of war do not offer; and (2) occupying powers can justify certain transformative policies on the basis that these are the best way to meet certain goals and principles enshrined in international human rights law, including the right of self-determination.

Illusions of Welcome as Liberators

Two propositions have contributed to the view that the laws of war are of limited relevance to transformative occupations. The first is that "liberation" and "occupation" are in some way opposites—when, in reality, liberators, to be effective, may need to observe rules of restraint that apply to occupying forces. The second is that a transformative project imposed by outsiders is likely to be, and to remain, universally welcomed by the inhabitants—when, in reality, trouble is likely to result when the outsiders are of a different religion and culture, and are intervening in a society that is already deeply fractured and is in a part of the world with extended experience of foreign domination and occupation. An appreciation of the limits of these propositions points to the continued relevance of the laws of war.

Compatibility Between Existing Law and Transformative Purposes

The seriousness and extent of any fault line between the conservationist thrust of the law and the transformative nature of some occupations should not be exaggerated. The requirement in the Hague Regulations that the occupant respect the laws in force in the territory "unless absolutely prevented" does not create a straitjacket. It was modified slightly in 1949—though much less than the United States had naively sought. Under the Hague rule, thus modified, certain occupants—and not only those with a generally transformative purpose—have been able to give cogent reasons why they were indeed "absolutely prevented" from maintaining each and every part of the existing legal system. For example, in the Israeli-occupied territories some significant changes were made to laws, including by abolishing the death penalty.

In addition, experience suggests that even overtly transformative occupants would be wise to recognize the strength and continuing validity of the law on occupations in general, and the conservationist principle in particular. Numerous errors in the occupation of Iraq arose from the failure to recognize that the laws of war can play a valuable role in focusing attention on certain perennial problems of armed conflicts and occupations—such as looting and the management of economic life—and do so in a sensible and constructive way. Ironically, Security Council Resolution 1546 of June 8, 2004, required the United States to accept a conservationist role for the new sovereign Interim Government of Iraq, which was obliged to refrain "from taking any actions affecting Iraq's destiny."[162]

[162] SC Res. 1546, *supra* note 75, para. 1.

Where, after an occupation has commenced, clashes take place between the conservationist principle and a perceived need for transformation, the occupant could seek specific authorization from international bodies. The UN Security Council has played such a role in Iraq, and has supported transformative projects in certain postconflict situations that, in some respects at least, are analogous to occupations. On occasion, the Security Council may be unable to reach agreement, in which case the question of whether other global or regional bodies can serve as a substitute will remain a matter of contention.

Distinguishing Between Transformative Projects

Just because the occupant has a transformative purpose does not mean that it is sensible to transform numerous aspects of a society at the same time. The Iraqi case counsels caution about proposals for sudden and large-scale transformations. It suggests that on a wide range of matters, including the economic structuring of society, fundamental decisions should be made by the sovereign institutions of a state after a system of representative government has been put in place, and cannot be imposed in a hurry by diktat from outside. An occupant, even one with transformative aims, needs to give priority to getting the basic infrastructure of society to work. On such matters, the demands of the conservative element in the laws of war, and of their humanitarian provisions, may coincide with the dictates of prudence.

Of all the elements of a transformative project, the ones likely to have the strongest appeal include the introduction of an honest electoral system as part of a multiparty democracy. To be sure, in Iraq the introduction of democracy necessarily involved contentious constitutional change on such fundamental matters as whether the structure of the state was to be federal in character, and if so on what model; and the imposition of such change may have contributed to the strength of the insurgency. The circumstances in which such change is imposable from outside are rare. Yet there is a serious case for such an approach—reflecting as it does the sense that democracy and self-determination, for all the difficulties of defining and applying them, constitute not only an important part of the human rights package, but also an acceptable means of hastening the end of an occupation. To the extent that a new and effective government emerges through such a process, an occupation may fade away progressively, rather than disappear suddenly at a set date.

The fact that democratic transformation has strong appeal does not mean that it is a panacea, or that occupants have a general entitlement to facilitate it. If an occupant invades part of a country to "liberate," say, an ethnic group inhabiting that area, the fact that the inhabitants are offered a democratic path will not assuage states' skepticism about such projects; nor will it dispel suspicions that power-political as well as idealistic motives may have informed the action. In other cases, there may be fears that the sudden imposition of democracy will result in chaos, civil war, or dictatorship.

A further hazard of any general advocacy of transformative occupation is that democracy is far from being the only transformative project on offer in the international marketplace of ideas. In the post–Cold War era, the predominant transformative projects have been based on liberal and democratic ideas, but other possible candidates exist.

Two Possible Legal Approaches to Transformation

Many developments in practice, and in decisions of international bodies, suggest that custom with respect to the law on occupations has undergone significant evolution. However, this evolution does not amount to a general recognition of the validity of transformative policies imposed by occupants. A more modest conclusion follows—that any expansion of the purposes of occupations beyond the narrow confines of existing occupation law could in principle be addressed by either of two legal approaches.

The first approach is essentially ad hoc, and follows some (but by no means all) aspects of the practice regarding Iraq. It seeks to secure a variation in the application of the law by obtaining a resolution from the UN Security Council (or other major international body) setting out the goals of the occupation. Such authorization can perform an important function. By imparting at least some measure of legitimacy to certain actions and goals, and by stressing the application of human rights law as well as humanitarian law, it can give law an important element of flexibility in response to exceptional situations; and it can reduce the intensity of international criticism of the occupant's actions. This approach raises the question of the extent to which the Security Council has a free hand to vary the application of even quite fundamental rules of international law—including, in this case, both the *jus ad bellum* and the *jus in bello.* In light of the powers vested in the Council, its capacity to act in such a way is hard to deny—especially in a case where what is at issue is reconciling divergent principles of international law on a specific and limited matter relating to the maintenance of peace and security. This course of action is very different from waiving the rules in some more general way.

The second approach would be to attempt to secure a formal modification of the Hague Regulations and the Fourth Geneva Convention to make allowance for transformative occupations, especially in the light of human rights law. The case for attempting to devise new law in this way is weak. The heart of occupation law remains a sensible and essentially conservationist set of rules to cover a type of emergency situation that frequently arises in war. Where the intent is transformative, there should be time to seek authorization from international bodies. A further reason for caution about making allowance in general terms for transformative occupation is that there are historically well-founded doubts about the extent to which foreign armed forces, arriving suddenly in a society with deep-seated problems, are really capable of bringing about fundamental change in that society. This situation has to be the exception rather than the norm. Military occupation remains a contentious issue on which differences of perspective and opinion, including on the extent to which transformative goals are legitimate, will inevitably emerge. The status of any given occupation vis-à-vis the principle of nonuse of force, and the right of self-determination, is necessarily problematical. An attempt to revise the laws of war provisions on occupations to accommodate the special and important case of transformative occupations would be open to criticism and likely to fail. It is simply not worth going down that road when other remedies for any claimed defects of the law on occupations are at hand in the form of human rights law, UN Security Council authorizations, and evolving custom about how the international community can properly assist in the transformation of damaged societies.

Name Index

www.ingramcontent.com/pod-product-compliance
Lightning Source LLC
LaVergne TN
LVHW080801011026
849160LV00015B/1498
9781138378643